Intra-European Litigation in Eighteenth-Century Izmir

Mediterranean Reconfigurations

INTERCULTURAL TRADE, COMMERCIAL LITIGATION, AND LEGAL PLURALISM

Series Editors

Wolfgang Kaiser (*Université Paris 1, Panthéon-Sorbonne*)
Guillaume Calafat (*Université Paris 1, Panthéon-Sorbonne*)

VOLUME 4

The titles published in this series are listed at *brill.com/cmed*

Intra-European Litigation in Eighteenth-Century Izmir

The Role of the Merchants' Style

By

Tijl Vanneste

BRILL

LEIDEN | BOSTON

The Open Access publication of this book has been funded by the ERC.

Cover illustration: View of Smyrna (Izmir) and the reception given to Consul de Hochepied (1657–1723) in the Council Chamber, anonymous, c. 1687–1723. From the collection of the Rijksmuseum, Amsterdam.

Library of Congress Cataloging-in-Publication Data

Names: Vanneste, Tijl, author.
Title: Intra-European litigation in eighteenth-century Izmir : the role of the merchants' style / by Tijl Vanneste.
Description: Leiden ; Boston : Brill, [2022] | Series: Mediterranean reconfigurations, 2494-8772 ; 4 | Includes bibliographical references and index.
Identifiers: LCCN 2021040803 (print) | LCCN 2021040804 (ebook) | ISBN 9789004382701 (hardback) | ISBN 9789004498235 (ebook)
Subjects: LCSH: Consular jurisdiction–Turkey–İzmir–History–18th century, | Commercial courts–Turkey–İzmir–History–18th century, | Dutch–Legal status, laws, etc.–Turkey–İzmir–History–18th century | Capitulations–Turkey–History–18th century,
Classification: LCC KKX1589 .V36 2022 (print) | LCC KKX1589 (ebook) | DDC 347.561/012–dc23
LC record available at https://lccn.loc.gov/2021040803
LC ebook record available at https://lccn.loc.gov/2021040804

Typeface for the Latin, Greek, and Cyrillic scripts: "Brill". See and download: brill.com/brill-typeface.

ISSN 2494-8772
ISBN 978-90-04-38270-1 (hardback)
ISBN 978-90-04-49823-5 (e-book)

This book is printed on acid-free paper and produced in a sustainable manner.

Contents

Acknowledgements

This book is the product of research I have done in the framework of an international project on intercultural trade, commercial litigation and legal pluralism between the fifteenth and nineteenth centuries in the Mediterranean basin, ConfigMed (Mediterranean Reconfigurations). It was hosted by the Université Paris 1 Panthéon Sorbonne and the Institut d'histoire moderne et contemporaine (IHMC) and funded by an ERC Advanced Grant (N°295868) from September 2012 to June 2018. Its principal investigator was Prof. Wolfgang Kaiser, and I am greatly indebted to him for giving me the opportunity to participate in his project and giving me all the academic freedom to pursue my own research while ensuring that I would not stray too far from the flock. And I want to thank that flock, my colleagues, for this project, for their suggestions, remarks and discussions during our project meetings in Paris: Andrea Addobbati, Sadok Boubaker, Guillaume Calafat, Mathieu Grenet, Güneş Işıksel, Manuel Lomas Cortés, Eloy Martín Corrales, Leila Maziane, Évelyne Oliel-Grausz, Johann Petitjean, Biagio Salvemini, Mafalda Ade Winter, Francisco Apellániz, Yavuz Aykan, Christopher Denis-Delacour, Ana Belem Fernández Castro, Michael Talbot and Rémi Dewière, who was also always patient and friendly when I was too late with paperwork.

I am thankful to Richard Blakemore for our discussions on early modern maritime law and litigation and to Bernard Allaire for sharing archival material. I am grateful to the always accommodating staff at the archives I visited, particularly at the National Archives in The Hague and the City Archives of Amsterdam.

A large part of this book was written behind a computer screen at the Vrije Universiteit Amsterdam, and I want to thank my colleagues there for support at times when I felt my manuscript would never see the light of day, thank you Erika Kuijpers, Ayla Krijnen, Inger Leemans, Petra van Dam, Ronald Kroeze, Frans Huijzendveld, Norah Karrouche, Wouter de Vries, Miel Groten, Lonneke Geerlings, Michel van Duijnen, Dienke Hondius, Bettine Siertsema, Ab Flipse, Caro Verbeek, Susan Legêne, Edwina Hagen, Ad Tervoort and Fred van Lieburg for making me feel at home.

I am particularly grateful to Maria Fusaro, who was the first to read the manuscript and was always spot on with her comments. Her inexhaustible and no-nonsense energy to go out there and be a historian is a continuing source of inspiration.

I also want to thank Maurits van den Boogert at Brill. Without his thorough reading of the manuscript and helpful suggestions, this book would never have existed, and the same can be said for his patience when I missed a deadline. I am very grateful for the revising of the manuscript by Rebekah Zwanzig and the help provided by Teddi Dols and Kavipriya V. It goes without saying that all remaining errors are my own.

A last work of thank goes to those who saw me struggle and who never failed to provide support. Thank you, first of all, Trees de Geest, for everything. Thank you also Rosa Sijben, Eva Schmitz, Lydia Aytogmus, Phil Baber, Andrea Capecci, Yassine Khoudja, Tracian Meikle, Al Angharad Williams, Gray Akotey, Erdem Meral, Adrian Olivet, Ignasi Solano Monner, Olivia Somsen, Nienke Elbertse, Elisabeth Enthoven, Orfee Melsen, Francisco Sousa, Alice Barthelemy, Henk Sleijfer, Chaim Wannet and Michel Hesp.

Figures and Tables

Figures

Tables

Introduction

In 1686, the Amsterdam Directorate of Levant Trade and Navigation in the Mediterranean (*Directie Levantse Handel en Navigatie in de Middellandse Zee*) drafted a proposal with which they hoped to settle all matters related to the jurisdiction of and the litigation done by the Dutch ambassador and consuls in the Levant.[1] It contained seven articles, the last one specifying that

> in order to prevent the inhabitants of this state [the United Provinces] in the Levant from annoying each other with lengthy trials, damaging trade and draining all its lifeblood, it is necessary that the States General order the resident [ambassador] and consuls in the Levant, together with their assessors [merchants acting as co-judges], to offer a prompt expedition of justice to the inhabitants of this state who air a dispute before them and to sentence in a short and tactful manner.[2]

The Directorate of Levant Trade was a board of merchants active in Levantine trade. It was established in 1625 as an institution supervising Dutch trade in the Levant.[3] It provided advice to the political organs in the Dutch Republic

---

1 In the early modern period, references to the Levant include the whole non-European eastern Mediterranean, including for instance Anatolia and its coast, contrary to today's interpretation of the term, which is limited to the lands along the coast between the Sinai desert and southeastern Anatolia.

2 Klaas Heeringa and J.G. Nanninga, *Bronnen tot de geschiedenis van den Levantschen handel (1590–1826)* (The Hague, 1917), 2: pp. 251–252, 'Ontwerp-reglement van justitie in de Levant', Amsterdam, 17/01/1686, on p. 252, 'en opdat de ingesetene van deesen staat in de Levante niet met langhdurige processen malkanderen en mogen vexeeren tot schaade van de negotie, en daartoe alle aderen mochte werden afgesneden, sal mede gansch dienstich sijn, dat H.H.M. den gemelte resident en consuls in de Levante serieuslijcken gelieven te gelasten, ten eyde deselve met haar assessoren, den ingesetenen van deesen staat voor haar eenige saake ventileerende, prompte expeditie van justitie komen te geven, mitsgaders cort en onvertooge recht te doen etc'. The work of Heeringa and Nanninga is an extensive publication of primary sources in Dutch archives related to the Dutch Levant trade. Its first two volumes were edited by Klaas Heeringa and published in 1910 and 1917. The other two were edited by J.G. Nanninga and were published in 1952, 1964 and 1966 (the last volume, like the second, appeared in two parts). The complete work can be consulted online at http://resources.huygens.knaw.nl/retroboeken/levantschehandel/#page=0&accessor=toc&view=homePane.

3 'The Low Countries is used to refer to both the Spanish/Austrian Netherlands and the Dutch Republic; Dutch refers to the Dutch Republic, or the United Provinces, while Holland only refers to the particular Dutch province of that name. In her work, Maartje van Gelder used 'Netherlandish' to indicate merchants coming from the Low Countries. I have chosen not to adopt that useful designation as the Dutch community of Izmir did not include merchants

and maintained contact with Dutch diplomatic representatives in the eastern Mediterranean.

Most of the Levant was controlled by the Ottomans, and by the time the proposal was drafted, the Dutch had maintained a diplomatic relationship with the Sublime Porte for almost seventy-five years in support of various Dutch trading communities active in several Levantine *échelles*, where they were active as commission traders, handling the merchandise of and for colleagues in the Dutch Republic as well as the Spanish Netherlands. Goods were bought and sold through Ottoman middlemen in Greece, Aleppo, Istanbul, Ankara and, most importantly, Izmir.[4] The Dutch, like other European trading communities, were guests, staying at the discretion of the Ottoman hosts, and their presence was regulated through an expanding set of privileges given by the Ottoman sultan that were known as the capitulations, or *ahdnames*.[5] These allowed for Europeans to stay indefinitely in Ottoman territory and provided them with several fiscal and commercial privileges, such as tax exemptions and lower custom tariffs. One of the main privileges that was granted to the Europeans was their right to legal autonomy. The capitulations stipulated that the various trading communities fell under the jurisdiction of consuls, vice-consuls or ambassadors, who also had the right to adjudicate disputes within their communities. This meant that Europeans could use their own 'national' laws, statutes and procedures in intra-community litigation, with the consul (or ambassador) acting as judge.

The Sublime Porte giving permission to trading communities to settle disputes amongst their members autonomously matched the European medieval custom of legal autonomy given to foreign trading communities headed by a consul. While the privilege of autonomy was thus not an exotic one for Europeans, it did not mean that the legal context within which European consuls in the Ottoman Empire needed to operate was always unambiguous and clearly delineated. Early modern European states did not have one codified

from the Austrian Netherlands. Maartje van Gelder, *Trading places: The Netherlandish merchants in early modern Venice* (Leiden and Boston, 2009).

4 This book has opted to refer to Ottoman cities under their current Turkish names. Early modern Smyrna is thus referred to as Izmir, Constantinople as Istanbul and so on. In quotes, the place name is kept the way it was written down, including its spelling.

5 The term 'capitulation', or *capitula* in Latin, was used for the 1304 treaty between Genoa and Byzantium and also designates late-medieval treaties concluded between Christian and Muslim states in the Mediterranean. Viorel Panaite, 'The legal and political status of Wallachia and Moldavia in relation to the Ottoman Empire', in *The European tributary states of the Ottoman Empire in the sixteenth and seventeenth centuries*, eds. Gábor Kármán and Lovro Kunčević (Leiden and Boston, 2013), p. 37.

body of national law.[6] Legal pluralism and a variety of local jurisdictions were commonplace. Thus, it was not so easy to transplant 'national' law onto the 'national' trading communities operating abroad.[7] An additional complication was the nature of disputes that were solved by consular litigation. European presence in the Ottoman Empire was a consequence of trade, and by far, most of the European individuals living in an Ottoman city were traders, and when they took each other to court, it was usually to settle a commercial dispute. There are two reasons why it was not so easy to use state law to settle such disputes.

The first one is that the legal autonomy granted by the Ottomans applied to intracommunity resolutions, and commercial relationships, almost without exception, extended beyond the community, which made legal autonomy insufficient and necessitated additional agreements between different actors, Ottoman as well as European, on jurisdiction. The second one is that there was no readily available corpus of written 'national' law that was developed enough to be used in all matters of commercial litigation, particularly when considering the increasingly international context of early modern trade.

Historians have pointed to the existence of an informal body of rules used by traders from different backgrounds to settle their disputes, the so-called 'law merchant', a concept that offers a solution for both problems mentioned above. The concept, which originated in the Middle Ages and was considered universal, or at least highly cosmopolitan, is still the subject of academic debate. While some scholars consider the law merchant one of the medieval institutions that helped revive and expand Europe's trade with the world, others have argued that the law merchant is an artificial concept introduced

6 While there were certainly European states with a strong degree of centralisation, such as France, others, such as the Dutch Republic, were fundamentally different. In general, the use of the term 'nation-state' for the period under study is complicated and does not do justice to the sophisticated political fragmentation and local autonomies that existed within the borders of many European states. For an analysis of the process of state formation in Europe, see Thomas Ertman, *Birth of the leviathan. Building states and regimes in medieval and early modern Europe* (Cambridge, 1997).

7 A national trading community abroad is more regularly referred to as a trading nation, both in contemporary and modern literature. It should not be equated with a nation-state – as the Dutch case makes abundantly clear. I will use both trading community and trading nation throughout the book. For an extensive study of the interaction of European trading nations with the institutions of a host society through a diplomatic and legal prism, see Roberto Zaugg, *Stranieri di antico regime. Mercanti, giudici e consoli nella Napoli del Settecento* (Roma, 2011).

by historians attempting to find the historical roots of early attempts at globalisation.[8]

This book argues that, while the law merchant did not exist in the way its advocates suggested, the international merchant community was nonetheless able to rely on a large and heterogeneous web of rules, customs and uses that merchants themselves labelled the 'merchants' style' (*koopmansstijl* is the term used in most Dutch sources).[9] Furthermore, analysis of several commercial disputes adjudicated by the Dutch consul in Izmir shows that the merchants' style was used in litigation as the central criterion on which the court based its legal verdicts. Legal procedure and the court's modus operandi were fully accommodating towards this merchants' style and the variety of merchants' customs, something that equally applied to various courts in different areas of the world – without there being an actual codified system of international law in existence.

The central thesis of this book is that the use of the merchants' style in courts adjudicating commercial disputes in an international context should be considered the legal equivalent of the commercial customs that underpinned early modern intercultural and international trade. It expressed what was

8 For criticism, see Emily Kadens, 'The myth of the customary law merchant', *Texas law review*, 90 (2012): pp. 1153–1206; and 'The medieval law merchant: The tyranny of a construct', *Journal of legal analysis*, 7:2 (2015): pp. 251–289; Stephen Sachs, 'From St. Ives to cyberspace: The modern distortion of the medieval "law merchant"', *American University international law review*, 21:5 (2006): pp. 685–812; Emily Kadens, 'Order within law, variety within custom: The character of the medieval merchant law', *Chicago journal of international law*, 5:1 (2004): pp. 39–65; and Albrecht Cordes, 'The search for a medieval lex mercatoria', *Oxford University comparative law forum* 5 (2003), consulted online at http://ouclf.iuscomp.org/the-search-for-a-medieval-lex-mercatoria/. For early defenders, see William Mitchell, *An essay on the early history of the law merchant* (Cambridge, 1904); and Levin Goldschmidt, *Handbuch des Handelsrechts* (Erlangen, 1868). Goldschmidt (1839–1897) was a professor in commercial law at Berlin University who studied with Max Weber. For an excellent recent analysis, see Dave De ruysscher, 'La lex mercatoria contextualisée: Tracer son parcours intellectuel', *Revue historique du droit français et étranger*, 90:4 (2012): pp. 501–504; see also J.H. Baker, 'The law merchant and the common law before 1700', *The Cambridge law journal*, 38:2 (1979): pp. 295–322; and for the argument on the revival of European trade, see Paul R. Milgrom, Douglass C. North, and Barry R. Weingast, 'The role of institutions in the revival of trade: The law merchant, private judges, and the champagne fairs', *Economics & politics*, 2:1 (1990): pp. 1–23. Historians have also considered the existence of a similar *lex maritima* for maritime law. For a discussion on this, see Dave De ruysscher 'Maxims, principles and legal change: Maritime law in merchant and legal culture (Low Countries, 16th century)', *Zeitschrift der Savigny-Stiftung für Rechtsgeschichte*, 138 (2021): pp. 260–275.

9 On the idea of a pluralism of custom, see Kadens, 'Order within law'.

considered reasonable and equitable *in law* as the legal consequence of what was considered reasonable and fair behaviour *in trade*.

A great deal of historiography on early modern intercultural trade has been motivated by an attempt to explain how such trade was possible in the absence of formal international institutions that could successfully sanction fraudulent behaviour. The absence of a legal framework able to adjudicate international mercantile disputes and the reluctance of traders to go to court are often considered givens in discourse on the development of commercial networks based on trust. Scholars such as Francesca Trivellato, Sebouh Aslanian, Gunnar Dahl, Xabier Lamikiz and others have all analysed such networks in the early modern period, demonstrating the efforts undertaken by the international merchant community to reduce risk and enhance trust. These efforts include the careful construction of long-lasting business correspondences, peer judgment through reputation and creditworthiness and the consideration of mutual interest.[10]

In recent years, a number of studies have begun to consider the importance of litigation as a way to solve commercial disputes. Scholars have asserted that litigation was not as uncommon or eschewed as hitherto has been thought, particularly after a boom that began in the late sixteenth century: 'almost every man – and more women than expected – went to law in England before the eighteenth century. Civil litigation was a common, almost universal experience in some areas, and many people appeared as prosecutors of suits as well as defendants, at least above the level of the desperately poor'.[11] This observation was not only true for England and it also applied to commercial disputes. Even though friendly settlement was often attempted as a first step, merchants frequently did take each other to court. Not only do archives contain a substantial amount of commercial litigation, merchants regularly, and without much questioning, acted on each other's behalf in court, carrying power of attorney

---

10 See for instance Sebouh Aslanian, *From the Indian Ocean to the Mediterranean: The global trade networks of Armenian merchants from New Julfa* (Berkeley and New York, 2011); Tijl Vanneste, *Global trade and commercial networks: Eighteenth-century diamond merchants* (London, 2011); Xabier Lamikiz, *Trade and trust in the eighteenth-century Atlantic world: Spanish merchants and their overseas networks* (Woodbridge, 2010); Francesca Trivellato, *The familiarity of strangers: The Sephardic diaspora, Livorno, and cross-cultural trade in the early modern period* (New Haven and London, 2009); and Gunnar Dahl, *Trade, trust and networks: Commercial culture in late medieval Italy* (Lund, 1998).

11 David Lemmings, *Law and government in England during the long eighteenth century. From consent to command* (Basingstoke and New York, 2011), p. 56.

for an overseas merchant who could be more of a stranger than the party they were facing in court.[12]

A growing number of studies have started to look at court cases between traders, providing a much-needed addition to the literature on the behaviour of merchants during the early modern period. These studies, however, often focus on a particular spatial context, such as early modern France, and thus do not fully address the possibility of litigation in an international and intercultural context.[13] More recently, a collection of essays on consuls operating in the Mediterranean between the seventeenth and twentieth centuries has addressed forms of litigation adjudicated by consuls in the contexts of major port cities like Livorno, Tunis, Barcelona, Cadiz and Sicily.[14]

While a 'merchant culture' is often recognised in these studies on commercial litigation, for instance in the excellent monograph on the Parisian merchant court by Amalia Kessler, its analysis is not fully reconciled with existing discourse on trade networks. The law merchant, the reliance on trust-generating mechanisms by the merchant community and litigation before a particular court have often been researched separately from each other in historiography. This book is meant as an attempt to cross the methodological and conceptual bridge that still exists between the law merchant, trust-generating mechanisms on which international trade was founded and commercial litigation by analysing trials between litigants of different backgrounds that were adjudicated at the Dutch consular court of Izmir during the second half of the eighteenth century. The central argument is that in places with a strong intercultural commercial presence, the customs of merchants involved in international trade, combined with political agreements and several bodies of 'national' and local law, were used to resolve legal disputes that arose as a consequence of international trade. The ability to resolve such disputes relied on

12 For powers of attorney as a form of support for international trade in a Mediterranean context, see Maria Fusaro, *Political economies of empire in the early modern Mediterranean: The decline of Venice and the rise of England, 1450–1700* (Cambridge, 2015), pp. 202–203, 234–235, and 254–255. For a short history on the context of Roman law, see Reinhard Zimmermann, *The law of obligations: Roman foundations of the civilian tradition* (Oxford, 1990), pp. 53–54.

13 See for instance Julie Hardwick, *Family business: Litigation and the political economies of daily life in early modern France* (Oxford, 2009); and Amalia D. Kessler, *A revolution in commerce: The Parisian merchant court and the rise of commercial society in eighteenth-century France* (New Haven, 2007); both focusing on France.

14 See the essays in *De l'utilité commerciale des consuls. L'institution consulaire et les marchands dans le monde méditerranéen (XVIIe-Xxe siècle)*, eds. Arnaud Bartolomei, Guillaume Calafat, Mathieu Grenet, and Jörg Ulbert (Rome and Madrid, 2017). The work is available through open access at http://books.openedition.org/efr/3253.

some sort of consensus amongst traders on what constituted the merchants' style and on an agreement between consular judges on the principles determining competence and jurisdiction.

Any attempt (this book included) to reconcile these three aspects of the regulation of intercultural trade in the early modern period encounters three important obstacles. First, the scholarly debate on the law merchant has obscured the role governments played in creating a legal environment in which litigation based on the customs and usages of merchants was possible, an omission further enlarged by the realisation that early modern European states harboured a hodgepodge of local laws, regulations and statutes inherited from the Middle Ages. This has rendered research more complicated, not least in areas that had a high degree of local legal autonomy and a large number of inhabitants participating in early modern international trade, such as the United Provinces. Concepts such as the law merchant and the merchants' style can only be applied if they were embedded within more formal systems of national or local law. In other words, merchants agreed upon the use of the merchants' style, but states still had to allow for its application in courts – analysis of the legal framework created to support the consular court of Izmir shows that states indeed did allow for this application. It is thus important to consider the development of state law in Europe to discover the exact place of the merchants' style and adjudication based on its use in the legal framework, but without making the mistake of considering the merchants' style as informal and subordinate to more formal systems of state and local law.

A second obstacle has to do with the legal fragmentation that was common in early modern Europe. It makes it hard to establish which jurisdiction applied in a particular commercial dispute, especially in an international context. In the United Provinces, traders could resort to urban institutions such as aldermen courts, and from the mid-seventeenth century onwards, they could also seek recourse at specialised courts, such as the maritime courts that were established in Amsterdam, Rotterdam and Zeeland. Additionally, merchants could bring cases before provincial and state courts, such as the States General, High Council (*Hoge Raad*) or Court of Holland (*Hof van Holland*).[15]

15 For an overview of courts in the Dutch Republic, see Oscar Gelderblom, *Cities of commerce. The institutional foundations of international trade in the Low Countries, 1250–1650* (Princeton and Oxford, 2013). The States General was also the representative governmental body of the United Provinces – each of the seven provincial states had representatives in it that dealt with matters of national interest, such as defence, military matters and foreign policy. Jan de Vries and Ad van der Woude, *Nederland: De eerste ronde van moderne economische groei* (Amsterdam, 1995), p. 125.

Additionally, Dutch merchants abroad could seek recourse to their consular representatives, if they had any. This fragmentation, combined with the growing international nature of trade, complicated adjudication, as it created a need to understand the sometimes complex agreements between different political entities on jurisdiction as well as a need to assert to what extent merchants had knowledge of different jurisdictions and the ways to access them.

A third obstacle is practical, as legal archives can be difficult to navigate. Even if a researcher knows which court to look at to find commercial litigation, archival records may be lost or destroyed. Most documents of the maritime courts in Rotterdam and Amsterdam, for instance, have not been preserved. When legal archives do exist, they are often hard to navigate. Often, for instance in the archives of the *Hof van Holland*, case documents have been preserved as series of the same types of documents and not as full cases in their entirety. This makes it hard to reconstruct the paper trail of a particular dispute, especially as a number of legal archives have not been properly inventoried. The possibility of appealing a sentence at a higher court further complicates the reconstruction of a full case.

When trial documents are found, it is a time-consuming affair to analyse even a relatively small case, as a minor dispute could produce a mass of documents, interrogations, memoirs, extracts of business books and accounts that can go on for dozens of pages in (frequently) hard-to-read handwriting in three or four different languages. Historians can get lost following this paper trail, which often includes sophisticated financial transactions, with payments in currencies that no longer exist and to which it might be complicated to attribute a modern value. And even if the logic of the case, and the string of events leading up to it, can be discerned, there will almost always be documents lost that could serve to contextualise it. If power of attorney was given to someone, we hardly know why it was given to that person. If an appeal was made, it is hard to find. If judges convened to discuss an outcome of a trial, they rarely left any documents related to it behind, and although proceedings at the Dutch consular court were based on written statements, and not on physical appearance in court and oral interrogations, the verbal aspect of the legal interaction between traders who lived near one another has mostly disappeared, references to it in written documents being the exception.

The Dutch consular court of Izmir was chosen for several reasons. Izmir was an important intercultural locale and a hub for international trade that involved Dutch traders, Englishmen, Frenchmen, 'Italians', 'Greeks', Armenians, Jews and Muslim Ottomans amongst others, rendering their constant interaction a suitable laboratory to test hypotheses on the use of litigation and the law in international commerce.[16] The functioning of European-Ottoman trade relied on those customary arrangements that were characteristic of intercultural international trade in the early modern period, but it was also subject to a legal context that was necessary in order to arrange the physical settlement of non-Ottoman subjects in Ottoman territories. This legal context consisted of privileges granted through capitulations as well as additional stipulations laid out through *fermans*, which were what decrees issued by the sultan were called. Although separate capitulations were concluded between the Ottoman Empire and the different European states present in the Ottoman Empire for centuries, the principle introduced in 1740 – that privileges granted to one European power became immediately active for the other powers as well – meant that there was a legal context that applied to all European nations, who further concluded a number of arrangements to regulate relationships between one another. The combination of legal arrangements between Europeans and Ottomans, but also between Europeans and Europeans, makes the Levantine context particularly interesting in the second half of the eighteenth century.

Contrary to French and English Levant trade, Dutch Levant trade was relatively open to foreigners, which led to the high participation of non-Muslim Ottoman traders, and subsequently to a higher amount of intercultural legal disputes.[17] The Dutch, like other European nations, took foreigners under their protection, and during the eighteenth century, the Dutch consul in Izmir extended diplomatic protection to traders from the Holy Roman Empire, Tuscany, Sweden, Denmark, Russia and Poland. Amongst his legal subjects, the Dutch consul also counted several non-Muslim Ottomans who had purchased protection. This added to the diversity of the litigants that entered litigation at the Dutch consular court.

Finally, there is a practical advantage to looking at the Dutch mercantile community of Izmir. Litigation that fell under Dutch jurisdiction was adjudicated by the Dutch consul, and the legal archives of the Dutch consular court

16 'Greeks' and 'Italians' are placed between quotation marks here because at the time there were no clear Greek or Italian nation-states with Greek or Italian subjects. Both terms, however, do carry important meaning related to ethnicity, language and religion and will be used throughout the book without quotation marks. For the Greeks, see Victor Roudometof, 'From Rum millet to Greek nation: Enlightenment, secularization and national identity in Ottoman Balkan society', *Journal of modern Greek studies*, 16:1 (1998): pp. 11–48.

17 Ismail Hakkı Kadı, *Ottoman and Dutch merchants in the eighteenth century. Competition and cooperation in Ankara, Izmir, and Amsterdam* (Leiden and Boston, 2012). For an overview of Dutch Levant trade prior to the eighteenth century, see Mehmet Bulut, *Ottoman-Dutch economic relations in the early modern period 1571–1699* (Hilversum, 2001).

in Izmir have been well preserved in the National Archives in The Hague. They consist of about 200 cases, which generally were kept in their entirety.[18] These archives provide excellent primary source material on which to build a historical analysis. Next to the richness of these archives, a great deal of diplomatic correspondence between consuls and ambassadors in the Levant and political institutions in the United Provinces has also been preserved and made accessible in a publication edited by Klaas Heeringa and J.G. Nanninga between 1910 and 1966. This work is now available online and is equipped with a search engine, which provides an invaluable addition to the primary sources of the consular court.[19] In addition, historians have already done crucial work studying the Dutch presence in the Ottoman Empire. Alexander de Groot is a pioneer when it comes to work on the Dutch capitulations and the history of Ottoman-Dutch relationships.[20] Ismail Hakkı Kadı has written an important work on Ottoman and Dutch traders in the eighteenth century, while Maurits van den Boogert has analysed the legal framework surrounding the Dutch presence in the eighteenth century in detail.[21] Without the existence of this body of work, it would have been impossible to manage the current study.

Something needs to be said about the time period. The consular archives only contain cases from the second half of the eighteenth century and a few from the early nineteenth century. Nothing has been preserved about litigation in earlier periods. The legal and commercial framework that was developed around the Dutch presence in the Levant and the Ottoman Empire, however, was created in the seventeenth century. This means that the theoretical part of this book focusses on seventeenth-century developments, while the cases studies that are examined in the more empirical section of the book all date from the eighteenth century. However, this time differential is not problematic for two reasons. First, the framework that was developed in the seventeenth century was still fully applicable in the eighteenth. Second, when analysing the position of commercial custom in the realm of law, it makes sense to look at it a substantial amount of time after the theoretical framework was

18 B.J. Slot, *Inventaris van het archief van het Nederlandse Consulaat te Smyrna, (1611) 1685–1811 (1837)* (The Hague, 1988), pp. 37–55, N°s 235–259 and N°s 316–462.They do not, however, include appeals very often.

19 See footnote 2 on page 1 for the full reference.

20 Alexander H. de Groot, *The Ottoman Empire and the Dutch Republic. A history of the earliest diplomatic relations 1610–1630*, revised ed. (Leiden, 2012). See the bibliography for more references to de Groot's work.

21 Hakkı Kadı, *Ottoman and Dutch merchants*; and Maurits van den Boogert, *The capitulations and the Ottoman legal system. Qadis, consuls and beratlis in the 18th century* (Leiden and Boston, 2005).

created – because it meant the legal framework surrounding consular litigation had fully matured in practice.

This book is divided into five chapters. The first chapter discusses the development of Dutch Levant trade and the establishment of the Dutch merchant community in Izmir from the late sixteenth to the eighteenth century. Dutch trade with the Levant was mostly commission trade, based on the import of raw materials used in the textile industry at home and the export of colonial merchandise, arms and finished textiles such as sheets and linen produced in Dutch cities. This traded expanded significantly in the early seventeenth century, leading to the establishment of the first Dutch Ottoman consulate in Aleppo in present-day Syria. By the middle of the seventeenth century, Izmir had become the main trading centre for Europeans, including the Dutch, and the development of the Dutch consulate there was plagued by periodic quarrels about competence, taxes and fraud between consuls and merchants, a phase that came to an end with the arrival of the first scion of the de Hochepied family, who would provide consuls in Izmir for the whole eighteenth century. The first chapter also discusses the institutional development of the consulate in Izmir by researching the legal framework produced in the United Provinces that aimed to settle disputes between the traders and consuls there. It ends with a brief description of the Dutch trading community of Izmir.

The second chapter is concerned with the development of the adjudicating authority of the Dutch consulate in Izmir. The laws establishing this authority all came about during the seventeenth century and can be said to have originated with the first Dutch capitulations given in 1612 by Sultan Ahmed I, which included the clause on legal autonomy. Additional laws on consular litigation were issued by the States General, the Dutch governing body concerned with international affairs, following the establishment of the first consulate in Aleppo in 1612. There were no formal arrangements that settled the specific argumentation European courts in the Ottoman Empire should follow to reach a verdict, except for the procedural aspect. This was codified in the seventeenth century in a number of ordinances specifically issued to assure the good functioning of Dutch consular courts in the Levant and can be labelled as the 'formal' aspect of litigation.[22] These ordinances defined the rules of

22 Cornelis Cau, *Groot placaet-boeck vervattende de placaten, ordonnantien ende edicten vande doorluchtige, hoogh mog: heeren Staten Generael der Vereenighde Nederlanden ende vande ed: groot mog: heeren Staten van Hollandt ende West-Vrieslandt mitsgaders vande ed: mog: heeren Staten van Zeelandt waer by noch ghevoeght wijn eenige placaten vande voorgaende graven ende princen der selver landen, voor soo veel de selve als noch in gebruyck zijn* (The Hague, 1664), 2: pp. 1335–1338, 'Acte, voor den consul van Aleppo, noopende

admission of written evidence, the options available for appeal and the system of written replies and counter-replies that traders submitted in court through the chancellor, who was responsible for communicating demands made by the judges, such as requests for information, and who also informed the parties of new developments and the final verdict. These regulations came from Roman law and in general can be identified with 'summary procedure'. Both concepts will be discussed in relation to the development of commercial litigation in the Dutch context.[23]

Procedure, next to jurisdiction, was considered important, but regulations on both issues did not necessarily deal extensively with content or argumentation. Surely summary procedure was based on the use of equity and natural law, but in theory, this could be made concrete in a number of ways. I will argue that for commercial courts, in practice, this resulted in a reliance on the principles of the merchants' style. It was crucial that the actions of a litigant were held up against the manner in which merchants were accustomed to doing business, which was based on shared usages and the reciprocal protection of mutual interests. The failure to adhere to the very important principle of reciprocity was at the basis of a great deal of commercial litigation. A trader's behaviour was judged through reputation and creditworthiness, instruments that served to establish trust within a wider international merchant community.[24] When litigating, a merchant not only put his financial balance on the

de judicature, &c.', 17/02/1616. Heeringa and Nanninga, *Bronnen tot de geschiedenis*, 2: pp. 156–158, 'Resolutie der Staten-Generaal tot nederlegging der geschillen in Izmir', 24/07/1658.

23 There is an extensive bibliography on the development of summary procedure, see the references in Maria Fusaro, 'Politics of justice/politics of trade: Foreign merchants and the administration of justice from the records of Venice's *Giudici del Forestier*', *Mélanges de l'École française de Rome – Italie et Méditerranée modernes et contemporaines*, 126:1 (2014), consulted online at https://journals.openedition.org/mefrim/1665.

24 On this connection, see Craig Muldrew, *The economy of obligation: The culture of credit and social relations in early modern England* (Basingstoke, 1998); and Natasha Glaisyer, *The culture of commerce in England, 1660–1720* (London, 2006); see also Francesca Trivellato, 'Credito e cittadinanza nella republica dei mercanti visti attraverso la diaspora sefardita nell'Europa moderna', *Mélanges de l'École française de Rome: Moyen Âge*, 125:2 (2013), consulted online at https://journals.openedition.org/mefrm/1447. On reputation, see also Luuc Kooijmans, 'Risk and reputation: On the mentality of merchants in the early modern period', in *Entrepreneurs and entrepreneurship in early modern times: Merchants and industrialists within the orbit of the Dutch staple market*, eds. Clé Lesger and Leo Noordegraaf (The Hague, 1995), pp. 25–34; and Nuala Zahedieh, 'Credit, risk, and reputation in the late seventeenth-century colonial trade', in *Merchant organization and maritime trade in the north Atlantic, 1660–1815*, ed. O.U. Janzen (St John's, 1998), pp. 53–74.

line, and thus his creditworthiness, but also his reputation, which could suffer severe damage depending on the outcome of a trial.

These first two chapters are heavily focussed on seventeenth-century developments in commerce and the legislative framework. As such, they analyse the development of the context within which consular litigation became institutionalised. The remaining three chapters will look into specific case studies to analyse to what extent the merchants' style was used in the cases adjudicated by the Dutch consul in Izmir during the second half of the eighteenth century. Chapter three deals with the least complicated form of commercial litigation, that between Dutch merchants alone. While intra-Dutch litigation did not occur very often, in the instances where Dutch traders took each other to court, we can see a discourse that is heavily influenced by notions of commercial friendship and reciprocal interest. These were crucial characteristics of the merchants' style, and when traders felt that their peers violated what was common amongst traders, their argumentation in the documents they sent to court could be quite explicit and emotional.

Traders did not fundamentally change their discourse in disputes involving peers that belonged to other communities. Occasionally, a merchant tried to obtain an advantage by pointing to differences between Europeans and Ottomans, but as a rule, merchants circumscribed their legal argumentation within the discourse on what was customary amongst them. Even the consuls, who looked out for the best interests of their subjects as well as the state they represented, refused to let any argument based on nationality weigh heavily in a decision regarding a commercial dispute. Chapter four will analyse how Europeans developed informal agreements to settle jurisdictional problems. Most importantly, European consuls agreed to use the Roman legal principle of *forum rei*, which stipulated that in a dispute the competent court was the one under whose jurisdiction the defendant stood. The principle was codified by the Ottomans in the capitulations granted to the French in 1740.[25] This had been the dominant principle to determine the competent court in cases involving traders of different jurisdictions since medieval times, and it was part of a more general effort to protect merchants – the use of summary procedure being another.[26] Intra-European litigation could be complicated by the presence of European *protégés*. These were European traders established in the Ottoman Empire whose nations did not have a proper consular or ambassadorial apparatus. The extension of protection over such merchants was used

25 Van den Boogert, *The capitulations*, pp. 35–36.
26 Fusaro, 'Politics of justice/politics of trade'.

by European nations to extend their influence, and at certain times, France, England and the United Provinces all had merchants operating under their flag and protection. In the period under study, the Dutch extended protection over Genoese, Tuscan and Habsburg merchants, and several of them can be found amongst the litigants that appeared before the Dutch consul. A special position was taken by the consular adjudication in maritime disputes. Maritime laws in Europe had developed early and were the result of various regional influences. Litigants were often subject to insecure jurisdiction due to the fact that many disputes occurred on moving vessels.

The fifth and last chapter deals with disputes that involved Ottoman subjects. In theory, these had to be judged by an Ottoman court.[27] There was one important exception to this rule. Non-Muslim Ottoman subjects who had purchased protection from a European state were, for legal purposes, considered subjects of that state and could thus appear as defendants before a European court under the *forum rei* principle. They could still opt to bring their case before an Ottoman court, but this was not obligatory. An Ottoman under Dutch protection in Izmir, for instance, could choose to sue a Dutch trader at the Dutch consular court, and if he was sued by a European trader, he was allowed to stand trial at the Dutch consular court as well. The jurisdictional issues related to the practice of protection might lead to confusion, and it certainly led to protests by Europeans who felt certain Ottomans were getting the best of two worlds. The controversy surrounding this practice was further fuelled by the adherence to commercial custom, as it was considered a violation of the merchants' style to foster individual gain over the interests of others. Modern scholars have debated the possibility of traders seeking recourse to different legal systems through the concept of 'forum shopping', which could be considered an analytical instrument for looking at the legal behaviour of traders rather than an actual practice.[28]

A last remark should be made in connection to the selection of cases. With over 220 different files kept in the archives of the Dutch consulate, selection

27 Van den Boogert, *The capitulations*, pp. 42–52. Europeans were also allowed to seek justice before an Ottoman court if they wanted.

28 For a debate on this, see 'Forum shopping reconsidered', *Harvard law review*, 103:7 (1990): 1677–1696; and Markus Petsche, 'What's wrong with forum shopping? An attempt to identify and assess the real issues of a controversial practice', *The international lawyer*, 45:4 (2011): pp. 1005–1028. For the Ottoman context, see also Paolo Sartori and Ido Shahar, 'Legal pluralism in Muslim-majority colonies: Mapping the terrain', *Journal of the economic and social history of the Orient*, 55 (2012): pp. 637–663; and Cihan Artunç, 'The price of legal institutions: The *beratlı* merchants in the eighteenth-century Ottoman Empire', *Journal of economic history*, 75:3 (2015): pp. 720–748.

was necessary. An attempt has been made to find a representative sample, particularly with regards to the legal identity of the litigants – Dutch, Dutch *protégés*, Europeans and Ottomans. Several names will return in different trials, as plaintiff, defendant, expert or as holding power of attorney for someone else. These names, such as Dirk Knipping, Pieter Ouckama, Manolaki di Panaiotis and Isaac Beaune, return not only because of the selection that was made. The cohesion between cases also shows that there was a high degree of interconnectedness. This has to do with the small size of the Dutch community as well as the nature of Dutch Levant trade, which was commission trade. It meant that often, when something went wrong, Dutch traders in Izmir were held accountable by their principals elsewhere, which made them defendants at the consular court. The same applied to the Ottoman *protégés*, who increasingly became commissioners for principals in the United Provinces in their own regard.

Eighteenth-century spelling was not consistent. I have opted to preserve the original spelling of the titles of the documents. A few documents did not have titles, in which case I gave them a descriptive title in English. The sources I used from Heeringa and Nanninga's work were given an English translation within Heeringa and Nanninga's description, except when they provided an original title, in which case I used that.

This study is part of a large and international project on intercultural trade, commercial litigation and legal pluralism between the fifteenth and nineteenth centuries in the Mediterranean basin.[29] The project's main aim is to look at commercial litigation to better understand the development of intercultural trade in a world characterised by legal pluralism: 'these issues will be investigated through the comparative analysis of commercial litigation and conciliation concerning trade in Mediterranean port cities, with a focus on disputes involving litigants who were not subjects of the local authorities, or whose legal status was linked to their religious identity. Encounters between Muslim, Jewish, Armenian, Protestant merchants and sailors with different legal customs and judicial practices appear as the social sites of legal and cultural creativity'.[30] This monograph fully inscribes itself in that mission statement. It means that part of its aim is to look at the Mediterranean basin as a space of legal and commercial innovation in a context that was not simply set by Europeans, and as such, it questions the classic assumption that the growing adaptation of legal institutions to foster international trade was a European

29 Funded by the ERC and headed by Wolfgang Kaiser. More details can be found at https://configmed.hypotheses.org/.

30 As stated at https://configmed.hypotheses.org/a-propos-2.

phenomenon that allowed (western) European societies to distinguish themselves from other places that were not able to incorporate similar changes. I am fully aware that I am doing this by focusing on European interaction within an Ottoman context and on the basis of European sources. I do think, however, that the agency of non-European actors, such as the Ottoman government and Ottoman traders, still takes a prominent place in the historical analysis undertaken in this work and that this analysis is valid for an environment in which Europeans played an important part alongside others.

FIGURE 1 Relief of a *Stretsvarer* or *Straatvaarder* (a ship active in Mediterranean navigation) on the facade of a building (Oude Doelenkade 21, Hoorn, Netherlands)
PHOTO BY GOUWENAAR

CHAPTER 1

The Dutch in the Levant

1 The Early Development of Dutch Levant Trade

1.1 Straatvaart: *Dutch Navigation into the Mediterranean*

During the last decades of the sixteenth century, ships originating from the Low Countries started to transport grain to Italian ports on a regular basis. This was the beginning of the so-called *straatvaart*, Dutch for 'navigation through the Strait [of Gibraltar]' (see figure 1). This involvement was part of a larger penetration of northern European commercial operations into the Mediterranean, often dubbed 'the northern invasion'.[1] Originally, Flemish merchants were behind many of these commercial voyages, but quickly, merchants from the Northern Netherlands equally became involved. This had to do with the migration of a substantial number of merchants from the Spanish Netherlands to cities in the north following the turmoil of the Eighty Years' War. The northern provinces had formally seceded from Spain in 1581 with the Act of Abjuration and proclaimed a Dutch Republic, the United Provinces, which quickly became an economic world power and experienced a 'golden age' during the seventeenth century.[2]

---

1 For the development of Dutch Mediterranean navigation, see Wilfrid Brulez, 'La navigation flamande vers la Méditerranée à la fin du XVIe siècle', *Revue belge de philologie et d'histoire*, 36:4 (1958): pp. 1210–1242; Maartje van Gelder, 'Supplying the *Serenissima*. The role of Flemish merchants in the Venetian grain trade during the first phase of the *straatvaart*', *International journal of maritime history*, 16:2 (2004): pp. 39–60; Z.W. Sneller, 'Het begin van den Noord-Nederlandschen handel op het Middellandsche Zeegebied', *Verslag Historisch Genootschap* (1935): pp. 70–92; and J.H. Kernkamp, 'Het begin van den Noordnederlandsche scheepvaart op Italië', *Tijdschrift voor geschiedenis*, 49 (1934): pp. 70–93; see also Molly Greene, 'Beyond the northern invasion: The Mediterranean in the seventeenth century', *Past & present*, 174:1 (2002): pp. 42–71.

2 This Dutch 'golden age' has been thoroughly studied. See, for instance, Maarten Prak, *The Dutch Republic in the seventeenth century* (Cambridge, 2005); Jonathan Israel, *The Dutch Republic, its rise, greatness and fall* (Oxford, 1995); John L. Price, *Holland and the Dutch Republic in the seventeenth century: The politics of particularism* (Oxford, 1994); Simon Schama, *The embarrassment of riches: An interpretation of Dutch culture in the golden age* (New York, 1987); and J.G. van Dillen, *Van rijkdom en regenten. Handboek tot de economische en sociale geschiedenis van Nederland* (The Hague, 1970). Today, the term 'golden age' has become controversial, and rightfully so, because this was a period with a heavy human toll caused by colonialism and the slave trade.

 | DOI:10.1163/9789004498235_003

The expansion of maritime trade and shipping to all corners of Europe, and across the Atlantic and Indian Oceans, played a central role in explaining Dutch economic advance during the seventeenth century.[3] In the public eye, no enterprise exemplified that expansion more than the Dutch East India Company (VOC), but historians have also put a high emphasis on the role played by the 'mother trade', the commerce in grain with the Baltic region.[4] Much of the imported grain was used in the United Provinces, where the older environment was not well suited for grain agriculture, but it was also reexported to Italian ports beginning in the 1590s.[5] Over time, Mediterranean navigation became more fully incorporated into the Dutch maritime enterprise as a whole and evolved into a structural branch of maritime commerce.

Dutch commercial activity at sea was expanding at a time of warfare and competition. In the Mediterranean, Dutch ships not only risked attacks from Spain or from corsairs operating out of the North African ports of Tunis, Algiers and Tripoli, but they also faced competition from French and English vessels. The young Dutch Republic quickly became aware of the need for legislation aimed at protecting its merchant marine. To that purpose, the convoys and licences (*konvooien en licenten*), a tax on foreign trade, was introduced by the States General in 1582.[6] The tax was used to finance the navy, which was 'necessary to protect the merchant ships with convoys, fight the pirates and enforce the principle of free navigation at sea'.[7] Contrary to popular ideas that the decentralised Dutch navy did not work efficiently, Marjolein 't Hart has asserted that the navy was able to protect Dutch commercial interests at

3 Jonathan Israel, *Dutch primacy in world trade, 1585–1740* (Oxford, 1989).

4 For the Baltic trade, see Milja van Tielhof, *The 'mother of all trades.' The Baltic grain trade in Amsterdam from the late 16th to the early 19th century* (Leiden and Boston, 2002). For the VOC, see Femme Gaastra, *The Dutch East India Company: Expansion and decline* (Zutphen, 2003). Next to analysing the economic importance of the VOC, as well as that of its Atlantic counterpart (the West India Company or WIC), recent scholarship has focussed more on the crucial issues of slavery and colonial oppression. See, for instance, Wim Klooster, *The Dutch moment: War, trade, and settlement in the seventeenth-century Atlantic world* (Ithaca, NY, 2016); and, for the Atlantic context, Karwan Fatah-Black and Matthias van Rossum, 'Beyond profitability: The Dutch transatlantic slave trade and its economic impact', *Slavery & abolition*, 36:1 (2015): pp. 63–83; and, for the Asian context, Markus P.M. Vink, 'Freedom and slavery: The Dutch Republic, the VOC world, and the debate over the "world's oldest trade" ', *South African historical journal*, 59:1 (2007): pp. 19–46.

5 Brulez, 'La navigation flamande'; and van Gelder, 'Supplying the *Serenissima*'.

6 These were taxes on imported and exported goods, installed by the States General but collected by the five Admiralties (Amsterdam, Rotterdam, West Frisia, Zeeland and Frisia) of the navy, each in their own jurisdiction. See Israel, *Dutch primacy*, p. 280.

7 De Vries and van der Woude, *Nederland*, p. 127.

sea: 'the five Boards [of Admiralty] were nominally under the authority of the States-General but they all evolved into rather independent institutions, with strong links to local mercantile elites. The Amsterdam Admiralty soon became the most prominent. Its customs officers gathered most revenues, which were obviously connected to the size and wealth of its district and reflected the trading strength of Amsterdam'.[8] It was quickly understood that naval protection should be complemented with a number of additional regulations for merchant marine vessels. In 1596, the States of Holland issued an ordinance that introduced standards for the armament of vessels undertaking commercial voyages through the Sound, the maritime strait between Denmark and Sweden.[9] Seven years later, the States General issued the first of a series of laws dealing with 'the armament and manning of the ships, merchant vessels as well as the fisheries, sailing from the United Provinces to the sea'.[10] The ordinance also included the establishment of a convoy system. Merchant marine ships were obliged to sail as a convoy under the protection of navy ships. Additional clauses stipulated that merchant marine ships needed to carry a minimum armament and crew, depending on a ship's freight capacities.[11] A ship able to carry between 190 and 200 *last*, for instance, was obliged to sail with at least twenty-two men, three

8 Marjolein 't Hart, *The Dutch wars of independence: Warfare and commerce in the Netherlands, 1570–1680* (London and New York, 2014), p. 127. Chapter six of this work deals with the early development of the Dutch navy and its role in protecting commercial interests (pp. 126–147).

9 National Archives The Hague (hereafter NA), 3.01.04.01 (Archief van de Staten van Holland en West-Friesland, 1572–1795), N°1357OO ('Ordonnantie van de Admiraal- Generaal en de Staten van Holland ter beveiliging van de handelsscheepvaart op het Oosten en de Sont', 1596).

10 *Nederlandtsche placcaet-boeck: Waerinne alle voornaemste placcaten, ordonnantien, accorden, ende andere acten ende munimenten, uyt-ghegeven by de EE. hoog-mogende heeren Staten Generael der Vereenigde Nederlantsche provintien; Sedert dat Philippus II. koninck van Spagnien eerst verclaert is, vervallen te wesen vande hoogh-overigheyt deser landen, in't jaer 1581, tot op den teghenwoordighen jaere 1644* (Amsterdam, 1644), 1: pp. 292–300, 'Placcaet ende ordonnantie, op de wapeninghe ende manninge van de schepen, soo ter koopvaerdye als visscherye uyt de Vereenighde Nederlanden over zee varende, midtsgaders op de ordre van de Admiraelschappen ende 't beleydt van dien, met het gene daer aen dependeert', 09/04/1603. This regulation was reissued on several occasions (23/02/1607, 22/07/1625, 16/01/1627, 17/03/1627, 20/10/1628, 19/03/1629, 24/12/1630 and 11/03/1632), with some slight modifications from time to time.

11 See, for instance, *Nederlandtsche placcaet-boeck*, 1: pp. 426–429, 'Ordre, by de hoogh-mogende heeren Staten Generael der Vereenighde Nederlanden, gemaeckt op het bevaren van de Middellantschse Zee, ende het zout-halen in West-Indien', 27/10/1621. The Dutch convoy system was even popular among non-Dutch skippers. See, for instance, NA, N°1.01.02, 'Archief van de Staten-Generaal, (1431) 1576–1796' (hereafter NASG), N°12561.151.4 ('Stukken betreffende het verlenen van convooi aan Hamburgse schepen varende op de Middellandse Zee, 1664'), which contains material concerning the assistance given by Dutch warships to merchantmen sailing to the Mediterranean under the

boys and sixteen cannons, as well as muskets and pikes.[12] The commercial routes that were mentioned included Norway and the Baltic, France, the East and West Indies, Guinea and the Mediterranean.[13]

Initially, vessels sailing through the Strait of Gibraltar were exempt from the convoy system. Dutch Mediterranean navigation was still in its infancy and relatively small in comparison to the fleet of herring fishermen or the merchantmen sailing to Scandinavia and the Baltic. The Twelve Years' Truce (1609–1621) between Spain and the United Provinces proved to be very beneficial for the development of Dutch navigation in the Mediterranean. The truce led to the lifting of Spanish embargoes against the Dutch, who managed to acquire an important piece of the carrying trade between Spain and Italy. Dutch vessels shipped wool and salt to Genoa, Livorno and Venice and became the most important carriers of salt from Valencia to Italy, and of grain from Sicily and Puglia to eastern Spain.[14] Amsterdam was becoming a staple market for Asian pepper and spices, and Dutch skippers increasingly exported these commodities to places such as Genoa, Livorno and ports in the Levant, successfully competing with English, Venetian and Genoese merchants and ship owners.[15]

Hamburg flag; see also Arie Bijl, *De Nederlandse convooidienst. De maritieme bescherming van koopvaardij en zeevisserij tegen piraten en oorlogsgevaar in het verleden* (The Hague, 1951).

12 One *last* was about 2,000 kilos. On the average volume of Mediterranean shipping, see Tijl Vanneste, 'Sailing through the straits: Seamen's professional trajectories from a segmented labour market in Holland into a fragmented Mediterranean', in *Labour, law, and empire: Comparative perspectives on seafarers, c. 1500–1800*, eds. Maria Fusaro, Bernard Allaire, Richard Blakemore, and Tijl Vanneste (Basingstoke, 2015), pp. 123–140.

13 *Nederlandtsche placcaet-boeck*, 1: pp. 292–300, 'Placcaet ende ordonnantie', 09/04/1603.

14 Israel, *Dutch primacy*, p. 97.

15 Ibid. Part of that success stemmed from lower Dutch freight charges. The war with Spain influenced the growth rate of Dutch commercial expansion, but historians do not fully agree on a timeline. Jonathan Israel provided an alternative narrative about Dutch economic growth during the war with Spain that was contended by Dutch historians such as Jan Luiten van Zanden and Leo Noordegraaf. Israel asserted that, contrary to common opinion, the period between 1621 and 1647 was a low point, partly owing to the end of the truce between the Republic and Spain, while the phase that followed, between 1647 and 1672, was the zenith of economic prosperity. Israel, *Dutch primacy*. For the criticisms, see Jan Luiten van Zanden, 'Een fraaie synthese op een wankele basis', BMGN – *Low Countries historical review*, 106:3 (1991): pp. 451–457; and Leo Noordegraaf, 'Vooruit en achteruit in de handelsgeschiedenis van de Republiek', BMGN – *Low Countries historical review*, 106:3 (1991): pp. 458–468. For Israel's reply, see Jonathan Israel, 'The "new history" versus "traditional history" in interpreting Dutch world trade primacy', BMGN – *Low Countries historical review*, 106:3 (1991): pp. 469–479. For a debate on the different phases of Dutch Mediterranean navigation during the early modern period, see Jonathan Israel, 'The phases of the Dutch straatvaart (1590–1713): A chapter in the economic history of the

Throughout the seventeenth century, Dutch ships also managed to obtain a higher share in intra-Mediterranean trade. Technological innovation, such as the *fluyt* ship, allowed the Dutch to ship at a lower cost than many of their competitors, and they increasingly acted as transport carriers for commercial journeys between Mediterranean cities, at the expense of Genoese, Greek and Venetian vessels.[16] These growing private successes in such an international and competitive region were recognised by the States General, which now granted their full support. Immediately after the resumption of hostilities with Spain in 1621, a new set of directives was issued that specifically aimed at regulating Dutch commercial navigation in the Mediterranean. Danger not only came from Spain but also from the North African corsairs, who wanted 'to rob the same good inhabitants [trading through the Strait of Gibraltar to the lands adjacent to the Mediterranean Sea in the Levant and the archipelago] of all commerce and traffic at sea, and to kill them, take their goods and make them bleed'.[17] The States General published a regulation instructing all ships leaving the United Provinces to register their cargos. Skippers who intended not to sail through the strait had to issue an explicit declaration confirming their destination.[18] Ships who did intend to sail into the Mediterranean were now also subject to the convoy system. The Boards of Admiralty were ordered to supply six well-armed warships, each at least 200 *lasts* in size, to assist strait-bound convoys composed of thirty to forty merchant vessels. Specific assembly points were stipulated, and skippers had to swear an oath with which they promised to fight the enemy when the convoy commanders asked them to do so.[19] From this moment onwards, private maritime enterprise through the

Mediterranean', *Tijdschrift voor geschiedenis* (1986): pp. 1–30. An analysis of Israel's division, in which his reliance on political events is questioned, is provided by P.C. van Royen, 'The first phase of Dutch straatvaart (1591–1605): Fact and fiction', *International journal of maritime history*, 2 (1990): pp. 69–102.

16 Marie-Christine Engels, *Merchants, interlopers, seamen and corsairs. The 'Flemish' community in Livorno and Genoa (1615–1635)* (Hilversum, 1997), pp. 118–119; and Jessica V. Roitman, *The same but different? Inter-cultural trade and the Sephardim, 1595–1640* (Leiden and Boston, 2011), p. 187. For the link between transport costs and intra-Mediterranean coastal trade, see de Vries and van der Woude, *Nederland*, pp. 447.

17 *Nederlandtsche placcaet-boeck*, 1: pp. 424–426, 'Placcaet, inhoudende verbodt dat niemandt varen en magh door de Strate van Gibraltar ofte near de zout-vaert, anders als in Admiraelschap, ende met convoy: Uytgegeven by de hoogh-mogende heeren Staten Generael der Vereenighde Nederlanden', 27/10/1621, on p. 425, '[...] omme deselve goede inghesetenen van alle commercien ende trafficque ter zee te berooven, ende deselve om lijf, goedt, ende bloedt te brenghen [...]'.

18 Ibid.

19 Evidence for the constant negotiating process between cities with regard to their national responsibilities, as well as Amsterdam's dominant role, can be found in the stipulation

Strait of Gibraltar was regulated by the States General. Dutch navigation into the Mediterranean became a matter of 'national interest', although the cities continued to play their role.[20]

1.2 *The Directorate of Levant Trade and European Competition*

The successes of the Dutch *straatvaart* led to expansion into the eastern Mediterranean, and Dutch vessels started to arrive with more regularity in ports in the Levant. Institutionally, this commercial expansion had two important consequences. First, the Dutch presence in the eastern Mediterranean warranted the establishment of diplomatic ties with the Ottoman Empire. An additional need for such ties was the growing presence of Dutch seamen amongst the Christian captives of corsairs from the North African city states, which formally fell under Ottoman control. Discussing terms of liberation for Christian captives was an essential part of the missions given to early Dutch envoys to Morocco and the Ottoman Empire. A second was the negotiation of military assistance in the fight against a common enemy – Spain.[21] In earlier years, attempts had been made to form an anti-Spanish alliance between the Ottoman Empire, the United Provinces and Morocco.[22] A Dutch envoy,

that the Admiralties of Westfrisia (Enkhuizen, Medemblik and Hoorn), Rotterdam and Zeeland each had to contribute one ship, while Amsterdam had to provide three. *Nederlandtsche placcaet-boeck*, 1: 426–429, 'Ordre, by de hoogh-mogende heeren Staten Generael', 27/10/1621. The text of the oath can be found on pp. 430–431.

20 The legislation concerned with maritime protection mentioned in the previous footnotes persistently labelled fraud in the payment of taxes that covered maritime protection and infractions against armament and crew size regulations as harmful to the 'national good'.

21 De Groot, *The Ottoman Empire*, pp. 55–58.

22 There was Dutch agent in Morocco, Pieter Coy, between 1605 and 1609 (in 1625 he was sent to Algiers). Coy had to promote Dutch trade and shipping as well as negotiate for the liberation of Dutch Christian captives. Otto Schutte, *Repertorium der Nederlandse vertegenwoordigers residerende in het buitenland 1584–1810* (The Hague, 1976), p. 381. This work provides a complete overview of Dutch diplomatic representation abroad until the first decade of the nineteenth century. Negotiations between Morocco and the Dutch took place through the involvement of Samuel Pallache, Morocco's Jewish agent residing in The Hague. See Otto Schutte, *Repertorium der buitenlandse vertegenwoordigers, residerende in Nederland 1584–1810* (The Hague, 1983), pp. 579–580. This work contains biographical information on diplomatic representatives of foreign rulers until the first decade of the nineteenth century and is the complement to Schutte's earlier publication on Dutch representatives abroad that was previously mentioned. For an analysis of the attempted military alliance, see Klaas Heeringa, 'Een bondgenootschap tussen Nederland en Marokko', *Onze eeuw*, 7:3 (1907): pp. 81–119. A recent biography of Pallache by Mercedes García-Arenal and Gerard Wiegers, *Samuel Pallache. Koopman, kaper en diplomaat tussen Marrakesh en Amsterdam* (Amsterdam, 2014) discusses the military alliance talks as

Cornelis Haga, was sent to Istanbul; he arrived in 1612 to negotiate a peace treaty with the sultan.[23]

Plans for a concrete alliance never resulted in a military partnership, but Haga quickly manage to befriend Grand Admiral Halil Pasha, which contributed to the rapid conclusion of an Ottoman-Dutch treaty only four months after Haga's arrival in the Ottoman capital. The treaty resulted in the establishment of the first Dutch capitulations, which arranged Dutch presence in the Ottoman Empire, following existing capitulations given to the French, English and Venetians.[24]

By the time of Haga's mission, the Dutch had already established a consular outpost in Syria, in Aleppo, to protect the interests of traders there, but Dutch Levant merchants made the need for the further institutionalisation of their commercial activities clear in advice to the States General and the provincial States, leading to further institutional innovation. In 1625, Amsterdam merchants successfully petitioned their burgomasters to install a Directorate of Levant Trade.[25] The directorate was not a company but a supervisory board of merchants, called into existence with the support of the Dutch ambassador in Istanbul, Cornelis Haga. Its main functions were to supervise ships' compliance with all existing legislation that regulated Mediterranean navigation, to control collection of maritime taxes, to verify ships' papers and to maintain correspondence with the Dutch ambassador in Istanbul and the consuls in the Levant and North Africa.[26] The Directorate of Levant Trade also played an

---

well, particularly on pp. 135–138 and 156–157; see also Hans Theunissen, ed., *Topkapi & turkomanie. Turks-Nederlandse ontmoetingen sinds 1600* (Amsterdam, 1989).

23 For a detailed description of the choice of Cornelis Haga, a diplomat with a law degree from Leiden University and son of rich parents originating from Schiedam, see de Groot, *The Ottoman Empire*, pp. 57–113. After his mission as envoy ended, Haga became the first Dutch ambassador in Istanbul, a function he occupied until 1639, when he returned to the United Provinces. For an overview of his tenure, see ibid., pp. 114–127. A recommendable recent biography of Cornelis Haga is Ingrid van der Vlis and Hans van der Sloot, *Cornelis Haga 1578–1654. Pionier en diplomaat in Constantinopel* (Amsterdam, 2012).

24 The capitulations are discussed in detail on pp. 28–39.

25 The burgomasters (*burgemeesters*) were the most influential magistrates in Amsterdam's governing body, the *vroedschap*, the thirty-six members of which came from the city's ruling elite, the so-called regent families. See Julia Lindemann, 'Dirty politics or "harmonie"? Defining corruption in early modern Amsterdam and Hamburg', *Journal of social history*, 45:3 (2012): pp. 586–588.

26 A copy of the original act establishing the Directorate of Levant Trade on 25 June 1625 can be found in the archives of the Directorate; NA, 1.03.01, 'Archief van de Directie van de Levantse Handel en de Navigatie in de Middellandse Zee, (1614) 1625–1826 (1828)' (hereafter NALH), 'Directie Amsterdam', N°86 ('Nominatieboek', 1625–1800), on the first six folios. On the history and functioning of the directorate, see also Heeringa and Nanninga, *Bronnen tot de geschiedenis*, 2: pp. 1–107.

important role in setting up the playing field for Dutch consuls; it 'drew up lists of nominees for consular appointments, set the consuls' salaries and drafted their instructions', while the final political responsibility for the consulates remained with the States General.[27]

Initially, there was only a directorate in Amsterdam, consisting of seven directors, all important Levant traders chosen by the burgomasters. Some of them were replaced on a yearly basis, but others stayed on for several years.[28] In 1644, a separate directorate was established in Hoorn, followed by new directorates in Rotterdam (1674) and Middelburg (1696). In 1668, the Amsterdam directorate had accepted the inclusion of one merchant from Leiden, as that city maintained an important cloth trade with Izmir.[29] The directors of each directorate met once a week, and once a year they all met in a general meeting. Besides their administrative and fiscal functions, the Directorate of Levant Trade also petitioned Dutch governmental bodies about the development of Levant trade. The States General often required their assistance and advice on all matters pertaining to navigational, commercial and political matters in the eastern Mediterranean, and the directorates also cooperated with the Admiralty Boards in matters of naval protection. In addition to the directors, the Directorate of Levant Trade engaged a number of civil servants. In 1749, for instance, documentation shows that the Amsterdam Directorate of Levant Trade employed a secretary, a tax collector, an appraiser and a clerk.[30]

The expenses of the Directorate of Levant Trade were funded by several taxes levied directly on shipping. The first was the *lastgeld*, a weight-based tax paid by each Dutch ship setting out to sail through the Strait of Gibraltar. It was set at sixteen pennies per *last* of cargo space, with two-thirds of the amount provided by the cargo owners and one-third by the ship's owners. Later, foreign vessels leaving Dutch ports were also subject to the tax, which was raised to twenty pennies.[31] A second tax, the *vrachtgeld*, was established in 1671. It was

---

27 Albert E. Kersten and Bert van der Zwan, 'The Dutch consular service: In the interests of a colonial and commercialised nation', in *Consular affairs and diplomacy*, eds. Jan Melissen and Ana Mar Fernández (Leiden, 2011), p. 277.

28 NALH, 'Directie Amsterdam', N°1 ('Resolutieboek', 04/10/1627–21/12/1663).

29 A.H.H. van der Burgh, *Inventaris van het archief van de Directie van de Levantse Handel en de Navigatie in de Middellandse Zee, (1614) 1625–1826 (1828)* (The Hague, 1882), pp. 18–20.

30 Hakkı Kadı, *Ottoman and Dutch merchants*, p. 155.

31 These taxes, based on the size of ships, were called 'lastgelden'. *Nederlandtsche placcaetboeck*, 2: pp. 13–17, 'Placcaet, ende ordonnantie vande hooge ende moghende heeren Staten Generael der Vereenighde Nederlanden, waer near de inghesetenen vande selve landen, varende near westen, door de Strate, ofte Engte van Gibeltar, om te negotieren op Levante, ende op de rijcken vanden grooten heere tot Constantinopolen, ofte mede binnen de voorsz. Strate, op Vranckrijck, ende Italien, hen sullen hebben te reguleren, ten

a levy of 5% on the value of all goods that arrived in Dutch ports from Izmir, and later also from other places in the Levant. Originally it only applied to Dutch ships, but in 1770, it was extended to include foreign vessels.[32] During the eighteenth century, a third tax existed, the *tanza*, or *levantrecht*. A decree by the States General issued in 1749 fixed this tax at 1.5% on Levantine goods arriving in all ports of the United Provinces under any flag.[33] These taxes were used as means of pressure in political conflict between cities. In 1630 and 1631, for instance, the city of Hoorn refused to pay the *lastgelden* unless their merchants would also receive a seat in the Directorate of Levant Trade, a demand that was met by the States General in 1633.[34]

---

regarde van hare zee-brieven, betalinghe van last-gelden, ende andersints', 24/06/1625. The tax receivers of the Admiralty colleges already collected the convoys and licenses tax (see p. 18); see also W.F.H. Oldewelt, *De oudste lastgeldrekening van Directeuren van de Levantse handel (1625–1631)* (Amsterdam, 1958).

32 Van der Burgh, *Inventaris*, pp. 21–23.

33 Hakkı Kadı, *Ottoman and Dutch merchants*, p. 156. Originally, the *tanza* had been raised on goods arriving in Dutch ports from Syrian Aleppo and Cyprus to cover the expenses of the consulates there. See Engels, *Merchants, interlopers*, p. 70. During the seventeenth century, it was used as a temporary tax on goods to cover a number of extraordinary expenses, such as the compensation demanded by the sultan after the Dutch vessel *Keizer Octavianus* had been taken by Christian corsairs in 1662, which caused a loss of cargo belonging to Ottoman traders. The demanded amount of 78,445 lion dollars was financed by a *tanza* of 1% on all goods shipped on Dutch vessels sailing from and to the Levant. NALH, 'Directie Amsterdam', N°238 ('Diverse stukken'), 'Extract resolutieboek vroedschap', f°45, 16/10/1663; see also the set of documents in NALH, 'Directie Amsterdam', N°238 ('Diverse stukken'), 'Stukken betreffende het geschil tussen de Admiraliteit te Amsterdam en de Directie over een schuld van ruim 37.000 gulden in het jaar 1633 door de ontvanger Hoefijser aangegaan', 1668–1669. The tax was levied for several years and caused friction between several directorates and admiralties. It even led to a discussion on urban competition and the difference between commercial navigation and commerce in the work of one of Holland's foremost early modern thinkers, Pieter de la Court, *Aanwysing der heilsame politike gronden en maximen van de Republike van Holland en West-Vriesland* (Leiden and Rotterdam, 1669), pp. 122–126. The *leeuwendaalder* (in English 'lion dollar') was a silver currency that was very popular in the Levant and often used by Dutch merchants to settle the balance of trade. See Ton Kappelhof, *Dukaten, daalders en duiten – Een geschiedenis van het geld* (Zwolle, 2006), pp. 34–35. New coins were no longer issued after 1712, and it was worth forty-two pennies of the Holland guilder. Willlem Sewel and Egbert Buys, *Volkomen woordenboek der Nederduitsche en Engelse talen; Névens eene spraak-konst van dezelven/A compleat dictionary Dutch and English to which is added a grammar, for both languages*, 4th ed. (Amsterdam, 1766 [1691]), 2: p. 443.

34 NALH, 'Directie Amsterdam', N°1, pp. 52–53, 68; and N°73 ('Remonstrantieboek', 1627–1649), pp. 94, 102–103, and 125. Hoorn, in West Frisia, was an important city in the *straatvaart*. See Hermann Wätjen, *Die Niederländer in Mittelmeergebiet zur Zeit ihren hochsten Machtstellung* (Berlin, 1909), p. 114.

It seems that the decentralised nature of the Dutch state helped Dutch commercial expansion in the Levant: 'the normal business environment in the Levant was not one where uniform policies [...] closely coordinated and controlled from central command in northern Europe, could hold sway [...]'.[35] That did not mean, however, that all the other European states with whom the Dutch competed adopted similar policies.[36] In 1569, the French had become the first western European power to obtain capitulations from the Ottoman sultan.[37] Merchants operating out of Marseille had obtained a quasi-monopolistic position in French Levant trade through the Chamber of Commerce, and after 1660, Louis XIV established firm control of the French Mediterranean port. The Marseille traders sent their representatives to important Levantine scales where they were supported by the French diplomatic network.[38] In this way they managed to expand their activities at the expense of other European nations, and by the 1750s, Marseille traders controlled over 60% of the volume of European Levant trade.[39]

The other important western European state to compete with the Dutch in the Levant was England.[40] The Levant Company was established in London in 1592 as the fusion of two older companies trading with the Mediterranean, the Venetian Company and the Turkey Company. Merchants who purchased membership to the company were allowed to act as independent traders, but nobody outside the company was allowed to trade directly with the Levant,

35 Rhoads Murphey, 'Merchants, nations, and free-agency: An attempt at a qualitative characterization of trade in the eastern Mediterranean, 1620–1640', in *Friends and rivals in the east. Studies in Anglo-Dutch relations in the Levant from the seventeenth to the early nineteenth century*, eds. A. Hamilton, A.H. de Groot, and M.H. van den Boogert (Leiden and Boston, 2000), p. 53.

36 For a general overview of the different efforts made by various European states in the Levant, see Alexander H. de Groot, 'The organization of western European trade in the Levant, 1500–1800', in *Companies and trade. Essays on overseas trading companies during the Ancien Régime*, eds. L. Blussé and F. Gaastra (Leiden, 1981), pp. 231–241.

37 These will be discussed in more detail on pp. 32–34.

38 For the establishment of Marseille as the centre of French trading activities with the eastern Mediterranean, see Juno T. Takeda, *Between crown & commerce: Marseille and the early modern Mediterranean* (Baltimore, 2011).

39 Edhem Eldem, 'French trade and commercial policy in the Levant in the eighteenth century', *Oriente moderno*, nuova serie, 18:1 (1999): pp. 27–47; see also Joseph Billioud and Raymond Collier, *Histoire du commerce de Marseille: de 1480 à 1599*, vol. 3 of *Histoire du commerce de Marseille*, ed. Gaston Rambert (Paris, 1951).

40 Already fierce enemies at sea for regular intervals during the three Anglo-Dutch wars of the seventeenth century, the English and the Dutch battled for Levantine primacy as well. See Jonathan Israel, 'Trade, politics and strategy: The Anglo-Dutch wars in the Levant (1647–1675)', in *Friends and rivals*, eds. Hamilton et al., pp. 11–23.

creating a monopoly for the group of mainly London-based traders who were its members.[41] Perhaps the main victim of the western European institutionalisation of their commercial operations in the Levant was Venice, which had long been a dominant factor in the eastern Mediterranean.[42]

The French and English Levant trades relied on centralisation and the establishment of monopolies, particularly successful in the French case, but the Dutch 'were the only nation among the major western European trade partners of the Ottoman Empire who pursued free trade policies in the Levant'.[43] This is a very important consideration, as it was the main cause behind the high participation of non-Muslim Ottoman traders in commerce between the United Provinces and the Levant. It also meant that, initially, trading communities of Dutch merchants were able to develop independently, without much interference from political institutions at home. Dutch communities had been established across the Mediterranean in Venice, Livorno, Genoa, Izmir and Syrian Aleppo. They all had developed with a certain degree of autonomy before requesting the States General for a formal diplomatic presence to better regulate Dutch trade.[44] Autonomy always remained an important feature of Dutch commercial communities abroad, in parallel to the political

41 See Fusaro, *Political economies*, particularly pp. 48–51 for the Venice and Turkey Companies, as well as pp. 64–88 for the Ottoman Levant; see also Despina Vlami, *Trading with the Ottomans. The Levant Company in the Middle East* (London and New York, 2014); Alfred C. Wood, *A history of the Levant Company* (Oxford, 1935); and Mortimer Epstein, *The early history of the Levant Company* (London, 1908). For a more general discussion of England's trading operations at the time, see Robert Brenner, *Merchants and revolution. Commercial change, political conflict, and London's overseas traders, 1550–1653* (Princeton, 1993); and David Ormrod, *The rise of commercial empires: England and the Netherlands in the age of mercantilism, 1650–1770* (Cambridge, 2008).

42 For an excellent analysis of this evolution, see Fusaro, *Political economies*; see also Suraiya Faroqhi, 'The Venetian presence in the Ottoman Empire (1600–1630)', *Journal of European economic history*, 15 (1986): pp. 345–384. For the competition between the English and the Dutch in eighteenth-century Izmir, see Elena Frangakis-Syrett, 'Commercial practices and competition in the Levant. The British and the Dutch in eighteenth-century Izmir', in *Friends and rivals*, eds. Hamilton et al., pp. 135–158.

43 Hakkı Kadı, *Ottoman and Dutch merchants*, p. 154.

44 For Venice, see van Gelder, *Trading places*; and Daniel Koster, *The conquering Dutch merchants and shipowners* (Venice, 2006). For Livorno and Genoa, see Engels, *Merchants, interlopers*; and 'Dutch traders in Livorno at the beginning of the seventeenth century. The company of Joris Jansen and Bernard van den Broecke', in *Entrepreneurs and entrepreneurship in early modern times. Merchants and industrialists within the orbit of the Dutch staple market*, eds. C. Lesger and L. Noordegraaf (The Hague, 1995), pp. 63–76. Not much scholarship exists for Izmir, the exception is Jan Willem Samberg, *De Hollandsche gereformeerde gemeente* (Leiden, 1928).

autonomy that existed in the United Provinces as well. Policies in the Levant were often discussed with the Directorate of Levant Trade, which meant that the functioning of Levant trade continued to receive strong impulses from the cities – Amsterdam first of all – even when Dutch commercial enterprise in the Levant, the Mediterranean and the Ottoman Empire became a matter of 'national interest'. The inheritance of local autonomy at times clashed with the efforts of Dutch institutional control, which was in any case divided by the urban institutions of the Directorate of Levant Trade and the national institution of the States General.

2 The Dutch Levantine Institutional Context

2.1 *A Short History of the European Capitulations*

With the establishment of the Directorate of Levant Trade, Levant trade was as regulated as it would ever be in the United Provinces. The establishment of a second institutional framework in the Levant was more important, but also more complicated. Throughout the early modern period, the legal, political and administrative context in which the Dutch and other European trading communities operated was created and controlled by the Ottoman Empire.[45] All European trading communities that wished to settle in an Ottoman city needed to obtain permission from the sultan. The continuous physical presence of Dutch traders on Ottoman soil was a privilege allowed by the Porte, and it was regulated on the basis of periodically renewed treaties that were called 'capitulations', or *ahdname*s. They provided a crucial part of the legal context within which these communities were permitted to operate and allowed for Dutch diplomatic representation to be established in the places where Dutch traders were active.

The capitulations applied to all members of the trading nation to whom they had been granted and were supplemented by additional legislation issued through *ferman*s, the sultanic decrees. These two, together with a third type of legal document called the *berat*, formed the written corpus that institutionalised the European presence in the Ottoman territories. Different from the capitulations, which were collective, and the *fermans*, which addressed particular issues, *berat*s were individual deeds of appointment to a position and were necessary for everyone who wanted to hold a bureaucratic position, Ottomans as well as Europeans. They described the authority and responsibility that

45 Van den Boogert, *The capitulations*, pp. 26–29.

came with the function and formed an official authorisation from the sultan for that person to take up the position for which the *berat* had been drafted.[46] Without these *berats*, European diplomats could not function in the Ottoman Empire, as their domestic appointments alone, in the Dutch case by the States General, were not considered sufficient by the Porte. Ottomans working for Europeans, such as interpreters, who were called 'dragomans', also needed a *berat*.[47]

But European employment was not the only reason an Ottoman subject might need a *berat*. The document also needed to be drafted for non-Muslim Ottomans who had purchased European legal protection.[48] These men were sometimes referred to as *beratlıs* (holders of a *berat*) but were also called *protégés* or 'honorary dragomans'. Only non-Muslim Ottoman subjects, particularly Jews, Greeks and Armenians qualified for protection status, and the title of honorary dragoman referred to the origins of the practice, which had grown out of the possibility of European diplomats hiring non-Muslim Ottomans as interpreters, or dragomans, who became then attached to European embassies and consulates in the Ottoman Empire. Dragomans enjoyed a number of privileges, which were described in the capitulations, such as tax exemption. Over

46 Bülent Arı, 'Early Ottoman diplomacy: Ad hoc period', in *Ottoman diplomacy: Conventional or unconventional?*, ed. A. Yuri Nurdusev (Basingstoke and New York, 2004), p. 41.

47 Dragomans were mediators, and as official interpreters, all European embassies and consulates had a number of them in their employment. See E. Nathalie Rothman, *The dragoman renaissance. Diplomatic interpreters and the routes of Orientalism* (Ithaca, NY, 2021); Éva Á. Csató, Bernt Brendemoen, Lars Johanson, Claudia Römer, and Heidi Stein, 'The linguistic landscape of Istanbul in the seventeenth century', in *The urban mind. Cultural and environmental dynamics*, eds. Paul J.J. Sinclair, Gullög Nordquist, Frands Herschend, and Christian Isendahl (Uppsala, 2010), pp. 415–439; E. Nathalie Rothman, 'Interpreting dragomans: Boundaries and crossings in the early modern Mediterranean', *Comparative studies in society and history*, 51:4 (2009): pp. 771–800; Alexander H. de Groot, 'Die levantischen Dragomanen. Einheimische und Fremde im eigenen Land. Kultur- und Sprachgrenzen zwischen Ost und West (1453–1914)', in *Verstehen und Verständigung: Ethnologie, Xenologie, Interkulturelle Philosophie*, ed. Wolfdietrich Schmied-Kowarzik (Würzburg, 2001), pp. 110–127; Frédéric Hitzel, ed., *Enfants de langue et drogmans* (Istanbul, 1995); and Alexander H. de Groot, 'Dragomans' careers: Change of status in some families connected with the British and Dutch embassies in Istanbul (1785–1829)', in *Friends and rivals*, eds. Hamilton et al., pp. 223–246. The position of dragoman came with certain privileges, and several families managed to make the position hereditary, creating dragoman dynasties.

48 Van den Boogert, *The capitulations*, pp. 25–26. For a French translation of such a *berat* given to Consul Haanwinkel in Aleppo in 1753, see Heeringa and Nanninga, *Bronnen tot de geschiedenis*, 3: pp. 249–251, 'Traduction du barat ou brevet imperial, que la Sublime Porte a accordé en faveur de mr le consul d'Alep Hannewinkel vers le 11 janv. 1753'. In the text, several of the capitulatory articles, which dealt with the consul's specific privileges, as well as his responsibilities, were repeated.

time, what had begun as employment developed into a status as *protégé* of a particular European state, bought by those interested in using the privileges attached to it.[49]

Initially, the capitulations had come into being for the benefit of southern European traders, who had become increasingly involved in Europe's trade with the Levant, even before the Ottoman conquest of Constantinople.[50] As early as 1082, the Byzantine emperor Alexius I Comenus had given the Venetians certain privileges, which included tax exemptions, right of Latin worship and Venetian jurisdiction over a Venetian quarter, including the establishment of judges who adjudicated in cases where Venetians were defendants.[51] Commercial relationships, and the diplomatic connections enabling these relationships, had been expanding since the Middle Ages, with a growing number of transactions taking place with merchants in Muslim territories. Both the import of European cloths and linen into the Muslim Levant and the export of Oriental textiles to Europe continued throughout the fourteenth century, with the heavy involvement of Catalan, Venetian and Genoese traders.[52] These three trading nations competed with one another, and Venice came out as the dominant European commercial actor in the eastern Mediterranean, including the Levant, during the first decades of the fifteenth century.[53] The expansion of the Ottoman Empire and the conquest of Constantinople in 1453 fundamentally altered Levant trade, leading European traders to forge stronger commercial ties with the Mamluk sultanate in present-day Egypt. At the same time, European diplomatic missions to the Porte attempted to obtain guarantees allowing European trading communities to continue their activities as before. Supplementing their treaties with Byzantium, Venice concluded a number of important peace treaties with the Ottomans in 1446, 1451 and 1454, all dealing with matters of territorial claims between the two and

49 For the *beratlıs*, see pp. 61–64. Litigation involving them will be discussed in chapter five.

50 For the long relationship between Venice and Byzantium, see S. Borsari, *Venezia e Bisanzio nel XII secolo: I rapporti economici* (Venice, 1988); and Donald M. Nicol, *Byzantium and Venice: A study in diplomatic and cultural relations* (Cambridge, 1988).

51 Marco Pozza and Giorgio Ravegnani, *I trattati con Bisanzio, 992–1198* (Venice, 1993), pp. 35–45.

52 Eliyahu Ashtor, *Levant trade in the Middle Ages* (Princeton, 1984), pp. 200–216. For a study of the early Venetian treaties, with translations of the capitulations between 1482 and 1641, see Hans Theunissen, 'Ottoman-Venetian diplomatics: The *'ahd-names*. The historical background and the development of a category of political-commercial instruments together with an annotated edition of a corpus of relevant documents', 2 vols. (unpublished PhD thesis, University of Utrecht, 1991).

53 Ashtor, *Levant trade*, pp. 216–269.

tribute payments.[54] The peace treaty that was made between Sultan Mehmed II and Venice in 1479 was crucial, as it not only settled frontier disputes but also allowed the Venetians exemption from certain customs duties. Additionally, it also gave them the right to appoint a *bailo*[55] in Istanbul, who was to hold internal jurisdiction over the entire Venetian trading community in the Ottoman Empire. Venice was also allowed to extend their protection to foreigners trading under the Venetian flag.[56] Most of these privileges – tax exemption, internal jurisdiction and the extension of protection – were to become standard in all future European capitulations, although the 1479 text was essentially still a peace treaty.

The privileges established in this treaty were confirmed in 1482, when Bayazid II rose to the throne. Renewal of treaties following the ascension of a new Ottoman sultan also became commonplace for the European capitulations. Bayazid II's agreement with the Venetians was more extensive, no longer a peace treaty, which is why Alexander de Groot has referred to it as the first set of capitulations (or *ahdnames*) in the proper sense – a document in which the Ottoman sultan grants fiscal, legal and commercial privileges to a European trading nation.[57] In 1513, Selīm I renewed the Venetian capitulations, which now included Venetian exemption from the poll tax, the *cizye* (or *haraç*),

54 Ibid., pp. 445–449.

55 In his article on the development of the capitulations, Alexander de Groot refers to the *bailo* as holding the same function as those of a consul (p. 577) while also referring to him as an ambassador (p. 588), 'The historical development of the capitulatory regime in the Ottoman Middle East from the fifteenth to the nineteenth centuries', *Oriente moderno*, nuova serie, 22:3 (2003): pp. 575–604. Maria Pia Pedani also likens the *bailo*'s function to that of the consul but considers him to be more important, 'Venetian consuls in Egypt and Syria in the Ottoman age', *Mediterranean world*, 18 (2006): pp. 7–8. Pedani mentions the appointment of a *bailo* as already present in the 1454 treaty.

56 De Groot, 'The historical development', pp. 588–589. For another general overview, see Viorel Panaite, 'Peace agreements in Ottoman legal and diplomatic view (15th–17th centuries)', in *Pax Ottomana: Studies in memoriam Prof. Dr. Nejat Göyünç*, ed. Kemal Çiçek (Ankara and Haarlem, 2001), pp. 277–308.

57 De Groot, 'The historical development', pp. 588–590; see also Maria Pia Pedani, 'Venezia e l'Impero Ottomano: La tentazione dell'impium foedus', in *L'Europa e la Serenissima. La svolta del 1509. Nel V centenario della battaglia di Agnadello*, ed. Giuseppe Gullino (Venezia, 2011), pp. 163–176. European trading nations in the Ottoman Empire, such as the Genoese, had obtained earlier treaties that were also referred to as 'capitulations', but these differed in scope and were different from the later capitulations that came to regulate European presence in the Ottoman Empire in a legally more detailed manner. For these earlier treaties, see Halil İnalcik and Donald Quataert, eds., *An economic and social history of the Ottoman Empire, 1300–1914* (Cambridge, 1994), pp. 192–195.

which was payable by all *zimmis*.[58] A *zimmi* was a non-Muslim subject of the Ottoman sultan – a concept that came from 'dhimma', which was 'a contractual bond between Muslim ruler and non-Muslim subject, stipulating the conditions under which certain groups would be allowed to live and practice their religion'.[59] These groups were referred to as the *ahl al-dimma*, or *zimmis* (plural). They had to be monotheistic and were subject to pay the *cizye* tax, while being exempt from the tithe, or *zakat*.[60] Exemption from the *cizye* meant the de facto abolition of an existing rule that said foreigners could legally stay one lunar year in Ottoman lands as *müste'min*. This was the name for the category of people holding an *aman*, which was a safe-conduct to travel through the Ottoman Empire. After the lunar year, foreigners had the choice to leave or to become *zimmis*, thus becoming Ottoman subjects.[61] Exemption from the *cizye* tax placed on these *zimmis* enabled European traders to stay for an indefinite period of time in Ottoman lands without becoming Ottoman subjects.

The conquest of the Mamluk sultanate by Selīm I in 1517 led to a rearrangement of Levantine commercial relationships. The Ottoman sultan now granted Venice a new, separate set of capitulations that dealt with the privileges and tributary payments agreed upon by the Mamluks and Venetians.[62] The existence of Mamluk treaties with European nations was in some cases an important precedent to the development of later Ottoman capitulations. French communities in Cairo and Alexandria had concluded treaties with the Mamluks, which were mentioned in the Egyptian capitulations Selīm I issued for the French in 1517, the same year as they were granted to the Venetians. Various stipulations expressed in the document were also present in the first French capitulations for the Ottoman Empire, which dated from 1569 and were granted by Selīm II – these included the legal responsibility of the individual, assistance in salvaging French shipwrecks, execution of wills and settling inheritances.[63] Such stipulations also resembled the existing Venetian capitulations,

58 De Groot, 'The historical development', p. 591. For the further development of Venetian trade networks in the Levant under Bayazid II's son, Selīm I, see Maria Pia Pedani, 'Venetians in the Levant in the age of Selīm I', in *Conquête ottomane de l'Égypte (1517)*, eds. Benjamin Lellouch and Nicolas Michel (Leiden and Boston, 2012), pp. 99–112.

59 Benjamin Braude, 'Introduction', in *Christians & Jews in the Ottoman Empire. The abridged edition*, ed. Benjamin Braude (Boulder, 2014), p. 3. In a way, this can also be considered as a form of protection. Salahi R. Sonyel, 'The protégé system in the Ottoman Empire', *Journal of Islamic studies*, 2:1 (1991): pp. 56–66.

60 Braude, 'Introduction', pp. 3–7.

61 Van den Boogert, *The capitulations*, p. 30.

62 De Groot, 'The historical development', p. 591.

63 The treaty of 1536 between François I and Süleymān the Magnificent was often considered to be the first French *ahdnames*, but more recent research suggests that this document

and its eighteen items also included the problem of Mediterranean slavery and exemption from the Ottoman *cizye*. Additionally, it established customs tariffs and made the presence of an interpreter (dragoman) obligatory in cases where a Frenchman was to appear before a *qadi* court. The *qadis* were judges presiding over certain districts, called *qada*.' They had a number of additional duties, which included drafting reports 'on the activities of high-ranking officials, the general situation and the mood of the population'.[64]

The French *ahdnames* were renewed in 1581, 1597, 1604, 1618, 1673 – the year in which customs tariffs were lowered to the 3% paid by the English and Dutch – and 1740.[65] In 1581, the privileges granted to the French were extended to other foreigners operating under the French flag – Venetians, Genoese, English, Portuguese and Catalans, as well as merchants from Ancona and Ragusa.[66] The possibility to extend protection to traders from other European nations was important, as it influenced the nature of intra-European relationships in the Levant. It led to competition between larger European nations in their struggle for dominance, all attempting to place merchant communities from smaller nations under their protection. It can also be seen as a precursor to the system of Ottoman *protégés* that was to become so important for Levant trade later on. This 'foreign protection' could be withdrawn in subsequent capitulations, depending on whether the nation of the former *protégés* had obtained a capitulatory regime of its own.[67]

Murād III granted the English their first capitulations in 1580. These followed earlier Venetian and French capitulations; the English were accorded the same customs tariff of 5%, the right to adjudicate disputes within their own community and exemption from *cizye*. English traders were allowed to travel and trade throughout the Ottoman Empire.[68] A renewal of these *ahdnames* in 1601

never obtained any legal validity. See Viorel Panaite, 'French capitulations and consular jurisdiction in Egypt and Aleppo in the late sixteenth and early seventeenth centuries', in *Well-connected domains. Towards an entangled Ottoman history*, eds. Pascal W. Firges, Tobias P. Graf, Christian Roth, and Gülay Tulasoğlu (Leiden and Boston, 2014), pp. 71–87. For specific contents on the Egyptian and Ottoman French capitulations, see de Groot, 'The historical development', pp. 595–596.

64 Gy. Káldy Nagy, 'Qadi', in, *Judicial practice. Institutions and agents in the Islamic world*, ed. Bogaç A. Ergene (Leiden and Boston, 2009), p. 202.

65 De Groot, 'The historical development', pp. 595–600. A renewal might contain new articles and clauses and did not occur often. When ascending the throne, every new Ottoman sultan also confirmed the existing capitulations, but these confirmations were not counted as renewals.

66 De Groot, 'The historical development', p. 596.

67 Ibid., p. 597.

68 For a study of early English-Ottoman relations, including the 1580 capitulations, see Susan Skilliter, *William Harborne and the trade with Turkey 1578–1582. A documentary study of the*

lowered the customs tariff to 3%, and the English were allowed to extend their protected status to merchants of certain nations who had not yet concluded capitulations of their own, a right the French already had. This protection also applied to traders coming from Holland, Zeeland, Friesland and Gelderland in the United Provinces and was the outcome of a dispute between the French and English ambassadors, who both tried to exercise influence over the other European trading nations in the Ottoman Empire.[69] In 1609, the Dutch entered a period of truce with Spain that was to last twelve years. The temporary halt to hostilities with Spain led to an expansion of Dutch trading activities in the Mediterranean to the extent that a special envoy named Cornelis Haga was sent to Istanbul in 1612 to establish official diplomatic relations and commercial privileges.[70] As a result, the first Dutch *ahdnames* were granted by Ahmed I the same year (see figure 2). Its fifty-nine articles included exemption from the *cizye* (article 32) and the establishment of a customs tariff of 3% (article 12), as well as the right for the Dutch ambassador and consuls to adjudicate intra-Dutch legal disputes (article 5; see p. 84). The Dutch also received permission to open vice-consulates in 'Alexandria, Tripoli of Syria, the Archipelago, Tunis, Algiers, Cairo and other places' (article 34).[71] The Dutch capitulations were renewed in 1634 and 1680, while the English ones were renewed in 1601 and 1675. The latter *ahdnames* resembled the Dutch capitulations of 1612, which

first Anglo-Ottoman relations (Oxford, 1977); see also V.L. Ménage, 'The English capitulation of 1580', *International journal of Middle East studies*, 12:3 (1980): pp. 373–383.

69 De Groot, 'The historical development', pp. 599–600; see also Arthur Leon Horniker, 'Anglo-French rivalry in the Levant from 1583 to 1612', *Journal of modern history*, 18:4 (1946): pp. 289–305. There is a debate on whether the French capitulations of 1569 formally authorised the French to protect other European traders under their flag, but in practice, both the French and English were indeed doing so, and later, the Dutch did so as well. Fusaro, *Political economies*, p. 70; Skilliter, *William Harborne*, pp. 1–3, denied the French were granted such privileges; while Domenico Sella disagreed, *Commercio e industrie a Venezia nel secolo XVII* (Firenze, 1961), p. 6; see also Hussein I. El-Mudarris and Olivier Salmon, *Le consulat de France à Alep au XVIIe siècle. Journal de Louis Gédoyn. Vie de François Picquet. Mémoires de Laurent d'Arvieux* (Aleppo, 2009), pp. 34–35. Alexander de Groot, the authoritative voice on the Dutch capitulations, believes the French capitulations of 1569 indeed enabled the Dutch to trade in the Ottoman Empire while protected under the French flag. De Groot, *The Ottoman Empire*, p. 52.

70 For Cornelis Haga, see footnote 23 on p. 23.

71 For an extensive overview of the first Dutch capitulations, see de Groot, *The Ottoman Empire*, which includes an English translation of these capitulations on pp. 138–157. For the article on the vice-consulates, see p. 154. A good account of Cornelis Haga's initial mission as well as the 1612 capitulations, relying extensively on Ottoman sources, is Bülent Arı, 'The first Dutch ambassador in Istanbul: Cornelis Haga and the Dutch capitulations of 1612' (unpublished PhD thesis, Bilkent University, 2003).

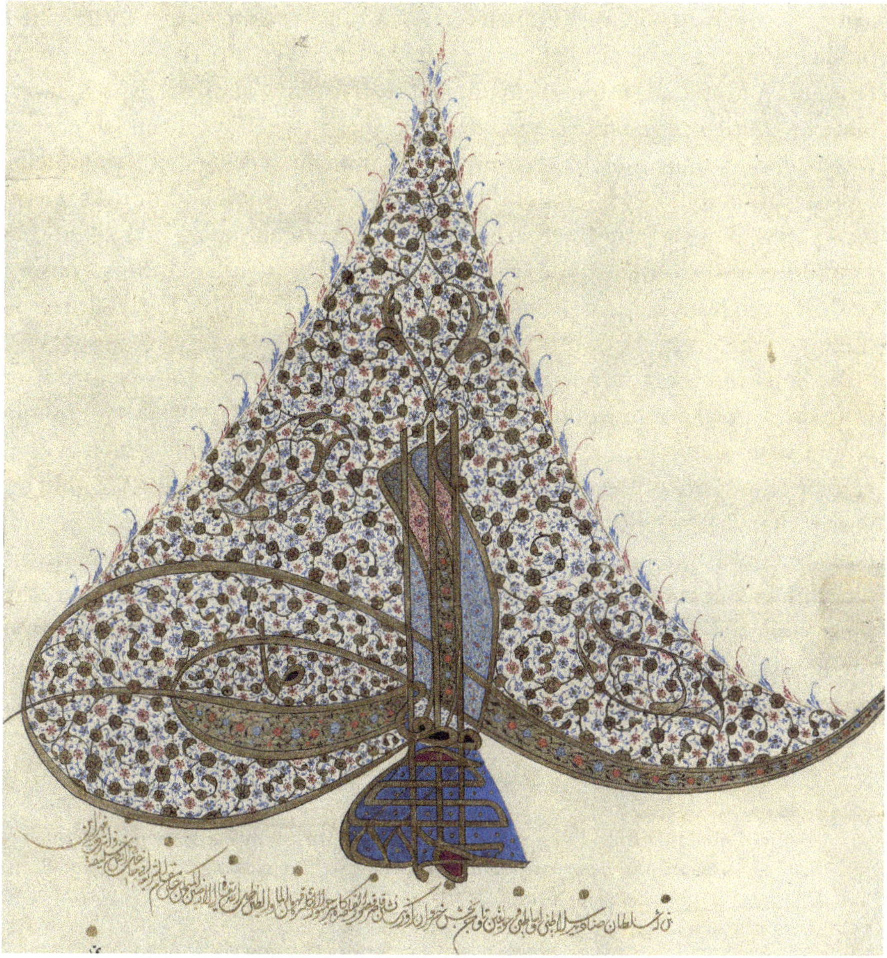

FIGURE 2 Tughra in the capitulations between Sultan Ahmed I and the Republic of the United provinces of 6 July 1612
FROM THE DUTCH NATIONAL ARCHIVES, THE HAGUE (ARCHIVES OF THE STATES GENERAL)

had been generous, and contained seventy-five articles that remained the legal basis for Anglo-Ottoman interaction until 1923.[72]

Interestingly, the English capitulations of 1675 still made a reference to the Anglo-French dispute on who was to protect the Dutch traders, even though the Dutch had obtained their own capitulations in 1612. For de Groot, it was an indication of the conservative nature of these capitulations in later stages,

72 De Groot, 'The historical development', pp. 600–603.

as well as of the desire of European nations to hang onto earlier established privileges (in this case protection over the Dutch), even if they were no longer relevant.[73] In 1694, fourteen years after the last renewal of the Dutch capitulations, the Porte issued a *ferman* stating that protection of the Dutch flag was extended to the merchant communities of Spain, Portugal, Ancona, Sicily, Florence, Catalonia and Flanders.[74] This was an important addition, as it covered Sephardi Jews from the Iberian Peninsula, who played an important role as middlemen in Dutch trade with the Levant.[75] It completed the ascension of the Dutch from being a protected trading nation to a protector, confirming their growing importance throughout the seventeenth century.

Perhaps the most important capitulations granted to a European power were those given to the French in 1740 by Sultan Mahmud I.[76] They were a recompense for the French assistance given by the Marquis de Villeneuve in concluding the Treaty of Belgrade between the Habsburg and Ottoman Empires a year earlier. With eighty-five articles that dealt with the jurisdiction of French diplomats, artisans, trade and taxes, religious personnel and services, maritime navigation and the problem of the corsairs, the 1740 capitulations were the most extensive set of capitulations issued. Very importantly, they referred to the French king as an equal, and the capitulations became permanent rather than renewable every time a new sultan ascended the throne.[77] This evolution

73 Ibid., p. 601.

74 Daniel Goffman, 'Izmir: From village to colonial port city', in *The Ottoman city between east and west. Aleppo, Izmir, and Istanbul*, eds. Edhem Eldem, Daniel Goffman, and Bruce Masters (Cambridge, 1999), p. 111.

75 See pp. 55–61.

76 It was with the understanding that the 1740 French capitulations were the definitive expression of European privileges as granted by the Ottoman sultan that Thomas-Xavier Bianchi, former translator in Oriental languages for the French king, included a translation of the whole body of French peace treaties and capitulations from 1535 to 1740 as the first part of an appendix to his work on French-Turkish conversation. These translations had been made in 1761 by a Monsieur Deval, first dragoman at the French embassy in Istanbul at the time, and appeared in print as 'Collection complète des capitulations ou traités de paix, de commerce et d'amitié entre la France et la Porte ottomane depuis 1535 (Hég. 942), c'est à dire depuis l'origine des relations entre les deux états, jusques et compris le dernier traité ou convention du 25 novembre 1838' in T.X. Bianchi, *Le nouveau guide de la conversation en français et en turc* (Paris, 1852), pp. 247–301, with the Turkish text following thereafter. The translation of the 1740 capitulations can be found on pp. 259–286. Another translation of the 1740 capitulations can be found in Gabriel Effendi Noradounghian, *Recueuil d'actes internationaux de l'Empire Ottoman, 1300–1789* (Paris, 1897–1903), 1: pp. 277–306.

77 Edhem Eldem, *French trade in Istanbul in the eighteenth century* (Leiden and Boston, 1999), p. 278.

can be interpreted as an almost open recognition that the Ottoman-European balance was tipping over in favour of the latter, and the effort can be seen, in a way, as an Ottoman normalisation of relationships along European lines. Another crucial change was that these capitulations formally recognised the principle of the 'most favoured nation' for the first time, which meant that privileges granted in the capitulations to one European nation now also automatically applied to the others.[78] This principle gave all European trading communities in the Ottoman Empire the same status, and it was an essential characteristic of the Ottoman vision that the various European capitulations were part of one large corpus of codified privileges. It meant that a member of one European trading nation, when defending his privileges towards Ottoman authorities, could invoke the capitulations granted to another nation.[79]

The practice of interconnecting capitulations was not new, but the French *ahdnames* of 1740 provided Europeans with a definitive version of the 'most favoured nation' principle. Earlier, capitulations for various European nations had influenced one another, as was for instance the case for the English ones of 1675, which were very similar to the Dutch ones of 1612. Additionally, capitulations for new nations at times referred to existing older ones – the English capitulations of 1580 confirmed privileges for the English that had already been granted to the French, Venetians and Poles.[80] The first capitulations granted to the Dutch in 1612 included an article stipulating that 'the points written and registered in the capitulation granted to the French and the English are also established in favour of the Dutch'.[81] Article 29 of the 1740 French capitulations confirms that all privileges given to the Venetians in earlier *ahdnames* also applied to the French.[82]

By the time the French obtained their 1740 capitulations, the European presence in a number of Ottoman cities had been long and was embedded in the context of social, legal, cultural and commercial norms and institutions, although these had not come about without conflict. The capitulations were just one aspect of this context. While Europeans considered them as acquired privileges, in the sense that they felt the privileges granted in these documents

78 There was only the formal need for European diplomats to obtain official *fermans* that confirmed these privileges for their own nation. It did give the French a short period of time in which they were the only European nation enjoying new privileges contained in renewed *ahdnames*. Van den Boogert, *The capitulations*, p. 25.

79 De Groot, 'The historical development', p. 603; see also van den Boogert, *The capitulations*, pp. 2, 25, 142, and 148.

80 De Groot, 'The historical development', p. 601.

81 The translation can be found in de Groot, *The Ottoman Empire*, p. 154.

82 Bianchi, *Le nouveau guide*, p. 268.

were sacrosanct, the Ottomans increasingly considered them as unilaterally given privileges, which could be revoked or adapted at their own desire. This meant Europeans needed official *fermans* that confirmed the practical execution of the specific regulations written down in the capitulations. The risk of revocation made Europeans careful not to create precedents that would lead to a retraction of a privilege given to a whole trading nation based on infringements committed by individuals, and protecting the capitulations always remained an important consideration for European diplomats who tried to keep their subjects in line.[83] The consul or ambassador could be held responsible for the actions of a particular merchant, as is for instance clear from article 69 of the French capitulations of 1740, which stipulated that no Frenchman could be prevented from travelling, as long as the consul or ambassador stood caution for his debts.[84] It was not uncommon for European diplomats to deny support to individual traders who had put the relationship with the Ottoman rulers at risk through their individual actions, as it might threaten the well-being of the whole trading community. An additional problem was that certain articles in the capitulations were open for interpretation, and at times, Ottoman authorities, both in Istanbul and elsewhere, issued *fermans* that, for Europeans, seemed to contradict the privileges described in the capitulations. Van den Boogert asserted that 'the *ahdnames* thus were nor immutable, and amendments, clarifications, and, sometimes, revisions, were part of the ongoing process of keeping the texts in tune with reality. The fact that the *ahdnames* allowed various interpretations was an uncomfortable reality for the Europeans to face'.[85] In short, the capitulations contained a number of fiscal and commercial advantages without which it would have been very difficult, if not impossible, for European traders to establish a profitable business, and the lowering of the customs tariff to 3% was perhaps the most important commercial measure benefitting the merchants.[86] A second important regulation was exemption from the *cizye* tax, not so much for financial benefit but because it allowed foreign merchants to remain in the Ottoman Empire for an indefinite amount of time without becoming a *zimmi*, or Ottoman subject. It was a very important stipulation and one that was generally accepted by Ottoman officials, although it was subject to controversy various times as well, most notoriously in the conflict that arose in the 1760s between Europeans and Greeks

83 For a discussion of the Dutch attitude in this regard, see pp. 287–289.
84 Bianchi, *Le nouveau guide*, p. 280.
85 Van den Boogert, *The capitulations*, p. 21.
86 Ibid., pp. 32–33.

when European traders started to marry Greek women, all *zimmis*.[87] The third element that made the capitulations so important for the European presence was the idea of legal autonomy. The *ahdname*s allowed for a consular apparatus that held jurisdiction over foreign communities. Legal disputes between members of the same European trading community could be adjudicated by the consul of that community.[88]

2.2 *The Dutch Consular System in the Levant*

The ability to exercise legal authority over a foreign trading community can be traced back to the medieval interpretation of consular responsibilities. In the Middle Ages, the office of 'consul' was not clearly defined, but generally, he acted as a mediator between a foreign merchant community and a host nation; the consul was generally a citizen of the city in which the foreign merchant community resided.[89] His role was different from that of the ambassador, who was a political representative. The consul defended commercial interests and was often a trader himself.[90] The principle that the consul represented merchants instead of states continued to define consular praxis during the early modern period and was of particular relevance to the development of the institution in the Levant. In his seminal article, Niels Steensgaard observed that in the Levant, 'the consuls' primary task was commercial. They were the leaders and representatives of a society of merchants of common origin, the

87 In 1678, for instance, the Dutch feared that the grand vizir wanted to subject all dragomans, but also Europeans married to Ottoman women, to the *cizye*. It caused distress, and the Dutch argued that it was against the capitulations. NASG, N°6913 ('Ingekomen ordinaris brieven en stukken van vorstelijke personen, gezanten, enz. betreffende Italië, Turkije en de Barbarijnse staten Algiers, Marokko, Tripoli en Tunis, 1596–1796'), Justinus Colyer to the States General, Istanbul, 18/01/1678. Olnon argued that European fears were exaggerated. Merlijn Olnon, *'Brought under the law of the land'. The history, demography and geography of crossculturalism in early modern Izmir, and the Köprülü project of 1678* (Leiden, 2013), pp. 206–207; see also his '"A most agreeable and pleasant creature"? Merzifonlu Kara Mustafa Paşa in the correspondence of Justinus Colyer (1668–1682)', *Oriente moderno*, nuova serie, 22:3 (2003): pp. 649–669.

88 A full understanding of the articles in the capitulations that deal with legal autonomy and litigation are important for the argument of this book and will be discussed in detail in chapter two, pp. 84–89.

89 An extensive bibliography exists on the function of the consul in medieval and early modern times. See for instance the references in Fusaro, *Political economies*, pp. 159–173. For a historiographical discussion of the Mediterranean context, see the introduction by Arnaud Bartolomei in *De l'utilité commerciale des consuls*, eds. Bartolomei et al. (Rome and Madrid, 2017), pp. 9–18.

90 Fusaro, *Political economies*, pp. 159–160.

so-called "nation"'.[91] This difference between consul and ambassador can also be observed in the initial lack of diplomatic immunity for the consul, who was subject to local jurisdiction. In the Ottoman context the first mention of consular diplomatic immunity can be found in the English capitulations of 1601 and the French capitulations of 1604.[92]

During the late sixteenth and early seventeenth century, four European states maintained a web of consuls in the Levant – Venice, France, England and the United Provinces.[93] The oldest consulates were those of Venice and France, which were well-established by the sixteenth century. Venetian consuls were part of the ruling aristocracy, very much tied to the Venetian administration, and not allowed to have commercial interests. The early French consuls in Egypt functioned on the medieval definition of the consulate. This difference between France and Venice might explain the difference in remuneration – the Venetian consuls received fixed salaries while their French colleagues were paid out of a consular fee, a tax paid by the merchants the consuls were representing.[94] The Dutch opted for the French model of remuneration on the basis of a tax that also was intended to cover consular expenses – a choice that was, according to Steensgaard, 'unsuccessful in most places but disastrous in the Levant'.[95] Throughout the seventeenth century, this choice led to a great deal of conflict between consuls and the merchants they represented.[96] The legislation issued by the States General throughout the seventeenth century aimed to quell conflicts between consuls and merchants but, at the same time, became

91 Niels Steensgaard, 'Consuls and nations in the Levant from 1570 to 1650', *The Scandinavian economic history review*, 15 (1967): pp. 14–15.

92 Fusaro, *Political economies*, p. 160; and Steensgaard, 'Consuls and nations', p. 18.

93 Steensgaard, 'Consuls and nations'. For an early history of the Venetian consuls in the eastern Mediterranean, see Benoît Maréchaux, 'Consuls vénitiens en Méditerranée orientale (1575–1645)', in *Los cónsules de extranjeros en la Edad Moderna y a principios de la Edad Contemporánea*, eds. M. Aglietti, M. Herrero Sánchez, and F. Zamora Rodríguez (Madrid, 2013), pp. 145–158. For France, see Géraud Poumarède, 'Naissance d'une institution royale: Les consuls de la nation française en Levant et en Barbarie aux XVIe et XVIIe siècles', *Annuaire-bulletin de la Société de l'Histoire de France* (2001): pp. 65–128.

94 Steensgaard, 'Consuls and nations'.

95 Ibid., p. 32. This was because the expenses were very unpredictable in the Levantine context. For a general overview of the establishment of Dutch consulates throughout the Levant, see Jonathan Israel, 'The Dutch merchant colonies in the Mediterranean during the seventeenth century', *Renaissance and modern studies*, 30 (1986): pp. 87–108.

96 Consular correspondence preserved in the archives of the Directorate of Levant Trade contains several references to quarrels between consuls and merchants; see also Fusaro, *Political economies*, pp. 159–173. Several examples in the Dutch context will be discussed below; see pp. 49–52, 91–95 and 100–101.

the legal foundation defining the mutual rights between consuls and traders for the remainder of the early modern period.

Van den Boogert has remarked that the text of the first Dutch capitulations of 1612 'seems to take the existence of consuls for granted'.[97] The first stronghold of Dutch Levant trade was a small trading contingent that had established itself in Aleppo, in present-day Syria. In 1607, a man from Dordrecht named Arnoult de la Valée was asked by Dutch merchants there to act as their consul. His salary would be paid by the merchants.[98] De la Valée's arrival in Aleppo was the first indication of a Dutch consulate in the Ottoman Empire, and it seems to have been on the basis of the medieval interpretation of what the consul was: 'the elected leader of a specific group of merchants, who often all came from one location, residing in a particular place abroad'.[99] De la Valée was not appointed by the States General but worked for the Dutch traders of Aleppo.[100] The choice for Aleppo was logical, as it was an important centre of trade and one of the stops of the silk caravan.[101] The Dutch trading community continued to expand, and it grew from two or three firms in 1604 to twenty in 1615, holding a share of the city's trade that was twice as large as what the English held.[102]

By this time, the Dutch consular system had undergone important changes following Cornelis Haga's arrival in Istanbul in March 1612. This was the period before the establishment of the Directorate of Levant Trade in Amsterdam, and the ambassador in Istanbul appointed consuls directly. Haga was involved in the early appointments of consuls on the Greek island of Chios and on Cyprus.[103] In Aleppo, the most important commercial centre for Dutch Levant trade, Cornelis Pauw was appointed consul in 1612.[104]

97 Maurits van den Boogert, 'Negotiating foreignness in the Ottoman Empire: The legal complications of cosmopolitanism in the eighteenth century', in *Exploring the Dutch Empire. Agents, networks and institutions, 1600–2000*, eds. Catia Antunes and Jos Gommans (London, 2015), p. 29.

98 Schutte, *Repertorium der Nederlandse vertegenwoordigers*, p. 349.

99 Van den Boogert, 'Negotiating foreignness', p. 29. The first English consulates seem to have been considered the same way.

100 Kersten and van der Zwan, 'The Dutch consular service', p. 276.

101 For the importance of Aleppo as a trading centre for western Europeans, see Bruce Masters, *The origins of western economic dominance in the Middle East: Mercantilism and the Islamic economy in Aleppo, 1600–1750* (New York, 1988); 'Aleppo: The Ottoman Empire's caravan city', in *The Ottoman city*, eds. Edhem Eldem et al., pp. 17–78.

102 Israel, 'The Dutch merchant colonies', pp. 91–92.

103 Schutte, *Repertorium der Nederlandse vertegenwoordigers*, pp. 346–347. For Haga's tenure as ambassador, see ibid., pp. 302–306.

104 Ibid., p. 349.

Pauw had been part of Haga's entourage in Istanbul, and his father Reynier had been a very important man in Amsterdam, a merchant who had been burgomaster, alderman, commissioner of the exchange bank and director of the Dutch East India Company.[105] Pauw was very important from an institutional point of view. While his predecessor had been in the private service of a group of merchants, Pauw was officially appointed by the States General. His appointment was confirmed by a regulation published by the States General in December 1612. It was the first time that legislation aiming to regulate consular appointments in the Levant was published. A first regulation instructed the head consul in Aleppo as well as the consuls in other quarters to deal with the inheritances of those who had died in their legal territory but had left no will. The consul had to make an inventory, register all the goods and inform the relatives.[106] A second regulation issued the same day authorised the head consul in Aleppo as well as the other consuls in the Levant to issue notarial acts with full legal powers, such as contracts, registrations of commercial transactions, wills, certifications and other documents at the demand of merchants, factors, skippers and all other individuals belonging to the United Provinces. These acts had to be drafted in the presence of witnesses.[107]

The right to levy consular and ambassadorial taxes was only codified in a regulation from 1615 – while Haga was still ambassador in Istanbul and Pauw was still consul in Aleppo.[108] The regulation stipulated a tax of 1.5% on all cash and goods that arrived in the Levant on behalf of Dutch merchants, which would be used to pay the salary of the ambassador in Istanbul, and a tax of 2% on the same commodities to pay for the salaries of the consuls. The salary of the consul in Cyprus, which amounted to 6,000 guilders per year and was paid by the Dutch merchant community there, was also subject to this new

105 Ibid., p. 11 and pp. 175–177.

106 Cau, *Groot placaet-boeck*, 2: pp. 1331–1332, 'Acte voor de consuls in de Levanten, noopende 't registereren der goederen vande overledene aldaer', 08/12/1612; see also van den Boogert, *The capitulations*, pp. 40–41.

107 Cau, *Groot placaet-boeck*, 2: pp. 1333–1334, 'Acte, waar by den secretaris vanden hooft-consul tot Aleppo, ende de andere secretarisen vande consuls inde andere quartieren van Levante gelast wert, te passeren alle contracten, compromissen, certificatien, &c. ten behoeve vande coopluyden, facteurs, schipperen, ende andere negotianten ende particuliere persoonen', 08/12/1612.

108 Ibid., pp. 1333–1336, 'Acte, waer by gheconsenteert wort ten behoeve vanden orateur tot Constantinopolen, ende consul van Aleppo, te lichten van alle de goederen inde Levante gebracht wordende anderhalf ende twee ten hondert, met authoriqatie tot het lichten der selver penningen, &c.', 06/06/1615. For Cyprus, see Schutte, *Repertorium der Nederlandse vertegenwoordigers*, p. 347.

regulation. To avoid fraud, merchants and skippers had to promise honesty about the goods they registered and shipping papers had to be shown to the consul.[109] Nine months later, additional legislation regulated the adjudicating powers of the consul in Aleppo.[110]

These regulations were accompanied by an expansion of the consular apparatus in the Mediterranean and the Levant. Between 1612 and 1618, the States General appointed consuls in Livorno, Venice, Genoa, Larnaca, Tunis, Algiers, Zante and Izmir.[111] By 1650, there were nine Dutch (vice-)consulates in the Levant, as well as three in Salé, Tunis and Algiers.[112] By 1700 the number of Dutch (vice-)consulates was lower, only eight, but by 1750 there were twenty-two. By 1800 the number had fallen to fourteen.[113] The consuls were officially appointed by the States General, but after 1625, they had to communicate with the Directorate of Levant Trade. There was thus a separation of the political appointment of the consuls by the States General and the consular accountability to the Directorate of Levant Trade. This system reflects the medieval distinction between the ambassador as a political state representative and the consul as a protector of the interests of merchants.[114] It was more explicit in the Dutch case because of the decentralised nature of the state apparatus and

109 Cau, *Groot placaet-boeck*, 2: pp. 1333–1336, 'Acte, waer by gheconsenteert wort ten behoeve vanden orateur tot Constantinopolen', 06/06/1615.

110 See pp. 93–94.

111 Israel, 'The Dutch merchant colonies'; and Steensgaard, 'Consuls and nations'. The end of the Eighty Years' War in 1648 was followed by Dutch consular appointments in Messina, Nice, Villafranca, Puglia, Naples and Ancona. See Tessa Agterhuis, 'Tot dienst, voordeel ende proffijt van de coopluyden ende schipperen van dese landen. Nederlandse consuls in Italiaanse havens, 1612–1672' (unpublished MA thesis, Leiden University, 2013), p. 12. Several of the early consuls in the Levant and North Africa, such as Lamberto Verhaer, the second consul in Tunis, had been part of Haga's entourage on his mission to Istanbul in 1612. See Schutte, *Repertorium der Nederlandse vertegenwoordigers*, p. 370.

112 For Algiers, see Gerard van Krieken, *Kapers en kooplieden. De betrekkingen tussen Algiers en Nederland* (Amsterdam, 1999); see also Schutte, *Repertorium der Nederlandse vertegenwoordigers*, pp. 368–380 for the different representatives in Tunis and Algiers, which started with Wijnant de Keyser's appointment in 1616. For Morocco, see ibid., pp. 381–388. For an analysis of Dutch diplomatic activities in North Africa, see Erica Heinsen-Roach, *Consuls and captives. Dutch–North African diplomacy in the early modern Mediterranean* (Rochester, NY and Suffolk, 2019).

113 Van den Boogert, 'Negotiating foreignness', p. 30. Vice-consulates were established in places considered less important, and they were considered as more informal than consulates. Steensgaard, 'Consuls and nations', p. 25.

114 Maria Fusaro remarked that this 'political asymmetry' was inherent to the medieval interpretation of the consulate. Fusaro, *Political economies*, p. 160.

existing competition between different cities and provinces.[115] Merchants were fully aware of the distinctive responsibilities of Dutch diplomats, and as early as 1612, Levant traders argued that the ambassador was serving the interests of the Dutch state (the United Provinces) and the consuls those of Dutch trade.[116]

The role played by Dutch urban governments and institutions makes it complicated to argue that consular appointments were part of a strategy to foster Dutch commercial interests rather than the particular interests of merchant communities. Maartje van Gelder argued that it is certain that there was an interplay between Dutch merchant communities and official Dutch representatives, with some overlap in personnel, and this interplay could foster particular interests, as well as national interest, without turning local Mediterranean Dutch trading communities into extensions of the United Provinces.[117] In the eighteenth century, the idea of 'national' interest became more central. In a memoir on Dutch trade written in 1754, Elbert de Hochepied, Dutch ambassador in Istanbul, discussed a reorganisation of Levant trade to bring back former glory to the homeland ('la patrie').[118] National interest started to figure prominently in discourse used by consuls in their letters to the Directorate of Levant Trade. At the same time, cities continued to play their role. Dutch consuls in the Mediterranean often had Amsterdam origins, and the States General had specifically transferred the responsibility of maintaining a diplomatic network in the Mediterranean to the Amsterdam Levant Directorate, the biggest of all the directorates.[119]

Archival material does not allow for a hypothesis that conflict between consuls and merchants can be explained by strife between factions coming from different Dutch cities. Reasons for the recurrent conflicts in the seventeenth century were personal and financial. From an early stage onwards, merchants attempted to avoid paying consular duties, and sometimes Dutch ships sailed

---

115 Oscar Gelderblom made a convincing argument for change in the Dutch institutions established to foster international commerce as driven by competition between cities. Gelderblom, *Cities of commerce*.

116 A.T. van Deursen, ed., *Resolutiën der Staten-Generaal*. Nieuwe reeks 1610–1670 (The Hague, 1971), 1: p. 793, Meeting States General 06/12/1612.

117 Van Gelder, *Trading places*, pp. 159–168.

118 NA, N°2.21.006.46 ('Archief van F.G. Baron van Dedem van de Gelder'), N°2 ('Mémoire pour le commerce d'Hollande en Levant. Composé par J. Chevrier, sécretaire de S.E. Monseigneur le Baron de Hochepied, ambassadeur d'Hollande à Constantinople, fait et écrit sur les idées de mondit seigneur et par son ordre', 1754).

119 G.T.H.C. Pieck, 'Francesco Gallacini, Florentijns koopman te Rotterdam 1647–1705', *Rotterdamsch jaarboekje*, 8 (1980): p. 207; see also the biographies of consuls in Schutte, *Repertorium der Nederlandse vertegenwoordigers*, passim.

under French, Venetian or English flags in order to avoid the higher Dutch duties.[120] Merchants felt taxes were too high, while the consuls felt they were not sufficient to cover both their salaries and the expenses they incurred when protecting the commercial interests of the Dutch merchants under their jurisdiction. The States General and the Directorate of Levant Trade concentrated on new regulations aimed at settling issues of taxes and remuneration, and they attempted to delineate clear rules on consular wages and expenses, particularly in Izmir, which had become the location of the most important Dutch trading community by the middle of the seventeenth century. A new regulation was published in October 1675 that aimed to settle this long-standing issue. The salaries of the ambassador in Istanbul at the time, Justinus Colyer, and the consul in Izmir, Jacob van Dam, were set at a fixed rate by law. The ambassador would receive 9,500 guilders a year as payment, as well as an additional 12,500 guilders every six months that came from the ambassadorial taxes on trade. The consul in Izmir would enjoy a remuneration of 10,000 guilders per year, funded by consular taxes on the Levant trade.[121] These sums were not only meant as salary but also had to cover household expenses as well as the salaries of other officials, such as the treasurer and chancellor, the chaplain, dragomans and janissaries.[122] A special administration needed to be

120 Mehmet Bulut, 'The role of Ottomans and Dutch in the commercial integration between the Levant and the Atlantic in the 17th century', *Journal of the economic & social history of the Orient*, 45:2 (2002): pp. 211–212.

121 Cornelis Cau, *Groot placaet-boeck inhoudende de placaeten, ende ordonnantien vande hoog mog. heeren Staten Generael der Vereenighde Nederlanden, ende van de groot mog. heeren Staten van Holland ende West-Vriesland; mitsgaders van de ed. mog. heeren Staten van Zeelandt* (The Hague, 1683), 3: p. 311, 'Extract uyt de resolutien van de Staten Generael der Vereenighde Nederlanden; reglement voor den resident tot Constantinopelen, Consul tot Smirna, ende Nederlantsche natie in de Levant', 07/10/1675. This followed earlier iterations of the same regulation published in April of the same year. Heeringa and Nanninga, Bronnen tot de geschiedenis, 2: pp. 204–207, 'Resolutie van de Staten-Generaal betreffende het reglement voor den resident te Constantinopel en den consul te Smirna', 12/04/1675.

122 The janissaries were enslaved soldiers, taken through the *devşirme system*, who had originally been serving as bodyguards for the sultan but who later became a well-respected and much-envied part of the Ottoman army, and a faction to be reckoned with within Ottoman political structures. See Gilles Veinstein, 'On the Ottoman janissaries (fourteenth–nineteenth centuries)', in *A comparative study of military labour (1500–2000)*, ed. Erik-Jan Zürcher (Amsterdam, 2013), pp. 115–134; see also Gülay Yılmaz, 'The economic and social roles of janissaries in a 17th century Ottoman city: The case of Istanbul' (unpublished PhD thesis, McGill University, 2011). Small contingents of janissaries were employed by European diplomats to ensure their physical protection.

kept in which all the duties on merchandise were to be registered and controlled by the treasurer.[123] Later, in 1724, the remuneration of the consul would be reduced from 10,000 to 6,000 guilders.[124]

The treasurer was a new post installed in 1675 to collect the ambassadorial and consular duties.[125] Along with the collection of these duties, the treasurer was also responsible for the arrangement of gifts to Ottoman officials and for all bookkeeping related to the consulate and the trading community as a whole. The consular accounts were also monitored by assessors, merchants elected by the community who also fulfilled crucial tasks in adjudication.[126] Officially, the treasurer was not allowed to trade – the exception was the treasurer in Aleppo. In 1729, the Dutch ambassador in Istanbul, Cornelis Calkoen, wrote a letter to a member of the illustrious Fagel family in which he suggested that the treasurers should be allowed to be merchants, but that the office should be rotated yearly, as was customary amongst the consulates of other European nations.[127] Calkoen felt this measure would prevent envy towards the treasurer, as the merchants were obliged to give accounts of their imports and exports to him, information he could exploit to gain an unfair advantage in trade.[128] Calkoen's suggestion was not followed, perhaps because the conflict of interest was still

123 Cau, *Groot placaet-boeck*, 3: p. 311, 'Extract uyt de resolutien van de Staten Generael der Vereenighde Nederlanden; Reglement voor den resident tot Constantinopelen, consul tot Smirna, ende Nederlantsche natie in de Levant', 07/10/1675.

124 Isaac Scheltus, *Groot placaatboek, vervattende de placaaten, ordonnantien en edicten van de hoog mog. heeren Staten Generaal der Vereenigde Nederlanden; en van de edele groot mog. Heeren Staaten van Holland en Westvriesland mitsgaders van de edele mog. heeren Staaten van Zeeland* (Amsterdam, 1795 [The Hague, 1746]), 6: p. 289, 'Resolutie, het tractement van den consul te Smirna van tien duisend guldens op ses duisend guldens vermindert', 28/01/1724.

125 The first treasurer was Jacob van der Merct, a commissioner for the Directorate of Levant Trade who had been stationed in Texel, and who arrived in Izmir in 1676. Schutte, *Repertorium der Nederlandse vertegenwoordigers*, p. 343.

126 See pp. 91 and 94–95.

127 It is not immediately clear to whom the letter was addressed. Members of the Fagel family, originally from Lokeren in Flanders, became clerks at the States General and attorneys and councillors at the *Hof van Holland*. *Nieuw Nederlandsch biografisch woordenboek*, eds. P.C. Molhuysen and P.J. Blok (Leiden, 1914), 3: pp. 385–394. At the time of writing, Cornelis Fagel was a councillor at the *Hof van Holland*, his son Hendrik was an official at the States General, as well as his brother François, who was a clerk there. As this and other letters sent by the ambassador to Fagel were kept in the archives of the States General, this letter – and others that will be mentioned later – must have been sent to either Hendrik or François, and thus they are addressed the States General.

128 Heeringa and Nanninga, *Bronnen tot de geschiedenis*, 3: pp. 21–24, Ambassador Cornelis Calkoen to Fagel, Istanbul, 30/11/1729.

considered too large, and the office of treasurer was only occupied by merchants in 1765 and 1766, by William Enslie and Daniel Fremeaux respectively, but both stints were only temporary replacements.[129] The responsibilities of the chancellor were crucial to the functioning of the consulate. More so than the office of treasurer, the chancellor had a full-time job; he was responsible for the drafting and registration of official documents at the chancery and the communication with other consulates and litigating parties in a trial. Because he did not handle the consulate's finances, he was allowed to trade.[130]

Consular and ambassadorial duties were put at 1.5% of the value of all imported and exported Levantine goods handled by Dutch merchants, but these were raised to 2% in 1692. Dutch traders shipping on foreign vessels had to pay a consular fee that was twice as high, although in the early eighteenth century Dutch merchants from Izmir demanded for that to be abolished, something which was done in 1750.[131] The concrete execution of the 1675 regulation was the subject of ongoing dispute, not only because the quarrels in Izmir between traders and consul continued but also because the regulation had first been drafted on the initiative of the Directorates of Levant Trade in Leiden and Rotterdam without prior knowledge of the more powerful directorate in Amsterdam.[132] The Amsterdam Directorate agreed but decided to draft a form, together with their colleagues in Leiden, that specified in twenty-two articles all the practical procedures related to remunerations for the ambassador in Istanbul and consul in Izmir and the levying of the consular and ambassadorial taxes on merchandise. This document also included texts for an oath demanded from the treasurers, who had to promise to register the taxes honestly and not to favour any particular merchant, as well as for the oath demanded from merchants and maritime personnel, in which they promised

---

129 Schutte, *Repertorium der Nederlandse vertegenwoordigers*, p. 344. Treasurers in Izmir had sometimes occupied administrative functions at other Dutch diplomatic institutions, such as Coenraad Schutz, who had been secretary (1752–1766) and chancellor (1756–1766) in Istanbul before becoming treasurer in Izmir, a post he held until 1802. Schutte, *Repertorium der Nederlandse vertegenwoordigers*, pp. 311 and 344.

130 Johan Frederik Mann, chancellor between 1751 and 1774, appears as a trader on the list of imports and exports of Dutch firms in Izmir between 1753 and 1765. See Heeringa and Nanninga, *Bronnen tot de geschiedenis*, 3: pp. 778–783, 'De Nederlandsche handelshuizen te Smirna en de waarde van hun invoer en hun uitvoer met Nederlandsche schepen in de periode 15 juli 1753–31 december 1765'. On Mann, see Schutte, *Repertorium der Nederlandse vertegenwoordigers*, p. 342.

131 Hakkı Kadı, *Ottoman and Dutch merchants*, pp. 150–151.

132 For the quarrels in Izmir, see pp. 49–52. A first resolution to settle the diplomatic remunerations had already been drafted in April 1675. See Heeringa and Nanninga, *Bronnen tot de geschiedenis*, 2: pp. 204–207.

to register their merchandise honestly and not commit fraud. The document was sent to the burgomasters of Amsterdam in January 1676 and to the States General in March. Shortly after their approval, copies were sent to the ambassador in Istanbul and the consul in Izmir with instructions that all had to observe the regulations stipulated in the twenty-two articles.[133] It would take another decade before the structural disputes in Izmir between consul and merchants were settled for good.

3 The Dutch Consulate of Izmir

3.1 *The Evolution towards Stability*

Aleppo in present-day Syria was the city with the first Dutch consul and with the most important Dutch trading community in the Levant. It is therefore not surprising that the first attempts to build a legislative framework around the Dutch Levantine consular system focussed on the situation in Aleppo. But by the end of the second decade of the seventeenth century, a few other consulates had been established as well. The most important one quickly turned out to be the consulate in Izmir. The first Dutch consul there was a Venetian named Nicolò Orlando, who was consul between 1618 and 1633. Before him, the English consul had acted as Dutch vice-consul. Orlando was succeeded by a Greek named Duca di Giovanni, who was consul between 1635 and 1657.[134] By the middle of the seventeenth century, Izmir had replaced Aleppo as the most important trading centre for Dutch traders in the Ottoman Empire. In their search for commercially viable cotton, merchants were looking for a port city with few regulations, and the choice fell on Izmir.[135] Izmir's growing importance came at the detriment of the Dutch community in Aleppo. Only one Dutch merchant was trading there during the 1640s, and for extended periods of time, there was no Dutch consul active in Aleppo. In 1684, a Dutch trader

133 Heeringa and Nanninga, *Bronnen tot de geschiedenis*, 2: pp. 207–217, 'Formulier, waernaer ende volgens hetwelcke den heer resident tot Constantinopelen, consul tot Smirna, aengestelt bij de H.M. heeren Staten-Generael der Vereenigde Nederlanden, en de gantsche Nederlantsche natie in de Levant residerende, respective, haer sullen hebben te reguleren omtrent den ontfanck en distributie van de ambassaet- en consulaetrechten', 1676.

134 Schutte, *Repertorium der Nederlandse vertegenwoordigers*, pp. 331–332. De Groot gives 1614–1629 as the period of Orlandi's consulship and 1630–1633 as the period when his brother Julio acted as Dutch consul, *The Ottoman Empire*, p. 129.

135 Elena Frangakis-Syrett, *The commerce of Smyrna in the eighteenth century (1700–1820)* (Athens, 1992), p. 24; see also Goffman, 'Izmir'; as well as his *Izmir and the Levantine world, 1550–1650* (Seattle, 1990) for an analysis of this development.

named Coenraet Calckberner addressed the Directorate of Levant Trade about the difficulties the Dutch community in Aleppo were experiencing because of the growing importance of Izmir.[136]

It is perhaps Izmir's rapid rise that made the States General decide to appoint a Dutchman as consul after di Giovanni's tenure, particularly as the Dutch traders in Izmir had already made such a request in 1653. The States of Holland proposed Michel du Mortier, one of two candidates selected by the Directorate of Levant Trade in Amsterdam. Du Mortier was a citizen of Leiden who was experienced in trade in the Levant. The States General accepted, and du Mortier was sent to Izmir, where he quickly attempted to enforce stricter control over the payment of consular duties while also claiming larger financial contributions from the merchants to the funds to purchase gifts for Ottoman officials. Unsurprisingly, the merchant community rebelled against him, leading to his dismissal in 1660 and the temporary return of di Giovanni.[137]

Dutch consuls and ambassadors in the Levant were not allowed to engage in commercial activities, but their income relied mainly on taxes paid by subjects whose commercial interests they represented. When quarrels about these taxes reached a zenith in 1658, the suggestion was made that the next appointment for consul should fall upon a merchant and not a legal scholar, as had hitherto been the case. Allowing a consul to trade would mean that he no longer depended on Dutch merchants for his salary, a dependence that had, according to a 1658 memorandum, led to jealousy on the part of the consul. The authors of the memorandum hoped that this change in policy would not only bring about a more harmonious relationship in Izmir between the consul and the merchants but also put a man in place who possessed knowledge and experience more apt for dealing with the demands of the Dutch trading community in Izmir.[138]

The traditional qualities required of consuls up to that moment were scholarly and not mercantile, and they included an acquaintance with Latin and the laws of the United Provinces. These were considered of lesser importance

---

136 NALH, 'Directie Amsterdam', N°161 ('Brieven van de vertegenwoordigers te Constantinopel, van de consuls en andere ambtenaren in de Levant en langs de Middellandse Zee. Aleppo en Cyprus', 1627–1826), Letter Coenraet Calckberner to Amsterdam Directorate of Levant Trade, Aleppo, 24/11/1684. Calckberner, from Amsterdam, was consul of Aleppo between 1689 and 1694. Schutte, *Repertorium der Nederlandse vertegenwoordigers*, pp. 351–352.

137 Heeringa and Nanninga, *Bronnen tot de geschiedenis*, 1: pp. 613–616, Directorate of Levant Trade to the States General, 06/08/1653. For more on both consuls, see Schutte, *Repertorium der Nederlandse vertegenwoordigers*, pp. 331–332.

138 Heeringa and Nanninga, *Bronnen tot de geschiedenis*, 1: pp. 1100–1102, 'Memorie en particuliere bedenkingen over de saken van Levanten', ca. 1658.

in the Levant, while knowledge of Spanish and Italian, common trading languages in the Mediterranean, was deemed far more important.[139] The suggestions made in the memorandum were not implemented, and for the remainder of the early modern period, the Dutch merchant community of Izmir continued to fall under the jurisdiction of men who were well versed in Latin and the laws of the Dutch Republic.

Even though the recommendations made in the memorandum were not implemented, the States General did issue a general regulation for Dutch consuls in the Mediterranean as well as another regulation that specifically applied to consuls active in the Ottoman Empire on the same day in July 1658. In its Ottoman regulation, the States General warned the merchants not to commit fraud in their declarations of goods subject to the payment of consular taxes – 1% on imported and exported goods that passed through Izmir.[140] The States General also hoped to end existing quarrels between the Dutch merchants in Izmir and their consul in the hopes that both parties would be thus able to 'preserve the honour of the nation and the prosperity of trade through a reciprocal harmony at all moments'.[141] In spite of these measures, the relationship between consul and traders in Izmir remained difficult until the end of the seventeenth century. After di Giovanni's short return, du Mortier was finally replaced by Gerard Smits, an old man who had great difficulties establishing his authority. His turn to become disputed by the traders came quickly, and he was dismissed in 1668 after complaints that he had raised unauthorised taxes for his own benefit. The merchants also accused him of neglecting his duty to provide Ottoman dignitaries with gifts.[142] He was replaced by Jacob

139 On the use of lingua franca in the Mediterranean, see Eric R. Dursteler, 'Language and identity in the early modern Mediterranean', in *Mediterranean identities in the premodern era: Entrepôts, islands, empires*, eds. John Watkins and Kathryn L. Reyerson (Farnham and Burlington, 2014), pp. 35–52; and 'Speaking in tongues: Language and communication in the early modern Mediterranean', *Past & present*, 217 (2012): pp. 47–77.

140 The general Mediterranean resolution can be found in Cau, *Groot placaet-boeck*, 2: pp. 1343–1344, 'Extract uyt 't register vande hoogh mogende heeren Staten Generael der Vereenighde Nederlanden, behelsende generael reglement voor de Nederlantsche consuls', 24/07/1658. The text for the Ottoman resolution can be found in Heeringa and Nanninga, *Bronnen tot de geschiedenis*, 2: pp. 156–158, 'Resolutie der Staten-Generaal tot nederlegging der geschillen in Smyrna', 24/07/1658.

141 Ibid., p. 157, '[…] door een overeenstemmende harmonie de eere van de natie ende den fleur van de negotie allenthalven te conserveren'.

142 For Smit's tenure, see Schutte, *Repertorium der Nederlandse vertegenwoordigers*, p. 332. On the dispute between him and the Directorate of Levant Trade, see NASG, N°12550.123 ('Stukken betreffende de geschillen tussen de Directeuren van de Levantse Handel en Gerardus Smits, gewezen consul te Smyrna, over nalatigheid in zijn functie, 1666').

van Dam, who did not want to suffer the same fate as his predecessors. He immediately asserted his authority, and in the end, it worked, as he stayed consul for almost twenty years.[143] One of his first decisions was to ban Dutch merchants from certain meetings, restricting them to himself and those merchants who held an official position. He also tried to stop one of the most common abuses: avoiding the payment of consular and ambassadorial duties. Van Dam felt his income was not high enough, particularly considering his expenses – for instance, purchasing gifts for Ottoman officials. The merchants in turn were quick to complain about the consul's excessive use of authority, which included the arrest of fraudulent traders.[144]

The atmosphere was already heated when the consul joined the Dutch ambassador on a trip to meet the sultan in Edirne at the end of 1668. The Dutch trading community in Izmir was instructed to cover the trip's expenses through a loan. Later, both the States General and the Directorate of Levant Trade refused to pay for the trip, and the Dutch traders in Izmir asked for exorbitant interest fees, complaining that nothing had been asked of their colleagues in Istanbul. This particular expense account was to cause trouble between the consul and Dutch merchants in Izmir for years to come. Between 1668 and 1672, both sides petitioned the Directorate of Levant Trade and the States of Holland to act, without much result. In a later phase, between 1672 and 1675, some traders tried to get the consul dismissed.[145] In those years, the English consul in Izmir mediated twice, but his efforts did not bring about any long-lasting solution. The authorities in the United Provinces recognised the gravity of the problem, for which they held the consul partially responsible. Nobody had any doubts that Dutch merchants avoided full payment of due taxes, out of which the consul gained his income, but it was also felt that the consul acted too harshly at times, which damaged Dutch commercial interests in the Levant. Several merchants complained to the burgomasters in

143 On the career of Jacob van Dam, see Schutte, *Repertorium der Nederlandse vertegenwoordigers*, pp. 332–334; see also Thierry Allain, 'L'information comme instrument de combat. Le consulat de Jacob van Dam à Smyrne (1668–1688)', in *Les consuls en Méditerranée, agents d'information XVIe-XXe siècle*, ed. Silvia Marzagalli (Paris, 2015), pp. 81–97.

144 For an extensive analysis of these conflicts and the main protagonists, including a summary of the problems in Izmir before van Dam's time, see W.E. van Dam van Isselt, 'Eenige lotgevallen van Jacob Van Dam, consul te Smirna van 1668–1688', in *Bijdragen voor vaderlandsche geschiedenis en oudheidkunde*, ed. P.J. Blok, 4th series, part 6 (The Hague, 1907), pp. 78–136; and 'De klachten, tusschen 1672 en 1675 ingebracht tegen Jacob van Dam, consul te Smirna (1668–1688)', in *Bijdragen voor vaderlandsche geschiedenis en oudheidkunde*, ed. P.J. Blok, 4th series, part 6 (The Hague, 1907), pp. 277–351.

145 Van Dam van Isselt, 'De klachten'.

Amsterdam about the 'tyrannical hardships' of van Dam, and they accused him of unjustly imprisoning several traders and sending them to Istanbul in chains and escorted by Ottoman soldiers. The merchants also complained that van Dam had extorted several of them to pay hefty fines.[146] Van Dam retired in 1687, was still in Izmir at the time of the fire of 1688 and arrived in the United Provinces in 1689, where he died in 1709.[147]

Stability was finally reached with the appointment of Daniel Jean de Hochepied (1657–1723) as consul in Izmir in 1688. Daniel Jean was the son of Jan Baptista de Hochepied, a silk merchant and director in the Directorate of Levant Trade of Amsterdam. De Hochepied married Clara Colyer, daughter of former Dutch ambassador Justinus Colyer and sister of Colyer's successor Jacob. Jacob Colyer was involved as a mediator in peace talks between the Habsburg emperor and the Ottoman sultan in 1699 and 1718 in Passarowitz. Colyer and de Hochepied had a good relationship, and it seems that, some years before 1699, Jacob had been counting on the assistance of de Hochepied in his attempts at mediation.[148]

With the appointment of Daniel Jean de Hochepied, a family dynasty began, as the consulate of Izmir remained in the hands of the de Hochepied family until 1824, passing on from father to son.[149] The de Hochepieds consolidated their position partially through marital alliances with family members of diplomats from other European nations and also with children of important Levant traders. Daniel Jean was succeeded by his son Daniel Alexander (1689–1759) in 1724, who already had been interim consul three years earlier when his father made a trip to Holland. Another son, Elbert, became ambassador in Istanbul between 1746 and 1763.[150] Daniel Alexander married Catharine, the daughter of Pietro Fremeaux. The Fremeaux family was to become one of the most distinguished families of the Dutch trading community of Izmir.

---

146 Ibid., pp. 315–316.

147 Schutte, *Repertorium der Nederlandse vertegenwoordigers*, pp. 332–334.

148 Ibid., pp. 308–309. For the relationship between Colyer and de Hochepied, see also Bianca Chen, 'Politics and letters: Gisbert Cuper as a servant of two republics', in *Double agents. Cultural and political brokerage in early modern Europe*, eds. Marika Keblusek and Badeloch Vera Noldus (Leiden and Boston, 2011), pp. 81–83.

149 Schutte, *Repertorium der Nederlandse vertegenwoordigers*, pp. 308–309 and 334–336. Family dynasties were not that uncommon. For a Venetian example, see Diego Pirillo, 'Venetian merchants as diplomatic agents: Family networks and cross-confessional diplomacy in early modern Europe', in *Early modern diplomacy, theatre and soft power. The making of peace*, ed. Nathalie Rivère de Carles (London and New York, 2016), pp. 183–204.

150 Schutte, *Repertorium der Nederlandse vertegenwoordigers*, pp. 311 and 335.

When Daniel Alexander passed away in 1759, his son Daniel Jean (1727–1796) became the next Dutch consul, a post he occupied until 1796. Daniel Jean was not married at the time of his appointment, but he later married Marie Dunant, the widow of the English consul Samuel Crowley.[151] Dunant had been born in Istanbul in 1728, and she was to bear several of Crowley's children, who were christened by the Dutch chaplain Jacob van der Vecht.[152] Their son Jacques became consul between 1796 and 1810 and then from 1814 to 1824.[153] This means the Hochepied family presided over the Dutch trading community of Izmir for a period of almost 150 years.[154] During that time, they established marital ties with some of the most important Dutch families active in Levant trade, not only the Fremeauxs but also the van Lennep family, as Jacques de Hochepied married a daughter of David van Lennep (1712–1797), perhaps the most important Dutch merchant in eighteenth-century Izmir (see figure 6).[155] Matrimonies also connected the de Hochepied family with Dutch and English diplomats.[156]

The stability that came with the de Hochepied family is not only demonstrated by the lack of new legislation for the Levantine consulates in the eighteenth century, which had now taken their definitive institutional form, but also by the role played by the Dutch consuls in Izmir as vice-consuls for other nations. As discussed above, it was not uncommon for nations with diplomatic representation in the Levant to extend the protection of their flag – and thus jurisdiction of their consul – over a merchant community with no diplomatic representation of its own. A consul of one nation could thus accumulate vice-consulates of other nations.

151 Ibid., p. 336. The marriage between Crowley and Dunant was mentioned in the handwritten notes by Crowley in a copy of the *Book of Common Prayer* he owned, which is now guarded in the Lambeth Palace Library in London. See http://www.levantineheritage.com/reg2.htm.

152 Such marriages, facilitated by religion, are an example of the social ties between the Dutch and English diplomatic elites in the Levant.

153 Schutte, *Repertorium der Nederlandse vertegenwoordigers*, p. 336.

154 On the de Hochepied family and their diplomatic presence in the Levant, see Marlies Hoenkamp-Mazgon, *Palais de Hollande te Istanbul. Het ambassadegebouw en zijn bewoners sinds 1612* (Amsterdam, 2002), pp. 61–67.

155 For David van Lennep, see pp. 70–71 and 157–158.

156 In 1763, for instance, Consul de Hochepied married the widow of the former English consul, Marie Dunant, who was the daughter of a French Protestant from Istanbul, see Schutte, *Repertorium der Nederlandse vertegenwoordigers*, pp. 335–336; and 'Crawley, Samuel (1705–1762)', *Oxford dictionary of national biography*, consulted online at http://www.oxforddnb.com/view/10.1093/ref:odnb/9780198614128.001.0001/odnb-9780198614128-e-109573.

Daniel Jean de Hochepied, the first consul from the de Hochepied family in Izmir and who held the position between 1688 and 1723, carried the title 'baron and magnate of Hungary' for his services to the Habsburg Empire as a diplomat after the war between the Ottoman Empire and the Holy League (1683–1699) and for the assistance he provided for the liberation of a number of Christian German slaves.[157] This is perhaps why the de Hochepied family was asked to represent Habsburg interests in Izmir. Vice-consulship not only had to be requested by a nation who did not have any consulships of their own, it also had to be allowed by the Dutch authorities, more specifically the States General. In 1742, the States General allowed Consul Daniel Alexander de Hochepied to be the agent for Maria Theresia of Austria but did not let him officially become vice-consul.[158]

In 1758 the States General also allowed Consul Daniel Alexander de Hochepied, to accept the office of Danish vice-consul. In their considerations to allow the request, which had come from the Danish envoy in Istanbul, the States General acknowledged that the Dutch consul in Izmir had already been allowed to act as vice-consul for several European nations in the past.[159] Material contained in the Dutch consular archives makes it clear that, towards the end of the eighteenth century, the Dutch consul in Izmir was also acting as vice-consul for the Holy Roman Empire, Tuscany and Sweden. He also looked after the interests of Russia and Poland.[160] Some of these additional consulships were strengthened through marriage. Gerhard Heidenstam, Swedish envoy in Istanbul, married Catharine de Hochepied, a daughter of the Dutch consul in Izmir, Daniel Jean de Hochepied. Daniel Jean was Dutch consul from

157 Schutte, *Repertorium der Nederlandse vertegenwoordigers*, p. 334; see also Heeringa and Nanninga, *Bronnen tot de geschiedenis*, 2: pp. 146–147.

158 Isaac Scheltus, *Groot placaatboek, vervattende de placaaten, ordonnantien en edicten van de hoog mog. heeren Staten Generaal der Vereenigde Nederlanden; en van de edele groot mog. heeren Staaten van Holland en Westvriesland mitsgaders van de edele mog. heeren Staaten van Zeeland* (The Hague, 1770), 7: p. 536, 'Resolutie van de Staaten Generaal, waar by aan den Consul Hochepied te Smirna word gelaaten, om den titel van graaf van Hungaryen aan te neemen, of niet, en dat hy de zaaken van de koningin van Hungaryen zal mogen bevorderen, zonder het caracter van consul of diergelyke aan te neemen', 10/05/1742.

159 Didericus Lulius and Joannes van der Linden, *Groot placaatboek, vervattende de placaaten, ordonnantien en edicten van de hoog mog. heeren Staten Generaal der Vereenigde Nederlanden; en van de edele groot mog. heeren Staaten van Holland en Westvriesland mitsgaders van de edele mog. heeren Staaten van Zeeland* (Amsterdam, 1795), 8: pp. 237–238, 'Resolutie van de Staaten Generaal, waar by aan den Consul de Hochepied te Smirna word toe gestaan de Deensche consulaire affaires aldaar waar te nemen', 13/11/1758.

160 Slot, *Inventaris van het archief*, pp. 64–72.

1759 until his death in 1796, while also being vice-consul for the Holy Roman Empire and Sweden.[161]

From an institutional point of view, it is important to note that, in cases where the Dutch consul acted as vice-consul for another nation, he did so independently from his office as Dutch consul. As Danish vice-consul, for instance, he could count on Danish personnel, such as a Danish chancellor, which ensured that administration belonging to the Danish vice-consulate remained completely separate from that belonging to the Dutch consulate.

3.2 *The Consular Protection of Jews*

The Dutch consul in Izmir not only exercised authority as consul over the Dutch traders in the city, and as vice-consul over a variety of other merchants, he also took a number of other groups under his protection. As will be seen, Dutch Levant trade relied to a great extent on Ottoman middlemen. By the mid-eighteenth century, this group had come to include Armenians and Greeks, but a century earlier, these were without exception Portuguese Jews who had migrated to the Ottoman Empire.[162] The Ottoman Empire's non-Muslim communities that were monotheistic fell under the *taife* system, allowing them protection and the ability to live as *zimmis* in the Ottoman Empire.[163] Different communities of *zimmis* were called *millets* or *taifes*. There is a slight difference between the two terms; the first meant 'religion' or 'religious community', while the second meant 'group' and was broader – it could also include professional groups.[164] According to Merlijn Olnon, *taife* resembled the European

161 After the end of Heidenstam's tenure, the couple moved to Izmir. Curiously, Heidenstam and his wife were involved in the first recorded opera performance in Istanbul – in 1786 at the Swedish Palace. Heidenstam had set the piece to music and acted as conductor of the orchestra, while his wife acted in it, next to the daughter of the Spanish ambassador, as well as Swedish, Venetian, Habsburg and Spanish embassy officials. Suna Suner, 'The earliest opera performances in the Ottoman world and the role of diplomacy', in *The age of Mozart and Selim III (1765–1808)*, vol. 1 of *Ottoman Empire and European theatre* (Wien, 2013), eds. Michael Hüttler and Hans Ernst Weidinger, pp. 187–191; see also Sture Theolin, *The Swedish palace in Istanbul: A thousand years of cooperation between Turkey and Sweden* (Istanbul, 2000), p. 194. The marriage between Gerhard Heidenstam and Catharine de Hochepied was announced in the *Hollandsche Historische courant*, 02/08/1783.

162 Olnon, *'Brought under the law of the land'*, p. 147. For the early history of Jews in the Ottoman Empire, see Joseph R. Hacker, 'The rise of Ottoman Jewry', in *The early modern world, 1500–1815*, vol. 7 of *The Cambridge history of Judaism*, eds. Jonathan Karp and Adam Sutcliffe (Cambridge, 2018), pp. 77–112.

163 Sonyel, 'The protégé system'.

164 The difference and different use over time, as well as in European and Ottoman documents, is further explained in Olnon, *'Brought under the law of the land'*, pp. 38–41.

early modern use of *nation*.[165] The Greek Orthodox, Armenian and Jewish communities were all *taifes*, which meant they enjoyed a certain degree of political and legal autonomy. This included the possibility of intracommunity adjudication. The European trading communities easily fell into this system after obtaining capitulations.

Merchants and brokers belonging to one of the *taifes* who were involved in commercial transactions with Europeans stood in a unique position that subjected them to vulnerabilities but also provided them with certain strengths. A good example of the pressure Izmir's Jews were able to exercise can be found in the problems faced by Dutch Consul van Dam in 1677, when a number of Jewish merchants standing under Dutch protection claimed the repayment of loans that had been given to Dutch merchants. The Jewish creditors threatened them with litigation before an Ottoman *qadi* court and petitioned the English to support their cause. They obtained the support of the grand duke of Tuscany through the Jewish community of the free port of Livorno, as well as that of one of the wealthiest Jewish traders in Amsterdam at the time, Jacob de Pinto. The situation led to a Jewish embargo and a standstill of Dutch trade in Izmir and angry letters from the States General to Consul van Dam. It was resolved by Dutch acceptance of repayment in the following years.[166]

The event might still have resonated in 1690, when the grand duke of Tuscany asked the Dutch consul to take several of his subjects, Portuguese Jews, under his protection. Van Dam had gone, succeeded as consul by Daniel Jean de Hochepied, who thought it was a good idea, writing to the States General that he would accept it unless they objected. It seemed a good way of expanding Dutch influence. Dutch traders in Izmir, however, had already objected to the idea, perhaps remembering the events that occurred two decades earlier. They feared the extension of Dutch protection to Tuscan Jews would cause a loss of commissions from Jewish traders, as well as from merchants established in Italy, but this was much to the consul's surprise, because several other European states, particularly France, were hoping for the opportunity to protect the same Tuscan subjects.[167] In his letters to the United Provinces, the consul explicitly stated that, if he refused protection to the Tuscan Jews, they would undoubtedly be 'received with open arms by the other consuls, particularly the

165 Ibid., p. 41.

166 Ibid., pp. 147–152.

167 Heeringa and Nanninga, *Bronnen tot de geschiedenis*, 2: pp. 254–255, Consul Daniel Jean de Hochepied to the States General, Izmir, 19/11/1690, and pp. 256–257, Consul Daniel Jean de Hochepied to the States General, Izmir, 04/07/1691.

French, who protect all persons without distinction'.[168] It would harm Dutch commercial interests, which he felt was a pity, especially considering it was a 'right and privilege permitted by the imperial capitulations'.[169] The Directorate of Levant Trade, whose advice was sought in the matter, agreed with the consul and felt it might benefit Dutch commercial interest, but they suggested the protection should only be given on the condition that the Tuscan Jews would agree to take the same oath as the Dutch nationals.[170]

The Dutch national oath was an instrument that was introduced in the Levant by the States General in their regulation from 6 June 1615. It was an oath destined to prevent fraud on the part of Dutch merchants, skippers and commercial agents active in Levant trade and shipping. The new regulation forced them to give Dutch consuls and vice-consuls, as well as the representative in Istanbul, access to their commercial documents and to give lists of everything – money and merchandise – that they received from the United Provinces or shipped to the Levant so that Dutch officials could determine the correct taxes to be paid on them, which included the consular taxes used to fund consulates. By taking the national oath, merchants, agents and skippers swore that their documents were sincere, honest and truthful.[171] The national oath, and who would be obliged to take it, was met with protest by Dutch merchants, who often argued that Ottoman traders involved in Dutch Levant trade had an unfair advantage because they were not obliged to take the oath. The practice remained controversial until the 1680s, a decade after new legislation had attempted to cement the obligation to take the national oath by making refusal a punishable offence. Further legislation in 1688 finally settled the matter.[172]

It seems that initially, the condition of the oath in the case of the Tuscan Jews was met, and Dutch protection was extended to the Tuscan Jews in Izmir but was challenged a few years later. In 1694, it was rumoured that the new grand vizier, Sürmeli Ali Pasha, wanted to expel the Portuguese Jews from

---

168 Heeringa and Nanninga, *Bronnen tot de geschiedenis*, 2: pp. 256–257, Consul Daniel Jean de Hochepied to the States General, Izmir, 04/07/1691, on p. 257, '[…] door de andere heeren consuls met open armen werden ontfangen, principaal door de Francen, die alle personen sonder onderscheyd beschermen […]'.

169 Ibid., '[…] een regt en privilegie is bij de kijserlijke capitulatie vergund […]'.

170 Heeringa and Nanninga, *Bronnen tot de geschiedenis*, 2: p. 257, Directorate of Levant Trade to the States General, Amsterdam, 14/09/1691.

171 Cau, *Groot placaet-boeck*, 2: pp. 1333–1336, 'Acte, waer by gheconsenteert wort ten behoeve vanden orateur tot Constantinopolen', 06/06/1615.

172 For the controversies surrounding the oath in the 1670s and 1680s, as well as the new legislation, see pp. 81–82 and 99–103.

Ottoman lands and perhaps even go so far as to confiscate their goods.[173] The Dutch ambassador in Istanbul, Jacob Colyer, warned the consul in Izmir, who informed the Jews under his protection.[174] According to the first letter the consul sent to the States General about this, the vizier had been instigated by the French ambassador. When informed of these plans, the Portuguese Jews under Dutch protection planned to send a delegation to Istanbul to discuss matters with the Dutch ambassador. The consul expressed his contentment about this, hoping the Jews would be able to arrange a solution so 'we can maintain, to the regret of our enemies, this point of the capitulations with regard to the protection of foreigners'.[175] Sürmeli's plans might have been motivated by the fact that he was heavily in debt, but the Dutch ambassador, supported by the Rais Effendi, managed to turn his mind, promising him financial compensation.[176] The Dutch ambassador and consul agreed that this compensation needed to be paid by the Portuguese Jews in Izmir, but they refused. For de Hochepied, it showed the 'ingratitude and little confidence those people have with regards to us, desiring to enjoy all privileges from our capitulations, without it costing them a penny'.[177] The consul concluded that, should the Jewish refusal continue, he would withdraw Dutch protection.[178]

While it cannot be explicitly proven that anti-Semitic motivations were behind the consul's remarks, it should be acknowledged that a certain animosity existed in regard to them as a community considered as different. Olnon acknowledges as much by stating that 'national sovereignty was clearly catching up with ethno-religious group identities as a determinant of legal status'.[179]

173 Heeringa and Nanninga, *Bronnen tot de geschiedenis*, 2: pp. 262–263, Consul Daniel Jean de Hochepied to the States General, Izmir, 24/06/1694. For Sürmeli Ali Pasha's tenure, see Michael Nizri, *Ottoman high politics and the Ulema household* (Basingstoke, 2014), pp. 105–107.

174 Jacob Colyer had succeeded his father Justinus as ambassador in 1688. Schutte, *Repertorium der Nederlandse vertegenwoordigers*, pp. 308–309. His brother-in-law Daniel Jean de Hochepied, who was to become Dutch consul in Izmir, initially was his secretary.

175 Heeringa and Nanninga, *Bronnen tot de geschiedenis*, 2: pp. 262–263, Consul Daniel Jean de Hochepied to the States General, Izmir, 24/06/1694, on p. 263, '[...] dit point van onse capitulatie, in spijt onser vijanden, in 't reguarde van het protigieeren der vreemdelingen sullen konnen maintineeren [...]'.

176 Heeringa and Nanninga, *Bronnen tot de geschiedenis* 2: pp. 263–264, Consul Daniel Jean de Hochepied to the States General, Izmir, 16/07/1694. This further confirms the thesis that the vizier was looking for a way to solve his financial troubles.

177 Ibid., on p. 264, '[...] de ondanckbaarheyd en het wijnig vertrouwen, soo dat volk op ons heeft, die wel te desideeren van alle onse voorregten en previligiën onser kapitulatie te jouïsseeren, sonder dat het haar een stuyver soude kosten'.

178 Ibid.

179 Olnon, *'Brought under the law of the land'*, p. 153.

The Dutch took action, and they petitioned for a *ferman* that revoked Jewish exemption from the poll tax if they were active as middlemen for the Dutch. Although they succeeded in getting it, it does not seem to have been used.[180] It did alienate the Jewish traders in question from the Dutch, and in September 1695, the Dutch ambassador wrote that the Jews had renounced Dutch protection and accepted that of France, claiming they were allowed to do so as free people who were acting in line with the relevant articles in the French capitulations. They had also obtained a sentence from the *qadi* in which he stated he would not interfere, as it was a matter of a dispute on protection between two foreign nations, which, the *qadi* stated, could not be adjudicated by the sultan.[181] By the time Colyer had sent this letter, Grand Vizier Sürmeli Ali Pasha had already been dismissed and executed for his inability to pay his debts.[182]

The problems with the Tuscan Jews did not stop Dutch efforts to extend their protection to Jews – who made several complaints that the Dutch consul in Izmir was charging them fees that were too high.[183] Several Jewish traders still figure amongst the lists of members of the Dutch community in Izmir for 1759 and 1766 (see tables 1 & 2), but nationality was not clearly delineated throughout the early modern period, and it is not clear whether they were foreigners under Dutch protection, as had been the case for the Tuscan Jews eighty years earlier, or whether they had ties to the United Provinces that qualified them as Dutch subjects in the Levant.[184] In 1758, a Jewish merchant who was established in Izmir, Daniel Chaves, petitioned the States General in an attempt to obtain the same rights as the Dutch merchants in Izmir. He explained that the Chaves firm had been established in Amsterdam 'for more than a hundred years' before his grandfather, a Dutch Jew, had relocated the

180 Ibid.

181 Heeringa and Nanninga, *Bronnen tot de geschiedenis*, 2: pp. 264–266, Ambassador Jacob Colyer to the States General, Istanbul, 07/09/1695. In his letter, Colyer mentioned the same Jews were the cause of an earlier dispute between the Dutch and the English in Izmir. This might be a reference to the events of 1668, as at the time, the Jewish creditors had complained to the English consulate about Dutch Consul van Dam.

182 This happened in May 1695. Nizri, *Ottoman high politics*, pp. 105–107.

183 Heeringa and Nanninga, *Bronnen tot de geschiedenis*, 2: p. 264. Of course, the possible protection of Jewish traders in this sense was only possible for non-Ottoman Jews and should not be confused with the protection bought by the 'honorary dragomans'.

184 Jews could become burghers of Dutch cities, but it did not pass on to their children, which necessitated the formal extension of Dutch protection, even if it was a Dutch Jew who went to the Levant. Dutch Jews only obtained full citizenship rights in 1796. Hans Daalder, 'Dutch Jews in a segmented society', in *Paths of emancipation. Jews, states, and citizenship*, eds. Pierre Birnbaum and Ira Katznelson (Princeton, 1995), pp. 37–59.

firm to Izmir.[185] There, he as well as his children had always enjoyed consular protection. Although he was born in Izmir, Daniel Chaves assumed he would enjoy the same protection 'ex natura', but he encountered a number of difficulties that made him think this was not the case.[186] The States General decided to grant Chaves' request and sent a letter to the consul and ambassador to protect Chaves and 'make him enjoy all freedoms, rights and privileges the free and ordinary merchants of these lands are enjoying there'.[187]

It seems, however, that in practice, this was not sufficient as, twenty-one months later, Daniel Chaves appeared on a list of members of the Dutch trading community in Izmir. He was described as born in Izmir but of Dutch extraction and married, with a house in the city as well as an outside residence in Bornova, eight kilometres northeast of Izmir (the place is mentioned as 'Burnabad' on figure 4).[188] He had done well apparently, but he also had purchased an official *berat* confirming he was an Ottoman under Dutch protection. His earlier petition had been made in the hopes of obtaining such protection free of charge but apparently that had not worked out. In comparison, a number of Jewish traders who had been born in the United Provinces managed to get such protection for free.[189] Chaves remained a respected member of the Dutch community, and when his firm went bankrupt in 1766, Consul Daniel Jean de Hochepied testified that Chaves was a 'good and honest man'.[190] The petition by Daniel Chaves is a good example of how merchants tried to best use a situation in which nationality was not immediately clear. The sometimes-blurry status of Dutchmen or persons born in the Ottoman Empire to Dutch parents was also a worry for officials, and the States General issued several laws confirming the Dutch nationality of their Ottoman-born consuls in Izmir and ambassadors in Istanbul. Elbert de Hochepied, for instance, was born in Izmir in 1706; son of the Dutch consul there, Daniel Jean de Hochepied, and Clara Colyer, daughter of the former Dutch ambassador in Istanbul. Elbert

185 NA, N°1.02.22 'Archief van het Nederlandse Consulaat te Smyrna, (1611) 1685–1811 (1837)' (hereafter NACS), N°30 ('Brieven en extract-resoluties Staten-Generaal'), 'Request Daniel Chaves', 18/01/1758, '[…] meer dan honderd jaar […]'.

186 Ibid. The request never specified what kind of difficulties.

187 Ibid., '[…] mitsgaders te doen goudeeren van alle zoodanige vrijheeden rechten en privilegien als vrije en ordinaris cooplieden deser landen aldaar zijn genietende'.

188 See table 2. A 1766 list refers to Chaves as the child of a mother and father from Holland. NACS, N°14 ('Uitgaande brieven, 1766–1774'), Daniel Jean de Hochepied to Ambassador Willem Dedel, Izmir, 08/12/1766.

189 See table 1.

190 Heeringa and Nanninga, *Bronnen tot de geschiedenis*, 4: p. 43, Consul Daniel Jean de Hochepied to Fagel, Izmir, 16/04/1766, '[…] een braaf ende eerlijk man […]'.

went to study law in Leiden in 1722 and was made secretary of the Orphan Chamber (*Weeskamer*) in Haarlem in 1735 before he became Dutch ambassador in Istanbul in 1746.[191] After he became secretary in Haarlem, he wanted to get his status as Hollander confirmed and petitioned the States General, which issued a resolution instructing that de Hochepied would be held as a born Hollander.[192]

3.3 *Purchasing Protection: The* Beratlıs *or Honorary Dragomans*

Men such as Chaves, an Ottoman with family ties going back to Amsterdam, could attempt to obtain Dutch protection on the basis of the status of their forefathers. This was a particularly complicated claim in Chaves' case because he was Jewish, and it seems it did not work out. There was, however, another option available to men in his position, and family ties to the United Provinces did not play a formal role in this option. Over time, it had become possible for non-Muslim Ottomans, such as Greeks, Jews or Armenians, who often acted as middlemen in European-Ottoman trade, to purchase European legal status through a *berat*. This practice was called the *protégé* system, and its beneficiaries were *protégés, beratlıs* or *barattaires*. The *protégé* system had grown out of the right for European nations to employ a number of Ottoman non-Muslims dragomans, who served as interpreters and legal brokers between themselves and Ottoman justice. It was the prerogative of ambassadors and consuls to appoint them, a privilege given by the sultan in the capitulations. These dragomans became attached to diplomatic European institutions and, as such, enjoyed a certain level of protection and insertion into European legal systems, including the right to be adjudicated by the consular court of the protecting nation.[193]

During the eighteenth century, the dragoman system was commercialised, and dragoman status was sold by European ambassadors, thereby gaining additional income. Although the Ottoman Empire always remained conscious of the number of *protégés* attached to the different European embassies and consulates, the system expanded, even leading to 'dragoman dynasties', where the post effectively became hereditary.[194] This followed an earlier practice in

191 Schutte, *Repertorium der Nederlandse vertegenwoordigers*, p. 311.

192 Scheltus, *Groot placaatboek*, 6: p. 73, 'Resolutie, Mr. Elbert de Hochepied, tot Smirna gebooren, te houden voor een Hollander', 11/07/1736. His brother Jacob had done the same in 1721. Ibid., p. 471, 'Resolutie, Jacob de Hochepied, in Turkyen gebooren, te houden voor een Hollander', 26/11/1721.

193 See footnote 47 on p. 29.

194 Van den Boogert, *The capitulations*, pp. 63–116. For the commercialization of the system and the price attached to obtaining dragoman status, see Artunç, 'The price of legal

which the position of dragoman as interpreter passed from father to son. In the seventeenth century, for instance, Venetian diplomats looked to replace dragomans with their sons, and a number of families employed different sons as dragomans for different European nations.[195] As official dragomans continued to be employed by diplomatic institutions, Europeans distinguished buyers of the status by labelling them honorary dragomans, *protégés* or *beratlıs*.[196] While this status gave them some of the same privileges that foreigners enjoyed in the Ottoman Empire, they remained subjects of the sultan. Beneficial as it could be, obtaining dragoman status was expensive. A Dutch *berat* cost 2,500 *kurus* in 1759, almost eighteen times the yearly income of an unskilled worker in Istanbul and almost nine times that of a skilled worker. By 1803, the price had risen to 4,500 *kurus*, or about thirty-two times the yearly income of an unskilled worker and sixteen times that of a skilled one.[197] At its zenith in 1757, the Dutch had thirty *beratlı*s, ten of them in Izmir. Both the French and English sold more *berat*s (forty-six and forty-three respectively) but less of them (four and five respectively) resided in Izmir.[198]

The purchase of a *berat* provided legal protection and fiscal exemptions for as long as the *beratlı* held his nominal position, and this included his sons as well as two 'servants'[199] for life. From the second half of the eighteenth century onwards, the *berat*s of the servants or *hizmetkâr*s were sold separately, at a lower price than the main *berat*s but offering the same privileges.[200] The two

institutions', pp. 20–48. An older version of the article is available as, 'The protégé system and berath merchants in the Ottoman Empire: The price of legal institutions', working paper, Yale University (2013), consulted online at http://www.econ.yale.edu/~egcenter/berats_third_draft.pdf. For these 'dragoman dynasties' in the late eighteenth and early nineteenth centuries, see de Groot, 'Dragomans' careers'; and 'The dragomans of the embassies in Istanbul 1785–1834', in *Eastward bound. Dutch ventures and adventures in the Middle East*, eds. Geert Jan van Gelder and Ed de Moor (Amsterdam and Atlanta, 1994), pp. 130–158.

195 Rothman, 'Interpreting dragomans', pp. 777–778 and 781.

196 Van den Boogert, *The capitulations*, pp. 76–77.

197 Artunç, 'The protégé system', p. 10.

198 Artunç, 'The price of legal institutions', p. 728.

199 Women (and thus daughters in this case) are often not mentioned in this context because they were not taxable, but the wives of *beratlıs*, for instance, did benefit from the legal protection of the husbands. See for instance the handling of the estate of Greek dragoman for the Dutch consulate, Dimitri Dallāl, discussed in van den Boogert, *The capitulations*, pp. 179–205.

200 Ibid., p. 70. Because servant status had to be confirmed by an official *ferman*, European sources often refer to these men as *firmanli*s (*fermanlıs*). Ottoman sources use the term *hizmetkâr* (servant). Van den Boogert, *The capitulations*, p. 68. Over time, these servant *berats* were sold to such an extent that they no longer automatically belonged to actual servants.

main advantages of buying a *berat* were exemption from certain taxes, including the *haraç*, and the lowering of others, such as Ottoman custom duties and access to the European legal system for settling disputes, which included the right to be judged as a defendant by the consular court of the European nation selling the protection. It meant that 'a *beratlı* was practically a European subject armed with extraterritorial rights'.[201] However, a number of differences remained. In the Dutch case, the Ottoman *beratlı*s were considered part of the Dutch trading community, but they did not have to take the national oath. They also paid higher consular duties than Dutch nationals.[202] The position of these *protégés* was often contested by Ottoman officials and Dutch diplomats and traders. There were times when the Ottomans attempted to curtail the practice of selling *berat*s in an attempt to exercise more control over their subjects, who had come under European protection for commercial or legal purposes.[203]

In the second half of 1766 the Dutch community increasingly came under Ottoman scrutiny concerning the Ottoman *protégés* attached to it (see table 1), and Consul de Hochepied wrote to the Dutch ambassador in Istanbul that he would never recommend anyone for a *berat* unless they were people of 'honour and reputation'.[204] In December, a *hatt-ı şerif* (sultanic writ) was issued in Izmir, warning consuls to no longer accept Ottomans under their protection and demanding all Ottoman subjects who had not purchased a *berat* to dress 'following the order of the Great Lord, wearing black vests'.[205] De Hochepied wrote that a similar *hatt-ı şerif* had been issued ten years earlier and that he had not accepted new *protégés* since then, sending his dragomans and the chancellor to the *qadi* with a list of members of the Dutch trading community as evidence. In return, he demanded from the *qadi* that no one was to lay a hand on his subjects who figured on the list nor to demand the *haraç*. He even declared he was willing to pay the *haraç* himself if the Ottomans insisted.[206] Apparently,

201 Artunç, 'The price of legal institutions', p. 725.

202 Contemporary sources confirm this status. See for instance a letter sent by the Dutch treasurer in Izmir to the Directorate of Levant Trade, in which he summed up these benefits. Heeringa and Nanninga, *Bronnen tot de geschiedenis*, 4: p. 186, Treasurer C.G.N. Schutz to the Directorate of Levant Trade, Izmir, 03/06/1774.

203 Van den Boogert, *The capitulations*, pp. 105–112.

204 NACS, N°14, Consul Daniel Jean de Hochepied to Ambassador Willem Dedel, Izmir, 16/10/1766.

205 Ibid.

206 Which demonstrates that there still remained a small contingent of Jewish traders with family ties to the United Provinces who stood under Dutch protection without purchasing it.

they did not, and de Hochepied only mentioned that two Livornese Jews had been released after they had been arrested by mistake.[207]

A few days later, Consul de Hochepied wrote to the Dutch ambassador in Istanbul that rumours were spreading in Izmir about the desire of certain Ottoman officials to turn all European-born Jews into Ottoman subjects, which would fit within a larger effort to reduce the number of Ottoman *beratlıs*.[208] The consul had obtained a list of names that the Ottomans were using for this purpose, which contained seven Jews and nine Ottomans who had been working for the Dutch.

De Hochepied wanted the ambassador to arrange a *ferman* allowing protection for the three Ottoman men who never had one, as well as for one of the Jews, Moise Pereira. He was an old man, born in the United Provinces, who had served the consulate for thirty-five years and whose life would be made easier with a *berat*.[209] In the end, it seems the Ottoman threats remained idle, but they did serve as a reminder to the Europeans that no privilege was permanently given and that they remained guests at the pleasure of the Porte.

4 The Dutch Trading Community of Izmir in the Eighteenth Century

4.1 *A Community of Competing Traders*

Izmir was conveniently located on the western coast of Anatolia near the Aegean Sea (see figures 3 & 4). It had been an important port city since Antiquity and was well suited for both overseas and overland trade because of its geographical position. It relied on its hinterland in Anatolia for the production of cotton and continued to play an important commercial role during the Middle Ages. It further expanded its commercial and industrial activities after the Ottoman conquest of 1426. By the end of the fifteenth century, the city had a flourishing trade in luxury items, such as cloth and decorated vases.[210] European traders had been active there since the Middle Ages and privileges were given to Venetians and merchants from Cyprus in 1207, to the Genoese in 1304, to members of the Holy League in 1348 and more extensive ones to Venetian and Genoese traders after 1350.[211] During this period, Izmir was still a

207 NACS, N°14, Consul Daniel Jean de Hochepied to Ambassador Willem Dedel, Izmir, 04/12/1766.

208 NACS, N°14, Consul Daniel Jean de Hochepied to Ambassador Willem Dedel, Izmir, 08/12/1766.

209 Ibid.

210 Frangakis-Syrett, *The commerce of Smyrna*, p. 23.

211 Olnon, *'Brought under the law of the land'*, p. 143.

TABLE 1 Ottomans working for the Dutch consulate in 1766

Name	Additional information	Status
Jacob Pisa	born in Amsterdam, not married	Jewish
Moise Pereira	born in Amsterdam, married in Izmir	Jewish
Judah Pereira	son of Moise Pereira	Jewish
Isaac Pereira	son of Moise Pereira	Jewish
Joseph Pereira	son of Moise Pereira	Jewish
Isaac Nunes	born in Amsterdam, not married	Jewish
Daniel Chaves (and son)	born and married in Izmir	Jewish holding a *ferman*
Diodato Abro	employed by the Directorate of Levant Trade	*beratlı*
Copruli Ammin	employed by the Directorate of Levant Trade	*beratlı*
Pitako Hagi Antonoğlu		*beratlı*
Tschellik Torcce		*beratlı*
Isaie di Massé		*beratlı*
Abram Assecri		*beratlı*
Januachi Malcozzi	tax collector for the Directorate of Levant Trade	neither *berat* nor *ferman*
Gualtieri Gallo	conducted visitation of ships for the Directorate of Levant Trade	neither *berat* nor *ferman*
Jorgachi Amira	employed at the consulate's chancery and treasury	neither *berat* nor *ferman*

SOURCE: NACS, N°14, CONSUL DANIEL JEAN DE HOCHEPIED TO AMBASSADOR WILLEM DEDEL, IZMIR, 08/12/1766

fairly modest town that would only transform into a trade hub of international proportions with the arrival of French, English and Dutch traders during the first half of the seventeenth century.[212]

212 For general analyses of European trade in Izmir that are indispensable, see Goffman, 'Izmir'; and Frangakis-Syrett, *The commerce of Smyrna*. For the establishment of Dutch trading relations with Izmir, see Fikret Yılmaz, *400 years in Izmir: Izmirian Dutch people and trade relations between Izmir and Holland* (Izmir, 2012).

FIGURE 3 View of Smyrna (Izmir) by N. Knop, 1779
FROM THE COLLECTION OF THE RIJKSMUSEUM, AMSTERDAM

It was this 'northern invasion' that made Izmir the most important centre for Ottoman trade with Europe. For some observers, it changed the city a great deal. The Ottoman traveller Evliya Çelebi (1611–1682) visited Izmir in 1671 and remarked that 'every year a thousand ships come and go to have their goods sold in this city of Izmir. Thus, this place has become a truly shining trading port adorned with bustling quays. And because of these malevolent Frankish ships arriving, half the city of Izmir resembles the land of the Franks'.[213] The observation that half the city looked European was an exaggeration; the European quarters were confined to an area in the lower part of the city near the seashore, around 'Street of the Franks' (see figure 4).[214] The area was surrounded by the Armenian and Jewish quarters, while the Greeks, often from Anatolia or the island of Chios, gradually incorporated themselves into the higher located Ottoman Muslim parts of the city.[215] The French artillery officer Claude Alexandre, Comte de Bonneval, wrote upon his arrival in Izmir in 1740 that 'the prettiest and most agreeable area of the city is the street that is called [street] of the Franks, because all the European merchants reside there. This street is filled with very pretty houses, all with very large galleries that extend

213 As quoted from and translated by Olnon, *'Brought under the law of the land'*, p. 141.
214 For an analysis of the geography of the city in the sixteenth and seventeenth centuries, see ibid., pp. 82–140.
215 Ibid., pp. 98–99.

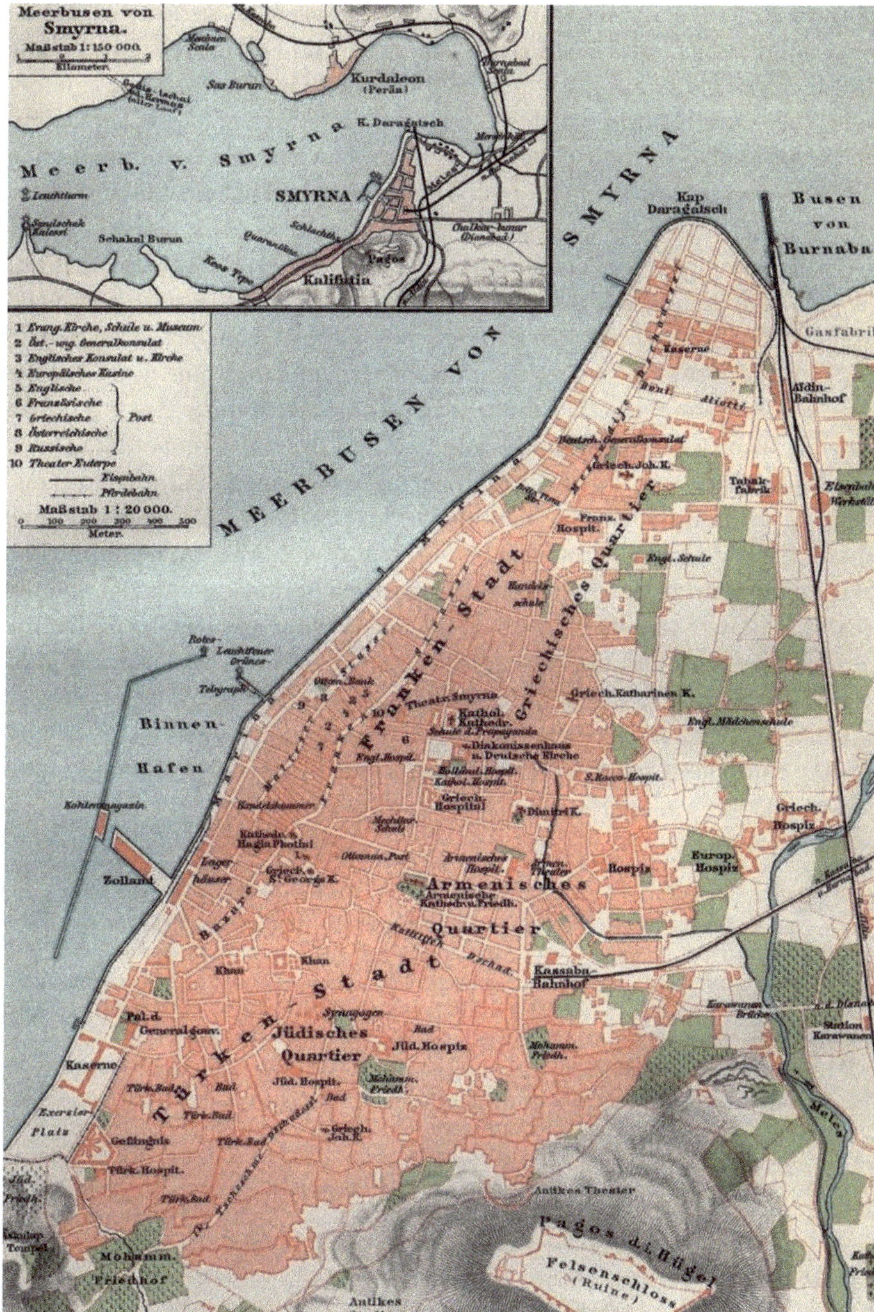

FIGURE 4 German map of Smyrna (Izmir). Lithograph, 25 cm x 16 cm.
FROM THE BROCKHAUS LEXIKON, 1895

all the way to the sea and particularly on the docks, which is strictly separated from where the galleries of the Great Lord are'.[216] When the Frenchman made his observation, the European population of Izmir was limited to a number between 700 and 800, of which 250 to 300 were French, of a total population that amounted to 100,000.[217] By that time, the three largest European trading nations in Izmir were, in order of importance, France, England and the United Provinces.

The Dutch mercantile community in Izmir was never very large. It is not easy to make estimates of the total European presence in the seventeenth and eighteenth centuries for lack of numbers, but Merlijn Olnon has collected data on the basis of several sources from the late seventeenth century. One of the most accurate reports on the European population seems to be that of Antoine Galland, who visited Izmir in 1672 and 1678 and counted twenty-three Dutch merchants, with three of them married to local women, and an additional eight clerks. Additionally, he mentioned that one Florentine merchant, one Florentine clerk and one trader from Siena all stood under Dutch protection. In comparison, the French community consisted of thirty merchants, and the English counted seventy.[218] A list of all members of the Dutch community compiled by Consul Daniel Jean de Hochepied in October 1759 included thirteen Dutch merchants, sixteen scribes, five artisans, three servants, a treasurer, chaplain, chancellor and physician.[219] The list also included two Genoese merchants, and one of them was married to a Dutch woman, who stood under

216 'Le plus bel endroit et le plus agréable de la ville est la rue qu'on appelle des Francs, parce que c'est où résident tous les négociants européens. Cette rue est remplie de très belles maisons toutes accompagnées de très grandes galeries qui avancent dans la mer, et particulièrement sur la darse, qui est fort séparé où l'on tient les galères du Grand Seigneur', quoted from NA, N°1.10.41 (Archief van de familie de Hochepied), N°101 ('Lezing, gehouden door Dr. Varenne voor de Alliance Française te Smyrna over Bonneval Pasja', S.d.). Later in his life, de Bonneval converted to Islam and worked for the Ottoman sultan. See Julia Landweber, 'Fashioning nationality and identity in the eighteenth century: The Comte de Bonneval in the Ottoman Empire', *The international history review*, 30:1 (2008): pp. 1–31.

217 Marie-Carmen Smyrnelis, 'Les européens de Smyrne du XVIIe au XIXe siècle: Citadins ou non?' in *L'urbain dans le monde musulman de Méditerranée*, ed. Jean-Luc Arnaud (Tunis, 2005), pp. 121–133.

218 Olnon, *'Brought under the law of the land'*, pp. 253–255. The French community was larger in total due to a large presence of people who were not merchants, such as artisans, doctors, pharmacists, surgeons and other personnel.

219 Heeringa and Nanninga, *Bronnen tot de geschiedenis*, 3: pp. 395–397, 'Lijst van Nederlanders en Nederlandse geprotegeerden te Smirna', 10/10/1759; see table 2. Daniel Chaves' profession was not mentioned, but we know from other sources that he was a merchant (see pp. 59–60).

Dutch protection. The total number of male members of the Dutch community of Izmir in 1759 amounted to forty-five persons, the forty-four that figured on the list and the consul. In 1766, the Ottoman authorities compiled a list of all the male members of the Dutch trading community of Izmir, reaching a number of forty-eight.[220]

Although the ages of the men appearing in both the 1759 and 1766 lists are not known, they must have varied. Some of the merchants, such as Dirk Knipping and Pieter Ouckama, were still young, while David da Costa had lived in Izmir for twenty-three years already. It was common practice for traders to send one of their sons abroad, as was for instance the case for the firm of Thomas de Vogel & Zoon. One of the sons, also named Thomas, was sent to Izmir, while another son, Leonard Thomas, remained a partner in Amsterdam.[221] In other cases, merchants' sons were employed by firms abroad with whom they corresponded so they could learn the ropes of the trade. When Pieter Ouckama and Dirk Knipping initiated a partnership in Izmir in 1759, they employed the son of Pieter Kikkert from Texel, but they sent him back to his parents due to bad behaviour.[222] It was fairly common for the larger Dutch partnerships in Izmir to employ scribes. It seems to have been far less common for these scribes to become independent traders in their own regard. Of the sixteen men registered as scribes in 1759, three had been there already for more than ten years. Only one of those three, Arnoldus Wissing, a scribe for the firm of Clement, van Sanen, van der Zee & C°, was still there in 1766. Keun and Slaars, scribes for Daniel Fremeaux, were also still there, as well as Frans Duytz, a scribe for the firm of van Lennep & Enslie, and Moses Pereira, who was a scribe in the service of the Dutch treasury. Only Jacob de Vogel, who had come from Rotterdam and was unrelated to Thomas de Vogel from Amsterdam, had moved up to become a partner in the firm of Jacob & George de Vogel – after a controversial association with an Ottoman Greek.[223] Everything suggests that the Dutch trading community was fairly stable in composition. What changed the most were the associations that these merchants formed with one another.

---

220 Heeringa and Nanninga, *Bronnen tot de geschiedenis*, 4: pp. 56–58, Consul Daniel Jean de Hochepied to Ambassador Willem Dedel, Izmir, 08/12/1766; see tables 2 and 3.

221 The business archives of the de Vogel firm in Amsterdam have been preserved for the period 1685–1804 in the family archives. City Archives Amsterdam (hereafter CAA), N°332 ('Archief van de familie de Vogel en aanverwante families') (hereafter CAA/ADV), containing the family's archives and business papers dated between 1608 and 1960.

222 NACS, N°490 ('Register van uitgaande brieven van het handelshuis Knipping & Ouckama, 1759–1761'), Knipping & Ouckama to Pieter Kikkert, Izmir, 20/10/1759.

223 For Jacob de Vogel, see pp. 283–288.

A second feature was the frequent bachelor status of the Dutch merchants in Izmir. This fits within classic interpretations of European merchants remaining single and is not surprising when considering that most of them must have been quite young.[224] It is, however, still somewhat remarkable in light of new research showing that, by the eighteenth century, it was not so uncommon for European merchants to bring wives with them to the Levant.[225] In spite of the growing presence of European women in Levantine cities, twenty-seven men, more than half the men that made up the Dutch community of Izmir, were not married, and table 2 shows that there is no clearly discernible correlation between the time merchants had resided in Izmir when the list was compiled and their marital status.[226] Of the men who were married, only three had Dutch wives: David van Lennep married Anne Marie Leystar, daughter of a Dutch trader (see figure 6), and Giovanni Giera, a Genoese merchant, and Clement van der Laan, a Dutch shopkeeper, both had Dutch wives. Seven men had European wives (French, Italian or German), one had a wife from Izmir, and the origins of the wife of Daniel Chaves were not mentioned. Five men had Greek wives, something that stirred great controversy in the 1760s. The Greek bishop in Izmir was afraid these marriages would come at the expense of the Greek Orthodox community and petitioned the Ottomans to forbid marriages between Greek women and western European men.[227] Although a formal restriction was never issued, the quarrels with the Greek bishop seriously troubled the Dutch community. Not everybody appreciated such interfaith marriages. Dirk Knipping had started out in Izmir working in the office of David van Lennep for seven months, until he was made partner in the firm that was renamed David van Lennep, Knipping & Enslie. The marriage of van Knipping to a local Greek woman angered David van Lennep, and Knipping's involvement in the firm was terminated following a clause in the partnership

224 Wood, *A history of the Levant Company*, p. 244.

225 Van den Boogert, 'Negotiating foreignness', p. 35.

226 Although it is possible that some of the merchants who had been there a long time were widowers.

227 NACS, N°223 ('Papieren raakende de Grieken met de Franken weegens trouw & veranderen der religie &c in maend meij 1767 t'laeste 25d'). Mixed marriages were often considered dangerous as they were considered to have the potential to upset the existing demographical balance between the different religious denominations. For a critical discussion of this, see van den Boogert 'Negotiating foreignness', pp. 35–40; as well as Ian Coller, 'East of enlightenment: Regulating cosmopolitanism between Istanbul and Paris in the eighteenth century', *Journal of world history*, 21:3 (2010): pp. 453–454.

contract that allowed van Lennep to do so in case of a marriage he did not approve.[228]

Changing partnerships, such as Knipping's involvement with van Lennep and Enslie and later with Pieter Ouckama, were not uncommon amongst the Dutch trading community of Izmir, and several partnerships were set up and dissolved within a few years. When they were not partners, it was rare for them to engage in business with one another. Firms were competitors with one another in their efforts to obtain commissions from Europe, but this did not necessarily make them antagonists. The Dutch community of Izmir was small, and traders not only competed with each other but also with the merchants of other trading nations. Additionally, every merchant needed a favour from a colleague every once in a while, and the mutual granting thereof was quite normal amongst early modern traders. While the Dutch merchants in Izmir were not accustomed to do business with each other, they could have shared interests with the same correspondents. The firm of David van Lennep, for instance, was a correspondent with and worked on commission for Thomas de Vogel & Zoon in Amsterdam. One of Thomas' sons resided in Izmir and also acted as an agent for him. Additionally, de Vogel's firm in Amsterdam did business on behalf of van Lennep as well as the son, while Thomas de Vogel in Amsterdam was also the accountant for a ship active in Levant navigation, the *Vogel Fenix* (*Phoenix Bird*), for which they owned a part, but van Lennep owned an equal part.[229]

Even though there were no marital alliances to strengthen ties within the Dutch community, or with other Protestant communities, the Dutch who lived in Izmir must have interacted socially with one another, and with other Europeans. They all lived in a particular neighbourhood, and at times they shared housing. Most merchants rented houses from Ottomans, which were located, together with the warehouses, in *khans*, and several of them lived together.[230] The Ottoman list of Dutch community members in 1766, for instance, mentioned Thomas de Vogel as living with van Lennep and Enslie.

---

228 CAA/ADV, N°36 ('Kopieboek', 1758-1759), pp. 56–58, Thomas de Vogel & Zoon to David van Lennep, Amsterdam, 06/06/1758; and pp. 175–177, Thomas de Vogel & Zoon to David van Lennep, Amsterdam, 21/07/1758.

229 Both owned three-sixteenths of the vessel. CAA/ADV, N°87 ('Redersboek van het schip De Vogel Phenix', 1752–1758). Later, they also owned parts in *De Vrouwe Catharina*. Heeringa and Nanninga, *Bronnen tot de geschiedenis*, 4: pp. 190–192, Thomas de Vogel & Zoon to David van Lennep & Enslie, Amsterdam, 23/08/1765; see also ibid., pp. 503–526 for several accounts of voyages made by the *De Vrouwe Catharina*.

230 *Khans* were communal buildings, large and square, built around a courtyard and owned by Muslim Ottomans, where Europeans rented living and warehouse space. See, for instance, Masters, 'Aleppo', p. 26; and de Groot, *The Ottoman Empire*, p. 131.

When their partnership was dissolved in 1792, David van Lennep's son Jacob expressed his contentment with being able to set up a new firm with a Swiss trader rather than having to deal with Enslie, who he felt was an 'angry, sore man', unmarried and living in the same house as the van Lennep family. Jacob van Lennep felt that Enslie had made their lives miserable, while he was spending most of his profit on a luxurious lifestyle.[231]

4.2 *Levantine Commission Trade*

Dutch trading communities such as the one in Izmir played a specific role in commerce. Hermann Wätjen asserted that in the seventeenth century, most Dutch traders in the Levant fell into two categories; they were either brokers working for a commission fee on behalf of merchants in the United Provinces or junior partners representing firms in the Dutch Republic.[232] The organisation of Dutch Levant trade at the time resembled the French and English systems that relied on 'factors', agents who were employed by firms at home. English Levant traders were united in the Levant Company, which maintained a monopoly over Anglo-Levant trade. The agents that the company sent abroad were often 'the sons of freemen or of gentlemen and cadets of noble families'.[233] In the French case, principals in Marseille employed French agents in the Levant to process their commissions. These agents, *régisseur*s, did not trade on their own as independent firms, and their number was limited by the Marseille Chamber of Commerce.[234]

French and English systems of hierarchy stayed essentially the same throughout the eighteenth century, but the Dutch system allowed for more freedom. By the mid-eighteenth century, Dutch Levant trade had evolved into a system in which most traders in the Levant worked as independent firms that were engaged in a variety of short-term and longer-term commercial partnerships, while still maintaining their role as commission agents.[235] A big difference between them and their French and English colleagues was that Dutch

231 Heeringa and Nanninga, *Bronnen tot de geschiedenis*, 4: pp. 1265–1266, Jacob van Lennep to Leonard Thomas de Vogel, Izmir, 17/11/1792. Not much is known of the general lifestyle of the Dutch merchant community in Izmir.

232 Wätjen, *Die Niederländer*, pp. 184–189.

233 Hakkı Kadı, *Ottoman and Dutch merchants*, p. 158. For the English factors, see Ralph Davis, *Aleppo and Devonshire Square. English traders in the Levant in the eighteenth century* (London, 1967).

234 For the French Levant trade in Izmir in the eighteenth century, see Sébastien Lupo, 'Révolution(s) d'échelles. Le marché levantin et la crise du commerce marseillais au miroir des maisons Roux et de leurs relais à Smyrne (1740–1787)' (unpublished PhD thesis, Aix-Marseille Université, 2015).

235 Hakkı Kadı, *Ottoman and Dutch merchants*, pp. 160–161.

TABLE 2 List of Dutch and Dutch-protected in Izmir, 10/10/1759

Name (as in source)	Profession	Marital status	Ownership	Time present in Izmir	Still present in 1766
Daniel Fremeaux	merchant	not married	no property	8 years	yes
Henrico Cassaing	merchant	not married	no property	14 years	
Daniel Hopker	merchant	not married	no property	3 years	
William Enslie	merchant	not married	no property	5 years	yes
Pieter Ouckama	merchant	not married	no property	2 months	yes
Dirk Knipping	merchant	Greek wife	no property	2 months	yes
Philipo de la Fontaine	merchant	not married	no property	5 years	
Abraham Mendes da Costa	merchant	Venetian wife	no property	11 years	
Johan Frederik Mann	chancellor	Venetian wife	house in Boudja	15 years	yes
David da Costa	merchant	not married	no property	23 years	
Pieter van Sanen	merchant	French wife	house in Hadjeloar [?]	6 years	
David van Lennep	merchant	Dutch wife	house in Sediköy	19 years	yes
Coenraad Borell	treasurer	not married	no property	3 years	
Justinus Johannes Leystar	merchant	not married	no property	2 years	yes
Bernardus Keun	chaplain	not married	no property	4 years	yes
Gaspar van der Sanden	merchant	Greek wife	no property	9 years	
Jan Jacob Cobbe	doctor	Greek wife	houses in Sediköy and Izmir	9 years	yes
Henrico van Tiel	scribe	not married	no property	2 years	

TABLE 2 List of Dutch and Dutch-protected in Izmir, 10/10/1759 (*cont.*)

Name (as in source)	Profession	Marital status	Ownership	Time present in Izmir	Still present in 1766
Abram Keun	scribe	not married	no property	2 months	yes, still as scribe
Giovanni Slaars	scribe	not married	no property	2 years	yes, still as scribe
James Enslie	scribe	not married	no property	1 year	
François Duytz	scribe	not married	no property	5 years	yes, still as scribe
Samuel Hebert	scribe	not married	no property	6 years	
Jan Theodoor Binman	scribe	not married	no property	5 years	
Willem Fourneau	scribe	Greek wife	no property	15 years	
Arnoldus Wissing	scribe	French wife	no property	12 years	yes, still as scribe
Michel Snell	scribe	Venetian wife	no property	13 years	
Frans Palau	scribe	not married	no property	4 years	
Jacob Pisa	scribe	not married	no property	7 years	
Salomon Rodrigo	scribe	wife from Livorno	no property	7 years	
Moses Perera	scribe treasury	wife from Izmir	no property	? Years	yes, with 3 sons
Jacob de Voogel	scribe	not married	no property	2 years	yes
Pietro Smirachi, Dutch	scribe	not married	no property	8 years	

Giovanni Carlo Giera (Genoa)	merchant	Dutch wife	house in Izmir	12 years	
Giuseppe Copurro (Genoa)	merchant	not married	no property	1 month	
Pietro de Rooy	Dutch servant	not married	no property	10 years	yes, still a servant
Jan Michel Sewalt	Dutch servant	not married	no property	3 years	yes
Jacob Kerner	Dutch servant	not married	no property	1 years	
Clement van der Laan	shopkeeper	Dutch wife	no property	9 years	
Frans Coenraad (Westphalia)	shopkeeper	German wife	no property	16 years	
Jacob Marchand (Geneva)	watchmaker	Greek wife	no property	12 years	
Estiene Cavalda (Geneva)	tailor	French wife	no property	10 years	
Johannes Ophuysen	tailor	not married	no property	3 years	
Daniel Chaves, born in Izmir, Dutch extraction	[merchant]	married	house in the city, house in Bornova	?	yes

SOURCE: HEERINGA AND NANNINGA, *BRONNEN TOT DE GESCHIEDENIS*, 3: PP. 395–397, 'LIJST VAN NEDERLANDERS EN NEDERLANDSCHE GEPROTEGEERDEN TE SMIRNA', IZMIR, 10/10/1759

TABLE 3 New members of the Dutch community in 1766

Name	Profession	Name	Profession
George de Vogel	Merchant	Jan van den Broek (Amsterdam)	Servant for van Lennep & Enslie
Diodato Abro	dragoman in the service of the Directorate of Levant Trade	Esaias Fercken (Liège)	scribe for van Sanen & van der Zee
Costala Amira	dragoman in the service of the Directorate of Levant Trade	J.M. Snell (Hessen-Cassel)	scribe for van Sanen & van der Zee
Pitako Hagi Anton Oglou	*beratlı*	Hendrik Bortendorf (Hamburg)	scribe for van Sanen & van der Zee
Missier di Jagia	*beratlı*	Christiaan Roodermeulen (Amsterdam)	?
Chelik Torec	*beratlı*	A. Beaune (Amsterdam)	?
Isaie di Massé	*beratlı*	Gerrit van Brakel	[merchant]
Adam di Morco	*beratlı*	Johan Antoni Coenraad (Bohemia)	glass seller
Abram Asecri	*beratlı*	Johan Fredrik Coenraad (Bohemia)	glass seller
Janatie Malgos	in the service of the Directorate of Levant Trade	Antoni Habel (Bohemia)	glass seller
Gualtero Gallo	in the service of the Directorate of Levant Trade	Auner van Zeevenbergen	surgeon
Jorgatie Amira	in the service of the Directorate of Levant Trade	Radman van Clef	cutter
Isaac van Oudermeulen	scribe for Fremeaux	Namer van Dresde	cutter

TABLE 3 New members of the Dutch community in 1766 (*cont.*)

Name	Profession	Name	Profession
Thomas de Vogel	lives with van Lennep and Enslie	Joh. Kraus	carpenter
Louis Stechman	scribe for van Lennep & Enslie	Ludecke van Halle	vicar

SOURCE: NACS, N°14, CONSUL DANIEL JEAN DE HOCHEPIED TO AMBASSADOR WILLEM DEDEL, IZMIR, 08/12/1766

merchants offered their services to a variety of firms in the United Provinces and elsewhere, rather than being employed by one particular firm. A second difference was that the Dutch institutional environment allowed for a much higher degree of freedom – which eventually led to the non-Muslim Ottoman penetration of Dutch trade networks with the Levant.[236]

The Dutch, like the other European merchants in Izmir, were involved in what was essentially an exchange trade. They received a variety of products from the United Provinces, which were sold in Izmir to Ottoman merchants. Goods included arms, spices, pepper, coffee, sugar, tin, steel, grain and wheat, but also textiles such as linen and blankets. In particular, woollen cloth, camlets and says produced in Leiden, the leading textile-producing centre of the United Provinces, were a popular export product sent to the Mediterranean.[237] In return, Dutch traders mainly bought raw materials for textile production in Dutch cities, such as cotton, silk, wool or mohair yarn, on behalf of firms in the United Provinces.[238]

Networks of trade developed that connected firms in the United Provinces not only to Dutch traders in Izmir but also to Ottoman non-Muslim merchants who

236 A process described in detail in ibid.

237 For an extensive study, see N.W. Posthumus, *De geschiedenis van de Leidsche lakenindustrie*, 3 vols. (The Hague, 1908). One substantial archive of a cloth merchant was preserved in Leiden, that of Daniël van Eys. He traded extensively with the Levant, and one of his younger brothers was a Director of Levant Trade. See J.W. Veluwenkamp, 'De Leidse lakenondernemer Daniël van Eys, 1688–1739', *Jaarboekje voor geschiedenis en oudheidkunde van Leiden en omstreken*, 84 (1992): pp. 109–124.

238 Bulut, *Ottoman-Dutch economic relations*, pp. 168–169.

acted as intermediaries, doing business on behalf of Europeans with Ottoman customers and suppliers, including Muslims. These intermediaries went by the name of *sensal* and came from the ranks of different non-Muslim Ottoman subjects well-versed in trade, such as Jews, Armenians and Greek.[239] They were brokers, buying goods from locals in various Ottoman cities destined for export and selling the merchandise that Europeans had shipped to the *échelles*.[240] They were paid a percentage of the transaction as fee that was raised by both parties. These *sensals* were thus a second type of intermediary in Dutch Levant trade, next to the Dutch traders in Izmir themselves. These men were traders in their own regard, and although they did not obtain any official privileges in the capitulations, the various Ottoman middlemen, which also included Ottoman scribes and warehousemen (*mahzencis*), obtained the same tax privileges as the Europeans and the dragomans during the eighteenth century.[241] It was important for Dutch and other European trading houses to find reliable *sensals* who could be trusted and stick with them. When Guillaume Cusson, one of the *régisseurs* of the Roux firm of Marseille, arrived in Izmir, he wrote that 'I do not have any *sensals* yet, because for [obtaining the services] this kind of persons one needs to make a careful approach and make the right choice, which is not a matter of one or two days'.[242]

This group of Ottoman *sensals*, which consisted of Armenian, Greek and Jewish Ottomans, managed to overcome their Dutch colleagues in Izmir as intermediaries between the United Provinces and the Levant. They controlled Izmir's internal trade and connections with Ottoman trade circuits further inland.[243] Several of these *sensals* became successful traders on their own, sometimes after they had been able to secure a *berat*. Some of them even started to employ Dutch scribes. In 1768, for instance, Manolaki di Panaiotis, a

239 The word derived from the Arabic 'simsār', meaning agent, and itself of Persian origin. It was altered to 'sensale' in Italian, used by Venetians, and became the term in other European languages to indicate the Ottoman intermediaries in Levantine trade. See S.D. Goitein, *Economic foundations*, vol. 1 of *A Mediterranean society. The Jewish communities of the world as portrayed in the documents of the Cairo Geniza* (Berkeley, Los Angeles, and London, 1967), p. 160.

240 Marie-Carmen Smyrnelis, 'Courtiers de Smyrne (fin du XVIIIe–milieu du XIX siècle). Médiateurs professionnels et médiations dans l'Empire ottoman', in *Hommes de l'entre-deux: parcours individuels et portraits de groupes sur la frontière de la Méditerranée, XVIe–XXe siècle*, eds. Bernard Heyberger and Chantal Verdeil (Paris, 2009), p. 120.

241 Van den Boogert, *The capitulations*, pp. 70–72; see also his 'Ottoman intermediaries in the 18th century: Analysis of a "dirty trade" ', *Oriente moderno*, 93:2 (2013): pp. 515–530.

242 Quoted in Lupo, 'Révolution(s) d'échelles', p. 98, 'Je n'ai pas encore des censseaux, pour ces sortes des gens il faut aller doucement et en faire un bon choix, ce qui n'est pas l'affaire d'un ou deux jours'.

243 Frangakis-Syrett, *The commerce of Smyrna*, p. 104.

Greek trader who purchased French protection, signed a contract with a man from Leiden named Nicolaas Johannes Boonhoff.[244] Boonhoff was to work for di Panaiotis for five years but was fired after less than two years. According to Boonhoff, di Panaiotis had refused to pay for a language instructor that Boonhoff had hired in order to learn French and Italian. This went against the terms agreed upon in the contract. He also did not understand why di Panaiotis accused him of using curse words and of being 'a traitor of his firm'.[245] Because di Panaiotis refused to pay for debts Boonhoff had made, Boonhoff could not leave Izmir, which is why he filed a complaint at the court of the Dutch consul.[246]

The outcome of the case was not registered, but the employment of Dutch scribes by Ottoman merchants involved in trade with the United Provinces was clearly visible. They could help with writing and translating letters and maintaining correspondence with firms in the United Provinces, lessening the need for these Ottomans to procure Dutch partners in Izmir. Some also formed intercultural partnerships with Dutch merchants, a practice the Dutch considered harmful to their national interests and was later forbidden.[247] The French and English commercial operations in the Levant were more tightly controlled, but the Dutch policies of freer trade allowed for the gradual overtaking of Dutch Levant trade by Armenian, Jewish and Greek Ottoman traders who attempted to bypass the Dutch traders in Izmir to deal directly with traders in the United Provinces, a process facilitated through the growing presence of their fellow countrymen in the United Provinces.[248] The Armenians were the first Ottomans to establish themselves in Amsterdam during the seventeenth century, and they were mostly active in the trade in mohair yarn. They found an existing Jewish community, and in the eighteenth century, they were joined by Greek merchants specialising in cotton.[249]

---

244 NACS, N°346 ('Proces tusschen de heeren M: K:r di Panajottis en haar schrijver Joh: Boonhoff van 6 tot 13 april 1770'), 'Contract van Boonhoff met M Kiriaco & C° 1768', Izmir, 22/12/1768.

245 NACS, N°346, 'Request van NJ Boonhoff weeg eenige differentie met Ml Kiriaco di Panajottis & C°', Izmir, 13/04/1770, '[…] een verrader van zijn huys […]'.

246 Ibid.

247 See pp. 281–290.

248 See the chapter 'Ottoman merchants in Amsterdam' in Hakkı Kadı, *Ottoman and Dutch merchants*, pp. 198–234.

249 Maurits van den Boogert, 'Ottoman Greeks in the Dutch Levant trade: Collective strategy and individual practice (c. 1750–1821)', *Oriente moderno*, nuova serie, 86:1 (2006): pp. 129–147. For Jewish traders in the United Provinces, see Daniel Swetschinski, *Reluctant cosmopolitans: The Portuguese Jews of seventeenth-century Amsterdam* (Oxford, 2000); Jonathan Israel and Reinier Salverda, eds., *Dutch Jewry: Its history and*

Dutch authorities quickly became worried about the growing presence of Ottoman merchants in their trade, and merchants in the United Provinces regularly expressed the fear that Ottomans would take over Dutch Levant trade completely in the letters they sent to their Dutch correspondents in Izmir.[250] An additional source for worry was the growing competition from other European trading communities. In 1688, Dutch exports of fine woollen textiles had risen from 3,000 to 6,000 half-pieces. This number had fallen to 3,000 again by the beginning of the eighteenth century, an evolution largely caused by competition from French textiles and English imitations of Dutch textiles.[251] After the War of Spanish Succession, the Dutch lost ground to the French in the Levant, and it was never recovered, partially due to protective tariffs established in Marseille.[252]

In a 1754 memoir on Dutch trade, Elbert de Hochepied, the ambassador in Istanbul, suggested that the Dutch traders in Izmir had been the victim of the success of the trade between the Ottoman Empire and the United Provinces. He stated that the volume of trade in Izmir was too big to be handled by the Dutch community there, so they started to count on foreigners (i.e., Ottomans) to sell their merchandise in Istanbul and Salonika. They also looked to these foreign contacts to purchase goods for the return voyage to the Dutch Republic, which led to the additional payment of commissions in Istanbul and Salonika, next to the payment of transport costs in Izmir, something that caused an unnecessary price rise. According to de Hochepied, this led to foreigners becoming rich from Dutch trade, while there were not even five Dutch traders who 'had been able to retire in the motherland with a not so considerable fortune'.[253]

---

secular culture (1500–2000) (Leiden and Boston, 2002); Jonathan Israel, *Diasporas within a diaspora: Jews, crypto-Jews and the world maritime empires (1540–1740)* (Leiden and Boston, 2002); and Herbert I. Bloom, *The economic activities of the Jews of Amsterdam in the seventeenth and eighteenth centuries* (Williamsport, 1937). For the Armenians, see René Arthur Bekius, 'The Armenian colony in Amsterdam in the seventeenth and eighteenth centuries: Armenian merchants from Julfa before and after the fall of the Safavid Empire', in *Iran and the world in the Safavid age*, eds. Willem Floor and Edmund Herzig (London and New York, 2012), pp. 259–284; Aslanian, *From the Indian Ocean*, pp. 80–81; and Kéram Kévonian, 'Marchands arméniens au XVIIe siècle, à propos d'un livre arménien publié à Amsterdam en 1699', *Cahier du monde russe et soviétique*, 16:2 (1975): pp. 199–244.

250 For a thorough discussion, see the chapter 'The Ottoman penetration of Dutch trading networks' in Hakkı Kadı, *Ottoman and Dutch merchants*, pp. 170–197.

251 Ibid., p. 165.

252 Frangakis-Syrett, *The commerce of Smyrna*, pp. 164–169.

253 NA, N°2.21.006.46, N°2 ('Mémoire pour le commerce', 1754), f°4v, '[…] depuis cinquante ans, se soyent retirez à la patrie, avec quelque fortune un peu considerable […]'.

Furthermore, de Hochepied suggested that firms in Amsterdam and Rotterdam no longer trusted the Dutch traders in Izmir to execute their commissions to satisfaction. De Hochepied felt the number of Dutch trading houses should be fixed, to stop competition between one another, and that partnerships needed to be rearranged to win back the trust that had been lost. The ambassador felt that 'the principal merchants could incorporate their family members or friends there [in the new partnerships in Izmir] and become involved there with knowledge, security and profit'.[254] De Hochepied blamed the independence of Dutch merchants in Izmir for their decline, and his text was meant as a call to go back to the situation of the seventeenth century, when Dutch traders in Izmir were employed as permanent agents by firms back home rather than acting as independent intermediaries working for everyone.

Elbert de Hochepied was not the only ambassador to consider the matter of Dutch national commercial interest and its decline in the face of a growing presence of Ottoman traders. In 1765, Willem Gerrit Dedel wrote to the Directorate of Levant Trade about the disadvantage Dutch merchants had in comparison to Ottoman traders. Dutch traders were obliged to take a national oath in which they promised to adhere to regulations. Dedel argued that the absence of such an oath for Ottoman traders such as the *protégés* made them resort to fraud much more frequently, creating a dishonest situation. Even though it is impossible to assess whether Dedel's observation was in any way correct, it is still an important consideration. An oath was a strong instrument that could be used in court as legal proof. While it is certainly naïve to think that Dutch merchants were hindered from committing fraud simply by taking an oath, it was a valid tool at the disposal of the authorities, and it was not for nothing that Dutch merchants had objected so strongly in the 1670s when they were forced to take it.[255]

Additionally, the national oath forced Dutch merchants to provide Dutch officials access to their commercial paperwork so the share of ambassadorial and consular taxes they needed to pay could be determined correctly. This was a financial burden that did not apply to Ottomans (unless they were *protégés*, but their status exempted them from certain Ottoman taxes), and Dedel felt it was time to make them pay a financial contribution for the institutions that had been introduced to foster the commerce in which they were now playing an integral part. Dedel explained that the oath had been introduced in 1675 at a time when Ottoman traders were still 'inexperienced in trade, and we did the

254 Ibid., f°5r, '[...] les principaux negociants pourront y incorporer de leurs parents, ou amis, et sy interesser avec connoissance, seureté, et profit [...]'.

255 For the disputes in the 1670s and 1680s, see pp. 81–82 and 99–103.

commerce here'.[256] Dedel referred to the overseas trade between the United Provinces and the Levant, and he added that since 1675, Ottoman traders had established themselves in the United Provinces, and Dutch firms at home had started to consign goods directly to Ottoman firms in the Levant, rather than only to Dutch firms.[257] The directors replied that freedom of trade was 'a very delicate matter', and they feared it would be difficult to put a stop to Ottoman influence over Dutch Levant trade.[258] By the 1770s, about half of the Dutch Levant trade was in the hands of Greek merchants, often with Chiot origins.[259]

The response of the directors demonstrated the disagreement within Dutch institutions on how to deal with the Ottoman presence. While many merchants and diplomats pressed for concrete measures, others did not want to obstruct the principles of free trade, and several actions undertaken in Izmir in the late eighteenth and early nineteenth centuries that were aimed against Ottoman traders met with disapproval from the Directorate of Levant Trade back home.[260] In spite of this difference of opinion, measures were taken in an attempt to protect Dutch merchants in the Levant. During the 1760s, the Dutch reacted by establishing new tariffs for consular duties, a restriction on intercultural partnerships between Dutch nationals and Ottomans, and the establishment of an additional duty of 5% on all goods that reached the United Provinces on foreign (non-Dutch) ships. At the end of the eighteenth century, several voices even advocated for the introduction of a monopoly to protect Dutch Levant trade, but this was never implemented. Throughout this century, the Dutch trading community in Izmir remained relevant in the trade between Europe and the Levant but never on the same scale as had been the case during the seventeenth century.[261] Between 1775 and 1789, the export out of Izmir to Dutch ports amounted to 22.5% of the total export of the city to Europe. On the import side, the Dutch share amounted to 18%.[262] During the

---

256 Heeringa and Nanninga, *Bronnen tot de geschiedenis*, 4: pp. 17–20, Ambassador Willem Dedel to the Directorate of Levant Trade, Istanbul, 02/11/1765, on p. 18, '[…] nog zeer onbedreeven in den handel en de negotie wierd hier door ons gedreeven'.

257 Ibid.

258 Heeringa and Nanninga, *Bronnen tot de geschiedenis*, 4: pp. 32–34, Directorate of Levant Trade to Ambassador Willem Dedel, Amsterdam, 24/12/1765, on p. 32, '[…] een seer delicaate saak […]'.

259 Frangakis-Syrett, *The commerce of Smyrna*, p. 100.

260 Hakkı Kadı, *Ottoman and Dutch merchants*, pp. 272–273.

261 On these measures, see the chapter on 'The transformation of Dutch trade policies in the Levant: From free trade to "faint" protectionism' in Hakkı Kadı, *Ottoman and Dutch merchants*, pp. 237–273.

262 Frangakis-Syrett, *The commerce of Smyrna*, p. 168.

Napoleonic wars, British sea blockades put a complete halt to Dutch maritime trade with the Ottoman Empire, and in the early nineteenth century, the Dutch shared the same malaise as the French. By 1820, it was American and British merchants that dominated Izmir's trade with the western world.[263]

263 Ibid., p. 186.

CHAPTER 2

The Dutch Consular Court of Izmir

1 Consular Jurisdiction

1.1 *Adjudication in the Capitulations*

The *ahdnames* allowed for European ambassadors and consuls to adjudicate legal disputes between the members of their nations, and European traders could count on certain privileges should they have to appear in an Ottoman court. This legal autonomy was already present in the early capitulations. The Ottoman-French treaty of 1535, which contained nineteen articles, stipulated that the French king was allowed to appoint bailiffs or consuls who were allowed to adjudicate disputes among Frenchmen without interference from an Ottoman tribunal.[1] Some of the early French capitulations included the clause that litigants belonging to the same European nation could appear before an Ottoman court, but only at the expressed wish of their ambassador. Trials between a Frenchman and an Ottoman subject were to be heard at an Ottoman court, but always in the presence of an interpreter.[2]

The English capitulations of 1580 contained similar clauses on legal autonomy, granting English ambassadors and consuls the right to adjudicate disputes between Englishmen on the basis of English legal custom.[3] Similar arrangements were given to the Dutch in the 1612 capitulations:[4]

> [Article 5] If lawsuits and hostility, cases of murder and blood money occur among those from the Dutch Provinces, their ambassador and consul should see to it according to their customs and decide the case; no qadis or legal officers should interfere.[5]

1 Paul Masson, *Histoire du commerce français dans le Levant au XVIIe siècle* (Paris, 1896), p. xii.

2 Ibid.

3 Skilliter, *William Harborne*, p. 88; see also Herbert J. Liebesny, 'The development of western judicial privileges', in *Origin and development of Islamic law*, vol. 1 of *Law in the Middle East*, eds. Majid Khadduri and Herbert J. Liebesny (Washington, 1955), pp. 309–333.

4 For a transcription into modern Turkish and an English translation of the Dutch capitulations of 1612, see de Groot, *The Ottoman Empire*, pp. 138–157. The translations included here are de Groot's.

5 Ibid., p. 150.

> [Article 6] When any persons enter upon a lawsuit [before the *qadi*] against the consuls appointed for the merchants' affairs, the consuls may not be put under arrest nor their houses be sealed. Their law suits involving consuls and dragomans must be heard at our threshold of felicity.[6]
> [Article 36] If, in the case of a dispute, someone goes to the qadi and the dragoman of the Dutch is not present, the qadi may not hear the case. If it is about important affairs, the case shall be adjourned till the coming [of the dragoman]. But they may not seek an excuse and try to cause delay by saying: 'our dragoman is not present'.[7]

These articles provided the formal expression of Dutch legal autonomy and allowed the consular and ambassadorial courts to operate independently from Ottoman justice, at least in cases involving members of the Dutch trading community. Several jurisdictional issues remained. Disputes involving Ottomans were to be heard at the local *qadi* courts, which were entitled to adjudicate both civil and criminal matters and which also had the competence to act as mediator and notary. The Imperial Council in Istanbul, the *dīwan-i hümayun*, was the Ottoman Empire's highest court, and any Ottoman subject was allowed to seek recourse to this court, although a plaintiff would have to travel personally to Istanbul, a practical impediment that led to decisions regularly being referred back to the *qadi* courts.[8] Several early capitulations specified that the Imperial Council was the competent court in a number of specific cases that involved foreigners. These included murder (first mentioned in the French capitulations of 1536), cases worth over 4,000 aspers (English capitulations of 1601) and cases involving consuls or dragomans (French capitulations of 1604).[9]

Because the capitulations were treaties between a specific European power and the Ottoman Empire, they did not include a solution to the problem of jurisdiction regarding a dispute that involved Europeans belonging to different nations. European consuls and ambassadors in the Levant had agreed to use the Roman principle of *actor sequitur forum rei*, meaning that the defendant was entitled to adjudication at the court under whose jurisdiction he fell.[10]

6 Ibid., pp. 150–151.

7 Ibid., p. 154.

8 Van den Boogert, *The capitulations*, pp. 47–52.

9 Ibid.

10 This was common European legal practice based on Roman law. It can be found in the *Codex* compiled by Justinianus, containing the imperial *constitutiones* from the second century until its publication in 534. It is referred to under the heading 'Imperatores

During the Middle Ages, when legal fragmentation was widespread, several bourgeoning European political entities adopted the *forum rei* principle as a means to determine jurisdiction regarding disputes that involved litigants coming from different towns or regions.[11] In the Ottoman context, *forum rei* was initially adopted on the basis of informal agreements between Europeans. They accepted to bring intra-European disputes in first instance before the consul of the defendant and to bring appeals before the ambassador of the defendant.[12] The first sign of recognition of the practice by the Porte can be found in the French capitulations of 1740:

> Article 52. S'il arrive que les consuls et les négociants français aient quelques contestations avec les consuls et les négociants d'une autre nation chrétienne, il leur sera permis, du consentement et à la réquisition des parties, de se pourvoir par-devant leurs ambassadeurs qui résident à ma Sublime Porte; et tant que le demandeur et le défendeur ne consentiront pas à porter ces sortes de procès par-devant les pachas, kadis, officier ou douaniers, ceux-ci ne pourront pas les y forcer, ni prétendre en prendre connaissance.[13]
> Article 52. If it should be so that the French consuls and merchants have some disputes with the consuls and merchants of another Christian nation, they will be allowed, with consent and at the requisition of all parties involved, to appear before their ambassadors who reside at my Sublime Porte; and in case the plaintiff and defendant do not consent to take such trial before the pachas, qadis, officers or customs officers, these [pachas, *qadis*, officers or customs officers] cannot force them to do so, nor pretend to take notice of it.[14]

Gratianus, Valentianus, Theodosius'. The full article is as follows: 'Actor rei forum, sive in rem sive in personam sit actio, sequitur. sed et in locis, in quibus res propter quas contenditur constitutae sunt, iubemus in rem actionem adversus possidentem moveri'. The *Codex*, as well as the two other Justinian compilations that make up the *Corpus iuris civilis*, can be consulted online at http://www.thelatinlibrary.com/justinian.html.

11 'Actor sequitur forum rei', in Aaron X. Fellmeth and Maurice Horwitz, eds., *Guide to Latin in international law* (Oxford, 2009), consulted online at http://www.oxfordreference.com/view/10.1093/acref/9780195369380.001.0001/acref-9780195369380-e-76.

12 Van den Boogert, *The capitulations*, p. 36. An early mention of the agreement between European consuls to apply the *forum rei* principle was in a letter sent by the Dutch consul in Aleppo, Cornelis Pauw, to the States General in 1615 about the abuses of the Dutch traders in that city against the consul's jurisdiction. See pp. 91–93.

13 Bianchi, *Le nouveau guide*, p. 274.

14 The last part of the phrase is unclear and would make more sense if another denial was added to it: 'these [pachas, *qadis*, officers or customs officers] cannot force them to do so, nor pretend not to take notice of it'.

This was the first time any capitulations contained a clear set of instructions on the proper handling of intra-European disputes. Several other articles of the 1740 capitulations dealt with adjudication:[15]

> Article 15. S'il arrivait quelque meurtre ou quelque autre désordre entre les Français, leurs ambassadeurs et leurs consuls en décideront selon leurs us et coutumes, sans qu'aucun de nos officiers puisse les inquiéter à cet égard.[16]
> Article 15. If a murder or any other disorder happens among the French, their ambassadors and their consuls will decide upon it on the basis of their usages and customs, and none of our officers can disturb them in that regard.
> Article 16. En cas que quelque personne intente un procès aux consuls établis pour les affaires de leurs marchands, ils ne pourront être mis en prison, ni leur maison scellée, et leur cause sera écoutée à notre Porte de félicité; et si l'on produisait des commandements antérieurs ou postérieurs contraires à ces articles, ils seront de nulle valeur, et il sera fait en conformité des capitulations impériales.[17]
> Article 16. In the case that anybody intends to go to trial against the established consuls regarding the affairs of their merchants, they [consuls] cannot be put in prison, their houses cannot be sealed, and their cause shall be heard at our Threshold of Felicity; and if one was to provide commandments, of an earlier or later date than these articles, they shall be of no value, and it will be done in conformity to the imperial capitulations.
> Article 26. Si quelqu'un avait un différend avec un marchand français, et qu'ils se portassent chez le kadi, ce juge n'écoutera point leur procès, si le drogman français ne se trouve présent; et si cet interprète est occupé pour lors à quelque affaire pressante, on différera jusqu'à ce qu'il vienne; mais aussi les Français s'empresseront de le représenter, sans abuser du prétexte de l'absence de leur drogman. Et s'il arrive quelque contestation entre les Français, les ambassadeurs et les consuls en prendront

15 These capitulations were chosen as an example because they were the first to contain the *forum rei* and the 'most favoured nation' principles, ensuring their relevance for capitulations of the other European nations. Additionally, the date they were issued is close to the dates of the disputes that will be investigated as case studies in this monograph, and a full and accurate translation of them into a European language has been published.

16 Bianchi, *Le nouveau guide*, pp. 264–265.

17 Ibid., p. 265.

connaissance, et en décideront selon leurs us et coutumes, sans que personne puisse s'y opposer.[18]

Article 26. If someone has a difference with a French merchant, and if they go to the *qadi*, this judge will not hear the trial unless the French dragoman is present. And if this interpreter is occupied at the time of a pressing matter, the case will be delayed until he comes; but the French will also hurry to represent the matter without abusing the pretext of the absence of their dragoman. And if any dispute occurs between the French, the ambassadors and consuls shall take notice of it, and they will decide according to their use and custom, without anyone able to oppose it.

Article 41. Les procès excédant quatre mille aspres seront écoutés à mon divan impérial, et nulle part ailleurs.[19]

Article 41. Trials concerning monetary sums exceeding 4,000 aspers will be heard at my Imperial Divan, and nowhere else.

Article 69. Si un marchand français voulant partir pour quelque endroit, l'ambassadeur ou les consuls se rendent sa caution, on ne pourra retarder son voyage, sous prétexte de lui faire payer ses dettes; et les procès qui les concernent, excédant quatre mille aspres, seront renvoyés à ma Sublime Porte, selon l'usage, et conformément aux capitulations impériales.[20]

Article 69. If a French merchant wants to leave for any place, the ambassador or the consuls will provide a security deposit for him, and his voyage cannot be delayed on the pretext of forcing him to pay his debts first; and trials concerning those debts higher than 4,000 aspers will be sent to my Sublime Porte, according to legal use, and the imperial capitulations.

Articles 15 and 26 were repetitions of the well-established legal autonomy that already existed in earlier capitulations for different nations.[21] Articles 16 and 69 had historical equivalents in earlier French, Dutch and English capitulations.

---

18 Ibid., pp. 267–268.

19 Ibid., p. 272. These values were quickly outdated as they were not adapted to the changing monetary value, and their presence in the capitulations lost relevance, something the translator of these capitulations was well-aware of.

20 Ibid., p. 280.

21 The Dutch equivalent of article 26, however, only mentioned the obligation to have dragomans present at *qadi* hearings involving a Dutchman. De Groot, *The Ottoman Empire*, p. 154.

Although European consuls and ambassadors were granted legal autonomy, there was nothing in the capitulations that prevented Europeans from seeking recourse to an Ottoman court.[22] Maurits van den Boogert pointed out that article 52 was used to reintroduce the option of appearing before an Ottoman court, should the involved parties desire to do so. It was an option that had been included in earlier French capitulations, but not in those granted to other states.[23] It was, however, an option that was strongly discouraged by European consuls and ambassadors, for fear of setting a precedent or having their subjects involved in trials under a foreign jurisdiction with unpredictable outcomes.

Even though European custom was clear, *forum rei* still led to quarrels; in 1730, the Dutch ambassador in Istanbul, Cornelis Calkoen, wrote to Fagel, an official at the States General, about the furious letters he received from the French ambassador concerning a dispute regarding damages suffered by the vessel of a Dutch skipper named Isaac Haverman.[24] Upon arrival in Salonika, he refused to unload before the issue of financial responsibility for the damage was settled, but the owners instructed him to unload first and promised to pay afterwards. Several French merchants whose goods were on board objected, which led to a legal dispute before the Dutch consul in Salonika. According to Calkoen, his sentencing did not please the Frenchmen, who then appealed before the Dutch ambassador in Istanbul. This made the French ambassador furious, writing to his Dutch colleague that he would never allow Frenchmen to seek justice before the Dutch ambassador; he wanted to try the Dutch ship owners himself.[25] Calkoen found the French ambassador's outrage unjustified, also because it might create legal confusion that the Ottomans might use to extend their jurisdiction to this type of dispute.[26]

1.2 *The Establishment of Consular Jurisdiction*

The capitulations made the Dutch consuls in the Ottoman Empire judges, able to adjudicate on the same basis as courts in the United Provinces. This was neither strange nor new as, since the Middle Ages, consuls had adjudicating powers in disputes involving members of the community over which they

22 Van den Boogert, *The capitulations*, p. 42.

23 Ibid., p. 36. A similar phrasing can be found in article 26, which confirmed the legal autonomy of Europeans, but not before pointing out the possibility of resorting to a *qadi* court.

24 Heeringa and Nanninga, *Bronnen tot de geschiedenis*, 3: pp. 27–29, Ambassador Cornelis Calkoen to Fagel, Istanbul, 08/11/1730.

25 Ibid.

26 Ibid.

had jurisdiction.[27] The institution of the consulate had developed in Venice, Genoa, Ancona and Florence to fill the need of a legal mediator between a host city and a foreign trading community.[28] Consular courts existed in several commercial cities in northwestern Europe as well. Foreign trading communities in Bruges, a crucial commercial centre in the late Middle Ages, had consular courts since 1309, and by 1450, ten of the fourteen foreign nations in Bruges were given their own consular jurisdiction by the city.[29] The granting of consular jurisdiction coincided with a late medieval expansion of adjudication, also in the Low Countries, which led to a growing need for specific legislation codifying the jurisdiction and procedure of litigation for specific courts. A great deal of this legislation was issued during the 'legal revolution' of the sixteenth century, which was also considered a peak period for litigation.[30] It was a period of the rationalisation of procedure, development of appeal procedures, bureaucratisation of the legal apparatus and development of the professional branch of lawyers.[31]

In 1612, when the first Dutch *ahdname*s explicitly allowed for Dutch legal autonomy, many of the legal procedures at local courts in the United Provinces had been codified in local law.[32] The next logical step was to integrate the consulates in the Ottoman Empire into existing legislation on how courts functioned in the United Provinces. The first consulate regulations, published by the States General following the appointment of Cornelis Pauw as consul of Aleppo in December 1612, were not very explicit on adjudication. One stated only that the consul's secretary, as well as those of other consuls, would have to pass along all requested documents on behalf of merchants – and these

27 See Paola Volpini, 'La trattatistica sulla figura del console nella prima età moderna. Spunti di ricerca', in *Los cónsules*, eds. Aglietti et al., pp. 35–45; and Géraud Poumarède, 'Le consul dans les dictionnaires et le droit des gens: Émergence et affirmation d'une institution nouvelle (XVIe–XVIIIe siècles)', in *La fonction consulaire à l'époque moderne. L'affirmation d'une institution économique et politique (1500–1800)*, eds. J. Ulber and G. Le Bouëdec (Rennes, 2006), pp. 23–36.

28 Mariya Tait Slys, *Exporting legality. The rise and fall of extraterritorial jurisdiction in the Ottoman Empire and China* (Genève, 2014), pp. 14–15.

29 Gelderblom, *Cities of commerce*, pp. 109–111.

30 The term 'legal revolution' was coined by Richard L. Kagan in reference to the expansion of litigation. Richard L. Kagan, *Lawsuits and litigants in Castile, 1500–1700* (Chapel Hill, 1981). For the Dutch case, see Marie-Charlotte Le Bailly, 'Langetermijntrends in de rechtspraak bij de gewestelijke hoven van justitie in de Nederlanden van ca. 1450 tot ca. 1800', *Pro memorie: Bijdragen tot de rechtsgeschiedenis der Nederlanden*, 13:1 (2011): pp. 30–67, particularly pp. 30–31.

31 Le Bailly, 'Langetermijntrends'.

32 See pp. 119–137.

included deeds of legal procedures as well as sentences.[33] The resolutions of the meetings held by the States General in that period are much clearer on the matter, and in a meeting that took place on 8 December 1612, it was decided that 'together with his assessors, he [Cornelis Pauw] will try to settle all disputes brought before him amicably, or, in case the parties want to adjudicate a dispute, to come to a sentence in a neutral manner'.[34] A new official letter of appointment for Pauw that was issued by the States General in May 1614 explicitly authorised him to adjudicate all civil and criminal matters brought before him and to choose assessors from amongst the Dutch merchants settled in Aleppo to assist him.[35] The assessors were assistant-judges, and as such, they fulfilled a crucial role in adjudication.[36] It is worth noting that the French had a similar system, in which the consul-as-judge was assisted by four notable merchants, but the French consul often had difficulties finding willing traders, which could have been related to the fact that these merchants were employees of larger firms in Marseille.[37]

It did not take long before Cornelis Pauw came into conflict with Dutch Levant traders, at home as well as in Aleppo. Pauw complained that his expenses were too high and his income through consular duties too low, while traders in the United Provinces felt Pauw was too young, incompetent and selfish. Levant traders in Zeeland were most adamant, criticising Pauw for not having gone to university and for having no experience in commerce. Several merchants felt Pauw had obtained his post because of his father's influence and not because of his own capabilities.[38] The conflict was further aggravated by Pauw's feelings that his adjudicating authority was challenged. In September 1615, he explained in a letter to the States General that it was common for Ottomans to turn to European consular justice in Aleppo because of the high cost involved

33 Cau, *Groot placaet-boeck*, 2: pp. 1333–1334, 'Acte', 08/12/1612.

34 Van Deursen, ed., *Resolutiën der Staten-Generaal*, 1: p. 794, Meeting States General, 08/12/1612, 'Hij zal met zijn assessoren trachten alle geschillen die hem voorgelegd worden in der minne te schikken, of, indien partijen de zaak berecht willen hebben, onpartijdig uitspraak te doen'.

35 Heeringa and Nanninga, *Bronnen tot de geschiedenis*, 1: pp. 444–446, 'Commissie voor Cornelis Reyniersz Pauw als consul in Aleppo, Syrie etc.', 30/05/1614.

36 The manner of their selection was part of the ongoing quarrels between Dutch consuls and merchants in seventeenth-century Izmir. See pp. 94–95.

37 Mason, *Histoire du commerce*, p. 446.

38 See several petitions made against Pauw in Heeringa and Nanninga, *Bronnen tot de geschiedenis*, 1: pp. 444–462. It seems the authorities did not agree, as Pauw was maintained as consul until 1625, after which he was active as envoy in Sweden and Germany. In 1632 he entered the service of Frederik Hendrik, prince of Orange. Schutte, *Repertorium der Nederlandse vertegenwoordigers*, pp. 176–177.

in going to the *qadi* court, and because of the European threat of issuing a boycott of Ottoman traders who refused to be tried by a European court.[39] The consul used the term *battelatie* to indicate an embargo issued by a community against trading with a specific merchant or group of merchants. While a known concept, the word is hard to translate: 'this procedure known as *battelation*, prohibited any contact with the boycotted merchant on pain of a fine. When one European community announced a battelation, solidarity was expected from all other European merchants until the embargo was lifted'.[40] It was not an exclusive European practice, but European trading communities in the Levant used it to discourage Ottomans from cheating European traders. At the end of his letter, Pauw included an example of a *battelatie*:

> We, Cornelis Pauw, on behalf of the gentlemen of the States General of the United Dutch Provinces consul in Syria etc. by our command and at the instance of the honourable Daniel van Goethem, [order that] Hagi Nureddin and Abdel Agi, Moorish merchants, remain battelated with all their goods and merchandise, [we] forbid all and everyone, particularly our own [subjects] to make a contract or trade with them, as well as the brokers, who will [not] conduct any brokerage with them, on the penalty that the transgressor shall pay 500 reals of eight.[41]

39 Heeringa and Nanninga, *Bronnen tot de geschiedenis*, 1: pp. 468–478, Consul Cornelis Pauw to the States General, Aleppo, 12/09/1615.

40 Maurits van den Boogert, 'European patronage in the Ottoman Empire: Anglo-Dutch conflicts of interest in Aleppo (1703–1755)', in *Friends and rivals*, eds. Hamilton et al., p. 214. It remains unknown where the word comes from. The only reference I found was in a work about the travels of a nobleman from Gent, Joos van Ghistele, that was first published in 1557. He travelled in North Africa, the Mediterranean and the Middle East between 1481 and 1485, and his experiences were written down by a certain Ambrosius Zeebout. When the text discusses marriage and divorce in Islam, it uses the word 'batteleren', a verb, to refer to a form of divorce, and a footnote compares this with the Arabic word *talāq*, which was historically a controversial form of divorce in which the man repudiated the woman. Ambrosius Zeebout, *Tvoyage van Mher Joos van Ghisele*, ed. R.J.G.A.A. Gaspar (Hilversum, 1998), p. 15; and Maaike Voorhoeve, Abed Awad and Hany Mawla, 'Divorce', in *The Oxford encyclopedia of Islam and women*, ed. Natana J. de Long-Bas (Oxford, 2013), consulted online at https://www.oxfordreference.com/view/10.1093/acref:oiso/9780199764464.001.0001/acref-9780199764464-e-0108?rskey=jinXdZ&result=1. It is possible that *battelatie* comes from *talāq* and has taken the negative connotation of 'repudiation' from it.

41 Itself published on 20 August 1615, the translation was included at the end of a long letter in Heeringa and Nanninga, *Bronnen tot de geschiedenis*, 1: pp. 468–478, Consul Cornelis Pauw to the States General, Aleppo, 12/09/1615, on p. 478, 'Wij, Cornelis Pauw, van wegen de H.M. heeren de Staten-Generael der Vereenichde Nederlantsche Provinciën consul in Soria etc., door ons bevel ende ter instantiën van den eersamen Daniël van Goetthem,

Five days later, the boycott was lifted after Nureddin and Agi gave 'satisfaction to our justice'.[42] Pauw's letter confirmed that Ottomans were aware of this practice and acted accordingly by choosing European over Ottoman justice. This acceptance of European courts, including the Dutch consular court, was good for the Dutch merchant community and for the consul, who could strengthen his legal authority by adjudicating a larger number of disputes. But according to Pauw, Dutch traders were abusing this practice. They litigated against 'Turks, Persians and Armenians', and even if they were in the wrong, they pressured their consul to issue a verdict in their favour.[43] In a case where the consul was unwilling to comply, several Dutch merchants threatened to take the matter before an Ottoman court, directly challenging the consul's legal authority, as well as his impartiality.[44]

Pauw made it clear that this posed a very serious threat to the consular system of adjudication, and the States General responded by issuing additional legislation in 1616, which was substantially more extensive than the paragraphs on adjudication that had been issued in 1612 and 1614. The States General's response to the conflict between the consul and the merchants in Aleppo became the model for all future legislation issued in regard to consular adjudication in the Levant, in the sense that regulations focussed on competence and procedure and were mostly issued as a posteriori responses to very concrete problems of jurisdiction and procedure as they occurred within the Dutch Levantine trading communities. A meeting held on 17 February made it clear that the States General felt that Pauw's authority needed formal support, and an ordinance on adjudication was published the same day.[45]

One of the first important stipulations was that consular sentences on litigation between Dutchmen and members of other communities (either European or Levantine) could not be appealed and would go into immediate effect. Verdicts in disputes that only involved Dutch subjects were to be executed under 'provision' (*provisie*) or 'caution' (*cautie*), meaning appeal was possible,

blijven gebatteleert Haggi Noredin ende Abdelagi, Moorsche cooplieden, met alle haere goederen ende coopmanschappen, verbiedende aen allen ende een yegelijcken in't besonder van de onse, met deselve te contracteren oft te handelen, van gelijcken aen alle de maeckelaers, die met deselve sullen doen eenige soorte van maeckelaerdije, op pene dat den overtreder van sijn eygen sall betaelen vijffhondert realen van achten'.

42 Ibid.

43 Ibid., p. 469, '[...] Turcken, Persianen, Armenen [...]'.

44 Ibid.

45 Van Deursen, ed., *Resolutiën der Staten-Generaal*, 2: p. 581, Meeting States General, 17/02/1616; Cau, *Groot placaet-boeck*, 2: pp. 1335–1338, 'Acte, voor den consul van Aleppo, noopende de judicature, &c.', 17/02/1616.

but a sum had to be deposited in the consular chancery by the convicted party as a guarantee. Appeal was not possible in cases concerning 'excesses, delicts, or public scandals'.[46] The exact meaning of these terms is not clear, but there was an important distinction in procedure between civil and criminal cases. In the latter, defined as 'delicts subject to corporal punishment', the consul was only authorised to arrest the offender, chain him in iron chains and send him back to the United Provinces on the first homebound vessel – a fate also awaiting those refusing to obey the consular orders.[47] In civil cases, he had to adjudicate on the spot.[48]

A third important element was concerned with the appointment of two assessors. The consul had to choose them from amongst the three foremost merchants – nominated by their peers – of the local Dutch trading community. Their task was to assist the consul in fostering commerce and in adjudicating legal disputes involving matters of 'greater importance'.[49] The decision to employ merchants as co-judges was not uncommon for a commercial court, and because the consul – who could not be a merchant himself – was first of all responsible for fostering trade and the Dutch community he held authority over was a community of merchants, the consular courts in the Levant were essentially commercial courts.[50] In the end, the 1616 ordinance was an exercise in balancing consular authority with commercial interest.

The appointment of the assessors continued to be used as currency in disputes between Dutch consuls and merchants, particularly in Izmir. In 1657, a new consul was appointed there, Michel du Mortier from Leiden.[51] Despite the fact that he was the first Dutch-born consul in Izmir, at the specific request of the Dutch merchants there, he quickly ran into conflict with the Dutch trading community when it came to his consular duties. In 1658, the States General issued legislation in an attempt to end the dispute, and part of it dealt with

46 Cau, *Groot placaet-boeck*, 2: pp. 1335–1338, 'Acte, voor den consul van Aleppo, noopende de judicature, &c.', 17/02/1616, on p. 1335, '[...] excessen, delicten ofte publijcque schandalen [...]'.

47 Ibid., p. 1337, '[...] delicten aenden lyve strafbaer [...]'.

48 Ibid.

49 Ibid., p. 1338, '[...] van grooter importantie [...]'. Although it is not clear from the text what these matters were, later adjustments indicate that it was determined on the basis of the monetary value of the dispute.

50 For an extensive analysis of the functioning of commercial courts in the early modern period, see Kessler, *The Parisian merchant court*. England did not establish such courts. Christian R. Burset, 'Merchant courts, arbitration, and the politics of commercial litigation in the eighteenth-century British Empire', *Law and history review*, 34:3 (2016): pp. 615–647.

51 Schutte, *Repertorium der Nederlandse vertegenwoordigers*, p. 332.

consular adjudication.[52] While the adjudicating role of the assessors, chosen as three of the 'most notable, most qualified and most modest merchants of the Dutch nation', was confirmed, their appointment was now fully the prerogative of the consul, and the procedure in which the trading community nominated them was abolished.[53] An additional stipulation was that the assessors were not allowed to adjudicate in cases in which they carried an interest; in the rare event that the whole Dutch trading community was involved in a case, the consul had to look for three of the most qualified merchants from another European trading community in Izmir.[54] Such requirement is further evidence of the pragmatism that easily crossed national boundaries and was attached to the merchants' style. It is clear that the States General, as they had done in 1616 during the Aleppo dispute, sided with the consul and protected his authority; as a consequence, the role of the trading community in choosing their own co-judges by nominating assessors was curtailed.

1.3 *A Proposal to Codify Adjudication in the Levant*

The measures taken by the States General in conflicts in Aleppo and Izmir were aimed at settling several issues within the Dutch trading communities, not only legal matters but also quarrels on taxes and remunerations. Particularly in the case of Izmir, legislation did not fully succeed in halting the quarrels until the arrival of the first consul from the de Hochepied family. Before then, Jacob van Dam had been the longest serving Dutch consul in Izmir, serving for almost twenty years.[55] His consulate was characterised by the most serious quarrels between Dutch consuls and merchants, and it was in reaction to his tenure that the States General decided to issue more profound legislation than they had done up to that moment. Next to van Dam's unjust claims on the merchants' money and his harsh treatment of some of his subjects, the Dutch traders in Izmir also accused the consul of sloppy adjudication.[56] Their complaint was taken seriously and led to an extensive attempt at codification of the legal powers of the Dutch consuls in the Levant.

---

52 For the quarrels in Izmir and the 1658 response to it, see pp. 49–51.

53 Heeringa and Nanninga, *Bronnen tot de geschiedenis*, 2: pp. 156–158, 'Resolutie der Staten-Generaal tot nederlegging der geschillen in Smyrna', 24/07/1658, on p. 158, '[...] drie van de notabelste, gequalificeerste ende bescheydenste coopluyden van de Nederlantsche natie [...]'. The regulation was reconfirmed on 18 September 1670.

54 Ibid.

55 See pp. 50–52.

56 Van Dam van Isselt, 'De klachten', p. 314.

New legislation was to serve a double purpose: first, it should settle once and for all the discussions on ambassadorial and consular duties by providing the diplomats with a fixed monetary recompense, to be paid out of a special register, for which several taxes would be collected; second, it had to define the duties and rights of diplomats and traders in the Levant, including regulations on litigation, in order to ensure a peaceful and smooth daily management of Dutch affairs, particularly in Izmir, which had by that time become the most important trading place for the Dutch.[57] In 1671, the States General ordered the Directorate of Levant Trade in Amsterdam to draft a new 'instruction' (*instructie*) that would fulfil these two goals. On 8 December 1673, a draft proposal was sent by the Directorate of Levant Trade in Amsterdam to the States General, which promptly expedited it to Consul Jacob van Dam in Izmir and Ambassador Justinus Colyer in Istanbul for comments.[58]

The version of the proposal included in Heeringa's *Levantschen Handel* was annotated by Consul van Dam, who sent a document with his comments back to the United Provinces in November 1674 and again in May 1675.[59] Although the instruction itself never became law, as the authorities decided to focus on the matter of consular income and tax fraud, the document containing the proposal as well as the consul's remarks is historically important because it is the most extensive text in which the authorities discuss legal procedures for Dutch consular jurisdiction in the Levant. They not only provide insight into the thought process of some of the actors behind Dutch consular adjudication in the Levant but also contain several procedures that were applied in litigation in the United Provinces and that must have been equally applied by the consul in his office as judge.

The draft contained twenty-three articles, and many of them, articles 9 and 12 to 19, addressed adjudicating procedures in great detail. Article 9 confirmed the existing arrangement of assessors, who had to assist the consul in judicial and political affairs. The local Dutch community was to nominate six persons, out of whom the consul would choose three men to be appointed as assessors for two years. In case they were personally involved in a legal dispute, the

57 W.E. van Dam van Isselt, 'Het ontwerp-regeeringsreglement voor de Levant van 1673 en het formulier van 1675', in *Bijdragen voor vaderlandsche geschiedenis en oudheidkunde*, ed. P.J. Blok, 4th series, part 6 (The Hague, 1907), pp. 379–429.

58 Ibid., pp. 387–390.

59 Heeringa and Nanninga, *Bronnen tot de geschiedenis*, 2: pp. 187–204, 'Reglement voor den resident tot Constantinopelen, consul tot Smirna, ende Nederlantsche natie in de Levant residerende respective, sooals hetselve bij de heeren Directeuren van den Levantschen handel aen H.H.M. is overgegeven, en bij deselve weder aen den Consul van Dam gesonden', 1675.

consul had to choose replacements amongst the other nominees or arrange for another round of nominations. As stipulated in earlier regulations, in case the whole local community was involved, temporary assessors would have to be chosen amongst the other Christian nations. Article 14 additionally stated that the assessors, when declaring not to be involved in the case they assisted to adjudicate, had to be believed at their word. Van Dam protested against this procedure to nominate assessors, and he argued that his problematic dealings with the trading community demonstrated that he should have absolute control over the nomination process. Furthermore, he felt that in all affairs he had to settle with the help of assessors, his voice should count double and would be decisive. Otherwise, he thought, the assessors could easily conspire against him. In the consul's opinion there was nothing in the draft that prevented partial judgment, as the assessors, who were merchants, could be motivated to judge on the basis of jealousy and their own commercial interests. The consul remarked that he had experience with many cases and that the merchants 'always advise according to their passions', while he was always without interest, as he was not allowed to engage in commerce himself.[60]

Article 12 stressed that, in order to avoid potential complaints on non-neutral sentencing, it was important to have clear regulations, which were explained in the articles that followed. It further stipulated that the consul and resident held the highest authority in their jurisdictions. Article 13 determined that, in case of a dispute, the consul and resident first had to try to settle matters amicably or have it referred to arbitrators, or 'good men of the nation'.[61] Adjudication was to follow only in the case that arbitration failed, and it should be brief, without hesitation, and rapid, without lengthy procedures.[62] Article 14 stipulated that the consul and assessors could adjudicate in cases up to 100 lion dollars, without the possibility of appeal before the ambassador in Istanbul. Cases involving an amount higher than 100 lion dollars or arising out of 'infamy or delict' could be appealed in Istanbul.[63] The party that was condemned received a maximum of three summations to obey the verdict, with a risk of confiscation of goods should the verdict not be respected within

60 Ibid., p. 194, '[...] maer altijd naer hare passie adviseren [...]'.

61 Ibid., p. 197, '[...] goede mannen van de natie [...]'.

62 For arbitration, see pp. 131–132 and 138–152.

63 Heeringa and Nanninga, *Bronnen tot de geschiedenis*, 2: pp. 187–204, 'Reglement voor den resident tot Constantinopelen, consul tot Smirna, ende Nederlantsche natie in de Levant residerende respective, sooals hetselve bij de heeren Directeuren van den Levantschen handel aen H.H.M. is overgegeven, en bij deselve weder aen den consul van Dam gesonden', 1675, on p. 197, '[...] infamie of delict [...]'.

fourteen days after the final summation. The consul agreed but demanded to be allowed to adjudicate without the assistance of the assessors in cases of 100 lion dollars or more. He also wished to be able to judge those who committed a crime against the consul himself – clearly in the hopes of establishing his authority more directly.[64]

Article 15 provided the consul with an extra vote in case the votes between him and the three assessors stalled. It also introduced the idea of weekly meetings, with fines for those who failed to attend. The consul repeated that he wished his extra vote to be permanent and dismissed the idea of weekly meetings, involving the whole nation, to discuss legal cases. Article 16 established fines for litigating parties not appearing at the court when due, which were half a lion dollar the first time and one lion dollar the second time. The third time, the case would be judged on the evidence brought forward by the plaintiff, unless the defendant had not been informed of everything in due time. Article 17 held that the consul and assessors had to pronounce their verdict within fourteen days after all the evidence had been presented, which was confirmed and further explained in article 19. As long as the sentence had not been issued, the party's demands to be heard by the court were to be allowed, but only if it could be demonstrated they had not been heard earlier because of the court's negligence.[65]

Article 18 dealt with the possibility of appeal against a consular verdict before the Dutch ambassador in Istanbul. The appeal itself had to be registered in the chancery in Izmir within ten days. If the appeal was for a case involving Dutch and non-Dutch merchants – disregarding whether they were European or Ottoman – the condemned party would have to put a deposit in the consular chancery, as negotiated between parties or as ordered by the consul and assessors. In addition, the person who demanded the appeal had to deposit twenty lion dollars, of which he would be reimbursed two-thirds in the case of the alteration of the verdict. Should the verdict remain the same, the money was forfeited. The ambassador was only allowed to adjudicate the appeal after the chancellor had confirmed the payment of all necessary sums. Article 18 further contained a very interesting specification on the citation of Ottomans. In case an Ottoman appeared before the consul and assessors, he had to declare in front of witnesses that he was willing to obey the verdict and would not seek appeal at an Ottoman court. Article 20 specified the financial

64 Ibid., pp. 196–198.

65 Ibid., pp. 198–199.

compensation the chancellor was to receive for all actions undertaken by him necessary for legal procedures.[66]

The proposed regulation was an impressive document and the most extensive written document dealing explicitly with legal procedures in the Levant. Some of the arrangements in the text had already been mentioned in the 1658 regulation, while others must have been an attempt to codify already existing procedures. Unfortunately, the implementation of these (or other seventeenth-century) rules dealing specifically with adjudication in the Levant and their concrete procedures cannot be tested by analysing concrete court cases that occurred at the same time, as no cases have been preserved for the period before 1732 (Istanbul) or 1743 (Izmir). There are no further indications that the draft proposal from 1673 was adopted. Instead, Dutch authorities concentrated their efforts on determining a fixed salary for the ambassador, consul and other officials attached to the embassy and consulates in the hopes of putting all disagreements between merchants and their representatives to rest. The States General had already issued regulations dealing with this matter in April and October 1675.[67] The lengthy proposal on adjudication was lost in the discussion. In December 1679, the regulation for the consul, ambassador and other officials was renewed but contained no specific articles on consular or ambassadorial adjudication. The legal task of consuls and ambassadors remained codified on the basis of the regulation issued on 24 July 1658 and was only replaced in October 1791.[68]

While the legislation introduced in 1675 had not addressed any matters on adjudication, it did introduce one novelty that was tangentially related to the competence of the consulate as a court. It finally laid down a procedure for taking the Dutch national oath.[69] All Dutch subjects, diplomatic personnel and merchants alike, had to swear to comply with regulations regarding the payment of tax duties on merchandise and to promise they would avoid all fraud. In an additional oath, the assessors had to pronounce that 'in all research, advice and adjudicating matters that shall happen, we shall behave

66 Ibid., pp. 199–200.

67 See pp. 45–46.

68 Van Dam van Isselt, 'Het ontwerp-regeeringsreglement', pp. 405–406. For the 1679 resolution, see Heeringa and Nanninga, *Bronnen tot de geschiedenis*, 2: pp. 234–236, 'Resolutie van de Staten-Generaal betreffende den Consul van Dam en het reglement voor de Levant', 14/12/1679.

69 Cau, *Groot placaet-boeck*, 3: p. 311, 'Extract uyt de resolutien van de Staten Generael der Vereenighde Nederlanden; Reglement voor den resident tot Constantinopelen, consul tot Smirna, ende Nederlantsche natie in de Levant', 07/10/1675.

ourselves neutrally, sincerely and loyally, as permitted as pious judges and assessors'.[70] The official inclusion of oaths was very important, as it was a formal subjection of the merchants to the jurisdiction of the consuls and ambassadors. Breaking an oath was an infraction that could be used against traders in court.[71]

The inclusion of an article forcing traders to take the Dutch national oath was an attempt to solve an old controversy. Consul van Dam had complained that, although the taking of an oath was obligatory for all merchants in the Levant since 1615, as decreed by the States General, many of them refused to take it, something the consul believed had to do with the high level of fraud. Van Dam pointed out that the introduction of a national oath had worked well in battling fraud within the English trading community of Izmir, and Dutch subjects should equally be forced to take one.[72] It remained a matter of dispute even after the 1675 regulation. Although W.E. van Dam van Isselt, one of the few historians who has written on the matter, asserted that the last Dutch merchant in Izmir who refused to take the oath did so in 1680, further States General legislation makes it clear that this was not the case. In 1687, thirteen merchants in Izmir still refused to take the oath in spite of the mediating efforts made by the consul's secretary, at the time Daniel Jean de Hochepied, and the Dutch ambassador in Istanbul. The merchants repeated older complaints about van Dam's inability to administer decent justice, a complaint apparently shared by the assessors, who wanted to be discharged from their office.[73] In spite of these complaints, no further efforts were made to compile a general regulation for

70 Heeringa and Nanninga, *Bronnen tot de geschiedenis*, 2: pp. 208–217, 'Formulier, waernaer ende volgens hetwelcke den heer resident tot Constantinopelen, consul tot Smirna, aengestelt bij de H.M. heeren Staten-Generael der Vereenigde Nederlanden, en de gantsche Nederlantsche natie in de Levant residerende, respective, haer sullen hebben te reguleren omtrent den ontfanck en distributie van de ambassaet- en consulaetrechten', 1676, on p. 213, '[...] soo belooven en sweeren wij mits desen, dat in 't ondersoeken, adviseeren en sententiëren van alle saeken, die sullen voorcomen, ons altos sullen dragen onpartijdich, oprecht en getrouw, als vroome rechters en assessoren toestaet [...]'.

71 See also pp. 133–135.

72 W.E. van Dam van Isselt, 'Het "in train brengen" van het in 1675 voor de Levant ontworpen formulier (1675–1680)', in *Bijdragen voor vaderlandsche geschiedenis en oudheidkunde*, ed. P.J. Blok, 4th series, part 7 (The Hague, 1909), pp. 289–333.

73 Jacobus Scheltus, *Groot placaet-boeck vervattende de placaten, ordonnantien ende edicten vande doorluchtige, hoogh mog: heeren Staten Generael der Vereenighde Nederlanden ende vande ed: groot mog: heeren Staten van Hollandt ende West-Vrieslandt mitsgaders vande ed: mog: heeren Staten van Zeelandt* (The Hague, 1705), 4: pp. 248–249, 'Resolutie van haer hoogh mog., tot voorkominge en weghneminge van de onlusten tot Smyrna, onder de koopluyden van de Nederlandtsche natie aldaer ontstaen', 11/08/1687.

adjudication, but dissenting merchants were forced to comply with the oath, on penalty of persecution and a hefty fine.[74]

In spite of this initial resistance, it became standard practice for newcomers to take the oath – without it, one was not able to participate in economic life in the Dutch Levantine trading communities. The consuls and ambassadors used the oath as an instrument to keep their subjects in line. When Dutch trader Isaac Beaune, upon arrival in Izmir in the 1760s, wanted to associate himself with an Armenian trader, something which was forbidden, he was not allowed to take the Dutch national oath unless he was willing to give up his partnership.[75] The problem of collecting consular duties was also dragging on. In 1683, the treasurer and assessors in Izmir informed the Directorate of Levant Trade that they finally had settled all accounts with van Dam on all financial matters. Nevertheless, when van Dam arrived back in the United Provinces in 1690, after he had been honourable discharged as consul, he still demanded reimbursement for various old expenses, reigniting long-standing animosities.[76] Finally, the end of van Dam's tenure put a halt to more than half a century of disputes between Dutch diplomats and merchants. Van Dam was succeeded by his secretary Daniel Jean de Hochepied, who never antagonised his subjects as van Dam had done and who founded a consular dynasty, as the Izmir consulate remained in the hands of the de Hochepied family until 1824.

In spite of the efforts made in the early 1670s, no extensive legal document ever came into being that fully settled the issue of adjudication by consuls and ambassadors. The adjudicating powers of consul and assessors were never questioned after the complaints lodged against van Dam. The States General might have felt that the most important matter was the establishment of consular and ambassadorial authority over their respective trading communities, and it was best ensured through regulations on taxes and the national oath. Authority as judge would then automatically follow, as the complaints on adjudication had been personal and were never aimed against the idea of consular adjudication itself. In addition, the national oath did include a promise to respect consular and ambassadorial jurisdiction and adjudication. Another

74 Ibid. Also in the same volume, see pp. 249–250, 'Resolutie van haer hoogh mog., regulerende de ambassaet- en consulaet-rechten tot Smyrna en Constantinopolen', 22/01/1688, and pp. 250–251, 'Resolutie van haer hoogh mog., noopende het vernieuwen van den eedt by den Levantschen handel, verhooging van ambassaet en consulaet-rechten tot Smyrna, Constantinopolen, &c.', 30/07/1692, which seems to have been the last legislation that was issued on the matter.

75 See pp. 288–289.

76 Van Dam van Isselt, 'Het "in train brengen" '.

reason why the States General never issued further regulations detailing legal procedures at the consular courts might be that the authorities in the United Provinces felt existing legislation was clear enough regarding the practice of litigation, or in any case, it did not need additional rules that applied specifically to adjudication in the Levant. The jurisdiction and the consuls' abilities to adjudicate were codified in Dutch and Ottoman laws – through the capitulations – and that might have been a sufficient basis for consuls to adjudicate according to the same principles as those used by their peers adjudicating commercial disputes in the United Provinces. There was, however, one exception. In 1686, the States General published a law dealing with sequesters and appeals in the Levant. It would be the last time a law on legal procedure in the Levant was issued, and much like the failed 1673 attempt, it followed a draft proposal issued by the Directorate of Levant Trade.[77]

Analysing the processes behind the drafting of the seventeenth-century resolutions concerned with consular adjudication in the Levant is important in order to understand the nature of Dutch lawmaking in the early modern period. A first observation is that Dutch legislative institutions acted only in response to concrete problems. The regulations of 1616 and 1658 and the proposal of 1673 all had been drafted as legal answers to practical problems and were examples of the a posteriori making of regulations that was so characteristic of the legal framework the Dutch developed around their Levantine communities. The absence of a comprehensive body of Dutch laws and regulations dealing with Dutch consular adjudication in the Levant can largely be explained by the fact that the Dutch consul was almost exclusively dealing with commercial disputes, and the adjudication of these was done according to a specific, widely used procedure, 'summary procedure', that aimed at a fast and cheap resolution of disputes between traders.[78] Naturally, summary procedure did not solve the issue of determining the legality of certain actions, such as a sequester in an international context, nor did it clarify automatically which court was competent to adjudicate a case, in first instance as well as in an appeal. Competence was generally solved by applying the custom of *forum rei*, but use of this principle could still be rendered difficult in cases where litigants were physically far removed from one another – or from the court against which decision a losing party wanted to appeal. It was to address these matters that Dutch legislation applicable to the consulates in the Levant had come into being throughout the seventeenth century.

77 The law is discussed on pp. 265–267.
78 Summary procedure is discussed in detail on pp. 119–138.

The 1688 appointment of Daniel Jean de Hochepied as Dutch consul in Izmir not only put an end to all conflict between the consul and his subjects, it also concluded the period during which legislation was drafted and issued on consular adjudication in the Levant. In theory, this is easy to explain; the capitulations granted the Dutch full legal autonomy, which they could then exercise by applying the regulations concerned with commercial disputes that existed in the United Provinces. After all, the different Dutch Levantine communities remained, thanks to the principles of legal autonomy and consular jurisdiction, fully Dutch.

Two problems remained. First of all, a normal application of Dutch laws abroad only worked in cases where all the litigating parties were Dutch, or at least willing to submit to Dutch adjudication. The actual number of cases brought before the Dutch consul in Izmir in which all litigants were Dutch was very limited. Foreign involvement, particularly of Ottoman merchants, in Dutch trading operations was high, and the Dutch consul also held legal authority over a significant number of non-Dutch subjects, such as the Ottoman *protégés*. Although certain informal arrangements existed, such as *forum rei* or the early seventeenth-century acceptance of Ottoman traders to be tried at Dutch courts, the Dutch consular courts in the Levant were still vulnerable to outside challenges to their jurisdiction and competence – particularly when Ottomans were involved, as Europeans generally did not like to be subjected to Ottoman adjudication.

The second problem is perhaps more fundamental. There was no such thing as 'Dutch' law – just as there was no 'Dutch' political nation.[79] The legal landscape of the United Provinces was a complicated web of local laws, rights and privileges next to provincial and 'national' legislation. Laws on sequesters, for instance, existed in the United Provinces to specify the cases when sequesters were legal and where they needed to be registered. Often, this was in the place where the goods were at that moment, but it could also be, depending

79 At least not in the sense of a unified, highly centralized state – the United Provinces was fundamentally different from monarchic states of the period for several reasons, but particularly for its highly decentralized political process, and the fundamental autonomy of its provinces. See Prak, *The Dutch Republic in the seventeenth century*, pp. 166–185. Often, 'Dutch' has been used as a synonym for 'from Holland'. While it is true that the province of Holland was the most powerful and the richest, and its inhabitants the most present in international trade, the 'Dutch' trading nation in the Levant was not simply the Holland trading nation. It seems important to stress that, during the early modern Dutch Republic, a sense of belonging seem mostly to have originated out of belonging to 'a family, neighborhood, club, guild, profession, church, city […]'. Christine Kooi, *Calvinists and Catholics during Holland's golden age: Heretics and idolaters* (Cambridge, 2012), p. 41.

on local custom, in the place of the plaintiff in cases where the defendant was in town. A number of restrictions existed and were defined in terms of privileges obtained by cities, such as the regulation that inhabitants of the bigger cities of Holland could not be subjected to a sequester of their goods in the countryside, unless they had been used as collateral.[80] It is easy to see that it would be difficult to transfer existing legislation on sequesters in the United Provinces to the Levantine context, and this is one of the reasons why a specific law on sequester was published for the Levant. It shows that the situation on the ground could be too complicated to be handled fully by the existing body of written law, which makes it remarkable that so little effort was made to complement this existing body with new laws that would be able to cover the situation on the ground better. It is, however, less remarkable than it seems at first sight. By far, most disputes adjudicated by the consul of Izmir were commercial in kind.

Their adjudication was not conducted on the basis of written law, not even in the United Provinces itself, but on the basis of something else. That 'something else' needed to be flexible enough to be applicable in an international and intercultural context and practical enough to ensure swift resolution of disputes. That 'something else' did indeed exist and was called the merchants' style – the way in which merchants were accustomed to do things. It underpinned the business correspondences merchants maintained with one another, it was embedded in the substance of the contracts they signed with each other, and it was part of the oral agreements they mutually agreed upon. All of these expressions of the merchants' style could be used in court, and the great success of international commercial litigation can be attributed to the manner in which the early modern legal and commercial contexts offered the necessary space to incorporate this merchants' style into the legal framework that was used in adjudicating commercial disputes. In the case of the United Provinces that legal framework was built upon a variety of foundations but nonetheless merits, according to most early modern scholars, the label 'Roman-Dutch law'.

---

80 For a summary of the established body of law and the procedure of how to deal with sequesters in the United Provinces, see Cornelis Willem Decker, *Het Roomsch Hollandsch recht; beschreeven door Mr. Simon van Leeuwen* (Amsterdam, 1783), 2: pp. 361–371. Cornelis Decker was an attorney and notary from Amsterdam. A.J. van der Aa, *Biographisch woordenboek der Nederlanden* (Haarlem, 1858), 4: p. 78. Simon van Leeuwen (1626–1682) was an attorney at the *Hof van Holland* and *Hoge Raad* and a member of the town council in Leiden. He published several influential works on Dutch law, some of which will be discussed in more detail on pp. 120–122. *Nieuw Nederlandsch biografisch woordenboek*, eds. P.C. Molhuysen and P.J. Blok (Leiden, 1911), 1: pp. 1261–1263.

2 The Dutch Legal Context

2.1 *Sources of Roman-Dutch Law*

'Premodern Europe was a patchwork of local and regional jurisdictions, each with its own legal traditions'.[81] This is a generally accepted statement amongst legal historians, and a historiographical tradition that has been particularly strong in Germany has turned this observation into the idea that a shared European law, based on a mixture of Roman and canonical law called *ius commune*, was residual and subordinate to local laws that had taken form in statutes, *consuetudines*, local customary laws and other expressions of 'proper law', also called *ius proprium*.[82] It seems clear now though that *ius commune*, as it developed after the fall of the Roman Empire and before the arrival of the Reformation in Christian Europe, 'created a shared legal tradition and a shared legal vocabulary that was more present in Europe than hitherto has been assumed and that influenced the "ius proprium" in such a way that it deserves a more formative position in the historiography of Europe's legal developments'.[83] The early Middle Ages was the formative period for this evolution, which took place in continental Europe and England in a parallel manner. In spite of later divergences and exaggerated claims regarding English exceptionalism, the English and continental European legal traditions are 'siblings'.[84] *Ius commune* relied strongly on Roman law but also was the result of an effort to overcome premodern Europe's legal patchwork, and it is hardly surprising that the post-Roman claim about a European 'common law' came from the church. Canonical law exerted a great influence on the European legal tradition.[85]

---

81 Gelderblom, *Cities of commerce*, p. 102; see also the collection of essays in Stephen Cummins and Laura Kounine, eds., *Cultures of conflict resolution in early modern Europe* (Farnham, 2016); and Dave De ruysscher, *Gedisciplineerde vrijheid. Een geschiedenis van het handels- en economisch recht* (Antwerp and Apeldoorn, 2014).

82 Emanuel G.D. van Dongen, *Contributory negligence. A historical and comparative study* (Leiden and Boston, 2014), pp. 227–228; and Manlio Bellomo, *The common legal past of Europe 1000–1800* (Washington DC, 1995), pp. 55–77.

83 This common 'legal culture' would disappear in the later stages of the early modern period due to 'national' projects of legal codification. See Bellomo, *The common legal past of Europe*, pp. 1–33; see also Peter Stein, *Roman law in European history* (Cambridge, 1999); and Randall Lesaffer, *Inleiding tot de Europese rechtsgeschiedenis* (Leuven, 2008), particularly pp. 306–331 and 399–432.

84 Tamar Herzog, *A short history of European law: The last two and a half millennia* (Cambridge, MA and London, 2018), p. 115. For an overview of the early development of this *ius commune* and the shared history of continental European law and early English common law, see ibid., pp. 45–115.

85 Ibid., pp. 45–72.

Roman law 'supplied the backbone for a common European legal tradition, [but] it could not solve the constant tensions between local and global, individual solutions and overreaching principles'.[86]

Later ideas about *ius commune* were of course influenced by the tendencies of nineteenth-century scholars to interpret European legal history as an evolution that led to the establishment of various sovereign 'national' legal systems. They might all have been related to each other, but more importantly, they were all considered fundamentally distinct from one another. The 'nationalist' lens through which historical developments are often distorted needs to be carefully adjusted, without immediately rejecting all efforts that were made to analyse the histories behind 'national' legal systems. The Dutch context is particularly interesting in this regard. In the early modern period, there was no codified 'national Dutch' legal corpus that was written down. The Netherlands has a civil law tradition, and Dutch law (*ius patrium*) was only codified in 1811, but this does not mean that any attempt to describe 'Dutch' law for the early modern period is useless.[87] The first attempt to fully describe 'Dutch' law was made by Hugo de Groot, or Grotius, in 1631 (see figure 5).[88] Several other early modern thinkers followed suit, and it was Simon van Leeuwen, an important Dutch legal scholar who invented the term 'Roman-Dutch law' (*Roomsch-Hollandts reght*) to describe the totality of the rule of law in the early modern United Provinces, which was Dutch but firmly rooted in the tradition of Roman law.[89]

In his treatise on Dutch law, Laurens Pieter van de Spiegel (1737–1800), who later became the last grand pensionary of Holland, distinguished five different origins for the totality of law in the United Provinces (*ius proprium* or *ius patrium*): old custom, which only became law because it had been in use for so long; old local laws (*keuren*) and privileges (*handtvesten*) issued by the counts of Holland; the laws of the highest central governments after independence, for van de Spiegel the States General and the prince of Orange; Roman law; and lastly, canonical law. For van de Spiegel, a number of laws existed that could not be categorised in any of the five categories mentioned above, and he specifically mentioned exchange law and the customs of Dutch commercial

86 Ibid., p. 7.

87 For an overview of the early modern sources of *ius patrium*, see Beatrix Jacobs, '*Ius patrium* en *ius commune*. Twee zijden van een medaille', *Pro memorie: Bijdragen tot de rechtsgeschiedenis der Nederlanden*, 19:1 (2017): pp. 22–46.

88 Hugo de Groot, *Inleiding tot de Hollandsche rechts-geleertheid* (The Hague, 1631).

89 Simon van Leeuwen, *Paratitula juris novissimi dat is een kort begrip van het Roomsch-Hollandts reght* (Leiden, 1652).

cities as exceptions that he labelled somewhat disdainful as part of a 'multorum camelorum onus' – a burden of various camels.[90]

What these scholars shared was the acknowledgement that 'Dutch' law consisted of a vast body of local and regional laws, and van de Spiegel's division is similar to divisions scholars make today in the early modern sources for Dutch law. In her article on Dutch law, Beatrix Jacobs equally distinguished between privileges and custom. A third category was legislation, which is the same as van der Spiegel's category of 'laws of the highest governments'. Fourthly, Jacobs distinguished 'learned law' (*geleerd recht*), a category covering van der Spiegel's Roman and canonical law categories. Jacobs, different from van der Spiegel, included jurisprudence as a category, reflecting the growing practice of collecting and publishing the sentences of higher courts. Jacobs argues that these collections became important in setting examples but also acknowledges that the significance of this category as source of law remains up for debate.[91]

These sources refer to the totality of civil law and thus include commercial law. Even if the categorisation of sources of law as used by van der Spiegel in the eighteenth century, Jacobs in the twentieth and many others does provide a relatively clear analytical division of the origins of Dutch law, reality was considerably more complex – and no area of law perhaps more so as commercial law. By nature, the development of laws of trade contains an element of foreign interaction, because transactions over distance are inherent to the nature of trade. This observation is explicitly made in what is still the most comprehensive work on commercial law before the modern period.[92] Its author, Wilhelm Franz Lichtenauer, did not categorise the origins of commercial law on the basis of theoretical labels, as Jacobs and van der Spiegel did. He was much more concerned with the places where commercial laws were written down. From the twelfth century onwards, the legal culture of the Low Countries increasingly became a written culture, leading to the growth of a written legal corpus.[93] This development of written culture did not cancel the 'Dutch' legal fragmentation, but it must have enhanced the knowledge of local legal cultures in a wider area. Lichtenauer identified nine locations for finding written-down commercial law. The first coincides more or less with

90 Laurens Pieter van de Spiegel, *Verhandeling over den oorsprong en de historie der vaderlandsche rechten, inzonderheid van Holland en Zeeland* (Goes, 1769), pp. 113–114.

91 Jacobs, 'Ius patrium en ius commune', p. 38.

92 W.F. Lichtenauer, *Geschiedenis van de wetenschap van het handelsrecht in Nederland tot 1809* (Amsterdam, 1968), p. 18.

93 Jacobs, 'Ius patrium en ius commune', p. 26; see also Wim van Anrooij, *Handschriften als spiegel van de middeleeuwse tekstcultuur* (Leiden, 2006), pp. 7–9.

FIGURE 5 Image of the court room of the *Hof van Holland* from the title page of the first edition of Hugo de Groot's *Inleiding tot de Hollandsche rechts-geleertheid*, Gillis van Scheyndel (I), 1631

FROM THE COLLECTION OF THE RIJKSMUSEUM, AMSTERDAM

'learned law' and consists of general publications by legal scholars, mainly discussing Roman law as well as other legal contexts where commercial legal stipulations can be found. Many are generalist and scientific, while some are moralistic – such as publications on bankruptcies. Two influential scholars publishing in the early modern period were Hugo de Groot in the seventeenth century and Cornelis van Bijnkershoek in the eighteenth century. Both wrote important works on the laws of Holland and Zeeland; de Groot's *Inleiding tot de Hollandsche rechts-geleertheid* (in English *Introduction to the jurisprudence of Holland*) was first published in 1631 (see figure 5), and Bijnkershoek wrote a *Corpus iuris Hollandici et Zelandici*, which was never published.[94] De Groot, as others after him, extensively dealt with bottomry loans, the use of brokers, exchange law, sales, sea law, insurance, contract law and bankruptcy, and his work was much commented upon by later scholars.[95] Next to scientific literature, Lichtenauer identified 'practical literature', such as manuals for notaries. In this category, he also included some well-known early modern monographs, such as Johannes Phoonsen's work on exchange law and Adriaen Verwer's work on maritime law.[96]

A third category is 'jurisprudence', under which Lichtenauer understood the instructions issued for specific commercial and maritime courts, such as the Commissioners of Maritime Affairs (*Commissarissen van Zeezaken*), which was an urban maritime court established in several Dutch cities in the seventeenth century, as well as collections of sentences and legal advice. Specific collections on commercial and maritime law were only published at the end of the eighteenth century, the first being J.M. Barels' *Opinions on commerce and maritime navigation*.[97] In the last decade of that century, an important collection

94 Lichtenauer, *Geschiedenis van de wetenschap van het handelsrecht*, p. 109.

95 Ibid., pp. 85–104.

96 Ibid., pp. 135–141. Johannes Phoonsen, *Wissel-styl tot Amsterdam. Vervattende niet alleen het geene dat men gewoon, maar oock wat een voorsichtigh koopman, tot sijn securiteit, in de wissel-handel dienstigh en noodigh is, te observeren. Mitsgaders de ordonantien, willekeuren, en reglementen van wisselen tot Amsterdam, Rotterdam, Antwerpen, Hamburg/Franckfurt/ Leipzig/Nürnberg /Augspurg/Brewlauw/Bologna, Bisenzone, Bolzano, en Lions. Als oock de ordonnances de Louis XIV. sur le commerce de negotians & marchands* (Amsterdam, 1676); and Adriaen Verwer, *Nederlants see-rechten; avaryen; en bodemeryen: begrepen in de gemeene costuimen vander see; de placcaten van Keiser Karel den Vijfden 1551 en Koning Filips den II 1563; 't tractaet van mr Quintyn Weitsen van de Nederlantsche avaryen: Ende daerenboven in eene verhandelinge nopende het recht der Hollantsche bodemeryen* (Amsterdam, 1711).

97 J.M. Barels, *Advysen over den koophandel en zeevaert. Mitsgaders verscheidene turbes, memorien, resolutien, missives enz. enz. daer toe behoorende*, 2 vols. (Amsterdam, 1781). An early example of a collection that was not focussed on commerce is *Consultatien, advysen*

of advice given by merchants on commercial disputes was published.[98] This publication provided advice to the reader in the form of various *turben* (singular *turbe*). *Turben* were essentially expert declarations that were invoked to prove the existence of certain rules or customs and were first used in medieval France. They were crucial in determining the applicability of certain customs in court.[99] In the Low Countries – they were used in Antwerp by the 1480s – declarations were registered in special books, *turbeboeken*, where they could be consulted later.[100] *Turben* were crucial in determining the applicability of specific customs. Merchants were aware of the existence of published collections of opinions and expert declarations, and sometimes, they explicitly referred to them during litigation.[101]

In addition to these publications, Lichtenauer further mentioned alphabetical registry books, a number of orations and W. Hessen's 1776 publication of legal forms related to commerce as sources for written law, but he did not discuss them much.[102] His last categories are laws – by which he meant the totality of written-down law in all its fragmented diversity; Hessen divided this category in local laws, regulations, ordnances, privileges, treaties, in which burghers of one city could count on certain privileges in another, and, lastly, custom and *desuetudo*.[103]

Lichtenauer made the crucial point that custom can be found in all of the other sources. For a good understanding of how the customs and usages of merchants found their way into court, it is important to realise that in certain environments, mercantile custom was incorporated into the law. The strong presence of foreign merchants in Antwerp contributed to the inclusion of merchant custom in local law; however, Dave De ruysscher has argued that the inclusion of custom and principles considered to be part of *ius commune* in the written corpus of Antwerp city law was primarily the work of aldermen

---

en advertissementen, gegeven ende geschreven bij verscheyde treffelijcke rechts-geleerden in Holland en elders, 6 vols. (Rotterdam, 1645–1666).

98 *Verzameling van casuspositien, voorstellingen en declaratien, betrekkelyk tot voorvallende omstandigheden in den koophandel, van tyd tot tyd binnen deeze stad beoordeeld en ondertekend*, 2 vols. (Amsterdam, 1793–1794).

99 L. Waelkens, 'L'origine de l'enquête par turbe', *Tijdschrift voor rechtsgeschiedenis*, 53 (1985): pp. 337–346.

100 Dave De ruysscher, 'From usages of merchants to default rules: Practices of trade, *ius commune* and urban law in early modern Antwerp', *Journal of legal history*, 33:1 (2012): pp. 12–16.

101 For an example, see pp. 189–192.

102 Lichtenauer, *Geschiedenis van de wetenschap van het handelsrecht*, pp. 149–151.

103 *Desuetudo* is the abolition, never in writing, of older laws or customs. Lichtenauer, *Geschiedenis van de wetenschap van het handelsrecht*, pp. 151–154.

and legal scholars. The absence of references to the 'customs of merchants' obscures the connection between custom and written law. De ruysscher concluded his analysis by stating that 'one may say that the City Court of Antwerp did not apply customs of merchants, but that the customs of merchants trading in Antwerp were the default rules imposed by the Antwerp City Court within a civil law framework'.[104]

There was certainly a tension between the application of merchant custom and local laws, or *ius commune* and *ius proprium*, in commercial litigation, and early modern legal scholars regularly underplayed the role played by merchant custom when writing their treatises, opting instead to focus on antecedents in Roman law.[105] It has been argued that in certain circumstances, it was a cooperation between these two legal cultures that contributed to the development of a legal apparatus. It seems that in the sixteenth century, jurists in the Low Countries were able to use merchant custom and merge it with existing statutes, leading to new and improved maritime laws.[106] De ruysscher's quote can also be considered as an expression of local city courts' efforts to retain their grasp over commercial litigation through *ius proprium*, rather than handing it over to forms of peer adjudication on the basis of *ius commune*. Such institutional competition was less of a problem in Izmir, where there was no local Dutch city court that might have challenged consular jurisdiction.[107]

The categorisation of the different sources for Dutch commercial law in the early modern period should not obscure the fact that there was a great deal of overlap and borrowing, not only through the insertion of custom into local laws but also through Roman legal principles that found their way into legislation. It should also not be forgotten that, while the law was made by local governments, and was in that sense an internal affair, it was influenced from the outside – and this is particularly relevant in the context of commercial and maritime law. A good example of these considerations is the history of the maritime ordinances issued by Charles V and Philip II in 1551 and 1563 respectively. These were ordinances that applied to all of the Burgundian Netherlands, as they were issued at a time when the Northern Netherlands were still part of the

104 De ruysscher, 'From usages of merchants to default rules', p. 29.

105 In the eighteenth century, for instance, Italian and German legal scholars were looking for the existence of credit contracts in Roman law. Francesca Trivellato, *The promise and peril of credit. What a forgotten legend about Jews and finance tells us about the making of European commercial society* (Princeton and Oxford, 2019), p. 113.

106 Dave De ruysscher 'Maxims, principles and legal change'.

107 There was, in some sense, competition from Ottoman courts, as merchants could choose to litigate before them, but it remained a choice rarely taken, and concrete competition was limited through the capitulations.

Spanish Empire. While several of the articles in these ordinances went out of fashion, others were observed in the United Provinces even after Dutch independence.[108] A good example is the practice of *voering*, private merchandise seamen could bring on the voyages on which they were employed, which was regulated by the maritime law issued by Philip II in 1563. The law stated that seamen could either bring private merchandise, to be put in the hold where the skipper indicated, or they could sell this right to the skipper who could then use the space to load more cargo.[109] Commenting on the relevant article in 1711, Adriaen Verwer (c. 1655–1717) stated that this choice was no longer formally included in agreements between skippers and seamen.[110]

In 1665, a century after Philip II's maritime ordinance had been published, a legal scholar named Taco van Glins published a comment on the ordinance.[111] In his address to the reader, van Glins evokes the men from the island of Rhodos, 'famous for their knowledge and experience in maritime navigation, and famous for their good sea laws and discipline on board'.[112] According to van Glins, Rhodian laws were so good that the Romans borrowed them, and Justinian acknowledged that his law on averages came directly from 'Rhodian law'. Van Glins continued to explain that the Rhodian example was followed by 'kings, princes and republics' and referred to famous old sea laws, such as the French Oléron laws and Scandinavian Wisby sea law, local regulations on maritime matters that were very influential in Europe.[113] Van Glins then proceeded

108 While these attempts are testimony of a larger but failed effort at codification, they did create, in certain areas, some sort of cohesion over different jurisdictions. Boudewijn Sirks, 'Sources of commercial law in the Dutch Republic and Kingdom', in *Understanding the sources of early modern and modern commercial law. Courts, statutes, contracts, and legal scholarship*, eds. Heikki Pihlajamäki, Albrecht Cordes, Serge Dauchy, and Dave De ruysscher (Leiden and Boston, 2018), p. 172.

109 Adriaen Verwer, *Nederlants see-rechten*, p. 91. Reference is made to the origins of this stipulation in medieval maritime law.

110 Ibid., p. 95.

111 Taco van Glins, *Aenmerckingen ende bedenckingen over de zee-rechten, uyt het placcaet van Koninck Philips uytgegeven den lesten octobris 1563. Alwaer der selver billickheyt uyt den gront van keyserlicke rechten, en krachtige beweeghreden bevestight, met andere zee-rechten over een gebracht, haer verschil aengewesen, en daer beneffens op verscheyden quaestien en voorvallen den koophandel en scheep-vaert aengaende, geantwoordt wordt. Den kooplieden en schipperen niet alleen, maer allen liefhebberen der rechts-geleertheydt seer dienstelick en profytelick* (Amsterdam, 1665). On van Glins, see A.J. van der Aa, *Biographisch woordenboek der Nederlanden* (Haarlem, 1862), 7: pp. 210–211.

112 Van Glins, *Aenmerckingen ende bedenckingen*, n.p., 'die van Rhodus […] eertydts in't bysonder vermaert van wegens haere groote kennisse en ervaerensheyt dewelcke ze hadden op de zeevaert, als mede van wegens haere goede zeerechten ende scheepstucht […]'.

113 Ibid., n.p., '[…] koningen, princen, en republiquen […]'. For the mix of custom and legal codes in European maritime law, see the afterword by Maria Fusaro in Fusaro et al., eds.,

to discuss the articles of the maritime ordinances of Charles V and Phillip II, and he traced the origins of articles on freight charges, damaged cargo and other navigational issues back to older laws, particularly Wisby sea law. Van Glins' example is interesting because it demonstrates borrowing from other legal cultures, demonstrating concretely how foreign laws become incorporated in Dutch law. This can also be observed in legal compilations made of all relevant laws for cities in Holland. In 1639, for instance, a compilation of all laws relevant for the city of Amsterdam in terms of trade and maritime navigation was published in Dutch, with a title that translates as *Charters or privileges, acts, custom and by-laws of the city of Amsterdam.*[114] These contained regulations taken from Wisby sea law, as well as from the Hanseatic cities, the ordinances of Charles V and Phillip II, charters of the counts of Holland, local by-laws from the city of Amsterdam and the rights and customs of the city of Antwerp, as well as other sources.[115] Scholars have acknowledged that there was a transfer of legal customs between cities, transfers facilitated by the migration of merchants.[116] In the case of Amsterdam, this can be related to the arrival of merchants from the Spanish Netherlands, Antwerp in particular, during the Dutch Revolt, but it also has to do with the nature of trade and the presence of foreign merchant communities.[117]

While it goes beyond the scope of this study to provide a detailed overview of the history of the origins of Dutch laws on commerce, it is important to note

---

Labour, law, and empire, pp. 304–310. For hybrid publications of local maritime law in the Spanish Netherlands before the revolt and their origins in legal texts from Scandinavia (Wisby), the *Rôles d'Oléron* and the Hanseatic towns, see Edda Frankot, *'Of laws of ships and shipmen' – Medieval maritime law and its practice in urban northern Europe* (Edinburgh, 2012), pp. 14–26. A detailed comparison between two of the most important medieval maritime law codes can be found in Julia Schweitzer, *Schiffer und Schiffsmann in den Rôles d'Oléron und im Llibre del Consolat de Mar – Ein Vergleich zweier mittelalterlicher Seerechtsquellen* (Frankfurt am Main, 2006).

114 The full Dutch title is *Handtvesten, ofte privilegien, handelingen, costumen, ende willekeuren der stadt Aemstelredam: Mitsgaders concept vande geraemde poincten op 't stuck vande iustitie, ofte maniere van procederen in civile saecken binnen deser stede: Met verscheyden placcaten dienstigh in diversche saecken. Als mede de zee ende scheeps-rechten van Wisbuy, vande oude Hanse steden, van Keyser Karel ende Koningh Philips: Met een tractaet van avarije. Alles verrijckt met een wijtloopig ende wel geordonneert register. Hier achter zijn by-gevoeght de rechten ende costumen van Antwerpen* (Amsterdam, 1639).

115 Ibid., passim.

116 Dave De ruysscher, 'Antwerp commercial legislation in Amsterdam in the 17th century. Legal transplant or jumping board?' *Tijdschrift voor rechtsgeschiedenis*, 77 (2009): pp. 459–479.

117 For the migration of traders from Antwerp, see Oscar Gelderblom, *Zuid-Nederlandse kooplieden en de opkomst van de Amsterdamse stapelmarkt (1578–1630)* (Hilversum, 2000).

that a great deal of the laws dealing with trade that found their way into written texts belonging to any of Lichtenauer's categories have their origins in old custom, and an important aspect of the commercial legal culture in the Low Countries was not just its fragmented nature but also its ability to incorporate foreign use and custom. It meant that merchants moving to a Dutch commercial city could, in certain instances, find a legal culture similar to the ones they had left behind in their places of origin. This familiarity not only applied to laws surrounding trade but can be somewhat extended to the courts themselves.It is not clear to what extent merchants were aware of the body of law within which the merchants' style that they did know was embedded, but by the eighteenth century, several notaries, attorneys and legal scholars had made compilations that contained useful information for traders.[118] In at least one of the cases that will be analysed later, one of the litigants invoked both natural and civil law to substantiate her argument.[119]

2.2 *The Diversity of Jurisdictions and the Similarity of Courts*

While Manlio Bellomo argued for a larger, shared European legal context than was commonplace amongst historians, he did not deny the existence of legal fragmentation in itself, and it was an early modern reality that litigants were faced with a multitude of jurisdictions. This was largely due to the absence of strong and centralised modern nation-states that relied on an extensive corpus of written-down national laws. In the United Provinces, this situation was even more extreme than in many other early modern European states. The Dutch Republic was a strongly decentralised state with divided political power. Cities and provinces had their own governmental system and possessed a great deal of political autonomy. The provincial states, such as the States of Holland, were composed of representatives of the nobility and the cities, and there was an agreement to protect existing local privileges. More central governmental institutions did exist, most importantly the States General, but its jurisdiction was limited to foreign affairs. Its composition did not reflect the political and financial power structures of the Dutch Republic, as all provinces had one

118 A good example in Dutch is Arent Lybreghts, *Burgerlyk, rechtsgeleerd, notariaal en koopmanshandboek; behelzende een korten grondslag van de rechtsgeleerdheid, notariaale practyq en van den koophandel zeer dienstig niet alleen voor advocaten, procureurs, solliciteurs, schouten en secretarissen ten platen lande, en practiseerende boekhouders; maar ook voor voogden, executeurs, administrateurs, en curateurs; die zich in den koophandel willen oeffenen, en voor yder burger van Nederlands gemeenebest*, 4th ed. (Amsterdam, 1764). In English, there was for instance G. Jacob, *Lex mercatoria: Or, the merchant's companion. Containing all the laws and statutes relating to merchandize* (London, 1718).

119 See p. 246.

vote, disregarding their real political and economic weight.[120] The absence of a strong centralised state apparatus was an elementary characteristic of the Dutch Republic, which had come into being in a region that already carried a long medieval tradition of decentralised territories and had resisted, ultimately successfully, the Spanish effort of incorporation into a global empire.[121]

This political fragmentation had important consequences for litigation. When merchants went to court in the United Provinces, they went first and foremost to a local court. Oscar Gelderblom has argued that the three most important commercial cities in the Low Countries, Bruges, Antwerp and Amsterdam, 'developed more inclusive commercial regimes in which all merchants were treated equally and the commercial infrastructure served the merchant community at large'.[122] This was part of a strategy aimed to keep foreign merchant communities in the city, without providing them with special status, and it included the development of legal instruments merchants could use to solve their disputes.[123] This long development originated in the Southern Netherlands, where cities had developed at an earlier stage than in the north. In Flanders and Brabant, several urban courts had managed to extend their jurisdiction into the countryside. In Holland, the most important of the northern provinces, the situation was different. Urban and rural courts each had their own jurisdictions, and ecclesiastical courts continued to play an important role as well. Initially, this fragmentation seems to have hindered the expansion of trade. Jessica Dijkman, for instance, argued that in cases of debt litigation, creditors had to physically travel to the debtor's jurisdiction to claim their money there, a situation that differed from practice in England and the Southern Netherlands.[124] It seems very plausible that the practical problems brought about by legal fragmentation contributed to the development of informal arrangements, which complemented the formal legal system, and these served as early and perhaps local examples of the merchants' style.

In the later Middle Ages, the growing power of the count of Holland changed the legal landscape of local and traditional forms of adjudication. By the end of the thirteenth century, Holland possessed a more centralised justice system,

---

120 De Vries and van der Woude, *Nederland*, p. 125.

121 For an overview of the Dutch political structures, see Prak, *The Dutch Republic in the seventeenth century*, pp. 166–185; see also Price, *Holland and the Dutch Republic*.

122 Gelderblom, *Cities of commerce*, p. 40.

123 For an extensive analysis of the development of conflict resolution mechanisms, see ibid., pp. 102–140.

124 Jessica Dijkman, *Shaping medieval markets. The organisation of commodity markets in Holland, c. 1200–c. 1450* (Leiden and Boston, 2011), pp. 265–268.

in which the count of Holland and a number of counsellors adjudicated certain disputes. This allowed for some important procedural innovations, such as clear instructions on the admittance of evidence.[125] Attempts were made to streamline the different jurisdictions in Holland and to further centralise a number of disputes. Duke Willem of Bavaria (1365–1417), count of Holland and Zeeland, released an order stating that 'our sheriff and aldermen administer justice and declare sentences concerning all those who are seaworthy and fleet-worthy, and the same of all seaworthy goods'.[126] This clause specifically aimed to cover potential problems of jurisdiction concerning people whose regular displacements made them cross legal boundaries, such as merchants who were, at the time, often still itinerant.

The count's efforts brought more unity to the different formats of local traditions, but the most important Dutch institutional framework dealing with maritime and commercial disputes was developed within urban jurisdictions, where it was needed the most – although local laws were periodically upheld by Burgundian and Spanish affirmations of privileges. In 1413, Amsterdam's magistrates had issued a law stating that conflicts between foreigners were to be adjudicated by the aldermen's bench (the court of aldermen).[127] Amsterdam organised the election and constitution of the council of citizens that ruled the city, the *vroedschap*, which included the aldermen and burgomasters coming from a number of elite urban families. Over time, regulations stipulated that out of the nine aldermen, several needed to be versed in commerce and maritime navigation. The reason given for this change was that the aldermen's bench had to adjudicate commercial disputes within its jurisdiction.[128] On days on which the bench convened, the city's sheriff opened the session by addressing the president of the court personally, instructing him to administer the law and justice 'to the old customs and privileges of this city'.[129]

Amsterdam continued to expand in the late sixteenth and seventeenth century, and the success of its legal institutions can perhaps be observed in the growing burden that litigation posed on the aldermen's bench, which was a general court that adjudicated all legal matters in Amsterdam. Contrary to

125 Ibid., p. 264.

126 *Handtvesten*, p. 20.

127 Gelderblom, *Cities of commerce*, p. 123.

128 Jan Wagenaar, *Amsterdam in zyne opkomst, aanwas, geschiedenissen, voorregten, koophandel, gebouwen, kerkenstaat, schoolen, schutterye, gilden en regeeringe beschreeven door Jan Wagenaar historieschryver der stad* (Amsterdam, 1768), 12: p. 17. Wagenaar (1709–1773) was a well-known Dutch chronicler and historian.

129 Ibid., p. 176, '[...] naar de oude coustumen en privilegien deezer stede', a phrase pronounced by the sheriff.

other commercial cities, such as Bruges and Antwerp, Amsterdam never admitted consular jurisdiction.[130] After the Dutch Revolt, the foreign communities in Amsterdam were not only groups of merchants but also religious refugees. Even though no consular courts existed in Amsterdam, the city did allow for religious leaders of certain groups to administer justice to members of their religious communities.[131] The leaders of the Portuguese Jewish community in Amsterdam, the *parnassim*, for instance, adjudicated a number of disputes between members of the community, and Amsterdam local courts could refer Jewish litigants to these leaders in order to reach an amicable settlement.[132]

In spite of the jurisdiction given to leaders of a number of religious communities, the city's legal institutions retained their primacy. It was perhaps out of this desire to control adjudication within the city that, from a very early moment onwards, Amsterdam's government considered the establishment of more specialised courts. As early as 1516, urban authorities had contemplated the foundation of a court aimed at settling disputes between merchants and seafarers, but it would take more than a century before such plans were finally realised. In the last decades of the sixteenth and the first half of the seventeenth century, more specialised civil courts were created to deal with specific types of disputes. A Chamber of Insolvent Estates (*Desolate Boedelskamer*) came into being in 1643, while the Bench of Minor Affairs (*Bank van Kleine Zaken*), established in 1611, took care of disputes limited to the sum of forty guilders, including those involving commerce. In 1650, the limit was raised to 600 guilders, which raised the number of cases to such an extent that cases related to violence were transferred to the Commissioners of Maritime Affairs (*Commissarissen van Zeezaken*).[133] This court was founded in 1641 to adjudicate all disputes between merchant and skipper, skipper and skipper, merchant and seaman and skipper and seaman.[134] Rotterdam, Middelburg and Vlissingen followed and established maritime courts of their own.

130 Gelderblom, *Cities of commerce*, pp. 121–123.

131 These communities could use social forms of punishment, such as exclusion from the group. Ibid., p. 122.

132 CAA, N°334 ('Archief van de Portugees-Israëlietische Gemeente'), N°s 875–877 ('Livros de citaçoes e resoluçoes', 1717–1816). These volumes are registries of parties appearing before the *parnassim*. N°s 878–880 contain *parnassim* sentences in affairs that were referred to them by the Bench of Minor Affairs between 1710 and 1806.

133 For the changes in the Bench of Minor Affairs during this period, see Hans Bontemantel, *De regeeringe van Amsterdam, soo in 't civiel als crimineel en militaire (1653–1672)*, ed. G.W. Kernkamp (The Hague, 1897), 2: pp. 453–463.

134 *Extract registers Amsterdam*, 31/01/1643. In England, this became the competence of the Admiralty Court. See George F. Steckley, 'Merchants and the Admiralty Court during the English Revolution', *American journal of legal history*, 22:2 (1978): pp. 137–175.

The maritime court took care of commercial disputes if they were directly related to maritime navigation, but it was not a commercial court. It is remarkable that, contrary to other cities in Europe, no specific court was established in the United Provinces that exclusively adjudicated commercial disputes; these remained divided amongst different local courts.[135] Johannes Phoonsen (1631–1702), who published a book on exchange law for merchants, argued that the establishment of a commercial court was highly necessary, and as he was convinced of the importance and centrality of bills of exchange in trade, he thought it best that the commissioners of the Amsterdam exchange bank were given legal authority as a court to adjudicate all commercial disputes involving bills of exchange and to extend it to deal with all trade disputes that were not explicitly the domain of the Commissioners of Maritime Affairs or the insurance chamber.[136] While this suggestion was never implemented, it does show the continuing effort to address problems of attempting to institutionalise commercial adjudication.

Local courts – particularly urban aldermen courts – continued to adjudicate commercial disputes. Additionally, merchants could also seek recourse to a central court. These were only established after Holland had become part of the Burgundian state in the middle of the fifteenth century. In the province of Holland, there were the *Hof van Holland* (see figure 5) and the *Hoge Raad*, while the highest court of all the Burgundian Netherlands was the *Grote Raad* in Mechelen.[137] The States General had some judicial authority, but its verdicts, subsequently turned into resolutions, were directly based on other courts' sentences.[138]

These centralised courts served as courts of appeal in commercial matters, but in the fifteenth century, the Burgundian rulers of the Low Countries offered foreign merchants the privilege to bring their disputes before these central courts first. It was a logical solution, as a more central court had a

135 See, for instance, Amalia Kessler's monograph on the Parisian merchant court, *A revolution in commerce*.

136 Phoonsen, *Wissel-styl tot Amsterdam*, pp. 235–236. 'Exchange law' was used by contemporaries to refer to regulations concerning bills of exchange.

137 For the Hof van Holland, see Marie-Charlotte Le Bailly, *Procesgids Hof van Holland, Zeeland en West-Friesland* (Hilversum, 2008); and *Recht voor de Raad. Rechtspraak voor het Hof van Holland, Zeeland en West-Friesland in het midden van de vijftiende eeuw* (Hilversum, 2001); for the Hoge Raad, see Marie-Charlotte Le Bailly and C.M.O. Verhas, *Hoge Raad van Holland, Zeeland en West-Friesland (1582–1795)* (Hilversum, 2006); see also Dijkman, *Shaping medieval markets*, p. 269.

138 N.M. Japikse and A. van der Poest Clement, *Inventaris van het archief van de Staten-Generaal (1431) 1576–1796* (The Hague, 1969), p. 25.

wider jurisdiction, meaning their verdicts could reach further – making them theoretically more apt to deal with trade. In spite of these efforts, local courts had no need to worry, as in the Low Countries, the central courts continued to only play a small role in the adjudication of commercial disputes, even when international trade was expanding. Oscar Gelderblom has shown that, for the fifteenth and sixteenth centuries, traders' recourse to the centralised courts of Flanders, Brabant, Holland and Zeeland was limited, which he attributed to the long timespan that was often needed to reach a verdict.[139] They did play a role as appeal courts, and in this sense, the *Hof van Holland* and the *Hoge Raad*, the two large centralised courts of the Dutch Republic, are relevant to this study. In the first instance, traders continued to rely on urban courts, preferably specialised ones. Thanks to the consular system, Dutch traders abroad could rely on similar access to adjudication in the manner they were used to, much like their foreign colleagues residing in the Low Countries, who expected the same.

3 Procedures in Commercial Litigation

3.1 *Dutch Regulations on Procedure*

The development of specialised local courts taking care of specific disputes was important and led to the adjudication of commercial disputes in urban courts. Instructions for these courts, as well as instructions for the more centralised ones, clearly delineated jurisdictions. There was, however, no guarantee of unity in procedure, as local courts had adopted their own ways of administering justice over time. This diversity grew after a 1577 regulation stipulated that all towns and villages in the province of Holland had to have their own aldermen court.[140] After 1572, the province of Holland was ruled by the States

139 Gelderblom, *Cities of commerce*, pp. 126–133. In spite of their relatively limited importance in commercial adjudication in relation to the urban courts, several scholars have looked into archival and handwritten material containing the notes and opinions of judges on sentences issued by the *Hof van Holland* and the *Hoge Raad*. See, for instance, H.C. Gall, *Regtsgeleerde decisien. Aan de raadsheer Pieter Ockers toegeschreven aantekeningen betreffende uitspraken van het Hof (1656–1669) en de Hoge Raad (1669–1678) van Holland, Zeeland en West-Friesland* (Amsterdam, 2002). While these notes do not focus on commerce, they do contain trade-related material. An extensive account of the legal context in which these courts operated in terms of trade disputes can be found in Christian Brom, *Urteilsbegründungen im 'Hoge Raad van Holland, Zeeland en West-Friesland' am Beispiel des Kaufrechts im Zeitraum 1704–1787* (Frankfurt am Main, 2008).

140 J.L. van der Gouw, 'Costumen betreffende land liggende gemener voor', in *Ter recognitie. Opstellen aangeboden aan Prof. Mr. H. van der Linden bij zijn afscheid als hoogleraar in de*

of Holland and Westfrisia, composed of eighteen representatives for the eighteen voting cities – which included Amsterdam, Leiden and Rotterdam – and the college of nobles, with one vote and which represented the countryside, as well as the cities with no vote of their own.[141] The States of Holland decided in 1580 that there was 'a great deal of confusion and diversity of rights and special custom in legal claims, procedures, sentencing and execution of sentences'.[142] They also noticed that there had been many complaints by the inhabitants of the province of Holland on the lack of a decent law regulating procedures.[143] To fill this lacuna, the States of Holland published an ordinance in 1580 that was to streamline civil procedure at all local courts in the province of Holland – the *Ordinance dealing with justice, within the cities as well as on the countryside, in the year 1580* (*Ordonnantie op 't stuk van de Justitie soo binnen de steden als ten platen Lande, in den jare 1580*).[144] It turned out to be the most important piece of legislation on procedure in Holland, but it was not the first one. Wagenaar mentioned the publication of a Burgundian ordinance rule as early as 1538 that aimed at shortening litigation.[145]

The 1580 ordinance was of crucial importance because its twenty-two articles laid out the procedural framework for civil law litigation, replacing 'all customs, uses and other styles [of administering justice] used so far that are contrary to this law and that are hereby derogated'.[146] Article 1 described the manner in which the plaintiff was to summon the defendant – with the crucial

Nederlandse rechtsgeschiedenis aan de Vrije Universiteit, eds. C. Streefkerk and S. Faber (Hilversum, 1987), p. 279.

141 See S.J. Fockema Andreae, *De Nederlandse staat onder de Republiek*, Koninklijke Nederlandse Akademie van Wetenschappen. Verhandelingen afd. Letterkunde. Nieuwe reeks, vol. 68, no. 3 (Amsterdam, 1978).

142 'Ordonnantie op 't stuk van de justitie, binnen de steeden ende ten platen landen van Holland, & c.', in *Manier van procedeeren in civile en crimineele saaken*, eds. Simon van Leeuwen, Henrik Verduyn, and Willem van Aller, 5th ed. (Amsterdam, 1721 [1666]), pp. 1–112, on p. 1, '[…] seer groote confusie ende verscheydenheyd van regten, soo vermids haar luider bysondere coustumen in de regtvordering, procedeeren, in 't sententieeren, als ook in 't executeeren van de sententien […]'.

143 Ibid., p. 2.

144 For legal procedures in criminal law, Phillip II had already issued a similar ordinance in 1570, the 'Ordonnantie, edict ende gebod van den jaare 1570 op 't stuk van de crimineele justitie in de Nederlanden', in *Manier van procedeeren in civile en crimineele saaken*, eds. Simon van Leeuwen et al., pp. 113–278. Both documents were collected and commented upon by the legal scholar Simon van Leeuwen and amplified later by lawyers and other scholars, with additional annotations.

145 Wagenaar, *Amsterdam in zyne opkomst*, 12: pp. 172–173. This volume was extended in 1656.

146 'Ordonnantie op 't stuk van de justitie', pp. 110–111, '[…] coustuymen, usantien ofte andere stylen tot nog toe contrarie desen gebruykt, die by desen werden gederogeert […]'.

observation that it was to take place at the court under whose jurisdiction the defendant fell.[147] Several of the articles thereafter dealt with the consequences of the nonappearance of either litigant – monetary fines for up to three nonappearances and ultimately sentencing. Article 10 codified the first proceedings when both parties physically appeared before court. The plaintiff had to bring his claim in writing, which had to be handed over to the secretary or clerk, who wrote it down. The plaintiff was allowed to claim a security deposit but could also wait to do that later during the trial.[148]

Article 11, which dealt with the distinction between written and oral procedure, was crucial. In court, the litigants had to reply to each other's arguments with their counter-arguments. This back-and-forth could be done in writing or by speaking directly in front of the judges. This article set the procedural choice between the two on the basis of the financial value of the claim; oral procedure applied for cases with claims under either 100 guilders (cities) or 50 guilders (villages). When oral procedure applied, written arguments were not allowed. A footnote stipulated that these were small affairs ('kleyne saaken') which were adjudicated in 'the summary manner'.[149] Simon van Leeuwen, one of the legal scholars commenting on this law in a later publication, explained what that meant – fast adjudication.[150] Lawyer Hendrik Verduyn, one of the other commenters, added a remark about the 1674 law from the States of Holland, which raised the monetary limit for the use of the 'summary manner' from 100 to 600 guilders in large cities, 300 in smaller cities (such as The Hague), and between 80 and 120 guilders in villages.[151] Further explanations by these two scholars made it clear that judges kept minutes of what was said by the litigants, but the latter were not allowed to submit written statements. The competent judges heard the litigants' replies and counter-replies and sentenced the case.[152]

In 1783, lawyer and notary Cornelis Decker edited a treatise on Roman-Dutch law originally written by Simon van Leeuwen. He commented in more detail on the nature of the oral procedure. First, he clarified it was indeed used for simple or pressing issues – cases that did not need further investigation or cases that could not be delayed. Decker added that the oral procedure was the most common legal procedure, used both in the cities and the countryside.

147 Ibid., pp. 5–14.
148 Ibid., pp. 35–53.
149 Ibid., p. 44.
150 Ibid., p. 45.
151 This corresponded, of course, to the rising importance of fast litigation. See pp. 124–131.
152 'Ordonnantie op 't stuk van de justitie', p. 45. Both litigants were generally allowed to reply twice, but not more.

It started with the plaintiff's narration of his claim and the reasoning behind it. This should be short. The defendant was then allowed to answer with his own version of events and refute the claim of the plaintiff. After that, it was the plaintiff's turn again to reply with a more in-depth argument in which he could refer to 'laws and doctors' and cite existing jurisprudence. This was officially called the reply (*replyq*), which was answered by a similar counter-reply (*duplyq*) from the defendant.[153] In this system of back-and-forth replies and counter-replies, there were two rounds – the law specified that an additional round, of a third reply (*triptycq*) and counter-reply (*quadruplycq*), was forbidden.[154] When the litigants had brought in all their arguments, the case was sentenced by the judges.

Cases that exceeded the financial limits for oral procedure were discussed in article 12. After the plaintiff made his claim, the defendant was given eight days to respond, either in writing or orally, in cases where a city court was concerned, and two weeks in cases where a village court was handling the case. According to van Leeuwen, the choice for submitting a written argument was based on the length of the answer. If the defendant's answer was too long to be written down by the clerk in the minutes of the court, it needed to be handed over in writing, in narrative form. After that, further replies and counter-replies could be presented orally if both litigating parties agreed to do so.[155] This article clearly indicates that even for cases involving a larger financial claim, the law explicitly allowed for an oral procedure – but in this case, litigation could only proceed in this manner should both plaintiff and defendant agree.

Articles 11 and 12 established slightly different procedures for different cases based on the value of the plaintiff's claim, but the exact nature of the cases themselves was never discussed in the 1580 ordinance. Only one type of dispute was mentioned, in articles 15 and 16, and that was a case that disputed facts ('saken in feyten') – this meant a witness was necessary in order to adjudicate. These needed to follow a different procedure, for the obvious reason that an additional party needed to be inscribed in the legal process – the witness.[156]

---

153 Decker, *Het Roomsch Hollandsch recht*, 2: pp. 548–550.

154 'Ordonnantien', p. 54. It seems, however, that it existed in certain situations and regions – the law for Overijssel, the region around Zwolle and Kampen, for instance, specifies the use of 'triplycq' and 'quadruplycq' in disputes with a sufficiently high financial claim. Christoffer Nessink, *Het landt-recht van Over-Yssel* (Kampen, 1747), pp. 333–334.

155 'Ordonnantie op 't stuk van de justitie', pp. 46–47. There are several examples of the use of the 'triptycq' and 'quadruplycq' in cases brought before the Dutch consul in Izmir.

156 Ibid., pp. 55–70.

Article 18 laid down rules on the admittance of copies in court – these needed to be compiled in a certain way and certified to be authentic. Article 21 stipulated the conditions to appeal a sentence, while article 23 determined that sentences needed to be executed within ten days if no appeal was made.[157] This 1580 ordinance was crucial, as it was the first law that attempted to regulate procedure within the whole province of Holland and go beyond local custom. Although the phrasing is not entirely clear, it seems that this law was also applied in Zeeland and Frisia.[158] Other provinces quickly followed suit. Utrecht issued its regulation on the system of civil legal procedures in 1583 and based it directly on the 1580 legislation. The States of Frisia issued a specific ordinance on legal procedures in 1602.[159]

All local courts within the jurisdiction covered by these laws had to abide by them. The central courts, such as the *Hof van Holland*, operated on the basis of their own separate sets of regulations.[160] Local courts included the specialised courts in the cities, as well as those litigating commercial disputes, such as the Commissioners of Maritime Affairs in Amsterdam and Rotterdam. The instructions published at their establishment dealt with the competence of these courts, members and dates of sessions. They also specified specific infractions and their penalties – in the case of the Commissioners of Maritime Affairs these ranged from seamen disobeying their captains to quarrels between freighters and shipowners about the shipped goods.[161] These instructions did not establish new procedures, as the courts had to follow the 1580 ordinance in terms of legal procedures.[162] As specified in that ordinance, trials at the urban courts began – similar to those at the *Hoge Raad* and *Hof van Holland* – with a request for summoning made by the plaintiff. The defendant was placed on a *rol*, a registry containing the cases to appear before the aldermen. Originally, there were different registries for different types of cases, but with the arrival of more specialised courts these different registries disappeared. Contrary to the higher provincial courts, the defendant, or someone on his behalf, had to

157 Ibid., pp. 71–72 (article 18), 85–87 (article 21), and 90–91 (article 23).

158 Ibid., p. 2.

159 Rembt van Boneval Faure, *Het Nederlandsche burgerlijk procesrecht* (Leiden, 1893), 1: p. 33.

160 See pp. 271–272.

161 See pp. 117 and 124.

162 For the instructions of the maritime courts of Amsterdam and Rotterdam, see *Extract keurboek Rotterdam*, 16/03/1655 and *Extract registers Amsterdam*, 31/01/1643. The Amsterdam instructions were renewed in 1731 and 1774. *Instructien en ordonnantien voor Commissarissen van Zee Zaken* (Amsterdam, 1731); and *Instructies en ordonnantien voor de Commissarissen van Zee Zaken* (Amsterdam, 1774).

appear in person. Then, the case was ready to be adjudicated following the legal procedures first set out in 1580.[163]

There were two reasons the oral procedure, set down in article 11 of the 1580 ordinance, took such a prominent place in litigation. Following the 'legal revolution' of the sixteenth century, litigation expanded enormously in various regions of Europe, and many people sought recourse to the court system – which had to be able to adjudicate a multitude of small disputes between people who could not necessarily read or write.[164] The oldest extant *rol* of the Commissioners of Maritime Affairs in Amsterdam contains more than 760 cases adjudicated between March and June 1641.[165] Judges would never be able to process that many disputes if all the arguments had to be brought to the court in writing, particularly as written replies and counter-replies could not be fabricated on the spot. A second reason for the use of the oral procedure was that it could guarantee speedy sentencing. This was not only relevant in the context of the rise of litigation – which did not continue through the eighteenth century – but was particularly important in the expanding number of commercial disputes that were also of an increasingly international nature. Merchants preferred fast sentences, so neither their time nor their resources were caught up in a trial. This aspect was referred to by Simon van Leeuwen as a 'summary' procedure – fast and simple adjudication without the involvement of professionals such as lawyers.[166]

3.2 *Summary Procedure and the Merchants' Style*

Summary procedure was considered a privileged form of procedure, the use of which was granted by Italian states to the category of the *misérables* – people who were low on the social ladder and needed legal protection as well as cheap and fast judgment. These people not only included the poor, widows, minors,

---

163 For a complete overview of normal as well as exceptional procedures, see Wagenaar, *Amsterdam in zyne opkomst*, 12: pp. 172–199.

164 See footnote 30 on p. 90.

165 CAA, N°5061 ('Archieven van de schout en schepenen, van de schepenen en van de subalterne rechtbanken'), N°2490 ('Rol voor Commissarissen van de Zeezaken', 21/03/1641–07/09/1641).

166 For van Leeuwen's definition of summary procedure, see 'Ordonnantie op 't stuk van de justitie', pp. 44–45. For an analysis of summary procedure, see Simona Cerutti, *Giustizia sommaria. Pratiche e ideali di giustizia in una società di Ancien Régime* (*Torino XVIII secolo*) (Milan, 2003); see also Mario Ascheri, *Tribunali, giuristi e istituzioni dal Medioevo all'età moderna* (Bologna, 1989), pp. 23–54; and Alessandro Lattes, 'Il procedimento sommario', in *Il procedimento civile nella legislazione statutaria italiana*, ed. Pietro Sella (Milan, 1927), pp. 216–267.

orphans and pilgrims but also foreigners and professionals such as soldiers and merchants – not coincidentally, people who displaced themselves regularly.[167] Foreigners or travellers could not be expected to be fully aware of local legal customs, making summary procedure an accessible and general alternative.[168] When several regions in Europe established specialised commercial courts throughout the early modern period, they usually relied on summary procedure.[169] This procedure was different from ordinary civil procedure that was used in European and Dutch civil courts, not only in practical terms but also in the theoretical justification that came from the principles of natural law and equity.

The development of legal procedures in medieval Europe was greatly inspired by canonical law.[170] One of the first publications that dealt with civil, criminal and canonical procedure was Guillaume Durand's *Speculum iudiciale*, compiled between 1271 and 1276.[171] Durand's work was a great influence on the subsequent development of the Roman canonical procedure that came to dominate European civil litigation until the nineteenth century. According to legal scholars, the influence of canonical law on civil litigation can be found in the importance given to written proof, the rational approach to evidence and the secrecy of legal deliberation.[172] These ideas were very welcome in the

167 See Cerutti, *Giustizia sommaria*; and Fusaro, 'Politics of justice/politics of trade'. In Venice, foreigners did not have access to the privilege of summary procedure – until it was granted to the English in 1698 – out of consideration for Venetian commercial interests.

168 For these considerations and a discussion of summary procedure in the context of the 'poor' in the Low Countries, see Griet Vermeesch, 'Access to justice: Legal aid to the poor at civil law courts in the eighteenth-century Low Countries', *Law and history review*, 32:3 (2014): pp. 683–714.

169 See for instance Kessler, *A revolution in commerce*; see also Knut Wolfgang Nörr, 'Procedure in mercantile matters: Some comparative aspects', in *The courts and the development of commercial law*, ed. Vito Piergiovanni (Berling, 1987), pp. 195–201; and Alessandro Lattes, *Il diritto commerciale nella legislazione statutaria delle città italiane* (Milan, 1884).

170 See Kenneth Pennington, *The prince and the law, 1200–1600: Sovereignty and rights in the western legal tradition* (Berkeley and Oxford, 1993), p. 189; and the part on 'Diritto canonico medievale' in Vito Piergiovanni, *Norme, scienza e pratica giuridica tra Genova e l'occidente medievale e moderno* (Genoa, 2012), 1: pp. 509–736.

171 Beatrice Pasciuta, 'Durantis, Speculum iudiciale', in *The formation and transmission of western legal culture*, eds. Serge Dauchy, Georges Martyn, Athony Musson, Heikki Pihlajamäki, and Alain Wijffels (Cham, 2016), pp. 37–40.

172 R.C. van Caenegem, 'History of European civil procedure', in *International encyclopedia of comparative law*, ed. Mauro Cappelletti (Leiden and Boston, 2014), 16: pp. 3–113 [first published in Tübingen in 1973]. For an analysis of the early modern development of the legality of various methods of proof, see Michael Macnair, *The law of proof in early modern equity* (Berlin, 1999), which traces the European history of proof from about 1550 to the eighteenth century.

fragmented European legal environment but did not necessarily deal with the legal basis that litigants could use to substantiate their arguments, nor with the theoretical apparatus judges could use to support their sentencing. This needed to come from the law – whether the abovementioned *ius proprium* or *ius commune*.

The *ius gentium* – a concept from Roman times that meant 'the law of nations' – is similar to the *ius commune*. It referred to laws applying to Romans and others – which meant it was useful for trade and found its origins in the idea of the law 'which natural reason establishes for all men'.[173] Several sixteenth- and seventeenth-century scholars saw the right to trade freely as part of the *ius gentium*. Scholars such as Hugo de Groot deemed it a natural right – natural law as a law applicable to all men was a Greek concept but thrived within Christian ideas of universal laws that could not be made by worldly rulers.[174] While free trade was not withheld as a natural principle, the idea that trade bound men together found strong expression in the work of de Groot and other advocates of natural law: 'for between the contracting parties, there is a closer union than ordinarily obtains [*sic*] in human society'.[175] In a manual on commercial law from the eighteenth century, it is argued that a contract of sale contains three sorts of commitments: first, those explicitly mentioned in the contract; second, those that are natural consequences of the transaction; and third, all those that are ascertained by 'laws, usages or customs'.[176] Trade is a form of contract and necessitated legal agreements and security that went beyond the *ius proprium*, the particular laws of individual territorial states, and belonged to the more universal domain of *ius gentium* or *ius natural*, but it nonetheless needed to be congruent with *ius proprium*.

When Hugo de Groot wrote down his ideas on natural law in *De iure belli ac pacis*, published in 1625, he based them on the idea of universal reason, but 'more often than not, reason's precepts happened to be found in the Roman law

173 Benn Steil, 'Globalism and natural law – A brief history', in *Natural law, economics and the common good*, eds. S. Gregg and H. James (Exeter, 2012), p. 66.

174 For a discussion of the connection between ideas on natural law and the development of international trade after Hugo de Groot, see Martti Koskenniemi, 'International law and the emergence of mercantile capitalism: Grotius to Smith', in *The roots of international law/Les fondements du droit international. Liber amicorum Peter Haggenmacher*, eds. Pierre-Marie Dupuy and Vincent Chetail (Leiden and Boston, 2013), pp. 1–37.

175 The quote is an English translation from the Latin original and can be found in Hugo Grotius, *Hugo Grotius on the law of war and peace*, ed. Stephen C. Neff (Cambridge, 2012), p. 205.

176 Lybreghts, *Burgerlyk, rechtsgeleerd, notariaal en koopmanshandboek*, p. 158, '[…] wetten, gewoontens, of gebruiken […]'.

texts of the *Digest*'.[177] Roman legal tradition allowed for sentencing based on shared rules, beyond *ius proprium*, and as such, natural law was not separated from it. This is an important consideration when analysing the idea that commercial litigation needed to be judged according to merchant custom. In the early seventeenth century, several English traders and scholars began to refer to a *lex mercatoria*, or law merchant, as a concept that referred to the universal customs that merchants agreed upon and used to conduct their manner of doing business. This interpretation was made famous by Gerard Malynes, one of the earliest and most vocal supporters of the idea of the law merchant: it 'may well be as ancient as any humane Law, and more ancient than any written Law. The very morall Law it selfe, as written by *Moses*, was long after the customary law of Merchants, which hath so continued and beene daily augmented successively upon new foundations'.[178]

Malynes' claims were exaggerated. He was not the first to use the term *lex mercatoria*, which was used in the English context of the development of royal jurisdiction through the Common Law in the twelfth century at the expense of local courts. It referred to these local courts' use of 'traditional' medieval legal norms and procedures and local competence. The same association with local uses and privileges, which included regulations for the marketplace, led to the use of the term *ius mercatorum* elsewhere in Europe. In its original meaning, the law merchant did not refer to an international law of merchants but to a multitude of local legal contexts.[179] The concept was only transformed in the seventeenth century to refer to, and discuss, a universal law of merchants applicable to regulate the development of international trade. Some have suggested that Malynes, a merchant himself, inflated the concept to use in the jurisdictional battles in England during this time, which saw courts concerned with commercial or maritime matters, such as the Court of Admiralty, lose competence to the common law courts, and the latter needed to be newly convinced of the importance of merchant custom in litigation.[180]

177 Benjamin Straumann, *Roman law in the state of nature. The classical foundations of Hugo Grotius' natural law* (Cambridge, 2015), p. 3. The *Digest* was one of the three legal compilations that are part of Justinian's *corpus iuris civilis*. See http://www.thelatinlibrary.com/justinian.html.

178 Gerard Malynes, *Consuetudo, vel lex mercatoria, or the antient law-merchant, divided into three parts: according to the essentiall parts of traffique. Necessarie for all states-men, judges, magistrates, temporall and civile lawyers, mint-men, merchants, mariners, and all others negotiating in all places of the world* (London, 1629 [1622]), p. 2.

179 De ruysscher, 'La lex mercatoria contextualisée', pp. 501–504; see also Baker, 'The law merchant'.

180 Maura Fortunati, 'La *lex mercatoria* nella tradizione e nella recente ricostruzione storico-giuridica', *Sociologia del diritto*, 32:2–3 (2005): p. 35. For an in-depth analysis of Malynes in

Some scholars still accept the idea that there was a *lex mercatoria* and that it carries a long history. While a narrowed-down definition of the concept – applied to forms of summary procedure able to deal with (international) commercial litigation – might still be fruitful, the idea of it as a universal and ancient legal system of commercial law based on reason seems ideologically biased as well as wishful thinking. Twentieth-century efforts supporting it can to an extent be summarised as an attempt to provide a historical legitimation of a system that was at some point considered to be the end of history – neoliberalism – and to be able to argue for a historical legal foundation for contemporary commercial globalisation.[181]

Both Malynes' enthusiasm and his claims to universalism should be questioned, as well as the almost timeless nature of the law merchant as hailed by several scholars, but his description is still revealing when considering the importance he attributed to reason and equity in commercial litigation. He concluded his introduction by stating that everything in his work was 'built upon the foundations of reason and justice'.[182] When describing the principles of litigation, Malynes asserted that 'the authoritie and proceedings of merchant courts, or priors and consuls, to decide their differences according to equitie in places where they are kept [...]'.[183] These aspects belonged, for Malynes, to the 'customarie law of merchants'.[184]

Carl Günther Ludovici (1707–1778), a German philosopher and economist who published several treatises and lexicons on trade in the second half of the eighteenth century, also mentioned the merchants' style, which he labelled as 'stylus mercatorum' or 'mercatorische Stylus'.[185] He used it to refer to 'usages

relation to the law merchant, see Stefania Gialdroni, 'Gerard Malynes e la questione della lex mercatoria', *Zeitschrift der Savigny-Stiftung für Rechtsgeschichte*, 126 (2009): pp. 38–69.

181 For the links between today and the past, see Oliver Volckart and Antje Mangels, 'Are the roots of the modern lex mercatoria really medieval?' *Southern economic journal*, 65:3 (1999): pp. 427–450; and Nikitas E. Hatzimihail, 'The many lives – and faces – of lex mercatoria: History as genealogy in international business law', *Law and contemporary problems*, 71:3 (2008): pp. 169–190. For an overview of twentieth-century historiography on the matter, see Stefania Gialdroni, 'Il *law merchant* nella storiografia giuridica del Novecento: una rassegna bibliografica', *Forum historiae iuris* (2008), consulted at https://forhistiur.net/2008-08-gialdroni/?l=it.

182 Malynes, *Consuetudo*, p. 8.

183 Ibid., p. 7.

184 Ibid.

185 Carl Günther Ludovici, *Grundik eines vollstandigen Kaufmanns-Systeme nebst den Unfangsgründen der Handlungswissenschaft un angehängter turzen Geschichte der Handlung zu Wasser un zu Lande woraus Man zugleich den gegenwärtigen Zustand der Handlung von Europe, auch bis in die andern Welttheile erkennen kann, zum Dienste der Handlungsbeslissenen* (Leipzig, 1768), passim. The work was translated into Dutch in 1771.

and customs' introduced by traders and considered it as one of several sources for commercial law. Ludovici distinguished all sorts of written regulations, ordinances, statues and treatises, including exchange law, the law of the sea, the Hanseatic statutes, particular legislation issued for the trade companies and, importantly, the laws rightfully made by emperors, kings and lords in commerce, 'to which also the Roman laws belong, in the sense that these include many commercial laws, which are still used today in our courts'.[186] The main distinction he made between the different sources of commercial law was between legislation that had been written down and legislation that had not, which consisted of usage and custom. Often, when arguing their case in court, merchants referred to this merchants' style. They sued colleagues in court because they had not respected the way in which merchants did things. The argument against the infraction was an argument of reason, as merchant custom had developed on the basis of reason that went beyond the codification of laws by man and stood on the principles of natural rights, exactly as Malynes had described. Considered this way, law merchant is perhaps best described as a term that indicated the use of 'natural law' in the legal evaluation of a merchant's behaviour. And, as shown by Straumann when discussing de Groot's interpretation of natural law, this law did not exist fully separated from the Roman law that was the foundation for the general laws of nations. In short, the idea of a law merchant, defined as a part of natural law that was applicable to adjudication between merchants, fits perfectly within the historical development of the national legal systems, at least in Europe, during the early modern period. In this sense, the merchants' style occupies the same terrain as universal reason governing human action, which is derived from natural law, and the reason of all men of all nations as reflected in the *ius gentium*. The incorporation of merchant custom in local laws governing trade ensured that the merchants' style can also be traced in the variety of *ius proprium*. It also means that Ludovici's division between written and unwritten sources for commercial law was perhaps too rigid, as they were more connected than it might seem at first, exactly because of the legal space preserved in Roman law for universal and reasonable principles of law.

The judges best qualified to adjudicate according to principles of commercial law were other merchants, and their importance in specialised commercial courts not only exemplifies the wish for speedy resolution through summary procedure but also confirms the reliance on the merchants' style. In her

186 Ibid., pp. 14–15, '[…] wohin auch die römischen Rechte gehoren, in so sern in denselben gar viele Commerciengesetze enthalten sind, die noch heut in Tage in unsern Gerichten gebrauchet werden'.

analysis of the Parisian merchant court, Amalia Kessler quoted a 1742 treatise that stated that 'the merchant courts […] distinguish better than others between the man of good faith and he who wants to deceive'.[187] This not only had to do with the merchants-as-judges' knowledge of commercial custom but also with the understanding that they might know the litigating parties personally or obtain personal information about them more easily.[188] This is more than a logical conclusion deriving from the fact that merchants were judged by their peers. It further connects the adjudicating process to the merchants' style, as successful trade in the early modern period functioned to an important extent on the basis of mechanisms of trust and reputation, expressed through recommendations merchants made to one another, the experience of past transactions, the reciprocity of commercial relations and the establishment of someone's creditworthiness following the growing use of negotiable bills of exchange.[189] In an early modern Dutch manual on commercial law, the most substantial part of commerce was described as 'the credit, the trustworthiness and the honesty'.[190] Natasha Glaisyer has argued that the term 'credit' could refer to three things: 'payments to be made later, one's capacity to pay later, and one's reputation'.[191] She also stressed that these meanings were all connected, as the capacity to pay was part of the reputation, which was fuelled by the concrete fulfilment of later payments, as well as by the assessment made about other traders' capacities to pay.[192]

The merchants' style can thus be defined as a concept that was applied to indicate the commonly accepted manner in which traders were doing their business. It referred to an often unwritten set of rules, habits, norms and values that were accepted by all involved in commerce to ensure its smooth running. In November 1786, Daniel Jean de Hochepied, Dutch consul in Izmir but also Swedish vice-consul, was asked to consider the claim of a Greek merchant in Amsterdam on the bankrupted house of Avierino & C°, Greek traders who stood under Swedish protection. De Hochepied sent a letter to the Directorate of Levant Trade in which he explained that he had appointed five merchants to investigate the claim and decide upon the merchants' style.[193] In

---

187 Kessler, *A revolution in commerce*, p. 66.

188 Ibid.

189 See pp. 293–294.

190 Lybreghts, *Burgerlyk, rechtsgeleerd, notariaal en koopmanshandboek*, p. 157, '[…] het Crediet, de goede Trouw, en de Eerlykheid'.

191 Glaisyer, *The culture of commerce*, p. 38.

192 Ibid.

193 Heeringa and Nanninga, *Bronnen tot de geschiedenis*, 4: pp. 391–392, Consul Daniel Jean de Hochepied to the Directorate of Levant Trade, Izmir, 17/11/1786.

their written arguments submitted before the consular court in Izmir, traders regularly referred to the same merchants' style as a set of rules that had been broken. An uncommon form of insurance could be referred to as 'unknown to the merchants' style', and actions of colleagues could be labelled as 'in conflict with all merchants' style'.[194] More than a commonly accepted way of doing business *in practice*, the merchants' style had legal significance and was, more than any written law, the foundation on which consular judges based their sentencing.

3.3 *Summary Procedure at the Dutch Consular Court of Izmir*

By the mid-eighteenth century, an institutional framework existed that allowed for equitable adjudication of disputes between traders within any Dutch jurisdiction. Judges, whether merchants or aldermen, adjudicated in local courts on the basis of the merchants' style and following summary procedure.[195] This framework not only applied within the geographical confines of the United Provinces but could be extended to include litigation within Dutch trading communities abroad. In the case of Dutch merchants residing in the Ottoman Empire, their disputes could be adjudicated by the consul and assisted by merchant-assessors because of the establishment of Dutch legal autonomy through the Ottoman capitulations and the Dutch legislation that provided consuls and ambassadors with adjudicating power.[196] But was there any specific legislation that codified that these consuls were to adjudicate according to the merchants' style and following summary procedure – or did the specific situation of adjudicating for Dutch merchants who lived abroad and who could get into legal troubles abroad warrant additional legislation?

In 1613, Cornelis Haga sent a letter to the consul in Aleppo, Cornelis Pauw, which included a set of instructions about adjudication.[197] Haga made it clear that, before accepting litigation, it was the consul's duty to first try to find an agreement between the quarrelling parties; by turning to arbitration, neutral

194 Both were used in a dispute between traders about the financial liability for burned cotton and damaged tobacco; see pp. 146–152.

195 In the early twentieth century, William Mitchell explicitly linked the *lex mercatoria*, which he defined as 'a kind of *ius gentium* known to all the merchants throughout Christendom', to the consulate's function as a commercial court. Mitchell, *An essay on the early history of the law merchant*, p. 1.

196 See pp. 84–95.

197 Heeringa and Nanninga, *Bronnen tot de geschiedenis*, 1: pp. 1115–1120, 'Ricordo voor den heer Cornelis Pau, Consul van Alleppo', 27/08/1613.

'good men' had to assess all the evidence to reach a verdict against which no appeal was possible.[198] Arbitrators were chosen according to a certain procedure, in which both parties were allowed to nominate one (or two), with an additional one nominated by the judges. In any case, parties could, and did, refuse the outcome of arbitration, even though there had to be a promise of acceptance beforehand.[199]

When that did not yield any results, the consul was instructed to hear both parties separately and examine all pieces of evidence, including statements by witnesses. The plaintiff had to provide evidence for his claim, otherwise the defendant was acquitted. This was a clear instruction to put the burden of evidence on the plaintiff, and the consul was allowed to dismiss a case at an early stage if there was not sufficient evidence to support the plaintiff's claim. If there was sufficient evidence, the consul should sentence the case, with the help of the assessors.[200] Cornelis Haga wrote further that the consul had to judge according to the 'custom of our lands, and the lands there [Ottoman Syria], the sea laws, and other ordinances made by the States General or Holland or Zeeland about trade, insurance and other matters. If no specific custom or other legal decision is known, you shall pay attention to equity and

198 For the origins of commercial arbitration, see Fabrizio Marrella and Andrea Mozzato, *Alle origini dell'arbitratio commerciale internazionale. L'arbitrato a Venezia tra Medioevo ed età moderna* (Padua, 2001); and Sheilagh Ogilvie, *Institutions and European trade: Merchant guilds, 1000–1800* (Cambridge, 2011), pp. 296–300. Amalia Kessler has pointed out that arbitration in the context of early modern commercial courts has not been analysed much. Amalia D. Kessler, 'Enforcing virtue: Social norms and self-interest in an eighteenth-century merchant court', *Law & history review*, 22:71 (2004): p. 82. Some studies exist, although they do not particularly focus on commercial litigation. For arbitration in late medieval England, see Edward Powell, 'Arbitration and the law in England in the late Middle Ages', *Transactions of the Royal Historical Society*, 33 (1982): pp. 49–67. For arbitration at Hanseatic courts, see Justyna Wubs-Mrozewicz, 'The late medieval and early modern Hanse as an institution of conflict management', *Continuity and change*, 32:1 (2017): pp. 59–84. For the use of arbitration in civil law disputes in an early modern Dutch city, see A.P.B. van Meeteren, *Op hoop van akkoord. Instrumenteel forumgebruik bij geschilbeslechting in Leiden in de zeventiende eeuw* (Hilversum, 2006), pp. 226–273. For a good analysis of the role played by the Dutch and English legal habits of arbitration in commercial disputes in eighteenth-century New York, see Eben Moglen, 'Commercial arbitration in the eighteenth century: Searching for the transformation of American law', *The Yale law journal*, 93:1 (1983): pp. 135–152.

199 For an example of an attempt at arbitration to settle a commercial dispute, see the analysis of the quarrel between Thomas de Vogel & Zoon and Clement, van Sanen, van der Zee & C° on pp. 146–152.

200 Heeringa and Nanninga, *Bronnen tot de geschiedenis*, 1: pp. 1115–1120, 'Ricordo', 27/08/1613.

natural justice'.[201] The last phrase is very important, as it was natural law that served as the underpinning of the merchants' style and summary procedure.

The documents preserved in the archives of the consular court allow for a good understanding of the practical mechanisms behind litigation. First, a merchant made a request, in which he briefly laid out his claim. In the margins, the consul and assessors noted their comments and instructed the chancellor to inform the defendant and provide him with a specific timeframe within which he had to provide his answer. After this, a dialogue of replies and counter-replies took place. As a rule, the replies and counter-replies were labelled by using the official legal terminology for them: *replyq*, *duplyq*, *triptycq*. The cases brought before the Dutch consul in Izmir counted several rounds of these dialogues – there was space for that in the legislation.[202]

These were not the only documents used in these cases. Written evidence was also admitted. This varied from expert reports and witness statements to excerpts from business books or commercial correspondence. These could be specifically demanded by the consul and assessors or produced by one of the parties within the framework of an argument. Their veracity had to be checked by the court before their admission in the case at hand. Haga summed up the three types of evidence the consul should allow: witness statements, instruments and strong presumptions.[203] Witnesses had to be asserted as neutral, honest and of good repute and needed to be at least two in number.[204] When the consul interrogated a witness, he should ask questions about the concrete case as well as about the wider context. He also had to make sure to exclude the witness declaration as coming from hearsay, as that rendered it invalid. It is clear that Haga's instruction to the consul was a first and important effort to codify procedures abroad, which is why he specifically asked Pauw to find out whether the consuls of other European nations allowed for witness statements made by 'Turks or Jews' ('Turcken off Joden') and whether their adherence to

---

201 Ibid., p. 1118, '[…] costuyme van onse en de landen aldaer, op de seerechten, sij andere placaten, bij mijnheeren de Staeten-Generael ofte Hollandt Seelant gemaect aengaende de negotie, soo van assurancie al sanders, die U.E. dienstich sullen sijn te ontbieden. Bovendien geen notoire costume ofte andere decisie van rechten U.E. bekent sijnde, sult principaelijck letten op de natuerlijcke billicheyt van de saeke ende van't recht […]'.

202 See p. 122.

203 Heeringa and Nanninga, *Bronnen tot de geschiedenis*, 1: pp. 1115–1120, 'Ricordo', 27/08/1613, on p. 1117.

204 Ulrik Huber, *Heedensdaegse rechtsgeleertheyt, soo elders, als in Frieslandt gebruikelijk*, 3rd ed. (Amsterdam, 1779), pp. 792–804 defines a number of necessary conditions for the use of witnesses in legal procedure.

their own religion was a sufficient reason to consider them trustworthy.[205] This was an important remark, considering the significance of the oath as a tool to establish the veracity of declarations: 'so the books of merchants, the matters therein about handling and delivering the goods were known, with good distinction of persons, affairs, year, month and day, are given full belief, if they are strengthened by oath'.[206] In one particular case brought before the consul in Izmir, a Dutch plaintiff declared himself willing to abandon a claim against Greek merchants if they were willing to take an oath in the presence of the Greek bishop, with their hands on the Bible.[207] The 1580 *Ordonnantie* – published thirty-three years before Haga wrote his instruction – contained a clause that specified that witness statements not supported by an oath were not valid in court.[208] As a general rule, Pauw was allowed to use the example of other European consuls in his manner of adjudication, particularly in a dispute between a Dutchman and a foreigner.

The second type of evidence Haga mentioned, 'instruments', consisted of public and private written documents. Public documents were drafted before a notary and witnesses at the consular chancery or in any court – this automatically validated their legal use. Private documents included all sorts of written documents made outside the public sphere or without help from a public official. Commercial correspondence and a merchant's business books were private documents, which meant they were not legally valid per se. Handwriting needed to be verified and the content of business books needed to be confirmed by an oath taken by the merchants to whom they belonged. In his comments on the 1580 ordinance that regulated civil procedure in Holland, Simon van Leeuwen wrote that it was a 'general custom' ('volgens generale costuymen') in Holland to accept business books in court.[209] When the legality of such documents had been verified, they could be used in court, similar to

205 Heeringa and Nanninga, *Bronnen tot de geschiedenis*, 1: pp. 1115–1120, 'Ricordo', 27/08/1613, on p. 1117.

206 Decker, *Het Roomsch Hollandsch recht*, 2: p. 443, 'So werden ook de boeken van koopluiden, van saken daar van de handeling en levering van het goed bekend werd, met goed onderscheid van personen, saken, jaar, maand, en dag gehouden, in het verder volkomen geloof gegeven, so die met eede gesterkt [...]'. A different religious background was sometimes considered problematic, while in other instances it was immediately accepted. See Francisco Apellániz, '"You cannot produce a Muslim witness": Early Ottoman attitudes towards proof and religious difference', in 'Litigation and the elements of proof in the Mediterranean (16th–19th c.)', eds. Wolfgang Kaiser and Johann Petitjean, *Quaderni storici*, special issue, 3 (2016): pp. 633–648.

207 See p. 297.

208 'Ordonnantie op 't stuk van de justitie', p. 70.

209 Ibid., p. 28.

'public instruments' ('publyque instrumenten') and debt declarations.[210] Once the instruments were accepted, they could be used to issue a temporary verdict (*bij provisie*), in which the defendant was condemned to deposit a security in the chancery worth the same amount as the plaintiff's claim before the dispute would be adjudicated fully (*ten principale*), resulting in a sentence.[211]

Haga's third category of evidence were presumptions (*presumtiën*). Legally, these were defined as 'probable causes' able to explain the facts after they had been established. Haga wrote that there were too many different presumptions to be written down, but scholars divided them into two categories. A strong presumption meant the party accused of wrongdoing had to prove the opposite. Under a light presumption, the role of the judge in assessing the evidence is more important.[212] Haga used these categories and indicated to Pauw that a very strong presumption was sufficient for the consul to consider the accusation proven. For less strong presumptions, the consul was allowed to take the oath from the person against whom the presumption was made. Should that person swear the presumption was wrong, the consul could acquit him, a mechanism that once again demonstrates the importance of the oath as a legal instrument to support or discard evidence.[213] Once all information had been gathered, the judges had to reach their verdict, which could be temporary or definitive. A temporary verdict was subject to change in cases where new information was provided, while a definitive verdict could only be changed through an appeal procedure at the competent court.[214]

Two years after Haga's letter, Cornelis Pauw sent a letter of his own from Aleppo to the States General in which he remarked that as far as adjudication was concerned, the European consuls were following the 'usages of these [Ottoman Syrian] lands'.[215] This might have been an answer to Haga's request for information about the use of witness statements by other European consuls.[216] It is clear from the content of Pauw's letter that he referred to the non-existence of lawyers or attorneys in the Ottoman context and the fact that the

---

210 Ibid.

211 Heeringa and Nanninga, *Bronnen tot de geschiedenis*, 1: pp. 1115–1120, 'Ricordo', 27/08/1613, on p. 1117.

212 Huber, *Heedensdaegse rechtsgeleertheyt*, pp. 805–806.

213 Heeringa and Nanninga, *Bronnen tot de geschiedenis*, 1: pp. 1115–1120, 'Ricordo', 27/08/1613.

214 Ibid.

215 Heeringa and Nanninga, *Bronnen tot de geschiedenis*, 1: pp. 468–478, Consul Cornelis Pauw to the States General, Aleppo, 12/09/1615, on p. 469, '[...] nae de usantie van dese landen [...]'.

216 Which he made in Heeringa and Nanninga, *Bronnen tot de geschiedenis*, 1: pp. 1115–1120, 'Ricordo', 27/08/1613.

trial was oral rather than in writing. Legal procedure, according to Pauw, was limited to hearing the litigants and witnesses and discussing written documents brought in as evidence, after which a sentence was pronounced orally. Pauw continued that 'this short style is necessary, because most disputes consist of misunderstandings between the buyer and seller, or a sinister interpretation of the brokers, also serving as interpreters, or also in the forgery of merchandise, deception and other differences regarding commerce, which demand to be settled immediately'.[217] What Pauw is describing is clearly a form of summary procedure ('short style'), and it is very similar to how Simon van Leeuwen described it half a century later.[218] It is possible that Cornelis Pauw, who received criticisms for being unexperienced, considered this sort of procedure as particularly 'Ottoman', even though it was not.

Even if Pauw was wrong about the origins of this summary procedure, he was not necessarily wrong in labelling them as Ottoman. Non-European courts also adopted forms of summary procedure. Evidence shows that the local seventeenth- and eighteenth-century Ottoman *qadi* courts relied less on written statements than on oral presentations of the arguments. This, however, did not mean that written documents were not relied upon or had no legal weight. They rather 'complemented the claims and allegations made by the litigants in court [...] these texts were designed to make space for the oral performance of the participants in the court process'.[219] This practice is not as different from the summary procedure used in the Dutch consular court in Izmir as it might seem. In theory, the role of written evidence was to support the claims that had been made. In the courts Boğaç Ergene studied, these claims were made orally and in person. In the consular court, it was done in writing, through the

---

217 Heeringa and Nanninga, *Bronnen tot de geschiedenis*, 1: pp. 468–478, Consul Cornelis Pauw to the States General, Aleppo, 12/09/1615, on p. 469, 'Dese corte stijl is te meer noodich, omdat de meeste questiën, die voorvallen, bestaen in misverstanden tusschen den cooper ende verkooper, door de sinistre interpretatie van de maeckelaers, gelijcksam voor taelmans dienende, item in vervalsinge van de coopmanschappen, bedroch ende andere differenten betreffende 't stuck van de negotie, dewelcke verheyschen datelijck worden gedecideert [...]'.

218 See p. 121.

219 Boğaç A. Ergene, 'Evidence in Ottoman courts: Oral and written documentation in early-modern courts of Islamic law', *Journal of the American Oriental Society*, 124:3 (2004): p. 487. For the notion that Eurocentric criticisms of how the Ottoman court functioned were unfounded, see Metin M. Coşgel and Boğaç A. Ergene, 'Dispute resolution in Ottoman courts: A quantitative analysis of litigations in eighteenth-century Kastamonu', *Social science history*, 38 (2014): pp. 183–202; Boğaç A. Ergene, *Local court, provincial society and justice in the Ottoman Empire. Legal practice and dispute resolutions in Çankiri and Kastamonu (1652–1744)* (Leiden and Boston, 2003).

system of replies and counter-replies. This was not just a matter of attributing more weight to the written word, it was also a consequence of long-distance trade; merchants could not be expected to appear in court personally, so it was a pragmatic choice to allow them to hand in written declarations. These were often compiled in a style that might as well have been oral, with sometimes hefty, emotional language, the building up of long narratives containing an argument that, more often than not, centred around the behaviour and degree of responsibility of the defendant.

CHAPTER 3

The Adjudication of Commercial Disputes within the Dutch Community

1 Adjudication amongst Peers: The Use of Arbitration

1.1 *The Friendly Settlement of Local Troubles*

As discussed in the first chapter of this book, the Dutch merchant community of Izmir was small, and merchants lived near one another around or on the so-called 'Street of the Franks' (see figure 4). While they certainly interacted with one another socially, Dutch traders in Izmir generally did not do business together. While Dutch commercial firms in Izmir certainly did favours for one another, their never-ending quest to obtain new commissions from their peers in the United Provinces or elsewhere also made them competitors. The only exception in this competition between peers was the establishment of an intra-Dutch partnership – and for long periods of time, some Dutch merchants were affiliated with one another before going their separate ways again. Firms such as Knipping & Ouckama; Lennep, Enslie & Knipping; and Clement, van Sanen, van der Zee & C° were all partnerships between Dutch traders, although their constellations varied over time, with some partners leaving to set up their own firms while others were fired. In 1753, for instance, the partnership of Belcamp, Begler & Clement figured on a list of Dutch firms in Izmir. The same list featured both Dirk Knipping and Pieter van Sanen as independent merchants.[1] The next year, Knipping partnered with David van Lennep, and van Sanen joined the partnership of Belcamp and Clement, while Begler di Joseph no longer appeared as a partner. In 1755, the partnership of van Lennep and Knipping was joined by William Enslie, while Belcamp, Clement & van Sanen continued to be in business together. In 1757, Belcamp ceased to be a partner, and in 1758, Knipping was fired from the partnership, leaving only van Lennep & Enslie.[2] In 1759, Knipping established a new partnership with Pieter Ouckama, a partnership that was dissolved in

1 Heeringa and Nanninga, *Bronnen tot de geschiedenis*, 3: pp. 778–783, 'De Nederlandsche handelshuizen te Smirna'; see also table 2.

2 Knipping was fired because he had married a Greek woman. See pp. 70–71.

DOI:10.1163/9789004498235_005

1762. In 1763, the partnership of Clement & van Sanen became Clement, van Sanen, van der Zee & C°.[3]

These changing constellations show the fragile nature of partnerships within the Dutch trading community of Izmir. Sometimes, these came about as calculated associations between established traders, but it was also possible for a younger merchant already employed by the firm as a scribe or accountant to be promoted to partner. Some of these partnerships worked well for several years, while others dissolved rapidly, sometimes following disputes between the partners or their representatives. Apart from forming partnerships, Dutch firms in the Levant regularly accepted employees to learn the specifics of Levant trade. These apprentices could be younger sons of well-established firms or simply young men aiming at a career of their own, but some of them never left the firm and remained employees for a long time. Several of Izmir's larger Dutch firms employed such men as accountants or scribes.[4] The list of the Dutch inhabitants of Izmir in 1759 contains the name of Arnoldus Wissing, who was a scribe (see table 2). According to the list, he had married a French woman and had been residing in Izmir for twelve years. He must have worked for the Dutch firm of Clement, van Sanen, van der Zee & C° since his arrival, because in 1771, he wrote that he had been in their service for twenty-five years, corresponding more or less with his arrival in 1747 – twelve years prior to 1759.[5] In 1760, Wissing travelled to Egypt on a mission to establish a branch of the firm Clement, van Sanen, van der Zee & C° in Cairo. In September of that year, the Dutch ambassador in Istanbul informed the States General that the Ottoman Porte had granted protection to Wissing, which enabled him to undertake the voyage to Cairo.[6] The venture did not work out, and Wissing's actions in Egypt were not appreciated by Robert Hughes, acting Dutch consul in Egypt at the time.[7] Following the debacle, Wissing seems to have gone back to Amsterdam, where he had been born. In 1763, a contract for six years was drafted before an Amsterdam notary in which Wissing, for a yearly salary of 750 guilders, was to

3 Heeringa and Nanninga, *Bronnen tot de geschiedenis*, 3: pp. 778–783, 'De Nederlandsche handelshuizen te Smirna'.

4 See tables 2 and 3.

5 NACS, N°348 ('Proces van N: van der Zee & C° voor Clement, van Sanen, van der Zee & C° met A: Wissing van 25 maert tot xbr. 1771'), 'Antwoord Arnoldus Wissing op d'intimatie der sententie van d'arbitter in differentie met Clement van Sanen van der Zee', Izmir, 01/10/1771.

6 *Verzameling van geheime brieven van en aan de gezanten der Nederlandsche Republiek, April 1756–April 1762* (The Hague, 1756–1762), 12: n.p., Consul Daniel Jean de Hochepied to the States General, Istanbul, 16/09/1760.

7 Heeringa and Nanninga, *Bronnen tot de geschiedenis*, 3: pp. 455–462, Robert Hughes to the States General, Alexandria, 15/03/1762.

work as an accountant for Clement, van Sanen, van der Zee & C° in Izmir, where he arrived at the end of January 1764. Wissing was allowed to conduct some trade affairs for his own benefit, or in commission for the benefit of others, as long as it did not exceed a certain value – in which case he would have to pay half of the profits to the firm.[8] It seems Wissing's employers were happy with his performance, as in 1766 they gave him power of attorney to act on behalf of the firm instead of Philippe Clement, the firm's main partner. Wissing was instructed to act as Clement would, according to the power of attorney that had been drafted before a French notary in Berlin. The reason this construction was necessary was the appointment of Philippe Clement a year earlier as president of the newly-founded Prussian Royal Levant Company, which had obtained a monopoly on all trade between Prussia and the Levant. His partner Pieter van Sanen was appointed as Prussian consul – later succeeded by the third partner, Nicolas van der Zee.[9] In December 1767, several of the scribes working for Clement, van Sanen, van der Zee & C° testified that Wissing was a well-behaved and honest person, and if required, they were willing to confirm under oath that Wissing, after coming back from Holland, had been the good fortune of the firm.[10]

As had been the case in the past, Wissing's work initially met with the approval of his principals, but things changed when Nicolas van der Zee boarded a Ragusan vessel to sail to Trieste, and from this city he would continue on to Berlin to discuss matters related to the consulship and the Prussian Royal Levant Company. Circumstances at that time were such that Arnoldus Wissing was left alone in charge of the firm in Izmir. Because the firm was so heavily involved in Prussian business, the Dutch consul did not know whether he should still consider it a Dutch firm, and he wrote the States General to ask how to treat Wissing in case the firm got involved in commercial or legal trouble.[11] The Directorate of Levant Trade sent a letter with their advice on the matter to the burgomasters of Amsterdam in February 1770. They decided that Wissing was no longer allowed to benefit from his Dutch status in matters

8 NACS, N°348, 'Contract van Wissing van Amsterdam', Amsterdam, 20/10/1763.

9 NACS, N°348, 'Copye procuratie van Philip Clement in faveur van Arnoldus Wissing', Berlin, 18/08/1766. This controversy must have led to the temporary removal of Philippe Clement from the partnership. See table 3; see also pp. 209–213.

10 NACS, N°348, 'Copye attestatie van de schrijvers van het huijs van Clement van Sanen van der Zee & Comp in faveur van Arnoldus Wissing', Izmir, 31/12/1767. One of these scribes was Esaias Fercken, who played a role in another dispute, see p. 247.

11 Both Pieter van Sanen and Philippe Clement had already lost their protected status as Dutch nationals in 1765. Heeringa and Nanninga, *Bronnen tot de geschiedenis*, 4: p. 137, Consul Daniel Jean de Hochepied to Fagel, Izmir, 01/11/1769.

related to the Prussian consulate, or to the house of Clement, van Sanen, van der Zee & C°, but that his national status could still be used in personal affairs.[12]

They equally informed the burgomasters that both van Sanen and Clement lost their Dutch protection and national status because of their involvement in Prussian trade matters, and van Sanen also needed to give up his assessorship. Nicolas van der Zee, the third partner in the firm, kept his Dutch status, as he was leaving the partnership – although he lost it later nonetheless, as he became Prussian consul after van Sanen.[13] This departure was confirmed only about a year later, in March 1771, in a request Nicolas van der Zee had filed with the Dutch consul in which he reclaimed certain monies from Wissing on behalf of his former company, because Wissing had not been performing well.[14] This was about a month prior to van der Zee's request to be relieved of his duties as Prussian consul because his firm was in such turmoil.[15] A direct link between the two requests was never explicitly made by the protagonists, but it is clear that van der Zee attributed the bad state of affairs of the house of Clement, van Sanen, van der Zee & C° at least partially to Wissing. By the time Wissing was taken to court, van der Zee had left the firm, which is why the plaintiff in the court case was Nicolas van der Zee & C° on behalf of Clement, van Sanen, van der Zee & C°.

Van der Zee accused Wissing of not having followed his instructions, particularly concerning a parcel of seventy bales of paper and a cargo of 'peauter', or pewter, a tin alloy, often made with lead, used in domestic objects such as cups, pans or bowls.[16] Van der Zee further accused Wissing of selling at too low a price in order to be able to apply the money as a loan for himself. Van der Zee claimed 3,210 lion dollars from Wissing. For the pewter, he wanted to be reimbursed with the product itself, as the selling price Wissing had obtained was too low, and van der Zee could not justify the sale to his friends, on whose behalf it had been sold. Additionally, he did not know who the buyer was.[17] Wissing disputed that he had broken the instructions and pointed out that no selling price had been set. He made a counterclaim, which included several current open accounts in his favour, and belated salary payments related to

12 Heeringa and Nanninga, *Bronnen tot de geschiedenis*, 4: pp. 138–139, Directorate of Levant Trade to the burgomasters of Amsterdam, Amsterdam, 21/02/1770.

13 Ibid.

14 NACS, N°348, 'Request Nicolas van der Zee om liquidatie te vragen aan Arnoldus Wissing van diverse interesten', Izmir, 25/03/1771.

15 See pp. 209–213.

16 J. Hatcher and T.C. Barker, *A history of British pewter* (London, 1974).

17 NACS, N°348, 'Request Nicolas van der Zee', Izmir, 25/03/1771.

his employment as accountant since 1763.[18] Copies of the contract and of a declaration on his good character made by scribes of Clement, van Sanen, van der Zee & C°, as well as excerpts from correspondence between Wissing and Philippe Clement in Berlin from 1768 were included in the trial files following Wissing's counterclaim, showing he had done nothing wrong.

On 11 April, both parties agreed to solve their dispute through arbitration. In the meantime, a sum of 590 lion dollars in the hands of Wissing had been sequestered, sparking a reaction from Wissing's French wife that it was her money and could therefore not be subjected to a sequester.[19] When the Dutch chancellor showed Constanzia Wissing's claim to van der Zee, he responded that he would release the sequester if Arnoldus Wissing was willing to declare under oath that it was his wife's money – a clear example confirming the importance of the oath as a legal instrument of evidence. At the same time that Constanzia's money was sequestered, so was the cargo of pewter, which had been kept in Wissing's house.[20] Van der Zee argued that the merchandise was not safe in Wissing's house, and he wanted Wissing to be held responsible should something – a fire or anything damaging the pewter – occur. Van der Zee also wanted Wissing to pay a security deposit to the Dutch chancery until the arbitrators had reached a conclusion.[21]

Wissing replied that he was more than happy to pay a security deposit if van der Zee was willing to do the same, writing that his own claim was legally as valid as van der Zee's but that he could neither agree nor disagree on the transport of the pewter, as it had been sold already to an Ottoman subject.[22] In the end, both conditions, the transport of pewter and the security deposit, were fulfilled, and the arbitrators were chosen by the litigants: van der Zee opted for the Englishman John Charnaud and the Dutchman William Enslie, while Wissing chose the Englishman Richard Lee and the Dutchman Christiaan

18 NACS, N°348, 'Request van A: Wissing tot antwoord aan van der Zee & Comp tot reclamatie van sijn saldo bij Clement van Sanen en van der Zee', Izmir, 30/03/1771.

19 NACS, N°348, 'Versoek van de huijsvrouwe van de heer Wissing tot het doen van een protest teegens de heer van der Zee', Izmir, 13/04/1771.

20 NACS, N°348, 'Replica Nicolas van der Zee weegens een arrest op 205 brooden spianten en het vragen van borgtocht voor de persoon van Arnoldus Wissing', Izmir, 13/04/1771. The end of the document contains a paragraph added by the consul in which he mentions that the sequester was made orally – which might be the reason no documents pertaining to the sequester can be found in the case file.

21 NACS, N°348, 'Replica Nicolas van der Zee', Izmir, 13/04/1771.

22 NACS, N°348, 'Antwoord van Arnoldus Wissing op vragen cautie', Izmir, 17/04/1771.

Rodemuller.[23] All the men were either merchants or persons experienced in trade and the commercial practices of Izmir.[24] As was common when arbitration was used, both parties agreed not to appeal the decision, on penalty of 3,000 lion dollars should they come back on that agreement.[25] The inclusion of a high penalty demonstrates the vulnerability of arbitration in an environment in which litigants had more than one court they could go to. The capitulations suggested that European traders could resort to an Ottoman court, even for a dispute with a fellow countryman.[26]

The arbitrators reached a decision in October – very late for such a solution. It was decided that Wissing needed to pay 593 lion dollars to Clement, van Sanen, van der Zee & C° as the outstanding balance of the current account between them, taking everything into account. Additionally, if the partnership wanted Wissing to take the oath declaring the sale of the pewter had occurred exactly as registered in the books, he would be obliged to do so.[27] Wissing answered that he could prove the sale had occurred exactly as he had registered it in the books by showing it in the handwriting of the buyer, who had passed away. In dramatic fashion, he added he believed that that evidence would be sufficient in front of the whole world.[28] He did not oppose the decision in which he was condemned to pay but needed more time than the three days he had been given. When van der Zee made his claim, he had ended Wissing's employment – for which he needed six months according to the contract – leaving him without much money. Wissing had some personal troubles as well and hoped a longer period of time would be granted to him.[29] He was given three months to pay, with his wife Constanzia standing as a security on behalf of her husband. The last document pertaining to the case was an act confirming the deposit in the Dutch chancery of a jewel with set diamonds

23 NACS, N°348 'Nader replicq van van der Zee tot versoek der executie van de transport der spianten in questie', Izmir, 27/04/1771; and NACS, N°348, 'Acte van cautie van Hagi Georgi voor de persoon van Arnoldus Wissing', 01/05/1771.

24 NACS, N°348, 'Compromis aengaende de differentie van Clement van Sanen van der Zee & Co en Arnoldus Wissing', Izmir, 06/05/1771.

25 Ibid.

26 See p. 89.

27 NACS, N°348, 'Copije der arbitraire sententie in de differentie van Wissing met van der Zee', Izmir, 01/10/1771.

28 NACS, N°348, 'Antwoord Arnoldus Wissing op d'intimatie der sententie van d'arbitter in differentie met Clement van Sanen van der Zee', Izmir, 01/10/1771. A month later, he took the oath about the pewter. NACS, N°348, 'Acte der eed van Arnoldus Wissing wegens de 205 spianten in questie met Clement van Sanen van der Zee', Izmir, 05/11/1771.

29 Ibid.

belonging to Constanzia Wissing.[30] As there was no more follow-up, Wissing probably paid before the due date of January 1772.

The type of dispute between Wissing and his principals was relatively easy to adjudicate in the sense that it concerned two Dutch parties, both residing in Izmir. The evidence that was used was related to the business relationship between Wissing and the firm that had employed him – correspondence, current accounts and a contract. The only evidence added to the case beyond those business documents, besides the replies and counter-replies by both parties, was the witness statement issued by Wissing's peers and the registration of the oath that he had been asked to take in order to prove that a sale he had made was indeed made exactly in the way he had registered it in the books. The fact that arbitration was chosen to solve this particular dispute seems not so easy to explain. Arbitration meant that a dispute was put before experts, also referred to as 'good men', or 'neutral men', who would decide the matter in a reasonable manner. Often, courts opted for this solution because the case could be too complicated to be left to judges who might not possess the know-how to adjudicate commercial disputes. A judge was not necessarily up to date with all the customs and habits merchants applied in their dealings with one another.

In principle, parties accepting arbitration also forfeited their right of appeal before another court. It was a particularly handy problem-solving mechanism in disputes between traders because it was cheap and because one could rely on the fact that it was one's peers who were making the decision – ensuring that the dispute was analysed by people who knew the rules of the game according to the merchants' style. According to Amalia Kessler, arbitration served a double purpose. First, it allowed the preservation of personal ties within the larger trading community – early modern trade relied heavily on social ties and mechanisms of trust.[31] When these were challenged because

30 NACS, N°348, 'Acte van cautie van juffr Wissing voor haer man Arnoldus Wissing voor Lx 593 23/100 tot saldo van reek: met Clement van Sanen van der Zee', Izmir, 08/11/1771; and 'Acte van een gedepositeerd stuk juweel van Arnoldus Wissing', Izmir, 21/11/1771.

31 Kessler, 'Enforcing virtue', p. 84. For an analysis of the concept of 'trust' in seventeenth-century discourse on commerce and the role trade and trust played in relationships between states, see the chapter on 'The *doux commerce* and interstate relations. Trust and mistrust in the emerging economic discourse', in Peter Schröder, *Trust in early modern international political thought, 1598–1713* (Cambridge, 2017), pp. 199–218. For a more general assessment of the role of trust in the relationship between individual and community, see Hans Blom, 'The meaning of trust: Fides between self-interest and *appetitus societatis*', in *The roots of international law/Les fondements du droit international. Liber amicorum Peter Haggenmacher*, eds. Pierre-Marie Dupuy and Vincent Chetail (Leiden and Boston, 2013), pp. 39–58.

of a dispute, it could harm the larger sociocultural tissue that bound traders together and allowed them to conduct long-lasting and mutually beneficial trade. Arbitration was a way the community itself, through peers, could solve its own disputes – the idea being that a solution would be mutually agreeable as it was not put upon the litigants from a higher judge or some higher legal rules. It is perhaps the purest expression of merchants' style, regulating a dispute and thereby keeping a whole community together. This corresponds to the second function fulfilled by arbitration according to Kessler, which was narrowing the distance between decision-makers and litigants.[32]

Generally speaking, those adjudicating commercial disputes could not be expected to know all the traders involved in them. The recourse to arbitration by peer experts allowed for adjudication by men who were personally acquainted with the litigants, enlarging the latter's trust in the decision but also making sure the parties would be better understood. Personal acquaintances might get better information to base their decision on. Amalia Kessler has pointed out that the element of intimacy and personal ties were so important that, in the case of French merchant courts, arbitration in rural villages was often executed by the village priest. In this case, his task was not simply to decide upon a resolution but to gather information and hear witnesses.[33]

In the context of the Dutch consular court, the choice to subject a dispute to arbitrators was made by the consul and assessors, but it had to be accepted by the litigating parties, who also needed to promise they would not appeal – that would render the whole choice to arbitrate a dispute obsolete. Both parties could appoint an equal number of arbitrators, and at times, the court chose an additional one to ensure that a majority of votes between arbitrators was always possible – a choice not taken in the dispute between Wissing and his principals. At first sight, it might seem remarkable that a dispute between Dutch litigants before a Dutch court was decided upon by a mixture of Englishmen and Dutchmen. But the merchants' style was internationally valid, and the nationality of those instructed to analyse whether it was observed or not was less important than the consideration that the merchants' style was followed. It might also have been an accepted custom in order to counterbalance too much intimacy. When a *national* community abroad as small as the Dutch contingent in Izmir quarrelled with one another – putting social and commercial cohesion at risk – and the solution of the quarrel lay in *international* merchant custom, it was not bizarre to rely partially on foreign involvement in

32 Kessler, 'Enforcing virtue', p. 84.

33 Ibid.

the solution-seeking process. It might provide a fresh but yet familiar look at a quarrel.

The claim made by Nicolas van der Zee against Arnoldus Wissing was of a very rare type – fully situated within the Dutch trading community of Izmir – but still, the solution was found in the international merchants' style, and English traders were involved in the arbitration process. By far, most cases were not so easily delineable where the litigants were concerned. Arnoldus Wissing had worked for the firm in which van der Zee was a partner, but most Dutch traders established in Izmir were not involved in trade with one another. They were independent and entered into business relationships with Ottoman traders and merchants in the Dutch Republic. They entered into legal disputes with members of both groups.

1.2 *A Failed Attempt at Arbitration*

As seen above, merchants often first tried to settle their disputes amicably. In the early seventeenth century, Dutch consuls had received specific instructions to ask litigants to first attempt friendly settlement through arbitration. This option could also be taken when one of the litigants was abroad, and the consular archives of Izmir contain an example of this, although the arbitration process failed in this case. The dispute in question arose between the firm of de Vogel & Zoon in Amsterdam and the firm of Clement, van Sanen, van der Zee & C° in Izmir. For the de Vogel firm, the first step was the choice of a power of attorney able to defend their legal interests before the Dutch consular court in Izmir.[34] The choice of who to give legal power of attorney to was easy, as he had a son, Thomas Junior, who lived in Izmir. The dispute was brought before the Dutch consul in Izmir in 1764 and included a claim on several outstanding debts. According to Thomas de Vogel Junior in Izmir, the total sum concerned was 1,922 lion dollars and 29 aspers.[35] In his claim, de Vogel explained that this included four different amounts. The first, 118:99 lion dollars, came from an *agio* of 10% demanded by Clement, van Sanen, van der Zee & C° on a purchase on behalf of Thomas de Vogel & Zoon in Amsterdam of fifteen bales of cotton.[36]

34 For the use of powers of attorney, see pp. 160–162.

35 The consulted sources always noted such sums in the following notation: 1,922:29 lion dollars. Future references to similar sums will be written down in the same manner.

36 NACS, N°333 ('Documenten van de proces tusschen Clement van Sanen van der Zee & C° & Th:s de Vogel over een parthij tabak &a begonnen 1764 eijndigt 11 febr 1765'), 'Repliek van Th:s de Vogel aan Clement en vansanen raakende de in kwestie zynde schaade der tabak verbrande cattoene & kwade schulden &ra', Izmir, 12/10/1764. The *agio* was the difference between two parallel domestic currencies, i.e., bank money and currency, and reflected an exchange price between the two. See Pit Dehing, *Geld in Amsterdam. Wisselbank en wisselkoersen, 1650–1725* (Hilversum, 2012), pp. 108–130.

Thomas de Vogel considered this percentage to be outrageous, particularly as it had only been brought into account seven months after all documents for the cotton transaction had been sent. De Vogel felt that no 'commissioning agent should be able to do business that way'.[37]

A second, larger sum stemmed from damage to a shipment of tobacco that had been on board the *Agatha*, which was sailing from Salonika to Livorno but had suffered shipwreck near the island of Ponza near the Italian coast.[38] The damage amounted to 1,200:50 lion dollars, and de Vogel objected to the conclusion of the transaction that had led to the shipment of the tobacco in the first place.[39] Apparently, two Ottoman traders, Hagi Emir Mustafa and 'Ali Aga, had delivered the tobacco to representatives of Clement, van Sanen, van der Zee & C° in Salonika in order to settle accounts with Thomas de Vogel & Zoon in Amsterdam. De Vogel claimed that his principals in Amsterdam had no interest in tobacco, particularly as Clement, van Sanen, van der Zee & C° had not originally mentioned this in their letters on the matter to de Vogel but had only referred to the debt being repaid. Additionally, Clement and his partners had agreed to the shipment of the tobacco without telling de Vogel and had not insured it, thus failing in their obligations as agents for the commission of de Vogel. They should never have 'subjected the interest of their friend to the sea without properly informing them'.[40] Van Sanen had offered to arrange matters with an insurer, but only for one-third of the value, and according to Thomas Junior such practices went against all merchants' style. The two other sums were 18:50 lion dollars for what de Vogel considered to be excessive postage expenses and a general outstanding balance of 584:30 lion dollars.[41]

When arbitration was suggested to solve this dispute, both parties accepted to subject themselves to the judgment of neutral merchants. Each party was allowed to appoint one. Thomas de Vogel Junior chose Daniel Hopker, a business correspondent of his father, while Pieter van Sanen nominated Jacob de

---

37 NACS, N°333, 'Repliek van Th:s de Vogel aan Clement en vansanen', Izmir, 12/10/1764, '[...] directien welke geen commissionair kan nog mag houden nog practiseeren'.

38 The trial files contain a twenty-two-page declaration made in Italian at the Chamber of Commerce in Livorno on this event. NACS, N°333, 'Zeeverklaaring en manifest, attest: van het keyss: schip de agatha galeij cap:t Christofer Romolj op Ponsa', Livorno, 21/09/1762.

39 There is some confusion in the documents as to whether the sum related to this event amounted to 1,250:50 lion dollars or 1,200:50 lion dollars, but only the latter makes the entire calculation correct. NACS, N°333, 'Repliek van Th:s de Vogel aan Clement en vansanen', Izmir, 12/10/1764.

40 Ibid., '[...] op geenerlij wijse vermoogen eenig intrest huner vriend ter zee te geeven sonder het behoorlijk advys ter regter tijd [...]'.

41 Ibid.

Vogel (from Rotterdam; he was not related to Thomas de Vogel). The arbitrators met at Hopker's house and investigated the accounts, but the procedure ended abruptly, according to van Sanen because de Vogel did not want to accept arbitration after all, but according to de Vogel because van Sanen had brought in an additional claim about seven bales of burned cotton.[42] The cotton had been in the hands of van Sanen but was destined for de Vogel in Amsterdam when a fire had damaged it. Originally, van Sanen had not wanted to charge de Vogel for the merchandise, as he believed himself to be responsible, but the outcome of another trial held the same year, in which van Sanen had acted on behalf of an Amsterdam firm that demanded compensation for damaged goods while they were in the hands of an agent, made him change his mind. The outcome of that case was that the agent could not be held responsible for damage to goods that were not his own. A crucial piece of evidence in that case was a declaration signed by various merchants with different nationalities in which they agreed to the commercial principle that an agent was not responsible for goods commissioned by a principal. As long as the agent had acted in accordance with his principal's instructions, and the cause of the damage was beyond the agent's responsibility, he could not be held accountable.[43] Van Sanen had lost that case, and he seemed to be determined to not be on the paying end twice. In his counterclaim, he made an explicit reference to the declaration issued by the merchants in March 1764 on behalf of his legal opponent at the time.[44] Van Sanen, who must have been in possession of a copy of the declaration, must have felt he had the merchants' style on his side this time. He justified his manoeuvre by stating that he only found out about his lack of responsibility later, because of the other trial, adding that he was happy to continue arbitration, but as the number of Dutch merchants was small and de Vogel refused to continue with Hopker and Jacob de Vogel, van Sanen proposed to look for arbitrators that were part of another trading nation.[45]

For de Vogel, his opponent's action was unheard of, going against that same merchants' style, because according to 'all rights and laws', an account that was approved by the involved traders and subsequently closed could not be

42 NACS, N°333, 'Attestatie voor dheer Pieter van Saanen, aangaande de geteekende compromis in de differentie met dh Th: de Vogel', Izmir, 15/09/1764; NACS, N°333, 'Antwoord van den heer van sanen aen dh: Th: de Vogel Junior weeg: eenige pretentie voor dh: Th: de Vogel & zoon d'Amsterdam', Izmir, [09/10/1764]; and NACS, N°333, 'Repliek van Th:s de Vogel aan Clement en vansanen', Izmir, 12/10/1764.

43 See pp. 162–189.

44 NACS, N°333, 'Antwoord van den heer van sanen aen dh: Th: de Vogel Junior', Izmir, [09/10/1764].

45 Ibid.

reopened to make new claims on it.[46] This was commercial custom that, according to de Vogel, Clement, van Sanen, van der Zee & C° would know about. De Vogel insisted he could not go into an arbitration process with van Sanen any longer, because the latter had 'formulated very unjust and unfounded claims against my principals, that have nothing to do with the case'.[47] De Vogel's refusal effectively ended the attempt at arbitration, and the case was brought before the Dutch consular court in Izmir, where de Vogel filed his claim of 1,922:29 lion dollars on behalf of his father and brother.[48]

Van Sanen, taking the defence on behalf of his partnership, had come up with a different calculation. He dismissed the problem of the *agio* and argued that de Vogel should know that the *agio* commonly calculated by the merchants in Izmir was not the same as the one in 'any Christian land', and although the defendant accepted that there were different ways of calculating the *agio* in Izmir, the end result was the same, the way he had done it was simply a little bit more advantageous for the commissioning agent.[49] He had a point, and the quarrel about the *agio* might be explained by the fact that de Vogel was used to a lower *agio* in Amsterdam – Pit Dehing has shown that, while it fluctuated, it was on average 4.23% during the eighteenth century, while Elena Frangakis-Syrett mentions *agio* rates in Izmir that did indeed reach 10% in 1761 and 1762.[50]

Perhaps, van Sanen argued, it was not always completely possible to follow merchant custom as it was applied in the United Provinces, as this would cause damage to friends in Izmir – by which he meant that if Thomas de Vogel applied *agio* on transactions in Izmir in the Dutch manner, it was his friend and agent van Sanen who would be disadvantaged. On the tobacco, van Sanen felt his former firm had done its best to recuperate the money owed to de Vogel by his Ottoman debtors in Salonika and concluded by stating that it was

46 NACS, N°333, 'Repliek van Th:s de Vogel aan Clement en vansanen', Izmir, 12/10/1764, '[...] in alle regten x wetten [...]'.

47 Ibid., '[...] kan niet met van Sanen in arbitragie treden, mag ook niet, aangezien hij zeer onrechtvaardige x ongefundeerde pretentien tegen mijn principalen formuleert die met de zaak niks te make hebben'.

48 NACS, N°333, 'Rekwest van dh Thomas de Vogel Junior teegens de heeren Clement vansanen vander zee & C°', Izmir, 26/09/1764.

49 NACS, N°333, 'Dupliek van dh van sanen op de Repliek van dheer deVogel gedagteekend 12 8bo', Izmir, 31/10/1764, '[...] nergens in't Christenrijck [...]'.

50 For other years no information was given. Frangakis-Syrett, *The commerce of Smyrna*, pp. 200–201; see also Dehing, *Geld in Amsterdam*, p. 116. For early modern *agio* rates in Amsterdam, see J.G. van Dillen, 'Bloeitijd der Amsterdamse wisselbank 1687–1781', in *Mensen en achtergronden*, ed. J.G. van Dillen (Groningen, 1964), pp. 403–404.

completely unreasonable that a commissioner should pay for 'damage caused by the Almighty', to goods that were not his own.[51]

In his counterclaim, van Sanen expressed the opinion that the firm in Amsterdam owed him money instead of the other way around.[52] He did not argue about the 584:30 lion dollars in the outstanding balance but added an amount of 860:28 lion dollars that he claimed de Vogel owed his firm. This sum consisted of debts to de Vogel of 360:28 lion dollars from Hagi Emir Mustafa and Salonali Mahmud Baraka and 500 lion dollars from Joseph de Bartolomeo, a merchant from Volos in Greece. These had been covered by obligations that Clement, van Sanen, van der Zee & C° had already settled in their accounts with Thomas de Vogel & Zoon in Amsterdam but that still needed to be paid. Thomas Junior wrote that van Sanen's claim had been made too late, and it was 'highly obscure and doubtful, going against all merchants' style'.[53] Furthermore, de Bartolomeo was a French *protégé* who had recently visited Izmir. At that time, van Sanen could have requested litigation at the French consular court, but he had failed to do so.[54] Unsurprisingly, van Sanen disagreed and stated that de Bartolomeo had acted as Swedish vice-consul in Volos, so it was impossible to put him under arrest. Van Sanen added that he preferred to do business with traders with conscience, who were looking after the interests of their friends as well as after their own interests, rather than dealing with merchants such as the father and son de Vogel, who 'use books of jurists and consult lawyers in order to follow the law, but at the same time they only looked at their own interest, and pushed that as far as possible, without consulting their conscience'.[55]

Van Sanen's juxtaposition of the letter of the law versus the respect for reciprocity and mutual interest is very revealing. Amalia Kessler has argued that merchant courts were referring to Christian virtue in the battle of good and evil fought out in court, and mentioning 'conscience' is evidence of a similar discourse here, but there is another reason behind it as well.[56] Van Sanen's

---

51 NACS, N°333, 'Replicq van dhr Clement & van Sanen in de differentie met den heer Th: de Vogel Junior', Izmir, 03/12/1764, '[…] schade door de allerhoogste […]'.

52 This sort of reversal of who owed who was quite common in this type of case. NACS, N°333, 'Antwoord van den heer van sanen aen dh: Th: de Vogel Junior', Izmir, [09/10/1764].

53 NACS, N°333, 'Repliek van Th:s de Vogel aan Clement en vansanen', Izmir, 12/10/1764, '[…] ten uitersten duister x twijfelachtig, strijdende tegens alle coopmansstijl […]'.

54 Ibid.

55 NACS, N°333, 'Dupliek van dh van sanen op de Repliek van dheer deVogel gedagteekend 12 8bo', Izmir, 31/10/1764, '[…] cooplieden die zig met regt geleerde boeken x advocaten consulteeren om de wetten te voldoen, x verders haar eijgen intrest door omweegen zoo ver pousseeren als maar kunnen, sonder haar gemoet te consulteeren'.

56 Kessler, 'Enforcing virtue'.

argument was that the letter of the law was less important than the mutual pursuit of interest, resulting in reciprocity, one of the cornerstones of the merchants' style and a mechanism on which most of early modern trade relied.[57] Even if the *agio* had not been calculated strictly according to Dutch law, the importance of mutual interest and the fact that the commercial world of Izmir rendered it impossible to respect Dutch law fully made that little infraction perfectly reasonable and equitable within the context of commercial custom. Taking care of one's friends was more important than adhering to the letter of the law. This is one of the few cases in which one of the parties made a legal argument out of a discrepancy between the law in the United Provinces and commercial custom as it was applied in the specific intercultural context of Izmir, where things worked slightly differently than in Amsterdam or Rotterdam: 'no merchant of any nation can agitate a trader here and direct all of his affairs according the merchants' style and laws of Holland or other countries in Europe, principally as one has to deal with persons of the land [Ottoman Empire]'.[58] This shows that, while the merchants' style was internationally applicable, it was also subject to interpretation in a local context. This made the role of foreign traders in the same city, as arbitrator or expert, more important than the role of certain national laws that had been issued far away.

The difference in commercial custom and adjudication in a context of interaction with Ottoman merchants was an important and tangible one, something that all traders in Izmir understood.[59] But these differences were never absolute, nor were they evidence that Ottomans or other non-Europeans were not well acquainted with the European way of doing trade – perhaps the merchants' style cannot be labelled as a specifically European way of doing trade. In a case that opposed a Dutch merchant to an Ottoman Muslim named Mehmed Araboğlu, the consul addressed an Ottoman official on Ouckama's behalf and wrote to him that 'you know perfectly the merchants' style, for having treated many affairs'.[60] The merchants' style was thus invoked as some

57 See pp. 173–181 for a more in-depth discussion of reciprocity.

58 NACS, N°333, 'Replicq van dhr Clement & van Sanen in de differentie met den heer Th: de Vogel Junior', Izmir, 03/12/1764, '[...] geen coopman van wat natie in staat is om een coopman hier te ageeren x alle zijn zaken te kunnen dirigeeren volgens den coopmansstijl en wetten van Holland of andre landen in Europa, x principaal zoo men met lieden van t land te doen heeft [...]'.

59 See chapter 5.

60 NACS, N°332 ('Brieven wegens de zaak tusschen Arab Ogloe & Ouckama'), 'Copije der brief int Turks geschreven aen Kútschuk Aga door de heer consul weegens d'affairen van de heer Ouckama & C° na Sanderlj [Çandarlı near Izmir]', Izmir, 11/09/1765, '[...] ed voi, cognoscendo, perfettamente il stile mercantile pr aver trattato molti affari [...]'. For the case itself, see pp. 319–323.

sort of generally agreed upon way of doing things amongst merchants but still could be subjected to varieties according to time and place, suggesting a commercial pragmatism that written law could not offer. Litigation based upon summary procedure and the merchants' style was better equipped to deal with relatively new situations, such as the development of intercultural trade in eighteenth-century Izmir.

After arbitration failed, the dispute between Thomas de Vogel Junior and Pieter van Sanen turned into a discussion of the merchants' style, and the consul decided to demand the advice of three neutral merchants, two of whom had been the original arbitrators in this case, Daniel Hopker and Jacob de Vogel, while the third, Daniel Fremeaux, was one of the most important Dutch traders.[61] Their opinion was that the *agio* could be charged, the open account with de Bartolomeo was indeed de Vogel's responsibility and van Sanen was allowed to ask a brokerage fee of 5% for the transaction in Salonika. On the other hand, Clement, van Sanen, van der Zee & C° did have to pay for the postage that had been disputed as well as for the burned cotton, while the damaged tobacco could not be used in settling the debts owed to de Vogel, meaning the damage was to be disputed between van Sanen and the merchants in Salonika he had gotten it from.[62] The consul and assessors agreed with all these elements, which led to a verdict confirming the suggestions of the three neutral merchants. As both parties were partially at fault, they were each condemned to pay half of the trial's expenses.[63] Both parties accepted, and no appeal was made, although it must have frustrated van Sanen, as he had now lost two cases dealing with burned cotton, even though he was plaintiff in one and defendant in the other. A dispute between parties did not necessarily mean that they would stop trading altogether. In September 1765, Thomas de Vogel wrote to his son to not do business with Philippe Clement any longer, because he had received the monopoly in Prussian trade with the Levant, which made him a traitor to the national cause. No mention was made of this trial or of any other legal or commercial disagreement between them.[64]

61 NACS, N°333, 'Rapport van dheeren gecommitteerden in de proces tusschen dheeren van Sanen Th:s de Vogel Jr', Izmir, 04/01/1765.

62 Ibid.

63 NACS, N°333, 'Sententie in de differentie van Clement & van Sanen & Th: de Vogel Junior', Izmir, 15/01/1765.

64 For the Prussian Royal Levant Company, see pp. 209–213.

2 The Mother of Levantine Trade Quarrels: Disputing Commission Trade

2.1 *The Principal-Agent Problem*

Dutch Levant trade was commission trade, and most Dutch merchants living in Izmir acted as agents on behalf of traders in the United Provinces. In this sense, they were competitors of one another, all striving to obtain new commissions. In order to stay in the picture of firms in the Dutch Republic, the merchants in Izmir cultivated lengthy business correspondences.[65] These often began with a request made by a principal to conduct a test transaction, or by an offer sent out by aspiring commissioning agents. The international trading community relied on a web of business correspondences, and one of the important characteristics was the reciprocity of services that were offered or sold through these letters. It was not uncommon that the services of certain merchants were recommended by mutual correspondents to other traders in need of a new business contact. In 1762, the firm of Jean Biolley in Verviers, in the Bishopric of Liège, addressed Thomas de Vogel & Zoon in Amsterdam because he hoped to obtain some information from his correspondent on the best way to establish a trade in sheets with the Levant. De Vogel answered him that Biolley was welcome to trade in his own name but that it was common for traders from Liège to send their sheets first to the United Provinces, where they would be packed as Dutch sheets. These were then sent to the Levant under de Vogel's name, who charged a commission fee on the service. A partnership between de Vogel and Biolley, as the latter had suggested, was impossible, and if Biolley did not want to make use of de Vogel's services, the latter was happy to provide the names of some friends who worked for him on commission. In Izmir, these friends consisted of three firms: David van Lennep, Enslie & C°;

65 For the importance of business correspondence in the establishment of durable commercial relationships, see Aslanian, *From the Indian Ocean*; Vanneste, *Global trade*; and Trivellato, *The familiarity of strangers*. Aware of the importance of business correspondence, early modern merchants had access to business manuals that came to include instructions on letter-writing. Early examples are Gabriel Meurier, *Formulaire de missives, obligations, lettres de change, d'asseurances* (Antwerp, 1558); Matthias Kramer, *Il segretario di banco* (Nürnberg, 1693); and Giovanni Domenico Peri, *Il negoziante* (Venice, 1638); see also essays in Roger Chartier, Alain Boureau, and Cécile Dauphin, eds., *Correspondence: Models of letter-writing from the Middle Ages to the nineteenth century* (Princeton, 1997); and Francisco Bethencourt and Florike Egmond, *Correspondence and cultural exchange in Europe, 1400–1700*, vol. 3 of *Cultural exchange in early modern Europe* (Cambridge, 2007). For the more technical aspects of early modern letter-writing, see James Daybell, *The material letter in early modern England. Manuscript letters and the culture and practices of letter-writing, 1512–1635* (Basingstoke, 2012).

Clement & van Sanen; and Fremeaux & Hopker. De Vogel added that the firm had other correspondents in Izmir, but those three were the most important ones, and their services had been good.[66]

Merchants always had to be careful to cultivate their correspondences; when the firm of Thomas de Vogel & Zoon sent some thread samples to the firm of Cauw in Leiden in 1757, the latter just sent them back, insulted by the fact that de Vogel had already sent similar samples to other firms in Leiden.[67] The cornerstones of a commercial friendship, expressed through a steady, regular and long-lasting correspondence, were reciprocity and the regard for mutual interests.[68] While reciprocity implies an idea of equality, it does not discard the possibility of finding mutual satisfaction in a relationship between a principal trader and an agent: first, because agent and principal could be partners in some transactions, and second, because roles could be reversed; for certain transactions, the principal in the United Provinces could become an agent for the agent-turned-principal in Izmir. It was exactly this sort of flexibility of roles that guaranteed reciprocity in early modern international trade. Avner Greif discussed reciprocity in information exchange between traders as a manner to avoid 'free riding'. In a world in which most merchants took on both the role of principal and agent, free riding was equally problematic and was solved through reciprocity.[69]

Not all initiatives to start up a business relationship were rejected. If a first sample was successfully sold, long-lasting relationships could develop. Shipments of samples between the United Provinces and the Levant were accompanied by negotiations on terms of sale in the accompanying letters. When they joined forces in 1759, Dirk Knipping and Pieter Ouckama immediately sent out letters of introduction in which they offered their services to merchants in Amsterdam, Haarlem, Zaandam, Rotterdam and Leiden, as well as Aken, Verviers, Liège, Aix-en-Provence and London. They informed potential business contacts that they had established a company together, with the permission of 'their blood relatives and their principals'.[70]

---

66 Heeringa and Nanninga, *Bronnen tot de geschiedenis*, 4: pp. 476–477, de Vogel to Jean Biolley Jr., Amsterdam, 10/12/1762.

67 CAA/ADV, N°85 ('Stukken betreffende de pretentie der compagnie op Missir di Eghia te Smirna'), Letter Cauw & C° to Thomas de Vogel & Zoon, Leiden, 10/03/1757.

68 Vanneste, *Global trade*, pp. 81–84.

69 Avner Greif, 'Contract enforceability and economic institutions in early trade: The Maghribi traders' coalition', *The American economic review*, 83:3 (1993): p. 529.

70 NACS, N°490, Knipping & Ouckama to Jan Bulte, Izmir, 03/09/1759, '[…] onder volkomen goetvindinge & toestemminge onser hoog g'achte bloetverwanten & principalen […]'.

If one of these potential contacts was interested, he sent small consignments of various goods to Izmir to test the market and the commercial abilities of the potential commissioning agents there. Knipping & Ouckama quickly sold nails belonging to Olof Jolles to Greek shopkeepers, some coffee and cochineal belonging to the Amsterdam trader Vasker Bake to several Jewish shopkeepers and thimbles coming from Rotterdam to Greeks. They also received sheets, linens, paper and pepper from Aron Joseph de Pinto, a member of a wealthy Sephardic family in Amsterdam, and guns, staple items regularly sold by them on behalf of others.[71] At the end of September, they confirmed to Floris Crol in Amsterdam that they had received three boxes of guns and that they would try to sell them as if they were their own, although there were many weapons in the city, thereby limiting the possibilities.[72] Knipping already had experience selling weapons on commission for traders in Holland, as the firm of Thomas de Vogel & Zoon of Amsterdam sent several consignments of guns to the firm of David van Lennep, Knipping & Enslie in Izmir. In 1756, for instance, the firm was involved in the sale of 2,000 pairs of pistols and eight boxes of flintlocks belonging to Thomas de Vogel & Zoon to Greek, Jewish and 'Turkish' merchants. These 'Turkish' merchants were Muslims, traders and shopkeepers with names such as Hagi Moussa, Brussali Soffia and Cheutajalj Hagi Soluman.[73] The firm also took care of de Vogel's textiles and sold them in Izmir and Salonika.[74] While these transactions were conducted on the basis of commission, de Vogel also dealt with non-Dutch merchant firms, such as the Jewish house of Chaves and Fernandes Dias, with whom he was involved as a partner, sending them textiles that were sold by them on condition of an equal sharing of the profits.[75] It is not so surprising that it was the de Vogel firm that had managed to branch out directly beyond the Dutch trading community, as they had a family member present in Izmir who was more likely to be trusted and who could set up such partnerships in person, without resorting to intermediaries, and it was practices like these that led to a decline in the Dutch merchants' share in the Dutch Levant trade.

One of the most interesting introductory letters the new firm of Knipping & Ouckama sent out went to Herman van Coopstad (1708–1772). Van Coopstad was an alderman in Rotterdam at the time and had been one of the directors

71 NACS, N°490, Knipping & Ouckama to Floris Crol, Izmir, 24/09/1759.

72 Ibid.

73 CAA/ADV, N°76 ('Factuurboek Thomas de Vogel & Zoon', 1756–1765), f°13r and f°18r.

74 Ibid., entries on f°13r, 14, 18, 48, to name a few examples.

75 Ibid., f°15, for instance, shows the sale of a parcel of cloth to Jusuf Scufi Kapostolaki by Chaves & Fernandes Dias, with an equal division of the profits.

of the local Directorate of Levant Trade. He had commercial interests the Levant since the 1730s but had gained most of his fortune and notoriety as a slave trader. The Dutch West India Company (WIC) had lost its monopoly on the slave trade in 1730, and van Coopstad's partnership with the husband of his niece was one of the private firms that jumped in.[76] When Knipping & Ouckama wrote to him, they wrote to a prominent man. By 15 September 1759, Knipping & Ouckama had sold 119 pairs of pistols in a joint account with Herman van Coopstad & C°.[77] Two weeks later, they announced further sales of pistols but expressed their regret that because of the captains bringing so many guns, selling them at almost any price, the prices they had obtained were not very good. Additionally, they had lost part of the shipment of weapons because of an encounter with an English ship, and the remainder of that shipment had been damaged. The chancellor of the Dutch consulate in Izmir had issued a certificate confirming the state of van Coopstad's shipment, so satisfaction could be obtained from the insurers. Knipping & Ouckama were aware that such misfortunes, even if they were not their own fault, could hinder the potentially promising relationship with a merchant such as van Coopstad, who obtained at least part of his weapons from arms dealers in Liège: 'we have to report to you with sorrow, that it saddens our soul, that our first enterprise with your honourable (for which we have to pay interest to your honourable) is so unhappy, being young merchants, who try to treat our respective friends with all loyal and honest dealings, fearing to lose a good sum of money in this, while we are convinced of your generosity, and we hope with God's help and according to your honourable promises to compensate the damage'.[78] Relations

76 Ineke Teunissen, *Herman van Coopstad en Isaac Jacobus Rochussen. Twee Rotterdamse slavenhandelaren in de 18e eeuw* (Rotterdam, 1996). The Rotterdam archives possess an archive on van Coopstad and Rochussen and related families, but it does not contain much information on van Coopstad's Levantine operations. For a recent investigation into Rotterdam's role in the slave trade, see Alex van Stipriaan, *Rotterdam in slavernij* (Amsterdam, 2020); see also Kwame Nimako and Glenn Willemsen, *The Dutch Atlantic. Slavery, abolition and emancipation* (London, 2011).

77 NACS, N°490, Knipping & Ouckama to Herman van Coopstad, Izmir, 15/09/1759.

78 NACS, N°490, Knipping & Ouckama to Herman van Coopstad, Izmir, 29/09/1759, '[…] wy moeten u ed met hertgrondig leetweezen melden, dat het ons in de ziel is smertende, onse eerste onderneeminge, met u ed (waarvoor wy aan u ed intrest moeten betaalen) x jonge cooplieden zyn, die onze respective vrinden met alle trouwe x eerlyke behandelingen tragten te bedienen, zoo ongelukkig zyn, zynde wy in vreezen hierby een goede somme gelde te zullen laten zitten, dan dewyl wy van u ed genereusiteit overtuygt zyn, zo hoope wy met gods hulp x volgens u ed belofften deze schade inderwaarts te doen winnen […]'.

with van Coopstad, and through him with merchants in Liège, continued but became very problematic later on.[79]

While Knipping & Ouckama wanted to provide their services to as many firms as possible, van Coopstad was equally interested in relying on several intermediaries who would try to get the best deals for him. This was not only a matter of spreading the risk, it was also a way of testing the competence of different trading houses and of empirically observing which firms would be able to obtain the best prices. As Cauw's reply to de Vogel has shown, this betting on multiple horses could create malcontent. The problem was not so much the practice per se but rather dishonesty or inequality. So, in 1759, Herman van Coopstad not only agreed to send merchandise to Izmir, but he was also conducting business with the Fernandes firm in Istanbul. Knipping & Ouckama had been informed that the Fernandes firm had merchandise ready to ship to van Coopstad and that the latter was sending two cases of textiles to Istanbul. This disturbed the young merchant house in Izmir, because they felt that an oral agreement had been made to send one case to Izmir, to be sold on a fifty-fifty partnership basis between Herman van Coopstad and Knipping & Ouckama. They stated that everyone was interested in van Coopstad's commission and that this way of favouring the Fernandes firm was not acceptable. They insisted that van Coopstad had to send one case to Izmir, after which they could show him the commercial advantages they could provide. Van Coopstad's actions, the young partners in Izmir felt, were 'no merchants' style, no sir'.[80] It is of crucial importance that the merchants themselves used this term to label commercial behaviour, inside as well as outside of court. The legal relevance of the concept meant that behaviour such as van Coopstad's could lead to a legal claim on the part of Knipping & Ouckama.

It seems that a legal claim was often the final step in a longer process of solution-seeking.[81] In the first instance, remarks from peers about breaking commercial custom were similar to threats to sue – it was meant as an incentive to set a wrongdoing right. Traders discussed their problems through their established business correspondence, as the example of a discussion between two major firms involved in Levant trade shows. The Amsterdam-based firm of Thomas de Vogel & Zoon was involved in a variety of business operations with the partnership between David van Lennep and William Enslie in Izmir.

---

79 See pp. 223–250.

80 NACS, N°490, Knipping & Ouckama to Herman van Coopstad, Izmir, 01/11/1759, '[…] neen myn heer, zulks is geen Coopmans styl […]'.

81 And disputes over the ownership of consigned goods were perhaps the most common type of disputes. See van den Boogert, *The capitulations*, pp. 220–224.

Thomas de Vogel was not only active in the Levant trade, with a son acting as his agent in Izmir, but also in import trade with South America as well as the pepper trade through the Dutch East India Company.[82] David van Lennep (1712–1797) was the most important trader in the Dutch business community in Izmir.[83] Van Lennep had arrived in the Levant to work for the firm of Muyssart and de la Fontaine in Istanbul before establishing his own firm in Izmir. In 1758, he married Anne Marie Leystar, the young daughter of a partner in another Dutch firm that was active in Istanbul and Ankara. Two of his daughters married English traders. One married the naturalised Swiss Isaac Morier, member of the Levant Company, who was to become the company's consul-general in Istanbul in 1806.[84] Another daughter married Jacques de Hochepied, son of Consul Daniel Jean de Hochepied and his successor as consul in Izmir, while one of Daniel Jean's daughters married Jacob van Lennep, the son of David van Lennep. Another of David van Lennep's sons married a daughter of the later Dutch treasurer in Izmir.[85]

In 1762 Thomas de Vogel & Zoon purchased the *Vrouwe Catharina*, with the intention to make journeys to the Levant. De Vogel & Zoon acted as bookkeeper and possessed one-eighth of the ship. Van Lennep & Enslie also held a share of one-eighth.[86] The latter's firm was crucial for using the ship in commercial voyages because out of the fifteen shareholders, it was the only firm that resided outside the United Provinces in Izmir and was very valuable in procuring cargos for the return voyages. When the *Vrouwe Catharina* arrived back home from a journey to the Levant in October 1765, part of the cargo of currants was found to have gone bad.[87] De Vogel wrote to van Lennep & Enslie that he thought that they surely had not seen it, as they never would

82 For the de Vogel firm, see Hakkı Kadı, *Ottoman and Dutch merchants*, pp. 183–197.

83 A painting of him and his family is preserved in the Rijksmuseum. See figure 6.

84 Two years earlier, he had also been appointed as ambassador, and both functions were unified in 1806. Wood, *Levant Company*, p. 184.

85 For a genealogy of the family branch in Izmir, see http://www.levantineheritage.com/pdf/The_Van_Lennep_Genealogy_Smyrna_Branch.pdf. Further information can be found in Mariëlle Hageman, *Amsterdam in de wereld. Sporen van Nederlandse gedeelde verleden* (Amsterdam, 2017); and Henry McKenzie Johnston, *Ottoman and Persian odysseys: James Morier, creator of 'Hajji Baba of Ispahan', and his brothers* (London and New York, 1998).

86 Heeringa and Nanninga, *Bronnen tot de geschiedenis*, 3: pp. 503–504, 'De Levantvaarder "De Vrouwe Catharina"', Amsterdam, 30/10/1762.

87 The story of the currants is narrated through a selection of letter fragments sent by Thomas de Vogel & Zoon (labelled by Heeringa and Nanninga as de Vogel & C°) to van Lennep & Enslie that are found in Heeringa and Nanninga, *Bronnen tot de geschiedenis*, 4: pp. 1194–1196 (07/10–05/11/1765), pp. 1204–1206 (07/03/1766), and pp. 1210–1213 (22/08/1766).

have shipped rotten currants that also had been very poorly packed. The other shareholders were angry, and in order to limit the financial damage, de Vogel had already written to Amsterdam's aldermen asking them to nominate three neutral persons to estimate the condition and value of the currants, which would immediately be sold at a loss at a public auction.[88] The event was seen as potentially harmful to de Vogel, who, in Amsterdam, had been responsible for the trip, and to van Lennep, who had obtained the cargo. Several letters were sent back and forth between the two firms, with van Lennep & Enslie reluctant to take responsibility until de Vogel ended the conversation by stating that he had observed van Lennep's desire to continue 'a friendly correspondence', something he also wanted to do, so the firm decided to let the whole affair pass, cancelling any further efforts to pinpoint responsibility.[89] During the whole conversation about responsibility, the authorities at no moment assumed a role, except for appointing neutral men – probably other merchants – who could determine the value of the cargo. At any given moment, though, de Vogel could have decided to look for a peer in Izmir to provide him with a power of attorney to act on behalf of the ship's shareholders and to take the firm of van Lennep & Enslie to court.

That he did not do so might be testimony to the importance of keeping van Lennep & Enslie as friends or to the doubts de Vogel had about a successful outcome. After all, he was also directly involved as the bookkeeper for the vessel. But it is not hard to see that the lack of physical contact between trading partners in international trade could create a multitude of problems. One had to do with the lack of ability to monitor the behaviour of agents or partners far away, a second was the problem of verifying information about markets abroad and a third was how to sue merchants living at a great distance. It was quite common that agents sold products at prices their principals were not happy about. Knipping & Ouckama wrote to van Coopstad in September 1759 that they were unable to sell some of the weapons he had sent them at a good price because of the competition from captains of a number of ships that had just arrived, who were selling 'à tout prix'.[90] A couple of days earlier, they had informed Benjamin and Samuel Symons, Jewish diamond traders in Amsterdam, that they had not sold their diamond rings because the price set by them was too high.[91] A principal who received letters with such remarks

88 Ibid.

89 Heeringa and Nanninga, *Bronnen tot de geschiedenis*, 4: p. 1210, Letter Thomas de Vogel & Zoon to David van Lennep & Enslie, Amsterdam, 22/08/1766, '[...] vriendelijke correspondentie [...]'.

90 NACS, N°490, Knipping & Ouckama to Herman van Coopstad, Izmir, 29/09/1759.

91 NACS, N°490, Knipping & Ouckama to Benjamin and Samuel Symons, Izmir, 24/09/1759.

could not automatically know whether they were true, whether the agent was incapable, or if, perhaps, the agent was cheating. Economic historians have labelled this the 'principal-agent problem'.[92] This problem could be solved in a number of ways, first of all by relying on the trust-generating mechanisms of credit and reputation to ensure the agent's behaviour would remain in check. Loss of access to credit or damage to personal reputation could be fatal blows for any trader. A second option was to maintain different correspondences in any given place and to make regular enquiries about colleagues and their economic circumstances. In spite of all measures taken to prevent problems, commercial transactions unavoidably did go wrong at times, and merchants did take each other to court. In the case of both litigants being Dutch, the court would be Dutch too. The problem was not so much 'national' competence but distance. In disputes between principals in the United Provinces and agents in Izmir or elsewhere in the Ottoman Empire, the competent court was that of the defendant according to the principle of *forum rei*. If a Dutch agent in Izmir was accused of wrongdoing, he had to defend himself at the Dutch consular court.

Generally, merchants tended not to travel to settle a dispute in court, particularly when it was far away. In cases brought before the consular court in Izmir, this meant the principal in the United Provinces, or elsewhere in Europe, would have a notary write a declaration stating his place of residence, and in it, he would give a merchant abroad the power of attorney. This was an old form of legal contract, made up before a notary, in which legal agency was transferred from a principal to an agent.[93] A notarial deed granting a fellow trader power of attorney was a common legal instrument in international trade, as with the expansion of commercial activities, since traders could not always attend to their affairs abroad in person. Several of the Dutch traders in Izmir acted as

92 Lamikiz, *Trade and trust*, p. 9. For additional literature on trust in a medieval and early modern context, see also Ana Sofia Ribeiro, *Early modern trading networks in Europe. Cooperation and the case of Simon Ruiz* (Abingdon, 2016); David Hancock, '"A world of business to do": William Freeman and the foundations of England's commercial empire, 1645–1707', *William and Mary quarterly*, 57:1 (2000): pp. 3–34; Dahl, *Trade, trust*; Ann M. Carlos and Stephen Nicholas, 'Agency problems in the early chartered companies: The case of the Hudson's Bay Company', *Journal of economic history*, 50:4 (1990): pp. 853–875; and Avner Greif, 'Reputation and coalitions in medieval trade: Evidence on the Maghribi traders', *Journal of economic history*, 49:4 (1989): pp. 857–882. For the importance of social and kinship ties in commercial relations of trust, see the classic text by Yoram Ben-Porath, 'The F-connection: Families, friends, and firms and the organization of exchange', *Population and development review*, 6:1 (1980): pp. 1–30.

93 Fusaro, *Political economies*, pp. 234–235; and van Gelder, *Trading places*, p. 169.

FIGURE 6 David George van Lennep (1712–1797), senior merchant of the Dutch factory at Smyrna (Izmir) with his wife and children, attributed to Antoine de Favray, 1769–1771
FROM THE COLLECTION OF THE RIJKSMUSEUM, AMSTERDAM

plaintiffs on behalf of traders elsewhere.[94] This meant that a firm that could be competing with the defendant for the same commercial opportunities was now called upon to defend the interests of a principal far away in the United Provinces. The granting of a power of attorney required trust, and the legal agent was expected to defend the principal's interests in the best way possible, just like a commercial agent was supposed to look after the best interests of the principal in business matters. While it can be argued that commercial agents were chosen based on a mixture of established reputation, credit and perhaps a sample sale, not all of these criteria could always be used to assess a legal agent. While commercial agents had a direct financial incentive to do their job well, through the commission fee, a similar direct financial incentive did not exist for legal agents.[95] Of course, there were positive incentives, as a principal satisfied with his representation in court could become a more important

94 Powers of attorney were not limited to litigation. Arnoldus Wissing received one to make commercial decisions on behalf of his principals. See p. 140.

95 I have found no evidence suggesting that legal agents were paid by those who had given them power of attorney.

business partner for the agent. It is hard to find clear reasoning behind a particular choice for a legal representative, also because existing source material is not always very informative on the different choices that traders made in this regard. But if a merchant had business interests in a place, and thus a number of correspondents he dealt with structurally, it seems not that big of a step to draft a power of attorney, have it notarised and send it abroad. Acting on someone's behalf in court must have been part of the reciprocal services traders rendered one another – refusing it might result in a loss of reputation, and a trader never knew when he could use a legal agent himself. Reciprocity, again, was key.

2.2 *Commission Trade Gone Wrong*

Not all disputes were resolved through arbitration. The criteria the judges adjudicating commercial disputes used to refer litigants to arbitration were not clearly defined; Kessler pointed out how it was related to the complexity of a case, as well as to considerations linked to maintaining cohesion within the merchant community.[96] Sometimes, arbitration was not considered, and the quarrel turned immediately into a trial. When Pieter Ouckama ended his partnership with Dirk Knipping, he started to take on commissions from the United Provinces in his own name. One of the merchant firms that had been working with him was the Amsterdam-based partnership of Wijnants & Cramer. Eventually, they felt that Ouckama had not served them well, and they had a power of attorney drafted in Amsterdam by notary Salomon Dorper on 19 November 1763, in which they provided Clement, van Sanen, van der Zee & C° with the power of attorney to close all accounts Wijnants & Cramer still had with Ouckama & C° in Izmir.[97] In case Ouckama was unwilling to close accounts or tried to slow down any final settlement, Philippe Clement and his partners had the authority to take him to court, 'rightfully following local style', and to request an advantageous sentence and appeal against a disadvantageous one.[98] If necessary, they were also allowed to demand sequesters on monies in Ouckama's hands in Wijnants & Cramer's name.[99] The reference to 'local style' is very revealing. It confirms that there was not one merchants' style that could be identified as a *lex mercatoria*, but rather the simultaneous development of converging usages, shared customs and the common use of

96 Kessler, 'Enforcing virtue'.

97 CAA, N°5075 ('Archief der notarissen standplaats Amsterdam'), Salomon Dorper, N°10812 ('Minuutacten', 01/11/1763–31/12/1763), 'Procuratie', Amsterdam, 19/11/1763.

98 Ibid., '[...] in regten na style locaal [...]'.

99 Ibid.

summary procedure – a development that had local variations, as well as differing local relationships to legal institutions. Emily Kadens has argued that such convergence was brought about by an increasing tendency to think about the law from the perspective of Roman law, which led to efforts 'to use definitions and procedure to try to turn custom into something more recognizable to them [trained lawyers] as law. In the process, they changed and colonized traditional conceptions of custom'.[100] To what extent the latter can be said to apply to early modern commercial adjudication is unclear, but it is true that in Dutch legislative efforts at regulating it, there was an exclusive focus on procedure – custom was left alone.

The remark in the procuration is exactly along the lines of van Sanen's reasoning in his dispute with the de Vogel firm, when he argued that one had to follow local rules more than habits that developed far away in the United Provinces.[101] The first action of Clement's firm was to go to Ouckama's house, where they demanded to see all accounts related to business with Wijnants & Cramer. Ouckama showed one current account that Clement found insufficient, so he wrote the consul to demand that Ouckama be forced to produce all the relevant business documents.[102] The consul ordered his chancellor to inform Ouckama of the request and to order him to provide the 'true and rightful current account' within seventy-two hours.[103] At this point, the dispute was not very concrete yet – in a way, the consular court was mediating between a principal demanding the closure of current accounts because of a general dissatisfaction with the agent's services and an agent who seemed reluctant to provide immediate clarity on his business dealings. Clement made his request in January 1764, and it was far from a strange one, as it was common for business documents to be used in trials. A series of written replies and counter-replies between the litigants followed until the consul and his assessors reached a verdict in May 1764. The case was of average length, containing twenty-five documents, although some of them were long narratives. It was

100 Emily Kadens, 'Convergence and the colonization of custom in pre-modern Europe', in *Comparative legal history*, eds. O. Moréteau, A. Masferrer, and K.A. Modéer (Cheltenham, 2019), p. 168.

101 See p. 151.

102 NACS, N°330 ('Stukken raakende de proces van Clement van Sanen van der Zee & C° als procurateuren vand heeren Wynants & Cramer d'Amsterdam teegens de heer Ouckama & C° alhier weegen 36 b verongelukte catt: in de brand van 6 aug l.l. van 17 jan: tot 21 juny anno 1764'), 'Request van Clement van Sanen van der Zee & Comp tot versoek van reek: courant aen Ouckama te vraagen weeg Wynants & Cramer', Izmir, 16/01/1764.

103 Ibid., '[…] de egte en regte reek: courant […]'.

resolved within five months, which was quite long, as the dispute quickly narrowed down to a single transaction.

When Ouckama handed over more detailed information to the court three days later as was required, he pointed out that on most points there was no disagreement. In fact, Ouckama reminded the court that he had already made an official declaration about his services to Wijnants & Cramer earlier, and his business books had already been subjected to an official viewing by the chancellor and several witnesses.[104] Apparently, Wijnants & Cramer had made an attempt to settle matters earlier, but no documents have survived of this, which might very well have been because it had been an amicable attempt to close accounts between two parties. The single transaction that was disputed was about thirty-six bales of cotton that had been purchased by Ouckama on behalf of Wijnants & Cramer in Amsterdam, for which he received a commission fee. Unfortunately, these bales were stacked in a Dutch warehouse on the night between 5 and 6 August 1763, when a fire ravaged parts of Izmir and destroyed almost all of the Dutch housing.[105] According to the monthly *Gentleman's and London Magazine*, the 'most dreadful fire [...] in less than 24 hours reduced to ashes the whole quarter occupied by the Christians. The *qadi* would by no means be prevailed upon to endeavour to stop the fury of the flames, as few of the Turks were affected by the disaster'.[106]

The quarrel between Wijnants & Cramer as plaintiff and Ouckama, who had worked for them on commission, as defendant turned into one of the most typical commercial disputes – responsibility for damages to goods that were part of commission trade. The central issue was to what extent an agent in Izmir could be held accountable for what happened to goods he had been trading on behalf of a principal in the Dutch Republic, or elsewhere in Europe – particularly considering the damage was due to an uncontrollable event. Ouckama had charged Wijnants & Cramer for the bales of cotton damaged or lost in the fire, but the latter felt that they should not assume financial responsibility for the cotton, as they argued it was not (yet) theirs. Wijnants & Cramer were of the opinion that Ouckama & C° had not acted as honest merchants

104 NACS, N°330, 'Antwoord van Ouckama & Comp weegens de pretentie van Clement van Sanen & C° voor dhr Wijnants & Cramer d'Amsterdam', Izmir, 19/01/1764.

105 It seems only Dirk Knipping's house was spared, as he lived in the Armenian neighbourhood (see figure 4). After the fire, the Dutch consul was forced to rent a house in the same neighbourhood, even though he still owned an out-of-town residence in Sediköy. Heeringa and Nanninga, *Bronnen tot de geschiedenis*, 3: pp. 483–484, Consul Daniel Jean de Hochepied to the States General, Izmir, 24/08/1763.

106 *Gentleman's and London magazine: Or, monthly chronologer* (Dublin, 1763), 32: p. 561.

during the fire, an accusation that could severely damage the latter's reputation. Wanting 'to show the whole world' that he was indeed an honest merchant, Ouckama was now more willing to show his books to the judge and to confirm their veracity under oath.[107] He would also allow the chancellor, in the presence of witnesses, to make copies and draw extracts from all the posts in the books that concerned business with Wijnants & Cramer, but this had to be paid for by Clement, van Sanen, van der Zee & C°. He would not provide the copies himself, as he felt that he was not obliged to do so legally, and his behaviour was evidence in itself that 'no suspicion of fraud remained'. Furthermore, 'he had other things to do'.[108] Ouckama clearly put the burden of proof on his opponent, who, as plaintiffs, indeed needed to demonstrate that something had gone wrong.

Clement, van Sanen, van der Zee & C° replied they were indeed satisfied about most of the transactions but not about the thirty-six bales of cotton that had been bought for Wijnants & Cramer and that Ouckama had marked in his books as burned by fire. These thirty-six had come out of a total purchase of sixty bales, made in two transactions; forty at first, of which sixteen had been damaged, and an additional twenty, all of which were damaged. The remaining twenty-four had been shipped to the United Provinces on board the ship of skipper Severus Zeegenberg. Clement, van Sanen, van der Zee & C° did not deny that the cotton had indeed been bought on behalf of Wijnants & Cramer, but they pointed to the fact that the Amsterdam-based traders had instructed Ouckama to ship it immediately, at the first opportunity. Ouckama, they continued, had been offered a shipping opportunity, and he refused to accept it. Both van Sanen and van der Zee had personally asked Ouckama to provide them with some return cargo for the *Maria Dorothea*, which was to sail back to the United Provinces with skipper Jacob Hilkes, who had been witness to these meetings. These demands had been made well before the fire occurred, and Ouckama ignored them, a negligence that made him responsible for the damage to the cotton. An additional argument to place the financial burden of the cotton on Ouckama was that the current account between Ouckama and Wijnants & Cramer showed that, at the time of the fire, Ouckama did not have enough of Wijnants & Cramer's money in his accounts to buy the cotton on their behalf with their money.[109]

107 NACS, N°330, 'Antwoord van Ouckama & Comp', Izmir, 19/01/1764, '[...] aan de geheele wereld te toonen [...]'.

108 Ibid., '[...] geen suspitie van fraude overblyft x omdat wy ook wel wat anders te doen hebben [...]'.

109 NACS, N°330, 'Replicq van dhn Clement, van Sanen van der Zee & Comp op het antwoord van Ouck & C° weegens Wijnants & Cramer', Izmir, 24/01/1764.

The core of the argument was that Ouckama had not acted as a good agent in several ways. His poor handling of Wijnants & Cramer's affairs made him liable for the damage done to the cotton. Philippe Clement continued his reply to Ouckama's claims by stating that he was most surprised about Ouckama's persisting refusal to show all documents related to his business with Wijnants & Cramer. His firm was entitled to see them as they held power of attorney from Wijnants & Cramer, which was an official legal instrument. Second, Ouckama had stated his desire to 'show the whole world they [Ouckama & C°] were honest merchants', and Clement argued this was the perfect occasion to do so.[110] Clement's firm, a partnership of honest people, would have taken it. Clement rebuffed Ouckama's claim that he had used the term 'suspicion of fraud' in his first request on 16 January but stated that he simply followed merchants' style (*coopmansstyl*), to be judged and satisfied according to justice and equity.[111] The connection Clement made between the merchants' style and equity is important, as it is the idea of equity as deriving from principles of reason and natural law that made the merchants' style such a logical and acceptable foundation for merchants to settles their commercial disputes.[112] For Clement, it was a matter of following commercial custom, and the outcome of a procedure doing so could, in his eyes, only lead to an equitable verdict that would naturally be accepted by all parties involved.

Clement's reply suggests that merchants considered litigation as more than the ultimate resort to disputes. Amalia Kessler has stressed the social function of arbitration, but litigation in general fulfilled an important social role within the international merchant community. Traders thought of the court as a place where a litigant's reputation was subject to 'peer-review'. The assessors, who were Dutch traders acting as assistant-judges, were not only there to ensure the adherence of the court to merchant custom but also to form an opinion on reputation, an opinion that might have had a bigger impact than the reputational judgment that took place in traders' business correspondences.

The court was a place where the (international) habits of merchants were subjected to national jurisdiction. It was perhaps the only institution that aimed to sanction the behaviour of traders that stood with one foot in the merchant community, where rules and habits were often international, informal and noncodified, and with another foot in the world of laws issued or recognised by a government. With regards to trade disputes, laws were not applied to settle a dispute but to provide the legal context in which the dispute could

110 Ibid., '[…] van aan de geheelen wereldt te toonen zy eerlyke lieden zyn […]'.
111 Ibid., '[…] geene minsten gewagh van suspitie van fraudes gemaakt […]'.
112 See pp. 128 and 132–133.

be settled. In other words, informal conflict-regulating solutions that derived from peer-review judgment could only be expected to carry sufficient weight to be accepted by all involved if such judgment came from a formal government-sanctioned institution that relied on procedure. It explains why great lengths were taken by the authorities to make sure that the Dutch consular court of Izmir was legitimate vis-à-vis the legal system in the United Provinces, the legal system in the Ottoman Empire and the legal systems under which merchants of other European trading nations found themselves.

2.3 *Whose Responsibility Is It?*

Ouckama's behaviour as an agent for others was under scrutiny here, and his liability in the matter of the damaged cotton was to be determined by the merchants' style. It was the court's task to assess the evidence in that light. To build their case, Clement and his partners insisted on having full access to all accounts related to the cotton. They felt it was crucial to find out whether the cotton had been bought with money that was unrelated to Wijnants & Cramer or whether the purchase had been financed with profits on goods sold on behalf of Wijnants & Cramer. The answer to this question would be crucial in determining responsibility for the damage, because the cotton was a return cargo that was theoretically paid for from the profits of the sales of Wijnants & Cramer's exports to Izmir. If it was proven that Ouckama had not used the latter's money, then Wijnants & Cramer could not be expected to take any financial responsibility for the cotton, as it would not be theirs. Secondly, Clement knew that Ouckama had not observed his principals' instruction to ship as fast as possible. He was given the option to load the cargo on board the *Maria Dorothea* of skipper Jacob Hilkes, in which the firm of Clement, van Sanen, van der Zee & C° was a shareholder. Pieter van Sanen, Nicolas van der Zee and Jacob Hilkes had personally informed Ouckama of that option, but he chose not to take it.[113] Later, Ouckama shipped the twenty-four bales that had not been damaged on the *Vrouwe Berendina* of skipper Severus Zeegenberg, and Clement knew that it had not been the first Dutch ship to leave Izmir for

113 NACS, N°330, 'Replicq van dhn Clement, van Sanen van der Zee & Comp op het antwoord van ouck & C°', Izmir, 24/01/1764. From the documents it is clear that the firm of Clement, van Sanen, van der Zee & C° was part-owner of Hilkes' ship, or at least responsible for logistics in Izmir. In 1760, Pieter van Sanen and Jacob Hilkes appeared before the *qadi* in Izmir, assisted by a dragoman for the Dutch nation and the consul, to be heard in a case in which the *Maria Dorothea* was allegedly used to transport money and jewels that belonged to a Tunisian prince from Naples to Izmir, and further to Istanbul. They denied any involvement. See *Verzameling van geheime brieven*, 13: n.p., Consul Daniel Jean de Hochepied to an unknown addressee, Izmir, 29/11/1760.

the United Provinces after the fire, again showing Ouckama's incapability to follow the orders he had been given.[114]

Lastly, Clement and his partners dismissed Ouckama's willingness to take a statement under oath and his proposal to obtain an official declaration of the truthfulness of his books from the chancellor, as they felt they could get sufficient information from the business papers. The oath was an important means of evidence, and if Ouckama was willing to take it, it could be a problem for Clement, but as the business documents contained enough evidence, the plaintiff did not see the necessity of taking one.[115] After reading Clement's statement, Consul de Hochepied ordered his chancellor to inform Ouckama and demand a reply from him within seventy-two hours. The reply came a bit earlier this time – two days later. He argued that he had not acted against the order for the prompt return of the shipment and claimed he had been unable to load the cotton on board a ship bound for the Dutch Republic immediately after having received the merchandise.[116] To demonstrate that he had been working as fast as he could, Ouckama referred to his correspondence with an uncle in Amsterdam, Sirp Ouckama. Because Wijnants & Cramer had instructed Ouckama to not bother them with every detail, he decided to keep his uncle up to date with all that was happening. That way, Pieter Ouckama had to write fewer letters to Wijnants & Cramer, saving postage.

At some point, Pieter Ouckama had asked his uncle to inform Wijnants & Cramer that he was busy procuring forty bales of cotton for a return cargo on their behalf. After the cargo was bought, he started to look for ships, but according to Ouckama, it was not possible to use the *Maria Dorothea*. Skipper Jacob Hilkes was supposed to leave by mid-July, when the cotton had not been secured yet. Ouckama tried to ship other merchandise on Hilkes' ship, but disagreements over the freight charges had brought an end to that. In the end, Hilkes had indeed stayed in port longer than foreseen, planning to sail on 6 August. But according to Ouckama, he had not postponed his departure to wait on the cotton but on the arrival of the caravan that brought Angora yarn. There would have been no place for Wijnants & Cramer's forty bales of cotton, nor for the twenty additional bales that Ouckama received on the afternoon of the fifth, which were also destined for Wijnants & Cramer. Ouckama had therefore started to negotiate with another captain, Adriaan Jansz Leuning, and Philippe

114 NACS, N°330, 'Replicq van dhn Clement, van Sanen van der Zee & Comp op het antwoord van Ouck & C°', Izmir, 24/01/1764.

115 For the establishment of the oath as legal proof in the Levantine context, see p. 134.

116 NACS, N°330, 'Replicq van Ouckama & C° aan Clement van Sanen, van der Zee & C° weegens Wijnants & Cramer d'Amstm', Izmir, 26/01/1764.

Clement had even promised to come into town on the sixth to assist in these talks. Ouckama could thus not have shipped earlier.[117]

A second argument to dismiss the claim that Hilkes was waiting for a return cargo of cotton was made by recalling certain events that happened the night of the fire. When Ouckama found out what was happening, he asked Pieter van Sanen and Nicolas van der Zee for assistance salvaging some of the cotton. He wanted them to send a sloop from Hilkes' ship, of which they were part-owners, so at least the twenty bales, which had only been received the day before and had not yet been properly stored, could be saved. In spite of their promise to help, Clement and van der Zee clearly 'preferred to break their word, leave a compatriot to his own devices and help a Frenchman instead'.[118] Ouckama had no choice but to throw the cotton in the water, hoping to save them from being fully consumed by the fire. Clement referring to the cotton as 'supposedly burned and perished' was insulting considering Ouckama's efforts, and Ouckama asked Clement to be careful about the words he used, or he would resort to other means.[119]

The question about whose money had financed the purchase of the cotton saddened Ouckama, because Wijnants & Cramer knew very well that Ouckama could not finance so many bales of cotton with the returns from sales on Wijnants & Cramer's behalf alone. The fact that he had been willing to use other money was an argument in favour of Ouckama's efforts to buy and ship rapidly. It was a generally known fact that the shopkeepers who bought the goods coming from Europe paid very slowly. Therefore, it would have been impossible to ensure a rapid return cargo by relying exclusively on the profits of the merchandise sold on behalf of Wijnants & Cramer. If Clement, van Sanen, van der Zee & C° felt Ouckama could only finance return cargos from the shopkeepers' payments, they had to understand that the consequence was that a return shipment could only be made two years later; three months were needed for buying, shipping and arriving in Izmir, twelve months for selling these goods from the United Provinces and receiving payment, two months for buying return goods and three months for the journey home. At that rate,

117 Ibid. Leuning, a skipper from Rotterdam, must have been one of the first Dutch skippers to leave Izmir after the fire, because he was one of the two skippers who had loaded goods belonging to Consul de Hochepied on board his vessel. Heeringa and Nanninga, *Bronnen tot de geschiedenis*, 3: pp. 483–484, Consul Daniel Jean de Hochepied to the States General, Izmir, 24/08/1763.

118 NACS, N°330, 'Replicq van Ouckama & C° aan Clement van Sanen, van der Zee & C°', Izmir, 26/01/1764, '[…] het heeft die heeren liever behaagt hun word niet te houden, een nationaal te verlaaten x een Fransman te helpen […]'.

119 Ibid., '[…] de zogenaamde verbrande off verongelukte cattoenen […]'.

Ouckama would have been long dismissed as agent by Wijnants & Cramer. In any case, if they only wanted their own money spent, they should have instructed Ouckama to do exactly that.[120]

Ouckama was also disappointed by Clement, van Sanen, van der Zee & C°'s refusal to have him take the oath. This, he argued, actually gave him the opportunity to commit 'the biggest fraud in the world', because even if he handed over the business papers now, as requested, the truthfulness of their contents would have to be taken for granted.[121] An oath would have added formal veracity to the business books, clearing Ouckama's name and confirming his honesty. Fully aware of the importance of reputation for merchants, but also of the importance of the oath as a means of evidence, Ouckama felt his adversaries had taken away a possibility for him to clear his name.[122]

This time, the plaintiff's reply took longer than usual – more than ten days. When it finally arrived, it expressed some strong sentiments. Clement and his partners felt that Ouckama had been childish for not choosing a ship for the return cargo, because their friends in Amsterdam – Wijnants & Cramer – could not have known which ships would leave first from Izmir.[123] Furthermore, all Ouckama needed to have done was give his word that he would ship his cargo on board the *Maria Dorothea*, and Clement, van Sanen, van der Zee & C° would have secured as much cargo space as necessary. To substantiate their point further, they added that their business books showed that they had purchased 130 bales of cotton after discussions with Ouckama about filling the ship, confirming that space had not been the problem. Clement was further disappointed that Ouckama mentioned a discussion on freight charges as the problem. They had promised him there was going to be space on their ship, and a promise, even when only made orally, had a clear and binding value in the merchant community. The discussions on freight charges, 'pertinent lies', were considered by Clement and his partners as an attempt to label them as deceitful.[124] Clement further complained about using Sirp Ouckama as an intermediary in the communication between Ouckama in Izmir and Wijnants & Cramer in Amsterdam. It meant that it could not be proven that the bales of cotton Pieter Ouckama referred to in his letters to his uncle had indeed been

120 Ibid.

121 Ibid., '[…] de grootste fraude der weereld […]'.

122 Ibid.

123 NACS, N°330, '2e replicq van dhn Clement van Sanen & C° in de differentie met Ouckama & C° weegens Wijnants & Cramer d'Amstm', Izmir, 07/02/1764. This shows that physical distance could create a particular problem: asymmetric information.

124 Ibid., '[…] impertinente x leugenaghtige expressies […]'.

purchased for Wijnants & Cramer, as that was not stated explicitly in the letters. Clement strongly believed that, had the fire not taken place, the cotton might very well have turned out to be Pieter Ouckama's, a severe accusation. In any case, Wijnants & Cramer were not personally informed by Pieter Ouckama about the cotton purchases, and Clement felt it went against all merchants' style for an agent to anticipate a return purchase without the approval of the principal, particularly cotton, which was not fetching great prices in the United Provinces at the time.[125]

Clement, van Sanen, van der Zee & C° persisted in their refusal to have Ouckama take the oath or have his business books checked by a public official, as they felt they could rely on witnesses to prove that Ouckama had not followed the orders of his principals, which they deemed as more than sufficient.[126] This persistence suggests Clement felt that Ouckama's position was stronger. Should he have been allowed to take the oath, it would have been difficult for the plaintiff to convince the court of his wrongdoing. In that sense, the refusal to have another party take the oath was part of the legal discussion about the nature of the case and not a refusal of the legal validity of the oath or public declarations as evidence, rather, to the contrary. An oath was considered such a strong form of evidence that it was not taken lightly.[127]

Clement also rebuffed the accusation that he had not helped a fellow countryman during the calamity of the fire. He recognised that at two o'clock in the night, van der Zee had gone to Ouckama, who had demanded the assistance of Hilkes' boat. But when both men tried to find Hilkes, they could not, because he had left with van Sanen to help a French trader, Majastre, whose house was on fire and who always had been 'a good friend' to the firm of Clement, van Sanen, van der Zee & C°.[128] After helping him out, Majastre returned the favour by sending a French sloop to help salvage goods (belonging to Clement, van Sanen, van der Zee & C°), a reciprocal favour that Ouckama would not have been able to provide. So Clement surely would have wanted to help a compatriot rather than a foreigner, but not under these circumstances. They also did not care much for Ouckama's threat to use other means if they did not

125 Ibid.

126 Ibid.

127 See also Kessler, 'Enforcing virtue', p. 93, 'Although from the modern perspective it seems extraordinary that the outcome of a lawsuit could turn solely on a litigant's oath, in the world of the Old Regime an oath made to God on penalty of eternal damnation remained a serious matter'.

128 NACS, N°330, '2e replicq van dhn Clement van Sanen & C° in de differentie met Ouckama & C° weegens Wijnants & Cramer d'Amstm', Izmir, 07/02/1764, '[...] een goede vriendt [...]'.

change their vocabulary, a threat that must have been meant to have an impact on their good name, because they replied that there was nothing that could harm their 'honour or reputation'.[129] In case Ouckama came up with 'follies and nonsense', they would counter with something to silence him.[130] In a similar manner to the understanding that the international merchants' style was stronger than national law in commercial litigation, the ability for merchants to reciprocate and observe each other's mutual interests was stronger than the loyalty created by sharing a nationality.

The reciprocal threats made by both parties are a reminder of what was at stake in these trials – beyond the financial aspect. Both sides being convinced that they were not to blame for what happened, they resorted to questioning each other's motives and actions, threatening to damage each other's public reputation. The disagreement continued but shifted to an argument about the nature of (commercial) friendship, and Ouckama turned the discussion into an attack on a more personal level. He stated that Clement, van Sanen, van der Zee & C° had 'so often declared to our Ouckama to be his intimate friend, but orally, never in business correspondence'.[131] Ouckama accused the firm of not helping him and that 'friends who are friends out of interest are our enemies, as interest makes many people unreasonable'.[132] Ouckama's accusations must have hit hard, and van Sanen felt obliged to write an additional letter the same day his company officially replied to refute Ouckama's characterisation of their friendship. He felt he had no choice but to consider Ouckama's remarks as slander and attributed them to 'his weak mind'.[133] He ended the letter by quoting a Latin expression, 'friends who want to sell my onions as lemons are not my friends', suggesting he was rejecting Ouckama's friendship.[134]

To question friendship was to put someone's reputation on the line. It was very important that friendship between two traders was recognised by their peers, as that way it could be evaluated against the standards applied in the international merchant community, not in the least those about reciprocity. A successful friendship demonstrated that friends adhered to the principles

---

129 Ibid., '[…] onse eer off reputatie […]'.

130 Ibid., '[…] bagatellen off gekheeden […]'.

131 NACS, N°330, 'Replicq van Ouckama & C° aan Clement van Sanen, van der Zee & C°', Izmir, 26/01/1764, '[…] die zo meenegmaal aan onse ouckama mondelings dan nooyt zaakelyk betuygt hebt, zyn intieme vriend te zyn […]'.

132 Ibid., '[…] vrienden die uyt intrest vrienden zyn, zyn by ons vyanden, want de intrest doet veele menschen buyten de reeden gaan'.

133 Ibid., '[…] zijn swakke geest […]'.

134 Ibid., '[…] vrienden die mijn oijens voor citroenen willen verkoopen mijn vrienden niet zijn […]'. The expression comes from 'selling turnips for lemons'.

of merchant custom, and the cultivation of friends amongst merchants not only enhanced one's reputation, but it also enlarged the network of peers that could testify of such a reputation. This was of crucial importance, as these testimonies were used to obtain new business opportunities, as well as to protect oneself in litigation. It was thus hardly surprising that van Sanen wrote an additional letter.

No friendship could survive without reciprocity. In that sense, van Sanen's choice to help out a French friend who was able to reciprocate, instead of a Dutch national who could not do the same, was fully in line with what could be expected from van Sanen according to the merchants' style. This idea of friendship might strike present-day readers as contradictory, but it was commonplace in the early modern conception of friendship.[135]

3 Friendship on Trial

3.1 *The Bond between Merchants*

The exchange between Pieter van Sanen and Pieter Ouckama arguing over friendship is highly relevant to the notion of a merchants' style. This has to do with the fact that both merchants attached a number of mutual duties to their relationship – related to the expectations on behaviour as inscribed in the merchants' style. A discussion on friendship necessitates a definition of friendship – one that is dependent on the historical context, as there is a great ideal of varying interpretations of what constitutes a friendship even today. A few characteristics that we would consider important today come to mind: the fact that a friend is chosen, instead of given in the way a family is, the fact that there are common interests and the idea that there is a certain intimacy and comfort in the presence of friends.[136] These elementary notions of friendship can equally be seen as 'cultural stereotypes', and scholars who

135 For an elaborate analysis, see Luuc Kooijmans, *Vriendschap en de kunst van het overleven in de zeventiende en achttiende eeuw* (Amsterdam, 1997). Adam Smith also developed economic ideas on the meaning of commercial friendship, particularly in his *Theory of moral sentiments* (Edinburgh, 1759). For differing interpretations of his ideas, see Lisa Hill and Peter McCarthy, 'On friendship and *necessitudo* in Adam Smith', *History of the human sciences*, 17:4 (2004): pp. 1–16; and Allan Silver, 'Friendship in commercial society: Eighteenth-century social theory and modern sociology', *American journal of sociology*, 95:6 (1990): pp. 1474–1504.

136 Liz Spencer and Ray Pahl, *Rethinking friendship. Hidden solidarities today* (Princeton and Oxford, 2006), p. 59.

look into the meaning of friendship often debate to what extent such characteristics can be taken out of a friendship without it necessarily losing its label.[137]

For our analysis, two things are important to consider. First, the concept of friendship is subject to change depending on the social and historical context. This means that when an early modern trader referred to a colleague as a friend, many people today might assume that they shared more, and more profound, things with one another than their profession. While it is certainly a possibility that van Sanen and Ouckama did share more – after all, they were part of a small community that was the guest in a city that was part of a different social, cultural and religious entity – the Ottoman Empire. The extension of business ties into the world of social ties was certainly a characteristic of commercial friendship during the early modern period – but it was not a necessary condition for us to accept their use of the concept of friendship as genuine.[138]

Second, discussions on elementary aspects of friendship have not led to the idea that there is only one type of friendship. Different types are considered, and often, these are ranked according to how much they relate to some 'ideal' form of friendship that is mostly related to the stereotypes mentioned above. Simpler forms of friendship considered within that scheme could be associates or useful contacts, while the most complex forms of friendship could be soulmates or confidants.[139] The ranking of types of friendship is old, and has already been promoted by Aristotle, who distinguished between advantage-friendship, pleasure-friendship and virtue-friendship, the latter being the most valuable.[140] It is further been argued that certain Greek ideas of friendship have persisted for a remarkably long time in western society and were still quite commonplace during the eighteenth century.[141] In this sense, one could easily consider the commercial friendships under discussion here as

137 Ibid.

138 For more on merchant sociability in the context of generating trust, see Tijl Vanneste, 'Commercial culture and merchant networks: Eighteenth-century diamond traders in global history' (unpublished PhD thesis, European University Institute, 2009), pp. 102–103. For the Mediterranean and Ottoman context, see Fusaro, *Political economies*, pp. 219–221; and Quentin van Doosselaere, *Commercial agreements and social dynamics in medieval Genoa* (Cambridge, 2009).

139 Spencer and Pahl, *Rethinking friendship*, p. 60.

140 'Introduction', in *Friendship: A history*, ed. Barbara Caine (London and New York, 2009), p. x. One of the most persistent Greek notions of friendship was that it was only possible amongst men. Ibid., p. xii.

141 Ibid., p. x.

advantage-friendships, but this does not mean they were merely driven by utility and self-interest.

For merchants to engage in business with one another, trust was important, as well as a certain degree of predictable behaviour. Such trust and predictability can be relied upon by constructing commercial friendship, which respects the rules of the merchants' style – otherwise, such friendship would not be possible. And one of the most crucial rules was to put mutual interest and reciprocity above self-interest and egoism. Peers were expected to follow this rule, and expectations were a crucial part of friendship. In an interesting analysis, P.E. Digeser has put forward the notion that, in all our discussions on friendship, 'language of duty gets in the way of describing what matters in our friendships'.[142] What he me meant is that, in our analyses, too much focus on the idea that duties and obligations do not mix with true friendships obscures the fact that they are not at all irreconcilable. Part of the answer lies in his notion that, while duty, obligation and self-interest might be part of a friendship, they cannot be explicitly invoked in the language of the friendship. This is inspired by Sarah Lynch's ideas about friendship. Digeser observes that 'in a friendship, one must act as if other aims (such as interest, personal advantage, pleasure) were "transcended" [...] Lynch is trying to capture the idea that we may be driven by duty, but the truth is corrosive of the relationship'.[143] It is a very interesting and useful line of thinking, as it would allow us to see the merchants' frequent expression that they adhered to the merchants' style, as well as their sometimes fierce and passionate language when accused of self-interest, as part of 'performing' a role. The whole cohesion of the merchant community as relying on commercial friendship is to a certain extent based on the way in which all participants are willing to accept that role, which, to a point, is a façade.

This façade was meant to guarantee that merchants always respected reciprocity and adhered to the idea of a mutual pursuit of profit, instead of following their self-interest. Lengthy formulations in business correspondences, mutual favours, letters of recommendation – these are all part of that same façade deemed a necessary support for the way in which merchants were able to interact with one another on a daily basis. Considered in this way, our modern doubts about the sincerity with which eighteenth-century merchants referred to each other as friends vanish, as these doubts were based on wrong assumptions.

142 P.E. Digeser, *Friendship reconsidered. What it means and how it matters to politics* (New York, 2016), p. 64.

143 Ibid., p. 68.

In his monograph on the friendly ties between different families in the seventeenth and eighteenth centuries, Luuc Kooijmans defined friends as the people who can be 'talked to in order to reach certain goals or to solve problems'.[144] This definition seems far removed from our modern notion of friendship, which is essentially interest-free, but Kooijmans successfully argues that we should not anachronistically judge early modern ideas of friendship as purely calculated relationships. The kind of relationship merchants maintained allowed for the pursuit of one's personal gain, but this also included a certain reciprocal privilege, which meant, in trade, the granting of favours and discounts. This kind of friendship required the careful cultivation of relationships, enabling traders to live up to their reputation by demonstrating their reliability. For merchants, there were several ways to do so, most importantly by maintaining a regular business correspondence.[145]

In the eighteenth century, the Scottish thinker David Hume (1711–1776) came up with the paradigm of interested and disinterested commerce. He considered 'interested' trade as modern, based on the idea that man acts out of self-interest. Since a mutually profitable transaction is generally not instantaneous, a convention is adopted to make sure the first receiver gives back. This convention is the explicit promise of looking out for the interests of the other in the future.[146] The expectation that a favour would be returned was an essential part of the merchants' style and part of the reason why traders could trust one another – they could trust them to adhere to the conventions of the merchants' style. Importantly, the reciprocity that comes from looking out for mutual interests can be rationalised within the framework of self-interest; not keeping one's promise goes against self-interest, since it makes a trader lose his reputation, his credit and thus his long-term possibilities of finding new trading partners.[147] There also existed an older form, 'disinterested' commerce, in which an exchange was rewarded by gratitude. The first receiver was not formally expected to return the favour.[148]

For Hume, the interested form of commerce was modern but had not abolished the older form of disinterested commerce that he attached specifically

---

144 Kooijmans, *Vriendschap*, p. 327, '[…] degenen die konden worden aangesproken om bepaalde doelen te bereiken of problemen op te lossen'.

145 Ibid., p. 327. For the use of business correspondence to establish friendly ties, see Vanneste, *Global trade*, pp. 84–88.

146 Pierre Force, *Self-interest before Adam Smith: A genealogy of economic science* (Cambridge, 2003), pp. 171–174.

147 For a discussion of commercial friendship and trust in the eighteenth-century, see Vanneste, 'Commercial culture', pp. 100–111.

148 Force, *Self-interest*, pp. 171–174.

to friendship (that would also come closer to our own view of friendship). But Hume's analysis leaves space for the notion that merchants did not see the reconciliation between (a modified form of) self-interest and friendship as problematic – as long as self-interest was mutually protected. Interested commerce, as Hume defined it, required reciprocity, and reciprocity (or, more generally, the creation of mutual expectations) can be thought of as one of the foundational elements that made early modern international trade possible. In this context, the commercial friendship that merchants referred to in their arguments was connected to the expectation of doing business along the lines of the merchants' style, or along the lines of Hume's interested, modern commerce.

The early modern notion of commercial friendship was important because it was attached to a merchant's reputation. Wijnants & Cramer probably never set foot in Izmir, nor did they meet Pieter Ouckama in person. But they needed to trust him, which was possible through setting up a business correspondence, but also through recommendations made by third parties. If traders A and C were interested in doing business together, person B, a friend in business to both of them, was a necessary intermediary. It was normal for merchants to endorse each other's reputations by writing formal letters of recommendation. The alternative was the collection of information from a series of correspondents about a series of potential business partners.[149] Ouckama must have come recommended to Wijnants & Cramer, perhaps through Clement, van Sanen, van der Zee & C°.

Disputes between two traders could have serious repercussions beyond the damage done to the relationship between those two traders. After his dismissal as the partner of David van Lennep and William Enslie, caused by his marriage to a Greek woman, Dirk Knipping travelled to the United Provinces in an attempt to ensure his contacts of his continued friendship and to look for new correspondents.[150] He met with Thomas de Vogel Senior at the Amsterdam exchange, but it was a rather frosty encounter. Nevertheless, Knipping was allowed to speak further with de Vogel at his house, but the encounter ended with de Vogel ceasing all business with Knipping, even though he did not want to think of him as an enemy. Knipping felt the marriage and the possible consequences thereof, were a private matter and that van Lennep had treated him

149 In the business archives of the firm of Hope & C°, based in Amsterdam and one of the most successful Dutch firms of the eighteenth century, several books have been preserved containing such information. CAA, N°735 ('Archief Hope & C°'), N°s 1404–1407; see also Vanneste, *Global trade*, p. 89.

150 See pp. 70–71.

unfairly. De Vogel took van Lennep's side. He expressed his surprise that someone who had received so many advantageous favours from David van Lennep could make himself so unworthy. He also promised van Lennep to ensure that their contacts in the United Provinces would be informed of the true reason of Knipping's ousting, the marriage, as Knipping had been spreading misinformation. De Vogel also told van Lennep that Knipping's behaviour in the United Provinces had been poor, and he should not worry that his credit or honour might suffer as consequence of this change, perhaps even to the contrary. Knipping, it seems, was not held in high esteem by de Vogel's correspondents, with his temper and his tendency to talk a lot, and his behaviour when he was in the United Provinces had made things worse.[151]

In a world in which trust and reputation were important commodities, and in which the private and professional spheres were not so easily delineated, one had to consider carefully how to interact with fellow merchants, and naturally, personal sympathies played a role next to considerations of commercial performance. In 1767, Thomas de Vogel wrote to his son in Izmir that Pieter van Sanen was offering advantageous terms to firms in the United Provinces, which meant that he would receive a great number of commissions, something that de Vogel was quite happy about.[152] But when he found out that William Enslie, partner of David van Lennep, planned to consign all his goods to his younger brother in Amsterdam, de Vogel was less happy and advised his son to do business with van Lennep but to ignore Enslie, whose friendship was 'worthless'.[153] Some years later, Leonard de Vogel informed his brother Thomas in Izmir that he intended to leave the world of trade but that another brother de Vogel had entered a partnership with the same brother of Enslie in Amsterdam.[154] Such shifting alliances, sometimes accompanied by hefty language in commercial correspondence, were not at all uncommon in the early modern world of international trade.

The exact relationship between Ouckama and van Sanen, Clement and van der Zee is not clear, but obviously they all knew each other. They lived near

151 CAA/ADV, N°36, pp. 56–58, Letter Thomas de Vogel & Zoon to David van Lennep, Amsterdam, 06/06/1758; and ibid., pp. 175–177, Letter Thomas de Vogel & Zoon to David van Lennep, Amsterdam, 21/07/1758. Hakki Kadi wrote that de Vogel even asked his correspondents not to engage in business with Dirk Knipping, *Ottoman and Dutch merchants*, p. 203.

152 Heeringa and Nanninga, *Bronnen tot de geschiedenis*, 4: pp. 1229–1230, Thomas de Vogel & Zoon to Thomas de Vogel Junior, Amsterdam, 06/10/1767.

153 Ibid., p. 1231, Thomas de Vogel & Zoon to Thomas de Vogel Junior, Amsterdam, 22/12/1767, '[...] niets waard'.

154 Ibid., p. 1261, Leonard de Vogel to Thomas de Vogel Junior, Amsterdam, 23/04/1771.

one another in the European quarter of Izmir, but no specific references were made in the court documents about any social interactions between them. It was important for the litigants to avoid the blame for the destruction of a hitherto mutually beneficial commercial friendship, which explains the emotional tone of some of the court documents. Reports on certain behaviour in Izmir quickly found their way to traders in the United Provinces by means of business correspondence, and as all Dutch merchants in Izmir lived off commission trade, it was important to not damage one's reputation back home – as it would be difficult to repair from a distance. This explains why van Sanen was so upset to be labelled a 'phony friend' that he felt obliged to address a personal statement to the court in which he countered the accusations against him, in addition to the normal replies that he had sent as partner of the firm that was involved in the lawsuit against Pieter Ouckama & C°.[155] Van Sanen made it very clear that he wanted Ouckama to respond to the question whether he thought it was in his interest to hurt van Sanen's 'honour' ('eer'), which meant, of course, his personal reputation.[156]

Friendship between traders, founded on the notion of reciprocity and maintained through the cultivation of a business correspondence, formed the fabric of the international merchant community. Webs of friendships flourished and declined, and their functioning was not only subjected to the informal judgment of peers within that community but also to formal evaluation in court. Legal challenges to reputation were part and parcel of commercial litigation, and they were always taken seriously, as happened in the litigation between Ouckama and Wijnants & Cramer. In his personal statement, van Sanen wrote that in his firm, Ouckama was always mentioned with praise, and often, van Sanen was told by his peers that he 'was a sincere friend of Ouckama and even much taken with him'.[157]

It is important that van Sanen specifically mentioned that other merchants had labelled him as such. The possibility of evaluating a commercial friendship in court was an essential feature of the merchants' style, as it allowed for a formal evaluation of the functioning of relationships within the international merchant community on the basis of informal rules. Commercial friendship was part of it and came with expectations attached to it that could be evaluated in court. Perhaps the most important task of the judges at the consular court, which included merchants, was to make an assessment of the behaviour

155 NACS, N°330, 'Antwoord van dhr P: van Sanen particulier aan P. Ouckama weegens onderlinge vriendschap', Izmir, 07/02/1764, '[…] een valse vriend […]'.

156 Ibid.

157 Ibid., '[…] U is een reghte vriend van Ouckema x selvers heel starck van hem ingenoomen'.

of litigants in relation to what could reasonably be expected from them. If such assessment turned out to be negative, it would be known to colleagues, and the repercussions to one's reputation could be large. Just as van Sanen had been upset for being called a false friend, Ouckama was distressed about Wijnants & Cramer's insinuations that he and his firm were 'being considered as dishonest people [...] that is the most unfriendly term that one could ever put in public writing'.[158]

In essence, commercial litigation should be considered as trial by peers on the basis of the merchants' style, which was accepted by the state under whose jurisdiction the particular court adjudicating the matter resided. This acceptance could take a formal form through the absorption of mercantile custom in written-down local law or through the confirmation that a certain court needed to adjudicate on the basis of commercial custom, an instruction explicitly given to the consul of Aleppo in 1613 for instance.[159] It was a form of legalising merchant custom through jurisdiction and procedure, but not through the codification of law.

In their written exchanges, Ouckama and van Sanen had raised the stakes. A dispute that evolved around financial liability for a cargo of damaged cotton turned into a formal evaluation of commercial friendship. Van Sanen had explicitly mentioned reciprocity, a crucial principle, as the reason behind him assisting the French trader Majastre instead of helping Ouckama. Majastre assisted van Sanen during the fire, but Ouckama could not offer any help. Additionally, van Sanen had already provided Ouckama with several favours. As discussed above, Dutch merchants in Izmir did not engage much in commercial transactions with one another. The reciprocal services they were able to provide to one another were thus not directly related to business transactions between each other but had to do with helping out one's business with third parties – the services consisted of offering credit, introducing one another to new potential correspondents, accepting to put one's name on a particular shipment to avoid taxes and acting as the power of attorney in disputes, etc.[160]

The firm of Clement, van Sanen, van der Zee & C° not only provided a service to Wijnants & Cramer by their willingness to act as plaintiff on their behalf in the case against Ouckama, but they also assisted Ouckama in his

158 NACS, N°330, '3e replicq van Ouckama & Comp weeg Wijnantz & Cramer', Izmir, 28/02/1764, '[...] ons voor oneerlyke lieden te houden [...] dat is de onvriendelykste term die men ooyt in publicque geschriften kan stellen[...]'.

159 See pp. 131–132.

160 A good example of such a service was Arnoldus Wissing's acceptance to act on behalf of Clement, van Sanen, van der Zee & C° in trade. See p. 140.

operations on behalf of Wijnants & Cramer. They promised Ouckama cargo space on a ship they were part-owners of. They also aimed to help Ouckama with the shipment of the twenty-four bales of cotton that had not been damaged in the fire.[161] Clement and his partners accused Ouckama of not obeying his principals' instructions by shipping the undamaged bales on the ship of Severus Zeegenberg, which had not been the first to leave.[162] While Ouckama agreed that might indeed have been the case, he argued that, at the time, his information was that Zeegenberg would be the first Dutch skipper to leave. He also suggested that Clement, van Sanen, van der Zee & C° raised this point not to defend the interests of Wijnants & Cramer but to defend their own. Apparently, Clement and his partners had suggested that Ouckama could load the twenty-four bales of cotton on the *Jonge Jacob* of skipper Richard Horneer, which was partially owned by Clement, van Sanen, van der Zee & C°.[163] Ouckama felt they were trying to press him to load on their ship against the interests of his principals. For him, this was not only an unfair interpretation of what had happened, it was also an ungrateful action on their part. Ouckama claimed that many firms in Izmir were able to confirm that, in the past, he often shipped return cargos on behalf of principles in the Dutch Republic on ships in which Clement, van Sanen, van der Zee & C° had a share. While van Sanen defended his actions as services given to Ouckama, the latter thought of them as breaching commercial custom in their lack of consideration for the interests of others: 'friends who are friends out of interest are our enemies'.[164] This phrase was perhaps the most important in the whole trial in terms of connecting commercial friendship and expected behaviour with the merchants' style and the role of reciprocity. To fully do justice to the importance of the latter, we need to look at the idea merchants had about the mutual pursuit of profit, a concept rated as more important than self-interest.

---

161 To resume the situation, Ouckama had purchased sixty bales for Wijnants & Cramer, of which thirty-six had been damaged (sixteen out of a first purchase of forty, and all twenty of a second purchase). This left twenty-four undamaged bales of cotton that had to be shipped to the United Provinces.

162 NACS, N°330, 'Replicq van dhn Clement, van Sanen van der Zee & Comp op het antwoord van ouck & C°', Izmir, 24/01/1764.

163 In 1766, another ship (or the same one under a different name), the *Smirniotta*, captained by Richard Horneer, commissioned by Clement and loaded by van Sanen, van der Zee & C° to sail from Izmir to Stettin, was considered an Izmir-based action of the Prussian Royal Levant Company, which stood under the general directorship of Philippe Clement and whose establishment was contested by the Dutch. Heeringa and Nanninga, *Bronnen tot de geschiedenis*, 4: p. 44; see also pp. 209–213.

164 NACS, N°330, 'Replicq van Ouckama & C° aan Clement van Sanen, van der Zee & C°', Izmir, 26/01/1764, '[…] vrienden die uyt intrest vrienden zyn, zyn by ons vyanden […]'.

3.2 *The Mutual Pursuit of Profit*

Merchants accepted each other's pursuit of profit as long as it took place within the well-established set of rules developed in the merchants' style, which dictated that reciprocity was a key element of any business relationship. Self-interest at the expense of others was a serious infraction. In 1721, Consul Daniel Jean de Hochepied sent a letter to the States General reporting a fraud committed by a Jewish merchant, who had attempted to sell wax from Marseille to Dutch traders by pretending it was Ottoman wax. This led to a commercial boycott in the form of a *battelatie* issued by the English, Dutch and Venetian trading nations, who agreed to not conduct any business with the Jewish merchant for three months. In his report, the consul stressed that the trader in question had attempted these 'intrigues' for 'his own particular profit'.[165] This example is very informative for the scholarly debate on the motives behind economic behaviour. Often, self-interest has been considered the prime motivator for the rational *homo economicus*. This is subject to debate nowadays, and can be nuanced by contemporaries' views on trade, in which there was hardly any place for self-interest as a respectable motive behind economic action, as well.[166] For contemporaries, self-interest only had a place in economic activity if it was balanced within a wider context of mutual interests.[167]

Ouckama's accusation of acting out of self-interest was a serious one, potentially very damaging to the reputation of van Sanen and his partners. At first, van Sanen's firm denied that his firm has asked Ouckama to load the cotton on board Horneer's ship.[168] In a letter van Sanen sent the same day in his own name, however, he did admit that he had tried to convince Ouckama to load merchandise on that ship. Firstly, he wrote that Ouckama often preferred the ships of others to load his return cargo on but that could not be held against him, considering it was a choice he had to make in agreement with his principals in the United Provinces. Secondly, he wrote that he had spoken with Ouckama around the time that the *Vrouwe Berendina*, Zeegenberg's ship, arrived in Izmir carrying several parcels of cloth that belonged to a partnership between Sirp Ouckama and Abraham Musquetier & Zoon of Leiden, who

165 Heeringa and Nanninga, *Bronnen tot de geschiedenis*, 2: pp. 381–383, Consul Daniel Jean de Hochepied to the States General, Izmir, 25/08/1721, on p. 381, '[…] intrigues […]' and '[…] om sijn particulire profijt […]'. For the concept of *battelatie*, see p. 92.

166 When self-interest was mentioned in cases adjudicated by the Dutch consular court in Izmir, it was always with a negative connotation.

167 Apart from the cases studied in this book, it is also clear from the analysis of early modern business networks of diamond traders, see Vanneste, *Global trade*, pp. 81–84. For a theoretical discussion on self-interest as cultural construct, see ibid., pp. 14–20.

168 NACS, N°330, '2^{e} Replicq van dhn Clement van Sanen & Co', Izmir, 07/02/1764.

were shareholders in the vessel. Pieter Ouckama was charged with finding a return cargo for that ship in Izmir.[169] In his letter, Pieter van Sanen admitted he had spoken to Ouckama in an attempt to load the goods he already had, such as the cotton, on Horneer's ship, in which they had a share, instead of on the *Vrouwe Berendina*. Their argument was that the former was already one-third loaded and there was a shortage of merchandise on the quays in Izmir. If Ouckama agreed to load on Horneer's ship, he could demand Zeegenberg make an intra-Mediterranean journey. Van Sanen promised to help procure a return cargo for Zeegenberg in the meantime. This way, both ships would arrive in the United Provinces faster than they would have without this mutual assistance.[170]

This was an important letter, as it rebuffed Ouckama's accusation that van Sanen had acted out of self-interest in detail. To the contrary, he argued that he had thought of a construction that would help himself, Ouckama and both of their principals in the United Provinces. It was a proposal that was fully congruent with the merchants' style, and the reciprocity it dictated was explicitly mentioned by van Sanen when he wrote that 'when Zeegenberg returned, [I] would have helped him reciprocally'.[171] Van Sanen felt that Ouckama had ignored this good idea because of a growing personal antipathy towards van Sanen, which seemed to have blurred his good vision.[172] It was a big mistake to make, especially considering the importance of supplying reciprocity. Trade could indeed not exist when its participants only relied on their self-interests. But in this case, it was Ouckama's personal sentiment that apparently got in the way of good (i.e., reciprocally advantageous) business. It turned out that the shipping suggestions of van Sanen and his partners were not so ill-advised. The *Jonge Jacob*, Horneer's vessel, left Izmir before 22 August, less than three weeks after the fire. Hilkes' *Maria Dorothea* left sometime between 22 August

169 There were problems with that return cargo on behalf of Abraham Musquetier and Sirp Ouckama because of the same fire that led to the dispute with Wijnants & Cramer, which led to a separate court case. See NACS, N°336 ('Ouckama & C°, Nederlandse kooplieden te Smyrna, tegen A. Musquetier, koopman te Leiden, 1766'), 'Copije depositie van Sirp Ouckama d'Amstm weegens d'intresten van Ab:m Musquetier te Leijden met Ouckama & C° alhier', Amsterdam. The document was stamped by the burgomasters of Amsterdam on 23 May 1766 and received in Izmir on 7 July 1766.

170 NACS, N°330, 'Antwoord van dhr P: van Sanen particulier aan P. Ouckama weegens onderlinge vriendschap', Izmir, 07/02/1764.

171 Ibid., '[…] als capt Zeegenberg weederom quam zouden hem weeder reciproquelijk helpen […]'.

172 Ibid.

1763 and 22 February 1764, similar to Leuning's ship. Zeegenberg's *Vrouwe Berendina* only left between 22 February and 22 November later that year.[173]

The litigants agreed on one thing: the twenty-four bales could indeed have been shipped earlier, and the discussion in court continued by the addition of a declaration made by Wijnants & Cramer about the damaged cotton, supported by extracts of correspondence between them and Ouckama. The latter had indeed stored sixty bales of cotton in his warehouse, first forty and then twenty more. After the fire, he sent an account for the sixteen that had been damaged during the fire. This was not disputed; only the matter of who should carry the financial responsibility was disagreed upon. The story was different for the twenty bales, all marked with the logo of Wijnants & Cramer. These twenty were part of a quantity of forty-eight bales that had not been stored in the warehouse yet but in the passage that gave access to it. According to Ouckama's correspondence to Wijnants & Cramer, he had thrown them in the water before the fire had reached the warehouse, which suggested they had not been burned. Ouckama stated they had been damaged by falling debris, in the form of burning nails and wood, something Wijnants & Cramer found unlikely considering they were wet. But worse was the fact that Ouckama claimed to have done his utmost to recuperate as many of the bales as he could from the water but that several had been stolen. Wijnants & Cramer found it most bizarre that none of the recovered cotton carried their logo. More absurd was Ouckama's explanation that the debris had burned the cotton bales exactly at the place of the markings. They concluded that Ouckama had forged accounts and lied about the true ownership of the cotton. The lost cotton could not have been theirs, and thus they could not be held responsible.[174]

These were very severe accusations, in a case that already had become quite emotional, and Ouckama specifically wanted to write a personal statement to address the remarks made by Wijnants & Cramer about the seeming paradox of cotton being burned while being thrown in the sea at the same time, just as van Sanen had done almost three weeks earlier. For him, the Amsterdam-based firm was deliberately using 'confused language, cowardly evidence and

173 Heeringa and Nanninga, *Bronnen tot de geschiedenis*, 3: pp. 764–773, 'De waarde der goederen, die door de nationale en door de vreemde handelshuizen te Smirna zijn ingevoerd en uitgevoerd met Nederlandsche schepen, geboekt in de periode 22 augustus 1760 – 22 augustus 1765'.

174 NACS, N°330, 'Remarkes der heeren Wijnantz & Cramer over de reek: & reek: courant &a van de hn Ouckama & C° vertoond op 07/02/1764'. These remarks, written in Amsterdam at an unknown date, were shown in court on 07/02/1764.

false conclusions'.[175] Pieter Ouckama did not accept the accusations of forgery and deceitful keeping of books and labelled Wijnants & Cramer's arguments as 'erroneous talk, follies' and even as 'fake evidence' – 'a disgrace for such merchants'.[176] This makes perfect sense, as his reputation as a merchant and commission agent was on the line, which is why he defended himself so forcefully; he ended by stating that it he would have preferred not to react to such 'childish expressions and reflections' but that he felt obliged to 'reveal their disgrace' to the court.[177] He concluded with a cynical address to the consul personally, excusing himself for bothering him with this matter but that the consul should 'thank' ('danken') Wijnants, Cramer, Clement, van Sanen and van der Zee, as they were all embarrassed, 'not knowing how to behave, to give an appearance of legality to their case'.[178]

One day later, most of the arguments Ouckama had made in his personal statement were repeated in a new counter-reply made by the firm of Ouckama & C°.[179] The words remained passionate, and Wijnants & Cramer were accused of calling Ouckama & C° dishonest, without bringing any evidence, a very severe accusation, particularly when made in a public space.[180] The court felt that perhaps the tone was getting a bit out of hand. In the margin of the text, a message from the consul had been written down, which stated that Clement, van Sanen, van der Zee & C° had ten days to come forward with a new reply but had 'to avoid all scandalous and offensive expressions, and that no more unorderly and legally unfitting writings and expressions, which have been used thus far, will be allowed'.[181]

For the consul, both parties were getting carried away, something the two parties accused each other of as well. Both parties argued their case in the

175 NACS, N°330, 'Contra remarkes van Ouckama & C° op de remarkes van Wijnants & Cramer weegens de verbrande cattoen', Izmir, 27/02/1764, '[…] verwarde taal laff bewys x valsche conclusie […]'.

176 Ibid., '[…] mis praaten, gekheeden […] x valsche bewyzen […]' and '[…] het is schande voor zulke cooplieden […]'.

177 Ibid., '[…] kinderagtige gezegdens reflectien […]' and '[…] om aan uw ed gestr hunne schande bloot te stellen […]'.

178 Ibid., '[…] niet weetende hoe het te draagen, om schyn van regt aan hun zaak te geeven […]'.

179 NACS, N°330, '3^{e} replicq van Ouckama & Comp weeg Wijnantz & Cramer', Izmir, 28/02/1764.

180 Ibid. The firm felt that dishonesty was the most unfriendly accusation one could possibly make. See pp. 179–180.

181 Ibid., '[…] met versuijminge van alle skandaleuse en aenstottelyke termen also afkomstig gene sulke onordentelijke en in regte onbetaemelijke geschriften & uijtdrukkinge, gebruijkt zijn van parthijen sullen worden g'admiteerd'.

conviction they were right, or at least in the realisation that it was important to escape both legal and financial responsibility for the damaged goods. It can only be expected for a legal argument to become somewhat heated.[182] While using forms of economic rationality that had to do with the calculation of risk, and consideration of one's own interests against those of both the competition and collaborators, merchants in the early modern period also operated within a sociocultural context that allowed for emotions in business. Ties were forged partially based on kinship, the sharing of religion or nationality, trust and reputation. These criteria for cooperation can be situated in some sort of overlapping area in which the impersonal nature of the modern market exchange coincided with the personal nature of individual transactions. This area was the framework within which early modern merchants operated, and while it is impossible to guess their thoughts, most of the material that survived regarding business letters, memoranda, etc. demonstrates clearly that emotions and passions were part of the nature of business.[183] A similar argument was made by Emma Rothschild when she analysed Turgot's writings on a famous case brought before the criminal jurisdiction of Angoulême in 1769, when several bankers were accused of charging usurious interest rates. While historians and economists have looked mostly at the theoretical parts of Turgot's *Mémoire* that dealt with the matter, Rothschild argued for the importance of understanding the presence of sentiment and emotion in economic history.[184]

Several eighteenth-century economic thinkers were concerned with the role of commerce in softening the passions of men. Montesquieu wrote in his *Esprit des Lois* that 'commerce [...] polishes and softens barbarian ways as we can see everyday'.[185] But, in times of expanding international trade, the idea of commerce in itself was not sufficient to tame the more violent passions of men. Commerce could also corrupt society and destroy its fabric based on religion and traditional hierarchies, some argued, through the quest of traders to strive for their own enrichment. Commerce could even harm society by bringing in foreign elements and merchandise, as well as foreigners, considered a

182 Others used similar emotional language; see several of the case studies in chapters four and five, passim.

183 Vanneste, *Global trade*, pp. 81–91.

184 Emma Rothschild, 'An alarming commercial crisis in eighteenth-century Angoulême: Sentiments in economic history', *Economic history review*, 51:2 (1998): pp. 268–293.

185 Quoted in Albert O. Hirschman, *The passions and the interests – Political arguments for capitalism before its triumph* (Princeton, 1977), p. 60.

negative development by various contemporary thinkers.[186] The debate over the relationship between commerce, politics and society goes back a long way and was certainly not restricted to the eighteenth century.[187] The expansion of international trade during the seventeenth and eighteenth centuries added a new dimension to the debate, and several thinkers constructed a worldview in which trade could fulfil a positive and constructive role in society and within human relationships, thereby opposing those believing the opposite to be true. Jean-Jacques Rousseau, Adam Smith, Bernard Mandeville, Edmund Burke and others all considered the position of trade in society and the nature of the men who formed society.[188] Two main visions were put forward. From a negative point of view, trade would destroy traditional and harmonious society by promoting selfish values and foreign involvement. Charles Davenant (1656–1714) wrote that 'trade, without doubt, is in its nature a pernicious thing; it brings in that wealth which introduces luxury; it gives rise to fraud and avarice and extinguishes virtue and simplicity of manners'.[189] In a positive assertion,

---

186 See, for instance, J.G.A. Pocock, *Virtue, commerce, and history. Essays on political thought and history, chiefly in the eighteenth century* (Cambridge, 1985) for an analysis of the challenges the expansion of trade brought to politics; see also the essays in Istvan Hont and Michael Ignatieff, eds., *Wealth and virtue – The shaping of political economy in the Scottish enlightenment* (Cambridge, 1983); and Albert O. Hirschman, 'Rival interpretations of market society: Civilizing, destructive, or feeble?', *Journal of economic literature*, 20:4 (1982): pp. 1463–1484. For a discussion on negative and positive aspects of trade, see Vanneste, 'Commercial culture', pp. 14–32.

187 For an analysis, see Schröder, *Trust in early modern international political thought*, pp. 199–218.

188 See, for instance, Jean-Jacques Rousseau, *Les confessions, suivies des rêveries du promeneur solitaire* (Genève, 1782); Edmund Burke, *Reflections on the revolution in France, and on the proceedings in certain societies in London relative to that event. In a letter intended to have been sent to a gentleman in Paris. By the right honourable Edmund Burke* (London, 1793) for rather negative visions on trade and self-interest; and Josiah Child, *A new discourse of trade: Wherein are recommended several weighty points*, 4th ed. (London, [1745?]); Bernard Mandeville, *The fable of the bees, or, private vices, public benefits* (London, 1714); Jean-François Melon, *A political essay upon commerce. Written in French by monsieur M***. Translated, with some annotations, and remarks. By David Bindon, Esq* (Dublin, 1738); and, of course, Adam Smith, *An inquiry into the nature and causes of the wealth of nations* (London, 1776) for a more positive approach, which led to the idea of *homo economicus* and classical economics. For criticism of this model, see Geoffrey Ingham, 'Some recent changes in the relationship between economics and sociology', *Cambridge journal of economics*, 20:2 (1996): pp. 243–275.

189 Charles Davenant, 'Essay upon the probable methods of making a people gainers in the balance of trade', in *The political and commercial works of the celebrated writer Charles D'Avenant, LL.D. relating to the trade and revenue of England, the plantation trade, the East-India trade, and African trade. Collected and revised by Sir Charles Whitworth, etc.* (Farnborough, 1967), 2: p. 275.

commerce would do exactly the opposite, and a commercial society was also a peaceful society that could not be ruled by a despot without taking the desires and needs of his subjects into account. When a Jewish diamond trader wrote an anonymous pamphlet to defend the idea of the naturalisation of Jews in England, one of his main arguments was the utility of the Jewish diaspora as traders.[190]

Both those who defended and those who attacked commerce could agree on one thing: societies needed laws so individual passions could be directed towards contributing to the public good. Jean-François Melon wrote in the 1730s that 'if men were so happy, as to regulate their actions, according to the pure maxims of religion, they would not have occasion for laws. Duty would serve, as a curb to vice, and an incitement to virtue. But, unhappily for us, we are swayed by our passions, and the legislature should only endeavour, to turn them to the best advantage of the community'.[191] This applied to society in general but also to well-regulated commerce, something that was clearly recognised by the Dutch ambassador in Istanbul, Elbert de Hochepied, in 1754, when he had his ideas on Levant trade put to paper in a *Mémoire*: 'men need laws to oblige them to practice that what is essential to their communal happiness, traders are essentially in need of them, they form the main body of the state, particularly in the United Provinces'.[192] De Hochepied was an advocate of trade and recognised its importance for the United Provinces as a state. He was of the opinion that it was the traders' habit to exalt freedom in commerce but, he added, too few of them paid attention to the fact that this freedom

---

190 Philo-patriae, *Considerations on the bill to permit persons professing the Jewish religion to be naturalized by parliament* (London, 1753); and *Further considerations on the act to permit persons professing the Jewish religion, to be naturalized by parliament* (London, 1753). The link made between commerce and Jews has often been used in anti-Semitic tropes and persisted over time, finding its way into academia as well. For an analysis, see, for instance, Benjamin Braude, 'The myth of the Sephardi economic superman', in *Trading cultures: The worlds of western merchants*, eds. Jeremy Adelman and Stephen Aron (Turnhout, 2001), pp. 165–194 and the references therein; as well as Benjamin Arbel, 'Jews in international trade: The emergence of the Levantine and Ponentines', in *The Jews of early modern Venice*, eds. R.C. Davis and B. Ravid (Baltimore and London, 2001), pp. 73–96. Francesca Trivellato has rightfully remarked that '[…] depictions of Jewish economic roles test the inclusivity of the Enlightenment trope of commerce as sociability'; Trivellato, *The promise and peril of credit*, p. 130.

191 Melon, *A political essay upon commerce*, pp. 173–174.

192 NA, N°2.21.006.46, N°2 ('Mémoire pour le commerce', 1754), f°4r, '[…] il faut aux hommes des loix pour les obliger à pratiquer ce qui est essential à leur bonheur commun, les commerçans en ont essentiellement besoins, ils forment le corps principal de l'état, surtout dans les Provinces Unies'.

caused disorder, which harmed the state. Freedom in trade, he continued, had to be limited by the state so the merchant's quest for individual profit would benefit the state.[193] This was the authorities' general attitude towards trade and a reason why commercial structures were developed by the state.[194]

It is no surprise then that the ambassador's nephew, Daniel Jean de Hochepied, consul in Izmir and thus responsible for adjudicating commercial disputes between Dutch merchants, aimed to preserve clear legal proceedings without the ballast of statements made by merchants about one another that were too passionate. Trade was crucial, and merchants had to be allowed to operate within a clear framework that allowed them to flourish. Limiting litigation, or at least restricting it to clear legal arguments that could be judged by the consul, assisted by his assessors who were, as fellow merchants, peers of the litigating parties, was a crucial part of this. Reflections on the regulating role the state should play in the world of international commerce were also behind efforts authorities made to enable a legal environment within which traders could litigate, even if the litigation itself took place on the basis of an operational context that was shaped by the merchants' style.

3.3 *International Support for the Merchants' Style*

In the trial between Ouckama and Wijnants & Cramer, litigation continued by turning to international merchant custom as confirmed by a group of traders from different backgrounds. The increasingly heated tone of both parties made it clear that the case was far from resolved, and in March 1764, the consul

193 Ibid. This was the authorities' general attitude towards trade and a reason why commercial structures were developed by the state. In the United Provinces, cities competed with one another to attract trade through the development of an institutional framework, see Gelderblom, *Cities of commerce*. Mercantilist policies can be considered a form of economic competition between states, a competition that grew throughout the early modern period. See Oscar Gelderblom, 'The organization of long-distance trade in England and the Dutch Republic, 1550–1650', in *The political economy of the Dutch Republic*, ed. Oscar Gelderblom (Farnham, 2009), pp. 223–254; and M.N. Pearson, 'Merchants and states', in *The political economy of merchant empires*, ed. James Tracy (Cambridge, 1991), pp. 41–116. For a profound analysis of trade, nations and economic thinking in the eighteenth century, see Istvan Hont, *Jealousy of trade. International competition and the nation-state in historical perspective* (Cambridge, MA and London, 2005).

194 Emma Rothschild, *Economic sentiments – Adam Smith, Condorcet, and the Enlightenment* (Cambridge, MA and London, 2007), p. 72. Providing assistance to the state was one of the motivations behind the developing field of political economy. See Terence Hutchison, *Before Adam Smith – The emergence of political economy, 1662–1776* (Oxford and New York, 1988); and for an eighteenth-century example, Etienne Bonnot (Abbé de Condillac), *Commerce and government considered in their mutual relationship*, trans. Shelagh Eltis (Indianapolis, 2008).

requested the opinion of French, English and Dutch firms in Izmir about the responsibility for damaged merchandise in a transaction between an agent and a principal. Most argued that it differed from case to case, particularly based on whether a specific order had been given, but that generally the agent was responsible.[195] That these declarations were collected by the plaintiffs did not seem to have affected their legal status. It is remarkable that even in a case involving only Dutch traders, the only evidence that was used outside of the respective traders' business papers and their declarations was a declaration by non-Dutch merchants. This, in combination with the various references to the merchants' style in the declarations, forms an important indication that a reliance on merchant custom was much more prevalent in legal procedures than a reliance on some formal, national body of law. In none of the more than thirty documents brought into this case was any reference made to Dutch law. The argumentation centred on responsibility according to the terms set by merchant custom, which had to be determined from the reasoning of the litigants, and additional declarations by the merchant community as a whole. This was an international matter because merchant custom was international, and in the legal reasoning, the nationality of the litigants did not play any role. It was normal for courts to rely on declarations from experts as evidence, particularly in courts dealing with commercial disputes – a judge, such as the consul, could not be expected to be aware of all current merchant custom. A reliance on merchants, either as assistant-judges or as outside experts, was crucial to a good functioning court.[196]

The use of expert declarations is directly related to adjudication on the basis of unwritten rules and custom. A litigant could question the legitimacy of the rule in question, which was considered proven in case a group of knowledgeable persons issued a declaration confirming the rule or custom. Such a declaration was called a *turbe*.[197] For Oscar Gelderblom, the use of *turben* in court was 'legislation from below', which revealed 'how sensitive urban magistrates, in this case from Antwerp and Amsterdam, were to demands from merchants'.[198] *Turben* had indeed also spread to Amsterdam, and the earliest example of their

195 NACS, N°330, 'Parere van Clement van Sanen van der Zee & C° weeg: de differentie met Ouckama & C°', Izmir, 21/03/1764.

196 For a recent historical overview on the role of experts in the Anglo-Saxon legal system, see Déirdre Dwyer, *The judicial assessment of expert evidence* (Cambridge, 2008).

197 See p. 110. For a contemporary discussion on the rules concerned with proving custom in the Dutch context, see Decker, *Het Roomsch Hollandsch recht* 1: pp. 30–31.

198 Gelderblom, *Cities of commerce*, p. 99. The use of expert declarations can be found in other commercial cities as well. For Venice, see Fusaro, *Political economies*, pp. 180–181.

use there dates from 1554, where they were used to deal with issues of payments to be made by creditors.[199] One of the discussions included in J.M. Barels' compilation of advice regarding trade and maritime navigation from 1781 centred on the relationship between principal and agent. Barels stated that no one could take any action or make any claim on merchandise in the hands of an agent unless the agent had been paid for what he was due. The reason behind this custom was the importance of commission trade and the central role of the agent, which needed to be protected. According to Barels, this rule was 'according to the notorious customs and usages generally observed amongst merchants', and it was confirmed in Amsterdam by a *turbe* from 1591.[200] A compilation of *turben* concerning commercial matters, published in Amsterdam at the end of the eighteenth century, was considered an important collection and was used to save time in court. The preface indicated that *turben* were used to avoid lengthy and costly procedures. Although they were considered as less crucial than laws made by sovereigns, they were founded on the basis of 'reason and equity' and were 'accepted by venerable courts'.[201] Because the drafting of such declarations took time, it was agreed in 1788 that merchants would only sign a *turbe* if it was clear that a copy of it would go to the publisher of the *Verzameling van casuspositien*.[202] Most interestingly, some of the declarations on the merchants' style issued by merchants in Izmir in legal disputes were not only signed by Europeans but also by Ottomans.[203]

The inclusion of Ottomans as experts or witnesses in European courts was neither very common nor exceptional. The case files in this dispute contain three translations concerning the registration of the payment of Ottoman export duties, the *bid'a*, on forty-eight bales of cotton delivered to Ouckama's warehouse the day before the fire. One came from an Armenian trader, Aszadur di Balta, who had received Ouckama's order to pay in cotton and who was one of the abovementioned Ottoman intermediaries. The second was a declaration by Mustapha, a scribe at the office for the *bid'a* on cotton in Izmir,

199 *Handvesten, privilegien, octroyen, costumen en willekeuren der stad Amstelredam* (Amsterdam, 1663), p. 187.

200 Barels, *Advysen over den koophandel en zeevaert*, 1: p. 78, '[...] alles agtervolgens de notoire costumenen usance onder de kooplieden alomme geobserveerd wordende, en waer van binnen deeze stad Amsterdam by forme van turbe bereids gedaen en verklaeringe genomen is in den jaere 1591'.

201 *Verzameling van casuspositien*, 1: pp. iii–iv, '[...] op de reden en billykheid gegrond [...] door zeer venerabele rechtbanken zyn aangenomen [...]'.

202 Ibid., p. v. This is a confirmation of the legitimacy of such compilations as sources for commercial law as argued by Lichtenauer. See pp. 109–110.

203 For an example, see figure 8.

confirming the forty-eight bales had been registered, which was confirmed by a declaration in Hebrew by three Jewish men who also worked for the Ottoman tax office.[204] The declaration of the men working at the *bid'a*, including one who was perhaps a Muslim man called Yūsuf, demonstrates that in a matter in which Ottoman-European relations were not at stake, it was not difficult to obtain official declarations from individuals within Ottoman fiscal structures, showing a willingness from Ottoman officials to cooperate with European demands, as long as they did not interfere with the functioning of Ottoman institutions.[205]

In March 1764, Ouckama was finally allowed to take an oath on the veracity of his earlier declarations, something he had insisted on giving but which he had not been allowed to do. The oath was not taken lightly, as it could be a crucial factor in determining the trial's outcome. On the fourteenth, Ouckama physically appeared before the consul, who agreed that the oath had become necessary, as Ouckama's honour and reputation were at stake.[206] It was taken one day after Ouckama sought the opinion of various merchants from Izmir on the whole matter. While Clement, van Sanen, van der Zee & C° had obtained a similar declaration in favour of Wijnants & Cramer, Ouckama managed to obtain signatures from several firms that had first testified on behalf of Wijnants & Cramer but changed their minds, and he also managed to obtain several more, seventeen in total, from Frenchmen, Italians, one Armenian and the Dutch firms of David van Lennep & Enslie and Panaiotis & de Vogel (see figure 7).[207] They all felt that Ouckama could not be blamed for using his own money to buy cotton for others, a fact used by the plaintiffs to argue it was Ouckama's cotton and not theirs. They further stated that, once the principal trader abroad had requested certain purchases, and his agent was keeping him informed about the process, the principal had to take full responsibility for them. It was both an argument of reason and fully in line with commercial practices that existed within the larger mercantile community, and the argument was well received by the consul. Together with the assessors, the consul finally reached a verdict in May 1764. Remarkably, one of assessors assisting on

204 NACS, N°330, 'Traductie van een Armeens en een Turks att: weeg: de bewuste 48 verloore B: cattoen van Ouckama & C°', Izmir, 27/02/1764; and NACS, N°330, 'Traductie van een hebrees att: van den Bedaetgi der catt: dat Ouckama & C° dags voor de brand 48 B: cattoen heefft ontfange', Izmir, 27/02/1764.

205 See also note 32 on p. 274.

206 NACS, N°330, 'Acte van de beeedigde declaratoir van P. Ouckama weegens zijn directie in de brand gehouden &a', Izmir, 14/03/1764.

207 NACS, N°330, 'Request van Ouckama & C° tot geleijde van eene parere', Izmir, 13/03/1764.

the case was Dirk Knipping, Ouckama's former business partner, while another was William Enslie, who had signed the merchants' declaration that was in Ouckama's favour. Normally, Pieter van Sanen should have been assisting in this case as assessor as well, but considering he was acting on behalf of the plaintiff, he was excused.

At several stages during the trial, merchants were demanded to give their opinion – as assessors assisting in the adjudication but also as experts offering declarations of their interpretation of commercial custom. Before agreeing on a verdict, the consul and assessors submitted all the paperwork involved in the case to three neutral persons, all merchants. They remained unnamed in all of the documentation, but their judgment was considered important in the process of reaching a final sentence, which concluded that 'justice and equity is in aspects on the side of the gentlemen Ouckama & C°'[208] Equity had indeed been an important consideration: 'considering that those gentlemen [Wijnants & Cramer], if all had ended well, would probably have gained a considerable profit, and considering that they would have enjoyed that profit all alone, without sharing with Ouckama & C°, so it seems just to us that they would have to carry and suffer all by themselves also the damages that came from above, without guilt of the gentlemen Ouckama & C°'.[209] The latter firm had 'defended and justified itself in all the necessary matters, in decent form, and with many demonstrations of truth'.[210] Clement, van Sanen, van der Zee & C° were given thirty days to pay the money that Wijnants & Cramer owed, as well as all legal expenses.[211]

The acquittal of Ouckama & C° and the confirmation of the liability of the principal are not remarkable and can be considered as evidence of the changing perceptions of European *ius commune* under the pressure of expanding trade. When international trade grew, the role of the agent became crucial. Roman law had no general concept of agency and did not recognise contracts made on behalf of third parties – even though situations involving middlemen

208 NACS, N°330, 'Sententie van de heeren consul & assessooren in de differentie van dh:n Clement v. sanen van der Zee & C° met dh:n Ouckama & C°', Izmir, 23/05/1764, '[…] soo is het regt en billijkhijd in allen deelen aen de zijde van de heeren Ouckama & C° […]'.

209 Ibid., '[…] considereerende dat die heeren, in dien alles wel affgeloopen was, en seer vermoedlijk een aensienelijke winst hadden affgeworpen, die winst alleen souden hebben genooten sonder de selve met de heeren ouckama & comp te deelen, soo schijnd het ons meede billijk dat zij de schaade als van hoogerhand sonder schuld van de heeren ouckama & C° gekoomen daar van ook alleen moeten draagen x lijden'.

210 Ibid., '[…] haer in alle het noodige in soo behoorelijke forma, en met soo veel blijken van waerhijd, hebben verdeedigt en geregtvaerdigt […]'.

211 Ibid.

were acknowledged.[212] The use of agents in international trade created a situation in which there were two legal arrangements instead of one – between the principal and the agent and between the agent and the buyer/seller. According to Reinhard Zimmermann, seventeenth-century Dutch scholars, influenced by natural law, developed the concept of the principal's liability in both arrangements, and they did so 'from the point of view of commercial practice and the mores hodierni'.[213] Thus, the concept of liability in the relationship between principal and agent had developed in spite of its absence in the Roman legal tradition and under pressure from the practices attached to early modern international trade. Adjudicating matters of liability for damage to merchandise in light of the principal-agent relationship is therefore not only a judgment about one of the most crucial characteristics of international trade, it is also a clear example of how the merchants' style came to full fruition as an internationally accepted legal concept situated between custom, as arising out of commercial practice, and law, as inspired by the context of *ius commune* but not limited by it. One can even argue that early modern juridical assessments of commercial agency led to a codification of the concept in the nineteenth century.[214]

It was not uncommon for the losing party to appeal, and they would generally do so by registering a demand for appeal at the consular court, after which, theoretically, the appeal procedure could start. This is what Clement, van Sanen, van der Zee & C° decided to do, and they sent a request for appeal, to be litigated 'before higher judges, where it should be treated'.[215] The general reference to higher judges, without specifying a particular court, was common amongst demands for appeal and might suggest that it was not always immediately clear which court was qualified to deal with the appeal. There were a number of seventeenth-century regulations, issued by the States General, clarifying which court had jurisdiction for appeals. According to a law issued in February 1686, the verdict of a case brought before the consular court that only involved traders from Holland could be appealed before the *Hof van Holland* or the *Hoge Raad*. Should there be other Dutchmen involved, particularly as defendants, the appeal had to be brought before the States General instead.[216]

---

212 For a detailed overview of Roman legal concepts of agency and third-party involvement and early modern changes, see Zimmermann, *The law of obligations*, pp. 45–58.

213 Ibid., p. 57. 'Mores hodierni' means modern manners.

214 Ibid., p. 58.

215 NACS, N°330, 'Appel der heeren Clement van sanen van der zee & C° op de sententie van 25 meij 1764', Izmir, 28/05/1764, '[…] voor hooger regters alwaar zulks dienen moeten'. For appeals, see pp. 265–272.

216 See pp. 266–267. The States General's sentencing relied on the advice issued at either the *Hof van Holland* or the *Hoge Raad*.

But in reality, there were hardly any cases brought before the Dutch consul in Izmir that only involved Dutchmen, and even less in which the litigants all came from Holland. Neither in the archives of the *Hof van Holland*, nor in those of the *Hoge Raad*, appeal cases on consular verdicts can be found. There were, however, a number of appeals that involved traders who were active in the Levant and who had been involved in litigation before a lower court in the United Provinces.

The archives do not reveal further traces of the appeal made by Clement, van Sanen, van der Zee & C°. The consul had accepted it under the condition that the sentence would be executed first, as stipulated in the February 1686 regulations.[217] The most interesting thing the request to appeal demonstrates is the grounds for appeal invoked in it: 'we the underwritten [Clement, van Sanen, van der Zee & C°] have proven sufficiently in our delivered writings that these gentlemen Ouckama & C° have, in this case, acted beyond their orders and disregarded the merchants' style'.[218]

Intra-Dutch litigation, as discussed in the cases in this part, was rare. Most cases involved a foreign plaintiff, and in the cases in which both litigants were Dutch, the plaintiff generally resided in the United Provinces, a consequence of the fact that Dutch Levant trade was commission trade – if a Dutch merchant was tried as defendant before the consular court in Izmir, it was often because a commission was disputed. Evidence shows that in none of these intra-Dutch disputes was there any mention of Dutch written law, except in arguments about procedure or the court's jurisdiction. The only concrete references these parties made were to the merchants' style, and these were regularly very specific and found explicit support through the declarations of experts. The latter were often foreign, and there were no indications that the nationality of the litigants was relevant for the trial. Dutch litigants who were tried by the Dutch consul in Izmir were merchants first and Dutchmen second. It was only when Ouckama complained that he was not helped by a fellow national during the August fire that nationality seems to have played a role in legal reasoning. In this case, it stood opposite the merchant custom of reciprocity, as was argued by Clement, van Sanen, van der Zee & C°. The lack of importance given to nationality by Consul Daniel Jean de Hochepied was never considered strange.[219]

---

217 NACS, N°330, 'Appel der heeren Clement van sanen van der zee & C° op de sententie van 25 meij 1764', Izmir, 28/05/1764.

218 Ibid., 'Wy ondergeschreeven genoeg aangetoondt hebben in onse overgeleeverden geschriften deesen heeren Ouckama & C° in deesen saak buyten orders x coopmansteyl te hebben te werk gegaan [...]'.

219 See also pp. 171–172 and 260–261.

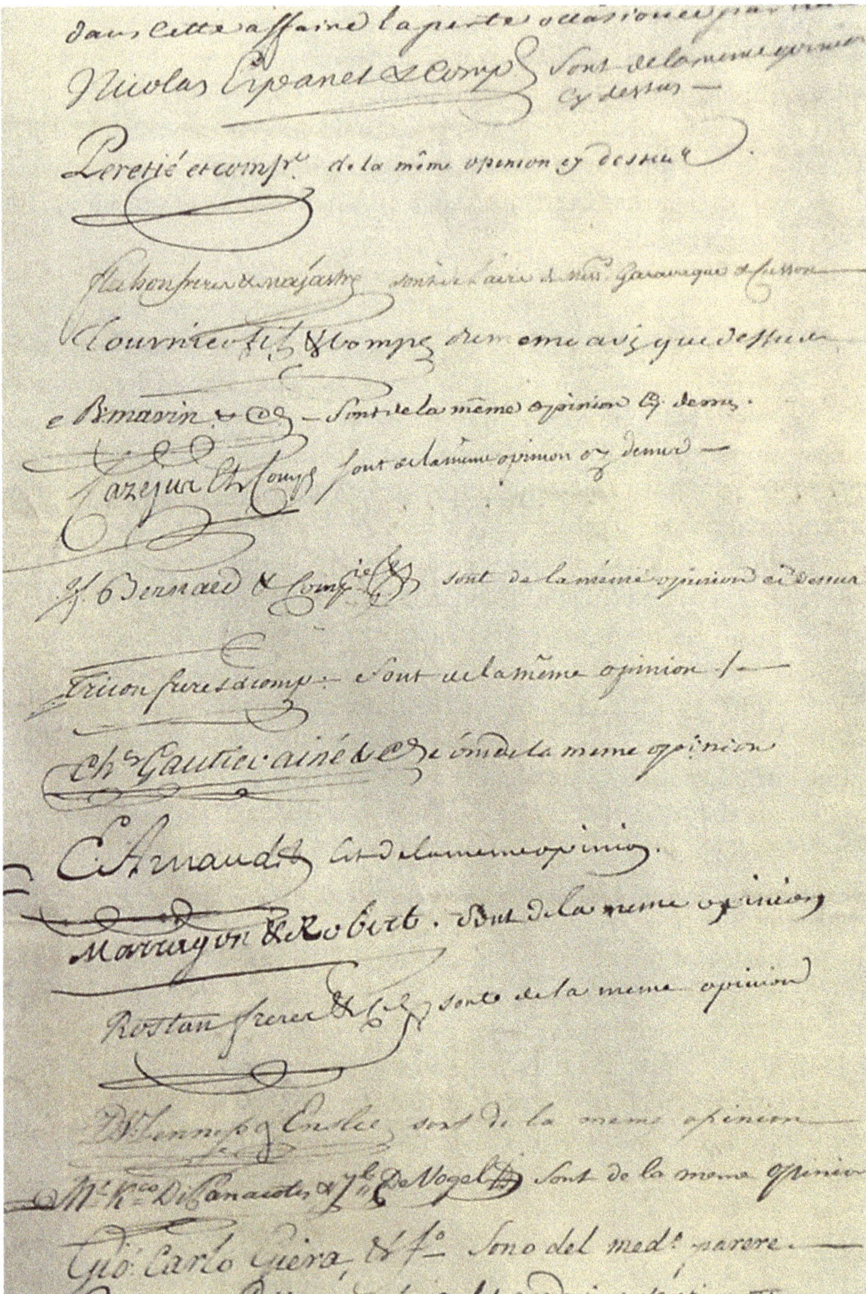

FIGURE 7 Signatures of merchants on an opinion [*parere*] in support of the argument of Pieter Ouckama, 13 March 1764

FROM THE DUTCH NATIONAL ARCHIVES, THE HAGUE (ARCHIVES OF THE DUTCH CONSULATE IN SMYRNA). PHOTO BY THE AUTHOR.

The ease with which merchants issued powers of attorney to ensure legal representation at a court far away is remarkable and further testimony to the successful integration of the merchants' style – here, expressed by the apparent, self-evident acceptance of powers of attorney as a commercial favour – into legal procedure. It is harder to estimate whether geographical distance played a role in punishment. Wijnants & Cramer was a firm established in Amsterdam, and both partners most likely never set foot in the Levant. The court's sentence, of course, led to a losing party who was made to pay. But the consul in Izmir could not force Wijnants & Cramer to pay. Should they refuse, the opposite party only had two options to force them: The first was the legal option, having their assets sequestered; the second was found in the merchants' style. A trader hoping to remain in business could not afford to ignore a legal verdict. In addition to legal and commercial pressure to force traders into compliance, there was also a social option that applied within merchant communities. Social forms of punishment for cheating traders existed when community leaders were bestowed with adjudicating powers. This was the case for several foreign trading communities in which unity was based on religion, such as the Jewish diaspora, but it also applied to European national trading communities in the Ottoman Empire, whose consuls equally had been bestowed with adjudicating powers by a host society. Some Dutch traders received forms of social sanctioning – although this seems to have been a very uncommon measure. Dirk Knipping, for instance, was thrown out of a partnership and ended up living in the Armenian neighbourhood (see figure 4).[220] Other Dutch nationals were (temporarily) stripped of their Dutch national status because of infractions they had committed – a fate that befell several partners of the firm of Clement, van Sanen, van der Zee & C°, who had become involved in official Prussian Levant trade and even took up diplomatic posts for Prussia.[221] Gerrit van Brakel ended up being a social pariah for several years because he could not afford to fulfil the financial requirements of a negative verdict.[222] It seems, then, that a plaintiff abroad had sufficient faith in his legal representative and the merchant community at large that a favourable sentence would indeed be upheld – and there could be social repercussions if a verdict was not respected. The options at the court's disposal to settle intra-Dutch disputes, including social ostracism, served less effectively in cases where one of the

220 See pp. 70–71 and 164.

221 See pp. 209–213.

222 See p. 237.

litigants was not Dutch.[223] Most court cases that the Dutch consul in Izmir adjudicated were international disputes between parties of different nationalities and religious affiliation.

---

223 Social ostracism as form of punishment for fraudulent merchants has often been studied in the context of diasporas, such as the Sephardic Jewish one. See, for instance, Yosef Kaplan, 'Political concepts in the world of the Portuguese Jews of Amsterdam during the seventeenth century: The problem of exclusion and the boundaries of self-identity', in *Menasseh Ben Israel and his world*, eds. Y. Kaplan, H. Méchoulan and R.H. Popkin (Leiden, 1989), pp. 45–62. It was a however a wider spread mechanism of punishment that was available to all foreign trading communities in a host society, and it is therefore unsurprising the Dutch in Izmir also made use of it.

CHAPTER 4

Europeans at the Dutch Consular Court

1 Belonging to a European Trade Nation Abroad

1.1 Forum Rei *and a Clash of Laws*

Because the consular court sentenced on the basis of the merchants' style, it was equipped to adjudicate disputes that involved fellow European traders as well as Ottomans. To avoid confusion or controversy over jurisdiction, the European merchants in the Levant relied on *forum rei*. This was a legal custom of that came out of Roman law and was usually the default principle that settled jurisdiction. It was part of *ius commune* and essentially meant that a dispute between litigants falling under different jurisdictions was adjudicated at the court under whose jurisdiction the defendant fell. By the middle of the eighteenth century, it already had a long tradition in Europe of adjudicating disputes that involved foreign merchants or traders coming from different localities. The United Provinces also made use of the principle, which had been codified in Burgundian law.[1] For *forum rei* to work in the Levant, however, it needed to be embedded in the Ottoman context. This happened in 1740, when the French received a renewed and very extensive set of capitulations, and *forum rei* became an officially Ottoman-sanctioned solution for determining which European consular court was to adjudicate a dispute – at a time when it had been in use for intra-European litigation for years.[2]

It seems that *forum rei* was generally accepted amongst litigants, even if it meant that a trader who felt his sentence had been unjust had to appeal at a court that could be far away. The general acceptance of this legal custom in the merchant community had not come about without some discussion and controversy, and at times, *forum rei* was challenged by diplomats who tried to bend the practice of law in favour of their subjects. Six months after the inclusion of the *forum rei* principle in the French capitulations, for instance, the Dutch ambassador in Istanbul, Cornelis Calkoen, wrote a letter to the States General about the fraudulent bankruptcy of two Venetian Jewish merchants.[3] Calkoen complained that the Venetian ambassador had sequestered goods

1 Decker, *Het Roomsch Hollandsch recht*, 2: pp. 353–354.

2 Van den Boogert, *The capitulations*, p. 36. See p. 86.

3 For an analysis of bankruptcy in the early modern Ottoman context, see van den Boogert, *The capitulations*, pp. 207–262.

DOI:10.1163/9789004498235_006

that had come from Holland, and had consigned them to the bankrupts, without informing Calkoen. The bankrupts had been ordered to sell these goods on commission. The Dutch ambassador also complained that his Venetian colleague had issued a judgment which rendered all Dutch traders in the Ottoman Empire liable for goods that the bankrupts had sent to Holland prior to their bankruptcy and that the value of these goods would serve to reimburse Ottoman creditors.[4]

Additionally, the fraudulent nature of the bankruptcy was considered enough reason to guarantee that the consigned goods remained in full ownership of the Dutch merchants who had sent them. Calkoen asked that the Venetian ambassador hand over these goods to the Dutch nation and suggested negotiating a further settlement of the bankruptcy, for which specific legal procedures existed.[5] He also proposed that two neutral merchants, neither Dutch nor Venetian, would be appointed jointly by himself and his Venetian colleague. Calkoen wanted the three administrators – two Venetians and a Frenchman – that had been dealing with the bankruptcy to be dismissed, as he had insufficient faith in these men 'on whose integrity much can be said'.[6]

The problem that had arisen was not so much a dispute on the legal custom of *forum rei*, nor was it caused by a different interpretation of the merchants' style; rather, it originated from the fact that bankruptcy procedures were part of national written laws. Their application in an international and intercultural context, in which existing national written laws had less use than international custom in practice, but could nonetheless be invoked in theory, made bankruptcy procedures particularly vulnerable for legalistic quarrels between consuls of different nations.[7] Different localities developed their own statutes

---

4 Heeringa and Nanninga, *Bronnen tot de geschiedenis*, 3: pp. 140–142, Ambassador Cornelis Calkoen to Fagel, Istanbul, 26/11/1740. Evidence shows that, much like the European diplomats looking out for 'national' commercial interests, Ottoman courts protected the commercial interests of Ottoman subjects. Van den Boogert, *The capitulations*, p. 261.

5 See pp. 201–206.

6 Heeringa and Nanninga, *Bronnen tot de geschiedenis*, 3: pp. 140–142, Ambassador Cornelis Calkoen to Fagel, Istanbul, 26/11/1740, '[...] op wiens integriteit al veel te zeggen zoude vallen [...]'.

7 There is the argument that an insolvent trader's problems with creditors could be projected on the community to which the trader belonged. Avner Greif, 'History lessons. The birth of impersonal exchange: The community responsibility system and impartial justice', *Journal of economic perspectives*, 20:2 (2006): pp. 221–236; 'On the social foundations and historical development of institutions that facilitate impersonal exchange: From the community responsibility system to individual legal responsibility in pre-modern Europe' (June 12, 1997), SSRN working paper No. 97-016, consulted online at https://ssrn.com/abstract=47178 or http://dx.doi.org/10.2139/ssrn.47178.

and laws on insolvency and bankruptcy, although there was a shared tradition through the medieval spreading of northern Italian bankruptcy laws by means of the system of European market fairs.[8] What is striking in these laws is the severe punishment it allowed for someone unable to pay back their debts – these included corporal punishment and imprisonment.[9] This can be traced back to Roman law, which considered an insolvent person automatically fraudulent, according to the principle *fallitus ergo fraudator* ('insolvent thus a swindler').[10] Bankruptcy procedures came into being to settle the different debts an insolvent person had towards different creditors. Without it, creditors competed with one another trying to get some of their money back, but bankruptcy law enabled an insolvent person to file for bankruptcy and to reach a legal settlement with the creditors.[11] The fact that definitions of insolvency in city regulations in Antwerp issued at the end of the sixteenth and beginning of the seventeenth century changed, not only demonstrates the continuing struggle to define exactly the legal meaning of insolvency and bankruptcy, it also puts the emergence of the idea that insolvency was not per definition fraudulent on display.[12] The nature of insolvency needed to be investigated, and what did become increasingly important, then, was to look at the reputation of an insolvent trader as part of the assessment of whether he had acted bona fide or in a fraudulent manner.[13]

A common denominator that applied to bankruptcy procedures in most of early modern continental Europe, but not in England, was the possibility

8 Jérôme Sgard, 'Bankruptcy, fresh start and debt renegotiation in England and France (17th to 18th century), in *The history of bankruptcy: Economic, social and cultural implications in early modern Europe*, ed. Thomas Max Safley (London, 2013), pp. 223–235; see also Umberto Santarelli, *Per la storia del fallimento delle legislazioni italiane dell'età intermedia* (Padova, 1964). For the common European origins through the development of bankruptcy laws in Italy in the thirteenth and fourteenth centuries, see Joseph Kohler, *Lehrbuch des Konkursrecht* (Stuttgart, 1892); and Maura Fortunati, 'Note sul diritto di fiera nelle fonti giuridiche di età moderna', in *Fiere e mercati nella integrazione delle economie europee secc. xiii–xvii*, ed. S. Cavaciocchi (Firenze, 2001), pp. 953–966. For England, see W.J. Jones, *The foundations of English bankruptcy: Statutes and commissions in the early modern period* (Philadelphia, 1979).

9 Karl Gratzer, 'Introduction', in *History of insolvency and bankruptcy from an international perspective*, eds. Karl Gratzer and Dieter Stiefel (Södertörn, 2008), p. 6.

10 Ibid. The translation is Gratzer's.

11 Ibid.

12 Dave De ruysscher, 'Designing the limits of creditworthiness: Insolvency in Antwerp banking legislation and practice (16th–17th centuries)', *Tijdschrift voor rechtsgeschiedenis*, 76 (2008): pp. 317–319.

13 Ibid., pp. 318–319.

for an insolvent trader to make private arrangements with his creditors that ensured the possibility of him continuing to do business – it made starting over again easier.[14] In the United Provinces, bankruptcy procedures were regulated according to city custom, even though Charles v had issued general legislation for the Spanish Netherlands in 1531 and 1540.[15] Antwerp had one of the most extensive bodies of city laws (*costumen*) with regard to bankruptcies, which may have been applied all over the Spanish Netherlands. They were written down in 1540, 1582 and 1609.[16] In the United Provinces, Amsterdam had the first codified bankruptcy law, based on city custom that was partially inspired by regulations in Antwerp.[17] In Amsterdam, a bankrupt's estate was controlled by the aldermen, who appointed administrators (who could be creditors or other able persons). The curators made an inventory, controlled, formalised and overseen by a sheriff (*schout*), two aldermen, a notary and witnesses. Curators had the authority to sell goods and to consign monies to the city. The growth of the city made it impossible for the aldermen to adjudicate all disputes in Amsterdam, which led to the establishment of specialised courts during the first half of the seventeenth century.[18] This included a specific court to deal with insolvencies and bankruptcy cases in 1643, the Chamber of Insolvent Estates (*Desolate Boedelskamer*). Later, other Dutch cities followed suit.[19] The Amsterdam Chamber of Insolvent Estates operated on the basis of an ordinance issued on 6 November 1643. It was replaced by a second, updated ordinance on 2 April 1659, which was confirmed by the States of Holland and remained in vogue until 1777. A third version came into being on 30 January of

---

14 Sgard, 'Bankruptcy'.

15 Goswin Moll, 'De Desolate Boedelskamer te Amsterdam – Bijdrage tot de kennis van het Oud-Hollandsch failliten-recht' (unpublished PhD thesis, Universiteit van Amsterdam, 1879), pp. 1–2.

16 M. Aukema, 'Andere tijden. Boedelafwikkeling in de 17e en 18e eeuw', in *De integere curator – Insolad jaarboek 2007*, eds. M.L.S. Kalff, R. Mulder, and S.H. de Ranitz (Deventer, 2007), p. 14.

17 Although Amsterdam had developed its own legal body dealing with bankruptcy, references to Antwerp laws were still frequent during the eighteenth century. See De ruysscher, 'Antwerp commercial legislation', pp. 459–479; see also Dave De ruysscher, 'Designing the limits of creditworthiness'.

18 See pp. 116–118.

19 Aukema, 'Andere tijden', pp. 15–16. This was part of the same specialization movement that also led to the development of the maritime court in the 1640s. For a look at this court and its functioning through a case study, see Maurits den Hollander and Remko J. Mooi, 'Protecting the foreign creditor – International insolvency in early modern Amsterdam and Frankfurt am Main', *TSEG/Low Countries journal of social and economic history*, 16:3–4 (2019): pp. 37–57.

that year and was applied until the arrival of the French *Code de Commerce* in 1811.[20]

When a bankruptcy was reported, a specific procedure was initiated. One or two commissioners were named, as well as the curators. The estate was sequestered, a list of creditors was made, and the commissioners summoned them to a meeting, where the debtor (or someone he gave power of attorney to) was present.[21] Time was provided for the debtor and creditors to reach an agreement, according to the 1777 ordinance this amounted to four weeks during which the estate could not be touched. The deal was deposed, generally at the orphanage (*burgerweeshuis*), and creditors could sign it. Those who did not want to sign it were publicly asked to make a claim.[22] If three-quarters of the creditors agreed on a proposed agreement, the remaining quarter had to comply with it as well. In cases where an agreement was reached, the bankrupt received full control over his estate again, at the condition that he would pay all the expenses that had arisen from his bankruptcy.[23] If no deal was reached within a month, the estate became officially insolvent and was registered as such. The administrators of the bankruptcy had to provide a list of monies still in their possession, and they had to provide the commissioners with their accounts. The declaration of insolvency ended the sequester, but the condition of bankruptcy remained. The administrators were replaced by curators.[24] Still, there was room for deal-making, but only if all creditors agreed, not one exception.[25] Creditors were asked three times to show their claim, and then curators went to liquidate the estate. The creditors had to show a balance, to be confirmed under oath by the bankrupt person.[26] A public sale was held, although furniture that was not too luxurious was allowed to be sold directly to family members. Other goods had to be sold within six weeks. After the sale, a list of sold items and profits was presented at the office of the curator.[27]

---

20 Ibid., p. 16.

21 For more on the sequester, mostly based on 1777 regulation, see Moll, 'De Desolate Boedelskamer', pp. 29–45.

22 Ibid., p. 57.

23 Ibid., pp. 58–59.

24 Although it was stipulated that the curators had to be the former administrators, something rarely challenged. Moll, 'De Desolate Boedelskamer', p. 68.

25 Ibid., pp. 66–67.

26 *Inventory of the archive 'Desolate Boedelskamer' in the City Archive Amsterdam*, pp. 4–8, consulted online at https://archief.Amsterdam/inventarissen/printversie/5072.nl.pdf.

27 This was according to Aukema, 'Andere tijden', pp. 15–16. Moll wrote that a surplus was divided pro rate between creditors who had subjected themselves to the agreement (but as he does not say when, this could be a post-1777 development). Moll, 'De Desolate Boedelskamer', p. 101.

Later, an advertisement called upon the creditors to be present at the division of the profits. First, the 'rightly preferred creditors' ('gejustificeerde preference schuldeisers') got their money, after which the 'concurrent creditors' ('concurrente schuldeisers') followed suit.[28] The privileged debts towards the preferred creditors were legal expenses, salary of curators, expenses made regarding the most recent illness of the debtor (but doctors' invoices and expenses for a funeral could be lowered by aldermen if they considered them to be too high), repair costs for ships, wages of seamen, salvage money and debts made for the purchase of masts, ropes and other shipping equipment.[29]

The Dutch interpretation of Roman law contained legislation on privileged debts that included women's dowries, although there were some restrictions, depending on whether it was a claim on goods or monies belonging to a commercial partnership the husband had been involved in.[30] The inclusion of claims of the wives of insolvent men as privileged debts was common in most early modern European bankruptcy statutes.[31] In the early modern period, there was a divide in approach towards the dowry, which was a daughter's share of her parents' inheritance, given to her at the time of her marriage; in northwestern Europe, it was more vulnerable to legal claims and insolvency issues, considering it was part of the conjugal goods. In the south, particularly in Italy, the dowry was placed in a separate fund, where it was protected from possible financial claims made on the husband; it was therefore an important instrument for transferring family fortunes from one generation to the next.[32] This type of protection was part of a more general European legal tradition in

28 *Inventory of the archive 'Desolate Boedelskamer'*, pp. 4–8.

29 Moll, 'De Desolate Boedelskamer', pp. 12–13.

30 Decker, *Het Roomsch Hollandsch recht*, 2: pp. 93–96. This was also part of the bankruptcy rules in Antwerp, which had a big influence on Dutch regulations. Dave De ruysscher, 'The struggle for voluntary bankruptcy and debt adjustment in Antwerp (c. 1520–c. 1550)', in *Dealing with economic failures: Extrajudicial and judicial conflict regulations*, ed. Margrit Schulte-Beerbühl (Frankfurt, 2016), p. 81.

31 As was, for instance, the case in Augsburg. Mark Häberlein, 'Merchants' bankruptcies, economic development and social relations in German cities during the long 16th century', in *The history of bankruptcy: Economic, social and cultural implications in early modern Europe*, ed. Thomas Max Safley (London, 2013), pp. 19–33.

32 Jan Luiten van Zanden and Tine De Moor, 'Mensen en economie in de Gouden Eeuw', *Leidschrift*, 23:2 (2008): pp. 15–26. On the situation in Italy, see Christopher F. Black, *Early modern Italy: A social history* (London and New York, 2001), pp. 111–115. For Spain, see Elizabeth A. Lehfeldt, 'Convents as litigants: Dowry and inheritance disputes in early-modern Spain', *Journal of social history*, 33:3 (2000): pp. 645–664; see also Martha C. Howell, *The marriage exchange: Property, social place, and gender in cities of the Low Countries, 1300–1550* (Chicago, 1998).

which dowries were sheltered from a number of crimes that were committed by husbands.[33]

The final repartition of the bankrupt's estate had to take place within eighteen months after the declaration of insolvency, but if there were any legal procedures pending on (parts of) the estate, this period could be extended. The creditors could not get their money unless they had deposited a caution in the presence of two aldermen. This was meant to make sure they would return the money they had received in case new creditors showed up with prioritised claims. The sum to be deposited differed, depending on whether they were preferred or concurrent creditors.[34] The 1659 ordinance made it clear that once the goods of an insolvent estate had been sold and the profits divided, the state of insolvency ended, and the merchant was again allowed to become active in commerce without his creditors having any right to stop him.[35] It is clear that this procedure was closely linked to local usages and regulations, and bankruptcies or temporary insolvencies, although they were frequent amongst traders, were not so easily resolved in cases where international creditors were affected. It was common in most early modern European bankruptcy procedures for creditors to make a majority decision, forcing dissenters to honour it.[36]

One of the basic steps was to compile a list of creditors in order of importance. The category of 'privileged creditors' was (and is) culturally specific, which caused problems.[37] A bankrupt could hardly be expected to pay all of his creditors back, and if these creditors fell under different jurisdictions, their political or diplomatic representatives could try to weigh in on the matter as a principle for defending the commercial interests of their respective nations.[38] This problem could only be solved in two ways: either through the existence

---

33 Hardwick, *Family business*, pp. 23–26.

34 According to Moll, this rule had been put into practice by the States of Holland and West Frisia. Moll, 'De Desolate Boedelskamer', p. 110; the archival inventory mentions the *Hoge Raad* as responsible for this.

35 For rehabilitation, see Moll, 'De Desolate Boedelskamer', pp. 134–142, and particularly p. 142 for the comment that the ordinances of 1643 and 1659 do not contain any specific clauses on rehabilitation.

36 Sgard, 'Bankruptcy'.

37 See Max Weber, *The history of commercial partnerships in the Middle Ages*, trans. Lutz Kaelber (Lanham, Boulder, New York and Oxford, 2003), pp. 76–78.

38 In their analysis of the insolvency case of Amsterdam merchant Gasparo Schellekens in 1701, Maurits den Hollander and Remko Mooi have argued that, rather than competing, there was cooperation between the Amsterdam Chamber of Insolvent Estates and the Frankfurt city council, a city in which Schellekens had creditors, and that such cooperation was not exceptional. Den Hollander and Mooi, 'Protecting the foreign creditor'.

of legislation apt at dealing with international disputes or through the establishment of certain customs that could be used as long as they were accepted by all sides as being an international norm. In the Ottoman context, some regulations and legislation did exist that could be used to solve international disputes. The capitulations had given legal autonomy to diplomats, but this was undermined by the frequent involvement of Ottoman creditors in bankruptcy cases. This involvement warranted the greater participation of Ottoman courts, who were just as concerned with their subjects' commercial well-being as European diplomats were instructed to be with theirs. Van den Boogert has shown that bankruptcy resolution in the Ottoman context relied on Ottoman law, but his research did not address the problematic nature of bankruptcy resolution amongst Europeans in an Ottoman context.[39] It seemed this was again left to customary agreements made amongst Europeans, and this could be problematic considering the importance of local bankruptcy laws, which could be irreconcilable with the various national commercial interests as defended by diplomats.

In the abovementioned argument between Ambassador Calkoen and his Venetian colleague, the former seemed convinced that the bankruptcy had been a fraudulent one, which had important legal repercussions. For Calkoen, this label of bankruptcy 'in infamia' led to the legal argument that the merchants in Holland should remain 'in plena possessione' and 'ad dispositionem' of their merchandise – rather than having it sequestered by the Venetian ambassador, whose sequester was a 'harsh and irregular manner of procedure'.[40] It is unsurprising that Calkoen called out the failure to adhere to procedure, as that was so essential in commercial litigation. But while the law was clear enough on this matter, it did not suffice to get Calkoen what he wanted, which is why he demanded the nomination of two neutral merchants to deal with the bankruptcy instead of the already appointed Venetians.

It seemed that, in the tension created by the juxtaposition of national interest and several bodies of local law, merchant custom, in the form of judgment by neutral traders, was called upon to solve the *imbroglio*. Rather than relying on any national law, which could surpass local regulations, but which was, according to van den Boogert, only seldomly invoked in eighteenth-century bankruptcy cases, judgment would have to come from within the merchant community and the 'universal' and rational principles of the merchants'

---

39 Van den Boogert, *The capitulations*, pp. 207–262.

40 Heeringa and Nanninga, *Bronnen tot de geschiedenis*, 3: pp. 140–142, Ambassador Cornelis Calkoen to Fagel, Istanbul, 26/11/1740, on p. 141, '[…] zoo harde en irreguliere wyze van procedeeren'.

style.[41] The appointment of neutral merchants was intended to avoid the unilateral pursuit of advantage, in this case not individual but national. Calkoen had to defend national interest, and in the case of a bankruptcy, it was a matter of limiting the losses of his countrymen to the greatest extent possible. The Venetian ambassador was doing the same, hence his nomination of Venetian merchants and his active efforts to lay claim on goods that were or had been in the hands of the bankrupts.

The Venetian ambassador's attempt to legally assert the financial liability of Dutch traders in Istanbul was based on an old custom, the community responsibility system. By using evidence from Flanders, England and Italy, Avner Greif has argued for the existence of a medieval system of punishment, based on the principle that all merchants belonging to a foreign trading nation could be held accountable for the actions of one merchant of that community.[42] It was one of the possibilities motivating a foreign trading community to prevent their members from cheating and a substitute for the absence of strong, neutral and centralised courts, and one could consider this a form of exogenous motivation. This co-existed – and was intertwined – with internal forms of control and retribution, in which the community itself punished a merchant for fraudulent behaviour. Perhaps the most popular measure was excommunication, a measure that seems to have been most effective in places where particular foreign communities did not interact all that much with host society.[43]

Endogenous forms of punishment relying on social ostracism do not necessarily need a legal justification – as long as there is a sense of being a separate community, community leaders, legally sanctioned by the host society or not, can punish cheaters. The collective responsibility system, however, was more closely tied to legal principles. Sheilagh Ogilvie has shown that collective punishment was a medieval custom that was only invoked when a legal claim on an individual had failed. The custom had developed in response to the problem of debt collection, and following *forum rei*, a creditor first had to seek justice against the debtor in the court under which jurisdiction the latter fell. Only when that failed, the creditor could seek recourse to collective responsibility.

41 Van den Boogert's remark on the absence of any reference to national law can be found in *The capitulations*, p. 259.

42 Greif, 'History lessons'; and 'On the social foundations'; see also Ogilvie, *Institutions and European trade*, pp. 272–276; and Gelderblom, *Cities of commerce*, p. 8.

43 Trivellato, *Familiarity of strangers*, pp. 165–167. An important example she gives is that of the Jewish diaspora – excommunication worked less as incentive in Amsterdam, where the Jewish community was fairly well-accepted, than in, for instance, Hamburg; see also Aslanian, *From the Indian Ocean*, pp. 171–174.

In that sense, 'a collective reprisal was formulated as a punishment not against a community of merchants but against a legal system that had failed to render justice'.[44] It is a crucial nuance to Greif's theory on collective responsibility – which gave too much credit to collective punishment as an autonomous institution supporting long-distance trade; Ogilvie manages convincingly to place collective punishment firmly within a formal legal context, rather than as an informal alternative to it – and individual responsibility remained an important component of it.[45]

While collective punishment helped to motivate a community to exercise pressure on their members to not commit fraud, it was also an important legal connection between foreign trading community and host society – particularly as it was common for foreign trading communities to be granted a degree of legal autonomy. Over time, collective responsibility in this strict sense of collective punishment disappeared, although remnants of the old custom for holding communities accountable for individual members' behaviour endured in certain contexts. Particularly in environments in which social ties such as kinship or religious affiliation were important as determinants for business, excommunication could be an important deterrent. Forms of punishment that relied on social ostracism have persisted into the twentieth century in specific closed environments such as New York's diamond district.[46]

The attempts of the Venetian ambassador in the bankruptcy case discussed above also demonstrate the persistence of some ideas on collective responsibility, although it was hardly surprising that these stirred controversy. The Venetian ambassador had not used old custom simply to obtain satisfaction from an offender who happened to belong to another nation but to defend the national interests of Venetian subjects in a matter of fraudulent bankruptcy. His Dutch colleague tried to do the same, and he defended the interests of his subjects. The matter pitted two communities against one another, so the recourse sought through the community responsibility system is not so strange in itself. What made it peculiar is that it had been out of use for so long. There is no information on how the issue was resolved, as the only further comment came from Calkoen's secretary in a letter to his brother, mentioning that the bankrupts had fled.[47]

---

44 Ogilvie, *Institutions and European trade*, p. 274.

45 Ibid., pp. 272 and 276.

46 Lisa Bernstein, 'Opting out of the legal system: Extralegal contractual relations in the diamond industry', *Journal of legal studies*, 21:1 (1992): pp. 115–157.

47 Heeringa and Nanninga, *Bronnen tot de geschiedenis*, 3: pp. 143–144, Secretary Jan Carel des Bordes to his brother, Istanbul, 30/11/1740.

1.2 *Competition from Within: The Prussian Royal Levant Company*

National competition was a tangible element of the interaction between European communities in Izmir. The consuls of the respective nations made no secret that one of their main responsibilities was to foster national commercial interests, and while traders were not necessarily motivated to look after the interests of the state to which they belonged, if they did well, the state also did well. Through custom duties and taxes, the state ensured it received its financial share of any success its merchants had. Because these taxes had been so disputed in the past, the state, in the Dutch case the States General, introduced other measures to ensure that Dutch traders were aware they were also serving Dutch interests and not simply their own or those of their correspondents and business partners. If a merchant undertook actions that were seen as harmful to the state, the consul intervened. A good example is the treatment of the firm of Clement, van Sanen, van der Zee & C° in the 1760s. In May 1765, the Prussian King Frederik gave Philippe Clement and his company the exclusive rights to trade between Prussia and the Levant for twenty years. This new Prussian Royal Levant Company was financed by the issuing of shares, and Philippe Clement was to be its director general and president in Berlin, while Pieter van Sanen, already Prussian consul in Izmir, was to serve as its director general in the Levant.[48] At the time, Pieter van Sanen was assessor at the Dutch consulate and thus closely involved in different matters of the consulate, particularly adjudication.

The Dutch ambassador in Istanbul, Willem Gerrit Dedel, sent letters to the States General and the States of Holland to explain the situation and ask them for advice. The problem was that Clement and van Sanen were Dutch, and as such, they would continue to enjoy Dutch protection and fall under Dutch jurisdiction. At the same time, their new Prussian functions also made them important agents in the development of an enterprise whose success would come at the expense of the Dutch, and Dedel wrote about van Sanen that 'under our protection and with his Dutch firm, he can give considerable support to his Prussian trade factory and as consul he can greatly suppress our trade'.[49] If the States General did not order him otherwise, he could not take away Dutch protection from these men, particularly as it was not uncommon

48 Heeringa and Nanninga, *Bronnen tot de geschiedenis*, 3: pp. 494–500, 'Octrooy van een exclusieven handel op den Levant, verleend door Frederik, koning van Pruisen, aan Philip Clement', Berlin, 17/05/1765.

49 Heeringa and Nanninga, *Bronnen tot de geschiedenis*, 4: p. 6, Ambassador Willem Dedel to Fagel, Istanbul, 16/09/1765, 'Onder onse bescherming en met zijn Hollandsch huis kan hij zijn Pruissise factorie merkelijk ondersteunen en als consul onze negocie zeer drukken'.

for European trading nations to extend protection to certain groups of nonnationals. Additionally, the Prussian envoy in Istanbul had asked Dedel to accept joint Dutch-Prussian protection for these men, something the ambassador found difficult to refuse.[50] Dedel, unsure how to act, also put the question directly before the States of Holland: 'shall these people be given the opportunity to destroy our trade here, established for a long time, while being under our protection?'[51]

The Directorate of Levant Trade, consulted on the matter, suggested that Pieter van Sanen should be convinced to renounce his assessorship voluntarily, while the status of Clement, van Sanen, van der Zee & C° as a Dutch firm should be discussed at a later time.[52] A meeting on this topic was indeed held in Izmir in February 1766, and the consul, assessors and treasurer decided that van Sanen could no longer be assessor and that the firm of Clement, van Sanen, van der Zee & C° would not be allowed to enjoy Dutch protection any longer. Only van der Zee, who had expressed his intention to leave the partnership, could remain under Dutch protection, unless he explicitly asked for it to be removed. Van Sanen and van der Zee were both further questioned about the Prussian Royal Levant Company and their interest therein, and when they indeed confirmed as much, van Sanen was dismissed as assessor and was no longer bound by the Dutch national oath. From this time onwards, he was to be considered a foreigner, and this also applied to the payment of consular fees.[53]

After this, apparently, things took a turn for the worse for van Sanen, who became ill, feverish and mad, denying he wanted to be consul. Rumours spread he was locked up in a warehouse, 'roaring like an ox' that there was a fire.[54] Van Sanen was succeeded as Prussian consul by his business partner van der Zee,

50 Ibid.

51 Heeringa and Nanninga, *Bronnen tot de geschiedenis*, 4: pp. 6–7, Ambassador Willem Dedel to the grand pensionary of Holland, Istanbul, 16/09/1765, 'Zal men die luiden geleegenheid geeven onder ons eige bescherming onze van oudsher hier gestelde koophandel te vernielen?'

52 Ibid., p. 8, Directorate of Levant Trade to Consul Daniel Jean de Hochepied, Amsterdam, 24/09/1765. This was confirmed in a meeting in Amsterdam in October 1765. Ibid., pp. 16–17, 'Extra-ordinaris vergadering met de buitenleden te Amsterdam', Amsterdam, 30/10/1765, when it was also decided that van Sanen could no longer attend meetings between consul, assessors and treasurer.

53 Ibid., pp. 35–36, 'Extract uyt de notulen ter gehouden bisoignes in de vergaaderinge van consul en assessooren etc. der Neederlandse natie', Izmir, 03/02/1766. Nicolas van der Zee was not involved as director or consul. Even though he held shares in the Prussian Royal Levant Company, Dutch protection was not taken away from him.

54 As quoted from a letter written by Consul Hochepied to the States General in a footnote in Heeringa and Nanninga, *Bronnen tot de geschiedenis*, 4: p. 139, '[...] hij bruld als een os [...]'.

who remained consul until 1771, when he renounced all his Prussian offices as well as his involvement in the firm of Clement, van Sanen, van der Zee & C° and asked permission to return under Dutch protection.[55] It was not given to him, because he could not give sufficient assurance that he had settled all his debts. A renewed request made by van der Zee at the end of 1773 was equally denied, even if all of his creditors were paid, because the States General needed assurance he had no further business engagements with Prussian or Ottoman subjects.[56]

The reasons for van der Zee's first request, as well as the refusal of the States of Holland to grant it, became clear very quickly to Daniel Jean de Hochepied, Dutch consul in Izmir. At around the time of van der Zee's first request, he turned down a petition from the Prussian envoy in Istanbul to act on his behalf in the settlement of the affairs of the house of Clement, van Sanen, van der Zee & C°. Following van Sanen's onset of madness, the company had been performing poorly and was indebted to many Ottoman subjects, including several Muslims.[57] The Royal Bank of Berlin had lent a good deal of money to the Prussian Royal Levant Company and withdrew their support. In March 1771, David van Lennep and William Enslie, prominent Dutch merchants, had already let the Prussian envoy in Istanbul know that, should the firm Clement, van Sanen, van der Zee & C° go bankrupt and the Royal Bank of Berlin wanted to press its claim against the firm, van Lennep and Enslie did not want to have anything to do with the affair.[58]

---

55 Ibid., pp. 153–154, *Chargé d'affaires* Frederik Johan Robert de Weiler to Fagel, Istanbul, 17/04/1771. After the death of Willem Dedel, the Dutch ambassador in Istanbul, in 1768, his secretary, Frederik Johan Robert de Weiler, was promoted to *chargé d'affaires*. In 1775 he was promoted to ambassadorship. Schutte, *Repertorium der Nederlandse vertegenwoordigers*, p. 312.

56 *Resolutien van de heeren Staaten van Holland en Westvriesland in haar edele groot mog. vergadering genoomen in den jaare 1774* (S.l., S.d.), pp. 325–326, 'Resolutie op de Missive van den Consul de Hochepied te Smirna omtrent het versoek van de geweese Pruissische Consul vander Zee, om weederom onder haar hoog mogende protectie te geraaken', 22/04/1774.

57 Heeringa and Nanninga, *Bronnen tot de geschiedenis*, 4: pp. 160–161, Consul Daniel Jean de Hochepied to Fagel, Izmir, 20/07/1771; and ibid., pp. 164–165, Directorate of Levant Trade to Consul Daniel Jean de Hochepied, 17/12/1771. The court case against Arnoldus Wissing, who had been responsible for the firm's affairs in a period of absence or the unavailability of all three partners, was part of this tumultuous affair; see pp. 139–144.

58 NACS, N°255 ('Stukken betreffende faillissementen. Clement, van Sanen & van der Zee, Nederlandse kooplieden te Smyrna, 1779'), 'Extrait d'une letter écrite par les soussignés [David van Lennep and William Enslie] a monsieur de Zegelin envoyé de sa majesté le roy de Prusse à la Porte ottomane', Izmir, 30/03/1771. The firm went bankrupt in 1770, and this letter was incorporated in the bankruptcy file.

To make matters worse, Nicolas van der Zee was behind with the payments he needed to make to the Ottoman administration on behalf of Prussia. De Hochepied refused to intervene in the manner, as he thought it would be a lengthy affair, with little to win. He felt that it would harm his work on behalf of Dutch national interests – a decision he was complimented for by the Directorate of Levant Trade.[59] The affair meant the end of the Prussian Royal Levant Company.[60] A year later, van Sanen's Dutch wife demanded Dutch protection for herself, but it was refused to her on the grounds that it had been taken away from her husband. Dutch assistance for her would involve the Dutch trading community in the handling of the closure of the Prussian Royal Levant Company, which nobody wanted.[61]

Prussian involvement had ended badly for all partners of the Clement, van Sanen and van der Zee partnership, partially because of poor commercial decisions, but also partially because their decision to work on behalf of Prussia cost them Dutch institutional protection. Matters turned out to be a bit different for the man who was later seen as partially responsible for those poor choices, Arnoldus Wissing, the firm's accountant with the power of attorney enabling him to conduct business in the partnership's name.[62] A compromise was reached about him. When he acted in the name of the firm of Clement, van Sanen, van der Zee & C°, his actions were not protected by a Dutch status, but when he acted as his own person, he continued, as a Dutch national, to fall under Dutch protection.[63] The decision was officialised in a resolution issued by the States of Holland, and part of the justification was the reasoning that if Wissing would not be allowed to enjoy Dutch protection when trading in his own name, it could harm the practice of foreign consuls who acted as Dutch consuls ad interim. The loss of protection when providing services for a firm belonging to another nation might make foreign consuls

59 Heeringa and Nanninga, *Bronnen tot de geschiedenis*, 4: pp. 160–161, Consul Daniel Jean de Hochepied to Fagel, Izmir, 20/07/1771; and ibid., pp. 164–165, Directorate of Levant Trade to Consul Daniel Jean de Hochepied, 17/12/1771.

60 A few decades earlier, the Prussian Asiatic Trade Company had met with same fate. These debacles led to King Frederik's decision to forbid all Prussian investment in overseas trading companies. See Florian Schui, 'Prussia's "trans-oceanic moment": The creation of the Prussian Asiatic Trade Company in 1750', *The historical journal*, 49:1 (2006): pp. 143–160.

61 Heeringa and Nanninga, *Bronnen tot de geschiedenis*, 4: pp. 172–173, Directorate of Levant Trade to the burgomasters of Amsterdam, 04/09/1772.

62 See pp. 139–144.

63 Heeringa and Nanninga, *Bronnen tot de geschiedenis*, 4: pp. 138–139, Directorate of Levant Trade to the burgomasters of Amsterdam, Amsterdam, 21/02/1770.

reconsider when asked to temporary take on a consular position on behalf of the Dutch.[64]

It is understandable that it took time for the States General, the Directorate of Levant Trade, the consul and the ambassador to reach a decision on the status of everyone involved. While the Prussian Royal Levant Company was a clear threat to the Dutch national interests that the institutions were meant to protect, these men were Dutch, and protection could not be taken away lightly, especially as the consequences reached further than loss of political protection. In September 1765, Thomas de Vogel in Amsterdam had already instructed his son Thomas Junior to not do any more business with Philippe Clement, as it would upset their other correspondents, who were likely to brand de Vogel as a traitor to the United Provinces and its commerce, an accusation already circulating in Amsterdam's commercial circles. Earlier, Clement, van Sanen, van der Zee & C° had litigated with de Vogel in Izmir, a matter that was not considered as sufficient reason to stop doing business with one another, as both firms continued to do so.[65]

What made this situation different was that Philippe Clement had entered Prussian service because he had financial difficulties. The crossing of national boundaries, from the United Provinces to Prussia, was not bad per se, but having done it for personal profit was a problem. Renouncing one's nation for reasons of personal profit was usually regarded as a severe misstep and could lead to serious damage to one's reputation.[66] When the pursuit of self-interest conflicted with the loyalty that was expected from merchants on the basis of reciprocity, which was part of merchant custom, a trader was attacked, and punished, for his choice. This is essentially why Clement and van Sanen were ostracised from the Dutch community for their involvement in the Prussian Royal Levant Company. It was not a matter of 'national' interest alone, it was also a matter of corroding one of the essential norms dictated by the merchants' style.

64 *Resolutien van de heeren Staaten van Holland en Westvriesland in haar edele groot mog. vergadering genoomen in den jaare 1770* (S.l., S.d.), pp. 337–338. 'Resolutie op de Missive van den Consul Hochepied te Smirna, om te weeten, hoe sig te gedraagen nopens den gesubstitueerden van den Pruissischen Consul vander Zee', 10/03/1770. Consul de Hochepied had sent a letter explaining the situation on 17 January 1770.

65 See pp. 146–152.

66 Heeringa and Nanninga, *Bronnen tot de geschiedenis*, 4: pp. 1193–1194, Thomas de Vogel to Thomas de Vogel Junior, Amsterdam, 20/09/1765.

1.3 *A Local European Dispute without any Dutch Involvement*

Another form of European competition was the desire of some of the more successful nations to take merchants without diplomatic representation in the Levant under their formal protection. European consuls could even become vice-consuls for other nations. Pieter van Sanen's combination of two consulships had not worked out because he had not received permission and because his actions were considered too selfish and detrimental to Dutch national interests, but this was not considered to be the case for the various vice-consulates occupied by members of the de Hochepied family in Izmir – at times, they acted as representatives for the Habsburg Empire, the Grand Duchy of Tuscany, Denmark, Sweden and later also Russia, while also protecting the interests of Polish traders at certain moments.[67]

During Daniel Alexander de Hochepied's tenure as consul, between 1720 (initially *ad interim*) and 1759, the Dutch were also protecting two Genoese traders.[68] It is unclear whether this stemmed from an agreement with the Genoese government or whether it was a form of individual protection. Giuseppe Copurro was a bachelor, but Gian Carlo Giera had married a Dutch woman, and in 1759, he had already lived in Izmir for twelve years.[69] A relative of Gian Carlo named Giovanni Lorenzo Giera was referred to in another trial as a 'négociant Genois protégé de France', and the name comes up on a list of French merchants in Izmir in 1751.[70] A certain Pietro Paolo Giera was said to be part of Livorno's Board of Commerce in 1717, and the Giera family can be found in Livorno in the early nineteenth century as a merchant family.[71] Another Pietro Paolo Giera appears in the archives of the Chamber of Commerce in Trieste amongst the records discussing relations between the Habsburg court in Vienna and the Dutch Republic in 1784, involving letters from vice-consuls and agents, in this case de Hochepied as Austrian vice-consul and Pietro

67 See pp. 53–55.
68 See table 2.
69 Ibid.
70 NACS, N°383 ('Paulo Poma, Grieks koopman te Smyrna, tegen Giovanni Lorenzo Giera, Toscaans koopman te Smyrna, 1790'), [Declaration of French consul Amoreux], Izmir, 29/08/1791. Michel Morineau, 'Naissance d'une domination. Marchands européens, marchands et marchés du Levant aux XVIIIe et XIXe siècles', *Cahiers de la Méditerranée*, 1 (1976): p. 184. The list is not without its problems, as it contains for instance the names of Fremeaux and van der Sanden, and members of those families were part of the Dutch trading community of Izmir; see table 2.
71 Alessandro Volpi, *Banchieri e mercato finanziario in Toscana (1801–1860)* (Firenze, 1997), p. 131; and David G. LoRomer, *Merchants and reform in Livorno 1814–1868* (Berkeley, Los Angeles and Oxford, 1987), p. 83.

Paolo Giera in Izmir as agent.[72] A *Memoria* published in Livorno by Carolina Bartoletti, the widow of Pietro Paolo Giera, in 1818 clarifies that her husband had been Austrian consul in the Levant, as well as deputy to the legislative body in Paris and president of the commercial tribunal in Livorno.[73] A number of other cases brought before the Dutch consular court involve Giera family members, such as Giuseppe and Gian Carlo Giera, Genoese merchants in Izmir (1745), Giancarlo Giera, Tuscan merchant (1792), and Jean-Laurent Giera, Tuscan merchant (1806).[74] It seems the Giera family was indeed an internationally settled merchant family and had, by the time Giovanni Lorenzo Giera became a defendant in this case, established themselves in Paris, possibly also in Genoa, Livorno and Izmir.

In any case, Gian Carlo Giera fell under Dutch jurisdiction. If a plaintiff wanted to summon him in court, Giera would be judged by the Dutch consul following the principle of *forum rei*. It is because of this principle that the firm of Giuseppe and Gian Carlo Giera found itself as the defendant at the Dutch consular court in Izmir in 1745. The plaintiff was the French firm of Séguier Père & Fils, also from Izmir. Jean Antoine Butini, the Swedish consul in Marseille, had shipped 120 bales of American coffee and eight bundles of cloth on the Swedish ship *Resolution* of the skipper Nils Svanson to Izmir and consigned it to the Giera firm. In a letter sent on 30 April 1745, Butini repeated a demand he had made three days earlier, when he asked the Giera firm to deliver the goods destined for Izmir to Séguier upon their arrival. Séguier had already received an order from Butini to sell them and to reimburse any expenses the Giera firm had made as intermediary. The plan to use the Giera firm as intermediary in the first place had come from Gian Carlo's brother and partner Giuseppe, who had freighted the ship in Marseille. He considered it a good way to avoid Mediterranean corsairs, who were considered more likely to plunder Butini's goods if they were addressed to a French firm. Butini had been trading with

72 Archivio di Stato di Trieste, Deputazione di Borsa poi Camera di Commercio e d'Industria di Trieste (1755–1921). Serie 7: Carteggio CXXX, 'Comunicazione del C.R. governo della sostituzione, visti i rapporti tra la corte di Vienna e la Repubblica d'Olanda' (1784).

73 Carolina Bartoletti, *Memoria per la signora Carolina Bartoletti vedova Giera, sacerdote sig. Luigi Cartacci suo maestro di casa e Maddalena Melani sua cameriera nella causa di preteso furto avanti la r. ruote criminale di Firenze* (Livorno, 1818), p. 3.

74 NACS, N°317 ('Stukken rakende het voldongen proces tusschen Seguier pere x fils en Giuseppe en Gio Carlo Giera, 1745'); N°396 ('Gian Carlo Giera, Toscaans koopman te Smyrna, tegen Govert Swenson, kapitein van het Nederlandse schip Clasina, 1792'); and N°454 ('Jean Laurent Giera, Toscaans koopman te Smyrna, tegen Daniel Fremeaux & Co., 1806').

Séguier for a long time, to his satisfaction, which is why he hoped the Giera firm would not make a problem of it. Additionally, they should exercise some caution, considering the Marseille Chamber of Commerce, in its role as controller of French Levant Trade, did not look favourably upon the consignment of goods coming from France to non-French firms in the Levant. Séguier had demanded the handover of the goods from Giera verbally, but they had refused, so Séguier turned to the competent judge, Consul Daniel Alexander de Hochepied, to obtain them.[75]

After the claim was registered, the Giera firm was given two days to come up with a written answer. In their reply, they claimed that Butini had given them the order to sell the goods and to purchase Angora yarn with the profits. Giera included an extract from Butini's letter from 27 April, in which the Swedish consul ordered them to receive and sell the goods and to look for some merchandise to be shipped on Svanson's vessel for the return voyage. In exchange, Butini claimed he might be able to obtain some good terms for future shipping on Swedish vessels as the consul. It must have been a tempting promise, as at the time, in the middle of the War of Austrian Succession, shipping on French vessels was dangerous, while Swedish ships were popular.[76] The Giera firm argued that the new orders for Séguier had come too late, as they had already sold the goods and decided to invest in Angora yarn.[77]

As with most commercial disputes brought before the Dutch consul in Izmir, the problem was with the middlemen, but what set this case apart was that the Giera firm was not supposed to engage in commercial transactions but only in the shipping. They were not used as agents but rather as an instrument to avoid problems with corsairs at sea. As in almost all cases, the consul asked for a second round of declarations and gave the French firm three days to reply. Séguier addressed all the points that Giera had raised and included extracts from Butini's letters to argue that the Giera firm had abused their role to appropriate a commission that was not theirs, acting '*mal à propos* and against the

75 NACS, N°317, 'Request van de messrs Seguier pere x filz, aen haer ho: mo: consul, a di 21 Juny 1745 g'apostilleert 22 detto en aen Giuseppe x Gio Carlo Giera g'intimeert en copije gelaten', Izmir, 21/06/1745.

76 Leos Müller, 'Commerce et navigation suédois en Méditerranée à l'époque moderne (1650–1815)', *Revue d'histoire maritime*, 13 (2011): pp. 45–70; and his 'Swedish shipping in southern Europe and peace treaties with North African states: An economic security perspective', *Historical social research/Historische Sozialforschung*, 35:4 (2010): pp. 190–205.

77 NACS, N°317, 'Antwoord van Giusepp x Gio Carlo Giera opt reqt van Seguier pater e figlio van dato den 21 d° dit g'intimeert den 28 aen seguier et volgens apostil, en copije gelaten', Izmir, 25/06/1745.

good faith of commerce'.[78] According to the Frenchmen, Giera had been verbally informed in Izmir by Séguier (the father) not to sell the merchandise received, as Butini's real intent had been to give the commission to the Séguier firm, and it was not the first time the Frenchmen had received commissions from Swedish merchants through an artificial intermediary intended solely to deceive corsairs. Three days after the commission order to Giera, Butini clarified that the real commissioning agents should be the Séguier firm. Giera refused to listen and quickly bartered the goods for Angora yarn. Additionally, Giuseppe Giera had been misleading, concocting a shipping plan with Butini without informing his brother in Izmir, something he easily could have done, as the Giera firm had sent a *commis* on Svanson's vessel who could (and should) have transmitted the message in person. Furthermore, the facts demonstrated that the Giera firm had committed a cardinal sin by not acting in Butini's interest, who had not asked for the barter transaction with the yarn. Even if the Giera firm had acted in good faith (which, according to Séguier, they clearly had not), they had acted as bad traders. It was thus a serious infraction against commercial custom, and Séguier insisted that either the goods, or their value in current money from Izmir, as valued by court-nominated experts, would be delivered to them.[79]

Gian Carlo Giera replied that he found the claims against his firm misleading and accused the Séguier firm of having 'the malicious idea to tarnish by their accusation the clarity of their true and candid motivations'.[80] They did not want to reply to all of the accusations, false as they were, but left that to those familiar with the firm's 'character'.[81] The Séguier firm insisted on its discourse and accused the Giera firm of manipulating things, referring back to the barter transaction the Giera firm had made so hastily but that was so disadvantageous for Butini, labelling their effort as exchanging 'a bar of gold for a bar of iron'.[82] The Séguier firm felt that the reason Giera had acted so speedily was to

78 NACS, N°317, 'Replicq van Seguier pere x filz opt antw:t van giusepp x Gio Carlo Giera van den 25 tevooren geapostileert den 6 julij en hetzelve g'intimeert, en copije gelaten', Izmir, 30/06/1745, '[…] mal a propoz et contre la bonne foy du commerce […]'.

79 Ibid.

80 NACS, N°317, 'Repliq van Giusep & Gio Carlo Giera, aen Seguier padre x figlio op het haere van 30 junij en den 6 july g'apostilleert en denzelve dag g'intimeert', Izmir, 10/07/1745, '[…] con l'idea maliziosa d'offuscare p tal mezzo la chiarezza delle vere, e candide nre. raggioni […]'.

81 Ibid., '[…] nostro carattere […]', referring to their reputation.

82 NACS, N°317, 'Treplicq van Seguier padre x figlio opt replicq van Giusep.e x Gio Carlo Giera van den 10 deezer g'appostileert den 14 detto en ook g'intimeert', Izmir, 13/07/1745, '[…] troquer une barre d'or, contre une barre de fer […]'.

secure a freight for Svanson's ship. The firm had been charged with the commission to procure merchandise for the return trip of the vessel from Izmir to Livorno. The faster the ship could leave, the better it was for Giera, and according to father and son Séguier, this was telling of Giera's true character – he had sacrificed Butini's interests to further his own, a very serious accusation in a world in which reciprocity was key to the good functioning of trade.[83]

Unsurprisingly, the Giera firm called the accusations lies, and they felt they had done nothing wrong. They insisted for Daniel Alexander de Hochepied to reach a verdict quickly so they would not have to suffer further insults.[84] Exactly one month after the initial request, de Hochepied, without seeking any recourse to his Dutch assessors or other traders, ruled that the Giera firm was to deliver all the Angora yarn to the Séguier firm. Should the later refuse to take it back, Giera had to sell it with the best interest of the owner, Butini, in mind.[85] The Séguier firm chose to appeal, but no traces of it were found. In the first instance, the reasoning of the plaintiff had been founded on the idea that the Giera firm had broken the rules of trade, and they had done so for their own profit and to the detriment of the person who had hired them to act as intermediary. This meant the reputation of the Giera firm was on the line, a crucial asset, particularly in the Levant, where European firms were mainly active as commission traders for merchants in Europe.

Luckily for them, the Swedish consul had employed the Giera firm as means of deception. The double order given by Butini to sell his merchandise in Izmir, on 27 April to Giera and on 30 April to Séguier, left enough space to doubt Butini's orders, a doubt that Séguier was not able to dispel. The Giera firm was aware they were used to disguise the true ownership of goods as insurance against corsairs. Butini's revelation about the actual consignment to Séguier had come too late, and Giera might have taken advantage of this to win a commission. Séguier tried to save the argument by stating that, even in the case that Giera had been the rightful commissioning agent, he had done a very bad job. This made the court assume its most common role – as a tribunal that had to judge the reputation and liability of an intermediary in trade. It is not clear whether Daniel Alexander de Hochepied was Swedish vice-consul at the

83 Ibid.

84 NACS, N°317, 'Treplicq van de ss.i Giusep:p & Gio Carlo Giera, op dat van de ss Seguier padre x figlio van den 13 July den 19 ditto g'appostilleert, en ook g'intimeert aen d.t s: Seguier x C', Izmir, 17/07/1745.

85 NACS, N°317, 'Sententie vant voldongen proces, van Seguier pere et fils en Giuseppe x Gio Carlo Giera gepronuncieert door haer Ho: mo: consul den 21 Julij 1745 en't appel van Seguier ex ondert zelve', Izmir, 21/07/1745.

time – his son would assume that function later, after he had also taken over his father's duties as Dutch consul. If this was indeed the case, Daniel Alexander de Hochepied at no moment mentioned it as relevant to adjudicating a case that involved goods belonging to a Swedish vice-consul in another locality.[86] It is possible that de Hochepied did not want to reward Butini's deceitful behaviour and therefore ruled in favour of Giera, although that need not be motivated necessarily by de Hochepied acting as Swedish vice-consul to keep a fellow Swedish vice-consul in check.

1.4 *The Possibility of Appeal*

For intra-European disputes, once the appropriate court was selected, the adjudicating process can hardly be distinguished from intra-Dutch proceedings. The fact that the plaintiff was not Dutch had no procedural consequences. The nature of documents submitted to the court stayed the same – requests, replies, counter-replies, witness statements and business documents. Most of the written evidence was filed in another language, but the court had ample experience with Italian, English and French. What was different was the manner in which the documents were registered. In intra-Dutch cases, both parties delivered their documents to the Dutch chancery. The chancellor was not only responsible for showing what was brought in by one litigant to the other, notifying the latter that a reply was due within a certain time, but also for registering all of the documents used in a trial in the chancery's registries.[87] When needed, the chancellor was also charged with selecting extracts from some of the material relevant to a particular case and with verifying that copies were identical to the original documents. Language could create an additional requirement – procuring a good and truthful translation.[88]

The responsibilities of the chancellor in instances of intra-European litigation were shared with his colleague at the consulate of the other litigant. Both parties were allowed to submit all of their materials to the court at the

---

86 For the consular functions of Daniel Alexander and his son Daniel Jean de Hochepied, see Schutte, *Repertorium der Nederlandse vertegenwoordigers*, pp. 335–336.

87 For the Dutch consular court, they have been preserved in eighteen volumes for the period between 1741 and 1810. All of case N°330, the dispute between Ouckama and Wijnands & Kramer, for instance, can also be found in NACS, N°204 ('Register der Nederlandsche kanzelary te Smyrna gehouden door den heer kanzelier Johann Fred.r Mann begonnen den 3 january 1764. Geeindigd den 4 april 1765'), pp. 84–187.

88 This was more important when Greek, Hebrew, Armenian or Turkish was concerned. There were sufficient shared languages between Europeans (and Ottomans) in the Levant, mainly Italian. On the use of shared language in the Mediterranean, see Dursteler, 'Language and identity in the early modern Mediterranean'; and his 'Speaking in tongues'.

chancery of their own consulate – if one existed.[89] The evidence clearly indicates that it was common practice for merchants to file a request, or a reply to a request, in the chancery of their own consulate, which would then ensure that the chancery of the Dutch consulate would get a copy of the document, which was subsequently added to the case documents preserved at the Dutch chancery and registered in the chancery's books. This made the role of the chancellor in ensuring the veracity of the submitted documents even larger than in intra-Dutch litigation.

The biggest difference with intra-Dutch litigation lay in the possibility of appeal. When a case between Dutch litigants that had been tried by the consul was appealed, it had to be done at a tribunal that stood higher in legal hierarchy. In the United Provinces, these were the *Hof van Holland* (see figure 5) and the *Hoge Raad*, and in the Levant, appeals were made at the court of the Dutch ambassador in Istanbul.[90] Matters were more complicated in litigation between Europeans, as these belonged to entirely different jurisdictions. In the United Provinces, such a matter was resolved by offering foreigners equal access to the higher courts. In the Levant, a parallel solution was not so easy. Some of the cases include a request of appeal, which was registered at the consular court, but to be adjudicated at another court. In intra-Dutch litigation, appeals were adjudicated by the Dutch ambassador, but in intra-European disputes, the choice was not so clear. The Ottomans offered Europeans access to their courts, which made it possible for Europeans to appeal there. They rarely seem to have done so, and the practice was actively discouraged by diplomatic representatives.[91] The other logical solution was the use of *forum rei* for the appeal. In the new trial, the losing party became the plaintiff and the winning party the defendant. As the appeal had to be adjudicated before a higher court, the likelihood of such court being situated abroad was high in the context of intra-European commercial litigation.

Adjudicating an appeal in a locality that might be far away was not an attractive option, and the path to it was restricted by additional regulations. One was to exclude certain cases from appeal – in 1675, it was determined that the consular court could adjudicate in cases up to 100 lion dollars' worth, and that in those cases, no appeal was possible.[92] A second restriction obliged the losing

89 Otherwise, it would have to be done at the consulate of the nation under whose protection the merchant stood, or under whose jurisdiction someone's power of attorney stood.

90 See also pp. 265–272.

91 See pp. 272–277.

92 Heeringa and Nanninga, *Bronnen tot de geschiedenis*, 2: pp. 187–204, 'Reglement voor den resident tot Constantinopelen, consul tot Smirna, ende Nederlantsche natie in de Levant

party to pay a caution equivalent to the money he had been sentenced to pay.[93] In practice, merchants requesting an appeal regularly had to be reminded that, in order for the appeal to happen, they had to pay first: 'Homero is master of the appeal, but he has to follow the laws of appeal, that is deposit the sum, or provide caution, and then he can appeal.'[94] These restrictions were not at all uncommon in the context of commercial litigation; the merchant court of Paris forbade appeals on sentences involving sums lower than 500 livres, and even in cases of appeal, the sentence would have to be executed without hindrance before the appeal took place, a measure that seems to have lessened merchants' desires to appeal unfavourable sentences.[95]

Another restriction – in the Dutch Levantine context – can be found in the early regulations issued by Cornelis Haga in 1616. These did not allow non-Dutch litigants to appeal a sentence issued by a Dutch court in the Levant, although, in practice, Haga's regulations were violated, and foreigners did appeal Dutch consular verdicts before the Dutch ambassador – the competent higher court.[96]

In 1787, a Greek Ottoman who was a Ragusan *protégé*, and thus legally considered a Ragusan subject, chose to appeal a sentence issued by the Dutch consul in Salonika in a dispute he had as plaintiff with another Greek, who was a Dutch *protégé* and the defendant in the case.[97] As the Dutch *protégé* had won the case, and was thus taken to court as a defendant again, *forum rei* dictated that the court of the Dutch ambassador was the competent tribunal. The Dutch ambassador at the time, Frederik Gijsbert van Dedem, went to administer justice 'en cas d'appel', assisted by the advice of 'four neutral and

---

residerende respective, sooals hetselve bij de heeren Directeuren van den Levantschen handel aen H.H.M. is overgegeven, en bij deselve weder aen den Consul van Dam gesonden', 1675, on p. 197.

93 Cau, *Groot placaet-boeck*, 2: pp. 1335–1338, 'Acte, voor den consul van Aleppo, noopende de judicature, &c.', 17/02/1616.

94 NACS, N°343 ('Papieren aangaande de process tusschen Alexander x Sottira x Gerrit van Brakel geboekt off geregistreerd op f°332 tot 345, 1769'), Note from the Dutch consul to the Dutch chancellor, Izmir, 30/05/1769, 'Homero is meester over 't appeleeren maar hij moet de wetten van 't appel volge dat is de somma dépositeere, of borgtogt geeven, dan kan hij appeleeren.' This note, which was written to discuss progress in a number of cases with the chancellor, was preserved in the documents of another trial.

95 Kessler, *A revolution in commerce*, pp. 51 and 102.

96 Such violations were not particularly uncommon either. The restriction of appeal to non-Dutch litigants of 1616 was replaced in the 1675 proposal by an article that specifically stated this possibility of appeal. Although it was not turned into law, several of its articles must have reflected legal practice; see pp. 95–104.

97 Which explains the competence of the Dutch consular court in Salonika.

irreproachable persons'.[98] The persons chosen were three consuls of other nations and an individual. Other evidence further confirms that the decision to follow *forum rei* in the case above was not a rarity. In 1766, the French firm of François Séquard & C° had filed a petition against the Tuscan chancellor Orazio Capirossi in a case related to protested bills of exchange, for which he held Capirossi responsible. As the Dutch consul was also vice-consul of the Grand Duchy of Tuscany (and Capirossi was, as chancellor, an employee of the Dutch consul in his position as the Tuscan representative), Capirossi was allowed to defend himself before the Dutch consular court following *forum rei*. He was found not liable for the bills, and Séquard was condemned to pay back a sum Capirossi had already paid, while his claim for payment of the four bills was dismissed. As Tuscan vice-consul (and consular judge), Daniel Jean de Hochepied did not rely on his usual Dutch assessors in this case. This did not mean, however, that he was adjudicating by himself. For this case, he was assisted by a Genoese, a Ragusan, and an English merchant – confirming the importance of using the expertise of merchants in the adjudicating process.[99]

Séquard appealed, and he followed *forum rei*, turning to the 'lords delegate judges of Florence or any other superior tribunal that was competent.'[100] Séquard even provided an address in Florence, with a fellow French trader, which was to serve as his domicile during the appeal procedure.[101] He must have been convinced that he could win the case. It might be that, in the absence of a Tuscan ambassador in Istanbul, the highest Tuscan court was the natural and legal choice for appeal, and the addition of 'tout autre tribunal superieur' suggests that Séquard simply was not sure under what jurisdiction this had to be tried. Research on the legal functions of the French consuls in the Mediterranean demonstrates that there was a degree of freedom in choosing

---

98 NA, N°1.02.20, 'Archief van de Legatie in Turkije, 1668–1810 (1811)' (hereafter NALT), N°1274 ('Pièces relatives au procès entre Hagi Nicola Papasoglou barattaire de Raguse mon beau fils Anastasio di Giovanni barattaire de Holl.de à Salonique, 1787'), Declaration by Ambassador Gijsbert Baron van Dedem, Istanbul, April 1787, '[…] quatre personnes impartiales et irreprochables […]'. For Ambassador van Dedem, see Schutte, *Repertorium der Nederlandse vertegenwoordigers*, p. 313.

99 NACS, N°337 ('Proces tusschen Capirossi & Francois Siquard & C° van 21 feb 1766 tot 30 maert 1767'), 'Request van Fran.co Sequard aen den Franse consul weeg: pretentie op Cappirossi', Izmir, 21/02/1766 (the request was made at the French consulate and sent to the Dutch/Tuscan consulate); and 'Sententie van den here Consul de Hochepied in de affairen tusschen Fran: Sequard & C° & Capirossi', Izmir, 19/02/1767.

100 NACS, N°337, 'Acte van appel van Fran: Sequard & C° teegens de sententie van dato 19 feb: anno courant', Izmir, 30/03/1767, '[…] les seigneurs juges deleguez a Florence, ou a tout autre tribunal superieur a qui la connoissance en apartiendra […]'.

101 Ibid.

an appeal court in intercultural litigation. French consular courts in Livorno and Tunis were used as appeal courts, both by French and non-French nationals. A treaty concluded in 1616 between Jacques de Vincheguerre, a knight of Malta working for the city of Marseille, and Yūsuf Dey, the dey of Tunis, contained a clause determining that the French consul in Tunis was allowed to adjudicate disputes between European Christians and those who recognised the French consul.[102] This apparently codified existing practice, as Italians had been issuing appeals at the Tunis consulate against sentences issued in Pisa or Livorno.[103] An alternative to this form of legal forum shopping was the establishment of the competence of specific courts for the appeal against sentences about commercial disputes amongst traders of various nations. When Ancona became a free port (*portofranco*) in 1732, hoping to attract foreign trading communities, regulations stipulated that traders who were dissatisfied with the sentences from their consuls were allowed to appeal at the *Consolato di Mare* of Ancona, 'without seeking refuge to any other tribunal'.[104]

2 Unravelling the Web of Commission Trade in Court

2.1 *Crossing Physical Distance by Power of Attorney*

The Giera case was relatively simple, with easily definable parties, a concrete action that was being disputed and clear jurisdiction. It took a total of three rounds of declarations and counter-declarations before the consul reached a verdict, and although excerpts from correspondence and accounts were included in the declarations, no additional evidence needed to be submitted. In many other cases, things were not so straightforward, as illustrated by a complicated case adjudicated in Izmir by Consul Daniel Jean de Hochepied in 1766. In August that year, Jacques Forêt, an arms dealer from Liège, gave a power of attorney to a Dutch merchant in Izmir, Gerrit van Brakel, to act on his behalf in a court case against the Dutch firm of Dirk Knipping & C°, also merchants in Izmir. The document allowed van Brakel to use all legal means he

102 Guillaume Calafat, 'La jurisdiction des consuls français en Méditerranée: litiges marchands, arbitrages et circulation des procès (Livourne et Tunis au XVIIe siècle)', in *De l'utilité commerciale des consuls*, eds. Arnaud Bartolomei et al.

103 Ibid., pp. 15–16.

104 *De Nederlandsche maandelyke post-ryder, medebrengende berigten van de voornaamste en gedenkwaardigste staat- en oorlogszaken, die in en buiten 't Christenryk zyn voorgevallen, beneffens de daar toe behoorende bewysstukken. Voor de maand may, 1732* (Amsterdam, 1732), p. 520, '[…] zonder toevlugt te neemen tot eenig ander geregtshof […]'; see also *Il consolato della città d'Ancona ovvero raccolta dei privilegj, e de' capitoli* (Ancona, 1777).

could to obtain satisfaction for his principal.[105] Forêt demanded restitution of some weapons he had sent to Knipping, as well as monetary compensation for several sales of weapons Knipping had concluded on his behalf, at prices lower than the minimum Forêt had set for them and for which he never would have given permission. The declaration had been drafted before a Liège notary and contained an official confirmation from the aldermen of Liège confirming the veracity of the deed.[106]

Liège was a Prince-Bishopric, part of the Holy Roman Empire, and the place became an important centre for arms production in 1492 when official 'letters patent' were issued by the French, the Burgundian Netherlands and the Habsburg Empire, in which they all recognised Liège's neutral status.[107] The Prince-Bishopric had regulations in place ensuring the quality of firearms production since 1672 and maintained important trade connections with the United Provinces, which had purchased a great number of weapons there during the Eighty Years' War, as had the Spanish.[108] It is not surprising that arms dealers in the Prince-Bishopric used middlemen in port cities in Holland to send their goods to destinations even further abroad, such as the Ottoman Empire. Dutch port cities were particularly interesting, as the Ottoman Empire had been the first state to recognise the independent United Provinces, and it even sent some support in the form of weapons and clothing for soldiers. These contacts were later expanded upon, and the Dutch sent maritime weaponry and ships to North Africa and exported handguns to the Ottoman Empire.[109]

Sometimes transactions went wrong, which happened in the case of Jacques Forêt in Liège and Dirk Knipping in Izmir. Knipping was an interesting member of the Dutch community of Izmir. He had been a partner in the firm of David van Lennep, one of the most important Dutch merchants in Izmir, and William Enslie until his marriage to a Greek woman in 1758 ended his involvement.

105 NACS, N°339 ('Gerrit van Brakel, Nederlands koopman te Smyrna, optredende namens Jacques Forêt te Luik tegen Dirk Knipping, Nederlands koopman te Smyrna, 1767'), 'Constitution general passée par monsieur Jacques Foret marchand d'armes sur la personne de monsieur Gerrit van Brakel negociant a Smirne', Liège, 25/08/1766.

106 Ibid.

107 W.S.M. Knight, 'Neutrality and neutralisation in the sixteenth century – Liège', *Journal of comparative legislation and international law*, 2:1 (1920): pp. 98–104.

108 See Steven J. Gunn, David Grummitt, and Hans Cools, *War, state, and society in England and the Netherlands 1477–1559* (Oxford, 2007). Liège's tradition as an arms fabrication and trade centre continues to this day.

109 Alexander H. de Groot, *Nederland en Turkije. Zeshonderd jaar politieke, economische en culturele contacten* (Leiden, 1986), p. 12. For the efforts of a Jewish diplomat serving in Morocco and brokering deals between the Moroccan ruler and the United Provinces, see the biography of Samuel Pallache by García-Arenal and Wiegers, *Samuel Pallache*.

After that, it seems Knipping and his wife embarked for Amsterdam, where he originally came from, but by August 1759, he was back in Izmir, where he established a new firm in partnership with Pieter Ouckama.[110] Jacques Forêt had been one of the first traders to answer their call for commissions, and he started to send them weapons, using the firm of Herman van Coopstad in Rotterdam as an intermediary. He was not the only arms dealer from Liège starting to conduct business with Knipping & Ouckama.[111] By 1762, the partnership between the two Dutchmen had been dissolved, shown by a power of attorney sent from Rotterdam to Pieter Ouckama in an effort to claim money from the disbanded partnership between Knipping & Ouckama.[112] Knipping was elected as assessor for the Dutch nation in February 1763, which not only rendered him an element of the adjudicating system but also provided him with experience in litigation.[113] Six months later, he became the only Dutch trader who managed to escape the fire of August 1763. He had not found housing in the 'Street of the Franks' (see figure 4), which was greatly damaged by the fire, but was living 'in a small house in the Armenian neighbourhood'.[114] In the years after, Knipping stayed an independent merchant. He had not remained assessor for very long, as he was referred to as the 'former assessor' in a Dutch meeting held in Izmir in February 1766.[115] The meeting discussed the appointment of Knipping as the provisional overseer for the payment of consular taxes by members of the Dutch nation, a service for which he was paid 600 lion dollars per year.[116] Knipping held that position for at least six years, as a special meeting of the Directorate of Levant Trade in Amsterdam renewed his contract for a period of three years in September 1769.[117] When he was summoned in court as defendant, he was thus a figure of distinction in the Dutch trading community of Izmir.

110 See p. 69; see also Hakkı Kadı, *Ottoman and Dutch merchants*, p. 203.

111 See pp. 155–157.

112 NACS, N°498, 'Volmacht van Looy & van Spaen te Rotterdam voor Pieter Ouckama om gelden te innen die Dirk Knipping nog onder zich heeft uit de boedel van Knipping & Ouckama', Rotterdam, 02/04/1762.

113 Heeringa and Nanninga, *Bronnen tot de geschiedenis*, 3: pp. 479–480, 'Notulen weegens installeeren der assessooren', Izmir, 17/02/1763.

114 Ibid., pp. 483–484, Consul Daniel Jean de Hochepied to the States General, Izmir, 24/08/1763, '[...] in een klijn huysje in de Armeense buurd'. This was also reported by newspapers in the United Provinces; see the *Middelburgsche courant*, 22/10/1763; see also figure 4.

115 The meeting is quoted in Heeringa and Nanninga, *Bronnen tot de geschiedenis*, 4, p. 27, '[...] geweesen assessor [...]'.

116 Ibid.

117 Ibid., pp. 136–137, 'Extra-ordinaris vergadering van de directeuren met de buitenleden te Amsterdam', 27/09/1769.

Jacques Forêt had been doing business with Dirk Knipping since at least 1759, and often together with a firm in Rotterdam, Herman van Coopstad & C°. It seems that it was van Coopstad who established the contact and through whose hands the weapons were sent from Liège to Izmir. There, the weapons were sold by Ottoman middlemen, rendering the whole chain of transactions quite intercultural. In November 1759 Knipping, still in partnership with Ouckama, wrote to van Coopstad about an order he had received in Izmir for 2,400 pairs of pistols mounted in copper and with a slightly bigger lock than the pistols they had received before. Knipping & Ouckama were interested in a deal in which they would be involved for a quarter, while the remainder was to be split equally between van Coopstad and his 'friends from Liège'.[118] They were certain that van Coopstad would place the order with the firm of Jacques Forêt, Comhaire & C°.[119] Later that day, Knipping & Ouckama wrote to the Forêt firm about the proposal, assuring them that van Coopstad would address them, even though a number of other arms producers in the Prince-Bishopric had already offered to produce weapons for van Coopstad at prices lower than those of Forêt and his partners.[120] Knipping & Ouckama were optimistic about Forêt's abilities to deliver the order, and they hoped it would lead to a more regular arms trade as friends. It seems that this initial transaction indeed led to the development of more durable business ties, and even after the partnership between Knipping & Ouckama had been dissolved, the former continued to do business with Jacques Forêt and Herman van Coopstad until their dispute in 1767.

A year after Forêt gave van Brakel power of attorney, the latter filed an official claim at the Dutch consular court in Izmir.[121] In it, he demanded, on Forêt's behalf, 10,396:8 guilders from Knipping & C°. This was to cover half the value of the 400 pairs of pistols sold in 1765 (f665:7 guilders), the value of the sale of 831 pairs of pistols sold to Pietro Ferrieri & C° (f5,606:5) in 1764 and, finally, the value of four boxes containing 532 pistols and two boxes containing 95 flintlocks (*snaphanen*) sold in 1765 (f4,121:16).[122] Efforts to settle this sum directly with Knipping, Forêt's agent in Izmir, had failed, and Dirk Knipping seems to

---

118 NACS, N°490, Knipping & Ouckama to Herman van Coopstad & C°, Izmir, 01/11/1759, '[...] Luykse vrienden [...]'.

119 Ibid. The partnership between Forêt, Comhaire and others must have disbanded by the time Jacques Forêt gave his power of attorney to Gerrit van Brakel, as no mention was made of that firm.

120 NACS, N°490, Knipping & Ouckama to Forêt, Comhaire & C°, Izmir, 01/11/1759.

121 NACS, N°339, 'Request van Gerrit van Brakel weegens de pretentie van Foret aen Knipping', Izmir, 21/08/1767.

122 For the 'snaphaan', an early modern improvement of the arquebus, invented in France around 1635, see Barry M. Berkovitch, *The Cape gunsmith: A history of the gunsmiths and*

have registered some of the information incorrectly. The 831 pairs of pistols had apparently been sold to the partnership of Pietro Ferrieri & Robert Farrar, not to Ferrieri & C°, at an acceptable price for Forêt, so van Brakel wanted to see the obligations showing the outstanding debt of the buyers.[123] The four boxes of pistols and two boxes of flintlocks had been sold for too low a price, so van Brakel argued that Knipping had to participate financially in the loss, particularly as he, as commissioned agent, had written a letter to Forêt in 1765 promising to await new orders from him.

Knipping's writing demonstrated he was fully aware that he was not allowed to sell below a specific price limit, but he had done so anyway. To make matters worse, the money from that sale had not even been remitted to Forêt. Van Brakel suggested that Knipping had perhaps kept it for his own advantage, a cardinal sin for a commissioning agent. A second aggravating circumstance was that Knipping knew he had been selling to merchants that lacked money, making him responsible for the failure of the buyers to pay. For this, van Brakel demanded that Knipping make up Forêt's loss on the six boxes. As 'magistrate of the Dutch nation' and 'competent judge for both parties', the consul was asked to demand payment or obligations from Knipping for these transactions.[124] De Hochepied and the assessors, who included two of Knipping's former business partners (David van Lennep and William Enslie), ordered Knipping to settle his accounts with Forêt within the next ten days and to provide an obligation concerning the unpaid order of Ferrieri & Farrar.[125]

The litigation that ensued quickly focussed on two of the claims: the sale of the 831 pairs of pistols to the firm of Ferrieri & Farrar and the four boxes containing 532 pairs of pistols and 95 flintlocks. The first transaction concluded in December 1764, but in July 1765, Knipping sent Forêt a letter informing him that Ferrieri & Farrar had not paid yet, citing general difficulties paying several of their creditors.[126] The second transaction had been made to a number of unspecified buyers, and Forêt had not yet received any money for that sale either, a sale which had been concluded against Forêt's orders and under the

---

gun dealers at the Cape of Good Hope from 1795 to 1900, with particular reference to their weapons (Stellenbosch, 1976).

123 The commercial relationship between Pietro Ferrieri, a Venetian, and Robert Farrar, an Englishman, is not exactly clear from the documents. They were mentioned as the buyers of Forêt's 831 pairs of pistols, and both were considered to be responsible for their payment. NACS, N°339, 'Request van Gerrit van Brakel', Izmir, 21/08/1767.

124 NACS, N°339, 'Request van Gerrit van Brakel', Izmir, 21/08/1767, '[…] magistraat der Nederlandse natie […]' and '[…] beijder parthijen competente regtere […]'.

125 Ibid.

126 NACS, N°490, Dirk Knipping to Jacques Forêt, Izmir, 21/11/1765.

minimum price he had set. An adjustment van Brakel made in September 1767 to the current account between Knipping and Forêt from February 1766 shows that the four boxes from the second transaction had been sent from Rotterdam to Izmir on 3 May 1765.[127]

By the time of that adjustment, van Brakel had already received the power of attorney from Forêt. There are no concrete indications that the two men knew each other or had established a business correspondence earlier. It seems that Forêt's first letter to van Brakel was sent on 1 September 1766, a week after he gave him the power of attorney. Forêt was staying in Rotterdam at the time, where he found lodging through van Brakel's recommendation.[128] In a letter to van Brakel written in May 1767, which included an earlier copy of a letter from December 1766, Forêt consistently referred to 'that miserable' Knipping ('ce miserable') as 'a rogue' ('un fripon'), a man who was 'unworthy of living' ('indigne de vivre'), and demanded that van Brakel, once he had received all the documentation he needed, take care of Forêt's interest as 'if it was his own' ('de vous emploier comme pour vous meme').[129] If Knipping refused to pay, he was to brought to justice. He had affected Forêt's business in such a way that his health and that of his children had suffered and promised that, should van Brakel manage to get Knipping convicted, he would reciprocate such a 'great work of charity' ('le plus grand oeuvre de charite') by offering him his own services – a pretty good return favour according to Forêt, who claimed to be so well-known in Holland that he was the man to go to in case of need.[130]

Clearly, Forêt's letter had been written in a state of emotion but also in the spirit of the merchants' style. At first sight, it might look like a call for help from someone who would not know who else to turn to, with Knipping being his main contact in Izmir. But there was more at play. One of the central characteristics of business correspondence was reciprocity.[131] Merchants were in business together because they believed it would be profitable for

127 NACS, N°490, Copy of a sales account, Izmir, 20/02/1766; and 'Reekening courant tusschen Knipping & Forêt', 1767.

128 Writing letters of recommendation on behalf of fellow merchants who were travelling so they could dispose of credit, lodging and even entertainment, was a common favour given by traders to one another, and as such, it was part of the merchants' style. See Vanneste, *Global trade*, pp. 82–84; and Sebouh Aslanian, 'The "quintessential locus of brokerage": Letters of recommendations, networks, and mobility in the life of Thomas Vanandets'i, an Armenian printer in Amsterdam, 1677–1707', *Journal of world history*, 31:4 (2020): pp. 655–692.

129 NACS, N°490, Jacques Forêt to Gerrit van Brakel, Liège, 14/05/1767.

130 Ibid.

131 See Vanneste, 'Commercial culture', pp. 106–111.

all parties involved. Essentially, of course, it was a manner of pursuing self-interest through a balanced consideration of everyone's interests, but there was a strong reliance within the business community on the idea that everyone's self-interest was best served through reciprocity.[132] In the early modern world of international trade, reciprocity was a generally accepted mechanism by which traders judged their peers' behaviour and by which they calculated the risks attached to future transactions. Whether a trader complied with the custom of reciprocity when engaging in trade with a fellow merchant or not influenced his reputation and the trust put in him by other traders. These in turn played a role in the merchant's efforts to build up an international network of business correspondents with whom the trader could engage in mutually advantageous and long-term commercial relationships. This is the reason why there are so many references in business letters to rendering service to one another and the importance of this as the basis for setting up mutually successful commercial enterprises.

All of this is evident in the rhetoric used by Knipping & Ouckama when offering their services to Dutch correspondents as a new trade firm in Izmir in such emotional terms, referring to their own desire to 'serve their friends with loyal and honest actions' while also reiterating their conviction about the 'generosity' of these same friends.[133] Forêt's offer of reciprocity to van Brakel was conditional, as it depended on van Brakel's performance before the Dutch consular court in Izmir, but it was a very real offer and most likely a valued one, as merchants were always on the lookout to expand their web of business contacts with new, trustworthy individuals. Reciprocity, perhaps, was the commercial equivalent of legal equity. Van Brakel was to be assessed by Forêt, which influenced his reputation, potentially in the eyes of every correspondent of Forêt, who, in case of a successful outcome, could vouch for van Brakel as a trader in Izmir who was able to defend the interests of a stranger.

It would have been unwise of Forêt to put all of his faith in van Brakel without trying to find an alternative source that could keep him up to date with the legal proceedings in Izmir. Forêt was also being informed of the state of his affairs in Izmir by the firm of Manolaki di Panaiotis and Jacob de Vogel.[134] They informed Forêt about the identity of at least one of the mysterious buyers of

132 Harold J. Berman, *Law and revolution: The formation of the western legal tradition* (Cambridge, MA, 1983), pp. 344–345; see also pp. 173–181.

133 NACS, N°490, Knipping & Ouckama to Herman van Coopstad, Izmir, 29/09/1759, '[…] die onze respective vrinden met alle trouwe x eerlyke behandelingen tragten te bedienen […]' and '[…] genereusiteit […]'.

134 See also pp. 248, 250, and 283–284.

the pistols and flintlocks that had come in the four boxes. This man, still nameless in the correspondence, seems to have been 'Turkish'. Di Panaiotis and de Vogel must have already established a longer relationship with Forêt, because they were the intermediaries who delivered all of the relevant accounts about the affair to van Brakel.[135] It is impossible, without the survival of all the relevant written evidence, to guess why Forêt did not choose Panaiotis & de Vogel to represent his interests at the court. Perhaps he asked, but they declined. Perhaps he wanted a more neutral party, or at least a third party he would be able to observe through his other contacts. In any case, van Brakel had been recommended to Forêt by correspondents the arms dealer had in Rotterdam, Gerrit van Brakel's city of origin.

The power of attorney that van Brakel accepted on behalf of Forêt could enhance his commercial reputation and expand his business networks, but it also meant a substantial amount of work. The positives seem to have outweighed the negatives, because I have only found one example in which a merchant from the Dutch trading community of Izmir refused to accept a power of attorney to represent a colleague in a legal dispute. In 1770, the traders Salomon Lamera and F.H. Heffert were asked to act on behalf of Isaac Beaune, a merchant in Izmir. The latter had left town temporarily but was sued in court by Daniel Fremeaux on behalf of an Amsterdam firm that demanded payments from Beaune that were overdue. When the Dutch chancellor, accompanied by several witnesses, went to the house where Beaune's firm had been established to summon the defendant, they found one fellow trader, F.H. Heffert, willing to act as power of attorney while the other, Lamera, refused. Lamera explained he did not want to have anything to do with Beaune's firm and insisted the chancellor note it in the margin of the letter he had brought with him. Lamera's refusal did not have any legal consequences, but it is unclear whether his reputation took a blow and his business suffered from his refusal.[136]

Lamera might not have felt in any way attached to the Dutch community of Izmir, and in that sense, it might have been easier for him to refuse the power of attorney. He had other options, but for Heffert, relying on commissions from the United Provinces, damage to his reputation could quickly spread from the Dutch trading community of Izmir to clients in the Dutch Republic, and his business might suffer accordingly. His fellow traders in Izmir might also stop

---

135 NACS, N°490, Jacques Forêt to Gerrit van Brakel, Liège, 14/05/1767.

136 NACS, N°349 ('Papieren der proces tusschen Fremeaux & Heffert, 19/02/1770–19/03/1771'), 'Acte van vertoonde procuratie aen de proc van Pieter Isaac Beaune & C° weegens de intresten van de heeren du long, De Conink & Elliot te Amst met protest weegens gewygerde verantwoord', Izmir, 19/02/1770.

doing him favours. In any case, van Brakel's immediate acceptance to legally represent a stranger from a foreign land in court was not at all exceptional, and the potential commercial advantages this legal effort could bring were substantial. Van Brakel was a relatively new member of the Dutch trading community of Izmir at the time, and he had a lot to win by obtaining the gratitude of Jacques Forêt, who would be able to ensure future commissions for him.

2.2 *The Trial*

After van Brakel filed his petition with the consular court in August 1767, a relatively short legal procedure ensued. Knipping disputed the claim of 10,396:8 guilders and sent a number of current accounts between him and Forêt along with his written reply to support his argument.[137] The main task of the consul and his assessors was to determine who was responsible for the two disputed transactions. The task was complicated by the fact that Knipping was in financial difficulties, with several of his creditors pressing him to pay his debts. It made all goods he was to receive on commission vulnerable. Knipping's financial difficulties were well-known, because Consul de Hochepied had issued a declaration in November 1766 in which he confirmed that Dirk Knipping was still fully in charge of his company (Dirk Knipping & C°) and that the management of his affairs had not been taken away from him, in spite of the financial troubles he was having.[138]

Van Brakel and Knipping were fellow merchants. Van Brakel not only knew Knipping personally, he also had been somewhat involved in Knipping's business activities on Forêt's behalf. Knipping stated that by the time the shipment of four barrels of pistols and two cases of flintlocks arrived, van Brakel was well aware of the financial difficulties Knipping was in. Gerrit van Brakel offered his help and suggested that the merchandise should be endorsed to him instead, and he would pay the import taxes on it.[139] Knipping accepted van Brakel's proposal, which might have been an attempt to take over as a commissioner for Forêt, hoping to gain more business prospects that way. While Knipping did not use this information to place van Brakel in a bad light, this part of the story is reminiscent of the discussion between Ouckama and Clement, van Sanen, van der Zee & C°. The latter stood in the same legal position as van

137 NACS, N°339, 'Request van Gerrit van Brakel', Izmir, 21/08/1767; and 'Antwoord van Knipping aen Braekel wegg: Forret te luijk', Izmir, 28/08/1767.

138 NACS, N°162 ('Minuten kanselarij, 1766'), 'Declaratie van den heere consul aen Dirk Knipping dat hem het bewind sijner saeken door niemand alhier is affgenoomen, maar alles ten volle is in handen gelaeten', Izmir, 19/11/1766.

139 NACS, N°339, 'Antwoord van Knipping aen Braekel wegg: Forret te luijk', Izmir, 28/08/1767.

Brakel, holding power of attorney for a geographically remote plaintiff, and also offered a commercial service to a fellow trader in the same community. That case sparked a debate on the nature of reciprocity. Here, Knipping used the discussion to shift part of the responsibility.

Whatever van Brakel's motives behind the proposal were, Knipping agreed, as it guaranteed the safety of Forêt's goods from Knipping's creditors in case he would go bankrupt. But when one of these creditors, a Turk named Hagi 'Abdullah, came to Knipping to claim his money, van Brakel put the weapons in the hands of Knipping's Jewish broker, Elia Hemzy, making them again vulnerable to any creditor's claim. Knipping insisted the weapons be put securely in the chancery, again to prevent any damage to Forêt's interests, but 'Abdullah became angry and threatened to take Knipping to an Ottoman court if he failed to pay his debts.[140] Knipping felt he had no choice but to hand over part of the weapons to 'Abdullah, defending his decision by remarking that they were living in 'a Turkish land and were exposed to all *avanias*'.[141] *Avania* was a term used by Europeans to label actions by the Ottoman authorities that they considered unjust; the meaning Europeans gave it was 'extortion'.[142]

Maurits van den Boogert, however, has shown that this negative interpretation was far from correct, inspired by a Eurocentric interpretation and incomplete understanding of Ottoman bureaucracy. It was derived from the idea that the capitulations, and the legal autonomy granted therein, were sacred, and every Ottoman action that could be interpreted as an infringement of the absolute nature of the capitulations was considered to be extortion. But this ignored the fact that the capitulations fit within the broader context of the Ottoman legal system and were balanced with a whole body of Ottoman *kanun* and Islamic law.[143] Mostly, it was used to refer to payments to Ottoman bureaucracy that Europeans mistakenly thought of as unfair 'extortion in the Turkish style', or with certain legal actions that Europeans feared, did not understand or did not consider honest.[144] The concept is thus often used in phrasing that

140 Ibid.

141 Ibid., '[…] dewyl wy alhier in een Turks lant zyn x voor alle avanies bloot staan […]'; see also pp. 308–312 for more on *avanias*.

142 For a detailed analysis of the concept of *avania* as used by Europeans, see van den Boogert, *The capitulations*, pp. 117–157; see also Merlijn Olnon, 'Towards classifying *avanias*: A study of two cases involving the English and Dutch nations in seventeenth-century Izmir', in *Friends and rivals*, eds. Hamilton et al., pp. 159–186.

143 Van den Boogert, *The capitulations*, pp. 117–157.

144 Heeringa and Nanninga, *Bronnen tot de geschiedenis*, 2: p. 10, '[…] geldafpersing in Turkschen stijl […]'. The language is Heeringa's and is a clear use of a prejudiced stereotype.

reflects the European perceptions of volatility and arbitrariness, such as 'out of fear of *avania*' or 'unheard of and tyrannical *avania*'.[145]

Europeans felt victimised by these *avanias* and never hesitated to express as much to their fellow Europeans. Knipping's observation that he had no choice because otherwise he might have suffered some unjust Ottoman extortion is but one of many examples. He continued his letter by stating that he sold the remainder of the weapons rapidly, indeed at too low a price, but he only had done to pay off his most pressing debts and out of necessity to live.[146]

Regarding the weapons that had been sold to Ferrieri & Farrar, Dirk Knipping insisted he continued to ask for their payment from the buyers. When that failed, he sought recourse to de Hochepied, who spoke with the English consul Anthony Hayes in an attempt to force Robert Farrar, an Englishman, to pay for the weapons. The conversation had some success, as Ferrieri issued two obligatory notes to cover the sale. The first was dated 24 December 1764 and was worth 2,039:50 lion dollars, while the other, dated 18 February 1765, initially had been worth 2,700 lion dollars but 1,000 had been paid already. The second of them had already been in van Brakel's possession since October 1765, long before the trial. With this in mind, Knipping was startled by the financial claim made by van Brakel in Forêt's name on that transaction.[147] Knipping's main argument was that he had always attempted to protect Forêt's interests, as a good agent, in spite of the financial difficulties he was going through. Knipping felt the accusation that he should have known better than to sell to a buyer with financial difficulties – Ferrieri & Farrar – was unjust and irresponsible, particularly as van Brakel himself had conducted business with Farrar ten months after the sale of the weapons, which was proof that van Brakel also had kept trust in the Englishman's creditworthiness. Knipping further stated that he was committed to repay all of his own creditors in full at a rate of ten percent per year over a period of ten years. He could, on the other hand, not provide any financial security for this promise, only his honesty, as he was living

145 Ibid., pp. 447–449, Theyls aan de directeuren, Cairo, 24/01/1664, on p. 447, '[…] uijt vreese van avenie […]' and Heeringa and Nanninga, *Bronnen tot de geschiedenis*, 3: pp. 379–390, 'De Nederlandsche kooplieden te Angora aan consul tresorier, assessoren en leden van de Nederlandscha natie te Smirna', Izmir, 01/12/1757, on p. 349, '[…] de ongehoorde en tirannise avania […]'.

146 NACS, N°339, 'Antwoord van Knipping aen Braekel wegg: Forret te luijk', Izmir, 28/08/1767.

147 Ibid. More information on the obligations can be found in the final verdict. NACS, N°339, 'Sententie &a weeg: de differentie van Knipping x van Brakel weegens Forret te Luijk', Izmir, 06/10/1767. Hayes was consul in Izmir between 1762 and 1794. Wood, *Levant Company*, p. 255.

parsimoniously with his wife and children, relying on the little income he was making as overseer of the Dutch consular taxes.[148]

Knipping's argument was crucial in the court's assessment of his responsibility. It seems that he had committed a cardinal sin for an agent by selling goods on behalf of his principal but under the minimum price that had been set.[149] If he was found guilty, Knipping's reputation would suffer. As his financial difficulties were already publicly known, he risked losing all of his reputational assets. It might incline other merchants to stop doing business with him, and Knipping might never fully recover. It was therefore very important that Knipping was able to fully explain his actions. The principal trader's lack of information on the market circumstances abroad was a common problem that agents faced. Traders complained regularly in their letters to correspondents that the prices fetched for their goods were too low. It made all the difference whether the agent could convince his principal, and the trading community at large, that such low prices had nothing to do with his commercial abilities but everything to do with the state of the market.[150] Agents sent long letters to their principals, explaining the circumstances behind transactions, and Knipping had done the same for Forêt.[151] In this particular case, Jacques Forêt had provided van Brakel with one such letter, so it could be demonstrated to the court that Knipping had gone against Forêt's orders. In the letter, Knipping argued that market circumstances were so bad he would wait on new orders from Forêt, because no transaction could be concluded at the price minimum that had been set.[152] Gerrit van Brakel argued that, contrary to what Knipping wrote in the letter, he continued to sell, but under the price minimum set by Forêt. This, of course, was motivated by Knipping's financial troubles. He continued to sell so he could use some of the money to pay off his debtors – something Knipping had already admitted – but also to secure the commission, which was in his own interest but not necessarily in that of his principal.[153]

The fundamental issue was about creditworthiness, not only Knipping's but also that of the buyers he had chosen. For the plaintiff, it all clearly

148 NACS, N°339, 'Antwoord van Knipping aen Braekel wegg: Forret te luijk', Izmir, 28/08/1767.

149 See also pp. 159–160.

150 Such claims could be hard to verify and traders tried other channels to obtain confirmation of such information. See also pp. 170 and 177.

151 See, for instance, NACS, N°490, Knipping & Ouckama to Herman van Coopstad, Izmir, 01/11/1759.

152 NACS, N°339, 'Request Gerrit van Brakel', Izmir, 21/08/1767 ; and 'Lettre de Vienne a Monsieur Jacques Foret Liege p adresse de messrs Bongaene & Panchaud a Constantinople le 21/11/1765 Vienne le 26/11 recu de vos tres hbles serv. p freres Smitmer', Izmir, 18/09/1765.

153 Ibid.

demonstrated that Knipping had acted as an incapable agent at best and as a fraudulent one at worst. One of the central questions that needed to be answered was to what extent Knipping had known about Ferrieri & Farrar's creditworthiness. The answer determined Knipping's liability in the financial fiasco of that transaction. It seems that Knipping's argumentation was convincing, because van Brakel accepted it. He expressed his willingness to procure payment for the two obligations in his hands. The other transaction, involving Hagi 'Abdullah, was not so easily resolved – and maybe this can be explained by the fact that Knipping had referred to van Brakel's involvement in it, which meant his reputation was now also at stake. Van Brakel replied to Knipping's narrative by writing that Knipping had been dishonest, because he had only given the weapons to the broker at Knipping's behest, not because he had been pressured by Hagi 'Abdullah. He further stated that Knipping's justification of selling below the set price so he could pay off his debts and live was completely unheard of: 'where in the world has it been heard of that someone might take the goods of another, and to dispose of them to his own liking, to pay preferential and other debts, and to survive, and to make a price to his own desire [...] I say nowhere in the world'.[154] Van Brakel found Knipping's proposal of reimbursement in ten years 'completely unreasonable', but he accepted it nevertheless so he could show the whole world that he was willing to settle affairs 'without having any desire to ruin the debtor and his family'.[155]

Van Brakel not only tried to salvage his own reputation, but his words also echo commercial morals from within the international trading community. Creditworthiness was a crucial asset for traders, because no international trade existed without credit.[156] They could always be broken because somebody got into trouble. Bankruptcy was not uncommon in the early modern period, and what happened to Knipping could easily have happened to van Brakel as well – particularly considering the fact that van Brakel had been doing business with

154 NACS, N°339, 'Replicq van Gerrit van Brakel weegens Knipping de affaires van Forret', Izmir, 12/09/1767, [...] waar is ooit in de weereld gehoort, dat imand het goed van een ander mag neemen, daar over na eigen wel behaage te disponeeren geprefeerde en andere schulden te betalen, en daar van t eleven &ca en dan dezelve nog in de prijze zoo maar na eijgen believe te stellen, ofte reguleeren [...] ik zegge nergens in de weereld'.

155 Ibid., '[...] geheel onreedelijk [...]' and '[...] zonder den debiteur off zijne familie te willen ruineeren [...]'.

156 John Smail, 'Credit, risk, and honor in eighteenth-century commerce', *Journal of British studies*, 44:3 (2005): pp. 439–456. For a case study linking credit and reputation, see Zahedieh, 'Credit, risk, and reputation'; see also Julian Hoppit, 'The use and abuse of credit in eighteenth-century England', in *Business life and public policy: Essays in honour of D.C. Coleman*, eds. D.C. Coleman and N. McKendrick (Cambridge, 1986), pp. 64–78.

the same insolvent clients. Fairness in judgment was important. In that sense, van Brakel's willingness to resolve the case without harming Knipping any further fits with the behavioural norm that dictated that one should look out for one's peers. While the self-sacrificing nature of van Brakel's easy acceptance of a solution might have been rhetoric; it was also a way of demonstrating to his peers that he had not set out to destroy a colleague's firm that was already in trouble. In other words, van Brakel was showing himself, and by association also the man he represented in court, Jacques Forêt, to be a man one could enter into business with. This might have been the most important aim van Brakel set out to achieve when he accepted Forêt's power of attorney. Forêt used very strong language against Knipping, Ferrieri and Farrar, calling all of them rogues.[157] Knipping was bankrupt. Amidst all of this, van Brakel could emerge as the voice of reason, a merchant one could count on for future commissions but also for upholding the merchants' style in all fairness and reciprocity.

In the same atmosphere of reason, the consul and assessors read all the written statements and asked both parties to appear before them in person for interrogation. The verdict that followed stipulated that Knipping endorse both of Ferrieri's obligations to van Brakel. This made Ferrieri and Farrar direct debtors to van Brakel, acting on behalf of Forêt, saving the latter from further involvement in Knipping's bankruptcy. The sentence continued that Knipping had to pay 4121:16 guilders, the amount claimed by van Brakel, for the 532 pairs of pistols and 95 flintlocks. At the same time, the court agreed on the ten-year plan Knipping proposed for repayment and on the plaintiff's claim for a caution, so they sentenced that half of Knipping's yearly reimbursements would have to come from his salary as overseer of the taxes. He had to promise 'as an honourable man' to pay the other half when due.[158] Should Knipping fail to pay, van Brakel could sequester his person and goods. Knipping was also sentenced to pay the expenses of the trial. Both parties agreed to this settlement of affairs.[159]

The sentence made Knipping partially responsible but still allowed him to try to save his business. He proceeded to do so, and when he attempted to reclaim money from a business partner in Rotterdam, Herman van Coopstad, in January 1769, Knipping asked legal help from the man who had been successful in defending Forêt's interests a little over a year earlier – Gerrit van Brakel. There clearly was no animosity between the two former adversaries.

157 NACS, N°490, Jacques Forêt to Gerrit van Brakel, Liège, 14/05/1767.

158 NACS, N°349, 'Sententie &a weeg: de differentie van Knipping x van Brakel weegens Forret te Luijk', Izmir, 06/10/1767, '[...] als een eerelijk man [...]'.

159 Ibid.

The transaction that Knipping disputed had to do with a sale of 912 pairs of pistols, which was concluded in January 1765 with Pietro Ferrieri. Van Coopstad had been involved for a quarter of the deal, and in 1769, he still owed Knipping money related to this transaction.[160] Knipping wanted to receive a bill of exchange, payable to Gerrit van Brakel, from van Coopstad, to settle affairs between them. Should van Coopstad refuse to furnish it, he authorised Gerrit van Brakel to act as a plaintiff on Knipping's behalf in court against van Coopstad.[161] This power of attorney must have meant that van Brakel had gone back to Rotterdam, a return that was most likely related to problems that arose between him and the consul. After Knipping, it was now van Brakel's turn to be plagued by financial problems: he failed to repay two Greek creditors and also was unable to meet his Dutch and Ottoman tax duties.[162]

Van Brakel's financial difficulties show that it had been a good decision to not press the case against Knipping too hard. The appeal Knipping made to van Brakel for his services also demonstrates that merchants did not bear resentment when they felt a case was handled fair and equitably. Beyond such considerations of mercantile custom, however, Van Brakel and Knipping might also have shared an understanding of the social problems one could get into in a foreign land. In 1767, Gerrit van Brakel married a Greek woman, something Knipping had also done almost a decade before. At the time, the marriage stirred controversy, because the Greek bishop in Izmir was fiercely opposing such marriages out of fear it might lead to the conversion of Greek women to the Roman Catholic or Protestant churches. The Dutch consul blamed van Brakel for some of the controversy.[163]

---

160 A declaration of debt had been left at the Dutch chancery, drafted in the presence of two witnesses, in which Ferrieri promised to pay Knipping for these pistols within six months. NACS, N°162, 'Attestatie van P: Ferrieri dat aen Knipping & C° voor gekogte pistoolen Lx 4332 schuldig is', Izmir, 18/11/1766.

161 NACS, N°345 ('Copye der documenten van D. Knipping teegens H. v. Coopstad in faveur van G. v. Brakel in Smirna'), 'Brieff aan Coopstad', Izmir, 07/01/1769.

162 Heeringa and Nanninga, *Bronnen tot de geschiedenis*, 4: pp. 191–192, 'Extra-ordinaris vergadering met de buitenleden te Amsterdam', Amsterdam, 26/10/1774. Van Brakel's financial difficulties led to temporary expulsions from the Dutch trading community of Izmir, but he managed to return to exercise different functions. He became tax overseer in 1774 (see p. 248), chancellor of the consulate between 1783 and 1804 and treasurer from 1805 until his death in 1817. Schutte, *Repertorium der Nederlandse vertegenwoordigers*, p. 342. For his financial difficulties and his various petitions to return to the community, see NACS, N°229 ('Stukken betreffende de schulden van de kanselier Gerrit van Brakel en diens tijdelijke schorsingen, 1770 & 1804').

163 See NACS, N°223, which contains documents on the quarrels arising out of the marriages between European Christians and Greek Orthodox women; see also pp. 70 and 299.

Van Coopstad's refusal to fully pay Knipping for the transaction was related to the fact that he had sold to Ferrieri, a buyer known to have poor creditworthiness. It was the same argument that Forêt had made, but van Brakel had accepted Knipping's argument that Ferrieri was not known to stand in poor credit at the time Knipping accepted the sale. The same issue was at stake here, and the case file contains two declarations drafted by several merchants that Ferrieri was still trusted and stood in good credit at the time Knipping was doing business with him. These documents could free Knipping of all responsibility for choosing Ferrieri as a buyer. The most interesting feature of these declarations was their international nature. They were signed by over twenty merchants in Izmir, and their backgrounds were diverse. There are signatures in Arabic, Latin and Hebrew script, and Turkish names such as 'Ali Effendi, Sale Aga and Mehmed Aga, Jewish names such as Chaim Albaglie and Joseph Leon & C°, and Greek firms such as Vitale, Zingrilara & C°, Jani Mavrogordatos and Michele Curmusi next to the French firm of Tricon Frères & C° and the name of Gerrit van Brakel (see figure 8).[164] This was a type of witness declaration that was frequently used in a court case as evidence. Often, these declarations indicated the opinion of part of the international merchant community on the behaviour of a fellow trader, and it was used to assess the individual responsibility of that trader in light of the merchants' style. Considering the international nature of the merchants' style, it was perfectly normal for such a declaration, even when issued in a specifically Dutch dispute, to contain the names of merchants with very different backgrounds.

The declarations were in support of Knipping, claiming he could not have known about Ferrieri's problems at the time of the sale. Additionally, these merchants confirmed they had also been doing business with Ferrieri at that time. This was perhaps the best weapon to use when defending someone's behaviour. It was hard to guess what an agent could and should know about a client he was doing business with. If twenty merchants wrote that they also continued to do business with the same client, it was very strong evidence that the agent could not have known and could thus not be held responsible. He should not pay for financial damages resulting from the transaction, and he should also not be branded as incompetent. These declarations were written to save Knipping's reputation, and the consul and assessors found them to be authentic. The remaining documents kept from this case do not include a final verdict, so the outcome remains unclear. It should be kept in mind that this

164 NACS, N°345, 'Acte hoe hy buyten myn door andre is vertrouwt geweest', Izmir, 08/12/1768; and 'Copije attestatie van diversen dat Feriere in gen: 1765 nog in buonis was', Izmir, 29/12/1768.

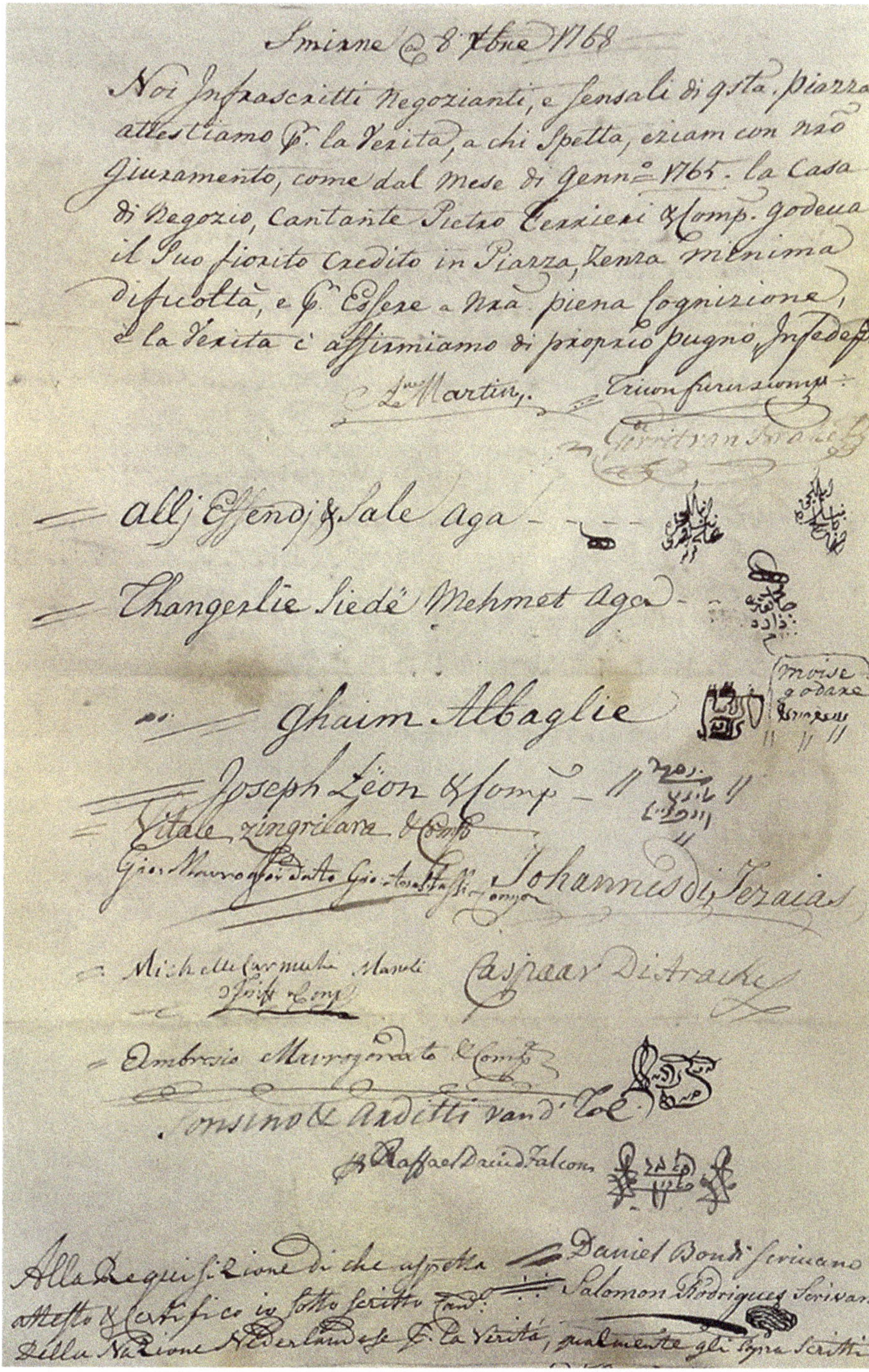

FIGURE 8 Signatures on a declaration of trust towards Pietro Ferrieri, 8 December 1768
FROM THE DUTCH NATIONAL ARCHIVES, THE HAGUE (ARCHIVES OF THE DUTCH CONSULATE IN SMYRNA). PHOTO BY THE AUTHOR.

was not a case in which the consul was adjudicating. These were documents concerning a case in which van Coopstad was the defendant. Thus, the case would have needed to be tried in Rotterdam, and the fact that a number of documents have been preserved in the archives of the Dutch consulate in Izmir might be related to the fact that Knipping had given them to the chancellor so they could be checked for veracity and sent to Rotterdam.

2.3 *A Complicated Web of Entanglement*

The outcome of the 1767 case between Knipping and Forêt was relatively straightforward. The verdict was not harsh on Knipping, and he was not blamed for selling quickly to cover his own financial problems. Perhaps these problems softened the judgment of the consular court, as he was not sentenced to pay for all of the trial's expenses. He was warned, however, that he would be forced to pay all future legal expenses that would occur as a consequence of a failure to repay Forêt. In 1774, however, it became clear that Forêt had not forgotten all of his claims against his former agent. Although Knipping had been paying off Jacques Forêt at set times, he was still indebted to the arms dealer. In addition, it became clear that Forêt was still disputing part of the payment of the 831 pairs of pistols that Knipping had sold to Ferrieri & Farrar, in particular the 1,000 lion dollars that had been part of the obligation of 2,700 lion dollars and had been registered as paid by the time the remaining 1,700 lion dollars had been endorsed to van Brakel to collect on Forêt's behalf.[165] The money never made it to Forêt, who felt Knipping, as the agent concluding the original sale, was still to blame.

Knipping was still in financial troubles but had been supported by the Dutch trading community in Izmir. At the time, all parties accepted the judgment in the first instance, and van Brakel had not appealed the consular sentence, which freed Knipping of all responsibility in the transaction of the 831 pairs of pistols. Jacques Forêt was apparently not happy with the outcome and perhaps also not happy with the position of van Brakel, who had acted on behalf of Knipping in the meantime, and this time, he decided to bring the case before a different court. He issued a power of attorney for legal representation to the Greek merchant Manolaki di Panaiotis, a *barattaire* of France and one of the merchants he had been in contact with to verify what was happening in Izmir at the time of the first trial against Dirk Knipping.[166] On 10 December 1773, di Panaiotis petitioned the judge under whose jurisdiction he fell, the

165 See p. 233.
166 For more on Manolaki di Panaiotis, see pp. 282–285.

French consul in Izmir, Charles de Peyssonnel, to sequester an obligation of 1,000 lion dollars that was in the hands of the Venetian consul, Luca Cortazzi (under whose jurisdiction Ferrieri fell), and represented Ferrieri's debt to Dirk Knipping.[167] Forêt was hoping that the sequester would help him to reclaim the money he was still owed. For Knipping, the manoeuvre came as a surprise. He knew that di Panaiotis had been looking after Forêt's interests in Izmir, and on 2 October 1773, he received di Panaiotis' permission to travel to Holland on a voyage to settle his remaining debts with Forêt, his last remaining creditor.[168]

The same day, Knipping endorsed the obligation of 1,000 lion dollars to his Greek wife, Marigo Sottira, so she could use it in his absence. The action was defended as a consequence of the marital contract made between the husband and wife in 1758. Two months later, di Panaiotis petitioned the French consul to place a sequester but still allowed Knipping to travel to Holland. Because he also accepted Knipping's latest repayment to Forêt, Knipping did not understand the actions of di Panaiotis.[169] Two weeks after the sequester, Marigo Knipping obtained a promise from the Venetian consul to pay her the 1,000 lion dollars of the obligation in his hands. But for that purpose, the sequester needed to be relieved. In January 1774, Marigo petitioned Dutch consul Daniel Jean de Hochepied to request that his French colleague lift the sequester.[170] The same day, di Panaiotis delivered a bundle of paperwork to the Dutch chancery with all the documents concerning the case between Pietro Ferrieri & C° and Dirk Knipping. These concerned all the information on the transactions involving Jacques Forêt.[171] When the French consul confronted him with the

167 As part of the larger obligation of 2,700 lion dollars. NACS, N°357 ('Affairen tusschen Pietro Ferrieri & Dirk Knipping'), 'Request van Dirk Knipping teegens Manuel Kiriako di Panajottis', Izmir, 07/02/1774. A short biography of Charles de Peyssonnel (1700–1790), born in Marseille, can be found in John Aikin, Thomas Morgan, and William Johnston, *General biography; or, lives, critical and historical, of the most eminent persons of all ages, countries, conditions, and professions, arranged according to alphabetical order* (London, 1813), 8: p. 109. His son succeeded him as consul.

168 Dirk Knipping explicitly mentioned that such permission was needed, considering the agreement made between himself and Forêt. NACS, N°357, 'Request van Dirk Knipping teegens Manuel Kiriako di Panajottis', Izmir, 07/02/1774.

169 NACS, N°357, 'Request van Dirk Knipping teegens Manuel Kiriako di Panajottis', Izmir, 07/02/1774.

170 NACS, N°357, 'Request van Marigo Knipping aan den wel ed Graaf de Hochepied om door de Franse consul te laate intimeeren aan Man K:° di Panajottis & Comp.a om de sequestro te ontlossen', Izmir, 19/01/1774.

171 NACS, N°357, 'Recief van my can aen M.K. di Panajottis weegens een verseegelde plicq papieren aengaende de affairen tusschen Pietro Ferrieri & Dirk Knipping', Izmir, 22/01/1774.

request, di Panaiotis agreed to lift it, but only if the Dutch consul was willing to pay a caution, which he refused.[172] Dirk Knipping, in the meantime, had informed the French consul, as well as a number of di Panaiotis' friends, that, if the latter refused to relieve the sequester, Knipping, whose clothes had already been transferred aboard a Dutch vessel, found himself obliged to declare bankruptcy, which would harm Forêt's interests as sole remaining creditor.[173]

Marigo Knipping's claim to lift the sequester, made on 19 January 1774 to de Hochepied, was the start of a trial that would be sentenced by the French consul. She and her husband had now become plaintiffs against the defendant Manolaki di Panaiotis, who, as a French *protégé*, fell under their jurisdiction. This was confirmed in the formulation of the sentence handed down by the French consul and his deputies a month later.[174] At first sight, it might seem remarkable that much of the trial's paperwork is preserved in the Dutch consular archives, considering the case was tried before the French consul. But on closer inspection, it can be understood as an expression of the procedural pragmatism that existed in the adjudication of international disputes. All European nations had accepted *forum rei*, so nobody disputed that di Panaiotis should defend himself before a French court. But the plaintiffs did not need to appear physically before the same court. The French consular adjudication, like the Dutch one, followed summary procedure, which stipulated that the core of the trial was formed by written statements, replies and counter-replies. Similar to the Dutch assessor system, the French adjudicated their disputes using a consular judge accompanied by a number of the most important French traders.[175]

172 NACS, N°357, 'Risposta di Manuel K:° di Panaiottis dimandando cauzione all console di Ollanda p soltare il sequestro fatto a Dirk Knipping', Izmir, 03/02/1774.

173 NACS, N°357, 'Request van Dirk Knipping teegens Manuel Kiriako di Panajottis', Izmir, 07/02/1774; and 'Versoekschrifft van Dirk Knipping om in de Franse cancel: te nottificeeren dat sijne conventie vernieuwd met Jacques Forret om in tien jaaren alles te betaelen, dog inteegendeel staende blijvende hij daer toe niet in staat was & alles moeste abandonneeren', Izmir, 19/02/1774.

174 NACS, N°357, 'Sentenza van de heere Franse consul & gedeputeerdens weegens de gesequestreerde Lx1000 van Dirk Knipping onder de heere Venetiaanse consul', Izmir, 21/02/1774.

175 For more on the French consuls, with specific attention paid to the Levant, see Anne Mézin, *Les consuls de France au siècle des lumières (1715–1792)* (Paris, 1997); see also the essays on French consuls by Jörg Ulbert, 'La dépêche consulaire française et son acheminement en Méditerranée sous Louis XIV (1661–1715)', pp. 31–57; Julien Sempéré, 'La correspondance du consulat français de Barcelone (1679–1716). Informer comme un consul ou comme un marchand?', pp. 121–140; and David Plouviez 'Puissance navale et réseaux consulaires. L'action des consuls français en Italie et sur les marges occidentales de l'Empire ottoman au XVIIIe siècle', pp. 179–199; all in *Les consuls en Méditerranée, agents d'information XVIe–XXe siècle*, ed. Silvia Marzagalli (Paris, 2015).

The plaintiffs, who fell under Dutch jurisdiction, were not forced to submit their documents to the French court. They were allowed to submit everything at the Dutch consulate, and in their statements, they specifically addressed the Dutch consul to inform his French colleague. When Marigo Knipping filed her claim, an additional paragraph added by the consul instructed the chancellor to keep a copy of it in the chancery and to send another copy to the French chancellor, 'asking them to do justice and to instruct Manolaki di Panaiotis to relieve the sequester and to condemn him to reimburse all expenses and interests'.[176] Di Panaiotis was doing the same but the other way around – he addressed the French consul. The only exception was that he had deposited some relevant paperwork concerning Forêt's transactions with Knipping and Ferrieri to the Dutch chancery.

This was a practice that created additional paperwork, as more copies needed to be made, and some of them might need additional translations. Knipping wrote in Dutch and di Panaiotis in Italian. Consul de Hochepied was also able to communicate in Italian, as was Knipping's wife. The French consul issued his documents in French. In disputes, the chancellor's task was to inform litigating parties of any statements filed by the opposition – this did not change – but an additional layer was created as it was not the Dutch chancellor but rather the French chancellor who would inform di Panaiotis of this in person. When visiting a litigant, the chancellors were often accompanied by witnesses. Sentencing, of course, was still the prerogative of the consular court of the defendant. In this case, the legal dispute was about the sequester that di Panaiotis had made through the French consul. Since 1686, a Dutch regulation existed that dealt with sequesters on goods in the Levant, but obviously, it did not directly cover the problem of an Ottoman merchant who was a French *protégé* laying a claim on monies in the hands of the Venetian consul, covering a debt of a Venetian subject (in partnership with an Englishman) to a Dutch subject and endorsed to that subject's Greek wife, in order to seek satisfaction for an outstanding debt the Venetian had with an inhabitant of Liège from a sale concluded by the Dutchman years earlier. With so many international parties, it might be considered remarkable that at no moment was competence or jurisdiction questioned. It was evidently a matter of French jurisdiction. Di Panaiotis laid out his arguments to the French consul and Dirk and Marigo

176 NACS, N°357, 'Request van Marigo Knipping aan den wel ed Graaf de Hochepied om door de Franse consul te laate intimeeren aan Man K:° di Panajottis & comp.a om de sequestro te ontlossen', Izmir, 19/01/1774, '[…] pregandola di fare giustizia & di ordinare a Manolaki di Panaiotis di levare il sequestro & di condannargli all'rifarcimento d'ogni danno spese x intresse […]'.

Knipping before the Dutch one. The consuls were in contact through their chancellors but also talked in person.[177] At a certain moment, Pietro Ferrieri was demanded to appear before both the Dutch and Venetian consuls, declaring that the 1,000 lion dollars in Cortazzi's hands arose from a debt Ferrieri owed Knipping for 400 lion dollars–worth of gunpowder and 600 lion dollars of cash.[178]

In his written reply to Dirk Knipping's summary of the case on 7 February, in which he restated his wife's claim to lift the sequester, Manolaki di Panaiotis mentioned he felt that Knipping had made an unreasonable threat, trying to claim money that did not belong to him in order to give it to his wife.[179] After receiving di Panaiotis' reply, the consul ordered his chancellor, Mann, to notify Dirk Knipping, as the French chancellor had asked. Mann went to Knipping's house that same day in the company of two witnesses. Knipping replied that he had nothing more to add, and he wanted the French consul to reach a verdict.[180] His wife must have known that the sentence would go against her and her husband, as on 23 February she issued a power of attorney to Gasparo Giovanelli to further look after her interests concerning the obligation and to interact on her behalf with 'justice, magistrate, tribunal and court'.[181] She did so because she argued that, as a woman, she was not a legally independent person.[182] She was well-informed, because later that day, the sentence of French Consul Charles de Peyssonnel was submitted to the Dutch chancery (the verdict itself had been pronounced at the French consulate on the twenty-first). The French consul and four 'negocians notables de la nation, assistans en jugement' had analysed all the evidence, including Cortazzi's obligatory note and the two older ones that Ferrieri had given to Knipping for 2,039:50 lion dollars and 2,700 lion dollars to cover the sale of the 831 pairs of pistols.[183] The

177 The documents contain additional written instructions from the consul to the chancellor, as well as comments from the chancellor concerning what he did, and when.

178 NACS, N°357, 'Memorie van Dirk Knipping tot het giudiceeren zijner saeken', Izmir, 23/02/1774.

179 NACS, N°357, 'Triplicq van M. K.co di Panajottis aan Dirk Knipping op zijn replicq', Izmir, 18/02/1774.

180 Ibid. The additional information also exists as a separate copy, NACS, N°357, 'Copia dell decreto dall illmo Hochepied su la supplica dall sigr Manolaki Kiriako di Panaiotis toccando la pretensione in riguardo dell seguestro di Lx1000 in mane dall Luca Cortazzi console Vento', Izmir, 18/02/1774.

181 NACS, N°357, 'Procuratie van Marigo Knipping in faveur van Gaspero Giovanelli', Izmir, 23/02/1774, '[…] giudizio, magistrate, tribunale e corte […]'.

182 Ibid.

183 NACS, N°357, 'Sentenza van den heere Franse consul & gedeputeerdens weegens de gesequestreerde Lx 1000 van Dirk Knipping onder den heere Venetiaanse consul data

French consular court had also investigated declarations by Gerrit van Brakel (who was not an involved party here and thus addressed his statement directly to the French consul), Cortazzi and Carlo Mudiano, the Venetian chancellor. The French consul and his assistant-judges decided that the obligation in the hands of Luca Cortazzi for 1,000 lion dollars did not belong to Marigo Knipping but to her husband Dirk, and it was part of the payment for the transaction of the 831 pairs of pistols that belonged to Forêt. This meant Marigo's request to relieve the sequester was denied. Dirk Knipping's argument about his payment plan with Forêt was also not relevant considering the sequester was made to recover debts from Ferrieri, which were separate from the agreement between Knipping and Forêt. Forêt was still owed money that was rightfully his, and the sequester was maintained.[184]

Knipping, who had been at the consul's house on the day of the verdict was very disappointed by the outcome and convinced that Charles de Peyssonnel had been partial. He also objected that Ferrieri's obligations had been subjected to examination by men belonging to a different nation while he had not been allowed to see them. He argued that a mistake had been made. It seems that the French sentence suggested that Ferrieri paid Knipping more than he actually had, and this suggestion created the misunderstanding about the obligation in the hands of Cortazzi. That obligation consisted of a debt of Ferrieri, which Ferrieri had admitted, but for money that Knipping insisted belonged to his wife. Knipping reminded the Dutch consul that his wife had declared as much under oath to 'her confessor', and she was willing to do that again.[185]

Confronted with the French sequester, Knipping entered a bankruptcy procedure before the Dutch consular court, as he was a Dutch subject. It must have been a blow for Knipping, who had almost managed to overcome his earlier financial difficulties. He offered his balance sheets to the consul, as the competent magistrate, who proceeded 'according to the law and laws in our [the United Provinces] lands'.[186] First, privileged debts were to be paid that were related to the dowry, doctor's bills and maid's wages, after which the remaining creditors were to be reimbursed as much as possible following a public sale of

---

21 feb: 1774 & geremitteerd in deese Neederlandse cancellerij heeden namiddag 23 feb:', Izmir, 21/02/1774.

184 Ibid.

185 NACS, N°357, 'Memorie van Dirk Knipping tot het giudiceeren zijner saeken', Izmir, 23/02/1774.

186 NACS, N°357, 'Ordinantie van den heere Consul Daniel Jan Graaf De Hochepied tot het verseegelen & opneemen p.r inventaris der meubelen & inboedel van Dirk Knipping', Izmir, 22/02/1774, '[...] volgens regt x wetten onser landen [...]'.

Knipping's goods.[187] In February 1774, the consul ordered the chancellor to seal Knipping's home, make an inventory of his goods and inform the creditors to appear the next day at ten o'clock at the consular house so curators could be chosen. Chancellor Mann went to several houses, including those of some of Knipping's Greek creditors, of which several did not consider it necessary to appear, claiming to accept all the magistrate's decisions. Somewhat ironically, Mann also paid a visit to Marigo Knipping, whose marital contract made her one of her husband's creditors, and she replied that she, as 'a woman in these Turkish lands, could not represent herself', so she would send one or two men in her stead – repeating what she had claimed earlier.[188]

The Knippings were not finished, as the fact that Marigo was her husband's creditor led her to request preferential payment out of Knipping's effects – to satisfy the debt arising out of the dowry – under the reasoning that 'women had a more particular right to public protection'.[189] Her argument, specifically addressed to Consul de Hochepied, was both legal and emotional, the latter not uncommon but the former more so, as her specific legal tone did not occur all that frequently amongst litigating merchants. She did not mention any particular law but instead spoke about 'the sanctity of the law' and the 'maximum of consecrated jurisprudence from the authority of so many illustrious legislators' amounting from 'a constant practice going back many centuries'.[190] She found it ridiculous that di Panaiotis continued to refuse to relieve the sequester without having heard from Forêt, as 'he wasn't the emperor of the moon'.[191] She felt it was rather the competent magistrate, Dutch Consul de Hochepied, who had to decide on it as 'custodian, vindicator and organ of the law'.[192] She concluded by stating that the superiority of de Hochepied's talents and the goodness of his heart unified the most sacred commitment to justice and the defence of oppressed innocence.[193]

187 For both the system of privileged debts and the dowry, see p. 204.

188 NACS, N°357, 'Ordinantie van den heere Consul Daniel Jan Graaf De Hochepied tot het verseegelen & opneemen p.r inventaris der meubelen & inboedel van Dirk Knipping', Izmir, 22/02/1774, '[...] als eene vrouw insonderheid in dese Turkse landen in haere persoon niet konde compareeren [...]'. The same day an inventory was made.

189 NACS, N°357, 'Suplicq van Marig: Knipping tot versoek van betaeling bij preferentie uijt de boedel van haar man', Izmir, 24/02/1774, '[...] che le donne hanno un diritto più particolare alla prottezione pubblica [...]'.

190 Ibid., '[...] la santità delle leggi [...]', '[...] l'massima di giurisprudenza consacrata dall'autorità di tanti illustri legislatori [...]' and '[...] dalla prattica constante di tanti secoli [...]'.

191 Ibid., '[...] l'imperator della luna [...]'.

192 Ibid., '[...] il custode il vindice e l'organo delle leggi [...]'.

193 Ibid.

While Marigo Knipping's argument did not really entail a questioning of jurisdiction, as she opposed di Panaiotis before the Dutch consul, it does point to the intermingling of cases under different jurisdictions – di Panaiotis' French sequester and Knipping's Dutch bankruptcy. Not surprisingly, her petition can be considered an attempt to make the sequester subordinate to the bankruptcy. The passion in her language might have represented a desperate final plea to the consul, but emotion was regularly present in legal reasoning, and in that sense, Marigo Knipping's petition was not exceptional.[194] Her request was neither without precedent nor without legal foundation. Dutch law contained stipulations on the privileged status of the dowry, and in Italy, wives could become creditors of their husbands' estates.[195] De Hochepied appointed two curators, Esaias Fercken, a merchant from Liège who had arrived in Izmir to work as a scribe in the Dutch firm of Clement & van Sanen (see table 3), and Gasparo Giovanelli, a Venetian physician who had also received power of attorney from Marigo Knipping to defend her interests regarding the 1,000 lion dollars.[196] In their report, they stated that Knipping was indebted for a total sum of 3,664:61 lion dollars but still was due 1,448:44 lion dollars, mostly from Luca Cortazzi, but which also included another 300 lion dollars he was owed by Ferrieri. Giovanelli and Fercken confirmed the preferential status of Marigo as a creditor, closely followed by the claims of the domestic servants, and they demanded that the Dutch consul contact the French consul in order to remove the sequester and that the Venetian consul make Ferrieri pay his 300 lion dollars.[197] Ferrieri declared he would not pay unless the sequester on Cortazzi's 1,000 lion dollars was relieved, while di Panaiotis maintained that Knipping had not been forced to declare bankruptcy. He insisted that the sequester had been legitimate and that the money was not Marigo's, contrary to what she and her husband had declared.[198] The situation, in short, remained the same, and the archives do not contain any hint about its final resolution.

194 For emotion in litigation, see pp. 185–188.

195 Julius Kirschner, 'Wives' claims against insolvent husbands in late medieval Italy', in *Women of the medieval world: Essays in honor of John H. Mundy*, eds. Julius Kirschner and Suzanne F. Wemple (Oxford, 1985), pp. 256–304.

196 NACS, N°357, 'Procuratie van Marigo Knipping in faveur van Gaspero Giovanelli', Izmir, 23/02/1774; and 'Sententie van den Hr Consul om te noemen 2 curatorij, den hr doctor Giovaneli & Ferken, op de zaaken van Dirk Knipping', Izmir, 03/03/1774.

197 NACS, N°357, 'Request van sig: Giovanellj & Esaias Ferken tot versoek van ontslag der gelden van Knipping bij den heere Venetiaanse consul in beneficie van geprivil schuld aen de huysvrouw Marigo Knipping', Izmir, 05/03/1774.

198 NACS, N°357, 'Antwoord van Pietro Ferrieri op de vraag der ssr curateuren van Dirk Knipping der bewuste Lx 300 in handen van Ferrierj adj 11/03/1774 ontf in deese Nederlandse can: & overgegeeven aen den heere consul Graaf Hochepied', Izmir, 11/03/

After 1774, the name Dirk Knipping no longer comes up in the consular archives. He voluntarily abandoned the position of tax overseer in January 1774, to be replaced by the man who had acted both as plaintiff against him as well as representative on behalf of him, Gerrit van Brakel.[199] In November 1795, a newspaper mentioned his death from the plague in Izmir, 'where he had lived for forty years', as well as the death of the widow of van Sanen.[200] Di Panaiotis' quarrels with Dutch merchants were far from over, and he reappeared later, when he denounced a former business partner, Jacob de Vogel, as someone who shipped goods from Ottoman merchants under his own name, an infraction of the national oath and a fraud against the payment of taxes.[201]

Although the final sentence in the case of Knipping, Forêt and Ferrieri – three subjects of different nationalities – remains unknown, complex trials such as this one, undertaken at the Dutch and French consular courts, are extremely useful for scholars as they show several things. The nature of Levant trade caused regular intercultural and international transactions. When something went wrong, it might lead to the involvement of the authorities and the justice systems of several European nations and potentially also of Ottoman justice. The references in the documents preserved at the Dutch consular court of Izmir make it clear that the French, Dutch and Venetian consuls all had their say on the case at hand. They used their abilities to sequester monies on behalf of their own subjects, and they were all part of the procedural aspects of the case through the involvement of the Venetian, Dutch and French chanceries. While litigants only rarely, if ever, raised a complaint about a court's jurisdiction, the involvement of various jurisdictions did bring Knipping to vent complaints about partiality, perhaps hoping for Consul de Hochepied's partisanship.[202]

The trial had been initiated to satisfy the claims of a man who was not Dutch, French or Venetian and who resided thousands of kilometres away

1774; and 'Antwoord van Manuel K:° di Panajottis op de vraag der h:n curateuren van Dirk Knipping der bewuste Lx 1000 in handen van den h:r venetiaanse consul Luca Cortazzi', Izmir, 14/03/1774.

199 NACS, N°357, 'Acte van eed van Gerrit van Brakel als opsiener aenden toll vande Nederlandse natie in Smirna', Izmir, 20/01/1774; see also Heeringa and Nanninga, *Bronnen tot de geschiedenis*, 4: p. 191, 'Extra-ordinaris vergadering van de directeuren met de buitenleden te Amsterdam', 26/10/1774.

200 *De Generaliteits-courant*, 07/11/1795, '[…] er 40 jaaren gewoond heeft […]'.

201 See pp. 283–285.

202 NACS, N°357, 'Memorie van Dirk Knipping tot het giudiceeren zijner saeken', Izmir, 23/02/1774.

from Izmir and probably never had set foot in the Ottoman Empire – Jacques Forêt from Liège. For Forêt, the system worked, and rulings at both the Dutch and French courts were in his favour, although it remained complicated to obtain financial satisfaction from a merchant far away, particularly as both his agent – Dirk Knipping – and at least one of his clients – Pietro Ferrieri – had financial troubles. But it is important to note that the consul's verdict was not based on a favourable approach towards the defendant, a Dutch national, who held an official position at the consulate and who had been living in Izmir for eight years. For de Hochepied, respecting commercial custom, as confirmed by a variety of other traders, was more important, as it was this attitude that held together the Europeans' system of trade in the Levant. The call to perform justice was the same, whether it was uttered at the Dutch or the French consular court, and cases were adjudicated by a mixture of peers, as both French and Dutch merchants had a voice in the final verdict of their respective consular courts, and of diplomats who, in the case of the United Provinces and France, were not allowed to engage in business, a situation which was very different from their English and Venetian counterparts.[203]

The role merchants played in the legal decision-making process at both the French and Dutch consular courts confirms the importance given to mercantile customs, as its legal application was best guaranteed through the involvement of those who understood it best, the traders, not simply as expert witnesses, although this occurred regularly, but as co-judges. None of the cases studied provide any support for the thesis that litigating traders had any problem with the involvement of colleagues, who were potential competitors, in their trials. Their competence was never questioned; Knipping only expressed his frustration about foreign merchants looking at obligatory notes he was not allowed to see. Jacques Forêt also needed to rely on the merchants' style, not only in his business dealings in Izmir but also when he felt forced to summon some of the merchants he had been dealing with in court. The commercial trust he placed in his middlemen had failed to protect him from trouble. He now had to hope his legal trust in first a Dutchman and then a Greek Ottoman trader would serve him better. He also would have to rely on the impartiality and expertise of the Dutch and French consular jurisdictions in Izmir, which might have been the biggest leap of faith of all. Commercial trust was constantly evaluated through reputational mechanisms upheld by the merchant community itself. The same

203 The French consuls often originated from established families in Marseille, which guaranteed a good understanding of French Levant trade, but they were not merchants themselves. Masson, *Histoire du commerce*, p. 447.

mechanisms applied when a trader was asked to protect a peer's interests in court. He had at least as much to offer to Dirk Knipping as Knipping to him, and Knipping risked, by not taking Forêt's interests to heart, losing an important commission, as well as other commissions from Liège and Rotterdam and perhaps elsewhere in the future. Similar mechanisms applied to ensure the best efforts of the traders he had provided with a power of attorney. A lack of effort by van Brakel or di Panaiotis in court would harm their reputations as traders as well, as no distinction was made between pursuing the best interests of a principal in trade or in court.

Forêt might have been less sure about the quality of the Dutch and French courts. He did not fall under their direct jurisdiction, and consuls were specifically expected to defend national interest. In that light, it is perhaps not a coincidence that, in a Dutch trading community that was dominated by Amsterdam traders and which maintained a strong connection with the Directorate of Levant Trade in Amsterdam, Jacques Forêt had first chosen Gerrit van Brakel to represent him, a trader who had come from Rotterdam, and later Manolaki di Panaiotis, who was a Greek Ottoman but who had formed an earlier association in Izmir with a merchant from Rotterdam, Jacob de Vogel. They might have had less to share with Knipping, and furthermore, Forêt had good connections in Rotterdam, which he also had visited personally. One of his main correspondents there, Herman van Coopstad, had been a director of Levant trade in Rotterdam since 1745 – and the directorate there was known to compete with their Amsterdam counterpart. His reliance on merchants from a relatively small circle in Rotterdam might have had as much to do with his familiarity with merchant circles there as with his fear that, in court, Amsterdam traders might protect each other too much from claims issued by the outsider Jacques Forêt.

2.4 *Invoking 'National' Law versus the Merchants' Style*

Solving a dispute regarding commission trade was common but could also be complicated because of the distance between litigants. The cases tried at the Dutch consular court that were concerned with a dispute between principals and their agents at times involved non-Dutch principals, such as Jacques Forêt. A non-Dutch agent rarely appears amongst the defendants tried at the Dutch consular court in Izmir, and if he did, it meant he was either an Ottoman holding a *berat* or a European belonging to one of the nations for which the Dutch consul officially acted as a diplomatic representative. Because European consulates allowed for litigating parties to file their documents at the chancery of their own consulate, the Dutch consular archives do contain a few documents related to court cases adjudicated by another European consular court, such as the dispute that arose between the Amsterdam-based firm of Weduwe Offerman & C° (Widow Offerman & C°) and the firm of André Chabeaud in Izmir. In June 1772, the Offerman firm sent four bales containing forty sheets of cloth to André Chabeaud, a French merchant in Izmir and agent for the house of Blanchenay & C° in Marseille.[204] The Offerman firm had been put in contact with the Frenchmen through a mutual acquaintance, and the cloth served as sample, to see what Blanchenay and their agents, the firm of André Chabeaud, would be able to achieve. The Offerman firm confirmed with Blanchenay that they hoped to send more parcels in case the first sample fetched a good price, and they concluded their first letter by stating that 'it shall be very pleasant for us, if we could conduct some business that is useful for both sides, from time to time'.[205] The Blanchenay firm expressed their happiness about the recommendation from their mutual friend and also hoped the first contact would lead to more: 'should we be able to serve you here or in another place, it would be most pleasurable to us, we do not only trade in Izmir, we also deliver many commissions for your lands, and friends there [the United Provinces] send us spices and other wares to sell'.[206]

It is not clear whether the Offerman firm had particular reasons for choosing a French intermediary beyond the recommendation they had received, but the choice meant that they accepted the possibility of French adjudication in case something went wrong. It seems that it was their first attempt at Levantine trade, so they might not have known any Dutch agents in Izmir. The Offerman firm probably sent the sample in an attempt to expand its business following the recent death of Pieter Offerman, head of the firm. In January 1772, an article in an Amsterdam newspaper informed its readers that the firm of Pieter

204 French Levant trade was a monopoly of trading houses in Marseille that all had their representatives in Levantine *échelles*. This meant that in contrast to the Dutch merchants in Izmir, their French colleagues were all working for firms in Marseille. See chapter one. NACS, N°354 ('André Chabaud & C°, Franse kooplieden te Smyrna, tegen Daniel Fremeaux & C°, optredend namens de weduwe Offerman & C° te Amsterdam, 1772–1773'), 'Wed: Offerman aen Blanchenay, Paul & C° a Marseille', Amsterdam, 18/06/1772. The actual document that has been preserved is a copy made on 15/10/1772.

205 NACS, N°354, 'Wed: Offerman aen Blanchenay, Paul & C° a Marseille', Amsterdam, 18/06/1772, '[...] zal het ons zeer aangenaam weezen, indien wy in vervolg van tyd aanzienlyke en voor weerskanten nuttige affaires met elkanderen konden doen [...]'.

206 NACS, N°354, 'Blanchenay Paul & C° aan hrn wed Pet Offerman & C°', Marseille, 03/07/1772. The actual document that has been preserved is a copy made on 15/10/1772, '[...] indien wy u ed in het eene of andere hier ter plaatze zoude konnen dienen, dit zou ons zeer aangenaam weezen, behalve onzen handel in smirna bezorgen wy veele comissies voor costige gewesten, en costige vrienden zenden on sook specereyen en andere waaren ter verkoop [...]'.

Offerman & Zoonen, trading in Amsterdam and Imgenbroich near Aachen in Germany, was dissolved, and its business would be continued by two separate firms, the Weduwe Offerman & C° in Amsterdam and Franz Pieter Offerman in Imgenbroich.[207] It was perhaps the new firm's inexperience in Levant trade that contributed to the fact that something did indeed go wrong. They had not sent the four bales themselves but had used an intermediary for the shipping named Philip Ludwig Bernhard, a trader also based in Amsterdam. Bernhard was the man who convinced them to use Chabeaud, Blanchenay's agent, as the intermediary for the transaction, as Bernhard and Blanchenay were friends in business. The latter expressly asked Bernhard to find clients they could get commissions for in the United Provinces.[208]

Unfortunately for all involved, Bernhard declared bankruptcy a few months after the shipment, and Blanchenay was one of his creditors. Offerman's problem arose from the fact that Bernhard had not specified to Chabeaud that the cloth belonged to Offerman. This meant that the merchandise was considered Bernhard's, and Offerman was running the risk of losing it. When they found out about Bernhard's bankruptcy, the Offerman firm petitioned the States General in the hopes of recuperating their goods, following legal advice given to them by specialists.[209] A declaration written by Bernhard, who confirmed that he had indeed expedited Offerman's goods to Izmir and not his own, was included in the petition.[210] The States General were sympathetic towards the petition and agreed to send the Dutch consul in Izmir instructions 'to offer a helping hand as much as possible'.[211] He was asked to contact his French colleague and to ensure either the recuperation of the cloth or the profits if they already had been sold.[212] A copy of the resolution issued by the States General, as well as copies of Offerman's request, Bernhard's declaration, an account of the shipment and extracts from correspondence exchanged between Blanchenay and Offerman were all sent to the Dutch consulate in Izmir. The shipped documents also included a power of attorney

207 *Amsterdamsche courant*, 21/01/1772.

208 NACS, N°354, 'Blanchenay Paul & C° aen hrn wed Pet Offerman & C°', Marseille, 03/07/1772.

209 NACS, N°354, 'Request voor de wed P Offerman en C°', Amsterdam, 13/10/1772, '[…] door advisen van rechtsgeleerden […]'.

210 Ibid.

211 NACS, N°354, 'Extract uit het register der resolutien van de ho mog heeren Staten Generaal der Vereenigde Nederlanden', The Hague, 13/10/1772, '[…] zoo veel mogelijk de behulpsaame hand te bieden […]'.

212 Ibid.

given to Daniel Fremeaux & C° in Izmir, a Dutch firm who was to represent Offerman's claims there.[213] The document specified that Fremeaux should 'seek justice if necessary, to arrest or sequester persons, monies and goods, to persist such sequesters and to lift them, to appear before all tribunals, courts and justice chambers, to observe all legal terms, and to request verdicts and sentences and their execution, as well as to appeal disadvantageous sentences'.[214] In December 1772, Fremeaux filed an official petition with the Dutch consul to demand payment from Chabeaud through the French consul, a letter that was written in Italian, like all of their subsequent written statements.[215] Fremeaux's petition started the procedure with Offerman as plaintiff and Chabeaud as defendant – meaning it was adjudicated by the French consul, Claude-Charles de Peyssonnel.[216]

Chabeaud was instructed by the French consul to reply to Fremeaux's statements, and he answered that Offerman's merchandise had already been sequestered following a sentence issued by the consular judges in Marseille at Blanchenay's behest to claim outstanding debts from Bernhard. This information was confirmed by the French consul.[217] Fremeaux remained in contact with the Offerman firm, which sent him an official *casuspositie* written by attorneys in Amsterdam in April, affirming the claim of the Offerman firm as proprietors of the goods and relying on Roman law as described in the *Hollandse Consultatien* and the work of van Leeuwen, an authority on Dutch-Roman law.[218] The recourse they sought to Dutch written law in a matter of sequester and bankruptcy is in itself not surprising, as it was one of the few

213 Fremeaux, born in 1714, was an important man, who had been assessor since 1752, a function he retired from in 1795, the year in which he died.

214 NACS, N°354, 'Verklaring voor notaris Nathanael Wilthuijzen & getuijgen', Amsterdam, 19/10/1772, '[...] desnoods regt te plegen, persoonen penningen en goederen te arresteeren dezelve arresten te vervolgen en na geraden wederom ontslaan, voor alle Hoven, geregten en kameren van Justitie te compareeren, alle termynen van regten te observeeren, vonnissen en sententien te versoeken obtineeren executeeren off van de nadelige te appelleeren [...]'.

215 NACS, N°354, 'Request van D: Fremeaux & C° tot versoek om aen de Franse consul te versoeken om Chabaud & C° te constiengeeren tot betaeling van het rend: van 4 pakken laeken intrest van de wed: Pieter Offerman &C° d'Amsterdam', Izmir, 09/12/1772.

216 Son of the previous consul, Charles de Peyssonnel. For Claude-Charles, see Pierre Larousse, *Grand dictionnaire universel du XIXe siècle* (Paris, 1874), 12: p. 740.

217 NACS, N°354, 'Antwoord van André Chabaud & C° aen D: Fremeaux weegens 4 pakken laakenen van de wed: P Offerman & C° d'Amsterdam ter deeser Nederlandse cancell: ontfangen op heeden 15xber en aen de heeren D: Fremeaux & C° g'intimeert op 16 ditto anno 1772', Izmir, 15/12/1772.

218 NACS, N°354, 'Casus positie', Amsterdam, 02/04/1773. A *casuspositie* was a declaration on the case by peers; see also p. 110.

types of commercial disputes for which written law existed.[219] Sequesters and bankruptcies, however, were not uncommon amongst merchants, and this document, containing the opinion of professional attorneys on a commercial dispute, is the only one of its kind found in the archives of the Dutch consulate of Izmir, contrary to the much more frequent use of reports signed by other merchants confirming commercial usage and custom. The rarity of the presence of such documents seems surprising considering the ease with which both the States General and the Dutch consul offered support to Weduwe Offerman & C°.

Perhaps the Offerman firm wanted more than a reliance on mercantile custom, considering they were far away, and the merchant holding their power of attorney had to argue their case by submitting written statements to a foreign consulate.[220] It is perhaps telling of the minor importance of written law in settling international trade disputes, in comparison to the role of the merchants' style, that the arguments brought forward by Fremeaux did not impress Chabeaud at all. On the contrary, he replied that the sequester and the French verdicts 'had been based on reason and equity and had been expressed in the most honest words, and that it was a truth that all the emphasis and bloatedness of the Italian language would not be able to destroy'.[221] Fremeaux had shown a document from Amsterdam that explained the legal fairness of Offerman's claim in terms of Dutch-Roman law, which theoretically could be recognised by the French litigants through *ius commune*, but Chabeaud & C° answered by referring to simple reason. Chabeaud & C°'s letter ended with an explicit refusal to reply to any further statements Fremeaux might make. They equally refused to let Fremeaux see any of their business documents.[222] Chabeaud's strong stance is particularly interesting in this case, as it seems his argument was that Fremeaux had relied on national Dutch written law in an attack on the French and had thus violated the merchants' style, which was based on reason and equity in an international context and thus could not be applied within a national framework. It was almost indecent, it seems, to use

219 See pp. 199–208.

220 The combination of bankruptcy and the involvement of other European diplomats, for instance, led to considerations on written law; see pp. 199–208.

221 NACS, N°354, 'Antwoord van Chabaud & C° weegens de in proces hangende 4 pakken laekens van de wed: Offerman & C°', Izmir, 14/09/1773, 'Il etoit fondé sur la raison et l'equité et exprimé dans les termes les plus honnêtes, c'est une vérité que toute l'emphase et tout le boursonflage de la langue italienne ne sauroit detruire'.

222 Ibid.

'national' arguments, such as a declaration drafted by attorneys in Holland and not by fellow merchants in Izmir, against a trader of a different nationality.

Chabeaud's argument resonated with the French consul and his assistant-judge, and after examining all the evidence that was brought over by the Dutch chancellor and the documents submitted with the French chancery, the French consular court sentenced against the plaintiff and in favour of the defendant, which meant the sequester was upheld.[223] About a week after the sentence was issued, the Fremeaux firm issued an appeal against the verdict, which was registered at the Dutch consulate and presented at the French consulate the next day.[224] The appeal was a natural consequence of the power of attorney they had received, but it remains unclear if the Offerman firm decided to proceed with it. Further adjudication would have taken place in Marseille, and the Offerman firm would have needed to send someone there or grant a power of attorney to a merchant established there. This turn of events was a risk the firm of Offerman, knowingly or unknowingly, had taken by employing French commissioners. The archives there do not contain any traces of further litigation, so it is impossible to say whether the Offerman firm really wanted to continue an appeal under French jurisdiction.[225]

Unlike what Jacques Forêt had done, the Offerman firm kept a close eye on proceedings in Izmir. While the final outcome of the dispute is not known, both the firms of Weduwe Offerman & C° and Philip Ludwig Bernhard went bankrupt after the case and deposited their accounts before the *Desolate*

---

223 NACS, N°354, 'Sententie van den heere france consul de Peijssonnell in de differentie weegens 4 pakken Laekenen onder Cabaud & C°', Izmir, 27/10/1773. For a discussion on the role of chanceries in formalizing commercial deeds in the context of early modern French consulates, see Arnaud Bartolomei, 'Actes notariés *versus* actes de chancellerie. Le rôle des chancelleries consulaires françaises dans la formalisation des actes commerciaux et civils (XVIIIe-XIXe siècle), *Mélanges de l'École française de Rome – Italie et Méditerranée modernes et contemporaines*, 128:2 (2016), consulted online at https://journals.openedition.org/mefrim/2801?lang=it.

224 NACS, N°354, 'Acte van appel der heeren Fremeaux & C° in de differentie van 4 pakken lakenen van de wed: Offerman & Comp:', Izmir, 05/11/1773.

225 The *Archives Départementales* in Marseille (ADM) contain a series of books in which legal deeds, claims and reports were registered, but no trace can be found of any litigation involving Offerman, Blanchenay and Chabeaud. The register for 1772 contains two reports on a dispute about a transaction of goat wool that involved André Chabeaud. ADM, XIII B 421, 'Verbaux et rapports divers' (1772), 'Rapport fait par les srs Vital Badere x Caurau Laina a la poursuitte detts Simon Lefleche x C° contre Chabaud & C°', Marseille, 26/09/1772 and ADM, XIII B 421, 'Raport de verification de 28 balles laine de chevron d les Belleville freres & Chabaud negts de cette vills contre les André Chabaud & C° negts a Smirne', Marseille, 30/09/1772.

Boedelskamer in Amsterdam, in 1784 and 1779 respectively.[226] Their creditors came from many places; in the case of Bernhard from Amsterdam, Bordeaux, Genoa, Mogador, Rostock, Köln, Leiden, London, Frankfurt, Paramaribo, Altona and Copenhagen, but no one from Marseille or Izmir figured on the list, suggesting that all matters between Offerman, Bernhard, Blanchenay and Chabeaud had been solved.[227]

3 Litigants at Sea and Maritime Jurisdiction

Disputes brought before the Dutch consul in Izmir most often involved merchants. Dutch Levant trade did not rely on intermediaries on land alone but also required the involvement of maritime personnel. In Mediterranean ports, where European ships could spend months selling merchandise and trying to secure a return cargo, it was often the skipper who negotiated with Dutch and foreign firms to find merchandise for the voyage back to the United Provinces. It was a crucial responsibility, as time that was spent idling in port was costly, particularly as crews continued to receive their wages.[228] Formally speaking, skippers and other maritime personnel were not part of the Dutch trading community of Izmir, but, upon arrival, they were obliged to take a national oath, with which they promised that the ship's manifests they had signed were truthful.[229] When they were in port, the Dutch consul had jurisdiction over them and was expected to help them draft documents that normally required a notary. While not the most visible part of the commercial chain connecting Dutch cities with Izmir, they were a crucial element in that chain.

Much like how merchants could have quarrels, things could also go wrong between traders and seamen. Settling maritime disputes was a special category of consular adjudication. Since the middle of the seventeenth century, the courts in the United Provinces qualified to adjudicate maritime disputes in first instance were the Commissioners of Maritime Affairs. These were urban

226 For the institution of the *Desolate Boedelskamer*, see pp. 202–203. Bernhard's bankruptcy was his second, after an earlier bankruptcy in 1772.

227 CAA, N°5072 ('Archieven van de Commissarissen van de Desolate Boedelskamer'), N°3764 (Offerman & Engler), as well as N°3139 and N°3536 (both for Philip Ludwig Bernhard).

228 For Dutch shipping in the Mediterranean context and the involvement of skippers and seamen, see Vanneste, 'Sailing through the straits'.

229 Heeringa and Nanninga, *Bronnen tot de geschiedenis*, 2: pp. 214–215, 'Formulier van den eedt voor de schippers, stuurlieden, supracargos en andre, die eenich bewint ofte directie ontrent 't lossen of 't laeden van scheepen sijn hebbende, respective', 1676. This is similar to the national oath merchants had to take; see p. 57.

courts, and their verdicts could be appealed at higher provincial courts such as the *Hof van Holland* (see figure 5).[230] Their jurisdiction covered conflicts involving sailors, skippers and freighters, without further specification of the origins of these men. The absence of any definition of geographical jurisdiction was logical, as most maritime disputes originated at sea or in a port where neither of the litigants was at home. It was easy to determine the consular jurisdiction in case of a maritime dispute between Dutch traders and sailors, but considering the frequent use foreign merchants made of Dutch shipping, there were obvious potential jurisdictional issues in case a dispute should arise.

In ports where there was a Dutch consul, Dutch skippers and sailors could go to a Dutch court, which they were entitled to as defendants according to the *forum rei* principle. There was no legislation that made a distinction between the consul's competence to adjudicate a dispute involving Dutch seafarers who happened to be in the city where the consul resided and a dispute involving Dutch merchants who lived in that city and thus fell under the consul's jurisdiction permanently. Intriguingly, regulations issued by the States General in 1658 covering consular responsibilities throughout the Mediterranean limited the fees consuls were allowed ask from skippers for the help given to them for their extra-ordinary needs (going beyond the drafting of notarial documents, for instance, which was a basic service). These needs included involvement in trials and adjudicating disputes.[231]

The adjudication of disputes that occurred on board a ship was not clearly defined in terms of jurisdiction. While, theoretically, *forum rei* could be chosen, leading to adjudication at the court of the defendant, such a court might be nowhere near the ship's nearest land location. This is perhaps why several early modern laws on maritime adjudication are not specific on jurisdiction in terms of geography but more so in terms of the people involved. The *Instructien* (*Instructions*) for the maritime court of Amsterdam specified that these were competent for conflicts between 'merchant and skipper, merchant and seaman, skipper and skipper, skipper and seaman, as also between merchant and pilot, freighters and freighters, ship owners and ship owners, as also skippers with their ship owners, in cases concerned with maritime navigation'.[232] The Rotterdam maritime court had issued the same phrasing,

230 See chapter two. For the earlier development of maritime law in the Low Countries, see De ruysscher, 'Maxims, principals and legal change'.

231 Cau, *Groot placaet-boeck*, 2: pp. 1343–1344, 'Extract uyt 't register der resolutien vande hoogh mogende heeren Staten Generael', 24/07/1658.

232 *Instructien* (1731), p. 4, '[…] tusschen koopman en schipper, tusschen koopman en bootsgezel, tusschen schipper en schipper, tusschen schipper en bootsgezel, item tusschen

as well as England's Admiralty Court.[233] No mention was made of a possible distinction between foreigners and Dutchmen or citizens of specific cities. Concerning jurisdiction, Louis XIV's influential *Ordonnance de la marine* from 1681 stated that 'the judges of the Admiralty will privately rule over all others, and between all persons of whichever quality they may be, even those who are privileged, Frenchmen and foreigners, both as plaintiffs and defendants, of all that concerns the construction, the tackle and gear, armament, provisioning and equipment, sale and tendering of ships'.[234] It is a particularly interesting statement as it not only suggests similar treatment at the court for Frenchmen and foreigners but also specifically went against the principle of *forum rei* by specifically stating that it would hear disputes between people regardless of their subject status. This has to do with the fact that during the *Ancien Régime*, two principles to organise legal jurisdiction co-existed: *ratione personarum*, meaning that jurisdiction is determined on the basis of the person, his or her legal status as subject; and *ratione materiae*, which determined jurisdiction on the basis of the matter – for instance a maritime dispute being adjudicated in a maritime court.[235] According to Maria Fusaro, the range of maritime jurisdiction was debated and depended on local circumstances and accidents of navigation. Jurisdiction could, to a certain extent, be negotiated, and in some instances, skippers could influence the choice of court that would try them by steering their ships to specific ports.[236]

---

koopman en lootsman, mitsgaders tusschen inladers en inladers, reeders en reeders, als ook schippers met haar reeders, in zaaken de zeevaart aangaande […]'.

233 See pp. 117–118; and Steckley, 'Merchants and the Admiralty Court', p. 137.

234 *Ordonnance de la marine du mois d'aoust 1681. Commentée & conferée avec les anciennes ordonnances, & le droit ecrit: Avec les nouveaux reglemens concernans la marine* (Paris, 1714), p. 15, 'Les juges de l'amirauté connaîtront privativement à tous autres, & entre tous personnes de quelque qualité qu'elles soient, même privilégiées, François et etrangers, tant en demandant qu'en deffendant, de tout ce qui concerne, la construction, les agrez & apparaux, armement, avictuaillement & equipement, vente & adjudication des vaisseaux'; for a more general discussion, see Bernard Allaire, 'Between Oléron and Colbert: The evolution of French maritime law until the seventeenth century', in *Labour, law, and empire*, pp. 79–99.

235 The development of commercial law has often been considered a straightforward process from *ratione personarum* to *ratione materiae*, for instance in Umberto Santarelli, *Mercanti e società tra mercanti* (Torino, 1998), pp. 18–29; and Dave De ruysscher, *Gedisciplineerde vrijheid*, p. 41, but there are strong indications this was not the case. See Cerutti, *Giustizia sommaria*, pp. 28–29; and Fusaro, 'Politics of justice/politics of trade'.

236 Maria Fusaro argued that the specified final port in a contract written up for a specific journey could play a role in these considerations, but this did not prevent maritime disputes from being adjudicated in cities that had not been specified as final ports of call. Personal communication with Maria Fusaro, 29 April 2019.

A good example is the 1743 dispute that arose between the Sicilian merchant Gasparo Marchetti and the Dutch skipper Cornelis Volkers. Volkers freighted his vessel, the *Sofia en Catarina*, in Trieste, and planned to sail to Messina and Livorno. On 14 June 1743 the ship arrived in Messina, where the plague was raging. According to the skipper and several of his crewmembers, the merchants to whom the merchandise was consigned did not want the goods to be unloaded because of the plague, but one of them, Gasparo Marchetti, declared that it was the skipper who had refused to unload because of the reigning chaos.[237]

In any case, a new charterparty was drafted in Messina in which it was specified that the goods should be unloaded in Livorno or elsewhere, but not in Messina. The charterparty was signed by a trader named Michele Panno and then endorsed to Marchetti, who had come aboard in Messina with his son and two servants, probably hoping to escape the plague. This was against all regulations, but Marchetti assured Volkers that he was taking full responsibility for it. On 25 June, the ship left Messina for Livorno, where they were refused entrance into the port as they were coming from a city stricken by the plague. A new pilot, also from Messina, came aboard in Livorno at the suggestion of Marchetti, and although a first attempt was made to sail to Marseille, the weather forced them elsewhere. As Marchetti was the freighter, he pretended to be in control of the voyage and wanted the ship to go to the Ambracian Gulf on the western coast of the Peloponnesus, but when the ship was near Stromboli, approaching the Strait of Messina, the crew got the feeling that Marchetti, a Sicilian, was planning to abandon the vessel and go ashore.[238] The skipper then decided to set sail for Izmir, according to the skipper and crew with Marchetti's consent, but Marchetti declared later that he was 'violently taken by Captain Volkers to this city of Smyrna [Izmir], against the law of his contract'.[239]

237 NACS, N°316 ('Alle de stukken rakende de zaken van capt. Cornelis Volkers van t fluijtschip de Soffia en Caterina, en sig. Gasparo Maria Marchetti Messinees adi ... stemb. tot 3 october 1743'), 'Verklaring van den capt Cornelis Volkers, zyn stuijrman en een matroos, wegens zijn vertrek van Messina en Livorno wegens de pest', Izmir, 13/09/1743; 'Consulaet der zee vant fluijtschip de Sofia en Caterina capt Cornelis Volkers', Izmir, 13/09/1743; Declaratie [by crewmembers], [Izmir], [11/09/1743]; and NACS, N°316, 'Protest van sig.r Gasparo Ma. Marchetti, teegen dheer Consul de Hochepied, en cap:to Cornelis volkers', Izmir, 02/10/1743.

238 NACS, N°316, 'Verklaring van den capt Cornelis Volkers, zyn stuijrman en een matroos, wegens zijn vertrek van Messina en Livorno wegens de pest', Izmir, 13/09/1743.

239 NACS, N°316, 'Eerste request van dheer Gasparo Ma. Marchetti', Izmir, [19/09/1743], '[...] esser stato violentem.te condotto dl cap Cornelis Wolkers 'n qsta città di smirne contro la leggi di suo contratto [...]'.

The choice of Izmir is interesting, as the skipper justified it by considering it the safest place to protect his ship and the merchandise on board in case troubles should arise. After the events in Messina and Livorno, he was expecting difficulties.[240] This claim was part of a statement skipper Volkers had drafted within two days after arriving in Izmir, which was co-signed by his helmsman and a sailor who understood Italian. The statement was drafted a week before Marchetti filed his petition at the Dutch consular court. The text of Volkers' statement clearly acknowledged that the skipper was well aware of the risks he had taken by accepting a change to the original freight contract, which included more traders than just Marchetti, and by continuing on the voyage after officials in Livorno had refused him entry – as Livorno had featured on the original charterparty. The skipper must have known which port cities in the Mediterranean had Dutch diplomatic representation and provided him with the possibility of defending himself before Dutch magistrates, which also explains the original choice to go to Marseille after Livorno.

Things might have been substantially more complicated in an Italian port, or in 'Chiarenza' (now known as Glarentza), an Ottoman port city south of the Ambracian Gulf (near Kyllini in present-day Greece), where Marchetti had first insisted on going.[241] The whole discussion demonstrates that merchants and skippers were well aware of their possibilities for adjudication in different places, and the conscious practice of navigating to a particular city in the hopes of getting adjudicated there might be the maritime counterpart of the practice of forum shopping. In this case, Cornelis Volkers knew there were Dutch legal institutions in place that were designed to adjudicate maritime and commercial disputes, and he wanted to navigate to a place that had access to such institutions rather than being forced into adjudication by Italian or Ottoman judges. Volkers also knew that, if he arrived in a port city with a Dutch consul, there might be fellow skippers there who could be asked to draft a witness statement, and he countered Marchetti's claims by stating that 'the captains of my nation in this port can testify to my character, and my honourable habits'.[242]

240 NACS, N°316, 'Verklaring van den capt Cornelis Volkers, zyn stuijrman en een matroos, wegens zijn vertrek van Messina en Livorno wegens de pest', Izmir, 13/09/1743.

241 NACS, N°316, 'Sonder datum schrift van Sig:r Gasparo Ma marchettj messinees met zijn Eerste Req:t overgeleeverd, inhoúdende zijn pretenzie en verantwoordinge tegen Cap:to Cornelis volkers zyn gedrag op de reyze', S.l., S.d.

242 NACS, N°316, 'Request antwt van cap Cornelis Volkers, op dat van sr Gasparo M:a Marchetti', Izmir, 24/09/1743, '[…] li cap.i di mia nazione in questo porto asistento possono testificare qualsia il mio carattere e quali li miei honorati costume […]'.

It is an interesting parallel to the importance merchants gave to reputation, although it is remarkable that, contrary to merchants, this skipper specifically referred to fellow nationals who were able to testify about his character. This might have to do with the fact that the skipper found himself physically distant from the place where he lived. He had an itinerant profession, while the merchants involved in eighteenth-century international trade were no longer physically moving about to conduct business but relied on a web of correspondents and agents. For them, reputation was an important instrument used to establish trust and assess the risks of engaging in business with a fellow trader who he might never see in person. For skippers, their activities were based more on physical encounters, lessening the need to develop some sort of usage that could validate behaviour through reputation. But in case of trouble, a skipper still wanted to prove that he was of a reliable character. There were only so many Dutch skippers sailing to Izmir, because Dutch navigation was specialised geographically, which meant that he must have known several of his Dutch colleagues in person. Considered this way, a skipper's recourse to fellow nationals is testimony to the importance of reputational mechanisms based on a shared occupation, in this case navigation to Izmir.

The fact that the *Sofia en Catarina* had come from a city where the plague was raging was an additional danger. It already had been refused entry in Livorno, something that could repeat itself elsewhere. Quarantine laws in the Ottoman Empire were non-existent – the Ottomans only adopted institutional reforms to battle the plague after 1800 – in spite of a similar scientific knowledge of the problem as the Europeans.[243] This provided Volkers with a second good reason to sail to Izmir, and the Dutch skipper wrote that it had been his purpose to find public officials from whom he could obtain clean bills of health for himself and his crew as well as permission to continue his voyage without further problems.[244] The problem was that Marchetti did not want to be in Izmir, but now that he was there, he wanted the goods consigned to him on board of Volker's ship to be unloaded immediately, while Volkers claimed he was not allowed to do so according to the terms of his contract.

As the dispute concerned contractual disputes as well as the complicated context of potential disease, the consul organised a meeting not only with the assessors but also with other Dutch merchants to ask their opinion. They

243 Birsen Bulmuş, *Plague, quarantines and geopolitics in the Ottoman Empire* (Edinburgh, 2012), pp. 39–40; see also Daniel Panzac, *La peste dans l'empire Ottoman, 1700–1850* (Leuven, 1985).

244 NACS, N°316, 'Request antwt van cap Cornelis Volkers, op dat van sr Gasparo M:a Marchetti', Izmir, 24/09/1743.

declared the second charterparty, which was made with Panno and endorsed to Marchetti, as void and denied the Sicilian's request to unload, first of all because he could not prove all the goods had been consigned to him, and secondly because it would take a long time to unload – at a time when the plague was already raging in Istanbul and might well arrive in Izmir. Unloading increased the risk that Volkers would run out of time and would not receive the clean bills of health he needed to continue his voyage. Marchetti's claim harmed the interests of the other freighters and only seemed to serve himself, a clear violation of the merchants' style. The consul gave Volkers two days to obtain the documents he needed, after which he was free to continue his voyage 'as was customary according to sailor's style'.[245] Similar to the multiple references to the merchants' style that were invoked to justify sentences concerning commercial disputes, the 'sailor's style' was equally used to suggest that there was a common way of doing things, generally accepted and understood by the involved parties, and by which they would have to behave themselves.

Not surprisingly, Marchetti protested this decision, and he filed his complaint with the consul of the Kingdom of the Two Sicilies in Izmir, Antonio Romiti.[246] Marchetti protested but did not appeal, and this might have had to do with his difficulty deciding where to appeal. Maritime disputes did not necessarily follow *forum rei* because navigational issues might play a role. An appeal would be equally hard to follow. Marchetti should appeal before a Sicilian court, but the skipper against whom he wished to litigate would probably already be at sea by then. The Dutch consul allowed Volkers to leave within the next two days, and Marchetti felt that 'the road to appeal to a superior tribunal in this city was closed', and thus he protested not only against Volkers but also against the consul himself.[247] It seems Marchetti attempted to keep the ship in port long enough for an official appeal to be filed, with the support of other merchants in Messina who were involved in the shipment. When the Dutch consul was informed of this, he filed a counter-protest in his own name. He felt that Marchetti had created the problem in the first place by illegally coming on board the ship in Messina, thereby endangering the whole crew. He also thought that Marchetti's legal challenge of the consular judge was

245 NACS, N°316, 'Extract ùijt de notulen van de gehoudene bisoignes ter vergadering van haer hoog mog consul midsgaeders de koopluyden vande nederlandse natie', Izmir, 30/09/1743, '[…] zoo alz near zeemanstijl gebrúijkelijk […]'.

246 NACS, N°316, 'Protest van sig.r Gasparo Ma. Marchetti, teegen dheer Consul de Hochepied, en cap:to Cornelis Volkers', Izmir, 02/10/1743.

247 Ibid., '[…] onde vedendosi il medemo preclusa la strada in qsta piazza di poter ricorrere ad altro tribunale superiore […]'.

an anomaly that was unheard of, particularly considering the agitated state in which Marchetti had expressed his sentiments.[248] The consul concluded by stating that the Dutch court did not owe Marchetti any explanation about its verdict, and he could appeal the verdict at another court in case he disagreed. His protest was therefore considered void and of no value, a decision that Daniel Alexander de Hochepied communicated to the consulate of the Kingdom of the Two Sicilies.[249]

Marchetti was thus free to appeal, but Volkers would have been long gone by then. In maritime disputes in which litigants of different territorial jurisdictions were involved, there was thus a potential clash of interests arising from the practical need for cooperation. Although de Hochepied had decided to free Volkers of any legal responsibility, he still had the option to keep him in port, allowing the plaintiff to file his appeal at the relevant (Sicilian) court. But the consul did not allow that option, perhaps because he was angry at Marchetti's behaviour or perhaps because he felt Dutch commercial interest was best served if Volkers was allowed to continue his journey without delay. This case brings to light a practical limitation when it came to the full exercise of all legal rights at all competent courts in the case of a maritime dispute when parties were often on the move, and it might even show the unwillingness of one court – the Dutch consular court – to cooperate with an appeal against its verdict at another, foreign, court. Particularly in litigation involving a plaintiff and defendant from separate jurisdictions, the execution of a sentence could be difficult.[250] This is why the Dutch had issued a regulation stipulating that traders submitting themselves to court judgments had to consent beforehand to respect the sentence, and also why, particularly in cases between Dutch and non-Dutch, the possibilities of appeal were formally restricted.[251] A proposal for a regulation of the legal powers of consuls and ambassadors as judges, first drafted in 1673, contained an article specifying that, in appeals made against the sentence of a dispute between a Dutch national and a non-Dutch, either European or Ottoman, the condemned party had to pay a caution to the Dutch chancery to the amount of the sum determined in the sentence, guaranteeing the execution of the verdict should it be upheld at another court, which might

248 NACS, N°316, 'Contraprotest van haer hoog mog: consul op dat van Gasparo M:a Marchetti Messinees, rakende 't fluijtschip de Soffia x Caterine cap:t Cornelis Volkers', Izmir, 07/10/1743.

249 Ibid.

250 See Calafat, 'La juridiction des consuls français', p. 16.

251 Heeringa and Nanninga, *Bronnen tot de geschiedenis*, 2: pp. 252–254, 'Resolutie der Staten-Generaal betreffende de rechtspraak in de Levant', 23/02/1686.

be far away. The condemned party might have left Izmir to never come back, rendering execution of a sentence impossible without a caution.[252]

This proposal never became a formal regulation, but it shows nonetheless that intercultural litigation was a difficult balancing act between the custom of merchants on the one hand and the duty and jurisdiction of consular judges on the other. The success of trade depended to an important extent on the degree of acceptance amidst traders, sailors and judges of customs and procedures. Marchetti's protest directly against the consul was a violation of such acceptance, and it was an infraction of the legal custom that had developed between the different European trading nations in the Levant. Marchetti had the option to appeal, but he was not to question the legitimacy of the Dutch consul as judge, particularly because he was considered to be responsible for the whole situation. From this point of view, it is perfectly explainable that the consul reacted so mercilessly to Marchetti's protest, even if, from a practical point of view, the Sicilian trader had a point: how could he possibly expect a successful appeal against a skipper who was sailing across the Mediterranean to other unknown ports? Marchetti's fate is not known, but the Dutch must have forgotten his personal attack on the consul. In 1774 he reappears in official documentation from the States of Holland as temporary Dutch consul in Messina.[253]

252 Ibid., pp. 187–204, 'Reglement voor den resident tot Constantinopelen, consul tot Smirna, ende Nederlantsche natie in de Levant residerende respective, sooals hetselve bij de heeren Directeuren van den Levantschen handel aen H.H.M. is overgegeven, en bij deselve weder aen den Consul van Dam gesonden', 1675, particularly on pp. 199–200.

253 *Resolutien van de heeren Staaten van Holland en Westvriesland in haar edele groot mog. vergadering genoomen in den jaare 1774*, pp. 494–495, 'Missive van G.M. Marchetti de Gaspere over de difficulteit in het waarneemen der saaken van de Hollandsche natie als interims consul, om dat vasal was van de Koning van Napels', 15/07/1774.

CHAPTER 5

Ottomans at the Dutch Consular Court

1 Levantine Confrontations with the Law

1.1 *Sequesters in 1686*

As mentioned before, virtually all Dutch legislative efforts to regulate legal procedure in the Levant were responses to concrete disputes over jurisdiction that occurred on the ground. A particular challenge to the existing Dutch legal framework presented itself in Izmir in 1685. That year, the States of Holland sent a letter to the Directorate of Levant Trade in Amsterdam, asking for clarification about a grievance brought before them by two Amsterdam-based traders, Gabriël and Pieter Eygels. They stated that 3,094 lion dollars and 95 aspers belonging to them had been sequestered in Istanbul from the accounts of a partnership between Abraham Vivier and Jan van Ris, both Dutchmen, and Gaspar Chazelles, a French Protestant. It was Vivier who had demanded the sequester, and the Dutch ambassador in Istanbul had complied with the request.[1] The States of Holland wanted to know from the directorate what their interpretation was of the 1616 article on the jurisdiction of the Aleppo consul, as that specific article had set the rules on litigation involving traders of different nations.[2]

Their first question was if the difference between conflicts within the Dutch community and between Dutch and non-Dutch merchants also applied to a case that affected merchants residing in the Netherlands. Secondly, they also wanted to know how the possibilities of appeal should be understood in this case. In their answer, the directors referred to a report that was issued by some of their members in Amsterdam during a meeting in March 1685, which stated that sequesters between 'the natural inhabitants of the Levant' were permitted, and appeals against them were equally permitted, but only in matters between Dutchmen.[3] Appeal was explicitly not allowed in cases between Dutchmen and 'Turks' that had been adjudicated in the Levant.[4] This was a specific clause

1 Heeringa and Nanninga, *Bronnen tot de geschiedenis*, 2: pp. 249–250, Directorate of Levant Trade to the States of Holland, Zeeland and West Frisia, Amsterdam, 19/04/1685.

2 For the 1616 regulation, see pp. 93–95.

3 Heeringa and Nanninga, *Bronnen tot de geschiedenis*, 2: pp. 249–250, Directorate of Levant Trade to the States of Holland, Zeeland and West Frisia, Amsterdam, 19/04/1685, on p. 250, '[...] naturelle inwoonders in de Levant [...]'.

4 Ibid.

in the 1616 regulation as well and had in all likelihood been introduced to avoid appeals before Ottoman courts.[5]

The problem was that, on the basis of the 1616 regulation, Gabriël and Pieter Eygels were not able to appeal the sequester, as the involved partnership in Istanbul was not exclusively Dutch. The States of Holland challenged this interpretation on the grounds that the regulation was only concerned with adjudication in the Levant and only applied to situations in which all the parties were physically in the Levant. If no appeal was possible on legal decisions made in the Levant, it was feared that traders in the United Provinces would stop sending money there, which would greatly harm trade. The directors proposed that all legal decisions by Dutch judges on sequesters made in the Levant would be open to a possible appeal, to be adjudicated at the *Hof van Holland* (see figure 5).[6]

The situation of Gabriël and Pieter Eygels and the possibility of multiple interpretations of the 1616 legislation were the motor behind the drafting of a new law in January 1686, which stipulated that sequesters on goods and monies in the Levant would be allowed, but the party demanding one had to provide a sufficient legal reason for it, which had to be presented to the resident or the consul and assessors, depending on jurisdiction. In cases where the person whose goods were claimed resided in the province of Holland, the sequester could not be adjudicated in the Levant but had to be brought before the Court of Holland (*Hof van Holland*) or the High Council (*Hoge Raad*), the two central courts of the province of Holland.[7] If the person whose goods were claimed live in one of the other provinces, the appeal would be treated by the States General. In cases where the person whose goods were claimed lived in the Levant, disregarding whether the claimant resided in the United Provinces or not, the case was to be adjudicated in the Levant by the resident or consul and assessors, 'according to the style and regulations traditionally used and established in these matters'.[8] Additionally, appeal before a higher judge was allowed on all verdicts and sentences issued in the Levant. If the verdict only concerned people from the province of Holland, or if the defendant in the appeal was from Holland, it was to take place at the *Hof van Holland* or the

5 For the 1616 regulation, see pp. 93–95.

6 Heeringa and Nanninga, *Bronnen tot de geschiedenis*, 2: pp. 249–250, Directorate of Levant Trade to the States of Holland, Zeeland and West Frisia, Amsterdam, 19/04/1685.

7 Heeringa and Nanninga, *Bronnen tot de geschiedenis*, 2: pp. 251–252, 'Ontwerp-reglement van justitie in de Levant', 17/01/1686, on p. 251.

8 Ibid., p. 252, '[...] volgens de stijl en de reglementen van outs voor deselve gebruyckelijck en vastgestelt sijnde'.

Hoge Raad. If the defendant came from another province, then the appeal had to be brought before the States General. All appeals needed to be registered within fourteen days at the court of first instance, and the appeal had to take place within eight months. The consul and resident were ordered to promptly expedite justice.[9]

A resolution issued by the States General on 23 February 1686 turned the draft into law and specified that 'sequesters requested by inhabitants of the Levant, either naturals, Turks or also other [from] other European nations, or the Dutch nation, shall be allowed, and cause effect [...] and the procedures have to be continued immediately and without delay [...] all according to the regulations, and the style in use there [the Levant]'.[10] This is a highly relevant passage in the resolution, which further specified that no appeal was possible against a verdict issued by a Dutch consul regarding a sequester that involved both Dutch merchants and those of other nations, disregarding whether they were European or Ottoman.[11]

The resolution also declared the sequester made by Vivier void, on the interpretation that the money belonged to a party who resided in Holland. The 1686 resolution was considered an addition to the February 1616 law, which codified the jurisdiction and adjudicating powers of the consul in Aleppo and had been applied to all the Dutch consulates in the Ottoman Empire.[12] In 1764, a dispute concerned with liability for several bales of burned cotton was brought before the Dutch consul in Izmir. At the end of the trial, the party sentenced to assume responsibility for the damaged goods wanted to appeal but was informed he could only do so after obeying the verdict issued by the consul and assessors. When that happened, the sentenced party could invoke the 1686 resolution to justify the appeal.[13] Of all the cases brought before the Dutch consul in Izmir and analysed for this book, this was the only one in

9 Ibid.

10 Heeringa and Nanninga, *Bronnen tot de geschiedenis*, 2: pp. 252–254, 'Resolutie der Staten-Generaal betreffende de rechtspraak in de Levant', 23/02/1686, on p. 253, '[...] dat de arresten die versocht sullen werden bij inwoonders in de Levant, hetsij naturellen, Turcken, off oock andere Europische ofte Nederlandtsche natie, sullen mogen werden verleent, ende effect moeten sorteeren [...] dat dien onvermindert aentstonts ende sonder uytstel sal moeten werden voortgevaren met de proceduren [...], alles volgens de reglementen, ende de stijle aldaer gebruyckelijk [...]'.

11 Ibid.

12 Ibid.

13 NACS, N°330, 'Appel der heere Clement, van Sanen, van der Zee & C° op de sententie', Izmir, 25/05/1764. The case, between the firms of Wijnants & Cramer of Amsterdam and Ouckama & C° of Izmir, is analyzed in detail on pp. 162–198.

which reference was made to a written Dutch law. It shows the continuing importance of the legislation issued in the seventeenth century, particularly as no further Dutch legislation on adjudication in the Levant was issued in the eighteenth century.

1.2 *Central Courts in the United Provinces*

The 1686 law was very timely. Sequester was a common legal means used in commercial disputes, and magistrates often laid legal claims on outstanding balances or consigned goods at the request of creditors to force debtors to take action. This book has focussed on litigation at the consular court of Izmir, thus, at a Dutch court in the Levant. As it was mostly concerned with international trade disputes, sequesters on money and goods were common, and they might take place in faraway territories. It has been argued that, although theoretically possible, commercial disputes were rarely brought before a centralised provincial court in the United Provinces.[14] Appeals against sequesters were an exception to this, and this had to do with the specific stipulation that these courts were to serve as appeal courts in this matter.

In June 1762, an Armenian merchant based in Amsterdam named Serkis Yazıcıoğlu demanded the aldermen court in Leiden lay a sequester on goods that were in the hands of the merchant Pieter Cauw, former aldermen of that city. These goods belonged to another Armenian trader, Melcum di Aretium, who lived in Izmir. Johan Frederik Mann, who was the chancellor of the Dutch consulate there, had sent di Aretium's goods, which included bales of yarn and cotton, to Cauw on five different ships. Yazıcıoğlu had some open accounts with di Aretium and demanded that the aldermen laid a sequester on goods of equal value to the money di Aretium owed him. Cauw was given the opportunity to respond and answered that he did not have any goods in his possession that had been sent by Mann or that belonged to di Aretium. In December 1762, Yazıcıoğlu petitioned the aldermen for a second sequester, this time on the money he thought was the profit made by Cauw in selling di Aretium's goods. Cauw insisted that he had no dealings with di Aretium, only with Mann. The sequester was permitted, however, and amounted to a value of 5,054 guilders and 16 pennies. When Mann was informed of it, he replied that he was still owed money by Cauw as well in relation to services he had offered in Izmir involving the same goods. Litigation concerning these sequesters ensued in Leiden, leading to a verdict that denied Yazıcıoğlu's claim in April 1764. An

14 Gelderblom, *Cities of commerce*, pp. 126–133.

appeal was made at the *Hof van Holland*, which confirmed the verdict issued by the aldermen in Leiden.[15]

There was a possibility for a second appeal, and on 28 July 1764, Amsterdam lawyer Pieter Ploos appeared before the *Hof van Holland*, holding a power of attorney given to him by Serkis Yazıcıoğlu, to appeal the sentence issued ten days earlier.[16] While the appeal had to be filed at the court that reached the sentence, the appeal itself took place at a higher court, in this case the *Hoge Raad*, which overturned the verdict in March 1765, for the first time confirming the legitimacy of the sequester. The different judges all provided written reasoning for their decision to allow the sequester, which was based on the evidence that Yazıcıoğlu was di Aretium's creditor and the goods sent to Cauw had indeed belonged to di Aretium, as Yazıcıoğlu claimed. These two conditions were considered sufficiently proven by the court following the admission of written evidence, which must have contained accounts and extracts from business books or commercial correspondence. The question of whether Mann could also lay a claim on the money subjected to the sequester was dismissed by the court, as Yazıcıoğlu had not been aware of this, and he only submitted his claim for a sequester on the money in response to Cauw's declaration that di Aretium's goods were no longer there (but had been sold).[17]

With the sequester considered legitimate, di Aretium and Yazıcıoğlu were expected to settle their dispute before the *Hoge Raad*. Di Aretium now was the defendant against claims made by Yazıcıoğlu to settle their accounts, something the latter had already demanded explicitly in December 1764 and March 1765, including a request for an additional payment of interest at 4%. Di Aretium tried to stall the procedure. He claimed the goods and monies on which a sequester had been laid in Leiden did not belong to him and that, consequently, the sequester should be released. But on the other hand, he also expressed his willingness to settle accounts with Yazıcıoğlu, but in Izmir rather than in the United Provinces, 'if necessary before the competent judge there'.[18] As the original sequester had been made by Yazıcıoğlu against Cauw, the person who had the goods in his hands, the *Hoge Raad* felt it was legitimate of di

15 NA, N°3.03.02, ('Archief van de Hoge Raad van Holland, Zeeland en (West-)Friesland, 1582–1797') (hereafter NA/Hoge Raad), N°678 ('Resoluties tot de sententies', 1763–1768), 19/03/1765.

16 NA, N°3.03.01.01 ('Archief van het Hof van Holland, 1428–1811') (hereafter NA/Hof), N°1729 ('Residentieboek', 16/12/1762–24/12/1775), f°52v-53r, 28/07/1764.

17 NA/Hoge Raad, N°678, 19/03/1765 and N°922 ('Register der dictums', 1761–1775), 30/03/1765.

18 Perhaps in the hope it would be brought before an Ottoman court. NA/Hoge Raad, N°678, 09/02/1768, '[…] des noods voor den bevoegden regter aldaar […]'.

Aretium to question ownership, but the court decided that di Aretium's ownership was sufficiently proven, considering there was evidence given by one of the toll officials in Izmir and by two fellow merchants in Izmir. The court also found di Aretium's legal efforts hard to reconcile with his denial of ownership of the sequestered goods.[19]

Di Aretium's questioning of ownership seemed to be a manoeuvre to avoid paying his debts more than anything else, and after considering the written evidence and the oral pleas, the judges of the *Hoge Raad* agreed to maintain their 1765 verdict, reiterating the legitimacy of the sequester and ordering di Aretium once more to settle his account with Yazıcıoğlu, including the payment of interest.[20] At this point, more than five years had passed since Yazıcıoğlu first attempted to turn to the Dutch legal system to force di Aretium to pay his outstanding debts, and the only thing Yazıcıoğlu had achieved was a sequester and a court order to settle debts.[21] Including two appeals, he had petitioned three courts, and he had been confronted with the threat of litigation far away in the Ottoman Empire as well. There are no specific indications that Yazıcıoğlu's case was particular, and while a path of litigation such as the one he experienced must have discouraged merchants from seeking recourse to legal action, they also must have felt that sequesters on open accounts or consigned goods abroad were part of the risk attached to international commission trade. The preserved court papers show that neither the physical distance between di Aretium and Yazıcıoğlu nor the fact that they were Armenians were considered as problematic. These were part of the particular circumstances of the case but had nothing to do with its essence, which was a mercantile problem to be resolved according to merchant custom; di Aretium owed Yazıcıoğlu money, and Yazıcıoğlu thus laid a claim on the profits of goods sold in Holland that belonged to di Aretium. The only relevant questions for the judges at the *Hoge Raad* were about ownership of these goods and the existence of a relationship of debt between di Aretium and Yazıcıoğlu.

This case was rendered more difficult and lengthier because it was brought before the centralised courts of the *Hof van Holland* and the *Hoge Raad* – caused

19 NA/Hoge Raad, N°678, 09/02/1768.

20 NA/Hoge Raad, N°922, 01/03/1768.

21 Such a long duration was not exceptional, and it was a widespread problem. The establishment of specialized courts and the use of summary procedure were two measures that were adopted to ensure speedier sentencing. Based on all the court cases considered in his work on the institutional foundations of long-distance trade, Oscar Gelderblom calculated an average length of 5.5 years. Gelderblom, *Cities of commerce*, p. 132. For Venice, see Fusaro, 'Politics of justice/politics of trade'.

by Yazıcıoğlu's desire to appeal a sentence that had not pleased him in the first instance. It is important to note the difference between procedures followed at the higher courts in the United Provinces – which were the formal procedures of a civil trial, presided over by professional judges and pleaded by professional attorneys – and those taking place at the consular court in Izmir, which were specifically designed to adjudicate commercial disputes and which relied on summary procedure and judgment by the consul assisted by peers.

The procedures of litigation at the *Hof van Holland* (see figure 5) were described in a series of instructions (*instructies*). The first one was issued by Charles the Bold in 1462 and described the jurisdiction, competence and composition of the court, and it also codified civil procedure. Other instructions followed, but it was only with the issuing of the *instructie* from 1531 that the court's functioning was set on firm foundations that remained unchanged until the court's abolition in 1811.[22] In a similar manner, the *Hoge Raad* operated on the basis of a large set of *instructies* – these were issued in 1582.[23] Civil procedures in these central courts relied on professional judges and were specific. When a case, either in first instance or as appeal, was brought before the *Hof van Holland*, a particular procedure, the *rolprocedure*, was followed. First, the plaintiff submitted a request, *rekest om mandement*, allowing an usher to summon the defendant in court. This request contained the plaintiff's motivation for the litigation. The judges then either allowed it, by writing *fiat ut petitur* on the request, which happened most of the time, or denied it (*nihil ut petitur*), in which case the plaintiff could attempt a second time in a hearing before all the judges. If the request was allowed, the writ had to be delivered to the defendant within fourteen days, or three weeks for inhabitants of Zeeland.

The defendant could then decide to either obey the demand or to defend himself. First, he could challenge jurisdiction of the court, ask for delay or provide reasons why the demand should be declared void. Second, he could defend himself regarding the demand itself in his answer or counter-request, which generally contained a formula demanding payment of legal expenses by the plaintiff. Theoretically, the court could sentence at this moment or demand additional information following a temporary verdict. Litigating parties could be asked to provide a *memoir* containing their legal reasoning or documents (*schrifturen*) that contained evidence supporting their view and deconstructing the other's view.[24] In case the defendant provided such

22 Le Bailly, *Procesgids*, pp. 18–19.

23 Le Bailly and Verhas, *Hoge Raad*, p. 18.

24 *Schrifturen* were written documents issued by the litigating parties explaining all the different points of the dispute.

reasoning to counteract the plaintiff's demand, the litigation entered a phase called *enqueste*, or evidential procedure, which meant that both parties had to support their viewpoint with evidence, led by one of the judges. Both parties had three months to produce evidence, after which the *enqueste* ended, and parties were allowed to look at the evidence produced by the opponent, against which they could protest and counter-protest. When this procedure ended, a specially appointed reporter had to control all the pieces of the case, after which he filed a report with the other judges, which started with his own advice for a verdict. The other judges equally provided advice, after which a verdict was reached by a majority of vote. After this, either a final sentence was reached, or it was decided that additional steps were necessary, such as for instance the obligation for parties to come to an agreement. The last element in the litigation was the taxation of the costs and sentencing who had to pay.[25] The whole procedure was formal, judged by professionals, and parties could be assisted by attorneys. It was also a procedure based on the delivery of written evidence, after which the judges discussed it orally between one another, which was written down in the report.

It is interesting to note that Yazıcıoğlu, as a foreigner, was allowed to bring his case directly before the *Hof van Holland* but had declined to do so, maybe because he was hoping a case brought before the alderman court against a local trader, in this example Pieter Cauw in Leiden, would be resolved faster and better, through a summary procedure rather than through the more complicated *rolprocedure* described above.[26]

1.3 *The States General and Ottoman Justice*

However, Yazıcıoğlu could have chosen a different path altogether. He could have asked for the sequester of goods belonging to di Aretium in Izmir. A first step would have been to file a claim at the States General, a regular practice with merchants involved in an international dispute, as the States General were the direct superiors of consuls and ambassadors abroad and could instruct them to take certain legal action, such as the sequester of goods. Yazıcıoğlu had not chosen that option, but other merchants who felt wronged did petition the States General. In April 1753, a group of merchants and clothmakers from Amsterdam and Leiden wrote the States General about Mattheus di Ovan, a Persian-born trader who had been living as a merchant in Amsterdam for

25 Le Bailly, *Procesgids*, pp. 29–41.

26 Although foreigners were allowed to litigate in first instance at a central provincial court, they rarely chose to do so. One of the reasons was that it took longer for these courts to reach a verdict. Gelderblom, *Cities of commerce*, pp. 126–133.

twelve years.[27] Di Ovan had bought cloth, silk and velvet from the petitioning merchants and had these further adapted by the clothmakers in question. The goods were then sent to St. Petersburg, Astrakhan and Izmir. The Persian subsequently disappeared from Amsterdam, still owing more than 45,600 guilders to that group of merchants and workers for payment of goods and wages. The petitioners immediately took measures to sequester di Ovan's goods but felt the case was so important that it should not be treated 'in the ordinary manner, without support from above'.[28] They demanded the States General to send letters to diplomats in St. Petersburg and Izmir, with a demand to sequester goods there that belonged to di Ovan. The States General consented and issued a resolution to that purpose.[29]

Consul Daniel Alexander de Hochepied in Izmir received a letter on the matter from the States General at the end of June 1753 and he wrote back within three days. He informed them that di Ovan had outstanding credit with two Armenian firms, Malcas di Carabeth and Aretun & Daniel Qatergıoğlu, and they both had already been asked to provide more information about di Ovan's credit by the correspondents of the petitioners in Amsterdam and Leiden as well as by other creditors of di Ovan. The Armenian firms refused to comply until they were summoned to appear at the consulate, where they showed their current accounts with di Ovan, which indeed contained more than 5,500 lion dollars belonging to di Ovan as well as a parcel of cloth. Additionally, a Dutch ship that arrived on 28 June, a day after de Hochepied received the first information on di Ovan from the States General, contained two boxes of merchandise that belonged to di Ovan, and sequester was laid on the ship, which the skipper accepted on the condition that it would be resolved before he had fully unloaded. According to the consul's calculations, the total sum of the sequestered assets surpassed 7,000 lion dollars.[30]

---

27 While the petitioners mentioned the period of twelve years, a petition issued to the Directorate of Levant Trade on a restriction to export ammunition in 1725 contains the name of Matteus di Ovan as merchant in Amsterdam. Heeringa and Nanninga, *Bronnen tot de geschiedenis*, 3: pp. 203–204, Amsterdam merchants to Directorate of Levant Trade, Amsterdam, 25/07/1725. For the 1753 petition, see NACS, N°30, 'Request Leonard Lups & Zoon, Willem Straalman, David Rutgers Jr & Henrick Buttelman c.s.', Amsterdam, 10/04/1753.

28 NACS, N°30, Request Leonard Lups & Zoon, Amsterdam, 10/04/1753, '[…] op ordinaire wijze en zonder steun van hogerhand […]'.

29 Ibid.

30 Heeringa and Nanninga, *Bronnen tot de geschiedenis*, 3: pp. 259–260, Consul Daniel Alexander de Hochepied to the States General, Izmir, 30/06/1753.

The consul, however, feared a successful outcome, because Malcas di Carabeth, Aretun Qatergıoğlu and Daniel Qatergıoğlu were all Ottoman subjects, and de Hochepied thought it would be very complicated to claim di Ovan's debts from the sequestered monies in their accounts, as those would be dealt with by Ottoman justice. De Hochepied wrote that the Ottomans accepted 'neither Frankish laws nor [do] *schrifturen* have any place according to the law and jurisdiction of the land [i.e., the Ottoman Empire]'.[31] European written evidence, such as business books or *schrifturen*, were indeed not allowed in Ottoman courts, and there was also no official sanctioning for lying or false testimony.[32] It is not difficult to understand why Europeans were not happy suing Ottoman subjects in an Ottoman court, as they felt they were at a disadvantage and the outcome was far less predictable for them.

It would, however, be a mistake to simply discard Ottoman courts as not apt for commercial litigation and to take European fear of Ottoman adjudication at face value. The *qadi* court and the consular court might not have been all that different in their adjudication of commercial disputes. Similar to the Ottoman refusal to accept European written evidence, European consular courts did not admit Ottoman written evidence unless it was translated into a European language. Additionally, the procedures at both courts were in writing. For the consular court, the system of written requests, replies and counter-replies was a written version of the oral summary procedure. For the *qadi* court, 'the ascendancy of written documents over witness statements' was 'a practical development [...] that was at odds with legal theory'.[33]

When Consul Cornelis Pauw in Aleppo described consular adjudication to the States General in 1615, he wrote that the consuls were following the use of these (Ottoman) lands, which meant they adopted a form of trial 'without admitting any lawyers, attorneys, or time to conduct a trial in writing, and only allowing dragomans to translate [languages of] foreign nations; and having heard the reasons of both parties, the declarations of witnesses who are knowledgeable about the about the affair or any other form of written evidence that

31 Ibid., on p. 260, 'Want Frankse wetten nog schrifftuuren vinden by het regt en justitie van 't land geen de minste plaetze [...]'.

32 Van den Boogert, *The capitulations*, p. 45; see also Apellániz, '"You cannot produce a Muslim witness"', pp. 633–648; and, for a later period, Mafalda Ade, 'The Ottoman commercial tribunal in Damascus and the use of testimony and evidence in mixed cases in the 19th century', *Quaderni storici*, 3 (2016): pp. 649–672. On Islamic legal ideas of distinctions between written and oral evidence, and the superiority of Muslim oral declarations over European written evidence, see Francisco Apellániz, *Breaching the bronze wall: Franks at Mamluk and Ottoman courts and markets* (Leiden and Boston, 2020).

33 Van den Boogert, *The capitulations*, p. 45.

mentions the case […] pronounce an oral sentence'.[34] Pauw's comments are interesting because he was describing summary procedure – a few lines further he referred to it as the 'short style' ('corte stijl') – and he explicitly connected this 'short style' to Ottoman procedures. He was not wrong in doing so, and the main difference with later Dutch consular adjudication in the Levant is that he described a procedure that seems to include physical appearance before court, while eighteenth-century adjudication at the Dutch consular court in Izmir was a written trial, similar in tone and structure to an oral one, allowing similar evidence, but without the obligation for litigants to physically appear before court. It seems then that, initially, Ottoman and European procedures concerning commercial adjudication were closer to one another than they would become later, but essentially, the European written trial kept its summary nature, making the later difference perhaps more about format than content, thus hiding continuing similarities between the two.

In spite of these similarities, in the case of di Ovan, Consul de Hochepied was clear that he wanted to avoid an Ottoman procedure, and he expressed the fear that di Ovan's Dutch creditors would end up paying double. He thought the best course of action would be for the States General to employ Ambassador Elbert de Hochepied, a younger brother of the consul, to obtain a *ferman* from the Porte ordering the sequestered assets of di Ovan be handed over to the Dutch creditors.[35] In September 1753, di Ovan's creditors in the United Provinces wrote to the States General again, as they had found out that the two sequestered boxes of merchandise on board the Dutch ship contained three of his sealed business books, which were sent away in an attempt to hide them from scrutiny and to avoid them being used in court. They demanded the consul open these books and have copies made of the extracts that were of relevance to them. The States General agreed.[36] In the meantime, Elbert de Hochepied did his best in Istanbul, and in December 1753, he informed

34 Heeringa and Nanninga, *Bronnen tot de geschiedenis*, 1: pp. 468–478, Consul Cornelis Pauw to the States General, Aleppo, 12/09/1615, on p. 469, '[…] de forme van procederen, daerin gouverneren haer de heeren consuls nae de usantie van dese landen, sonder t'admitteren advocaten, procureurs oft tijt om eenige schrifftelijcke processen te formeren, amer alleenlijck H.E. turchemans tot vertalinge van de vrembde natiën; ende aenhoort hebbende de redenen van partijen ten wedersijden, de verklaringe van de getuygen, die van de saecke kennisse hebben, oft eenich ander schriftelijck bewijs, dat daervan soude mogen sprecken, gevisiteert hebbende, geven daerop mondelinge sententie […]'.

35 Heeringa and Nanninga, *Bronnen tot de geschiedenis*, 3: pp. 259–260, Consul Daniel Alexander de Hochepied to the States General, Izmir, 30/06/1753.

36 NACS, N°30, Request Leonard Lups & Zoon, Willem Straalman, David Rutgers Jr & Henrick Buttelman c.s., Amsterdam, 24/09/1753.

his older brother in Izmir that he had obtained a *ferman*, of which he sent a translation. The *ferman* was to force the Armenian firms to appear at the Ottoman court and to have a *hüccet* (legal deed) issued there, which would oblige them to deposit the sequestered goods with the Dutch chancery according to agreements made in the capitulations. In case the Armenians denied the presence of di Ovan's assets under their account, it would be easy to find evidence to the contrary, either from declarations by toll officials or in the business correspondence from the Armenian firms. In any case, considering the role Ottoman justice would play, Elbert advised his brother to speak to the Ottoman judge beforehand.[37] Later writing by Ambassador de Hochepied was more pessimistic; he possessed information that di Ovan was in Astrakhan and feared nothing could be done for his creditors unless they would be able to obtain some official statement from di Ovan.[38]

In 1754, Consul Daniel Alexander de Hochepied ordered for copies of the relevant business documents of di Ovan that had been found in Izmir to be sent back to the United Provinces. Van Lennep and Knipping, holding a power of attorney, and Belcamp, Clement & van Sanen addressed the parcel to one of the principal creditors in Amsterdam, Willem Straalman. In the meantime, they had been researched 'confidentially, without having changed, obscured, added or left out anything' by three Armenian merchants in Izmir, and these three men were willing to confirm as much under oath. They made copies of the documents, and after this they handed them back to the Dutch chancellor in a bag that was sealed, bound together with a rope and subsequently kept in the chancery.[39] A separate document confirmed that in total, the documents in question numbered thirteen and included balances in Armenian and Italian, a booklet summing up all goods sent to di Ovan from Astrakhan, a contract made with Armenian traders in Astrakhan, several obligations and notes, a business ledger written in Armenian and a letter book containing copies of 232 letters.[40] As part of the documents had been written in Armenian, it might

---

37 Heeringa and Nanninga, *Bronnen tot de geschiedenis*, 3: pp. 267–268, Ambassador Elbert de Hochepied to Consul Daniel Alexander de Hochepied, Istanbul, 16/12/1753.

38 Ibid., p. 268.

39 NACS, N°240 ('Matheus di Ovan, Armeens koopman, uit Amsterdam naar Smyrna gevlucht, 1754'), 'Acte wegens de terug ontfangen Armeense boeken en schriftuuren van Matt di Ovan als meede weegens de versendingh der copije met capt Elias Hendriks', Izmir, 16/08/1754, '[...] vertrouwelijk gedaan zonder het minste te hebben achtergelaten, verandert, verdonkert, vermeerdert nog vermindert [...]'.

40 NACS, N°240, 'Notta der g'extraheerde Armeense schrifturen de welken met het schip van de capt Elias Hendriks na Amst[erda]m versonden sijn aen den heer Willem Straelman', Izmir, 16/08/1754.

have been unavoidable to demand Armenian traders to assist in translating the relevant material. The role of merchants as co-judges and court experts was crucial in legitimising the merchants' style in court and ensuring its incorporation in the Dutch legal system. Here, they were needed to assess the legitimacy of the written evidence, which was then sent back to the United Provinces, where it could be used in court.[41]

In spite of these efforts, the case remained unresolved, and di Ovan was not found. Further communications on the matter between the States General and Ambassador Elbert de Hochepied several years later referred to new instructions the ambassador had obtained from the Porte, in which the *qadi* in Izmir was demanded to hand over di Ovan's goods and monies in the hands of the Armenian traders to di Ovan's creditors in the United Provinces. Consul de Hochepied was not pleased, as according to the terms of the instruction, the goods would be delivered only if the consul and all the Dutch traders of Izmir provided security on these goods, a practice that was dangerously close to getting the whole Dutch trading community of Izmir involved in a dispute that did not really concern them. The States General did not see the problem and instructed de Hochepied to comply.[42]

It is not clear whether, and how, the case was resolved, but six years later, the goods belonging to di Ovan remained sequestered.[43] The cases involving Serkis Yazıcıoğlu and Mattheus di Ovan are telling for a number of reasons. First of all, they demonstrate that merchants did petition the States General for intervention, and the States General was sensitive to these petitions, even when they were made by non-Dutch traders. It confirms, however, the difficulty of a speedy resolution in a context in which summary procedure was not used, with di Ovan's goods still under sequester six years after the initial claim had been made. Perhaps di Ovan's creditors were not able to seek recourse at a local court in the United Provinces, where the procedural context would have led to faster sentencing. It seems likely that, before disappearing, di Ovan made sure not to have left any goods in the United Provinces. He had been careful to consign merchandise to himself and others abroad and attempted to hide his business books. It might have been a conscious strategy to obstruct adjudication in the United Provinces.

41 On legal evidence, see pp. 132–137.

42 NACS, N°30, 'Resolutie Staten Generaal', 23/12/1757.

43 Heeringa and Nanninga, *Bronnen tot de geschiedenis*, 3: pp. 402–404, Consul Daniel Jean de Hochepied to the States General, Izmir, 15/09/1760.

2 Legal Issues of Dutch Protection and Subject Status

2.1 Beratlı *Problems*

In May 1774, Frederik Johan Robert de Weiler, the Dutch *chargé d'affaires* in Istanbul, sent a letter to the United Provinces in which he objected to a resolution issued by the States General that granted a Greek trader a number of privileges he was not naturally entitled to.[44] The Greek trader was Demetrio Fronimo, and he acted as an agent in Istanbul and Izmir on behalf of a Greek firm that was established in Amsterdam, the partnership of Brink & Curmulli.[45] The resolution had come in response to a request made by them, wanting Fronimo to have the same 'freedoms, liberties and privileges' as the Dutch merchants.[46] The problem was that they justified their request by arguing Fronimo was an agent for a firm established in Amsterdam, while he was, as a born Greek, an Ottoman subject. De Weiler objected, stating that the original request had falsely portrayed Fronimo as Dutch and the house of Brink & Curmulli was not officially established in either Istanbul or Izmir. On the other hand, de Weiler admitted that Fronimo was indeed working on commission as an agent for Brink & Curmulli. De Weiler also sold Fronimo 'an imperial *berat* by which he [Fronimo] has come under your [States General's] protection, under the moniker of interpreter and in the service of the minister [representative in Istanbul]'.[47]

---

44 Heeringa and Nanninga, *Bronnen tot de geschiedenis*, 4: pp. 183–185, *Chargé d'affaires* Frederik Johan Robert de Weiler to the States General, Istanbul, 17/05/1774.

45 A 1784 registry included Johannes Brink as a Levant trader who was established at the Trippenburgwal near the Nieuwmarkt, as well as Demetrio Curmulli & C°, whose company was registered on the Keizersgracht. *Naamregister van alle de kooplieden voornaame handeldryvende of negotiedoende winkeliers en fabricanten der stad Amsterdam* (Amsterdam, 1784), pp. 16 and 30. In the 1770s, Curmulli also had an insurance firm in Venice; see also van den Boogert, 'Ottoman Greeks', pp. 133–138; and Hakkı Kadı, *Ottoman and Dutch merchants*, p. 249. Johannes Brink, whose diary was kept, was a Greek trader whose original name was Ioannis Pringos. Hasan Çolak, 'Amsterdam's Greek merchants: Protégés of the Dutch, beneficiaries of the Russians, subjects of the Ottomans and supporters of Greece', *Byzantine and modern Greek studies*, 42:1 (2018): p. 116.

46 Heeringa and Nanninga, *Bronnen tot de geschiedenis*, 4: pp. 183–185, *Chargé d'affaires* Frederik Johan Robert de Weiler to the States General, Istanbul, 17/05/1774, on p. 183, '[…] vrijheeden, rechten en priviligiën […]'; see also *Resolutien van de heeren Staaten van Holland en Westvriesland in haar edele groot mog. vergadering genoomen in den jaare 1774*, p. 495, 'Missive met sijne bedenkelykheid teegens haar hoog mog. resolutie van 16 maart, op het versoek van Brink en Morré, tot protectie van seekeren Fronimo: commiss', 15/07/1774.

47 Heeringa and Nanninga, *Bronnen tot de geschiedenis*, 4: pp. 183–185, *Chargé d'affaires* Frederik Johan Robert de Weiler to the States General, Istanbul, 17/05/1774, on pp. 183–184, '[…] een keyzerlijk barat, waardoor hij onder de naam van tolk en als in dienst van den

De Weiler continued that, as a Dutch *protégé*, Fronimo was exempt from the *cizye* and enjoyed several other privileges, which were already very advantageous for his principals but that the *berat* allowed him 'neither to be withdrawn from the supreme authority of his legal lord the sultan, nor to enjoy all such rights, liberties and privileges as the free and national Dutch merchants here do, who are under immediate protection from you as their lords [the States General] and under your same jurisdiction, as if they were in Holland'.[48] De Weiler further mentioned that the French and English did not even allow their Ottoman *protégés* to trade with France and England, a right Dutch Ottoman *protégés* did have, and those who had obtained a *berat* as a Dutch *protégé* could always forfeit it whenever they wanted.[49] De Weiler suggested that Brink & Curmulli had only made the request in order for Fronimo to enjoy the same advantageous fiscal regime as a Dutch merchant, and he advised against granting the request, as it could motivate other *protégés* to demand the same privileges, which would be harmful for Dutch Levant trade.

Two weeks after de Weiler's letter to the States General, the consul in Izmir, Daniel Jean de Hochepied, sent a letter to the Directorate of Levant Trade in which he agreed with de Weiler. He also referred to earlier problems that occurred after a similar request had been granted to Antonio Zingrilara. Zingrilara had been one of the first Ottoman Greek merchants to establish himself in Amsterdam, where he married a Dutch woman. He successfully petitioned the States General to consider his firm in Izmir as Dutch in 1759, in spite of protests from the Dutch community there, who considered the decision as harmful for their national trade. The Directorate of Levant Trade took the side of the Dutch traders in Izmir, while Zingrilara became an official citizen of Amsterdam in 1760. Zingrilara returned to Izmir in 1765, determined to divorce his Dutch wife and revert back to his Greek roots. The Dutch status of his firm was withdrawn, and Zingrilara's wife had his goods in Holland sequestered, leading to a conflict between Zingrilara and the Dutch that lasted for several years.[50]

---

minister staande onder uw hoog mogende protectie gekomen [...]'. The phrasing reflects the origins of the *berat* system given to Ottoman interpreters; see pp. 28–29.

48 Ibid., on p. 184, '[...] dog door welke hij nooyt kan nòg worden onttrokken aan 't opperste gezag van zijnen wettigen heere, den sultan, nòg kan gaudeeren van alle zodanige regten, vrijheeden en privilegiën als vrije en nationaele Nederlandsche kooplieden alhier, die onder de immediate protectie van uw hoog mogende als hunne heeren staan en onder hoogstderzelver jurisdictie, even alsof zij in Holland waren [...]'.

49 The *chargé d'affaires* is hinting here at the large Ottoman involvement in Dutch Levant trade that has been discussed on pp. 79–83.

50 Zingrilara had resided in Holland, but returned to Izmir later, hoping to be considered a Dutch national. See van den Boogert, 'Ottoman Greeks', pp. 131–133. Heeringa and

De Hochepied pointed to the Zingrilara case in order to explain that official Dutch recognition of a Greek firm as Dutch could be highly problematic and cause a great deal of protest from Dutch traders.[51] Such recognition would cost the Dutch community money, because Greek firms paid more consular duties than Dutch traders. A favourable decision for Fronimo would create a dangerous precedent.[52] De Hochepied's concerns were shared by his treasurer, Coenraad Schutz, who sent a letter to the Directorate of Levant Trade the same day: 'if such a resolution would take effect, all Greek and other merchants here who have a *berat* will try, together with their correspondents in the mother country [United Provinces], to bring our nationals to ruin and suppression'.[53] The Directorate of Levant Trade took these fears serious and advised the States General to deny Fronimo the request, as 'no dragomans, either ordinary salaried ones [the employees at the consulate] or the honorary ones are permitted to trade as nationals'.[54] Fronimo's request was denied, and he continued to do business as a *protégé*. Perhaps Brink & Curmulli felt that the privileges that came with the *protégé* status were not sufficient, and they might have made the request out of desperation, as Demetrio Fronimo was not doing well commercially - one year after the request had been made, he went bankrupt.[55]

Even if the status of Dutch national merchants, as well as that of the non-Muslim Ottoman traders who had purchased Dutch protection, was clearly defined by legislation, it did not mean that traders did not try to bend the rules to their advantage and approach officials and diplomatic representatives in attempts to obtain privileges. Antonio Zingrilara, for instance, went to

Nanninga, *Bronnen tot de geschiedenis*, 4: pp. 185–186, Consul Daniel Jean de Hochepied to the Directorate of Levant Trade, Izmir, 03/06/1774.

51 Heeringa and Nanninga, *Bronnen tot de geschiedenis*, 4: pp. 185–186, Consul Daniel Jean de Hochepied to the Directorate of Levant Trade, Izmir, 03/06/1774.

52 Ibid.

53 Ibid., p. 186, C.G.N. Schutz to the Directorate of Levant Trade, Izmir, 03/06/1774, '[...] wanneer voormelde resolutie effect sorteeren sal, alle met barat voorsiene Griekse en andere kooplieden, hier gestabileert, door hunne correspondenten in het vaderland mede diergelijke naedelige previlegiën tot ruïne en onderdrukkinge onser nationaalen sullen tragten te obtineeren [...]'.

54 Ibid., pp. 189–190, Directorate of Levant Trade to the States General, Amsterdam, 04/08/1774, on p. 189, 'dat het daerenboven nooyt aan eenige draaglieden, hetsij ordinaris gesalarieerde of honoraire, gepermitteert is geweest eenige negotie als nationale te drijven [...]'.

55 Ibid., p. 190. Fronimo continued to trade, although it seems that he left Izmir to start a firm of his own in Vienna. A commercial registry for 1797 contains an entry for 'Demetrio Fronimo und Comp. sudetto Olandese' amongst the list of 'Turkish' subjects settled in Vienna. It seems, thus, Fronimo had managed to keep his protected status. *Allgemeiner Handelstands-kalender für das Jahr 1797 welches ein gemeines Jahr von 365 Tagen ist* (Wien, 1797), n.p.

Amsterdam as a Greek trader. After he arrived, he married a Dutch woman and managed to become officially recognised as an Amsterdam citizen. When he went back to Izmir years later, he tried to use his marriage and citizenship in a failed attempt to get his firm accepted as a Dutch national firm. As a result, Zingrilara needed to get an official Ottoman *berat*, without which the Dutch were not able to protect him.[56] In the end, he decided to turn away from the Dutch community. He divorced his Dutch wife and rejoined the Greek community. In 1768 he attempted another switch of allegiance by becoming partner in a Dutch firm. A second demand to get Zingrilara recognised as Dutch national failed, after which no further efforts seem to have been taken.[57]

The demands to be recognised as Dutch nationals made by Zingrilara, Fronimo and others were caused by the growing Greek and Armenian Ottoman presence in Amsterdam. Several Ottoman merchants settling in Amsterdam managed to obtain citizen status in Amsterdam, which strengthened their petitions to become Dutch or to become accepted as a partner in a Dutch firm.[58] The advantages their situation could bring were heavily contested by Dutch traders, who felt they were denied the same beneficial situation, and the Dutch authorities denied Ottoman traders' requests to be considered Dutch and eventually decided to forbid Dutch nationals from accepting Ottoman partners in their firms.

2.2 *Ottoman-Dutch Intercultural Partnerships*

Even though an intercultural partnership was disadvantageous in terms of nationality and protection, it could still be beneficial to all involved traders. The Dutch partner could associate his interests more closely with those of his Ottoman partner, who was more likely to possess better local commercial know-how and a more extensive commercial network in the Levant. While Dutch traders already relied on Ottoman expertise, a formal association through a partnership would motivate the Ottoman intermediary to put his full weight in the transactions he was involved in by becoming a stakeholder in its success. For the Ottoman partner, it could open the possibility of forging closer links with traders in the United Provinces and building up a network that extended well into western Europe. It also opened up the possibility of

---

56 NACS, N°14, Consul Daniel Jean de Hochepied to Ambassador Willem Dedel, Izmir, 16/10/1766.

57 Van den Boogert, 'Ottoman Greeks', pp. 131–133.

58 This evolution was analysed by van den Boogert, 'Ottoman Greeks'; see also Çolak, 'Amsterdam's Greek merchants'.

access to Dutch privileges regarding legal protection and tax exemptions, without having to pay for an official *berat*.

The first known intercultural Ottoman-Dutch partnership was the association in Izmir between the Dutch firm of Belcamp & Clement and Panaiotis & Begler di Joseph, a Greek trading house, established sometime between 1726 and 1730.[59] Although both di Panaiotis and Begler di Joseph eventually managed to purchase Dutch protection, their association with Belcamp & Clement might predate this. In his work on Dutch and Ottoman traders, Ismail Hakkı Kadı refers to Ottoman official documents to demonstrate that di Panaiotis received his first *berat* in May 1731 but also that Begler did not receive one between 1730 and 1740, a period during which all Dutch *berat*s were renewed.[60] At a later date, the intercultural partnership was renamed as Belcamp, Begler & Clement, probably following the departure of Panaiotis, and their firm came up as one of the freighters of a ship sailing with a Dutch captain that had been sent out to buy wheat in Algiers in the late 1740s. The captain had not brought back sufficient wheat, particularly not considering the money he had been given in advance, and as a result, he was summoned for adjudication at the Dutch consular court in Izmir. The consul decided to refer the case to arbitration, with unknown results.[61]

It is interesting to note that, while the legal documents described Begler di Joseph as a 'merchant of our nation', he was not allowed to take the national oath.[62] The reason given for this was that it would have given him permission to attend meetings held by the Dutch trading community in Izmir and provide him access to Dutch assistance in case of problems with the Ottoman administration.[63] This shows that, while Ottoman *beratlı*s were recognised as members

59 In his study on Ottoman-Dutch relations during the embassy of Cornelis Calkoen between 1726 and 1744, Gerard R. Bosscha Erdbrink refers to this association. G.R. Bosscha Erdbrink, *At the threshold of felicity. Ottoman-Dutch relations during the embassy of Cornelis Calkoen at the Sublime Porte, 1726–1744* (Ankara, 1975), p. 199. Ismail Hakkı Kadı refers to the partnership as in business by 1730. Hakkı Kadı, *Ottoman and Dutch merchants*, p. 178.

60 Hakkı Kadı, *Ottoman and Dutch merchants*, p. 178.

61 NACS, N°318 ('Belcamp, Begler en Clement, Nederlandse kooplieden te Smyrna en Crisoganni en Curmusi, Griekse kooplieden te Smyrna tegen Reyer Hoogtreed, kapitein van het Nederlandse schip Santa Maria, 1747').

62 NACS, N°318, 'Sententie provizioneel weegens t proces tusschen Belcamp, Begler & Clement, als Hagi Nicolo Gruscheni, en Jami Crumusi, requiranten, en capt Reyer Hoogtreed geacquireerde gepronuncieert', Izmir, 07/04/1747. Di Joseph was labelled with two others as 'koopluijden onzer natie'. Heeringa mentioned Dutch protection given to 'Pannotti Josuf' and 'Joseph di Josuf' in 1719 but mistakenly thought these men were Jewish. Heeringa and Nanninga, *Bronnen tot de geschiedenis*, 2: p. 155.

63 Hakkı Kadı, *Ottoman and Dutch merchants*, p. 179.

of the Dutch trading community with regards to their legal and (mostly) their fiscal status, they remained foreigners who paid higher consular duties.[64] Not allowing *protégés* to take the national oath was part of the Dutch attempt to keep foreigners at a distance from the Dutch trading community following the regular complaints made by Dutch nationals to the consul in Izmir about the position of Ottoman *protégés*, which they considered as too advantageous.[65] At an unknown date, the partnership ended. Begler di Joseph went to Trieste, where he was held in 1755 because he went bankrupt, leaving behind considerable debts with Dutch traders. It caused a stir, and four years later, after an intervention on di Joseph's behalf by a Greek in the service of the dey of Algiers, he was let go as the creditors agreed there was nothing to be recovered anymore.[66]

At first, Dutch authorities saw commercial partnerships between Ottoman and Dutch traders as a way to make money. In 1741 the States General formally allowed such partnerships but introduced additional tariff rates of 2% on the value of imports and exports of all goods belonging to such a partnership that were shipped on Dutch vessels and 1% of goods that were shipped on foreign vessels.[67] Several Ottoman-Dutch partnerships came into being in the following years, apparently functioning well, such as the one between Manolaki di Panaiotis, a Greek Ottoman who had purchased French protection, and Jacob de Vogel in 1760. Manolaki di Panaiotis was the son of the man who had partnered up with Belcamp, Begler and Clement, while Jacob de Vogel was a merchant from Rotterdam who had originally come to Izmir in 1757 as a scribe.[68] By August 1767 the partners had decided to separate, but the split was not amicable.[69] Later, the former partners met at the French consular court, with di

64 For the national oath, see pp. 57, 81 and 99–100.

65 See also pp. 300–307.

66 News on the bankruptcy was published, for instance, in *The Whitehall evening post, or London intelligencer*, 13–15/11/1755. News about the resolution was sent in a letter from Bartold Douma van Burmania, the Dutch envoy in Vienna dated 25 February 1759, in *Verzameling van geheime brieven*, 9: n.p. A claim of one of the Dutch creditors is preserved in the archives of the Dutch envoy in Vienna. NA, N°1.02.05 ('Archief van de Legatie bij de Duitse keizer'), N°134 ('Stukken betreffende een vordering van Cornelis van der Oudermeulen, koopman in Amsterdam, op Begler de Joseph in Triëst, gewezen Grieks koopman in Smyrna, 1755–1757').

67 Scheltus, *Groot placaatboek*, 7: pp. 1588–1589, 'Resolutie van de Staaten Generaal, waar by vastgesteld word een generaal reglement over alle de schaalen van de Levant, Salonica daar onder begreepen', 27/06/1741.

68 Jacob de Vogel from Rotterdam was not related to the de Vogels of Amsterdam.

69 Heeringa and Nanninga, *Bronnen tot de geschiedenis*, 4: p. 1226, Thomas de Vogel to Thomas de Vogel Junior, Amsterdam, 07/08/1767; and ibid., pp. 200–201, Directorate of Levant Trade to C.G.N. Schutz, Amsterdam, 21/03/1775.

Panaiotis a defendant against the firm of Jan Ackerman & Zoon in Amsterdam, from whom Jacob de Vogel had received a power of attorney to act as plaintiff.[70]

In 1766, the consul, treasurer and assessors had confirmed that only men who were Dutch nationals were allowed to take the Dutch national oath and that neither foreign traders nor foreign clerks or scribes could take it, which was a measure to prevent these foreigners from paying lower consular duties.[71] On 16 January 1769, the national oath was formally extended to include the promise that 'no one of the land [Ottoman Empire], subjects of the great lord or other foreigners would carry an interest, directly or indirectly, in their trade firms or commission houses', formally forbidding partnerships between Ottoman and Dutch traders.[72]

In 1775, di Panaiotis decided to denounce his former business partner, who had been shipping goods belonging to Ottomans under his own name, breaking existing regulations as well as the Dutch national oath. Di Panaiotis further complained about poor treatment from his former partner, but this was considered of no concern to Dutch authorities.[73] Jacob de Vogel was summoned to defend himself in a meeting in Izmir, during which he admitted that he indeed received goods from foreigners in commission but claimed that this was not

70 NACS, N°356 ('Proces stukken tusschen gebroeders de Vogel & Comp als procureurs van Jan Ackerman & Zoon in Amsterdam & Ml Kiriaco di Panajotti & Comp, begonnen 24/01/1775 gaande tot 06/11/1775').

71 NACS, N°162, 'Notulen van consul, tresorier en assessoren weegens diverse orders & reglementen vande heeren directeuren', Izmir, 14/11/1766.

72 Joannes van der Linden, *Groot placaatboek, vervattende de placaaten, ordonnantien en edicten, van de hoog mog heeren Staaten Generaal der Vereenigde Nederlanden en van de edele groot mog. heeren Staaten van Holland en Westvriesland; mitsgaders van de edele mog. heeren Staaten van Zeeland* (Amsterdam, 1796), 9: p. 1296, 'Resolutie van de Staaten Generaal, houdende verbod aan de ingeseetenen van deesen staat, in de Levant geëtablisseert, om zig in hunnen handel of commissien met de onderdanen van de Grooten Heer of met andere vreemden te mogen associeeren', 16/01/1769, '[…] en zonder dat er iemand van het land, onderdaanen van den Grooten Heer, of andere vreemden in onse commissien direct of indirect mogen zyn geinteresseert'.

73 Heeringa and Nanninga, *Bronnen tot de geschiedenis*, 4: pp 200–201, Directorate of Levant Trade to C.G.N. Schutz, Amsterdam, 21/03/1775. Di Panaiotis had litigated against de Vogel before the Dutch consular court between 1770 and 1773 in an attempt to claim money he felt Jacob de Vogel owed him in relation to an earlier affair that concluded the partnership of the two men. The consul's sentence dismissed the claim made by di Panaiotis, who intended to bring an appeal before the Dutch ambassador, the competent court. The ambassadorial archives do not contain such an appeal case. NACS, N°225 ('Proces tusschen Ml Kco di Panajottis & Jacob de Vogel aengaende eene avania van 1770 tot 16 maert 1773'), 'Sententie in faveur van Jacob de Vogel & teegens Manuel Kiriako di Panaiotti', Izmir, 16/03/1773.

forbidden. It caused a debate amongst merchants, and several agreed with de Vogel, according to the chancellor because they were in the same situation. In his letter to the Directorate of Levant Trade, the chancellor wrote that de Vogel's fate could not be decided and that he waited for the judgment of the directors. It did not stop him from choosing a side, and he labelled Jacob de Vogel as a 'very honest man, known as such to everyone', while he described di Panaiotis as 'that Greek, known to everybody as a very bad person' with a 'filthy and evil character'.[74]

The Directorate of Levant Trade, however, was not convinced of de Vogel's defence. In his written statement, de Vogel maintained that he had not broken the national oath, but he did not mention the addition made to the national oath in January 1769, which stipulated that no Ottoman subjects were allowed to have a commercial interest in the trade of a Dutch national if it was the latter who had paid the (lower) consular duties and other taxes. The problem was that de Vogel had indeed lent his name to hide transactions in goods belonging to Ottoman traders, who tried to avoid the higher tariff on their goods when shipped on Dutch ships and sent to the United Provinces. At the same time, this merchandise, officially Dutch, was exempt from certain Ottoman taxes according to the capitulations. De Vogel was not the only trader involved in this case, and the illegal practice of using Dutch firms as cover for Ottoman trade harmed both Dutch commercial interests and the Ottoman treasury, and the directors wanted the consul to put a stop to this abuse.[75] In response to the matter, the States General issued a regulation in 1769 which prohibited partnerships between Dutch merchants in the Levant and Ottoman subjects or any other foreigners active there.[76] The case dragged on for years, with consul, assessors and treasurer concluding in a meeting on the matter held in December 1775 that, although the addition to the national oath did not prevent associations between Dutch and foreigners, the practice of using Dutch firms to cover up Ottoman commercial activities was illegal.[77]

---

74 Heeringa and Nanninga, *Bronnen tot de geschiedenis*, 4: pp. 204–205, C.G.N. Schutz to the Directorate of Levant Trade, Izmir, 18/05/1775, on p. 205, '[…] dat hij een dooreerlijk man is en daarvoor ook bij een yder bekent is […]' and 'het vuyl en boosaardig character van die Griek, die van een yder voor een seer slegt subject bekent is […]'.

75 Heeringa and Nanninga, *Bronnen tot de geschiedenis*, 4: pp. 215–216, Directorate of Levant Trade to Consul Daniel Jean de Hochepied, Amsterdam, 19/09/1775.

76 Van der Linden, *Groot placaatboek*, 9: p. 1296, 'Resolutie van de Staaten Generaal', 16/01/1769.

77 Heeringa and Nanninga, *Bronnen tot de geschiedenis*, 4: pp. 218–219, 'Vergadering consul, thesaurier en assessoren', Izmir, 18/12/1775.

It is interesting to note that Dutch merchants themselves played a role in resolving this problem, as the assessors were chosen yearly amongst the Dutch traders of Izmir.[78] The commercial experience of traders was considered as a crucial element in commercial litigation, and their involvement as assessors was not exceptional.[79] Still, Dutch authorities realised that conflicts of interest might occur. The merchant community in Izmir was small, and merchants were competing with one another over commissions. This is why assessors had to swear an oath of neutrality. Assessorship rotated, but some merchants were able to hold on to the position for years, giving them a great deal of power in the Dutch community. In all cases studied for this book, the consul followed the advice given by the assessors. On the other hand, the assessors were kept in check by the rotation system, the oath they had taken and by the consequences their reputation could suffer if it was perceived that they might have been motivated by personal interest. Additionally, an assessor with poor judgment might find himself in court as defendant on day, judged by his peers. The importance given to the legal reasoning provided by the assessors, who were Dutch nationals, was also balanced by the recurrent use of expert reports. These experts were always chosen from amongst different trading communities.

A potential conflict of interest was most likely one of the reasons why, in an earlier letter, the directors had made an enquiry about the possibility of having 'neutral merchants', by which they meant other Europeans or even Ottomans, investigate whether Jacob de Vogel could have taken the national oath 'with a pure conscience'.[80] Correspondence between the directors and the consul makes it clear that the national oath was not intended to prevent Dutch houses in Izmir from taking commissions from foreign firms, but only to stop the practice of letting Ottoman traders in Izmir use a Dutch merchant's name for shipping or receiving goods in an attempt to avoid taxes. In August 1777 the consul became tired of the whole discussion and wrote in frustration to the States General that 'never anything is clear enough for our gentlemen merchants here, and they always try to find excuses [...] some continue to load

78 See pp. 91 and 94–100.

79 See for instance Kessler, *A revolution in commerce*.

80 Heeringa and Nanninga, *Bronnen tot de geschiedenis*, 4: pp. 215–216, Directorate of Levant Trade to Consul Daniel Jean de Hochepied, Amsterdam, 19/09/1775, on p. 215, '[...] neutraele lieden [...]' and '[...] met een suijver gemoed [...]'. While the practice of using foreign experts was normal enough for the directors to not make such an enquiry, this situation was different, as it considered an opinion on the national oath and not on the merchants' style.

and receive goods under their name, on behalf of foreigners and *rayas* living in Izmir'.[81]

In April 1778, the Dutch chancellor in Izmir visited the firms of the assessors as well as that of Esaias Fercken, a merchant originally from Liège, asking them whether they agreed to pay consular duties and *dragomanagie* as if they were foreigners in cases where they were handling goods of foreigners.[82] They all agreed, and they also recognised that any troubles with Ottoman fiscal authorities resulting from this practice would fall under each firm's personal responsibility, which meant that the Dutch consul would not interfere to help and the Dutch community as a whole would not pay.[83] The problem was finally put to rest at a meeting of the Directorate of Levant Trade in Amsterdam, who suggested the addition of another phrase to the text of the national oath, namely that the merchants promised to accept all *avanias* resulting from the practice of name-lending to Ottomans at the Ottoman tax administration and to deal with them individually, without seeking recourse to the consulate or to any money in the common register.[84]

In the context of *avanias*, the new addition to the national oath meant that if the practice of name-lending would lead to additional taxation by the Ottoman authorities, it was an individual problem. The word *avania* reflects the European idea that any additional taxation not specified in the capitulations was a form of extortion.[85] Europeans were extremely fearful that individual behaviour led to collective consequences – a fear that is very reminiscent of the functioning of the medieval mechanism of collective responsibility.[86]

---

81 Heeringa and Nanninga, *Bronnen tot de geschiedenis*, 4: pp. 240–242, Consul Daniel Jean de Hochepied to the States General, Izmir, 09/08/1777, on p. 240, 'Nooyt is er yets klaars genoeg voor sommige onser heeren cooplieden alhier en zij tragten altoos eenige capties te vinden [...] sommige gaan daarop voort met goederen op hunne naam te laaden en te ontfangen voor de vreemde en rayas hier te Smirna woonagtig [...]'. 'Raya', or 'Re'âyâ', was the term for a tax-paying member of the lower class in the Ottoman Empire but was often also used to refer to Ottoman non-Muslim subjects who paid the *haraç* and was thus synonymous with *zimmi*. See van den Boogert, *The capitulations*, pp. 43 and 189.

82 *Dragomanagie* was a tax of 2.5% of the value of consular fees payable on goods and was used to pay the ordinary dragomans who worked as interpreters. Hakkı Kadı, *Ottoman and Dutch merchants*, p. 157.

83 Heeringa and Nanninga, *Bronnen tot de geschiedenis*, 4: p. 254, 'Extract registers kanselarij Smyrna', Izmir, 14/04/1778.

84 Heeringa and Nanninga, *Bronnen tot de geschiedenis*, 4: p. 260, 'Vergadering directeuren', Amsterdam, 29/07/1778. In August, this suggestion was communicated to the burgomasters of Amsterdam. Ibid., pp. 260–263, Directorate of Levant Trade to the burgomasters, Amsterdam, [?]/08/1778.

85 See pp. 232 and 308–312.

86 See pp. 207–208 and 311–312.

It is, of course, understandable that European traders in the Ottoman Empire preferred no collective consequences and less taxation, but that, of course, does not necessarily mean that additional taxation by Ottoman authorities was in any way unjust.

By the time Jacob de Vogel was defending himself before his peers, partnerships between Dutch and Ottoman traders had already been forbidden, which was probably the reason why Ottomans had started to ship their goods under the names of Jacob de Vogel and several other Dutch traders in the first place. It seems the first concrete steps leading to restrictions on intercultural partnerships had come from Consul Daniel Jean de Hochepied, who expressed his doubts about allowing any Ottoman partner into a Dutch firm in a letter to Holland in 1766. He feared these practices would lead to the whole firm passing as Dutch, enjoying all commercial advantages that came with the Dutch status. De Hochepied stated that 'our national meetings would be swarming with all sorts of people' and claimed that 'our interests would be mingled with theirs', something he felt would be a bad evolution.[87] While the association between di Panaiotis and de Vogel had come into being before his tenure, his letter was inspired by events that were happening at that time. A young man named Isaac Beaune was expected to arrive in Izmir from Amsterdam, and he had agreed to form a partnership with the Armenian trader Malcas di Carabeth.[88] Beaune, the consul argued, surely expected to benefit from the protection offered to him as a Dutch subject and all the national privileges that derived from the payment of the consular duties. The consul would not be able to decline Beaune protection, as he was Dutch, but he was not willing to extend the same status to his Armenian business partner, because he would not allow national protection to foreigners.

The consul refused to validate any Ottoman-Dutch partnership, because he felt that the interests of the national and the foreigner would become inseparable, and the Ottomans would certainly consider the firm as Dutch. This, de Hochepied felt, would harm Dutch national interests. He seemed to be afraid that Beaune would not be the only foreign merchant to benefit from the Dutch privileges but also 'many of his friends and acquaintances', perhaps again a reference to the practice of Ottomans shipping under a Dutch name.[89]

87 NACS, N°14, Consul Daniel Jean de Hochepied to unknown addressee, Izmir, 03/07/1766, '[...] de nationale vergaderingen zouden krioelen van alle soorten mensen' and '[...] souden onse intresten met de haere gemengt werden [...]'.

88 For Isaac Beaune, see also pp. 101 and 230.

89 NACS, N°14, Consul Daniel Jean de Hochepied to the States General, Izmir, 19/08/1766, '[...] veele zijnder vrienden en kennissen [...]'.

But for de Hochepied, the most detrimental consequence was the exposure an Ottoman-Dutch firm would get in case the Ottoman was summoned before an Ottoman court. Europeans generally held a negative attitude towards the option of litigation before an Ottoman court, where they were 'vulnerable to suffering many difficulties and even great disadvantages'.[90] While the European idea that Ottoman courts were somehow less reasonable and equitable in their sentencing was false, there was also the general European fear that the Ottomans might ignore at will some of the privileges granted in the capitulations. One of these privileges was legal autonomy, and the inclusion of Ottoman partners in Dutch firms and a subsequent summoning of an Ottoman partner at an Ottoman court might provoke a challenge to this authority. De Hochepied concluded that allowing di Carabeth and Beaune to form an association would harm the Dutch community as a whole, while it would only be beneficial to di Carabeth, a foreigner. Furthermore, allowing the business association meant that di Carabeth would receive similar advantages as a Dutch Ottoman *beratlı* without paying for them.[91] This, of course, went against recirprocity and mutual interest, cornerstones of the merchants' style.

Beaune, convinced of di Carabeth's value as a partner, insisted, but when he wanted to take the Dutch national oath after his arrival, this was refused unless he was willing to trade in his name alone without di Carabeth as partner. Beaune did not want to comply, but when his name appears later in official documents, it is as an independent trader, which suggests that in the end, he might have had little choice if he wanted to remain part of the Dutch trading community of Izmir.[92] The national oath had evolved from a controversial instrument that no trader wanted to take in the seventeenth century, to a mechanism that could be used to pressure Dutch nationals into respecting the consul's decisions in the eighteenth century.[93]

The objection Dutch authorities had towards intercultural partnerships was partially justified by the damage done to the national interest, the protection of which was a crucial consular task. But this did not mean that such partnerships did not work or that no merchants tried to form Ottoman-Dutch partnerships after Beaune and di Carabeth. Several others, mostly between

90 Ibid., '[…] daer door aen veel strubbelingen en selffs aen groot nadeel werden blootgesteld […]'.

91 For the *beratlıs*, see pp. 61–64.

92 See p. 230.

93 For the national oath, see pp. 57, 81 and 99–100.

Ottoman Greeks and Dutch merchants, were known to exist.[94] It has been argued that intercultural partnerships in Izmir were less important than the totality of returning transactions between Dutch and local traders, one-off or repeated, particularly when considering the total volume of trade.[95] This does not diminish the importance of looking at intercultural partnerships and the manner in which they were dissolved. Several of these partnerships ended on bad terms, such as the one between di Panaiotis and de Vogel, but hardly any evidence exists amongst the Izmir court cases that suggests the partners blamed each other for having a different origin, religious adherence or nationality. In court, traders only blamed each other for personal behaviour that went against the reason and equity of the merchants' style. In the rare cases where di Panaiotis was called 'that Greek' and Jews were referred to negatively, such references without exception came from chancellor and consul, not from fellow merchants. The only trader to attempt a legal argumentation on the lines of national background was Gerrit van Brakel, who constructed a discourse in which he complained about the unfair treatment of Europeans in comparison to Ottomans, but the consul dismissed his argumentation completely.[96]

The lack of 'national' animosity between merchants of different origins is also reflected in the fact that Dutch consular jurisdiction offered a sufficient legal framework within which disputes between business partners of different origins could be settled. This is an argument in favour of the idea that intercultural trade could develop and be fostered through the development of a set of increasingly international norms and habits regulating the business relationships between merchants. A merchant needed to remain trustworthy, well-reputed and financially sound. His background was not so important, except when it gave him an unfair advantage, as that would go against the commercial custom of reciprocity and mutual interest. This is why Ottoman traders who had associated themselves with Dutch nationals or who had obtained Dutch protection either through the purchase of a *berat* or through requests made to the States General in the United Provinces only came under criticism from their Dutch fellow traders in the context of discussions on fiscal and legal advantages.

---

94 Various other partnerships are mentioned in Hakkı Kadı, *Ottoman and Dutch merchants*, pp. 182–197; and Artunç, 'The protégé system', pp. 17–18.

95 Hakkı Kadı, *Ottoman and Dutch merchants*, p. 183.

96 See the case discussed on pp. 291–300.

3 The Most Cosmopolitan Form of Quarrelling

3.1 *Gerrit van Brakel's Bill of Exchange*

Non-Muslim Ottoman traders who had purchased *berat*s figured frequently amongst the parties involved in commercial litigation before the Dutch consular court, next to a small number of Ottoman traders who had not purchased a protected status. The difference was that the Dutch Ottoman *protégés* could be tried by a Dutch court as defendant while Ottomans without such status did not have that legal privilege and could only appear in the court records as plaintiffs against Dutch nationals or Dutch *protégés*. It was as plaintiff that the Greek firm of Alexander & Sottira was involved in a dispute that was tried at the Dutch consular court in 1769. In May that year, they filed a request for restitution from the Dutch merchant Gerrit van Brakel, who had issued a bill of exchange of 939 guilders to Alexander & Sottira, to be paid out by correspondents in Rotterdam. The bill of exchange bounced and came back to van Brakel, who was asked to redeem it as well as pay for interest and expenses.[97]

The court documents do not make any mention of a protected status for the Greek partners, and as Ottoman subjects, they could have attempted litigation before the *qadi* in Izmir. Perhaps they had declined to do so because the European-style bill of exchange was not commonly used in the Ottoman Empire and litigating on the basis of non-Ottoman exchange law before a *qadi* court seemed much less practical than seeking recourse to the Dutch consular court. There was an Ottoman-style bill of exchange, the *suftaja*, which was a letter of credit that differed from the European bill because repayment was in the same currency as the original payment. Its payment, however, was sanctioned by the state, and *qadi* courts were used for disputes involving *suftaja* payments.[98] It is also possible that Alexander & Sottira preferred to avoid a *qadi* court because Islamic law forbade loans with interest, and it was commonly known that the European-style bill of exchange indirectly charged interest by

97 NACS, N°343, 'Request van Alexander en Sottira weeg: een geret. wisselbrief aen G: v Brakel van f939', Izmir, 08/05/1769.

98 Abraham L. Udovitch, *Partnership and profit in medieval Islam* (Princeton, 1970), pp. 268–269; Eliyahu Ashtor, 'Banking instruments between the Muslim east and the Christian west', *Journal of European economic history*, 1 (1972): pp. 554–562; and Şevket Pamuk, *A monetary history of the Ottoman Empire* (Cambridge, 2000), p. 84. For Islamic financial instruments, see chapter six on 'The medieval *hawale*: The legal nature of the *suftaja* and other Islamic payment instruments', in Benjamin Geva, *The payment order of Antiquity and the Middle Ages. A legal history* (Oxford and Portland, 2011), pp. 252–306.

including it in the exchange rate.[99] In their claim, Alexander & Sottira were specifically asking for an interest payment from van Brakel, a claim that was perhaps impossible to ask at a *qadi* court. In the late Middle Ages, Islamic legal scholars had come to object to the bill of exchange on the grounds that it placed liability on the payee, who received the money, as well as on the person that had accepted the bill – the taker. This double liability gave an advantage to the payee because, the bill of exchange was considered a loan, and Islamic law had it that full liability for a loan was with the borrower or payee alone – and thus not shared.[100]

Van Brakel defended himself by stating that the protest of the bill had arisen out of the refusal by Alexander & Sottira to contribute to the damages on certain goods, which had been sent to Holland in a joint operation by Gerrit van Brakel and Alexander & Sottira. Each party had benefitted, and since the transaction, the partnership between the Dutchman and the Greek traders had been dissolved, with an oral agreement that each party would carry a part of the potential damage and loss. As this had not happened, van Brakel answered the claim from his former Greek partners by petitioning the consul, treasurer and assessors of the Dutch nation to grant him restitution of 200 *bordaten* in recompense for the unpaid damages on the transaction.[101]

A week after van Brakel's reply, the consul, treasurer and assessors issued a temporary verdict in which they sentenced van Brakel to deposit the value of the protested bill of exchange at the chancery and to comply with 'the

99 Formally, Christianity also forbade loans with interest, the pope still sanctioning it in 1745. See, for instance, Jerry Z. Muller, *The mind and the market – Capitalism in modern European thought* (New York, 2002), p. 9. Restrictions, however, did not mean the practice did not exist, and, similar to the Christian world, Islamic societies had systems of borrowing with interest. See, for instance, Şevket Pamuk, 'Institutional change and longevity of the Ottoman Empire', *Journal of interdisciplinary history*, 35:2 (2004): pp. 231–232; and Ronald C. Jennings, 'Loans and credit in early seventeenth century Ottoman judicial records: The sharia court of Anatolian Kayseri', *Journal of the economic and social history of the Orient*, 16:2–3 (1973): pp. 168–213.

100 Murat Çizakça, *Islamic capitalism and finance. Origins, evolution and the future* (Cheltenham and Northampton, MA, 2011), pp. 47–48.

101 NACS, N°343, 'Request antwoord van Gerrit van Brakel aen Alexander & Sotira weeg: een geretourneerde wissel van f939', Izmir, 11/05/1769. It is unclear what a 'bordaat' actually was, but in all likelihood, it was cloth with hems. It was a regularly imported item from the Levant to the United Provinces, see René Bekius, 'Avet Jeremias. Een Levantijns koopman in achttiende-eeuws Amsterdam', in *De Nederlands-Turkse betrekkingen*, eds. Maurits van den Boogert and Jan Jonker Roelants (Hilversum, 2012), p. 67.

exchange law and custom in this type of case.'[102] The bill of exchange was a financial instrument necessary for conducting international business, as it allowed for payment in different currencies, and it was a contract involving three or four parties in two countries. With the growing recognition of its importance for trade, and the growing realisation that trade was important for the economic development of states, an exchange law developed that codified aspects of international merchant custom into local, and later also 'national', legal statutes and ordinances.

Since the Middle Ages, bills of exchange had been crucial instruments in international trade, because they allowed for the financial remittance of profits on transactions abroad. From the early eighteenth century onwards, bills could be endorsed to other traders, a possibility that had turned them into negotiable commodities.[103] They were regulated through written law, the so-called 'exchange law'. As the bill of exchange was an international device, the laws regulating their handling were international, and already in 1629, it was argued in the United Provinces that exchange law was uniform and valid in all Christian countries.[104] Various legal scholars, such as Laurens Pieter van der Spiegel and Carl Günther Ludovici, attributed a special place for exchange law in their analysis of the sources for commercial law, and exchange law occupies an interesting position between written law and merchant custom, not unlike bankruptcy procedures.[105]

The importance of the bill of exchange as a credit instrument in international trade was not disputed, and as such, all regulations surrounding it

---

102 NACS, N°343, 'Vonnis van consul, th:r x assessooren tot het depositeeren van de waerde van een met protest geret: wisselbrief van f939 aen Gerrit van Brakel', Izmir, 19/05/1769, '[…] het wisselregt x gebruijk in sulke gevallen […]'.

103 About the evolution of the endorsement, a practice that may have started in the late sixteenth century and had become common by the middle of the seventeenth century, see Geoffrey Poitras, *The early history of financial economics, 1478–1776 – From commercial arithmetic to life annuities and joint stocks* (Cheltenham, 2000), pp. 231–232; and Raymond de Roover, *L'évolution de la lettre de change XIVe–XVIIIe siècles* (Paris, 1953), pp. 220–221.

104 Martin van Velden, *Fondament vande wisselhandeling: onderrichtingh ghevende van alle voornaemste wisselen van Christenrijck, so van trates remessen, vergelijcking van prysen, verscheyden commissien te vormen* (Amsterdam, 1629). On the use of the bill of exchange in the Ottoman Empire, see Maria Christina Chatziioannou and Gerlina Harlaftis, 'From the Levant to the city of London: Mercantile credit in the Greek international commercial networks of the 18th and 19th centuries', in *Centres and peripheries in banking. The historical development of financial markets*, eds. Philip L. Cotrell, Even Lange, and Ulf Olsson (Abingdon, 2016), pp. 13–40. On the history of the bill of exchange, see the first chapter in Trivellato, *The promise and peril of credit*, pp. 19–35.

105 See pp. 106–109 and 129.

were fundamentally international, but it would be a mistake to assume that exchange law was a clear and simple example of international law. There were local varieties, and disputes on bills of exchange referred to the locality of the competent law. Several cases brought before the *Hoge Raad* are discussed in an eighteenth-century compilation of the private notes of Willem Pauw, counsellor at the *Hoge Raad* and later its president. Fifty-eight of the disputes were concerned with bills of exchange, and Pauw mentions the use of Amsterdam exchange law in fifteen cases and Rotterdam exchange law in six. Local exchange laws of other Dutch cities are mentioned in other cases.[106] Amsterdam exchange law took a central place because that city played a crucial role in the traffic in bills of exchange.[107]

Because exchange law was so well-developed, it is not a coincidence that one of the very few references made to a particular law in any of the trial documents preserved in the archives of the Dutch consulate in Izmir was to it. In that context, it seems logical that the dispute between Alexander & Sottira and Gerrit van Brakel was solved quickly. Alexander & Sottira filed their petition, van Brakel provided a written reply and the Greek traders provided a counter-reply, after which a sentence instructed van Brakel to obey the law.[108] There were eleven days between the initial claim and the verdict. But the dispute was not resolved, as Gerrit van Brakel did not feel satisfied with its outcome, because no mention was made of the merchandise he felt he was entitled to. He remarked that he would have no problem subjecting himself to the verdict, but only if the opponents 'were subjects of any European sovereign, who would also be judged according to European laws, but as they were subjects of the land [Ottoman Empire], who only wanted to profit from European rights and laws for as long as these matched their interests, but who, when they considered it otherwise, would call upon the rules and laws of these lands [Ottoman Empire]'.[109] It is important to note that in one of the few instances

---

106 C.H. Bezemer, 'Tussen wal en schip. Het wisselrecht ten tijde van de Republiek der Verenigde Nederlanden', *BW-krant jaarboek*, 29 (2015): pp. 22–23.

107 See, for instance, Phoonsen, *Wissel-styl tot Amsterdam*; and Wagenaar, *Amsterdam in zyne opkomst*, 4: pp. 425–446. For an early modern study on exchange law, see Johann Gottlieb Heineccius, *Grondbeginselen van het wisselrecht* (Middelburg, 1774).

108 NACS, N°343, 'Vonnis van consul, th:r x assessooren tot het depositeeren van de waerde van een met protest geret: wisselbrief van f939 aen Gerrit van Brakel', Izmir, 19/05/1769.

109 NACS, N°343, 'Antwoord van Gerrit van Brakel op het vonnis tot depositeeren van f939 weegens Alex & Sottira', Izmir, 22/05/1769, '[…] menschen waaren van eenige Europese souverainen, die ook na Europese wetten konde geoordeeld werden, maar onderdanen van dit land zijnde, die maar van de Europese regte x wette willen profiteeren, voor zoo lange zulx met hare interesse overeenstemd, maar het contrarie ziende, zij zig op de regten, en wetten deezer landen komen te beroepen […]'.

in which a concrete and codified law could be invoked, van Brakel attempted to delegitimise the verdict that was based upon it by pointing to the fact that his opponents were not Europeans. Because the merchants' style upon which trade disputes were settled generally was international, the different nationality of an opponent could not be invoked as a counter-argument to a verdict. But this was different, exactly because of the verdict's reliance on codified law.

Van Brakel's remark was not atypical for the way European traders looked upon Ottoman merchants who sought recourse to European legal institutions, and it shows a more general discomfort with the idea that some traders attempted forum shopping for individual advantage, an action that contradicted the reciprocity of the merchants' style.[110] Van Brakel's argument did not help him, and the consul insisted that he had to comply with exchange law, deposit the money and, in case he wanted to prosecute Alexander & Sottira for the *bordaten*, make a separate claim within twenty-four hours. The consul was sure that van Brakel would file a separate claim and ordered Alexander & Sottira to deposit the *bordaten* at the Dutch chancery.[111]

Alexander & Sottira requested immediate execution of the verdict instead, but van Brakel reiterated his earlier appeal.[112] The language he adopted became quite emotional, not uncommon in litigation.[113] He labelled Sottira as 'a thief of honour and an ungrateful creature', complaining 'riffraff had better access [to a favourable sentence] than an honest man'.[114] The terms of the verdict were not suitable for the honest merchant that van Brakel considered himself to be, as they were those given to bankrupts, which he was not.[115] With these comments, the case was steered into a familiar direction – using attacks on the opponent's reputation as a central legal argument. What was unusual, though, was that van Brakel took it one step further when he started to question the

110 For the practice of forum shopping, see pp. 14 and 308–312.

111 NACS, N°343, 'Antwoord van Gerrit van Brakel op het vonnis tot depositeeren van f939 weegens Alex & Sottira', Izmir, 22/05/1769; and 'Recieff van ter deposito ontfangen 200 p.s bordaten van Alex: & Sottira', Izmir, 27/05/1769.

112 NACS, N°343, 'Request van Alex:r & Sottira tot versoek van executie van het vonnis tot de deposito der f939', Izmir, 29/05/1769; and 'Origineele missive van Gerrit van Brakel in ant op die van den heere consul van heeden aen mij cancel geschreeven', Izmir, 30/05/1769.

113 See pp. 185–188.

114 NACS, N°343, 'Origineele missive van Gerrit van Brakel in ant op die van den heere consul van heeden aen mij cancel geschreeven', Izmir, 30/05/1769, '[...] Sottira die eerdief, en ondankbaar creatuur [...]' and '[...] een canailie meer ingang heeft als een braaf mens [...]'.

115 Ibid. Van Brakel's pejorative use of 'bankrupt' is hardly surprising considering the long association between fraud and bankruptcy – even though legally that automatic association was disappearing; see pp. 199–208.

consul's decisions.[116] He expressed his surprise at the twenty-four-hour period he was given to comply and suggested that it was not fully honest, but this time, he addressed his letter directly to the chancellor, who he asked to be his protector, and not to the consul. He reminded him of the case between Jacques Forêt and Dirk Knipping, in which he had acted as plaintiff on Forêt's behalf, the time it took to resolve the matter and the leniency then granted to Knipping: 'how I was treated then, verify it with your own conscience'.[117] He concluded that he would not obey the verdict but bring his 'equitable and righteous case' to competent judges, who would 'not need 24 hours but only one minute to satisfy me'.[118] He concluded his letter to the chancellor with a threat: 'they are *rayas*, slaves of the Great Lord, and I will make these gentlemen dance differently'.[119]

The consul, treasurer and assessors read van Brakel's letter and expressed their surprise. The consul claimed that it did not matter who the involved parties were, the problem was with a bill of exchange, so exchange law applied no matter where the case was taken to. Should it have been brought before a court in Holland, Daniel Jean de Hochepied continued, van Brakel would already have been judged for not paying. The consul gave him forty-eight hours to pay, otherwise the Dutch community would treat him as an 'unwilling and disobedient person'.[120] This meant he might lose his status of Dutch national in Izmir and the protection of the Dutch authorities. It would be communicated as such to the other European chanceries and the Ottoman authorities too. De Hochepied added that 'it does not bother us what Sottira is, and we have to be content if the people of the land [Ottoman Empire] are willing to accept our law, and not their own' – a phrase that confims that Sottira might very well have chosen to litigate before a *qadi* court.[121] The consul concluded his letter by reminding van Brakel that he had already created problems when he owed some money to the Dutch treasury, which had forced the consul to threaten

116 A similar manoeuvre ended badly for the Sicilian merchant Gasparo Marchetti; see pp. 259–264.

117 NACS, N°343, 'Origineele missive van Gerrit van Brakel in ant op die van den heere consul van heeden aen mij cancel geschreeven', Izmir, 30/05/1769, '[…] hoe ben ik behandelt, gaat het in u eyge conscientie na […]'.

118 Ibid., '[…] mijn billike en regtvaardige zaak […]' and '[…] geen 24 uure maar een minuut tijd om mij direct te voldoen […]'.

119 Ibid., '[…] t zyn reaas slaven van den grooten heer zal ik die messieurs anders doen danze'.

120 NACS, N°343, 'Twee copijen der brieven van van Brakel & de heere consul', Sediköy, 30/05/1769, '[…] als onwillige en ongehoorzaame […]'.

121 Ibid., '[…] wat of Sottira is doet ons niets, en wij moeten al wel te vreeden zijn, als de lieden van het land aan ons regt wille koomen, en zig niet aan het hare houden […]'.

him with a sequester of his goods, and by stating that he wished honourable, young and esteemed men would not let affairs get that far. He regretted that van Brakel had written such an insulting letter to his own judges.[122] Confronted with these threats, van Brakel complied under protest but pursued his claim against Alexander & Sottira before the Dutch consular court in Izmir.[123]

The remainder of the case documents deal with van Brakel's claim and focus on the dissolution of the partnership between him and Alexander & Sottira. The chancellor issued a declaration confirming that in April 1769, a notarial deed ending the partnership had been passed before him and several witnesses. It did not, however, specify the concrete terms of the dissolution, which had been agreed upon verbally and which included the possible reimbursement of the bill of exchange under scrutiny, in case it would bounce. A solution had also been discussed verbally about the division of the damages on the goods that the partnership had sent to the United Provinces.[124] Chancellor Mann's declaration served van Brakel better than Alexander & Sottira, who denied that verbal agreements on the dissolution of their partnership with van Brakel had been made, and they suggested that van Brakel had manipulated the chancellor's written statement.[125] Van Brakel replied that the chancellor was an official who was bound to the truth by an oath, which was a valid legal instrument in Dutch law, and his declaration should be evaluated by the consular judge and not by the plaintiff. Van Brakel made the additional comment that he was willing to abandon his claim if Alexander & Sottira swore under oath, with their hands on the Bible and in the presence of the Dutch chancellor and the Greek bishop, that no verbal agreement had been made between themselves and van Brakel.[126] It was a very strong request, given the tight connection between religion, truth and natural law, and it clearly demonstrates how seriously oaths were taken as instruments to establish the truth.[127]

122 NACS, N°343, 'Twee copijen der brieven van van Brakel & de heere consul', Sediköy, 30/05/1769; and 'Origineele missive van den heere consul aen van Brakel tot het depositeeren offte andere dispositie', Sediköy, 01/06/1769.

123 NACS, N°343, 'Request van Gerrit van Brakel beloften van het deposito der g'ordonneerde f939 voor een geretourneerde wissel', Izmir, 02/06/1769; 'Recieff van de ter deposito ontfange waerde van f 939 van Gerrit van Brakel weegens Alexander & sottira', Izmir, 05/06/1769; and 'Replicq van Gerrit van Brakel aen Alex:r & Sottira', Izmir, 24/07/1769.

124 NACS, N°343, 'Declaratie van mij can: weegens het gepasseerde tusschen van Brakel & Alexander & Sottira aengaende de reservatie van eene nog loopende wisselbrieff', Izmir 02/08/1769.

125 NACS, N°343, 'Replicq d'Alex:r en Sottira teegens van Brakel met verwerping der declaratie van mij Cancell:', Izmir, 08/08/1769.

126 NACS, N°343, 'Replicq van Gerrit van Brakel aen Alexander & Sottira', Izmir, 12/08/1769.

127 For the role of the oath as legal evidence, see pp. 134–135.

A similar remark pointing to the importance of religion can be found in a 1760 dispute in which Herman van Coopstad in Rotterdam demanded Knipping & Ouckama in Izmir have the monies they still had of Marcus Koch, an arms dealer in Liège, sequestered in order to recover debts the latter had to van Coopstad. Knipping & Ouckama answered that they would comply, but they also remarked that they were not surprised, as 'one has never something good to expect from those who renounce their god and their faith', the reason why they had advised van Coopstad not to engage in business with them.[128] In a world in which a person's reputation was one of his most important business assets and the trust placed in a fellow trader was a necessary step for engaging in business, questioning someone's change in religious affiliation was not so strange. A change of religion might have been considered as evidence of a lack of loyalty, which was a crucial part of commercial reputation. If one was willing to renounce one's god, one might just as easily discard business partners.

When Chancellor Mann and two witnesses went to the house of Alexander & Sottira to ask whether they were willing to take an oath, they were met with a refusal.[129] Van Brakel's demand must have been familiar to Alexander & Sottira, considering they were Ottoman subjects. The oath was a common practice in Ottoman courts as a means of evidence as well.[130] Now that the case would not be judged on the basis of the oath, a declaration before God, which would have to be accepted as the truth by Gerrit van Brakel, the consul and assessors decided to request the opinion of other merchants, in other words, peers would have to provide advice based on merchant custom. French, Italian, English and Ragusan merchants were consulted, and all concurred that, in cases where a partnership was dissolved and a general closure of accounts had been accepted by both parties, as in this case, no party could go to a court trying to obtain a different settlement concerning matters that had occurred before the dissolution.[131] The consul and assessors agreed with this opinion, and the sentence was simple: neither party got what they wanted, as the bill of exchange had to be given back to van Brakel, and he had to bear the damages' costs incurred on the joint shipment of goods. Both parties were to pay

128 NACS, N°490, Knipping & Ouckama to Herman van Coopstad, Izmir, 31/01/1760, '[…] men heeft nooit iets goets te wachten van iemand die syn god x gelooff versaackt […]'.

129 NACS, N°343, 'Acte tot het vraagen van een eed aen Alexander & Sottira van diferente pointen', Izmir, 31/08/1769.

130 Ergene, *Local court*, pp. 64–65.

131 NACS, N°343, 'Parere weegens de differentie van Alex:r & Sottira met Gerrit van Brakel', Izmir, 01/09/1769.

half of all the expenses made.[132] Van Brakel accepted, but Alexander & Sottira made their intention to appeal the verdict before the competent court very clear.[133] It is unclear whether the Greek firm filed an appeal and, if so, at which court. Theoretically, appeals against consular verdicts should be adjudicated by the Dutch ambassador in Istanbul, but Dutch records contain no further references to this dispute.

Even though the sentence did not put the full blame on Gerrit van Brakel, his discourse troubled the consul, and not for the first time. A few years earlier, in 1767, he had married a Greek woman at a time when the Greek bishop was disputing such marriages. At the time, de Hochepied considered van Brakel as careless, because he had celebrated his marriage in public.[134] After van Brakel's behaviour at the trial with Alexander & Sottira, de Hochepied called him a 'stubborn creature', and he wrote to the States General that he wanted to expel van Brakel from the Dutch community to set an example.[135] When this was communicated to the Directorate of Levant Trade, its directors concurred, even though it was an unusual decision. Van Brakel lost his Dutch-protected status but would later return to the fold. He even became chancellor of the Dutch consulate between 1783 and 1804 and then treasurer until his death in 1817.[136]

This case is remarkable for a number of reasons. Although Alexander & Sottira were Ottoman subjects, they accepted the principle of *forum rei* and initially took the case to the Dutch consular court, most likely because they felt their case was strong and the existence of Dutch exchange law would be in their favour. It does indicate that certain traders had the option of forum shopping and took it. Van Brakel was not the only European merchant to complain about Ottomans seeking the best of both worlds. On several occasions, Europeans complained of the legal actions undertaken by several Ottomans who could choose either a European or an Ottoman court for litigation.[137] This choice was formally also open to European traders, as by the middle of the eighteenth

132 NACS, N°343, 'Sententie in de differentie van Alex:r & Sottira & C° x g: van Brakel', Izmir, 02/09/1769.

133 NACS, N°343, 'Annotatie van appel van Alex:r en Sottira teegens van Brakel', Izmir, 04/09/1769.

134 Something he expressed in a letter sent on 01/08/1767, mentioned in a footnote in Heeringa and Nanninga, *Bronnen tot de geschiedenis*, 4: p. 192.

135 The quote comes from a letter written by Consul de Hochepied to the States General, Izmir, 03/07/1769, mentioned in a footnote in Heeringa and Nanninga, *Bronnen tot de geschiedenis*, 4: p. 192, '[...] soo een koppig schepzel [...]'.

136 See footnote 162 on p. 237.

137 See pp. 308–312.

century all European capitulations contained options for Europeans to choose litigation at an Ottoman court. The fact that Europeans did not appear eager to do so does not take anything away from their option to do so.[138] The case of Alexander & Sottira proves that Ottomans did not even need to be a European *protégé*. By remaining silent vis-à-vis Ottoman authorities and simply accepting Dutch competence, a nonprotected Ottoman could be tried at a European court in cases where he wanted to prosecute a European as plaintiff. *Protégés* had the same option, but it was expanded, with the right to seek legal recourse as defendant due to their protected status, an option several of them took.

3.2 *Ottoman Justice and European Protection*

In 1766, an Ottoman Armenian trader in Amsterdam named Alexander di Massé started having difficulties paying bills of exchange drawn on him by the firm of Massé, di Herabeth & Sons in Izmir, in which one of the partners was Isaie di Massé, Alexander's brother. The inability of Alexander to pay for the bills issued by Massé, di Herabeth & Sons created a huge problem for Isaie di Massé in Izmir.[139] In May 1768 Consul Daniel Jean de Hochepied wrote to the States General about the return of unpaid bills of exchange drawn by Massé, di Herabeth & Sons on Alexander di Massé. Isaie di Massé was a Dutch *protégé* (see table 3), which is why seven merchants holding his bills turned to the consul to demand payment from him. The consul gave di Massé twenty-four hours, 'according to usage in those cases', or the option to find a surety for the amount he owed.[140] Di Massé replied he was unable to pay, as too many protested bills had returned from different places at once. He needed time, but the merchants were adamant and demanded that the consul seal di Massé's effects and order his business books to be handed over. The consul replied that he could not do this, because di Massé was an Ottoman subject, and even though he was also a Dutch *protégé*, the consul stated he 'could not

---

138 It has been argued, for Ottoman courts in seventeenth-century Istanbul, that a bias existed against non-Muslim litigants, which might explain the lack of European enthusiasm to appear before an Ottoman judge; on this see Timur Kuran and Scott Lustig, 'Judicial biases in Ottoman Istanbul. Islamic justice and its compatibility with modern economic life', *Journal of law and economics*, 55 (2012): pp. 1–48.

139 For Alexander di Massé and the financial problems created by the bills, see Ismail Hakkı Kadı, 'On the edges of an Ottoman world: Non-Muslim Ottoman merchants in Amsterdam', in *The Ottoman world*, ed. Christine Woodhead (London and New York, 2012), pp. 276–288; see also Hakkı Kadı, *Ottoman and Dutch merchants*, pp. 215–223.

140 Heeringa and Nanninga, *Bronnen tot de geschiedenis*, 4: pp. 99–100, Consul Daniel Jean de Hochepied to the States General, Izmir, 18/05/1768, on p. 99, '[…] volgens gebruyk in dusdaenige gevallen […]'.

act completely according to the laws of our lands – in order to avoid the *avanias* that might result from this'.[141]

This is an important remark for understanding the dual position of the Ottoman *protégés*. They had obtained certain privileges, similar to those granted to the European trading communities, including the right to be tried as defendant before a European court, but at the same time, they also remained Ottoman subjects. This could offer them protection from European action. It might have been formally possible for the consul to follow European legal practice and seal di Massé's effects, but he feared that it might lead to the involvement of Ottoman officials who would counteract such a decision to protect Ottoman interests.[142] These interests were not only with the person of Isaie di Massé. After denying the request of the European merchants, de Hochepied decided to receive all of di Massé's creditors in his house. There were fifty-four in total, forty-seven Ottomans, which included 'Turks, Jews, Greeks and Armenians', and 'seven Frankish firms'.[143] The Ottomans took a united stance by allowing di Massé the fifteen-day period he had asked for to come up with a payment plan. The Ottomans expected the Europeans to agree but stated that if they did not, they would file an official protest against the Europeans at an Ottoman court and hold them responsible in case the firm of Massé, di Herabeth & Sons went bankrupt. De Hochepied continued by stating that the Europeans were forced to give in, considering there was a majority of forty-seven against seven. When the Europeans asked Isaie, who was also present at the meeting, how much he owed, the Ottomans protested, claiming di Massé should be left alone. The consul concluded by writing that di Massé had showed a great deal of courage and hoped he would be able to pay and save himself.[144]

The Ottoman majority amongst the creditors must have worried the consul, as it brought the risk of litigation before an Ottoman *qadi* court. Europeans generally hoped to avoid this. When Pieter Ouckama entered into financial difficulties in 1769 that led to his bankruptcy, for instance, the consul explained

141 Ibid., '[…] konde ik niet volkoomen ageeren volgens de wetten onser landen – om de avanies, die er mogten opkoomen, te eviteeren […]'.

142 The capitulations do not contain much on the involvement of Ottoman courts in bankruptcy cases, but they did include stipulations protecting European traders and *protégés* from 'unexpected financial demands as a result of debts incurred by others'. Van den Boogert, *The capitulations*, pp. 212–213.

143 Heeringa and Nanninga, *Bronnen tot de geschiedenis*, 4: pp. 99–100, Consul Daniel Jean de Hochepied to the States General, Izmir, 18/05/1768, '[…] Turken, Jooden, Grieken, en Armeenders […] seeven Frankse huysen […]'.

144 Ibid.

to Hendrik Fagel, then working at the States General, that Ouckama was lucky he did not have any 'Turkish' (i.e., Muslim) creditors, only Jews, Greeks and Armenians. They all came to visit the consul to find a solution but 'did not have the heart' to seek recourse at an Ottoman court.[145] De Hochepied seemed to have been too optimistic, because Ouckama fled from Izmir not much later, claiming his creditors had threatened to have him arrested by the 'Turks' and bring him in chains to Istanbul, in spite of an earlier agreement allowing him to travel to Holland to procure funds.[146]

In the case of Massé, di Herabeth & Sons, it is clear that the Ottoman creditors were in the majority and were also aware that, although they accepted to negotiate an outcome at the Dutch consul's house, they used the option of Ottoman justice as means of pressuring the Europeans into following their solution, which was to extend time to di Massé. The granted time period of fifteen days ran from 6 to 15 June, and when it ran out, the Dutch *chargé d'affaires* in Istanbul, Frederik Johan Robert de Weiler, wrote to the Directorate of Levant Trade that Massé, di Herabeth & Sons had declared bankruptcy, which immediately caused a great deal of trouble in Istanbul and Izmir. Several goods ready to be shipped by the bankrupt firm from Izmir to the United Provinces had been sequestered by the Ottoman authorities. De Weiler was trying to liberate the goods by obtaining a *ferman* from the Porte, but he feared that the 'Turkish' and Ottoman subjects would not lose so much in the bankruptcy, contrary to the Europeans.[147]

Not much later, the consul arrested Isaie di Massé, and while the latter was still in custody, some of the 'Turkish' creditors informed de Hochepied that they had agreed with the firm to get paid 25% of their debts within six months and that subsequently, di Massé should be released. The consul refused on the grounds that he had not only been arrested on demand of the *qadi* but also at the request of three French firms. This angered the 'Turkish' creditors, who gathered with a group of forty and a number of men of the Ottoman justice and appeared before the consul's house to threaten him and demand di Massé's liberty. The consul replied that 'our laws' impeded this, and he could not agree unless the French firms consented.[148] The group then moved to the

145 Heeringa and Nanninga, *Bronnen tot de geschiedenis*, 4: pp. 127–129, Consul Daniel Jean de Hochepied to Fagel, Izmir, 17/03/1769, on p. 128, '[…] hadden zij 't hart niet […]'.

146 See the documents in NACS, N°254 ('Stukken betreffende faillissementen. Pieter Ouckama, Nederlands koopman te Smyrna, 1769').

147 Heeringa and Nanninga, *Bronnen tot de geschiedenis*, 4: p. 103, *Chargé d'affaires* Frederik Johan Robert de Weiler to the Directorate of Levant Trade, Istanbul, 15/06/1768.

148 Heeringa and Nanninga *Bronnen tot de geschiedenis*, 4: pp. 108–109, Consul Daniel Jean de Hochepied to Fagel, Izmir, 18/07/1768, '[…] onse wetten […]'.

house of the French consul, who wanted some time to consider, so everyone returned to the Dutch consul's house, who then agreed to liberate di Massé on the double condition that two Armenians stood as surety for him and that he would not run away.[149]

The news had already spread to the United Provinces, and in June 1768, the firm of Thomas de Vogel & Zoon wrote to David van Lennep in Izmir that they were not surprised about the bankruptcy, as they felt the firm had been poorly run. They heard the 'Turks' had taken possession of everything, with nothing left for the Christians. They feared Alexander di Massé in Amsterdam would suffer the same fate, and it seems that he indeed went bankrupt too, but managed to repay most of his debts, meaning his reputation remained intact. De Vogel was sorry for Alexander di Massé, who he felt he was a good man.[150]

The Directorate of Levant Trade used the example of Massé, di Herabeth & Sons to warn Dutch traders to think twice before entering into business with Ottoman firms, suggesting that any advantage that derived from it would be 'twice destroyed by unforeseen damages later'.[151] Two days later, the Directorate of Levant Trade expressed disappointment that the 'Turkish' creditors had taken everything from the bankrupt firm, even several goods that belonged to Dutch traders, which had been consigned to Massé, di Herabeth & Sons.[152] It is difficult to verify if European complaints about arrangements that turned out well for Ottomans were justified in each individual case, but Maurits van den Boogert has demonstrated that many negative European comments on Ottoman practice were evidence of a particular European way of thinking and did not point to the existence of an unjust Ottoman legal system. He demonstrated that settlements that were unfair in European eyes were 'a pragmatic method of dispute resolution between Ottomans and Europeans that was more common in this period than many Europeans cared to admit'.[153]

Two years later, the firm of Massé, di Herabeth & Sons found itself in another predicament in spite of the good standing the di Massé brothers enjoyed. Alexander's business in Amsterdam had picked up again, and Isaie

149 Ibid.

150 Ibid., pp. 1239, Thomas de Vogel to David van Lennep, Amsterdam, 21/06/1768. It seems that Alexander di Massé fully recovered. When he died in 1803, he left a considerable estate. Hakkı Kadı, 'On the edges of an Ottoman world', p. 282.

151 Heeringa and Nanninga, *Bronnen tot de geschiedenis*, 4: pp. 112–113, Directorate of Levant Trade to consul, treasurer and assessors in Izmir, Amsterdam, 20/09/1768, on p. 113, '[…] naderhand door onversiene schaadens dubbeld werden vernietigt […]'.

152 Ibid., pp. 113–115, Directorate of Levant Trade to the States General, Amsterdam, 22/09/1768.

153 Van den Boogert, *The capitulations*, p. 157.

stood in good contact with the Dutch ambassador in Istanbul, to whom he sent several gifts.[154] The problem was that, in an effort to counter the effect of their bankruptcy, the Armenian firm had summoned one of their debtors, Caspar di Carabeth, before Ottoman justice. On 25 November 1770, Caspar and Simon di Carabeth made a request to the Dutch consul to take away all Dutch assistance to Isaie di Massé in his dealings with Ottoman justice, as well as his protected status. They felt di Massé had made 'vain pretentions and unjust demands' and that he had every opportunity to bring the dispute before the Dutch consul.[155] They found his actions to be particularly inexplicable considering he was a debtor to Simon di Carabeth himself. So, as Caspar di Carabeth was brought before Ottoman justice, they felt that di Massé should also be brought before Ottoman justice, as a *raya*, and with 'the greatest respect' they asked the consul to remove the protected status from di Massé.[156]

The Dutch ignored this request, as they were fully sympathetic to the cause of di Massé. A remark added by chancellor Mann underneath the request shows that the Dutch were keen on avoiding Ottoman justice altogether. Mann, who was still hoping to bring the case before arbitrators, had asked di Massé to contact Ottoman justice in an effort to obtain the release of Caspar di Carabeth, who had been arrested, but di Massé refused.[157] Di Massé must have felt strongly about his chances at Ottoman justice, but Consul de Hochepied expressed 'his great surprise', as he could not understand how Isaie di Massé, principal partner in the firm and Dutch *protégé*, could bring anyone before an Ottoman court without first consulting him or the first dragoman of the Dutch consulate

154 The ambassador felt obliged to accept some fish and fifty watermelons, and to return fifty-two bottles of red wine, as his general feeling was that he could only accept gifts of limited value. He had to assure di Massé that this was not because he held di Massé in low esteem. Heeringa and Nanninga, *Bronnen tot de geschiedenis*, 4: p. 13, Ambassador Willem Dedel to Isaie di Massé, Istanbul, 11/10/1765.

155 NACS, N°347 ('Massé di Carabeth, Armeens koopman te Smyrna, tegen zijn broer Caspar di Carabeth, 1770'), 'Request van Caspar & Simon di Carabeth om aen Masse de assistentie & protectie te onttrekken', Izmir, 25/11/1770, '[…] vane pretenzionij e ingiuste dimande […]'. The reference to this case in the catalogue of the Dutch national archives mistakenly identifies the litigants in this case as Massé di Carabeth and Caspar di Carabeth, two brothers. It was a case between the firm of Massé, di Herabeth & Sons and Caspar di Carabeth. While the documents also mention a Simon di Carabeth, his exact relationship to Caspar is unclear; but at least the two were not opposing parties. To further complicate matters, the firm of Massé, di Herabeth & Sons remains mysterious in terms of partners. Hakkı Kadı consistently refers to it as Massé, di Carabeth & Sons. See for instance Hakkı Kadı, *Ottoman and Dutch merchants*, p. 218.

156 NACS, N°347, 'Request van Caspar & Simon di Carabeth om aen Masse de assistentie & protectie te onttrekken', Izmir, 25/11/1770, '[…] con il maggior rispetto […]'.

157 Ibid.

in Izmir, a Greek named Diodato Abro.[158] De Hochepied's surprise was not as remarkable as it seems, because it was granted in the Dutch capitulations that Dutch litigants, which di Massé was due to his *berat*, could be assisted by a dragoman of the Dutch nation as his interpreter before an Ottoman court.[159] Perhaps di Massé thought that, as an Ottoman subject, he did not need such assistance, but de Hochepied expressed the fear of creating a precedent which could lead to a general practice of litigation before an Ottoman court involving Dutch *protégés* without the assistance of dragomans.[160]

Part of di Carabeth's goods had been sequestered by the Ottomans, which was not to de Hochepied's liking, and he wanted his chancellor to speak to Abro so a way could be found to lift the sequester. De Hochepied felt the dispute should either be examined by himself or by 'good men', referring to the possibility of settling through arbitration.[161] In a way, it was a remarkable choice. Di Carabeth had no connection to the Dutch community through a *berat*, and di Massé could at least claim some debts, which in turn might be used to pay off European creditors who had not found satisfaction in the resolution of the bankruptcy two years earlier. It seems likely that the consul was motivated by a desire to preserve the autonomy of legal procedures as granted to him in the capitulations, and litigation before an Ottoman court posed a threat to that autonomy, at least in the consul's eyes.

After the consul's letter to Chancellor Mann, a meeting was organised between Isaie di Massé and five other Armenians, Babi di Arun, Aretun di Minas, Lucas di Marcos and Malcas and Simon di Carabeth. These last two were relatives of Caspar di Carabeth, and Malcas was not unknown to the Dutch consul, as he was the Armenian trader with whom the Dutch merchant Isaac Beaune had hoped to establish a intercultural partnership in Izmir before the consul forbade him to do so.[162] In the meeting, an agreement was reached to put the dispute before four arbitrators, each party choosing two, and an eventual fifth should their opinions be divided. Their judgment should be accepted without the possibility of appeal. It was also agreed that Isaie di Massé should pay for the expenses related to the Ottoman sequester and its lifting, as well as for the

158 NACS, N°347, Consul Daniel Jean de Hochepied to chancellor Johan Frederik Mann, Izmir, 25/11/1770, '[…] tot mijne groote verwondering […]'. For the appointment of Abro as dragoman between 1765 and 1797, see Schutte, *Repertorium der Nederlandse vertegenwoordigers*, p. 345.

159 See pp. 84–85.

160 NACS, N°347, Consul Daniel Jean de Hochepied to chancellor Johan Frederik Mann, Izmir, 25/11/1170.

161 Ibid., '[…] goede mannen […]'.

162 See p. 288.

release of Caspar, who was held by the Ottoman authorities. Di Massé's actions should be considered an '*avania* caused by him', but since he had no funds, the four other Armenians were to advance it, and it would be subtracted from di Carabeth's debts.[163] If di Carabeth was not found to be indebted to di Massé, the latter had to pay for all expenses. As surety, di Massé was asked to deposit the actual document of the *berat* he had bought and that had given him Dutch protection.[164] The four other Armenians stood as surety for di Carabeth.[165]

On 29 November 1770, Chancellor Mann, who had been present at the meeting, informed the consul about the events that had occurred. He reported about the compromise to send the case to arbitration but added that several of the Armenians had changed their minds, declaring that they were *rayas* who had nothing to do with Dutch justice.[166] Mann had apparently confronted the Armenians directly, asking them why they had sent a request to the Dutch consulate if they did not want to have anything to do with its justice. They ignored the question, not knowing that Mann had the actual request in his pocket.[167] They claimed to only have come out of friendship, but Mann concluded that their attitude made it clear that they did not want to be judged. The chancellor was convinced that they would be unwilling to pay anything if the arbitrators concluded that di Carabeth owed money to di Massé. The chancellor continued his report by stating that, after they had spoken to him, the Armenians had physically assaulted di Massé, after which he had agreed to subtract all expenses made from the debt. He also agreed to help to secure the release of Caspar.[168]

It is not clear how the case was resolved, but the Dutch authorities fully stood behind Isaie di Massé. The consul felt that he and di Massé had justice at their side and demanded that Caspar provide the surety asked from him, sign the compromise and accept arbitration or fully declare himself a *raya* and accept the consequences, which would be a continuation of the case before Ottoman justice. Should this happen, the consul instructed Mann to talk to Diodato Abro, who had to go to di Massé, because 'I absolutely want di Massé

163 NACS, N°347, undated and unsigned declaration, '[…] avania da lui causato […]'.

164 *Berats* were commodities that could be bought and sold; see pp. 61–64.

165 NACS, N°347, undated and unsigned declaration.

166 NACS, N°347, Chancellor Johan Frederik Mann to Consul Daniel Jean de Hochepied, Izmir, 29/11/1770.

167 Some, or all, of the four Armenians must thus have brought the case before the Dutch consulate, which was not strange considering two of them were di Carabeth's relatives, but the actual request has not been preserved.

168 NACS, N°347, Chancellor Johan Frederik Mann to Consul Daniel Jean de Hochepied, Izmir, 29/11/1770.

to be assisted'.[169] Di Massé was a well-respected *protégé*; his earlier bankruptcy had led some Dutch merchants to sympathise with him, expressing their hopes that he would recover.[170]

The consul's remark about Caspar di Carabeth having to declare his status as *raya* suggests that the man had some choices to make. No evidence was found, and no mention was made, however, of any privileged status for di Carabeth. The choice to turn to arbitration was not strange, as the peaceful resolution of conflict was often attempted before litigation, but it seems peculiar that di Massé addressed Ottoman justice then refused to withdraw his request when the consul asked, only to then agree to arbitration. The consul and Armenian friends of di Carabeth must have pressured him. It is not clear how the case was resolved, but in 1784, Caspar di Carabeth travelled to Amsterdam to visit Alexander di Massé, demonstrating that he had an interest in Dutch Levant trade (which might have created the initial quarrel on the debt).[171] Di Carabeth might have been trading with the United Provinces on his own account, through di Massé, which would be an additional reason to seek peaceful resolution through the consulate.

As the assistance provided to di Massé, in spite of his earlier bankruptcy and his choice of turning to Ottoman justice, shows, the Dutch took their protection duties seriously. The status of the *protégés* provided them with certain privileges, and rather than seeking recourse at Ottoman courts, they did resort to consular justice when they felt that these privileges were harmed or threatened. In 1782, for instance, a Chiot trader named Jani Mavrogordatos complained to the Dutch consul that he was subjected to taxes and custom duties by Chios magistrates, while as a *protégé* he was exempt from them. Clearly, traders used their expensively bought *protégé* status as means to gain commercial profit, and when that did not work out because of the different administrative legal and administrative systems, they sought what was to their best advantage. These developments furthered the opportunities for forum shopping mentioned earlier, in this case allowing a Greek Ottoman subject to turn to Dutch diplomacy trying to avoid paying tariffs.[172]

169 NACS, N°347, Consul Daniel Jean de Hochepied to Chancellor Johan Frederik Mann, Izmir, '[...] ik wil apsolut hebben dat men masse assisteert [...]'. The note is undated and only mentions that it was written on a Thursday afternoon.

170 See p. 301.

171 Hakkı Kadı, 'On the edges of an Ottoman world', p. 282.

172 NALT, N°626 ('Memoire par les affaires des barataires de Scio'), 'Mémoire présenté a la Porte', S.l., 17/12/1782.

4 An Islamic Merchants' Style?

4.1 *European Fear of Ottoman Abuses*

In 1760, Consul Daniel Jean de Hochepied wrote to the States General about the case of Yaqub Çelik, an Armenian merchant based in Izmir who had gone bankrupt. De Hochepied had received directives from the States General to assist the merchant firm of van Lennep & Enslie, who carried a power of attorney from the creditors of Çelik's son Serkis, based in Amsterdam. Van Lennep & Enslie had been instructed to claim some of Yaqub's goods that had been sequestered by the consul. Yaqub Çelik, it was specified, was an Ottoman subject who enjoyed Dutch protection through the purchase of a *berat* with help from the Dutch ambassador in Istanbul and which had been accepted by the Porte. While reflecting on Çelik's case, Consul de Hochepied condemned the practice of forum shopping:

> those people of the land [Ottoman Empire] serve themselves effectively from the *berats* and protections of the Europeans, for as long as it coincides with their interest, and as soon as they observe, particularly in bankruptcies, that those *berats* do not coincide with their own particular interests, they abandon *berats* and protections, and return to Turkish protection, in which case no ambassador or consul has the power to interfere, unless with the risk of opening the whole nation to unbelievable and unthinkable inconveniencies, *avanias* and liability.[173]

The consul then wrote to the ambassador in the hope that the Porte would acknowledge the need for Çelik's Ottoman creditors to fully understand the rights of the creditors in the United Provinces and thus accept a settlement that included them all. The ambassador replied that such a thing would only be possible if Yaqub Çelik would declare, at the instigation of *all* his creditors, in an Ottoman court that his bankruptcy was not fraudulent and that he had

173 Heeringa and Nanninga, *Bronnen tot de geschiedenis*, 3: pp. 402–404, Consul Daniel Jean de Hochepied to the States General, Izmir, 15/09/1760, on pp. 402–403, '[…] welke menschen van 't land sig effective maer soo lang van de baratten en protextiën der Europeëren bedienen, als het haar met derselver belangen conveniëert, en soo ras sy bespeuren, insonderhijd by faillissementen, dat die baratten met haere bysondere belangen niet overeenkoomen, soo laeten sy baratten en protextiën vaeren en begeeven haer weederom onder de Turkse protextiën, wanneer dan geen ambassadeur off consul meer de magt heefft sig het allerminste meer met haer te bemoeyen, tenzy sig en de gansche natie in de gevolgen aen ongeloofelyke en onbedenklyke inconveniëntiën, havaniën en verantworrdinge bloot te stellen […]'.

no other possessions than the goods that were already sealed off by the Dutch. According to de Hochepied, this was not possible, because it had become clear that Yaqub's Ottoman creditors did not agree with those of Serkis Çelik in the United Provinces. The Ottoman creditors, who were positioning themselves as the competitors of the Dutch creditors, expressed no interest in prosecuting Yaqub Çelik, expecting to obtain more money from him by waiting.

In the meantime, a third party had entered the stage, the Ottoman proprietors of the *khan* in which Yaqub Çelik's warehouse was located. As was normal in bankruptcy procedures, Çelik's warehouse had been sealed off by the Dutch authorities, awaiting inventory and possibly a public sale to cover his debts. The *khan* proprietors were claiming unpaid rent from the Armenian and threatened to get it by petitioning the local Ottoman court to break the seal so they could take goods as compensation. De Hochepied argued that this was not only disadvantageous to the Dutch creditors, it also went against the legal autonomy stipulated in the capitulations, which also held in the case of a bankruptcy procedure. In a meeting amongst Dutch merchants in Izmir, it was decided to hold off the Ottoman creditors for the time being. The *khan* proprietors protested, and afraid of the possible repercussions, the consul wanted van Lennep & Enslie to pay the rent or cancel the sequester.[174]

This example clearly shows that European jurisdiction was challenged by Ottoman traders and that Europeans were afraid of the consequences such challenges could bring. On the one hand, the capitulations ensured European legal autonomy, which also applied to Yaqub Çelik as a Dutch *protégé*. On the other hand, the bankruptcy involved Ottoman creditors in the Ottoman Empire. While attempting to safeguard the interests of Dutch creditors, as specifically demanded by the States General, de Hochepied also knew that the Dutch lived as 'guests' of the sultan and that, while trying to point to the capitulations to keep a maximum of legal agency, they had to accept that there were limits, and these limits were not set according to a Dutch logic, but to an Ottoman one. There was always a risk in objecting too much to an Ottoman resolution to a particular dispute, and it could be harmful to the Dutch trading nation as a whole.

Forum shopping in Izmir was different for Ottomans and Europeans. Europeans had agreed on the unwritten rule of *forum rei*, an existing principle stipulating that the jurisdiction of the defendant would be chosen for adjudication. Europeans were allowed, through the capitulations, to choose to appear before an Ottoman court, as long as both litigating parties agreed.

174 Ibid.

While evidence shows that European diplomats discouraged their subjects from litigation before an Ottoman court, the use European merchants made of Ottoman courts, such as the *qadi*, has not been analysed.[175] Before the appearance of European traders in Ottoman courts is better understood, no assertion can be made about the advantages Ottomans had over Europeans. But the latter often felt that the *protégés*, because of their dual legal identity as Ottomans and Europeans, had an unfair advantage over them. This also included the assumption that Ottoman Jewish or Christian *protégés* who had bought European protection through a ferman were, unlike the Europeans themselves or members of their communities without ferman, free of *avanias*: 'fermans or orders, which liberate them of all *avanias* brought upon their nations'.[176]

These perceived competitive advantages of the *protégés* led to frequent requests from Dutch traders to their diplomatic representatives, in which they demanded that *protégés* would be forced to choose their legal status, either European or Ottoman – although such a choice was not possible.[177] Added to this was the fear that the appearance of a Dutch Ottoman *protégé* before an Ottoman court rendered the Dutch community as a whole vulnerable to *avanias*. While there are no indications that such a thing happened, Dutch diplomats feared that Ottoman adjudication involving their *protégés* could lead to a situation in which Ottoman justice would attempt to exercise jurisdiction over *all* Dutch merchants based on the situation created by the *protégé*.[178]

The fear fitted within the general European concern that the Ottoman authorities would violate the privileges specified in the capitulations, which Europeans considered as sacrosanct.[179] This fear meant that, in their assessment of interactions with Ottoman officials, European diplomats often expressed themselves in very strong terms in their correspondence, labelling Ottoman actions as unfair, unjust or unpredictable. The problem for Europeans was perhaps the feeling that, no matter how they interpreted the capitulations, they were still living under an Ottoman administration that could alter the terms of the relationship when they wanted. As such, use of the pejorative

---

175 Van den Boogert, *The capitulations*, p. 44.

176 Heeringa and Nanninga, *Bronnen tot de geschiedenis*, 3: pp. 357–358, Van Asten to Elbert de Hochepied, Aleppo, 09/02/1757, on p. 357, '[…] firmans of commandementen, die haarlieden bevryd van alle avanies, die op haare natsies gebragt werden […]'.

177 See also pp. 61–64 and 277–281.

178 Heeringa and Nanninga, *Bronnen tot de geschiedenis*, 3: pp. 27–29, Ambassador Cornelis Calkoen to Fagel, Istanbul, 08/11/1730.

179 Van den Boogert, *The capitulations*, p. 21.

term *avania* was nothing more but the expression of European vulnerability. This was further fuelled by the understanding that a whole trading community could be made to pay the consequences of an individual action.

European diplomats were well aware of this vulnerability, particularly when dealing with Ottoman merchants, and the Dutch consul in Izmir warned his merchants to be conscious of their actions, fearing the creation of a precedent in which the whole Dutch community would be held accountable for individual missteps. When Pieter Ouckama declared bankruptcy in 1769, the Dutch consul suggested a public sale of Ouckama's furniture in order to raise money to pay off as much debt as possible. Local creditors had refused, as they wanted Ouckama's furniture stored in a warehouse until the bankrupt's future intentions were clear. Daniel Jean de Hochepied remarked that he did not need to listen to the desires of the creditors, as he was 'authorised by our laws as magistrate of our nation here' to proceed with the public sale, but he would nevertheless respect the wishes of the local creditors in order to 'not be exposed to any *avania* that they could bring on us or on our nation'.[180]

Just like the embeddedness of collective punishment in European medieval legal context, the principle that a whole community of foreigners (in this case a European trading community in the Ottoman Empire) could be held accountable by the host society for the individual behaviour of one of its members is fully in line with Ottoman legal tradition.[181] According to Işık Tamdoğan, who analysed a sodomy trial brought before the *qadi* court of Adana, 'the evolution of the notion of collective responsibility in Ottoman jurisprudence has a long history'.[182] According to Tamdoğan, Ottoman use of forms of collective responsibility not only applied in both Islamic and *kanun* law but also found their way into eighteenth-century taxation systems.[183] The understanding that there was an old legal tradition, both in Europe and the Ottoman Empire, of collective responsibility – one that did not exclude individual accountability – provides

180 NACS, N°254, 'Order van de heeren consul thes x assessooren tot het bergen der boedel van Ouckama & C° tot nader dispositie in een brandvrij magazijn', Izmir, 24/05/1769, '[…] schoon door onse wetten daer toe g'authoriseert als magistraat der Nederlandse natie alhier]' and '[…] niet bloot te stellen, aen deese of gene avania, die sij aen ons off onse natie soude konnen maaken […]'.

181 For European legal embeddedness, see Ogilvie, *Institutions and European trade*, pp. 272–276.

182 Işık Tamdoğan, 'The Ottoman political community in the process of justice making in the 18th-century Adana', in *Forms and institutions of justice. Legal actions in Ottoman contexts*, eds. Yavuz Aykan and Işık Tamdoğan (Istanbul, 2018), consulted online at https://books.openedition.org/ifeagd/2323.

183 Ibid.

an additional argument for the idea that European views on Ottoman corruption and extortion were false.

A good example is the Ottoman reaction to the growing involvement of Ottoman Greeks in Dutch Levant trade in the 1760s. To avoid paying higher customs duties, some of these Greeks covered their transactions by borrowing the name of Dutch traders, with their consent.[184] When Ottoman officials discovered this practice, they threatened to hold the whole Dutch community responsible, not just the merchant who had lent out his name.[185] It seems that in certain potential disputes, measures had been taken to avoid the unwished use of collective responsibility mechanisms. Article 28 of the 1612 Dutch capitulations specified that 'if a Dutchman becomes a debtor, the debt must be demanded from the one who owes it and no other may be arrested or required to pay unless he has stood as surety'.[186] The inclusion of such an article suggests that an opposite practice could be imagined. Indeed, in 1767, the Dutch ambassador in Istanbul wrote to the States General to obtain advice about potential Ottoman infractions against the capitulations. One of the examples he used was the practice in which powerful Ottomans purchased certain debts that were owed by Dutchmen and intended to hold the ambassador or the whole Dutch trading community responsible for them.[187]

4.2 *Greek Community Resolutions*

The mechanism of collective responsibility was not the only option available within the Ottoman legal context to avoid or punish the cheating behaviour of traders without immediately going to court. The Ottoman legal system also allowed for forms of friendly community settlements in much the same way as certain European societies did. The obvious example is the legal autonomy granted to European consuls through the capitulations, but Ottomans allowed for intracommunity resolutions for their *millets* as well. On occasion, documents related to such processes found their way to European chanceries in the Levant, because Ottoman traders with a *berat* were able to challenge community resolutions by resorting to consular adjudication. An example is the resolution of the dispute between two Greek traders, both holders of a European *berat*. In 1760, French *protégé* Manolaki di Panaiotis was taken to court by a

184 See pp. 248 and 284–285.

185 Heeringa and Nanninga, *Bronnen tot de geschiedenis*, 4: p. vi.

186 Quoted from de Groot, *The Ottoman Empire*, p. 153.

187 Heeringa and Nanninga, *Bronnen tot de geschiedenis*, 4: pp. 73–77. Ambassador Willem Dedel to Fagel, Istanbul, 15/09/1767.

fellow Greek trader, Panaiotis Pittaco, who was a *protégé* of the Dutch consulate, for unpaid debts.[188]

Initially, the case was subject to judgment within the Greek community by the Greek bishop and three merchants, who sentenced di Panaiotis to pay his debts. When the French *protégé* stalled his payments for too long, Pittaco went to court. Because di Panaiotis was a French *protégé*, the case had to be tried by the French consul. Some documents pertaining to this case have been preserved in the archives of the Dutch consulate because Pittaco, as a Dutch *protégé*, was allowed to deposit his documents at the chancery of the consulate under whose jurisdiction he fell. The Dutch chancellor brought copies of the documents to his French colleague and vice versa. In this case, the French chancery withheld several documents, because the title on the trial documents explicitly mentions that paperwork was in the French chancery and had not been shown to the Dutch consulate, which was not the normal procedure.[189]

The case's first document kept in the Dutch chancery is a declaration in Italian, made by Pittaco on behalf of the Dutch consul and signed by the Greek bishop and the three Greek merchants involved in the original sentencing, Leone Prasacachi, Demetrio Vitale and Giovanni Zingrilara.[190] The dispute and the original sentencing was explained, as well as the recourse sought at the French consulate. A day after it had been drafted, Dutch chancellor Haan added a paragraph declaring he had gone to see the bishop and the three merchants in the presence of two witnesses – Gualtiero Gallo and Luca Homero, both well acquainted with the Dutch community in Izmir.[191] This personal visit confirmed the situation, and de Hochepied ordered that both the Greek declaration and Haan's addition should be copied and sent to the French chancery so di Panaiotis could read it and reply.

The problem was that a man named Ağa Esse was indebted to Pittaco for a sum of 2,500 lion dollars. The first 1,500 lion dollars came from an older debt that remained unspecified, but the second came from a loan given by Pittaco after mediation with Manolaki di Panaiotis, who had insisted for Pittaco to grant Esse the loan and who was willing to stand as surety. When

188 This was the same di Panaiotis who was later involved in the case between Dirk Knipping and Jacques Forêt and who also had a dispute with Jacob de Vogel. The papers of the case can be found in NACS, N°324 ('Papieren der proces van Manolachi de Panajottis x Panajotti Pittaco, welke door den Grieksen bischop zijn uijtgesprooken & de sententie in de Franse cancellerij berust, sonder ter deeser cancellerij te zijn vertoond, 1761').

189 Ibid.

190 The choice of these three merchants might not be a coincidence, as at least two of them, Vitale and Zingrilara, had been or still were under Dutch protection at the time.

191 Gallo was working for the Directorate of Levant Trade in 1766. See table 1.

di Panaiotis promised that he would pay Pittaco the 1,000 lion dollars back within a year, should Ağa Esse not be able to, Pittaco was convinced, as he immediately accepted these terms.[192] Unfortunately, Ağa Esse went bankrupt, and his creditors agreed to try to recuperate 70% of Esse's debts. Pittaco did not want to side with that claim, in the hopes to fully reclaim his money. Di Panaiotis seemed to agree and convinced him to remain patient and not go to court. No agreement was reached, and eventually, Ağa Esse's son turned to the Greek bishop in Izmir for help, who summoned Pittaco before him in person. In the meantime, a man from Ankara named Ağa Raz promised to pay off part of the debt to Pittaco, but nothing happened, so the case was put before the Greek bishop and three Greek merchants, who decided that Manolaki di Panaiotis, as surety, was liable. He promised to pay the 1,000 in cash, and the remaining 1,500 would be satisfied by a delivery of cochineal at twenty lion dollars per *ocque*.[193] Pittaco was willing to forget the interest of 116 lion dollars, but when di Panaiotis kept postponing payment, Pittaco and his father decided to go to the French consulate to obtain payment from its *protégé* di Panaiotis.[194]

Manolaki di Panaiotis replied by stating that Pittaco had written almost nothing that was true and that he was ingrateful, and he disputed Pittaco's claim about the caution for the 1,000 lion dollars, for which he claimed there was no evidence. According to the French *protégé*, Pittaco was committing 'pure chicanery, deprived of all common sense' by claiming he had a caution for the 1,000 from both Manolaki di Panaiotis and Ağa Raz, which was not possible.[195] For the 1,500, Pittaco should be grateful that it was thanks to di Panaiotis that he had managed to salvage 1,500 from the bankruptcy of Ağa Esse. If Pittaco did not want to buy the cochineal at the set prices, that was not di Panaiotis' problem, and he could not be held responsible for the lowering of the prices for cochineal on the market. It was, according to Manolaki di Panaiotis, a matter of Pittaco who 'complains about broth rich in fat', as the lower price of 2.5 lion dollars per *ocque* on the 50 di Panaiotis had offered would cause a loss of 125 lion dollars, which was better than the loss of 300 lion dollars on 1,000 had he sided

---

192 NACS, N°324, 'Antwoord van Panajotti Pittaco op het schrift van Manuel Kiriako di Panajotti', Izmir, 29/10/1760, '[…] subito o acetate la sua parola […]'.

193 This was an Ottoman weight measurement and equalled about 1.284 kilograms. A.C. Barbier de Meynard, *Dictionnaire turc-français* (Paris, 1886), 2: p. 602; see also Jacques Savary des Bruslons, *Dictionnaire universel de commerce* (Copenhagen, 1765), p. 987.

194 NACS, N°324, 'Antwoord van Panajotti Pittaco', Izmir, 29/10/1760.

195 NACS, N°324, Replicq van Manuel Kiriako di Panajotti weeg: zijn proces met Panajotti Pittaco', Izmir, 13/11/1760, '[…] une chicane toute pure et depourveûe du bon sens […]'.

with the other creditors of Ağa Esse.[196] Pittaco in turn labelled these claims as 'useless words without any true foundation', while his own declarations were substantiated by the Greek bishop and the three Greek merchants, Prasacachi, Vitale and Zingrilara, men 'who were known in the entire city'.[197] He insisted on the 2,500 lion dollars plus the 116 of interest in a declaration made on 14 November and brought by the Dutch Chancellor Mann to the French consulate the same day.[198] Di Panaiotis replied by demanding from Pittaco that 'he should once and for all produce either one or the other [referring to the Greek bishop's sentence and to the promissory note of Manolaki di Panaiotis] and all will be over [...] for good, that the said gentleman Pittaco would cease to blacken [meaning putting ink on] paper without use and that he [Pittaco] would take care to not file any requests with the court without having the documents authorising you to do so'.[199] Pittaco retorted that the bishop's sentence had not been issued in writing, so he could not produce that document, but insisted that he had already provided the declaration of the witnesses.[200] The legal discussion of the two Greek merchants thus centred around the production of written evidence, and di Panaiotis did not confirm or deny many of the claims made by Pittaco but decided to concentrate his defence on the claim that Pittaco had to prove di Panaiotis' responsibility in writing. It created a stalemate, and the case was taken to arbitration.[201] The seventy-five *ocques* of cochineal that di Panaiotis wanted to give and that Pittaco did not want had already been deposed at the Dutch chancery in October 1760. In January 1761 it was decided that di Panaiotis had to take fifty of them back and pay 1,000,

196 NACS, N°324, Replicq van Manuel Kiriako di Panajotti, Izmir, 13/11/1760, '[...] si lamenta del brodo grasso [...]'. Comments on an earlier request (that has not been preserved) were made by di Panaiotis and registered at the French chancery on 28/10/1760.

197 NACS, N°324, 'Request van Panajotti Pittaco aen den heere Boyer eerste Franse deputée, weeg: een differentie met sig: Manuel Kiriako di Panajottis', Izmir, 14/11/1760, '[...] parole inutile e senza verun fondamento [...]' and '[...] da tutta la città pr tali cognosciuti [...]'. The French consul was out of town at the time, so the request was addressed to the first deputy.

198 NACS, N°324, 'Request van Panajotti Pittaco', Izmir, 14/11/1760.

199 NACS, N°324, 'Replicq van Manuel Kiriako di Panajotti aen Panajotti Pittaco', Izmir, 17/11/1760, '[...] une fois pour toutes qu'il produise ou les unes ou les autres et tout sera fini [...] pour une bonne fois que le dit sr pitako cesse de noircir du papier inutilement x qu'il fasse attention qu'on ne forme pas de demandes en justice lors qu'on na pas des titres qui vous y authorisent [...]'.

200 NACS, N°324, 'Copije van een suplicq replicq van Panajotti Pittaco aen den eersten Franse deputé', Izmir, 19/11/1760.

201 No documents directly related to this arbitration were preserved in the Dutch consular archives.

while Pittaco had to accept twenty-five at the price of twenty lion dollars each, making up the remaining 500. The other 1,000 would have to be collected by Pittaco at the French chancery, where di Panaiotis must have been instructed to depose them.[202] Manolaki di Panaiotis did not intend to pay that last sum so easily, perhaps convinced he would be able to argue with French officials, as he was a French *protégé*. He had attempted the same with the Dutch, in vain, and two undated notes of his hand have been preserved at the Dutch consulate, both written to an official, probably the chancellor. In the first, he stated that he had brought the cochineal to the addressee and would send someone with the note, who would take the fifty *ocque* back. He also wrote that he did not want to see Pittaco at the chancery. In the second, he wrote that he thought Pittaco would go straight to the French chancery, and was hoping that he would not be received before di Panaiotis had the possibility to speak in person with the consul and the addressee of the note later the same day or the next. He wanted to ask about the interest and time period he would have to pay.[203] It is unclear whether this personal approach had any success, but it seems unlikely.

The insertion of the earlier sentencing by the Greek bishop demonstrates the ease with which informal intracommunity judgment – a common practice since the Middle Ages – was also applied within an Ottoman-European context.[204] At no moment was the legitimacy of the bishop's sentencing or his subsequent declaration questioned. The only element that was questioned was the nature of the sentencing, which had been communicated orally and not in writing. It might suggest an opposition between out-of-date community sentencing, with a Greek bishop adjudicating orally, and a modern, more rational sentencing necessitating written evidence. The contrast, however, is false and should be seen as a strategic attempt by di Panaiotis to challenge Pittaco's claim irrespective of the background of the system that had produced the sentencing.

4.3 *The Merchants' Style through Muslim Eyes*

Inspired by the institutional turn in analyses on the development of international trade and early modern capitalism, it has been argued that, while European legal instruments developed in such a way that they managed to

202 NACS, N°324, 'Quitantie van M. Kiriako di Panajotti weegens den ontfang van 50 /o/ [*ocques*] couchenille uijt deese cancellerij', Izmir, 15/01/1761; 'Quitantie van Panajotti Pittaco weegens den ontfang van 25 /o/ couchenille uijt deese cancellerij', Izmir, 16/01/1761; and [Declaration about the payment of the 1,000 lion dollars], Izmir, 16/01/1761.

203 NACS, N°324, two undated and unaddressed notes by Manolaki di Panaiotis.

204 See pp. 55–56 and 207–208.

support the expansion of international trade, Islamic legal systems did not undergo a similar evolution. In this view, Europe grew ever more exceptional, while the Ottoman Empire already went into decline after the sixteenth century – an interpretation not everyone adheres to.[205] More recent research into the Ottoman legal context has demonstrated that such a juxtaposition is overly simplistic. Léon Buskens has argued that Islamic law was only one aspect of the legal context of the Ottoman Empire, next to state law and legal custom, which, van den Boogert contended, can be said to have included 'European'-style legal practices, including merchant custom, through the legal privileges granted in the capitulations.[206] Evidence has also shown the European fear of suffering *avanias* was based on a desire to hang on to the privileges that had been established in the capitulations. In their discourse on Ottoman justice, early modern European commentators neglected the intricacies of the Ottoman legal system, which prevented them from understanding the nature of the *avanias* properly.[207] In his book on the functioning of the *qadi* courts of Çankırı and Kastamonu between 1652 and 1744, Ergene has asserted that, in spite of European assertions of corruption and unpredictability, 'we can identify a legal system with relatively concrete boundaries, pre-established procedure of litigation, and well-known evidentiary standards'.[208]

Secondly, Europeans protested against some of the procedural practices upheld at Ottoman courts, such as restrictions to the submission of European written evidence and the lack of punishment for false statements, but they did not fundamentally question the Ottoman understanding of the most important adjudicating principle in commercial litigation, sentencing according

205 For the idea of Islamic underperformance, see Kuran and Lustig, 'Judicial biases in Ottoman Istanbul'; Timur Kuran, *The long divergence. How Islamic law held back the Middle East* (Princeton, 2011); 'Why the Middle East is economically underdeveloped: Historical mechanisms of institutional stagnation', *Journal of economic perspectives*, 18:3 (2004): pp. 71–90; and 'The Islamic commercial crisis: Institutional roots of economic underdevelopment in the Middle East', *Journal of economic history*, 63:2 (2003): pp. 414–446. Opposing views were expressed in Pamuk, 'Institutional change and longevity of the Ottoman Empire'; as well as in Benjamin Braude, 'Christians, Jews, and the myth of Turkish commercial incompetence', in *Relazioni economiche tra Europa e mondo islamico, secc. XIII-XVIII* (*Atti della trentottesima settimana di studi 1 – 5 maggio 2006*, ed. Simonetta Cavaciocchi (Firenze, 2007), pp. 219–239. In Bryan S. Turner, 'Islam, capitalism and the Weber theses', *British journal of sociology*, 61:1 (2010): pp. 147–160, the author deconstructs a number of Weberian ideas on the incompatibility of Islam and capitalism.

206 Léon Buskens, 'An Islamic triangle. Changing relationships between *sharīʿa*, state law, and local customs', *ISIM newsletter*, 5/00, 8, consulted online at *The capitulations*, pp. 58–61.

207 See van den Boogert, *The capitulations*, pp. 155–157.

208 Ergene, *Local court*, p. 115.

to the merchants' style.[209] Declarations by Ottoman merchants and officials were accepted at the Dutch consular court, and it was not strange for expert statements to include signatures of Muslim traders.[210] Europeans knew that Ottoman courts adjudicated commercial disputes – the capitulations even allowed for quarrels between European merchants to be settled at an Ottoman court.[211] Not much is known about the actual functioning of a *qadi* court in the settlement of commercial disputes, but a few elements point to similarities with adjudication as it took place at the Dutch consular courts. It was common for the *qadi* to first attempt to settle matters amicably and informally, and the *qadi* judge seems to have often acted as arbitrator and mediator.[212]

Comparisons between European law and Islamic law regarding the role of individual rights generally make the point that, in the latter, individual rights (*ḥaqq*) are subordinate to obligations (*wājib*), an observation that has led to a rather negative perception on the less modern nature of Islamic law and its lesser adaptability to the requirements of international trade than western European models of law.[213] In his work on Moroccan Islamic courts, Lawrence Rosen discussed the concept of *ḥaqq* as an organising principle for networks of mutual indebtedness and obligation, networks in which individual legal persons could participate.[214] While such concepts have contributed to the common reading of western concepts of 'rights' versus Islamic concepts of 'obligations', another interpretation is possible. In the context of early modern commercial litigation, Islamic concepts of mutual obligations and reciprocity as binding people together are easily reconcilable with the same concepts used in the merchants' style. The language and reasoning with which commercial disputes were adjudicated were not so different, it seems, from language and reasoning relying on *ḥaqq*. While he does not make this point explicitly, Ergene,

209 See the contributions in Wolfgang Kaiser and Johann Petitjean, eds., 'Litigation and the elements of proof in the Mediterranean (16th–19th C.)', *Quaderni storici*, special issue, 3 (2016).

210 For an example of the signatures of Muslim traders on a declarations, see figure 8.

211 See p. 89.

212 Van den Boogert, *The capitulations*, p. 43.

213 Mohammad H. Kamali, 'Fundamental rights of the individual: An analysis of *haqq* (right) in Islamic law', *American journal of Islamic social sciences*, 10:3 (1993): pp. 340–366. The concept of *ḥaqq* has several meanings, including 'established fact', 'right, power or claim', 'certainty or proof'. In the legal context, its primary meaning is 'truth' and reflects a positive assertion of an individual right, given by a lawgiver and attributable if it can be proven. Right of ownership, for instance, is a typical *ḥaqq*, considered an exclusive assignment. Kamali, 'Fundamental rights', pp. 342–345.

214 Lawrence Rosen, *The anthropology of justice. Law as culture in Islamic society* (Cambridge, 1989), pp. 16–17.

using Rosen's insights, steers his analysis in a similar direction by arguing that 'if the main function of the court is the regulation of reciprocity among members of the community, as Rosen argues, then mediation and arbitration are the primary means to achieve it'.[215] This quote could just as easily have been applicable to the nature of the European consular court system, whose task was essentially the same – considering the centrality of reciprocal interest in the concept of the merchants' style and the mechanisms that regulated the relationships between merchants.

While the consular court archives from Izmir do not contain litigations involving Muslim Ottomans, as such cases would have been brought before an Ottoman court, the archives of the consular court contain documents belonging to a debt affair that provides a glimpse into how one Muslim Ottoman attempted to obtain satisfaction for money owed to him. In 1765, Mehmed Araboğlu, a Muslim Ottoman gentleman who resided in Bergama, near Izmir, was owed 500 lion dollars by the Tuscan merchant Pietro Ferrieri. He accused the Tuscan of deceiving him by breaking his word and suggested this practice could have serious consequences, with 'no one trusting the Frankish nations to give them merchandise'.[216] While Araboğlu claimed to have a great friendship with Consul Daniel Jean de Hochepied, he felt he also needed to insist on receiving his money back.[217]

To obtain satisfaction, Araboğlu refused to release an obligation belonging to 'Capirossi', probably Orazio Gaetano Capirossi, Tuscan chancellor at the time. Araboğlu had also sequestered goods located in Çandarlı belonging to a Dutch merchant, Pieter Ouckama, and he had Ouckama's Jewish *sensal* arrested.[218] This alarmed the Dutch consul, who made an effort to protect Ouckama's interests. Letters were sent back-and-forth, translated from and to Turkish, some of them given to a janissary named 'Ali Başa, who travelled between Izmir and Bergama, for delivery to Araboğlu. Several letters were sent to other persons in Bergama, who were thought to have an influence over Araboğlu, to try to convince him to release the sequestered goods as well as the *sensal*.[219]

215 Ergene, *Local court*, p. 193.

216 NACS, N°332, 'Translaat copije der brieff van Arab Oglu met de janitsar Allj Bassa weegens d'affairen van Ouckama & C° aug: 1765', S.l., S.d., '[...] alla Nazione Franca nisuno non fida a dare mercanzie [...]'.

217 Ibid.

218 A *sensal* was a middleman in trade; see p. 78.

219 NACS, N°332, 'Copije der brief int Turks geschreven aen Kútschuk Aga', Izmir, 11/09/1765, 'Copije brief van de heeren consul assessooren en cooplieden van de Nederlandse natie aen Monsr Etienne in Sanderlk [Çandarlı near Izmir] weeg: d'affairen van de hn Ouckama & C° met Arab Oglu', Izmir', 11/09/1765; and 'Copije translaet der brieff aen Arab Oglou met sig: Masgana', Izmir, [?]/11/1765.

Ouckama had also contacted correspondents in Bergama, who explained that Ferrieri would need to pay or nothing could be done. Once Ferrieri reimbursed Araboğlu, all remaining issues between the Europeans could be settled in Izmir 'by way of justice and according to our capitulations, and who is in the wrong will pay the penalty'.[220] Central to the argument developed by the Dutch consul was that Araboğlu, in his attempt to obtain satisfaction, had resorted to a form of community responsibility: rather than taking Ferrieri to an Ottoman court, he had sequestered goods of subjects belonging to the same nation – or at least he thought he had. Ferrieri was Tuscan, Capirossi as well, and the Tuscan merchants stood under protection of the Dutch consulate at the time, so for Araboğlu, they fell under the same jurisdiction as Ouckama, who was Dutch. In a reply to the Ağa of Çandarlı, who was thought to have influence over Araboğlu, the consul did not question the sequester as a means to obtain reimbursement in itself, but he argued that it was applied to the wrong person, 'as one [Ouckama] is Dutch and the other imperial [Ferrieri], one has nothing to do with the other and you, perfectly aware of the merchants' style for having dealt with many affairs, you know very well that this is not right'.[221]

In a letter sent the same day to a Frenchman in Çandarlı, Consul de Hochepied, his assessors and the community of Dutch merchants of Izmir wrote that they had only suggested to Araboğlu to seek recourse to an Ottoman court so he could seek reimbursement through Ottoman adjudication on the basis of Ottoman equity.[222] At no moment were Araboğlu or the Ağa of Çandarlı considered strangers to the informal laws and usages governing international trade. In letters addressed to them, terms such as equity and justice were mentioned, as well as the merchants' style, and the context or meaning was no different than when these concepts were used in a purely European context of litigation. When Araboğlu resorted to the common legal action of sequestering goods, he justified his actions with the principle of liability through collective responsibility, the mechanism in itself was not questioned by the Dutch diplomats. This might have been a strategic choice, as it was, admittedly, a bit outdated by the mid-eighteenth century, but forms of collective liability had

220 NACS, N°332, 'Andrea Cardona aen dh: Ouckama in Smirne', Bergama, 14/08/1765, '[…] con via di giustizia e secondo nostre capitulationi, e chi avera torto paghera la pena […]'.

221 NACS, N°332, 'Copije der brief int Turks geschreven aen Kútschuk Aga', Izmir, 11/09/1765, '[…] come l'uno [Ouckama] è olandese ed l'altro imperiale [Ferrieri], l'uno non a che fare con l'altro ed voi, cognoscendo perfettamente il stile mercantile pr aver trattato molti affari sapete molto bene, che questo non è giusto […]'. Nominally, the Grand Duchy of Tuscany fell under the Holy Roman Empire, making Ferrieri indeed an imperial subject.

222 NACS, N°332, 'Copije brief van de heeren consul assessooren en cooplieden van de Nederlandse natie', Izmir, 11/09/1765.

not fully disappeared from commercial custom.[223] The sequester of Ouckama's goods was questioned because of jurisdiction, not out of a fundamental misinterpretation of legal custom.

In the end, the *sensal* and Capirossi's obligation were released, but the sequester of Ouckama's goods remained unresolved. Ferrieri was given eight months to pay, in which time he hoped his uncle, arriving from Livorno, could ensure him the necessary funds.[224] Muslim Ottomans, who could resort simply to Ottoman justice, were willing to communicate with European consuls on legality and the merchants' style, and they even adhered to similar mechanisms that had been in use to solve commercial disputes. Araboğlu showed, in the two letters he wrote and that were translated in Italian, that he was indeed fully aware of the merchants' style. He referred to name and reputation as very important commodities for traders.[225] Ferrieri was equally aware of it, and he wrote a lengthy and secretive letter to a certain Andrea Cardona in Bergama, who had to deliver a message to Araboğlu for him, in which he asked to give him time to pay and to release Capirossi's and Ouckama's belongings. He also considered the debt 'a futility' ('una bagatella') and feared the actions of Araboğlu might lead to the end of all of Ferrieri's business in Christian lands, while, with a little bit of time, he could, with the assistance of friends, reestablish himself with more honour.[226] It was a matter of commercial life or death for him, and Ferrieri realised that his name as well as his commercial reputation was at stake.[227] The means that Araboğlu used affected Ferrieri's relationship with his diplomatic representative, de Hochepied, who apparently had threatened to throw Ferrieri in prison. Additionally, Ferrieri's inability to fulfil his obligations had negative consequences for his fellow traders.

While the letters pertaining to this quarrel preserved in the archives of the Dutch consulate of Izmir indicate that an agreement was reached, it still meant that Ferrieri had to pay and that Araboğlu had to wait. A second set of documents kept in the archives of the Dutch embassy in Istanbul suggests that

---

223 See pp. 207–208.

224 NACS, N°332, 'Translaat copye der briefj van Araboglú aen den heere consul met sig. Masgana', [Bergama], 25/09/1765; and 'Translaat der Turkse brieff aan Araboglú met dhr Ouckama & de can: Mann afgegaan', [Bergama], 03/10/1765. Araboğlu's frequent references to 'obligations', not just in the technical sense of a financial obligation but more generally as well, are reminiscent of the *ḥaqq* concept discussed earlier.

225 NACS, N°332, 'Translaat copije der brieff van Arab Oglu met de janitsar Allj Bassa weegens d'affairen van Ouckama & C° aug: 1765', S.l., S.d.

226 NACS, N°332, 'Copije van een brief van P: Ferrieri aen Andrea Cardona in Bergamo', Izmir, 22/08/1765.

227 Ibid.

Araboğlu was not able to remain patient. About five months after the agreement with Ferrieri had been reached, a memorandum was sent to the Porte, which stated that the Ottoman was harassing Ferrieri, not letting him breathe, bringing the Tuscan to bankruptcy. Even though Araboğlu had been ordered by a *ferman* to keep quiet and wait for Ferrieri's payment, he had defied such orders by molesting the imperial vice-consul (Daniel Jean de Hochepied), the chancellor and Ferrieri, who was thrown in prison. Araboğlu even threatened to publicly disrepute the vice-consul. The memorandum, unsigned but in all likelihood written by someone at the imperial vice-consulate, probably in the name of the vice-consul, asked for a second *ferman* to control Araboğlu's actions. It reminded the sultan of the principle of reciprocity by stating that

> I can assure the Sublime Porte that in Vienna, and in all of Germany, as well as in Hungary and Tuscany, many Turkish traders can be found, subjects of the Porte, amongst whom many are indebted to various German merchants, and some of them who cannot satisfy their debts flee, while others declare bankruptcy; but this does not mean that my Porte allows ours to attack other Turkish merchants or subjects of the Porte, to ask them reimbursement of the debts of those who fled or declared bankruptcy, as that would go against all the capitulations, and all justice, and our capitulations are reciprocal in all its articles, I am convinced that the Sublime Porte will not allow that his subjects act against the tenor of them and commit similar illicit excesses as those that the voivode of Bergama dares threaten to commit.[228]

The memorandum argues that forms of collective responsibility were indeed outdated and that rulers in Europe would not resort to such a mechanism.

---

228 NALT, N°1262 ('Affaire du négociant Ferrieri à Smyrne avec le voivode Arabzade de Pergame Dedel. NB tocca le affare di Smirne per Ferieri 1 iuglio 1766'), 'Memoria alla fulgida Pte. Ottma.', S.l., S.d., '[…] mentre posso assicurare la fulgida Porta, che tanto à Vienna ed in tutta la Germania, quanto in Hungaria e nella Toscana si trovano moltissimi mercanti Turchi, e suddite della Porta, frà li quali molti hanno contrattati debite con differente sudditi e mercanti Todeschi, e non potendo sodisfare li loro debiti sono parte fuggiti, parte falliti; mà non per questo la mia Porte hà permesso ai nostri, di atttaccare altri mercanti Turchi, o sudditi della Porta, per dimandare da loro il pagamento delle debiti dei fuggitivi o falliti, mentre questo sarebbe un agire contro le capitolazioni, ed contro ogni giustizia, e le nostre capitolazioni essendo reciproche in tutti li articoli, sono più che sicuro, che nemeno la fulgida Porta permetterà, che li suoi dipendenti agischino contro il tenore di quelle, e commettino simili illeciti Eccessi, delle quale ardisce minacciare il voivoda di Bergamo […]'.

While Araboğlu's actions can thus be considered not only as an infraction against the capitulations, a common argument used by European diplomats when trying to counteract Ottoman actions they felt were against the interest of their subjects, they can also be considered as violating the merchants' style in the sense that these actions can be interpreted as fitting within a mechanism of collective liability that in medieval times was an element of mercantile custom, but could no longer be considered as such in the second half of the eighteenth century. Araboğlu's actions should thus not be interpreted as belonging to a system unacquainted with or hostile to the merchants' style per se but should be seen as evidence that the content of the merchants' style is subject to change over time.

It seems only logical that the elements belonging to an international and informal set of customs used by merchants are disputed at times, which is part of the reason why adjudication was done by peers and relied on the use of *turben* in which peers explain what did belong to the merchants' style. But such mechanisms were harder to use in the Ottoman context, particularly considering the lack of use of European evidence. The Porte did, however, issue a second *ferman* in which Araboğlu's actions were condemned as going against all laws and rights, as well as against the tenor of the 'sacred capitulations'.[229] It would have pleased all adherents of the merchants' style to read that in justifying the *ferman*, one of the most essential characteristics of commercial custom was used: it was pointed out that Araboğlu had no right to seek satisfaction from Ferrieri through third persons, as he had 'put trust in the said merchants of his own spontaneous will'.[230] While the documentation belonging to one particular quarrel involving a Muslim Ottoman cannot serve as definitive evidence of Muslim adherence to the merchants' style, the reasoning used by all parties allows for the suggestion that Muslim Ottomans were willing to discuss disputes in terms dictated by the merchants' style.

229 NALT, N°1262, 'Traduzione di fermano toccante il Ferieri', Istanbul, 30/06/1766, '[...] sacri capitolazioni [...]'.

230 Ibid., '[...] di sua spontanea volontà mise nel sudetto mercante confidenza [...]'.

Conclusion

In May 1769, an Armenian merchant named Beniat di Eghia initiated a lawsuit before the Dutch consul in Izmir against a Dutch skipper named Jan Theodorus. The two men had signed a contract in which di Eghia promised to supply Theodorus with several bales of raw cotton from Kırkağaç in western Anatolia.[1] When di Eghia allowed Theodorus to inspect the cotton, the skipper invoked the assistance of a fellow merchant, who marked the bales according to their quality. Following this selection, the Dutch skipper refused several bales of the cotton that he considered too low in quality. Di Eghia protested and wanted Theodorus to take all of the cotton, on the grounds that by having them marked, he had accepted them. Di Eghia addressed himself to all reasonable merchants in Izmir, of every nation, to do him justice by confirming that it was not permitted to examine and mark bales without taking them afterwards.[2] Theodorus' reply was straightforward. He wanted di Eghia to obey the terms of the contract, which specified the delivery of cotton of a certain quality, and he was willing to submit himself to the judgment of three neutral persons who, on the consul's authorisation, should re-examine the thirty-seven bales he already had examined. Di Eghia, however, refused arbitration.[3] As was common in commercial disputes, both parties substantiated their arguments with declarations by their peers confirming their position. This case contained three such documents (in Dutch labelled as *casusposities*), in which the marking of merchandise was rendered an abstract problem by labelling the litigants 'A' and 'B' or 'Marco' and 'Antonio'.[4] The different declarations did not agree, as one, signed by eleven firms, argued that Jan Theodorus had the right to cancel the contract, particularly following di Eghia's refusal at arbitration, while another, signed by twelve firms, argued that, according to 'the merchants' style' ('l'uso mercantile') and the 'rule of commerce' ('regola di commercio'), the

1 NACS, N°342 ('Benjat di der Eghia, Armeens koopman te Smyrna, tegen Jan Theodorusz, kapitein van het Nederlandse schip Archipel, 1769'), 'Protest van Benjat di der Eghia aen capt Jan Theodorus weg het merken eenige baelen cattoenen &a', Izmir, 16/05/1769.

2 Ibid.

3 NACS, N°342, 'Antwoord van capt Jan Theodorus weegens het merken eenigen b cattoen aen Benjant der Eghia &a', Izmir, 16/05/1769.

4 NACS, N°342, 'Parere over de differentie tusschen capt Jan Theodorus & Benjat di der Eghia weegens een parthij cattoene', Izmir, 20/05/1769, 'Parere di Benjat weeg: de cat: met capt Theodorus', [Izmir], [20/05/1769]; and 'Nog een parere van zijde van capt Theodorus weegens de catt van Benjat', Izmir, 20/05/1769. The declarations were signed by several European and Ottoman firms.

skipper had to accept the bales because they had been marked. A third declaration, signed by four merchant firms, took Theodorus' side.[5]

It is unclear whether anything happened following these statements, but a few days after they had been delivered at the chancery of the Dutch consulate in Izmir, di Eghia sent a letter to the consul, treasurer and assessors of the Dutch nation to complain about Theodorus' approach to the case: 'who has ever in his life heard of such behaviour, but I am informed that the captain does not want to have this case judged according to the merchants' style and according to the use of the traders in this city, but seeks a way out following the laws of Turkish justice'.[6] Di Eghia continued by stating that, even though he was an Ottoman subject who was also willing to obey Ottoman justice, he preferred to be sentenced according to the 'customs and usages of the merchants'.[7] He also stated that he refused the re-examination of the cotton because they had already been examined by a famous expert, Mister Manolaki.[8] He felt he had observed all that was customary in these cases, and he felt Theodorus should not be allowed to 'bring a new style in an old city, bringing shame to the seller without any legal reason'.[9]

It seems the consul and assessors did not know how to sentence this case, and they opted for the case to be examined by four neutral merchants. Each litigant had to choose two names out of the firms that had signed the declarations on their behalf. The reason given for this solution was that the consul and assessors 'found the affair in question without precedent and the sentiments of the merchants differ greatly on the same matter, so we did not want to decide'.[10] The Dutch skipper chose merchants from France and Ragusa, while the Armenian trader opted for English and Livornese traders. These four merchants gave the sentence that an experienced cotton merchant had to examine the bales of cotton, and the Dutch skipper had to accept all the bales that

5 Ibid.

6 NACS, N°342, 'Antwoord van Benjant aen capt Theod', Izmir, 24/05/1769, '[...] en wie heefd ooit van zyn leeven zo'n gedrag gehoort maar ik verneem, als dat de capt deeze zaak niet naa de koopmansstyl wil afgemaakt hebben, & volgens t'gebruik der negotiaante te deezer steede, maar den uitvlugt zoekt naa de wette & regt vande Turkse justitie [...]'.

7 Ibid., '[...] de gewoonte x usantie der negotiaante [...]'.

8 Ibid. Perhaps this was Manolaki di Panaiotis.

9 Ibid., '[...] het staat haar niet toe een nieuwe moode in een oude stad te bouwen en daar meede een schande aan den verkooper opbrengen, zonder een wettige reeden te hebben [...]'.

10 NACS, N°342, 'Vonnis tot overgeeving der proces van Benjat & capt J.T. weeg: eenige cattoen', Izmir, 27/05/1769, '[...] en vindende de saeke in questie sonder voorbeeld, en op een x de selve saeke de sentimenten der cooplieden soo verschillende, hebben wij daer op niet willen disponneeren [...]'.

this examiner would judge to be of sufficient quality.[11] After this final sentence, the quarrel disappeared from the consular archives, so it remains a mystery whether the experienced cotton merchant came up with an assessment that was acceptable to both litigants, but this case nonetheless contains all the elements that confirm this book's hypothesis.

This book has set out to demonstrate that in places in which trade was essentially cross-cultural, legal institutions existed to adjudicate commercial disputes. These institutions were installed and regulated by governments, sanctioned by official regulations, and relied on the use of summary procedure and legal arguing on the basis of the merchant's style.Consular adjudication of disputes between traders in eighteenth-century Izmir was done according to the rules that were customary amongst merchants, summarised in the concept of the merchant's style. Merchants were aware of its existence and referred to it in their written argumentation before court. If necessary, their peers confirmed certain rules through written expert statements, or *turben*. Cases in which the consul had doubts, he referred them to be judged by merchants – he would never invoke a Dutch law or his own legal authority to sentence a case. The government's law was only ever applied to set up the legal framework within which adjudication was possible, and in the case of Izmir, this framework had two lawmakers, as consular legal authority was given through the Ottoman capitulations by the sultan, while Dutch regulations allowed then for the consul, assisted by merchants, to adjudicate disputes according to summary procedure, following merchant custom.

The reliance on the merchants' style was the main reason why the consul, who was not a merchant, was assisted by merchants who would help him reach a verdict. As the Dutch community in Izmir was small and confined to a particular part of the city, merchants knew each other, and of each other, rendering the advice of fellow traders even more pertinent, while also creating a potential problem of a conflict of interest. This explains the regular recourse to have foreign traders confirm custom, and this is also why the assessors had to swear an oath promising to be impartial. While motivations for gaining a competitive advantage cannot be completely excluded from being behind the sentencing of the assessors, the fact that they operated in a commercial culture in which it was almost a deadly sin to pursue one's individual profit at the expense of mutual interest, it was a risky endeavour to try to manipulate a verdict to harm a competitor.

11 NACS, N°342, 'Sententies soo arbitraal als finaal in de differentie tusschen capt Th & Benjat', Izmir, 01/06/1769.

Often, litigants did not share the same nationality and fell under a different jurisdiction. This was solved by formal and informal agreements based on shared principles, such as *forum rei*, to ensure the international applicability of courts. Beyond determining who was to be tried where, different nationalities or religious affiliations played little to no role in the adjudicating process. What bound litigants together, their profession as merchants, was bigger than what separated them. Litigants such as Gerrit van Brakel, who attempted to gain an advantage in court by lamenting that he, a European, was poorly treated by the consul in a case against Ottomans, were quickly put in their place and reminded that nationality was not relevant but adherence to commercial custom was.

As demonstrated by the quarrel between Theodorus and di Eghia, litigants often invoked the merchants' style. Often, they referred to the reason and equity they felt were essential components of the merchants' style. While there is no a priori reason to assume that reason and equity are universal, or that geographical or cultural differences disappear in light of them, the analysis of concrete court cases between merchants of varying backgrounds confirms that commercial custom, as it was upheld in an international port city such as Izmir, was surprisingly unhindered by borders of geography, culture or religion.

Ottoman subjects who were not Muslim had some space to adjudicate before a European court, particularly if they had purchased *beratlı* status allowing them to appear as defendant before a European court, but as the case between di Eghia and Theodorus shows, Ottoman merchants decided to subject themselves to European adjudication. This did not mean, however, that they did not opt for Ottoman courts nor that these were by definition less able to adjudicate commercial disputes. A reliance on summary procedure and commercial custom has generally been considered as European, and proof of European institutional advance that allowed for the development of early modern capitalism, but on several occasions, Dutch diplomats referred to Ottoman procedures aimed at swift sentencing. Ottoman courts were well-equipped to adjudicate commercial disputes in a similar summary manner. Dutch merchants traded with Ottoman Muslims, and there are some indications that they were well aware of the merchants' style and some of its central characteristics, such as reputation. In the case of a Tuscan trader who was indebted to Mehmed Araboğlu, an Ottoman Muslim, the latter wrote a letter to the Dutch consul in Izmir in which he remarked that 'the name that they [the merchants] carry, is like a true god'.[12] He was not exaggerating all that much, considering the

12 NACS, N°332, 'Translaat copije der brieff van Arab Oglu met de janitsar Allj Bassa weegens d'affairen van Ouckama & C° aug: 1765', S.l., S.d., '[…] il nome loro riguarda è como iddio vero […]'.

lengthy and emotional replies and counter-replies merchants addressed to the court in an effort to save their reputation or that of their peers when a power of attorney demanded them to do so. In a world in which success in trade greatly depended on the maintenance of correspondence, credit and reputation, it was the reasonable thing to do.

Bibliography

1 Websites

https://configmed.hypotheses.org/.

Inventory of the Archive 'Desolate Boedelskamer' in the City Archive Amsterdam. Consulted online at https://archief.amsterdam/inventarissen/printversie/5072.nl.pdf.

http://www.levantineheritage.com/pdf/The_Van_Lennep_Genealogy_Smyrna_Branch.pdf.

https://www.rijksmuseum.nl/en/collection/SK-A-4127.

'Crawley, Samuel (1705–1762)', *Oxford Dictionary of National Biography*, consulted at http://www.oxforddnb.com/view/10.1093/ref:odnb/9780198614128.001.0001/odnb-9780198614128-e-109573.

http://www.levantineheritage.com/reg2.htm.

http://www.thelatinlibrary.com/justinian.html.

'Actor sequitur forum rei'. In *Guide to Latin in International Law*, edited by Aaron X. Fellmeth and Maurice Horwitz. Oxford, 2009. Consulted online at http://www.oxfordreference.com/view/10.1093/acref/9780195369380.001.0001/acref-9780195369380-e-76.

2 Archival Material

2.1 *Archivio di Stato di Trieste*

Deputazione di Borsa poi Camera di Commercio e d'Industria di Trieste (1755–1921). Serie 7: Carteggio CXXX, 'Comunicazione del C.R. Governo della sostituzione, visti i rapporti tra la corte di Vienna e la Repubblica d'Olanda', 1784.

2.2 *Archives Départementales Marseille*

ADM, XIII B 421, 'Verbaux et rapports divers' (1772).

2.3 *City Archives Amsterdam* (CAA)

Archief van de familie de Vogel en aanverwante families (CAA/ADV) (N°332)

N°36 ('Kopieboek', 1758–1759).

N°76 ('Factuurboek Thomas de Vogel & Zoon', 1756–1765).

N°85 ('Stukken betreffende de pretentie der compagnie op Missir di Eghia te Smirna').

N°87 ('Redersboek van het schip De Vogel Phenix', 1752–1758).

Archief van de Portugees-Israëlietische Gemeente (N°334)

N°s 875–877 ('Livros de citaçoes e resoluçoes', 1717–1816).

N°s 878–880 ('Uitspraken inzake schikkingen door de parnassim in zaken die door de stedelijke Commissarissen van Kleine Zaken aan parnassim gerenvoyeerd', 1710–1806).

Archief Hope & C° (N°735)

N°s 1404–1407 ('Registers van verstrekte inlichtingen over handelshuizen in binnen- en buitenland. Met indexen', 1778-1819).

Archieven van de schout en schepenen, van de schepenen en van de subalterne rechtbanken (N°5061)

N°2490 ('Rol voor Commissarissen van de Zeezaken', 21/03/1641–07/09/1641).

Archieven van de Commissarissen van de Desolate Boedelskamer (N°5072)

N°3139 ('Philip Ludwig Bernhard', 1779).

N°3536 ('Philip Ludwig Bernhard', 1782).

N°3764 ('Maria Agnes Offerman en Christoph Engler', 1784).

Archief der notarissen standplaats Amsterdam (N°5075)

Salomon Dorper, N°10812 ('Minuutacten', 01/11/1763–31/12/1763).

2.4 *National Archives The Hague* (NA)

Archief van de Staten-Generaal (1.01.02) (NASG)

N°12561.151.4 ('Stukken betreffende het verlenen van convooi aan Hamburgse schepen varende op de Middellandse Zee, 1664').

N°12550.123 ('Stukken betreffende de geschillen tussen de Directeuren van de Levantse Handel en Gerardus Smits, gewezen consul te Smyrna, over nalatigheid in zijn functie, 1666').

N°6913 ('Ingekomen ordinaris brieven en stukken van vorstelijke personen, gezanten, enz. betreffende Italië, Turkije en de Barbarijnse Staten Algiers, Marokko, Tripoli en Tunis, 1596–1796').

Archief van de Legatie bij de Duitse Keizer (1.02.05)

N°134 ('Stukken betreffende een vordering van Cornelis van der Oudermeulen, koopman in Amsterdam, op Begler de Joseph in Triëst, gewezen Grieks koopman in Smyrna, 1755–1757').

Archief van de Legatie in Turkije (1.02.20) (NALT)

N°626 ('Memoire par les affaires des barataires de Scio').

N°1262 ('Affaire du négociant Ferrieri à Smyrne avec le voivode Arabzade de Pergame Dedel. NB tocca le affare di Smirne per Ferieri 1 iuglio 1766').

N°1274 ('Pièces relatives au procès entre Hagi Nicola Papasoglou barattaire de Raguse mon beau fils Anastasio di Giovanni barattaire de Holl.de à Salonique, 1787').

Archief van het Nederlandse Consulaat te Smyrna (1.02.22) (NACS)

N°14 ('Uitgaande brieven, 1766–1774').

N°30 ('Brieven en extract-resoluties Staten-Generaal').

N°162 ('Minuten kanselarij, 1766').

N°204 ('Register der Nederlandsche kanzelary te Smyrna gehouden door den heer kanzelier Johann Fred.r Mann begonnen den 3 January 1764. Geeindigd den 4 april 1765').

N°223 ('Papieren raakende de Grieken met de Franken weegens trouw & veranderen der religie &c in maend meij 1767 t'laeste 25d').

N°225 ('Proces tusschen Ml Kco di Panajottis & Jacob de Vogel aengaende eene avania van 1770 tot 16 maert 1773').

N°229 ('Stukken betreffende de schulden van de kanselier Gerrit van Brakel en diens tijdelijke schorsingen, 1770 & 1804').

N°240 ('Matheus di Ovan, Armeens koopman, uit Amsterdam naar Smyrna gevlucht, 1754').

N°254 ('Stukken betreffende faillissementen. Pieter Ouckama, Nederlands koopman te Smyrna, 1769').

N°255 ('Stukken betreffende faillissementen. Clement, van Sanen & van der Zee, Nederlandse kooplieden te Smyrna, 1779').

N°316 ('Alle de stukken rakende de zaken van capt. Cornelis Volkers van t fluijtschip de Soffia en Caterina, en sig. Gasparo Maria Marchetti Messiness adi ... stemb. tot 3 october 1743').

N°317 ('Stukken rakende het voldongen proces tusschen Seguier pere x fils en Giuseppe en Gio Carlo Giera, 1745').

N°318 ('Belcamp, Begler en Clement, Nederlandse kooplieden te Smyrna en Crisoganni en Curmusi, Griekse kooplieden te Smyrna tegen Reyer Hoogtreed, kapitein van het Nederlandse schip Santa Maria, 1747').

N°324 ('Papieren der proces van Manolachi de Panajottis x Panajotti Pittaco, welke door den Grieksen bischop zijn uijtgesprooken & de sententie in de Franse cancellerij berust, sonder ter deeser cancellerij te zijn vertoond, 1761').

N°330 ('Stukken raakende de proces van Clement van Sanen van der Zee & C° als procurateuren vand heeren Wynants & Cramer d'Amsterdam teegens de heer Ouckama & C° alhier weegen 36 b verongelukte catt: in de brand van 6 aug l.l. van 17 jan: tot 21 juny anno 1764').

N°332 ('Brieven wegens de zaak tusschen Arab Ogloe & Ouckama').

N°333 ('Documenten van de proces tusschen Clement van Sanen van der Zee & C° & Th:s de Vogel over een parthij tabak &a begonnen 1764 eijndigt 11 febr 1765').

N°336 ('Ouckama & C°, Nederlandse kooplieden te Smyrna, tegen A. Musquetier, koopman te Leiden, 1766').

N°337 ('Proces Tusschen Capirossi & Francois Siquard & C° van 21 feb 1766 tot 30 maert 1767').

N°339 ('Gerrit van Brakel, Nederlands koopman te Smyrna, optredende namens Jacques Forêt te Luik tegen Dirk Knipping, Nederlands koopman te Smyrna, 1767').

N°342 ('Benjat di der Eghia, Armeens koopman te Smyrna, tegen Jan Theodorusz, kapitein van het Nederlandse schip Archipel, 1769').

N°343 ('Papieren aangaande de process tusschen Alexander x Sottira x Gerrit van Brakel geboekt off geregistreerd op f°332 tot 345, 1769').
N°345 ('Copye der documenten van D. Knipping teegens H. v. Coopstad in faveur van G. v. Brakel in Smirna').
N°346 ('Proces tusschen de heeren M: K:r di Panajottis en haar schrijver Joh: Boonhoff van 6 tot 13 april 1770').
N°347 ('Massé di Carabeth, Armeens koopman te Smyrna, tegen zijn broer Caspar di Carabeth, 1770').
N°348 ('Proces van N: van der Zee & C° voor Clement, van Sanen, van der Zee & C° met A: Wissing van 25 maert tot xbr. 1771').
N°349 ('Papieren der proces tusschen Fremeaux & Heffert, 19/02/1770–19/03/1771').
N°354 ('André Chabeaud & C°, Franse kooplieden te Smyrna, tegen Daniel Fremeaux & C°, optredend namens de weduwe Offerman & C° te Amsterdam, 1772–1773').
N°356 ('Proces stukken tusschen Gebroeders de Vogel & Comp als procureurs van Jan Ackerman & Z6oon in Amsterdam & Ml Kiriaco di Panajotti & Comp, begonnen 24/01/1775 gaande tot 06/11/1775').
N°357 ('Affairen tusschen Pietro Ferrieri & Dirk Knipping').
N°383 ('Paulo Poma, Grieks koopman te Smyrna, tegen Giovanni Lorenzo Giera, Toscaans koopman te Smyrna, 1790').
N°396 ('Gian Carlo Giera, Toscaans koopman te Smyrna, tegen Govert Swenson, kapitein van het Nederlandse schip Clasina, 1792').
N°454 ('Jean Laurent Giera, Toscaans koopman te Smyrna, tegen Daniel Fremeaux & Co., 1806').
N°490 ('Register van uitgaande brieven van het handelshuis Knipping & Ouckama, 1759–1761').
N°498 ('Volmacht van Looy & van Spaen te Rotterdam voor Pieter Ouckama om gelden te innen die Dirk Knipping nog onder zich heeft uit de boedel van Knipping & Ouckama', Rotterdam, 02/04/1762).

Archief van de Directie van de Levantse Handel en de Navigatie in de Middellandse Zee (1.03.01) (NALH)

'Directie Amsterdam', N°1 ('Resolutieboek', 04/10/1627–21/12/1663).
'Directie Amsterdam', N°73 ('Remonstrantieboek', 1627–1649).
'Directie Amsterdam', N°86 ('Nominatieboek', 1625–1800).
'Directie Amsterdam', N°161 ('Brieven van de vertegenwoordigers te Constantinopel, van de consuls en andere ambtenaren in de Levant en langs de Middellandse Zee. Aleppo en Cyprus', 1627–1826).
'Directie Amsterdam', N°238 ('Diverse stukken').

Archief van de familie de Hochepied (1.10.41)

N°101 ('Lezing, gehouden door Dr. Varenne voor de Alliance Française te Smyrna over Bonneval Pasja', S.d.).

Archief van F.G. Baron van Dedem van de Gelder (2.21.006.46)

N°2 ('Mémoire pour le commerce d'Hollande en Levant. Composé par J. Chevrier, sécretaire de S.E. Monseigneur le Baron de Hochepied, ambassadeur d'Hollande à Constantinople, fait et écrit sur les idées de mondit seigneur et par son ordre', 1754).

Archief van de Staten van Holland en West-Friesland' (3.01.04.01)

N°1357OO ('Ordonnantie van de Admiraal- Generaal en de Staten van Holland ter beveiliging van de handelsscheepvaart op het Oosten en de Sont', 1596).

Archief van het Hof van Holland (3.03.01.01) (NA/Hof)

N°1729 ('Residentieboek', 16/12/1762–24/12/1775).

Archief van de Hoge Raad van Holland, Zeeland en (West-)Friesland (3.03.02) (NA/Hoge Raad)

N°678 ('Resoluties tot de sententies', 1763–1768).

N°922 ('Register der dictums', 1761–1775).

3 Literature

Ade, Mafalda. 'The Ottoman commercial tribunal in Damascus and the use of testimony and evidence in mixed cases in the 19th century'. *Quaderni storici*, 3 (2016): pp. 649–672.

Agterhuis, Tessa. 'Tot dienst, voordeel ende proffijt van de coopluyden ende schipperen van dese landen. Nederlandse consuls in Italiaanse havens, 1612–1672.' Unpublished MA thesis, Leiden University, 2013.

Aikin, John, Thomas Morgan, and William Johnston. *General biography; or, lives, critical and historical, of the most eminent persons of all ages, countries, conditions, and professions, arranged according to alphabetical order*, vol. 8 of 10. London, 1813.

Allain, Thierry. 'L'information comme instrument de combat. Le consulat de Jacob van Dam à Smyrne (1668–1688)'. In *Les consuls en Méditerranée, agents d'information XVIe–XXe siècle*, edited by Silvia Marzagalli, pp. 81–97. Paris, 2015.

Allaire, Bernard. 'Between Oléron and Colbert: The evolution of French maritime law until the seventeenth century'. In *Labour, law, and empire: Comparative perspectives on seafarers, c. 1500–1800*, edited by Maria Fusaro, Bernard Allaire, Richard Blakemore, and Tijl Vanneste, pp. 79–99. Basingstoke, 2015.

Allgemeiner Handelstands-kalender für das Jahr 1797 welches ein gemeines Jahr von 365 Tagen ist. Wien, 1797.

Amsterdamsche courant. 21/01/1772.

Apellániz, Francisco. *Breaching the bronze wall: Franks at Mamluk and Ottoman courts and markets.* Leiden and Boston, 2020.

Apellániz, Francisco. '"You cannot produce a Muslim witness": Early Ottoman attitudes towards proof and religious difference'. In 'Litigation and the elements of proof in the Mediterranean (16th–19th C.)', edited by Wolfgang Kaiser and Johann Petitjean, *Quaderni storici*, special issue, 3 (2016): pp. 633–648.

Arbel, Benjamin. 'Jews in international trade: The emergence of the Levantine and Ponentines'. In *The Jews of early modern Venice*, edited by R.C. Davis and B. Ravid, pp. 73–96. Baltimore and London, 2001.

Arı, Bülent. 'Early Ottoman diplomacy: Ad hoc period'. In *Ottoman diplomacy: conventional or unconventional?*, edited by A. Yuri Nurdusev, pp. 36–65. Basingstoke and New York, 2004.

Arı, Bülent. 'The first Dutch ambassador in Istanbul: Cornelis Haga and the Dutch capitulations of 1612'. Unpublished PhD thesis, Bilkent University, 2003.

Artunç, Cihan. 'The price of legal institutions: Beratlı merchants in the eighteenth-century Ottoman Empire', *Journal of economic history*, 75:3 (2015): pp. 720–748.

Artunç, Cihan. 'The protégé system and berath merchants in the Ottoman Empire: The price of legal institutions'. Working paper, Yale University, 2013. Consulted online at http://www.econ.yale.edu/~egcenter/berats_third_draft.pdf.

Ascheri, Mario. *Tribunali, giuristi e istituzioni dal Medioevo all'età moderna*. Bologna, 1989.

Ashtor, Eliyahu. *Levant trade in the Middle Ages*. Princeton, 1984.

Ashtor, Eliyahu. 'Banking instruments between the Muslim east and the Christian west'. *Journal of European economic history*, 1 (1972): pp. 553–573.

Aslanian, Sebouh. 'The "quintessential locus of brokerage": Letters of recommendations, networks, and mobility in the life of Thomas Vanandets'i, an Armenian printer in Amsterdam, 1677–1707'. *Journal of world history*, 31:4 (2020): pp. 655–692.

Aslanian, Sebouh. *From the Indian Ocean to the Mediterranean: The global trade networks of Armenian merchants from New Julfa*. Berkeley and New York, 2011.

Aukema, M. 'Andere tijden. Boedelafwikkeling in de 17e en 18e eeuw'. In *De integere curator – Insolad jaarboek 2007*, edited by M.L.S. Kalff, R. Mulder, and S.H. de Ranitz, pp. 13–26. Deventer, 2007.

Baker, J.H. 'The law merchant and the common law before 1700'. *The Cambridge law journal*, 38:2 (1979): pp. 295–322.

Barbier de Meynard, A.C. *Dictionnaire turc-français*, 2 vols. Paris, 1886.

Barels, J.M. *Advysen over den koophandel en zeevaert. Mitsgaders verscheidene turbes, memorien, resolutien, missives enz. enz. daer toe behoorende*. 2 vols. Amsterdam, 1781.

Bartoletti, Carolina. *Memoria per la signora Carolina Bartoletti vedova Giera, sacerdote sig. Luigi Cartacci suo maestro di casa e Maddalena Melani sua cameriera nella causa di preteso furto avanti la r. ruote criminale di Firenze*. Livorno, 1818.

Bartolomei, Arnaud. 'Introduction'. In *De l'utilité commerciale des consuls. L'institution consulaire et les marchands dans le monde méditerranéen*, edited by A. Bartolomei, G. Calafat, M. Grenet, and J. Ulbert, pp. 9–18. Rome and Madrid, 2017.

Bartolomei, Arnaud, Guillaume Calafat, Mathieu Grenet, and Jörg Ulbert, eds. *De l'utilité commerciale des consuls. L'institutions consulaire et les marchands dans le monde méditerranéen (XVIIe–Xxe siècle)*. Rome and Madrid, 2017.

Bartolomei, Arnaud. 'Actes notariés *versus* actes de chancellerie. Le rôle des chancelleries consulaires françaises dans la formalisation des actes commerciaux et civils (XVIIIe–XIXe siècle). *Mélanges de l'École française de Rome – Italie et Méditerranée modernes et contemporaines*, 128:2 (2016). Consulted online at https://journals.openedition.org/mefrim/2801?lang=it.

Bekius, René Arthur. 'The Armenian colony in Amsterdam in the seventeenth and eighteenth centuries: Armenian merchants from Julfa before and after the fall of the Safavid Empire'. In *Iran and the world in the Safavid age*, edited by Willem Floor and Edmund Herzig, pp. 259–284. London and New York, 2012.

Bekius, René. 'Avet Jeremias. Een Levantijns koopman in achttiende-eeuws Amsterdam'. In *De Nederlands-Turkse betrekkingen,* edited by Maurits van den Boogert and Jan Jonker Roelants, pp. 65–69. Hilversum, 2012.

Bellomo, Manlio. *The common legal past of Europe 1000–1800*. Washington DC, 1995.

Ben-Porath, Yoram. 'The F-connection: Families, friends, and firms and the organization of exchange'. *Population and development review*, 6:1 (1980): pp. 1–30.

Berkovitch, Barry M. *The Cape gunsmith: A history of the gunsmiths and gun dealers at the Cape of Good Hope from 1795 to 1900, with particular reference to their weapons.* Stellenbosch, 1976.

Berman, Harold J. *Law and revolution: The formation of the western legal tradition.* Cambridge, MA, 1983.

Bernstein, Lisa. 'Opting out of the legal system: Extralegal contractual relations in the diamond industry'. *Journal of legal studies*, 21:1 (1992): pp. 115–157.

Bethencourt, Francisco, and Florike Egmond. *Correspondence and cultural exchange in Europe, 1400–1700*. Vol. 3 of *Cultural exchange in early modern Europe*. Cambridge, 2007.

Bezemer, C.H. 'Tussen wal en schip. Het wisselrecht ten tijde van de Republiek der Verenigde Nederlanden'. *BW-krant jaarboek*, 29 (2015): pp. 21–33.

Bianchi, T.X. *Le nouveau guide de la conversation en français et en turc*. Paris, 1852.

Bijl, Arie. *De Nederlandse convooidienst. De maritieme bescherming van koopvaardij en zeevisserij tegen piraten en oorlogsgevaar in het verleden*. The Hague, 1951.

Billioud, Joseph, and Raymond Collier. *Histoire du commerce de Marseille: de 1480 à 1599*. Vol. 3 of *Histoire du commerce de Marseille*, edited by Gaston Rambert. Paris, 1951.

Black, Christopher F. *Early modern Italy: A social history*. London and New York, 2001.

Blom, Hans. 'The meaning of trust: Fides between self-interest and *appetitus societatis*'. In *The roots of international law/Les fondements du droit international. Liber amicorum Peter Haggenmacher*, edited by Pierre-Marie Dupuy and Vincent Chetail, pp. 39–58. Leiden and Boston, 2013.

Bloom, Herbert I. *The economic activities of the Jews of Amsterdam in the seventeenth and eighteenth centuries*. Williamsport, 1937.

Bonnot, Etienne (Abbé de Condillac). *Commerce and government considered in their mutual relationship*, translated by Shelagh Eltis. Indianapolis, 2008.

Bontemantel, Hans. *De regeeringe van Amsterdam, soo in 't civiel als crimineel en militaire (1653–1672)*, edited by G.W. Kernkamp, vol. 2 of 2. The Hague, 1897.

Borsari, S. *Venezia e Bisanzio nel XII secolo: I rapporti economici*. Venice, 1988.

Bosscha Erdbrink, G.R. *At the threshold of felicity. Ottoman-Dutch relations during the embassy of Cornelis Calkoen at the Sublime Porte, 1726–1744*. Ankara, 1975.

Braude, Benjamin. 'Introduction'. In *Christians & Jews in the Ottoman Empire. The abridged edition*, edited by Benjamin Braude, pp. 1–49. Boulder, 2014.

Braude, Benjamin. 'Christians, Jews, and the myth of Turkish commercial incompetence'. In *Relazioni economiche tra Europa e mondo islamico, secc. XIII–XVIII (Atti della trentottesima settimana di studi 1–5 maggio 2006*, edited by Simonetta Cavaciocchi, pp. 219–239. Firenze, 2007.

Braude, Benjamin. 'The myth of the Sephardi economic superman'. In *Trading cultures: The worlds of western merchants*, edited by Jeremy Adelman and Stephen Aron, pp. 165–194. Turnhout, 2001.

Brenner, Robert. *Merchants and revolution. Commercial change, political conflict, and London's overseas traders, 1550–1653*. Princeton, 1993.

Brom, Christian. *Urteilsbegründungen im 'Hoge Raad van Holland, Zeeland en West-Friesland' am Beispiel des Kaufrechts im Zeitraum 1704–1787*. Frankfurt am Main, 2008.

Brulez, Wilfrid. 'La navigation flamande vers la Méditerranée à la fin du XVIe siècle'. *Revue belge de philologie et d'histoire*, 36:4 (1958): pp. 1210–1242.

Bulmuş, Birsen. *Plague, quarantines and geopolitics in the Ottoman Empire*. Edinburgh, 2012.

Bulut, Mehmet. 'The role of Ottomans and Dutch in the commercial integration between the Levant and the Atlantic in the 17th century'. *Journal of the economic & social history of the Orient*, 45:2 (2002): pp. 197–230.

Bulut, Mehmet. *Ottoman-Dutch economic relations in the early modern period, 1571–1699*. Hilversum, 2001.

Burke, Edmund. *Reflections on the revolution in France, and on the proceedings in certain societies in London relative to that event. In a letter intended to have been sent to a gentleman in Paris. By the Right Honourable Edmund Burke*. London, 1793.

Burset, Christian R. 'Merchant courts, arbitration, and the politics of commercial litigation in the eighteenth-century British Empire'. *Law and history review*, 34:3 (2016): pp. 615–647.

Buskens, Léon. 'An Islamic triangle. Changing relationships between *sharīʿa*, state law, and local customs'. *ISIM newsletter*, 5/00, 8. Consulted online at https://core.ac.uk/download/pdf/15605032.pdf.

Caine, Barbara, ed. *Friendship: A history*. London and New York, 2009.

Calafat, Guillaume. 'La jurisdiction des consuls français en Méditerranée: litiges marchands, arbitrages et circulation des procès (Livourne et Tunis au XVIIe siècle)'. In

De l'utilité commerciale des consuls. L'institutions consulaire et les marchands dans le monde méditerranéen (XVIIe–Xxe siècle), edited by Arnaud Bartolomei, Guillaume Calafat, Mathieu Grenet, and Jörg Ulbert. Rome and Madrid, 2017. Consulted online at https://books.openedition.org/efr/3293.

Carlos, Ann M., and Stephen Nicholas. 'Agency problems in the early chartered companies: The case of the Hudson's Bay Company'. *Journal of economic history*, 50:4 (1990): pp. 853–875.

Cau, Cornelis. *Groot placaet-boeck vervattende de placaten, ordonnantien ende edicten vande doorluchtige, hoogh mog: heeren Staten Generael der Vereenighde Nederlanden ende vande ed: groot mog: heeren Staten van Hollandt ende West-Vrieslandt mitsgaders vande ed: mog: heeren Staten van Zeelandt waer by noch ghevoeght wijn eenige placaten vande voorgaende graven ende princen der selver landen, voor soo veel de selve als noch in gebruyck zijn*. Vol. 2 of 10. The Hague, 1664.

Cau, Cornelis. *Groot placaet-boeck inhoudende de placaeten, ende ordonnantien vande hoog mog. heeren Staten Generael der Vereenighde Nederlanden, ende van de groot mog. heeren Staten van Holland ende West-Vriesland; mitsgaders van de ed. mog. heeren Staten van Zeelandt.* Vol. 3 of 10. The Hague, 1683.

Cerutti, Simona. *Giustizia sommaria. Pratiche e ideali di giustizia in una società di Ancien Régime (Torino XVIII secolo)*. Milan, 2003.

Chartier, Roger, Alain Boureau, and Cécile Dauphin, eds. *Correspondence: Models of letter-writing from the Middle Ages to the nineteenth century*. Princeton, 1997.

Chatziioannou, Maria Christina, and Gerlina Harlaftis. 'From the Levant to the city of London: mercantile credit in the Greek international commercial networks of the 18th and 19th centuries'. In *Centres and peripheries in banking. The historical development of financial markets*, edited by Philip L. Cotrell, Even Lange, and Ulf Olsson, pp. 13–40. Abingdon, 2016.

Chen, Bianca. 'Politics and letters: Gisbert Cuper as a servant of two republics'. In *Double agents. Cultural and political brokerage in early modern Europe*, edited by Marika Keblusek and Badeloch Vera Noldus, pp. 71–94. Leiden and Boston, 2011.

Child, Josiah. *A new discourse of trade: Wherein are recommended several weighty points*. 4th ed. London, [1745?].

Çizakça, Murat. *Islamic capitalism and finance. Origins, evolution and the future.* Cheltenham and Northampton, MA, 2011.

Çolak, Hasan. 'Amsterdam's Greek merchants: Protégés of the Dutch, beneficiaries of the Russians, subjects of the Ottomans and supporters of Greece'. *Byzantine and modern Greek studies*, 42:1 (2018): pp. 115–133.

Coller, Ian. 'East of enlightenment: Regulating cosmopolitanism between Istanbul and Paris in the eighteenth century'. *Journal of world history*, 21:3 (2010): pp. 447–470.

Il consolato della città d'Ancona ovvero raccolta dei privilegj, e de'capitoli. Ancona, 1777.

Consultatien, advysen en advertissementen, gegeven ende geschreven bij verscheyde treffelijcke rechts-geleerden in Holland en elders. 6 vols. Rotterdam, 1645–1666.

Cordes, Albrecht. 'The search for a medieval lex mercatoria'. *Oxford University comparative law forum* 5 (2003). Consulted online at http://ouclf.iuscomp.org/the-search-for-a-medieval-lex-mercatoria/.

Coşgel, Metin M., and Boğaç A. Ergene. 'Dispute resolution in Ottoman courts: A quantitative analysis of litigations in eighteenth-century Kastamonu'. *Social science history*, 38 (2014): pp. 183–202.

Csató, Éva Á., Bernt Brendemoen, Lars Johanson, Claudia Römer, and Heidi Stein. 'The linguistic landscape of Istanbul in the seventeenth century'. In *The urban mind. Cultural and environmental dynamics*, edited by Paul J.J. Sinclair, Gullög Nordquist, Frands Herschend, and Christian Isendahl, pp. 415–439. Uppsala, 2010.

Cummins, Stephen, and Laura Kounine, eds. *Cultures of conflict resolution in early modern Europe*. Farnham, 2016.

Daalder, Hans. 'Dutch Jews in a segmented society'. In *Paths of emancipation. Jews, states, and citizenship*, edited by Pierre Birnbaum and Ira Katznelson, pp. 37–59. Princeton, 1995.

Dahl, Gunnar. *Trade, trust and networks: Commercial culture in late medieval Italy*. Lund, 1998.

Davenant, Charles. 'Essay upon the probable methods of making a people gainers in the balance of trade'. In *The political and commercial works of the celebrated writer Charles D'Avenant, LL.D. Relating to the trade and revenue of England, the plantation trade, the East-India trade, and African trade. Collected and revised by Sir Charles Whitworth, etc.*, 2 vols. Farnborough, 1967. [A facsimile of the 1771 edition.].

Davis, Ralph. *Aleppo and Devonshire Square. English traders in the Levant in the eighteenth century*. London, 1967.

Daybell, James. *The material letter in early modern England. Manuscript letters and the culture and practices of letter-writing, 1512–1635*. Basingstoke, 2012.

de Groot, Alexander H. *The Ottoman Empire and the Dutch Republic. A history of the earliest diplomatic relations 1610–1630*. Revised ed. Leiden, 2012.

de Groot, Alexander H. 'Die levantischen Dragomanen. Einheimische und Fremde im eigenen Land. Kultur- und Sprachgrenzen zwischen Ost und West (1453–1914)'. In *Verstehen und Verständigung: Ethnologie, Xenologie, Interkulturelle Philosophie*, edited by Wolfdietrich Schmied-Kowarzik, pp. 110–127. Würzburg, 2001.

de Groot, Alexander H. 'The historical development of the capitulatory regime in the Ottoman Middle East from the fifteenth to the nineteenth centuries'. *Oriente moderno*, nuova serie, 22:3 (2003): pp. 575–604.

de Groot, Alexander H. 'Dragomans' careers: Change of status in some families connected with the British and Dutch embassies in Istanbul (1785–1829)'. In *Friends and rivals in the east. Studies in Anglo-Dutch relations in the Levant from the seventeenth to the early nineteenth century*, edited by A. Hamilton A.H. de Groot, and M.H. van den Boogert, pp. 223–246. Leiden and Boston, 2000.

de Groot, Alexander H. 'The dragomans of the embassies in Istanbul 1785–1834'. In *Eastward bound. Dutch ventures and adventures in the Middle East*, edited by Geert Jan van Gelder and Ed de Moor, pp. 130–158. Amsterdam and Atlanta, 1994.

de Groot, Alexander H. *Nederland en Turkije. Zeshonderd jaar politieke, economische en culturele contacten*. Leiden, 1986.

de Groot, Alexander H. 'The organization of western European trade in the Levant, 1500–1800'. In *Companies and trade. Essays on overseas trading companies during the Ancien Régime*, edited by L. Blussé and F. Gaastra, pp. 231–241. Leiden, 1981.

de Groot, Hugo. *Inleiding tot de Hollandsche rechts-geleertheid*. The Hague, 1631.

de la Court, Pieter. *Aanwysing der heilsame politike gronden en maximen van de Republike van Holland en West-Vriesland*. Leiden and Rotterdam, 1669.

de Roover, Raymond. *L'évolution de la lettre de change XIVe–XVIIIe siècles*. Paris, 1953.

De ruysscher, Dave. 'Maxims, principles and legal change: Maritime law in merchant and legal culture (Low Countries, 16th century)'. *Zeitschrift der Savigny-Stiftung für Rechtsgeschichte*, 138 (2021): pp. 260–275.

De ruysscher, Dave. 'The struggle for voluntary bankruptcy and debt adjustment in Antwerp (c. 1520–c. 1550)'. In *Dealing with economic failures: Extrajudicial and judicial conflict regulations*, edited by Margrit Schulte-Beerbühl, pp. 77–95. Frankfurt, 2016.

De ruysscher, Dave. *Gedisciplineerde vrijheid. Een geschiedenis van het handels- en economisch recht*. Antwerp and Apeldoorn, 2014.

De ruysscher, Dave. 'La lex mercatoria contextualisée: Tracer son parcours intellectuel'. *Revue historique du droit français et étranger*, 90:4 (2012): pp. 499–515.

De ruysscher, Dave. 'From usages of merchants to default rules: Practices of trade, *ius commune* and urban law in early modern Antwerp'. *Journal of legal history*, 33:1 (2012): pp. 3–29.

De ruysscher, Dave. 'Antwerp commercial legislation in Amsterdam in the 17th century. Legal transplant or jumping board?' *Coutum*, 77 (2009): pp. 459–479.

De ruysscher, Dave. 'Designing the limits of creditworthiness: Insolvency in Antwerp banking legislation and practice (16th–17th centuries)'. *Tijdschrift voor rechtsgeschiedenis*, 76 (2008): pp. 307–327.

de Vries, Jan, and Ad van der Woude, *Nederland: De eerste ronde van moderne economische groei*. Amsterdam, 1995.

Decker, Cornelis Willem. *Het Roomsch Hollandsch recht; Beschreeven door Mr. Simon van Leeuwen*. 2 vols. Amsterdam, 1783.

Dehing, Pit. *Geld in Amsterdam. Wisselbank en wisselkoersen, 1650–1725*. Hilversum, 2012.

den Hollander, Maurits, and Remko J. Mooi. 'Protecting the foreign creditor – International insolvency in early modern Amsterdam and Frankfurt am Main'. *TSEG/ Low Countries journal of social and economic history*, 16:3–4 (2019): pp. 37–57.

Digeser, P.E. *Friendship reconsidered. What it means and how it matters to politics*. New York, 2016.

Dijkman, Jessica. *Shaping medieval markets. The organisation of commodity markets in Holland, c. 1200–c. 1450*. Leiden and Boston, 2011.

Dursteler, Eric R. 'Language and identity in the early modern Mediterranean'. In *Mediterranean identities in the premodern era: Entrepôts, islands, empires*, edited by John Watkins and Kathryn L. Reyerson, pp. 35–52. Farnham and Burlington, 2014.

Dursteler, Eric R. 'Speaking in tongues: Language and communication in the early modern Mediterranean'. *Past & present*, 217 (2012): pp. 47–77.

Dwyer, Déirdre. *The judicial assessment of expert evidence*. Cambridge, 2008.

'Edict en ordonnantie van Koning Philips op 't stuk van de crimineele justitie in de Nederlanden'. In *Manier van procedeeren in civile en crimineele saaken*, edited by Simon van Leeuwen, Henrik Verduyn, and Willem van Aller, pp. 113–240. 5th ed. Amsterdam, 1721 [1666].

Eldem, Edhem. *French trade in Istanbul in the eighteenth century*. Leiden and Boston, 1999.

Eldem, Edhem. 'French trade and commercial policy in the Levant in the eighteenth century'. *Oriente moderno*, nuova serie, 18:1 (1999): pp. 27–47.

El-Mudarris, Hussein I., and Olivier Salmon. *Le consulat de France à Alep au XVIIe siècle. Journal de Louis Gédoyn. Vie de François Picquet. Mémoires de Laurent d'Arvieux*. Aleppo, 2009.

Engels, Marie-Christine. *Merchants, interlopers, seamen and corsairs. The 'Flemish' community in Livorno and Genoa (1615–1635)*. Hilversum, 1997.

Engels, Marie-Christine. 'Dutch traders in Livorno at the beginning of the seventeenth century. The company of Joris Jansen and Bernard van den Broecke'. In *Entrepreneurs and entrepreneurship in early modern times. Merchants and industrialists within the orbit of the Dutch staple market*, edited by C. Lesger and L. Noordegraaf, pp. 63–76. The Hague, 1995.

Epstein, Mortimer. *The early history of the Levant Company*. London, 1908.

Ergene, Boğaç A. 'Evidence in Ottoman courts: Oral and written documentation in early-modern courts of Islamic law'. *Journal of the American Oriental Society*, 124:3 (2004): pp. 471–491.

Ergene, Boğaç A. *Local court, provincial society and justice in the Ottoman Empire. Legal practice and dispute resolutions in Çankırı and Kastamonu (1652–1744)*. Leiden and Boston, 2003.

Ertman, Thomas. *Birth of the leviathan. Building states and regimes in medieval and early modern Europe*. Cambridge, 1997.

Extract keurboek Rotterdam. 16/03/1655.

Extract registers Amsterdam. 31/01/1643.

Faroqhi, Suraiya. 'The Venetian presence in the Ottoman Empire (1600–1630)'. *Journal of European economic history*, 15 (1986): pp. 345–384.

Fatah-Black, Karwan, and Matthias van Rossum, 'Beyond profitability: The Dutch transatlantic slave trade and its economic impact'. *Slavery & abolition*, 36:1 (2015): pp. 63–83.

Fockema Andreae, S.J. *De Nederlandse Staat onder de Republiek*. Koninklijke Nederlandse Akademie van Wetenschappen. Verhandelingen afd. Letterkunde. Nieuwe reeks, vol. 68, no. 3. Amsterdam, 1978.

Force, Pierre. *Self-interest before Adam Smith: A genealogy of economic science*. Cambridge, 2003.

Fortunati, Maura. 'La *lex mercatoria* nella tradizione e nella recente ricostruzione storico-giuridica'. *Sociologia del diritto*, 32:2–3 (2005): pp. 29–41.

Fortunati, Maura. 'Note sul diritto di fiera nelle fonti giuridiche di età moderna'. In *Fiere e mercati nella integrazione delle economie europee secc. xiii–xvii*, edited by S. Cavaciocchi, pp. 953–966. Firenze, 2001.

'Forum shopping reconsidered'. *Harvard law review*, 103:7 (1990), pp. 1677–1696.

Frangakis-Syrett, Elena. 'Commercial practices and competition in the Levant. The British and the Dutch in eighteenth-century Izmir'. In *Friends and rivals in the east. Studies in Anglo-Dutch relations in the Levant from the seventeenth to the early nineteenth century*, edited by A. Hamilton, A.H. de Groot, and M.H. van den Boogert, pp. 135–158. Leiden and Boston, 2000.

Frangakis-Syrett, Elena. *The commerce of Smyrna in the eighteenth century (1700–1820)*. Athens, 1992.

Frankot, Edda. *'Of laws of ships and shipmen' – Medieval maritime law and its practice in urban northern Europe*. Edinburgh, 2012.

Fusaro, Maria. *Political economies of empire in the early modern Mediterranean: The decline of Venice and the rise of England 1450–1700*. Cambridge, 2015.

Fusaro, Maria. 'Politics of justice/politics of trade: Foreign merchants and the administration of justice from the records of Venice's *Giudici del Forestier*', *Mélanges de l'École française de Rome – Italie et Méditerranée modernes et contemporaines*, 126:1 (2014). Consulted online at https://journals.openedition.org/mefrim/1665.

Fusaro, Maria 'Afterword'. In *Labour, law, and empire: Comparative perspectives on seafarers, c. 1500–1800*, edited by Maria Fusaro, Bernard Allaire, Richard Blakemore, and Tijl Vanneste, pp. 304–310. Basingstoke, 2015.

Gaastra, Femme. *The Dutch East India Company – Expansion and decline*. Zutphen, 2003.

Gall, H.C. *Regtsgeleerde decisien. Aan de raadsheer Pieter Ockers toegeschreven aantekeningen betreffende uitspraken van het Hof (1656–1669) en de Hoge Raad (1669–1678) van Holland, Zeeland en West-Friesland*. Amsterdam, 2002.

García-Arenal, Mercedes, and Gerard Wiegers. *Samuel Pallache. Koopman, Kaper en Diplomaat tussen Marrakesh en Amsterdam*. Amsterdam, 2014.

Gelderblom, Oscar. *Cities of commerce. The institutional foundations of international trade in the Low Countries, 1250–1650*. Princeton and Oxford, 2013.

Gelderblom, Oscar. 'The organization of long-distance trade in England and the Dutch Republic, 1550–1650'. In *The political economy of the Dutch Republic*, edited by Oscar Gelderblom, pp. 223–254. Farnham, 2009.

Gelderblom, Oscar. *Zuid-Nederlandse kooplieden en de opkomst van de Amsterdamse stapelmarkt (1578–1630)*. Hilversum, 2000.

Gentleman's and London magazine: Or, monthly chronologer. Vol. 32. Dublin, 1763.

Geva, Benjamin. *The payment order of Antiquity and the Middle Ages. A legal history*. Oxford and Portland, 2011.

Gialdroni, Stefania. 'Gerard Malynes e la questione della lex mercatoria'. *Zeitschrift der Savigny-Stiftung für Rechtsgeschichte*, 126 (2009): pp. 38–69.

Gialdroni, Stefania. 'Il *law merchant* nella storiografia giuridica del Novecento: Una rassegna bibliografica'. *Forum historiae iuris* (2008), consulted online at https://forhistiur.net/2008-08-gialdroni/?l=it.

Glaisyer, Natasha. *The culture of commerce in England, 1660–1720*. London, 2006.

Goffman, Daniel. 'Izmir: From village to colonial port city'. In *The Ottoman city between east and west. Aleppo, Izmir, and Istanbul*, edited by Edhem Eldem, Daniel Goffman, and Bruce Masters, pp. 79–134. Cambridge, 1999.

Goffman, Daniel. *Izmir and the Levantine world, 1550–1650*. Seattle, 1990.

Goldschmidt, Levin. *Handbuch des Handelsrechts*. Erlangen, 1868.

Goitein, S.D. *Economic foundations*. Vol. 1 of *A Mediterranean society. The Jewish communities of the world as portrayed in the documents of the Cairo Geniza*. 5 vols. Berkeley, Los Angeles, and London, 1967.

Gratzer, Karl. 'Introduction'. In *History of insolvency and bankruptcy from an international perspective*, edited by Karl Gratzer and Dieter Stiefel, pp. 5–12. Södertörn, 2008.

Greene, Molly. 'Beyond the northern invasion: The Mediterranean in the seventeenth century'. *Past & present*, 174:1 (2002): pp. 42–71.

Greif, Avner. 'History lessons. The birth of impersonal exchange: The community responsibility system and impartial justice'. *Journal of economic perspectives*, 20:2 (2006): pp. 221–236.

Greif, Avner. 'On the social foundations and historical development of institutions that facilitate impersonal exchange: From the community responsibility system to individual legal responsibility in pre-modern Europe'. June 12, 1997. SSRN working paper No. 97-016. Consulted online at https://ssrn.com/abstract=47178 or http://dx.doi.org/10.2139/ssrn.47178.

Greif, Avner. 'Contract enforceability and economic institutions in early trade: The Maghribi traders' coalition'. *The American economic review*, 83:3 (1993): pp. 525–548.

Greif, Avner. 'Reputation and coalitions in medieval trade: Evidence on the Maghribi traders'. *Journal of economic history*, 49:4 (1989): pp. 857–882.

Grotius, Hugo. *Hugo Grotius on the law of war and peace*, edited by Stephen C. Neff. Cambridge, 2012.

Gunn, Steven J., David Grummitt, and Hans Cools. *War, state, and society in England and the Netherlands 1477–1559*. Oxford, 2007.

Häberlein, Mark. '"Merchants" bankruptcies, economic development and social relations in German cities during the long 16th century'. In *The history of bankruptcy*, edited by Thomas Max Safley, pp. 19–33. London, 2013.

Hacker, Joseph R. 'The rise of Ottoman Jewry'. In *The Cambridge history of Judaism*. Vol. 7: *The early modern world*, edited by Jonathan Karp and Adam Sutcliffe, pp. 77–112. Cambridge, 2018.

Hageman, Mariëlle. *Amsterdam in de wereld. Sporen van Nederlandse gedeelde verleden*. Amsterdam, 2017.

Hakkı Kadı, Ismail. *Ottoman and Dutch merchants in the eighteenth century. Competition and cooperation in Ankara, Izmir, and Amsterdam*. Leiden and Boston, 2012.

Hakkı Kadı, Ismail. 'On the edges of an Ottoman world: Non-Muslim Ottoman merchants in Amsterdam'. In *The Ottoman world*, edited by Christine Woodhead, pp. 276–288. London and New York, 2012.

Hancock, David. '"A world of business to do": William Freeman and the foundations of England's commercial empire, 1645–1707'. *William and Mary quarterly*, 57:1 (2000): pp. 3–34.

Handvesten, privilegien, octroyen, costumen en willekeuren der stad Amstelredam. Amsterdam, 1663.

Handtvesten, ofte privilegien, handelingen, costumen, ende willekeuren der stadt Aemstelredam: Mitsgaders concept vande geraemde poincten op 't stuck vande iustitie, ofte maniere van procederen in civile saecken binnen deser stede: Met verscheyden placcaten dienstigh in diversche saecken. Als mede de zee ende scheeps-rechten van Wisbuy, vande oude Hanse steden, van Keyser Karel ende Koningh Philips: Met een tractaet van avarije. Alles verrijckt met een wijtloopig ende wel geordonneert register. Hier achter zijn by-gevoeght de rechten ende costumen van Antwerpen. Amsterdam, 1639.

Hardwick, Julie. *Family business. Litigation and the political economy of daily life in early modern France*. Oxford, 2009.

Hatcher, J., and T.C. Barker. *A history of British pewter*. London, 1974.

Hatzimihail, Nikitas E. 'The many lives – and faces – of lex mercatoria: History as genealogy in international business law'. *Law and contemporary problems*, 71:3, (2008): pp. 169–190.

Heeringa, Klaas, and J.G. Nanninga. *Bronnen tot de geschiedenis van den Levantschen handel (1590–1826)*. 4 vols. The Hague, 1910–66.

Heeringa, Klaas. 'Een bondgenootschap tussen Nederland en Marokko'. *Onze eeuw*, 7:3 (1907): pp. 81–119.

Heineccius, Johann Gottlieb. *Grondbeginselen van het wisselrecht*. Middelburg, 1774.

Heinsen-Roach, Erica. *Consuls and captives. Dutch – North African diplomacy in the early modern Mediterranean.* Rochester, NY and Suffolk, 2019.

Herzog, Tamar. *A short history of European law: The last two and a half millennia.* Cambridge, MA and London, 2018.

Hill, Lisa, and Peter McCarthy. 'On friendship and *necessitudo* in Adam Smith'. *History of the human sciences*, 17:4 (2004): pp. 1–16.

Hirschman, Albert O. 'Rival interpretations of market society: Civilizing, destructive, or feeble?' *Journal of economic literature*, 20:4 (1982): pp. 1463–1484.

Hirschman, Albert O. *The passions and the interests – Political arguments for capitalism before its triumph.* Princeton, 1977.

Hitzel, Frédéric, ed. *Enfants de langue et drogmans.* Istanbul, 1995.

Hoenkamp-Mazgon, Marlies. *Palais de Hollande te Istanbul. Het ambassadegebouw en zijn bewoners sinds 1612.* Amsterdam, 2002.

Hollandsche historische courant. 02/08/1783.

Hont, Istvan. *Jealousy of trade. International competition and the nation-state in historical perspective.* Cambridge, MA and London, 2005.

Hont, Istvan, and Michael Ignatieff, eds. *Wealth and virtue – The shaping of political economy in the Scottish enlightenment.* Cambridge, 1983.

Hoppit, Julian. 'The use and abuse of credit in eighteenth-century England'. In *Business life and public policy: Essays in honour of D.C. Coleman*, edited by D.C. Coleman and N. McKendrick, pp. 64–78. Cambridge, 1986.

Horniker, Arthur Leon. 'Anglo-French rivalry in the Levant from 1583 to 1612'. *Journal of modern history*, 18:4 (1946): pp. 289–305.

Howell, Martha C. *The marriage exchange: Property, social place, and gender in cities of the Low Countries, 1300–1550.* Chicago, 1998.

Huber, Ulrik. *Heedensdaegse rechtsgeleertheyt, soo elders, als in Frieslandt gebruikelijk.* 3rd ed. Amsterdam, 1779.

Hutchison, Terence. *Before Adam Smith – The emergence of political economy, 1662–1776.* Oxford and New York, 1988.

İnalcık, Halil, and Donald Quataert, eds. *An economic and social history of the Ottoman Empire, 1300–1914.* Cambridge, 1994.

Ingham, Geoffrey. 'Some recent changes in the relationship between economics and sociology'. *Cambridge journal of economics*, 20:2 (1996): pp. 243–275.

Instructien en ordonnantien voor Commissarissen van Zee Zaken. Amsterdam, 1731.

Instructies en ordonnantien voor de Commissarissen van Zee Zaken. Amsterdam, 1774.

Israel, Jonathan, and Reinier Salverda, eds. *Dutch Jewry: Its history and secular culture (1500–2000).* Leiden and Boston, 2002.

Israel, Jonathan. *Diasporas within a diaspora: Jews, crypto-Jews and the world maritime empires (1540–1740).* Leiden and Boston, 2002.

Israel, Jonathan. 'Trade, politics and strategy: The Anglo-Dutch wars in the Levant (1647–1675)'. In *Friends and rivals in the east. Studies in Anglo-Dutch relations in the Levant from the seventeenth to the early nineteenth century*, edited by A. Hamilton, A.H. de Groot, and M.H. van den Boogert, pp. 11–23. Leiden and Boston, 2000.

Israel, Jonathan. *The Dutch Republic, its rise, greatness and fall*. Oxford, 1995.

Israel, Jonathan. 'The "new history" versus "traditional history" in interpreting Dutch world trade primacy'. *BMGN – Low Countries historical review*, 106:3 (1991): pp. 469–479.

Israel, Jonathan. *Dutch primacy in world trade, 1585–1740*. Oxford, 1989.

Israel, Jonathan. 'The Dutch merchant colonies in the Mediterranean during the seventeenth century'. *Renaissance and modern studies*, 30 (1986): pp. 87–108.

Israel, Jonathan. 'The phases of the Dutch straatvaart (1590–1713): A chapter in the economic history of the Mediterranean'. *Tijdschrift voor Geschiedenis* (1986): pp. 1–30.

Jacob, G. *Lex mercatoria: Or, the merchant's companion. Containing all the laws and statutes relating to merchandize*. London, 1718.

Jacobs, Beatrix. '*Ius patrium* en *ius commune*. Twee zijden van een medaille'. *Pro memorie: Bijdragen tot de rechtsgeschiedenis der Nederlanden*, 19:1 (2017): pp. 22–46.

Japikse, N.M., and A. van der Poest Clement. *Inventaris van het archief van de Staten-Generaal (1431) 1576–1796*. The Hague, 1969.

Jennings, Ronald C. 'Loans and credit in early seventeenth century Ottoman judicial records: The sharia court of Anatolian Kayseri'. *Journal of the economic and social history of the Orient*, 16:2–3 (1973): pp. 168–213.

Johnston, Henry McKenzie. *Ottoman and Persian odysseys: James Morier, creator of 'Hajji Baba of Ispahan', and his brothers*. London and New York, 1998.

Jones, W.J. *The foundations of English bankruptcy: Statutes and commissions in the early modern period*. Philadelphia, 1979.

Kadens, Emily. 'Convergence and the colonization of custom in pre-modern Europe'. In *Comparative legal history*, edited by O. Moréteau, A. Masferrer, and K.A. Modéer, pp. 167–185. Cheltenham, 2019.

Kadens, Emily. 'The medieval law merchant: The tyranny of a construct'. *Journal of legal analysis*, 7:2 (2015): pp. 251–289.

Kadens, Emily. 'The myth of the customary law merchant'. *Texas law review*, 90 (2012): pp. 1153–1206.

Kadens, Emily. 'Order within law, variety within custom: The character of the medieval merchant law'. *Chicago journal of international law*, 5:1 (2004): pp. 39–65.

Kagan, Richard L. *Lawsuits and litigants in Castile, 1500–1700*. Chapel Hill, 1981.

Kaiser, Wolfgang, and Johann Petitjean, eds. 'Litigation and the elements of proof in the Mediterranean (16th–19th C.)'. *Quaderni storici*, special issue, 3 (2016).

Kamali, Mohammad H. 'Fundamental rights of the individual: An analysis of *haqq* (right) in Islamic law'. *American journal of Islamic social sciences*, 10:3 (1993): pp. 340–366.

Kaplan, Yosef. 'Political concepts in the world of the Portuguese Jews of Amsterdam during the seventeenth century: The problem of exclusion and the boundaries of self-identity'. In *Menasseh Ben Israel and his world*, edited by Y. Kaplan, H. Méchoulan, and R.H. Popkin, pp. 45–62. Leiden, 1989.

Kappelhof, Ton. *Dukaten, daalders en duiten – Een geschiedenis van het geld*. Zwolle, 2006.

Kernkamp, J.H. 'Het begin van den Noordnederlandsche scheepvaart op Italië'. *Tijdschrift voor geschiedenis*, 49 (1934): pp. 70–93.

Kersten, Albert E., and Bert van der Zwan. 'The Dutch consular service: In the interests of a colonial and commercialised nation'. In *Consular affairs and diplomacy*, edited by Jan Melissen and Ana Mar Fernández, pp. 275–302. Leiden, 2011.

Kessler, Amalia D. *A revolution in commerce: The Parisian merchant court and the rise of commercial society in eighteenth-century France*. New Haven, 2007.

Kessler, Amalia D. 'Enforcing virtue: Social norms and self-interest in an eighteenth-century merchant court'. *Law & history review*, 22:71 (2004): pp. 71–118.

Kévonian, Kéram. 'Marchands arméniens au XVIIe siècle, à propos d'un livre arménien publié à Amsterdam en 1699'. *Cahier du monde russe et soviétique*, 16:2 (1975): pp. 199–244.

Kirschner, Julius. 'Wives' claims against insolvent husbands in late medieval Italy'. In *Women of the medieval world: Essays in honor of John H. Mundy*, edited by Julius Kirschner and Suzanne F. Wemple, pp. 256–304. Oxford, 1985.

Klooster, Wim. *The Dutch moment: War, trade, and settlement in the seventeenth-century Atlantic world*. Ithaca, NY, 2016.

Knight, W.S.M. 'Neutrality and neutralisation in the sixteenth century – Liège'. *Journal of comparative legislation and international law*, 2:1 (1920): pp. 98–104.

Kohler, Joseph. *Lehrbuch des Konkursrecht*. Stuttgart, 1892.

Kooi, Christine. *Calvinists and Catholics during Holland's golden age: Heretics and idolaters*. Cambridge, 2012.

Kooijmans, Luuc. *Vriendschap en de kunst van het overleven in de zeventiende en achttiende eeuw*. Amsterdam, 1997.

Kooijmans, Luuc. 'Risk and reputation: On the mentality of merchants in the early modern period'. In *Entrepreneurs and entrepreneurship in early modern times: Merchants and industrialists within the orbit of the Dutch staple market*, edited by Clé Lesger and Leo Noordegraaf, pp. 25–34. The Hague, 1995.

Koskenniemi, Martti. 'International law and the emergence of mercantile capitalism: Grotius to Smith'. In *The roots of international law/Les fondements du droit international. Liber amicorum Peter Haggenmacher*, edited by Pierre-Marie Dupuy and Vincent Chetail, pp. 1–37. Leiden and Boston, 2013.

Koster, Daniel. *The conquering Dutch merchants and shipowners*. Venice, 2006.

Kramer, Matthias. *Il segretario di banco*. Nürnberg, 1693.

Kuran, Timur, and Scott Lustig. 'Judicial biases in Ottoman Istanbul. Islamic justice and its compatibility with modern economic life'. *Journal of law and economics*, 55 (2012): pp. 1–48.

Kuran, Timur. *The long divergence. How Islamic law held back the Middle East*. Princeton, 2011.

Kuran, Timur. 'Why the Middle East is economically underdeveloped: Historical mechanisms of institutional stagnation'. *Journal of economic perspectives*, 18:3 (2004): pp. 71–90.

Kuran, Timur. 'The Islamic commercial crisis: Institutional roots of economic underdevelopment in the Middle East'. *Journal of economic history*, 63:2 (2003): pp. 414–446.

Lamikiz, Xabier. *Trade and trust in the eighteenth-century Atlantic world: Spanish merchants and their overseas networks*. Woodbridge, 2010.

Landweber, Julia. 'Fashioning nationality and identity in the eighteenth century: The Comte de Bonneval in the Ottoman Empire'. *The international history review*, 30:1 (2008): pp. 1–31.

Larousse, Pierre. *Grand dictionnaire universel du XIXe siècle*. Vol. 12 of 17. Paris, 1874.

Lattes, Alessandro. 'Il procedimento sommario'. In *Il procedimento civile nella legislazione statutaria italiana*, edited by Pietro Sella, pp. 216–267. Milan, 1927.

Lattes, Alessandro. *Il diritto commerciale nella legislazione statutaria delle città italiane*. Milan, 1884.

Le Bailly, Marie-Charlotte. 'Langetermijntrends in de rechtspraak bij de gewestelijke hoven van justitie in de Nederlanden van ca. 1450 tot ca. 1800'. *Pro memorie: Bijdragen tot de rechtsgeschiedenis der Nederlanden*, 13:1 (2011): pp. 30–67.

Le Bailly, Marie-Charlotte. *Procesgids Hof van Holland, Zeeland en West-Friesland*. Hilversum, 2008.

Le Bailly, Marie-Charlotte. *Recht voor de Raad. Rechtspraak voor het Hof van Holland, Zeeland en West-Friesland in het midden van de vijftiende eeuw*. Hilversum, 2001.

Le Bailly, Marie-Charlotte, and C.M.O. Verhas. *Hoge Raad van Holland, Zeeland en West-Friesland (1582–1795)*. Hilversum, 2006.

Lehfeldt, Elizabeth A. 'Convents as litigants: Dowry and inheritance disputes in early-modern Spain'. *Journal of social history*, 33:3 (2000): pp. 645–664.

Lemmings, David. *Law and government in England during the long eighteenth century. From consent to command*. Basingstoke and New York, 2011.

Lesaffer, Randall. *Inleiding tot de Europese rechtsgeschiedenis*. Leuven 2008.

Lichtenauer, W.F. *Geschiedenis van de wetenschap van het handelsrecht in Nederland tot 1809*. Amsterdam, 1968.

Liebesny, Herbert J. 'The development of western judicial privileges'. In *Origin and development of Islamic law*, edited by Majid Khadduri and Herbert J. Liebesny, pp. 309–333. Vol. 1 of *Law in the Middle East*. Washington, 1955.

Lindemann, Julia. 'Dirty politics or "harmonie"? Defining corruption in early modern Amsterdam and Hamburg'. *Journal of social history*, 45:3 (2012): pp. 582–604.

LoRomer, David G. *Merchants and reform in Livorno 1814–1868*. Berkeley, Los Angeles and Oxford, 1987.

Ludovici, Carl Günther. *Grundik eines vollstandigen Kaufmanns-Systeme nebst den Unfangsgründen der Handlungswissenschaft un angehängter turzen Geschichte der Handlung zu Wasser un zu Lande woraus Man zugleich den gegenwärtigen Zustand der Handlung von Europe, auch bis in die andern Welttheile erkennen kann, zum Dienste der Handlungsbeslissenen*. Leipzig, 1768.

Lulius, Didericus, and Joannes van der Linden. *Groot placaatboek, vervattende de placaaten, ordonnantien en edicten van de hoog mog. heeren Staten Generaal der Vereenigde Nederlanden; en van de edele groot mog. heeren Staaten van Holland en Westvriesland mitsgaders van de edele mog. heeren Staaten van Zeeland*. Vol. 8. Amsterdam, 1795.

Lupo, Sébastien. 'Révolution(s) d'échelles. Le marché levantin et la crise du commerce marseillais au miroir des maisons Roux et de leurs relais à Smyrne (1740–1787)'. Unpublished PhD thesis, Aix-Marseille Université, 2015.

Lybreghts, Arent. *Burgerlyk, rechtsgeleerd, notariaal en koopmanshandboek; behelzende een korten grondslag van de rechtsgeleerdheid, notariaale practyq en van den koophandel zeer dienstig niet alleen voor advocaten, procureurs, solliciteurs, schouten en secretarissen ten platen lande, en practiseerende boekhouders; maar ook voor voogden, executeurs, administrateurs, en curateurs; die zich in den koophandel willen oeffenen, en voor yder burger van Nederlands gemeenebest*. 4th ed. Amsterdam, 1764.

Macnair, Michael. *The law of proof in early modern equity*. Berlin, 1999.

Malynes, Gerard. *Consuetudo, vel lex mercatoria, or the antient law-merchant, divided into three parts: According to the essential parts of traffique. Necessarie for all statesmen, judges, magistrates, temporall and civile lawyers, mint-men, merchants, mariners, and all others negotiating in all places of the world*. London, 1629 [1622].

Mandeville, Bernard. *The fable of the bees, or, private vices, public benefits*. London, 1714.

Maréchaux, Benoît. 'Consuls vénitiens en Méditerranée orientale (1575–1645)'. In *Los cónsules de extranjeros en la Edad Moderna y a principios de la Edad Contemporánea*, edited by M. Aglietti, M. Herrero Sánchez, and F. Zamora Rodríguez, pp. 145–158. Madrid, 2013.

Masson, Paul. *Histoire du commerce français dans le Levant au XVIIe siècle*. Paris, 1896.

Marrella, Fabrizio, and Andrea Mozzato. *Alle origini dell'arbitratio commerciale internazionale. L'arbitrato a Venezia tra Medioevo ed età moderna*. Padua, 2001.

Masters, Bruce. 'Aleppo: The Ottoman Empire's caravan city'. In *The Ottoman city between east and west. Aleppo, Izmir, and Istanbul*, edited by Edhem Eldem, Daniel Goffman, and Bruce Masters, pp. 17–78. Cambridge, 1999.

Masters, Bruce. *The origins of western economic dominance in the Middle East: Mercantilism and the Islamic economy in Aleppo, 1600–1750*. New York, 1988.

Melon, Jean-François. *A political essay upon commerce. Written in French by Monsieur M*** Translated, with some annotations, and remarks. By David Bindon, Esq.* Dublin, 1738.

Ménage, V.L. 'The English capitulation of 1580'. *International journal of Middle East studies*, 12:3 (1980): pp. 373–383.

Meurier, Gabriel. *Formulaire de missives, obligations, lettres de change, d'asseurances.* Antwerp, 1558.

Mézin, Anne. *Les consuls de France au siècle des lumières (1715–1792)*. Paris, 1997.

Middelburgsche courant. 22/10/1763.

Milgrom, Paul R., Douglass C. North, and Barry R. Weingast. 'The role of institutions in the revival of trade: The law merchant, private judges, and the champagne fairs'. *Economics & politics*, 2:1 (1990): pp. 1–23.

Mitchell, William. *An essay on the early history of the law merchant*. Cambridge, 1904.

Moglen, Eben. 'Commercial arbitration in the eighteenth century: Searching for the transformation of American law'. *The Yale law journal*, 93:1 (1983): pp. 135–152.

Moll, Goswin. 'De Desolate Boedelskamer te Amsterdam – Bijdrage tot de kennis van het Oud-Hollandsch failliten-recht'. Unpublished PhD thesis, Universiteit van Amsterdam, 1879.

Morineau, Michel. 'Naissance d'une domination. Marchands européens, marchands et marches du Levant aux XVIIIe et XIXe siècles'. *Cahiers de la Méditerranée*, 1 (1976): pp. 145–184.

Muldrew, Craig. *The economy of obligation: The culture of credit and social relations in early modern England*. Basingstoke, 1998.

Muller, Jerry Z. *The mind and the market – Capitalism in modern European thought*. New York, 2002.

Müller, Leos. 'Commerce et navigation suédois en Méditerranée à l'époque moderne (1650–1815)'. *Revue d'histoire maritime*, 13 (2011): pp. 45–70.

Müller, Leos. 'Swedish shipping in southern Europe and peace treaties with North African states: An economic security perspective'. *Historical social research/ Historische Sozialforschung*, 35:4 (2010): pp. 190–205.

Murphey, Rhoads. 'Merchants, nations, and free-agency: An attempt at a qualitative characterization of trade in the eastern Mediterranean, 1620–1640'. In *Friends and rivals in the east. Studies in Anglo-Dutch relations in the Levant from the seventeenth to the early nineteenth century*, edited by A. Hamilton, A.H. de Groot, and M.H. van den Boogert, pp. 25–58. Leiden and Boston, 2000.

Naamregister van alle de kooplieden voornaame handeldryvende of negotiedoende winkeliers en fabricanten der stad Amsterdam. Amsterdam, 1784.

Nagy, Gy. Káldy. 'Qadi'. In *Judicial practice. Institutions and agents in the Islamic world*, edited by Boğaç A. Ergene, pp. 198–203. Leiden and Boston, 2009.

De Nederlandsche maandelyke post-ryder, medebrengende berigten van de voornaamste en gedenkwaardigste staat- en oorlogszaken, die in en buiten 't Christenryk zyn voorgevallen, beneffens de daar toe behooeende bewysstukken. Voor de maand may, 1732. Amsterdam, 1732.

Nederlandtsche placcaet-boeck: Waerinne alle voornaemste placcaten, ordonnantien, accorden, ende andere acten ende munimenten, uyt-ghegeven by de EE. hoogmogende heeren Staten Generael der Vereenigde Nederlantsche provintien; Sedert dat Philippus II. koninck van Spagnien eerst verclaert is, vervallen te wesen vande hooghoverigheyt deser landen, in't jaer 1581, tot op den teghenwoordighen jaere 1644. 2 vols. Amsterdam, 1644.

Nessink, Christoffer. *Het landt-recht van Over-Yssel*. Kampen, 1747.

Nicol, Donald M. *Byzantium and Venice: A study in diplomatic and cultural relations*. Cambridge, 1988.

Nieuw Nederlandsch biografisch woordenboek, edited by P.C. Molhuysen and P.J. Blok. Vol. 3 of 10. Leiden, 1914.

Nieuw Nederlandsch biografisch woordenboek, edited by P.C. Molhuysen and P.J. Blok. Vol. 1 of 10. Leiden, 1911.

Nimako, Kwame, and Glenn Willemsen. *The Dutch Atlantic. Slavery, abolition and emancipation*. London, 2011.

Nizri, Michael. *Ottoman high politics and the Ulema household*. Basingstoke, 2014.

Noordegraaf, Leo. 'Vooruit en achteruit in de handelsgeschiedenis van de Republiek'. *BMGN – Low Countries historical review*, 106:3 (1991), pp. 458–468.

Noradounghian, Gabriel Effendi. *Recueuil d'actes internationaux de l'Empire ottoman, 1300–1789*. 4 vols. Paris, 1897–1903.

Nörr, Knut Wolfgang. 'Procedure in mercantile matters: Some comparative aspects'. In *The courts and the development of commercial law*, edited by Vito Piergiovanni, pp. 195–201. Berlin, 1987.

Ogilvie, Sheilagh. *Institutions and European trade: Merchant guilds, 1000–1800*. Cambridge, 2011.

Oldewelt, W.F.H. *De oudste lastgeldrekening van Directeuren van de Levantse handel (1625–1631)*. Amsterdam, 1958.

Olnon, Merlijn. *'Brought under the law of the land'. The history, demography and geography of crossculturalism in early modern Izmir, and the Köprülü project of 1678*. Leiden, 2013.

Olnon, Merlijn '"A most agreeable and pleasant creature"? Merzifonlu Kara Mustafa Paşa in the correspondence of Justinus Colyer (1668–1682)'. *Oriente moderno*, nuova serie, 22:3 (2003): pp. 649–669.

Olnon, Merlijn. 'Towards classifying *avanias*: A study of two cases involving the English and Dutch nations in seventeenth-century Izmir'. In *Friends and rivals in the east. Studies in Anglo-Dutch relations in the Levant from the seventeenth to the early nineteenth century*, edited by A. Hamilton, A.H. de Groot, and M.H. van den Boogert, pp. 159–186. Leiden and Boston, 2000.

Ormrod, David. *The rise of commercial empires: England and the Netherlands in the age of mercantilism, 1650–1770*. Cambridge, 2008.

Ordonnance de la marine du mois d'aoust 1681. Commentée & conferée avec les anciennes ordonnances, & le droit ecrit: Avec les nouveaux reglemens concernans la marine. Paris, 1714.

'Ordonnantie op 't stuk van de justitie, binnen de steeden ende ten platen lande, in den jare 1580'. In *Manier van procedeeren in civile en crimineele saaken*, edited by Simon van Leeuwen, Henrik Verduyn, and Willem van Aller, pp. 1–112. 5th ed. Amsterdam, 1721 [1666].

Pamuk, Şevket. 'Institutional change and longevity of the Ottoman Empire'. *Journal of interdisciplinary history*, 35:2 (2004): pp. 225–247.

Pamuk, Şevket. *A monetary history of the Ottoman Empire*. Cambridge, 2000.

Panaite, Viorel. 'French capitulations and consular jurisdiction in Egypt and Aleppo in the late sixteenth and early seventeenth centuries'. In *Well-connected domains. Towards an entangled Ottoman history*, edited by Pascal W. Firges, Tobias P. Graf, Christian Roth, and Gülay Tulasoğlu, pp. 71–87. Leiden and Boston, 2014.

Panaite, Viorel. 'The legal and political status of Wallachia and Moldavia in relation to the Ottoman Empire'. In *The European tributary states of the Ottoman Empire in the sixteenth and seventeenth centuries*, edited by Gábor Kármán and Lovro Kunčević, pp. 9–42. Leiden and Boston, 2013.

Panaite, Viorel. 'Peace agreements in Ottoman legal and diplomatic view (15th–17th centuries)'. In *Pax Ottomana: Studies in memoriam Prof. Dr. Nejat Göyünç*, edited by Kemal Çiçek, pp. 277–308. Ankara and Haarlem, 2001.

Panzac, Daniel. *La peste dans l'Empire ottoman, 1700–1850*. Leuven, 1985.

Pasciuta, Beatrice. 'Durantis, speculum iudiciale'. In *The formation and transmission of western legal culture*, edited by Serge Dauchy, Georges Martyn, Athony Musson, Heikki Pihlajamäki, and Alain Wijffels, pp. 37–40. Cham, 2016.

Pedani, Maria Pia. 'Venetians in the Levant in the age of Selīm I'. In *Conquête ottomane de l'Égypte (1517)*, edited by Benjamin Lellouch and Nicolas Michel, pp. 99–112. Leiden and Boston, 2012.

Pedani, Maria Pia. '*Venezia e l'Impero ottomano: La tentazione dell'impium foedus*'. In *L'Europa e la Serenissima. La svolta del 1509. Nel V centenario della battaglia di Agnadello*, edited by Giuseppe Gullino, pp. 163–176. Venezia, 2011.

Pedani, Maria Pia. 'Venetian consuls in Egypt and Syria in the Ottoman age'. *Mediterranean world*, 18 (2006): pp. 7–21.

Pearson, M.N. 'Merchants and states'. In *The political economy of merchant empires*, edited by James Tracy, pp. 41–116. Cambridge, 1991.

Pennington, Kenneth. *The prince and the law, 1200–1600: Sovereignty and rights in the western legal tradition*. Berkeley and Oxford, 1993.

Peri, Giovanni Domenico. *Il negoziante*. Venice, 1638.

Petsche, Markus. 'What's wrong with forum shopping? An attempt to identify and assess the real issues of a controversial practice'. *The international lawyer*, 45:4 (2011): pp. 1005–1028.

Philo-patriae. *Further considerations on the act to permit persons professing the Jewish religion, to be naturalized by parliament*. London, 1753.

Philo-patriae. *Considerations on the bill to permit persons professing the Jewish religion to be naturalized by parliament*. London, 1753.

Phoonsen, Johannes. *Wissel-styl tot Amsterdam. Vervattende niet alleen het geene dat men gewoon, maar oock wat een voorsichtigh koopman, tot sijn securiteit, in de wissel-handel dienstigh en noodigh is, te observeren. Mitsgaders de ordonantien, willekeuren, en reglementen van wisselen tot Amsterdam, Rotterdam, Antwerpen, Hamburg/Franckfurt/Leipzig/Nürnberg/Augspurg/Brewlauw/Bologna, Bisenzone, Bolzano, en Lions. Als oock de ordonnances de Louis XIV. sur le commerce de negotians & marchands*. Amsterdam, 1676.

Pieck, G.T.H.C. 'Francesco Gallacini, Florentijns koopman te Rotterdam 1647–1705'. *Rotterdamsch jaarboekje*, 8 (1980): pp. 204–235.

Piergiovanni, Vito. *Norme, scienza e pratica giuridica tra Genova e l'occidente medievale e moderno*. 2 vols. Genoa, 2012.

Pirillo, Diego. 'Venetian merchants as diplomatic agents: Family networks and cross-confessional diplomacy in early modern Europe'. In *Early modern diplomacy, theatre and soft power. The making of peace*, edited by Nathalie Rivère de Carles, pp. 183–204. London and New York, 2016.

Plouviez, David. 'Puissance navale et réseaux consulaires. L'action des consuls français en Italie et sur les marges occidentales de l'Empire ottoman au XVIIIe siècle'. In *Les consuls en Méditerranée, agents d'information XVIe–XXe siècle*, edited by Silvia Marzagalli, pp. 179–199. Paris, 2015.

Pocock, J.G.A. *Virtue, commerce, and history. Essays on political thought and history, chiefly in the eighteenth century*. Cambridge, 1985.

Poitras, Geoffrey. *The early history of financial economics, 1478–1776 – From commercial arithmetic to life annuities and joint stocks*. Cheltenham, 2000.

Posthumus, N.W. *De geschiedenis van de Leidsche lakenindustrie*. 3 vols. The Hague, 1908.

Poumarède, Géraud. 'Le consul dans les dictionnaires et le droit des gens: Émergence et affirmation d'une institution nouvelle (XVIe–XVIIIe siècles)'. In *La fonction consulaire à l'époque moderne. L'affirmation d'une institution économique et politique (1500–1800)*, edited by J. Ulber and G. Le Bouëdec, pp. 23–36. Rennes, 2006.

Poumarède, Géraud. 'Naissance d'une institution royale: Les consuls de la nation française en Levant et en Barbarie aux XVIe et XVIIe siècles'. *Annuaire-bulletin de la Société de l'Histoire de France* (2001): pp. 65–128.

Powell, Edward. 'Arbitration and the law in England in the late Middle Ages'. *Transactions of the Royal Historical Society*, 33 (1982): pp. 49–67.

Pozza, Marco, and Giorgio Ravegnani. *I trattati con Bisanzio, 992–1198*. Venice, 1993.

Prak, Maarten. *The Dutch Republic in the seventeenth century*. Cambridge, 2005.

Price, John L. *Holland and the Dutch Republic in the seventeenth century: The politics of particularism*. Oxford, 1994.

Resolutien van de heeren Staaten van Holland en Westvriesland in haar edele groot mog. vergadering genoomen in den jaare 1774. S.l., S.d.

Resolutien van de heeren Staaten van Holland en Westvriesland in haar edele groot mog. vergadering genoomen in den jaare 1770. S.l., S.d.

Ribeiro, Ana Sofia. *Early modern trading networks in Europe. Cooperation and the case of Simon Ruiz*. Abingdon, 2016.

Roitman, Jessica V. *The same but different? Inter-cultural trade and the Sephardim, 1595–1640*. Leiden and Boston, 2011.

Rosen, Lawrence. *The anthropology of justice. Law as culture in Islamic society*. Cambridge, 1989.

Rothman, E. Nathalie. *The dragoman renaissance. Diplomatic interpreters and the routes of Orientalism*. Ithaca, NY, 2021.

Rothman, E. Nathalie. 'Interpreting dragomans: Boundaries and crossings in the early modern Mediterranean'. *Comparative studies in society and history*, 51:4 (2009): pp. 771–800.

Rothschild, Emma. *Economic sentiments – Adam Smith, Condorcet, and the enlightenment*. Cambridge, MA and London, 2007.

Rothschild, Emma. 'An alarming commercial crisis in eighteenth-century Angoulême: Sentiments in economic history'. *Economic history review*, 51:2 (1998): pp. 268–293.

Roudometof, Victor. 'From Rum millet to Greek nation: Enlightenment, secularization and national identity in Ottoman Balkan society'. *Journal of modern Greek studies*, 16:1 (1998): pp. 11–48.

Rousseau, Jean-Jacques. *Les confessions, suivies des rêveries du promeneur solitaire*. Genève, 1782.

Sachs, Stephen. 'From St. Ives to cyberspace: The modern distortion of the medieval "law merchant"'. *American University international law review*, 21:5 (2006): pp. 685–812.

Samberg, Jan Willem. *De Hollandsche gereformeerde gemeente*. Leiden, 1928.

Santarelli, Umberto. *Mercanti e società tra mercanti*. Torino, 1998.

Santarelli, Umberto. *Per la storia del fallimento delle legislazioni italiane dell'età intermedia*. Padova, 1964.

Sartori, Paolo, and Ido Shahar. 'Legal pluralism in Muslim-majority colonies: Mapping the terrain'. *Journal of the economic and social history of the Orient*, 55 (2012): pp. 637–663.

Savary des Bruslons, Jacques. *Dictionnaire universel de commerce*. Copenhagen, 1765.

Schama, Simon. *The embarrassment of riches: An interpretation of Dutch culture in the golden age*. New York, 1987.

Scheltus, Isaac. *Groot placaatboek, vervattende de placaaten, ordonnantien en edicten van de hoog mog. heeren Staten Generaal der Vereenigde Nederlanden; en van de edele groot mog. heeren Staaten van Holland en Westvriesland mitsgaders van de edele mog. heeren Staaten van Zeeland*. Vol. 7. The Hague, 1770.

Scheltus, Isaac. *Groot placaatboek, vervattende de placaaten, ordonnantien en edicten van de hoog mog. heeren Staten Generaal der Vereenigde Nederlanden; en van de edele groot mog. heeren Staaten van Holland en Westvriesland mitsgaders van de edele mog. heeren Staaten van Zeeland*. Vol. 6. Amsterdam, 1795 [The Hague, 1746].

Scheltus, Jacobus. *Groot placaet-boeck vervattende de placaten, ordonnantien ende edicten vande doorluchtige, hoogh mog: heeren Staten Generael der Vereenighde Nederlanden ende vande ed: groot mog: heeren Staten van Hollandt ende West-Vrieslandt mitsgaders vande ed: mog: heeren Staten van Zeelandt*. Vol. 4. The Hague, 1705.

Schröder, Peter. *Trust in early modern international political thought, 1598–1713*. Cambridge, 2017.

Schui, Florian. 'Prussia's "trans-oceanic moment": The creation of the Prussian Asiatic Trade Company in 1750'. *The historical journal*, 49:1 (2006): pp. 143–160.

Schutte, Otto. *Repertorium der buitenlandse vertegenwoordigers, residerende in Nederland 1584–1810*. The Hague, 1983.

Schutte, Otto. *Repertorium der Nederlandse vertegenwoordigers residerende in het buitenland 1584–1810*. The Hague, 1976.

Schweitzer, Julia. *Schiffer und Schiffsmann in den Rôles d'Oléron und im Llibre del Consolat de Mar – Ein Vergleich zweier mittelalterlicher Seerechtsquellen*. Frankfurt am Main, 2006.

Sella, Domenico. *Commercio e industrie a Venezia nel secolo XVII*. Firenze, 1961.

Sempéré, Julien. 'La correspondance du consulat français de Barcelone (1679–1716). Informer comme un consul ou comme un marchand?' In *Les consuls en Méditerranée, agents d'information XVIe–XXe siècle*, edited by Silvia Marzagalli, pp. 121–140. Paris, 2015.

Sewel, Willem, and Egbert Buys. *Volkomen woordenboek der Nederduitsche en Engelse talen; Névens eene spraak-konst van dezelven/A compleat dictionary Dutch and English to which is added a grammar, for both languages*, 4th ed., 2 vols. Amsterdam, 1766 [1691].

Sgard, Jérôme. 'Bankruptcy, fresh start and debt renegotiation in England and France (17th to 18th century)'. In *The history of bankruptcy: Economic, social and cultural implications in early modern Europe*, edited by Thomas Max Safley, pp. 223–235. London, 2013.

Silver, Allan. 'Friendship in commercial society: Eighteenth-century social theory and modern sociology'. *American journal of sociology*, 95:6 (1990): pp. 1474–1504.

Sirks, Boudewijn. 'Sources of commercial law in the Dutch Republic and Kingdom'. In *Understanding the sources of early modern and modern commercial law. Courts, statutes, contracts, and legal scholarship*, edited by Heikki Pihlajamäki, Albrecht Cordes, Serge Dauchy, and Dave De ruysscher, pp. 166–184. Leiden and Boston, 2018.

Skilliter, Susan. *William Harborne and the trade with Turkey 1578–1582. A documentary study of the first Anglo-Ottoman relations*. Oxford, 1977.

Slot, B.J. *Inventaris van het archief van het Nederlandse Consulaat te Smyrna, (1611) 1685–1811 (1837)*. The Hague, 1988.

Slys, Mariya Tait. *Exporting legality. The rise and fall of extraterritorial jurisdiction in the Ottoman Empire and China*. Genève, 2014.

Smail, John. 'Credit, risk, and honor in eighteenth-century commerce'. *Journal of British studies*, 44:3 (2005): pp. 439–456.

Smith, Adam. *An inquiry into the nature and causes of the wealth of nations*. London, 1776.

Smith, Adam. *Theory of moral sentiments*. Edinburgh, 1759.

Smyrnelis, Marie-Carmen. 'Courtiers de Smyrne (fin du XVIIIe–milieu du XIX siècle). Médiateurs professionnels et médiations dans l'Empire ottoman'. In *Hommes de l'entre-deux: Parcours individuels et portraits de groupes sur la frontière de la Méditerranée, XVIe–XXe siècle*, edited by Bernard Heyberger and Chantal Verdeil, pp. 117–131. Paris, 2009.

Smyrnelis, Marie-Carmen. 'Les européens de Smyrne du XVIIe au XIXe siècle: Citadins ou non?' In *L'urbain dans le monde musulman de Méditerranée*, edited by Jean-Luc Arnaud, pp. 121–133. Tunis, 2005.

Sneller, Z.W. 'Het begin van den Noord-Nederlandschen handel op het Middellandsche Zeegebied'. *Verslag Historisch Genootschap* (1935): pp. 70–92.

Sonyel, Salahi R. 'The protégé system in the Ottoman Empire'. *Journal of Islamic studies*, 2:1 (1991): pp. 56–66.

Spencer, Liz, and Ray Pahl. *Rethinking friendship. Hidden solidarities today*. Princeton and Oxford, 2006.

Steckley, George F. 'Merchants and the Admiralty Court during the English Revolution'. *American journal of legal history*, 22:2 (1978): pp. 137–175.

Steensgaard, Niels. 'Consuls and nations in the Levant from 1570 to 1650'. *The Scandinavian economic history review*, 15 (1967): pp. 13–55.

Steil, Benn. 'Globalism and natural law – A brief history'. In *Natural law, economics and the common good*, edited by S. Gregg and H. James, pp. 58–92. Exeter, 2012.

Stein, Peter. *Roman law in European history*. Cambridge, 1999.

Straumann, Benjamin. *Roman law in the state of nature. The classical foundations of Hugo Grotius' natural law*. Cambridge, 2015.

Suner, Suna. 'The earliest opera performances in the Ottoman world and the role of diplomacy'. In *The age of Mozart and Selim III (1765–1808)*, edited by Michael Hüttler and Hans Ernst Weidinger, pp. 155–222. Vol. 1 of *Ottoman Empire and European theatre*. Wien, 2013.

Swetschinski, Daniel. *Reluctant cosmopolitans: The Portuguese Jews of seventeenth-century Amsterdam*. Oxford, 2000.

't Hart, Marjolein. *The Dutch wars of independence: Warfare and commerce in the Netherlands, 1570–1680*. London and New York, 2014.

Takeda, Juno T. *Between crown & commerce: Marseille and the early modern Mediterranean*. Baltimore, 2011.

Tamdoğan, Işık. 'The Ottoman political community in the process of justice making in the 18th-century Adana'. In *Forms and institutions of justice. Legal actions in Ottoman contexts*, edited by Yavuz Aykan and Işık Tamdoğan. Istanbul, 2018. Consulted online at https://books.openedition.org/ifeagd/2323.

Teunissen, Ineke. *Herman van Coopstad en Isaac Jacobus Rochussen. Twee Rotterdamse slavenhandelaren in de 18e eeuw*. Rotterdam, 1996.

Theolin, Sture. *The Swedish palace in Istanbul: A thousand years of cooperation between Turkey and Sweden*. Istanbul, 2000.

Theunissen, Hans. 'Ottoman-Venetian diplomatics: The *'ahd-names*. The historical background and the development of a category of political-commercial instruments together with an annotated edition of a corpus of relevant documents'. 2 vols. Unpublished PhD thesis, University of Utrecht, 1991.

Theunissen, Hans, ed. *Topkapi & turkomanie. Turks-Nederlandse ontmoetingen sinds 1600*. Amsterdam, 1989.

Trivellato, Francesca. *The promise and peril of credit. What a forgotten legend about Jews and finance tells us about the making of European commercial society*. Princeton and Oxford, 2019.

Trivellato, Francesca. 'Credito e cittadinanza nella republica dei mercanti visti attraverso la diaspora sefardita nell'Europa moderna', *Mélanges de l'École française de Rome: Moyen Âge*, 125:2 (2013). Consulted online at https://journals.openedition.org/mefrm/1447.

Trivellato, Francesca. *The familiarity of strangers: The Sephardic diaspora, Livorno, and cross-cultural trade in the early modern period*. New Haven and London, 2009.

Turner, Bryan S. 'Islam, capitalism and the Weber theses'. *British journal of sociology*, 61:1 (2010): pp. 147–160.

Udovitch, Abraham L. *Partnership and profit in medieval Islam*. Princeton, 1970.

Ulbert, Jörg. 'La dépêche consulaire française et son acheminement en Méditerranée sous Louis XIV (1661–1715)'. In *Les consuls en Méditerranée, agents d'information XVIe–XXe siècle*, edited by Silvia Marzagalli, pp. 31–57. Paris, 2015.

van Anrooij, Wim. *Handschriften als spiegel van de middeleeuwse tekstcultuur*. Leiden, 2006.

van Boneval Faure, Rembt. *Het Nederlandsche burgerlijk procesrecht*. Vol. 1 of 4. Leiden, 1893.

van Caenegem, R.C. 'History of European civil procedure'. In *International encyclopedia of comparative law*, vol. 16, edited by Mauro Cappelletti, pp. 3–113. Leiden and Boston, 2014. [First published in Tübingen in 1973.].

van Dam van Isselt, W.E. 'Het "in train brengen" van het in 1675 voor de Levant ontworpen formulier (1675–1680). In *Bijdragen voor vaderlandsche geschiedenis en oudheidkunde*, edited by P.J. Blok, 4th series, part 7, pp. 289–333. The Hague, 1909.

van Dam van Isselt, W.E. 'Het ontwerp-regeeringsreglement voor de Levant van 1673 en het formulier van 1675'. In *Bijdragen voor vderlandsche geschiedenis en oudheidkunde*, edited by P.J. Blok, 4th series, part 6, pp. 379–429. The Hague, 1907.

van Dam van Isselt, W.E. 'De klachten, tusschen 1672 en 1675 ingebracht tegen Jacob van Dam, consul te Smirna (1668–1688)'. In *Bijdragen voor vaderlandsche geschiedenis en oudheidkunde*, edited by P.J. Blok, 4th series, part 6, pp. 277–351. The Hague, 1907.

van Dam van Isselt, W.E. 'Eenige lotgevallen van Jacob Van Dam, consul te Smirna van 1668–1688.' In *Bijdragen voor vaderlandsche geschiedenis en oudheidkunde*, edited by P.J. Blok, 4th series, part 6, pp. 78–136. The Hague, 1907.

van den Boogert, Maurits. 'Negotiating foreignness in the Ottoman Empire: The legal complications of cosmopolitanism in the eighteenth century'. In *Exploring the Dutch Empire. Agents, networks and institutions, 1600–2000*, edited by Catia Antunes and Jos Gommans, pp. 27–42. London, 2015.

van den Boogert, Maurits. 'Ottoman intermediaries in the 18th century: Analysis of a "dirty trade"'. *Oriente moderno*, 93:2 (2013): pp. 515–530.

van den Boogert, Maurits. 'Ottoman Greeks in the Dutch Levant trade: Collective strategy and individual practice (c. 1750–1821)'. *Oriente moderno*, nuova serie, 86:1 (2006): pp. 129–147.

van den Boogert, Maurits. *The capitulations and the Ottoman legal system. Qadis, consuls and beratlis in the 18th century*. Leiden and Boston, 2005.

van den Boogert, Maurits. 'European patronage in the Ottoman Empire: Anglo-Dutch conflicts of interest in Aleppo (1703–1755)'. In *Friends and rivals in the east. Studies in Anglo-Dutch relations in the Levant from the seventeenth to the early nineteenth century*, edited by A. Hamilton, A.H. de Groot, and M.H. van den Boogert, pp. 187–221. Leiden and Boston, 2000.

van der Aa, A.J. *Biographisch woordenboek der Nederlanden*. Vol. 7. Haarlem, 1862.

van der Aa, A.J. *Biographisch woordenboek der Nederlanden*. Vol. 4. Haarlem, 1858.

van der Burgh, A.H.H. *Inventaris van het archief van de Directie van de Levantse Handel en de Navigatie in de Middellandse Zee, (1614) 1625–1826 (1828)*. The Hague, 1882.

van der Gouw, J.L. 'Costumen betreffende land liggende gemener voor'. In *Ter recognitie. Opstellen aangeboden aan Prof. Mr. H. van der Linden bij zijn afscheid als hoogleraar in de Nederlandse rechtsgeschiedenis aan de Vrije Universiteit*, edited by C. Streefkerk and S. Faber, pp. 275–294. Hilversum, 1987.

van der Linden, Joannes. *Groot placaatboek, vervattende de placaaten, ordonnantien en edicten, van de hoog mog. heeren Staaten Generaal der Vereenigde Nederlanden en van de edele groot mog. heeren Staaten van Holland en Westvriesland; mitsgaders van de edele mog. heeren Staaten van Zeeland.* Vol. 9. Amsterdam, 1796.

van der Vlis, Ingrid, and Hans van der Sloot. *Cornelis Haga 1578–1654. Pionier en diplomaat in Constantinopel.* Amsterdam, 2012.

van de Spiegel, Laurens Pieter. *Verhandeling over den oorsprong en de historie der vaderlandsche rechten, inzonderheid van Holland en Zeeland.* Goes, 1769.

van Deursen, A.T., ed. *Resolutiën der Staten-Generaal.* Nieuwe reeks 1610–1670. 2 vols. The Hague, 1971.

van Dillen, J.G. *Van rijkdom en regenten. Handboek tot de economische en sociale geschiedenis van Nederland.* The Hague, 1970.

van Dillen, J.G. 'Bloeitijd der Amsterdamse wisselbank 1687–1781'. In *Mensen en achtergronden*, edited by J.G. van Dillen, pp. 385–415. Groningen, 1964.

van Dongen, Emanuel G.D. *Contributory negligence. A historical and comparative study.* Leiden and Boston, 2014.

van Doosselaere, Quentin. *Commercial agreements and social dynamics in medieval Genoa.* Cambridge, 2009.

van Gelder, Maartje. *Trading places: The Netherlandish merchants in early modern Venice.* Leiden and Boston, 2009.

van Gelder, Maartje. 'Supplying the Serenissima. The role of Flemish merchants in the Venetian grain trade during the first phase of the straatvaart'. *International journal of maritime history*, 16:2 (2004): pp. 39–60.

van Glins, Taco. *Aenmerckingen ende bedenckingen over de zee-rechten, uyt het placcaet van Koninck Philips uytgegeven den lesten octobris 1563. Alwaer der selver billickheyt uyt den gront van keyserlicke rechten, en krachtige beweeghreden bevestight, met andere zee-rechten over een gebracht, haer verschil aengewesen, en daer beneffens op verscheyden quaestien en voorvallen den koophandel en scheep-vaert aengaende, geantwoordt wordt. Den kooplieden en schipperen niet alleen, maer allen liefhebberen der rechts-geleertheydt seer dienstelick en profytelick.* Amsterdam, 1665.

van Krieken, Gerard. *Kapers en kooplieden. De betrekkingen tussen Algiers en Nederland.* Amsterdam, 1999.

van Leeuwen, Simon. *Paratitula juris novissimi dat is een kort begrip van het Roomsch-Hollandts reght.* Leiden, 1652.

van Meeteren, A.P.B. *Op hoop van akkoord. Instrumenteel forumgebruik bij geschilbeslechting in Leiden in de zeventiende eeuw.* Hilversum, 2006.

van Royen, P.C. 'The first phase of Dutch straatvaart (1591–1605); fact and fiction'. *International journal of maritime history*, 2 (1990): pp. 69–102.

van Stipriaan, Alex. *Rotterdam in slavernij*. Amsterdam 2020.

van Tielhof, Milja. *The 'mother of all trades'. The Baltic grain trade in Amsterdam from the late 16th to the early 19th century*. Leiden and Boston, 2002.

van Velden, Martin. *Fondament vande wisselhandeling: onderrichtingh ghevende van alle voornaemste wisselen van Christenrijck, so van trates remessen, vergelijcking van prysen, verscheyden commissien te vormen*. Amsterdam, 1629.

Vanneste, Tijl. 'Sailing through the straits: Seamen's professional trajectories from a segmented labour market in Holland into a fragmented Mediterranean'. In *Labour, law, and empire: Comparative perspectives on seafarers, c. 1500–1800*, edited by Maria Fusaro, Bernard Allaire, Richard Blakemore, and Tijl Vanneste, pp. 123–140. Basingstoke, 2015.

Vanneste, Tijl. *Global trade and commercial networks: Eighteenth-century diamond merchants*. London, 2011.

Vanneste, Tijl. 'Commercial culture and merchant networks: Eighteenth-century diamond traders in global history'. Unpublished PhD thesis, European University Institute, 2009.

van Zanden, Jan Luiten. 'Een fraaie synthese op een wankele basis'. *BMGN – Low Countries Historical Review*, 106:3 (1991): pp. 451–457.

van Zanden, Jan Luiten, and Tine De Moor. 'Mensen en economie in de Gouden Eeuw'. *Leidschrift*, 23:2 (2008): pp. 15–26.

Veinstein, Gilles. 'On the Ottoman janissaries (fourteenth–nineteenth centuries)'. In *A comparative study of military labour (1500–2000)*, edited by Erik-Jan Zürcher, pp. 115–134. Amsterdam, 2013.

Veluwenkamp, J.W. 'De Leidse lakenondernemer Daniël van Eys, 1688–1739'. *Jaarboekje voor geschiedenis en oudheidkunde van Leiden en omstreken*, 84 (1992): pp. 109–124.

Vermeesch, Griet. 'Access to justice: Legal aid to the poor at civil law courts in the eighteenth-century Low Countries'. *Law and history review*, 32:3 (2014): pp. 683–714.

Verwer, Adriaen. *Nederlants see-rechten; avaryen; en bodemeryen begrepen in de gemeene costuimen vander see; de placcaten van Keiser Karel den Vijfden 1551; en Koning Filips den II 1563; 't tractaet van mr Quintyn Weitsen van de Nederlantsche Avaryen: Ende daerenboven in eene verhandelinge nopende het recht der Hollantsche bodemeryen*. Amsterdam, 1711.

Verzameling van casuspositien, voorstellingen en declaratien, betrekkelyk tot voorvallende omstandigheden in den koophandel, van tyd tot tyd binnen deeze stad beoordeeld en ondertekend. 2 vols. Amsterdam, 1793–1794.

Verzameling van geheime brieven van en aan de gezanten der Nederlandsche Republiek, April 1756–April 1762. Vols. 9, 12, and 13. The Hague, 1756–1762.

Vink, Markus P.M. 'Freedom and slavery: The Dutch Republic, the VOC world, and the debate over the "world's oldest trade"'. *South African historical journal*, 59:1 (2007): pp. 19–46.

Vlami, Despina. *Trading with the Ottomans. The Levant Company in the Middle East*. London and New York, 2014.

Volckart, Oliver, and Antje Mangels. 'Are the roots of the modern lex mercatoria really medieval?' *Southern economic journal*, 65:3 (1999): pp. 427–450.

Volpi, Alessandro. *Banchieri e mercato finanziario in Toscana (1801–1860)*. Firenze, 1997.

Volpini, Paola. 'La trattatistica sulla figura del console nella prima età moderna. Spunti di ricerca'. In *Los cónsules de extranjeros en la Edad Moderna y a principios de la Edad Contemporánea*, edited by M. Aglietti, M. Herrero Sánchez, and F. Zamora Rodríguez, pp. 35–45. Madrid, 2013.

Voorhoeve, Maaike, Abed Awad, and Hany Mawla. 'Divorce'. In *The Oxford encyclopedia of Islam and women*, edited by Natana J. de Long-Bas. Oxford, 2013. Consulted online at https://www.oxfordreference.com/view/10.1093/acref:oiso/9780199764464.001.0001/acref-9780199764464-e-0108?rskey=jinXdZ&result=1.

Waelkens, L. 'L'origine de l'enquête par turbe'. *Tijdschrift voor rechtsgeschiedenis*, 53 (1985): pp. 337–346.

Wagenaar, Jan. *Amsterdam in zyne opkomst, aanwas, geschiedenissen, voorregten, koophandel, gebouwen, kerkenstaat, schoolen, schutterye, gilden en regeeringe bescreeven door Jan Wagenaar historieschryver der stad*. Vol. 12. Amsterdam, 1768.

Wagenaar, Jan. *Amsterdam in zyne opkomst, aanwas, geschiedenissen, voorregten, koophandel, gebouwen, kerkenstaat, schoolen, schutterye, gilden en regeeringe bescreeven door Jan Wagenaar historieschryver der stad*. Vol. 4. Amsterdam, 1766.

Wätjen, Hermann. *Die Niederländer in Mittelmeergebiet zur Zeit ihren hochsten Machtstellung*. Berlin, 1909.

Weber, Max. *The history of commercial partnerships in the Middle Ages*, translated by Lutz Kaelber. Lanham, Boulder, New York and Oxford, 2003.

The Whitehall evening post, or London intelligencer. 13–15/11/1755.

Wood, Alfred C. *A history of the Levant Company*. Oxford, 1935.

Wubs-Mrozewicz, Justyna. 'The late medieval and early modern Hanse as an institution of conflict management'. *Continuity and change*, 32:1 (2017): pp. 59–84.

Yılmaz, Fikret. *400 years in Izmir: Izmirian Dutch people and trade relations between Izmir and Holland*. Izmir, 2012.

Yılmaz, Gülay. 'The economic and social roles of janissaries in a 17th century Ottoman city: The case of Istanbul'. Unpublished PhD thesis, McGill University, 2011.

Zahedieh, Nuala. 'Credit, risk, and reputation in late seventeenth-century colonial trade'. In *Merchant organization and maritime trade in the north Atlantic, 1660–1815* (Research in maritime history 15), edited by O.U. Janzen, pp. 53–74. St. John's, 1998.

Zaugg, Roberto. *Stranieri di antico regime. Mercanti, giudici e consoli nella Napoli del Settecento.* Roma, 2011.

Zeebout, Ambrosius. *Tvoyage van Mher Joos van Ghisele*, edited by R.J.G.A.A. Gaspar. Hilversum, 1998.

Zimmermann, Reinhard. *The law of obligations: Roman foundations of the civilian tradition*. Oxford, 1990.

Index

www.ingramcontent.com/pod-product-compliance
Lightning Source LLC
Chambersburg PA
CBHW071327230926
51849CB00002B/328
9789004382701